HISTORY OF ISLAMIC ORIGINS OF WESTERN EDUCATION

A.D. 800-1350

HISTORY OF ISLAMIC ORIGINS OF WESTERN EDUCATION
A.D. 800-1350

WITH AN INTRODUCTION TO MEDIEVAL MUSLIM EDUCATION

MEHDI NAKOSTEEN

PROFESSOR OF HISTORY AND
PHILOSOPHY OF EDUCATION
UNIVERSITY OF COLORADO

UNIVERSITY OF COLORADO PRESS
BOULDER, COLORADO

Library of Congress Catalog Card No. 63-22473.

DEDICATION

To the memory of my mother, Ozra Khanum, whose life was a flawless model of womanhood,
and
to my brother, Mirza Ahmad Khan Nakhosteen—a gentleman, a scholar, and a humanitarian.

INTRODUCTORY NOTE

IN ANY SURVEY of the history of Western education, we may bypass the Sino-Japanese civilizations and refer only occasionally to Hindu culture without doing considerable damage to our knowledge and understanding of the evolution of educational theory and practice in Europe and the United States. But to overlook the complex of cultural patterns that comprised the Middle Eastern civilizations of the pre-Christian and early Christian centuries and to neglect the phenomenal development of Muslim learning and educational institutions during the "Medieval" centuries, between 750 and 1350, is to ignore some of the basic foundations of our Western traditions and the lasting significance which they have in our Western mode of life.

The pre-Christian and early Christian Middle Eastern cultures and nations are important to us, for, in addition to giving the religious, linguistic, and perhaps aesthetic beginnings of our Western cultures, they also preserved for us through the Alexandrian, Syrian, and Persian institutions of learning the substance of the Greco-Hellenistic traditions of science, mathematics, philosophy, and technology, as well as the educational ideals and methods which created them.

At a time when European monarchs were hiring tutors to teach them how to sign their names, Muslim educational institutions were preserving, modifying, and improving upon the classical cultures in their progressive colleges and research centers under enlightened rulers. Then, as the results of their cumulative and creative genius reached the Latin West through translations of Arabic versions of classical works as well as of Muslim writings in medicine, philosophy, geography, history, technology, pedagogy, and other disciplines, they brought about that Western revival of learning which is our modern heritage.

Greek and Hellenistic learning and education did not terminate with the closing of the schools of Athens by Justinian in 529 A.D. It was re-routed through Syrian-Nestorian scholarship to make contacts with Persian and Hindu thought under Sassanian monarchs and Zoroastrian teachers and then passed through Muslim hands, which enriched and modified it, finally to reach the Latin schoolmen and the modern world. No doubt this transmission was irregular and selective, "original and capricious," adding here and subtracting there. But it put the West in touch with its own heritage, to which much had been added. Sarton says:

> The Muslims were standing on the shoulders of their Greek forerunners much as the Americans are standing on the shoulders of their European ones. . . . Arabic was the international language of science to a degree which has never been equalled by another language except Greek and has never been repeated since. It was the language not of one people, one nation, one faith, but of many peoples, many nations, many faiths. The Muslim culture was . . . and to some extent still is, a bridge, the main bridge between East and West. . . . Latin culture was Western, Chinese culture was Eastern, but Muslim culture was both. . . . It was stretched out between the Christianism of the West and the Buddhism of the East and touched both.[1]

Indeed there is no important aspect of the development of Western civilization since the twelfth and thirteenth centuries in which the decisive impact of Islamic culture is not discernible. This is particularly true of our institutions of higher learning and their curriculums and methodologies. Hence the great need for incorporating the development of Muslim institutions of learning and their intellectual products in any comprehensive survey of the history of Western education.

The treatment of "medieval" Muslim education as a fundamental phase of educational progress in Western Europe and America is seriously neglected in our textbooks on the history of education today. This study, therefore, attempts to present the development of "medieval" Muslim educational institutions, their extensive scholarly products, and their important contributions in shaping modern Western education. If its efforts, however introductory, may result in directing appropriate attention to the intimate and far-reaching relation of "medieval" Muslim learning to Western educational thought and practice, it has fulfilled its main task.

One idea that should be kept clearly in the reader's mind at the outset is the proper use of the label Muslim. The term is not necessarily synonymous with such other ones as Arabic or Persian. Nor are these terms interchangeable. Not all Arabs are Muslims; there are Christian Arabs, Hebrew Arabs, Syrian Arabs, and so on. And not all Muslims are Arabs; there are non-Arab Muslims from Spain to China and southwest Asia, among them Persians, Afghans, Turks, Pakistanis, Indians, varieties of southeast Asians, even Filipinos, Japanese, and so forth.

Again, not all that is in Persian culture is necessarily Muslim. First of all, Persian culture antedates Islam. Zoroastrian (Sassanian) civilization reached the peak of its cultural renaissance in the sixth century before the advent of Islam. It had then become the torchbearer of Western civilization, bringing together into a new creative synchronism the scientific and philosophic conclusions of the Greeks, Hebrews, Indians (Hindus), Syrians, and Zoroastrians. Its nerve center was the greatest academy of its time—the Academy of Jundi-Shapur in southeastern Persia. Not only that, but even after the birth of Islam and the conquest of the Persians by the Arabs, the most important cultural developments in Islam (in areas of science, technology, mathematics, logic, philosophy, the basic arts, astronomy, chemistry [alchemy], music, mechanics, ethics, perhaps history and geography, even theology, and literature) were the contributions of Persian thinkers and scholars who in the early centuries of Islam wrote in the Arabic language and in the name of Islam. Even the political patterns and concepts prevailing during the long Abbasside period of the Muslim rule were basically Persian in origin and in application. In fact most of the greatest statesmen of the Abbasside Islam were either natives of Persia or of Persian origin. "Take from what is generally called Arabian Science," says Edward G. Browne in his famous *Literary History of Persia,* "the works contributed by Persians, and the best part is gone."[2]

To the contributions of the Persians may be added those made by Hebrews, Spaniards, Italians, Portuguese, Turks, Indians, Sabaeans (such as scholars of the Hunayn family), Syrians, Harranese, Berbers, and others. For example, Avicenna, al-Ghazzali, Biruni, Tabari, Nasir-al-Din, Abul-Wafa, al-Battani, and Omar Khayyam were Persians. Al-Kindi was Arab; al-Khwarizmi was a native of Khiva; al-Farghani was from Transoxiana; al-Farabi, though listed as a Turk, was originally from Khorassan; Arzachel (al-Zarkali), Albetragius (al-Bitruji), and Averroes (ibn Rushd) were Spanish Arabs.[3]

The confusion created from using the term Muslim loosely comes from the fact that almost all the translations and works of creative scholarship during the ninth and tenth centuries were written in the Arabic language, although the Persian language competed successfully with Arabic during the latter half of the eleventh and throughout the twelfth and thirteenth centuries. The common denominator, as we shall see, was nonetheless the Arabic language in the same sense that Latin was in the development of learning and education in medieval Western Europe. But more of this in the context of this study.

The reader should also remember that medieval Muslim education and scholarship were sustained by a spirit of scholasticism not unlike that of the Christian West. While this scholasticism resulted, in the hands of Latin Christian theologian-scholars, in erudite efforts to reconcile and synthesize Greek philosophy, particularly Aristotelianism and neo-Platonism, with church doctrines, reaching its peak in St. Thomas Aquinas, Muslim scholasticism attempted to reconcile Greco-Hellenistic thought with Muslim religious doctrines, reaching its peak in the works of al-Ghazzali. In both educational schemes, scholastic knowledge, logic, and method were skillfully employed to reconcile secular or lay scholarship with religious dogma, to harmonize reason with faith. In the same manner and for the same reason, Jewish scholasticism, stimulated by Muslim scholarship, reached its peak in Maimonides in the second half of the twelfth century, half way between the heights reached by Islam under al-Ghazzali in the eleventh and by Christianity under Aquinas in the thirteenth century.

In the struggle for intellectual maturity, scholasticism appears to be a necessary transition from faith unaided by scholarship and logic to science unhampered by religious dogma and restriction. Scholasticism is neither pure faith nor empirical science: While loyal to doctrine, it employs the resources of reason to sustain the premises of religion. Although appearing to be rational, it is at heart dogmatic. While professing adherence to basic dogmas, it gives the appearance of reasonableness and makes at times important intellectual contributions, as is evident particularly in Muslim scholasticism.

Islamic learning made impressive advances during the "medieval" period through such creative men as al-Kindi, al-Razi, al-Farabi, ibn Sinan, ibn Sina (Avicenna), al-Masudi, al-Tabari, al-Ghazzali, Nasir Khusru, Omar Khayyam, and others. It made far-reaching investigations in medicine, technology, mathematics, geography, and even history. But all this was done within the framework of faith and scholasticism.

One reason Islam produced so much in scholarship in so short a time and then became so sterile so rapidly is to be found in the very nature of this Islamic scholasticism, which was dynamic and creative on the one hand, reactionary and finalistic on the other. While some of the caliphs and "crusaders" of Islam burned libraries and hushed scholars, others took pride in employing copyists and bookdealers to assemble fabulous libraries and make them centers of public education and scholarship.

However, Islam remained creative and progressive as long as freedom of thought and investigation prevailed over fatalism. As long as Islam considered the world an open book for all men to read and understand, the elements of fanaticism and orthodoxy, imbedded in scholasticism, remained subdued and could not exert a decisive influence. But once the dynamic and liberal elements gave way to total submission to orthodoxy and the concepts of pre-determinism and pre-destination, and overcame the impulse to investigate, innovate, and create, the torch was passed from Islam to the men of the European Renaissance.

The Purpose of the Study

Specifically, the purpose of this study is to determine the scope and extent of Muslim scholarship between 750 and 1350, and to indicate the influence and impact of this scholarship on Latin Christian schools in western Europe. The study is controlled by, and endeavors to provide answers to, *four* basic questions:

1. Through what channels and to what extent did the contents of classical scholarship—Greco-Hellenistic, Syriac-Alexandrian, Zoroastrian, and Indian—reach the Muslims?

2. What cumulative and creative additions, modifications, or adaptations of this classical learning took place in the hands of Muslim scholars and schoolmen from the eighth through the eleventh centuries?

3. Through what channels and to what extent did the results of classical scholarship so preserved, enriched, and enlarged by the Muslims reach the Western world, mainly during the twelfth and thirteenth centuries?

4. Finally, what were some of the basic contributions of this scholastic transmission to the expansion and reconstruction of the West European curriculum, particularly on levels of higher and professional education?

Before entering upon this four-fold task it is necessary to outline, however briefly, the political, religious, and geographic settings in which this development took place, and through which its origins, progress, and termination may be identified.

The Transliteration System Used in This Study

As shown in the general bibliography, a number of Persian and Arabic sources have been consulted in preparation of this work. The sources in English, French, and German which have been consulted also contain in many instances words, phrases, names of authors, and titles of books transliterated from Arabic and Persian materials. Since there is no uniform and universal method of transliteration, German, French, and English transliteration methods do not always agree. Even transliterations from these languages into English vary considerably by the method each author employs. The problem is further complicated by the fact that the Persian language is saturated with Arabic terms involving modifications of sound and transliteration to fit Persian usage. Finally, since the Persian alphabet is an adaptation of the Arabic, with the addition of four purely Persian letters (p پ, ch چ, s as in *Persian* ژ, and g as in *God* گ) transliteration of Arabic phrases from Persian sources and transliteration of purely Persian words written in Arabic characters constitute another problem. It is also of interest to note that the Arabic alphabet also contains eight characters which have been added to the original Persian alphabet of twenty-four characters to make the modern Persian alphabet of thirty-two letters.

In view of such unresolvable problems, my original impulse was to bypass the different transliteration systems and adopt as nearly as possible a transphonetic system of my own. I found out soon enough that this method had a fatal disadvantage: Without solving any of the problems, it added new ones of its own. For one thing, many Arabic and Persian words have evolved into more than one phonetic usage among Persian- and Arabic-speaking peoples, and to have changed the phonetic sounds of these words into English according to many historic and contemporary usages would have appeared inconsistent and merely added to the reader's confusion. Another problem is the impossibility of transphonetization of certain Arabic and Persian words into English for the simple reason that both Arabic and Persian alphabets contain certain sound characters for which we have no equivalents in the English alphabet. Finally, all the authorities I consulted discouraged me from the unorthodox use of a transphonetic system, strongly advising me to adhere to one of the traditional methods and make the best of it. This warning was formidable enough to intimidate me into orthodoxy in quick order.

There is to my knowledge no system of transliteration that can always fit both Persian and Arabic terms, although the *Table of Arabic Transliteration* approved and adopted by the Library of Congress and the American Library Association seems to come closest to meeting this need. The important features of this system are as follows:

ا	Alif	a (as a long vowel)	ض	Dad	d
ب	Ba	b	ط	Ta	t
ت	Ta	t	ظ	Za	z
ث	Tha	th	ع	'Ayn	
ج	Jim	j	غ	Ghayn	gh
ح	Ḥa	h	ف	Fa	f
خ	Kha	kh	ق	Qaf	q
د	Dal	d	ك	Kaf	k
ذ	Dhal	dh	ل	Lam	l
ر	Ra	r	م	Mim	m
ز	Zayn	z	ن	Nun	n
س	Sin	s	ه	Ha	h
ش	Shin	sh	و	Waw	w
ص	Sad	s	ى	Ya	y

Vowels and Diphthongs

َ	Fathah (short)	a	(long)	a	َا
ِ	Kasrah (short)	i	(long)	i	ِى
ُ	Dhammah (short)	u	(long)	u	ُو

(See also Dodge, Bayard, *Moslem Education in Medieval Times*, The Middle East Institute, Washington, D. C., 1962, p. 91.)

Other Items:

1. *Shaddah* or lengthening of a consonant such as *bb* in *abba* is transliterated by doubling the consonant. Example:
   أُمّ (mother) *omm*
2. Except in the construct state, the final *Ha* is transliterated *h*. For the construct state, the final *Ha* is transliterated *t*.
3. *Alif* (ا), *Waw* (و) and *Ya* (ى) are not transliterated whenever they are used to support the *Hamzah* (ء). In initial position, *Hamzah* (ء) is not transliterated, whether at the be-

ginning of a word, following a prefixed preposition or conjunction, or following the definite article. It is transliterated whenever it is medial or final.

4. *Maddah* (~) is translitered *a*. When medial it is transliterated *a* as in تآليف *ta'alif*.

It is important to remember that Arabic and Persian letters have more than one phonetic use among Arabic- Persian- and Turkish-speaking peoples, depending on the area. In such cases an effort is made to adapt transliteration whenever necessary or reasonable to local use, particularly in adaptations of Arabic characters in Persian, and vice versa.

(For other transliteration details consult *Arabic Transliteration,* Cataloguing Service, The Library of Congress, Processing Department, Bulletin 49, November, 1958, Washington 25, D. C., pp. 1-10.)

A few names such as Baghdad and al-Ghazzali have not been transliterated because of their established spelling in works dealing with Islamic culture. The phonetic transliteration of certain Persian words of Arabic origin, such as Nizam (Arabic Nidham), has also been maintained throughout this work whenever these words are taken or quoted directly from Persian sources.

One other factor may have contributed to the appearance of transliteration inconsistencies in this work. Whenever materials in English, German, or French sources are used, transliterated Persian or Arabic terms or names are quoted as they appear in these works, however inconsistent they may be. This is particularly true in the general and topical bibliographies and in direct quotes from these sources.

Also, in the lists of authors and their works appearing in Appendix IV, only important titles are translated into English, some of them indicating only the subject matter of the work, or stating the title in abbreviated form. There are cross references for some authors, such as ibn Sina or al-Ghazzali, who wrote on many subjects.

The chances of errors of judgment, inconsistencies in transliteration of words from Persian and Arabic sources, and inadequate translations, are readily admitted in a complex study such as this.

ACKNOWLEDGMENTS

THE RATHER EXTENSIVE bibliography which appears at the end of this work is a partial witness to a long list of eminent scholars whose works have given light and substance to the contents of this study. To each a special acknowledgment is due. I am particularly indebted to the extensive volumes of Dr. George Sarton and Dr. Thabih-Allah Safa for factual and interpretive materials on Islamic learning from the eighth to the thirteenth centuries. I am indebted to my brother, Mirza Ahmad Khan Nakhosteen, for suggesting and sending many valuable Persian and Arabic works from Teheran which have been consulted and quoted in this research. I am grateful to Dr. Bayard Dodge, President of the University of Beirut—now at Princeton—for his counsel on the *Al-Fihrist* of ibn-al-Nadim, and for his advice on problems of transliteration of Arabic and Persian names into English. The Library of Congress transliteration method employed in this work has been due to his recommendation. I cannot adequately thank Dr. Karl Hulley, Professor of Classics and former Editor of the University of Colorado Press, for his continuous guidance in preparation of the manuscript and for his editing of the entire work, and to Mr. J. K. Emery, Director of University Publications, for his skillful guidance of the manuscript through the arduous tasks of publication. I wish to extend my thanks also to our specialist on Islamic history, Dr. Charles Geddes, for reading the entire manuscript and making many valuable organizational and other suggestions; and to my friend, Dr. Alfred Crofts, Professor of History at the University of Denver, for his careful reading of the entire work and for drawing attention to the need for explaining certain Arabic and Persian terms, and expanding certain historical backgrounds.

The author is grateful to the Council on Research and Creative Work of the University of Colorado for several grants-in-aid in connection with this research; and to Harvard University Press for allowing the use of Al-Gazzali's "My Child," appearing in Dr. Robert Ulich's *Three Thousand Years of Educational Wisdom.*

A work of this nature goes through several typings and involved mechanical tasks requiring background and care. I should especially mention in this connection my wife, Frances, who assumed the lion's share of these difficult tasks.

MEHDI NAKOSTEEN

TABLE OF CONTENTS

CHAPTER I *

THE CULTURAL, POLITICAL, AND RELIGIOUS SETTING

THE INTELLECTUAL life of the medieval period, particularly from the ninth century through the thirteenth, is marked by developments which took place in five recognizable geographic areas—the Sino-Japanese world (or should we say Chinese and Japanese worlds?), India, Greek Christendom, Latin Christendom, and Eastern and Western Islam. The Hebrew culture, though it maintained its identity throughout this period, had been incorporated politically within the Christian and Muslim domains. By adhering to its own faith and yet adapting itself politically, linguistically, and culturally to both societies, Hebrew scholarship proved itself an invaluable instrument of cultural exchange in both Muslim and Christian intellectual circles. We shall note later how much Latin schoolmen owed the Hebrews in transmitting the substance of the Greco-Muslim learning to the West by translations from Arabic into Latin and Hebrew, or into Latin from Hebrew translations of Arabic works.

The five areas may be looked upon geographically as two grand cultural worlds—India, China, and Japan in the East, and the Christian and Muslim worlds in the West. The two worlds—East and West—were separated by distance as much as by ideals, and any intellectual association between them was too small during the medieval period to bridge the wide gap which geography had imposed upon them. It is true that the art of manufacturing paper and the use of gunpowder and the compass may have reached Europe from China through the Muslims; and the Persians, Syrians, and Arabs transmitted Hindu medical, mathematical, and astronomical knowledge. It is true also that certain elements of Greek science reached India during the Alexandrian period, as they may also have reached China through Khiva. But such contacts between East and West were too infrequent and their influence too sparse to constitute any penetrating East-West cultural intercourse. Islam, as we shall see later, constituted nonetheless the bridge, however narrow, over which cultural traffic and exchange between East and West were maintained.

The Muslim and Christian worlds on the other hand, though each defined and maintained its own identity on religious and political

*All dates refer to A.D. unless otherwise specified.

grounds, shared in various degrees and for different purposes some common cultural elements. They were both sustained at different times and through different channels by the intellectual life of the Greco-Hellenistic world, and they claimed a common religious heritage from Judaism. They shared a religious basis for life and society. Also, in relations between religious and temporal powers certain similarities existed between the two cultures. In the Christian world two opposing trends developed: In Eastern, or Greek, Christianity the emperor appointed the patriarch of Constantinople and had the power to reduce or remove his jurisdiction. In Western, or Latin, Christianity the two centers of power, the pope and the emperor, competed for supremacy, the pope maintaining the upper hand throughout the Middle Ages. In Islam, too, the caliphs, and later the sultans, played the role of defenders of the faith, allowing the religious leaders a degree of autonomy in civic and religious matters but reducing their powers when they exceeded predetermined limits. But spiritual leadership in Islam was never centralized as in the Roman papacy, nor was it brought under political jurisdiction as in the Byzantine world. That is perhaps why religious stability was of such short duration in Islam, and gave way to politico-religious nationalistic identifications, such as Persian-Islam, Egyptian-Islam, and Hispano-Islam, while it remained of long duration in the Christian world, particularly in the Latin West.

The factors which kept Islam and Christianity apart and mutually ignorant of each other were far stronger than common elements which may have brought them together. The barriers of language, political rivalries and conquests, and of religious conflicts were formidable and moved each faith to use its intellectual facilities to destroy or misrepresent the other. The crusades were politically wasteful for both Islam and Christianity and bred the inevitable obstacles of ignorance, suspicion, fear, force, and bloodshed. For centuries the Muslims resisted the political power of the West in Italy, Sicily, Spain, and North Africa, and for the same number of centuries the Byzantines resisted the power of the Muslims in the East. As the crusades exhausted both the Muslims and the Christians, the Latin West expanded deep into Europe, the Greek East into southern and eastern Slavic areas, the Nestorian and Monophysite religious factions eastward into Arabia, Persia, and some of the fringes and centers of Asia. During this period the Muslims moved deep into Afro-Asia while remaining loosely on the edges of the three continents of Europe, Asia, and Africa.

On the intellectual plane the three powers and cultures—Latin, Greek, and Muslim—remained perpetually suspicious of each other, and suspiciousness led to mutual indifference and ignorance. Greek Christianity broke away from the Roman and was in turn divided into antagonistic religious sects of which Nestorianism proved the most formidable. Latin Christianity also isolated itself gradually but decisively from Greek orthodoxy, from Islam, and from the Hellenistic heritage which Eastern Christianity kept alive, mainly through Nestorian and Monophysite scholarship. Both Eastern and Western Islamic cultures, though founded upon Greco-Hellenistic, Persian, and Indian knowledges and skills, remained out of touch with the Latin Christian world for several centuries, save for contacts with Syriac Christianity in Eastern Islam and with certain elements of Christianity in Western Islam, mainly in Sicily and Spain.

Both Latin and Greek Christianity looked upon Muslims as infidels and upon Islam as a pagan faith. It took Western Europe until the twelfth century, or five hundred years after the birth of Islam, to develop respect for Muslim scholarship, and it took an additional five hundred years for the Muslim world to begin to examine the intellectual consequences of the European Renaissance, which their own intellectual contributions had largely initiated. The factors which kept Muslim and Christian cultures apart are evidenced in some of the views of Greek and Latin Christian writers of Islam and its prophet Muhammad.* John of Damascus calls Muhammad, to whom he refers as Mamed, a false prophet.[1] Theophanes Confessor, the Byzantine historian, refers to him as the prophet Mouamed, a poor epileptic, who indoctrinated the Arabs in immoral and foolish fables about man and the hereafter.[2] As late as the thirteenth century Bartholomew of Edessa writes about Mouchamet, (as Bartholomew called him), "a voluptuary, defiled to the very core, a brigand, a profligate, a murderer and a robber."[3]

The Latin world, which read its first text of the *Qur'an* (*Koran*) in the translation by Peter of Cluny in 1141, was hardly more charitable toward Islam than were the Byzantine writers. Eulogius of Cordova, martyred in 859, relates that Muhammad's corpse was devoured by dogs after his death, and that his soul "descended to hell," after the angels abandoned him.[4] Ginbert of Nogent (died 1124) tells us that Muhammad's body was devoured by pigs while he was in one of his epileptic fits. In *Chanson de Roland* Muhammad is confused with Allah, suggesting that the Muslims were the heathens who prayed to many gods, mainly to their God Muhammad.[5] With this error, Latin ignorance of Islam reached its lowest low! Even while the bulk of Muslim writings were reaching the schoolmen of Latin Europe, William of Tripoli could write a work on Islam in 1273 entitled *Tractate on the State of the Saracens, Muhammad The False Prophet, Their Law and Their Faith!*

The Muslims, on the other hand, were more charitable toward the Christians. For one thing, they had derived the substance of their own faith largely from Judaism and Christianity. Both Christians and Jews were accepted as *Ahl al-Kitab,* or the People of the Book, meaning the Old and New Testament. They accepted all the Judaeo-Christian

*Incidentally, the many spellings and pronunciations of Muhammad's name throughout Christian Europe's Medieval period indicate unfamiliarity with Muslim sources in Latin writings. He is referred to, among other names, as Moameth, Mahomet, Mahoun, Mouamed, Mouchamet, Moamed, and Mehmet.

prophets from Adam to Jesus, though they rejected the doctrine of Christ's divinity, as they also renounced the concept of the Trinity as polytheistic and therefore contrary to the belief in the absolute oneness of God.

Educated Muslims respected Jewish and Christian scholars during the formative and maturing centuries of their cultural development. Nestorian scholars, including medical theorists and practitioners, held positions of respect at the courts of the Muslim caliphs. From them the caliphs and their subjects received, in part, their first knowledge of Greek learning. To Nestorians they delegated the extensive task of translating classical works into Arabic, and remunerated them handsomely for the service. They accepted Nestorian leaders as teachers, heads of hospitals and medical academies, interpreters, and creative writers. They gave them freedom of faith and, with understandable limitations, freedom of action.

It was this Muslim attitude of limited charity which in the end well repaid both Muslim and Christian cultures. It opened the treasures of classical knowledge to creative minds within the culturally heterogeneous Muslim world. When the forces of hatred, isolation, and ignorance gradually gave way in the Latin West to an era of understanding, the substance of this classical learning, preserved and advanced by the Muslims, reached Latin Europe to pave the way for the Renaissance of the fifteenth and sixteenth centuries.

Geographic and Political Factors

In terms of geographic and political factors, the materials to be examined in this study entail some consideration of the Islamic Empire, including the eastern and western wings, and the Christian world—the Byzantine Empire in the East with Constantinople as its capital and the Holy Roman Empire in the West dominated by Rome. It may, therefore, help the reader if we take a brief glance at the political structure and geographic extents of these two political powers—the Christian and the Muslim, East and West, particularly from the eleventh century to the thirteenth.

Before the beginning of the Christian era, the Roman ruler Octavian assumed the title of *imperator* and the name *Augustus.* The grandeur that was Rome's reached its climax in the first two centuries A.D., under some of Octavian's successors, such as Vespasian, Trajan, Hadrian, Antoninus Pius, and Marcus Aurelius. After Aurelius, the Empire began a decline which continued throughout the third and fourth centuries, with long successions of short-lived and second-rate emperors, the army remaining in real control of affairs. In a period of one hundred and fifty years, 235 to 385 A.D., Rome witnessed twenty-six emperors.

By the fourth century, Diocletian initiated and Constantine founded an eastern wing of the empire with Byzantium, renamed Constantinople, its new seat. There developed one empire in name but in reality two empires with two emperors with two seats of government. Constantine made Christianity the state religion in 325. Both the Eastern and Western Empires were overrun by German invasions in the fourth, fifth, and sixth centuries. Greece, Macedonia, and Asia Minor fell in the East; Italy, France, England, and Spain in the West, though the Church continued to carry on under Germanic kings. Theodosius was the last emperor to rule over the whole extent of the Roman Empire, though Emperor Justinian, himself a zealous Christian, revived some of the power of the Eastern, or Byzantine, Empire during the sixth century, conquered Italy, and extended his empire through northern Africa to southern Spain. In 529, he closed the secular academies of Athens, thereby initiating an establishment of religion and the abandonment of classical culture.

Under Justinian's successors the Byzantine Empire was reduced again (with some exceptions which will be pointed out later) to the eastern Mediterranean areas, but held itself together against Eastern powers—the Sassanian Persians, the Eastern Umayyad and Abbasside Muslim caliphs, the Ottoman rulers, and the crusaders (1095-1291) until the fifteenth century.

The Roman bishops had assumed power as popes over the Western church by the end of the fifth century, and Rome was recognized more and more as the religious center of the Western Empire. However, Italy had been weakened by the Germanic invasions, and the center of political power had shifted gradually to the Frankish kingdoms of central and western Europe, particularly under Merovingian kings. Charles Martel further unified the Frankish domain in the eighth century and strengthened the power of the Roman church. His son, Pepin the Short, continued this close tie with the Roman papacy by protecting the pope against the Lombard kings and the Byzantine emperor. Charlemagne, his son, succeeded him and expanded Frankish sovereignty to the North Sea, the Mediterranean, and the Elbe River.[6]

Meanwhile, during the seventh and eighth centuries the Muslim Umayyads, Abbassides, Fatimids, Aghlabites, and others had reduced the Byzantine Empire in the east, in North Africa, and in southern Europe. Eastward, they had spread their control into Transoxiana and India. Spain had already fallen to the Muslims in the first decades of the eighth century. Sicily and southern Italy were being overrun by Muslims from North Africa early in the ninth century, after Christianity had been split into two empires politically and theologically.

In 800 A.D. a great politico-religious event took place in Rome which changed the course of European and Islamic history for centuries to come. In that year Charlemagne, having united the warring factions of western and northern Europe, was proclaimed by Pope Leo III as Charlemagne Augustus, "crowned by God, the great and peace-bringing emperor of the Romans." In this decisive and historic stroke, the pope transferred to him the homage which had been reserved since 476 for the Eastern emperor. By 812 Charlemagne was recognized in Constantinople as co-emperor on condition that he allow Venice and southern Italy to be under the sovereignty of Byzantium. The "Holy" Roman Empire was thus inaugurated, and the stage was set for the great schism between Greek and Latin Christianity.[7] Before the end of his reign, Charlemagne ruled an empire greater in size than the Byzantine but surpassed by the Muslim.

This grand separation within Christendom, the schism, was in itself a complex phenomenon: It involved time, geography, language, political conflicts, and theological, liturgical, and perhaps even emotional differences. In point of *time* the events which brought about a final and complete division within the church began with the coronation of Charlemagne and were completed in July of 1054, three months after the death of Pope Leo IX, when the legates deposited a bull on the altar of St. Sophia, excommunicating Michael Cerularius, the Patriarch of Constantinople.

Geographically, the schism divided Europe between Greek and Latin orthodoxies, with Greek orthodoxy establishing itself in the lands around the eastern Mediterranean and spreading its doctrines among the Slavs, and Latin orthodoxy more or less dominating the rest of Europe.

Linguistically, it identified Eastern orthodoxy with the Greek language and Western with the Latin. This kept Greek orthodoxy closer to Greco-Hellenistic thought and cultural environment, and the Latin world relatively out of touch with this heritage until the twelfth and the thirteenth centuries. This is evidenced by the encyclopaedic work, the *Myriobiblion,* of Ignatius in the ninth century, which contained 280 chapters in which were preserved many passages of classical literature.[8]

Politically, Greek orthodoxy attached itself closely to Byzantine emperors, who regulated church affairs by secular laws and appointed and deposed the patriarchs, while the Latin church dominated into the thirteenth and fourteenth centuries the political fortunes of western Europe.

Theologically, the differences involved the Monothelite controversy over the point of origin for the Holy Ghost. The Nicene Creed had accepted the Holy Ghost as proceeding from the Father (*ex patre procedit*). In 589 a council of the church in Toledo declared that the Holy Spirit proceeds from the Father and the Son (*ex patre filioque procedit*), a view which was soon accepted by Charlemagne and the churches in Gaul. It was adopted in the eleventh century by

Roman orthodoxy. Greek orthodoxy declared that the Holy Ghost proceeds from the Father and not from the Son.

Liturgically, ecclesiastical ornaments, vessels, and vestments were more ornate in Greek orthodoxy than in the Western church; the Latins knelt at prayer, while the Greeks stood up; the Latins baptized by aspersion, but the Greeks by immersion. Western priests shaved, Eastern priests grew beards; Latin orthodoxy forbade marriage to its priests, Greek orthodoxy allowed it; Latin papacy was more involved in politics, Greek patriarchy in theology.[9]

And finally, *emotionally,* Greek orthodoxy looked upon the Western papacy as too worldly, politically oriented, and uncouth, and the Western peoples (Germans, Franks, and Anglo-Saxons) as illiterate barbarians. The Latins, the papacy in particular, characterized the Greeks as heretics and schismatics, perhaps more pagan than Christian.

In the centuries following Charlemagne and the division of Christendom into co-empires, the Eastern or Byzantine Empire remained harassed with internal discord and external attack from the Muslims, whom they resisted and held back for centuries. What cultural contacts were made between Europe and the Muslim East in this period came largely through Syria in arts and crafts during the crusades (1095-1291). In the West the Muslims had pushed the Byzantines out of North Africa and were, by 732, in control of the Iberian Peninsula and threatening to cross the Pyrenees into Gaul and central Europe.

After Charlemagne, the Western Empire was split into three kingdoms: The eastern Frankish (Germany), the western Frankish (France), and the southern (Italy). It was against this tri-centered empire that three weakening invasions were directed in the ninth century: From the north, the Vikings; from the east, the Magyars; and from the south, the Muslims.

Otto the Great challenged this division in 962, conquered Italy, and ruled as Charlemagne before him, as the head of the Holy Roman Empire. The struggle between the church and state, the papacy and the emperors, continued, however, far into the thirteenth century, with the papacy constantly expanding and deepening its powers at the expense of the kings of France and England. The climax was reached with Pope Innocent III against Frederick II. After Frederick's death, the papacy was the dominant religious and political power for the remainder of the thirteenth century, with vast economic and educational controls over western, northern, and southern Europe.[10]

By 1000, the Byzantine Empire had reached another peak of political and cultural life which it had once experienced in the sixth century under Emperor Justinian. Territorially, the Eastern Empire included southern Italy, the Balkans, Asia Minor, northern Syria,

Rhodes, Crete, Cylades, and Cyprus. Constantinople, its capital, had become one of the four great centers of medieval culture west of India, the other three being Baghdad, the Eastern cultural center of Islam; Rome, the theological-cultural center of Western Christendom; and Cordova, the political and cultural capital of Western Islam. Greek orthodoxy had by this time expanded throughout the Balkans and into Russia.

The Eastern Roman Empire and the Muslims, by the end of the First Crusade, were bitterly guarding against each other, with the Byzantines controlling the lands adjoining the Mediterranean shores from Al-Iskandaruna in the north between the Tigris and Euphrates Rivers, and southward to Antioch and Jerusalem. The rest of Europe (except for the island of Sardinia, most of Spain, and parts of Sicily) was in control of the Western Roman Empire.

As for Islam, it controlled, in addition to most of Spain (exclusive of Leon, Castile, and Navarre), all of North Africa from Tangier on the Atlantic coast to Egypt and the Red Sea, Sardinia, parts of Sicily, and all of the Middle East, extending north to the Caucasus Mountains, the Aral and Transoxiana; eastward, including the areas of Punjab, Sind, and Cujart in India; northeast, including Ferghana; south, including all of the Arabian Peninsula; and westward to the Byzantine line.

Now a word on the Muslim conquest of Sicily, southern Italy, and Spain. The Aghlabites from Qayrawan in North Africa initiated the first real conquest of Sicily by the Muslims at the beginning of the ninth century. Ziadat-Allah (818-838), the third Aghlabite, undertook a full-fledged conquest of the island in 827 under the command of Asad ibn-al-Furat, his vizier, followed by waves of invasion under other commands.[11] Palermo was captured in 831; Messina in 843; Syracuse in 878 by Ibrahim II (874-902). By 902, all of Sicily was under Muslim rule and remained so, in whole or in part, until the last decade of the eleventh century.

Ibrahim II had also crossed the straits in 902 just before his death and put Calabria in southern Italy under Aghlabite control. By 841 the same Aghlabites had captured Bari on the Adriatic and reached Venice. Five years later, Aghlabite squadrons had landed at Ostia and threatened Rome but failed to capture it. By 869 they had captured Malta. The peak of Muslim rule in Sicily was reached under the Kalbite Amir al-Futuh Yusuf ibn-Abd'ul'lah (989-998).

The downfall of the Kalbites, brought about by the Norman conquest of Sicily in 1060 with the capture of Messina by Count Roger and completed by 1091, did not terminate the continuity of Muslim cultural activities in the island and in Italian cities. In fact, the Norman kings (Roger I, Roger II, and Frederick II of Hohenstaufen, 1215-1250) cultivated Muslim culture and learning and lived semi-Muslim royal lives. The Emperor Frederick patronized Muslim arts, architecture, sciences, philosophies, and translations of Muslim scientific works from Arabic into Latin. Palermo became a center for such translations. This cultural assimilation made Sicily one of the three centers of transmission of Muslim culture to European society and of Muslim learning to European schools and universities.[12]

The second, and by far the most far-reaching, center of Muslim culture and scholarship in Europe was Spain. How did the Muslims reach Spain? The year 732 was the centennial of the death of Muhammad, the founder of Islam. His followers had already reduced the territories and powers of the Byzantine Empire; the Sassanian Persian Empire had met a humiliating defeat and liquidation. Hajjaj-ibn Yusuf had marched through Persia into India; Musa-ibn Musayr, on orders from Damascus, had pushed westward from Egypt through North Africa to Qayrawan, the farthest west to Maghrib (the west land), subduing the Berbers all the way to Tangier and to the Atlantic coast; Tariq-ibn Ziyad had crossed the strait into Spain on orders of ibn Nusayr in 711; under new leaders Arabs and Berbers had then marched up the Iberian Peninsula toward the Pyrenees and Gaul; Spain had fallen to the invaders, and in 732 Muslim soldiers, led by Abd-al-Rahman (ibn-Abd'ullah al-Shafiqi), had advanced through the western Pyrenees and were threatening to push farther north, to turn eastward and march perhaps through central Europe, to reach Damascus and complete the encirclement of North Africa and Europe. But they were halted in that year between Tours and Poitiers in southern Gaul by the Frank, Charles Martel. The Battle of Tours marked the farthest extent of Muslim invasion of Latin Europe. Not that a victory for the Muslims through the Pyrenees would necessarily have led to their conquest of Europe, but the new faith was on the march. Anyone looking back today can wonder what would have been the fate and future of Europe and the world had the crescent replaced the cross. We can only suggest in the light of this study what might have been the intellectual and educational consequences for the Western world if our universities had developed as *bait-al-ilms* and our schools into *madrasahs* and *kuttabs*.

Although the first invasion of the Spanish Peninsula took place in 711, the new Umayyad dynasty in Spain was begun by Abd-al-Rahman I, who had escaped the tragic fate of the Umayyads in Damascus in 750-751. He established himself in Cordova, and this Muslim dynasty, which changed titles from amir to caliph under Abd-al-Rahman III, lasted until 1031, or two and three-quarters centuries. To Abd-al-Rahmans I and III, Muslim Spain owes some of its richest cultural and educational developments, reaching its peak under Abd-al-Rahman III (912-961), the eighth amir and new caliph. Muslim rule in Spain after this period began to decline, and Cordova lost its distinction as the cultural capital of Spain. In 1492, with the fall of Granada to Ferdinand II, Islam lost its last foothold on the peninsula after 581 years. And when the end came, it was as final as the beginning had been sweeping. Not only was Spain at last liberated from its Muslim invaders, but Muslim culture and education became, in turn, targets of attack, ending in closing Muslim schools and burning Muslim libraries. Hundreds of thousands of Muslims emigrated to North Africa, Egypt, and the Middle East; many thousands who failed to emigrate met their fate in the tragic Inquisition.

In 1609, Phillip III signed the last of a number of orders of expulsion, resulting in the deportation of almost all recognized Muslims, totalling 500,000, from Spain, but by that time some three million Muslims had been either expelled from Spain or executed. This situation in Spain had allowed Christian communities to exercise their faith freely and under their own ecclesiastical jurisdiction.[13]

Islam, therefore, failed to establish itself as a new faith in Spain, and it had at no time seriously imposed the faith upon the Spaniards. Relatively few Arabic works were translated into Spanish. Spain at the end regained its national pride, its Latin faith, its native language, and its cultural identity.

As the Muslims were being uprooted from European soil, they were compensating for their Western losses by moving ahead of Europeans into southeast Asia: Malaya, Java, Sumatra, parts of Indonesia, and some of the islands of the Pacific, including the Philippines.[14] This eastward expansion was checked, however, by European penetration into Asia at the beginning of the fifteenth century.

Cultural Diversity in Islam

Some Muslim historians believe that the geographic expansion of Islam was an evolution rather than a pre-determined action. But evidence in the *Qur'an* and in early political practices in Islam, both in the East and the West, suggests that the religion of Muhammad aspired to expand in time into a world political system as well as a world faith. Muhammad himself sent emissaries to the king of Ethiopia and the emperors of Iran and Byzantium, inviting them to adopt Islam. Also the imperialistic ambitions of the first politico-religious leaders of the faith seem to reflect the acceptance of a concept of universalism rather than of regionalism. In less than a century, Islam extended its economic-politico-religious power over a territory matched in magnitude only by the Roman Empire. That the faith spread in so short a time over three continents, persuading or compelling diverse peoples and cultures from Spain to China either to adopt the new faith or accept its political jurisdiction, reveals the partial success of Islam's original design. Islam, like its Christian prototype, labored to bring the world under one system of religion, one form of government, one way of life.[15] Islam's experiment in empire-building, however, was more dramatic than lasting and in the end expressed its genius in building a religion with widespread appeal rather than a political order ruled by common consent.[16]

Nor did Islam develop into one world culturally. At the outset, Islamic culture was as cumulative as it was heterogeneous. At a period when European civilization seemed to be at a standstill, when it forsook, particularly in the Latin West, its Greek and Hellenistic heritage in science and philosophy, Islam assumed the responsibility for carrying on and enriching that heritage. Intellectually, the Muslims took over the Hellenistic heritage, primarily through the medium of Syriac-Nestorian thought which already was enriched through an acquaintance with some of the principal works of Greek science and philosophy.[17]

The Umayyads allowed the sciences of the Hellenistic world to flourish in Syria: Christian, Sabaean, and Persian schools were patronized at Alexandria, Beirut, Jundi-Shapur, Nisibis, Harran, and Antioch. The Abbassides followed the Umayyads in encouraging the translations of Greek works into Arabic, often by Jews and Nestorian Christians. Al-Ma'mun in 830 established a research and translation center called Bait-al-Hikmah (House of Wisdom), where translations from Syriac, Greek, Sanskrit, and Pahlavi were made until the tenth century. Among the great translators and compilers of the early centuries of Islamic culture were Hunain ibn-Is'haq (809-873) and his son, Is'haq ibn-Hunain, whose combined translations included works by Aristotle, Galen, Plato, Hippocrates, Dioscorides, Ptolemy, and Alexander of Aphrodisias. The works of al-Khwarizmi and al-Biruni were also important, the former compiling astronomical tables, introducing Hindu numerals, formulating the oldest known trigonometrical tables, and cooperating with sixty-nine other scholars in preparing a geographic encyclopaedia. How extensive both original and translated materials were at this early period can best be exemplified by the *Fihrist-al-Ulum* (*Index of Sciences,* 987) of Mahmud ibn-al-Nadim, an annotated bibliography of original and translated works in Arabic running into thousands of titles, most of them lost.

A religious culture, which began in the early decades of the seventh century as purely Arabic in origin, developed by the fifteenth century into a unique culture "created through the blending of elements from the civilizations of the highly advanced peoples who had been conquered. There were elements from Persian and Indian sources, from Turkish and even, through them, from Chinese sources; there were strong elements from the ancient Roman and Greek civilizations, and strong elements in Spain and Sicily from the preceding Roman and Visigothic German cultures."[18] Let us see how much of this complex of classical cultures and learning was assimilated into Muslim culture, to be in turn given back to Europe to enrich its schools and revive its progress.

CHAPTER II *

CLASSICAL FOUNDATIONS OF MUSLIM EDUCATION

THE CONQUESTS OF THE ARABS during the earlier centuries of Islam (Umayyad and Abbasside) brought them into close contact with some of the great civilizations of the world. The old theory that the early Muslims were enemies of learning and science and that except in their own *Qur'an* and tradition they showed no tolerance of the beliefs and intellectual treasures of other nations is without historical basis. It is true that one could point out a particular person or age and charge him or it with intolerance, as happened with the burning of libraries by the early Muslim conquerors in Egypt and in Iran. But such exceptions or early short-sightedness should not conceal the spirit of inquiry and creativity which characterized the early centuries of Islam, particularly under the Abbassides. The Muslims of the Arab world, as well as those of Persia, Spain, Egypt, India, Afghanistan, Transoxiana, and so forth, produced great scholars who were not blind to the wealth of science and literature of each other and of the Hellenistic and Christian worlds. The famous al-Jahiz (869), speaking of the nature of these influences, especially Grecian, writes in the following manner:

> Did we not possess the books of the Ancients in which their wonderful wisdom is immortalized and in which the manifold lessons of history are so dealt with that the past lives before our eyes, did we not have access to the riches of their experience which would otherwise have been barred to us, our share in wisdom would be immeasurably smaller, and our means of attaining a true perspective most meager.[1]

Factors in Transmission of Classical Culture

The transmission of Greek learning, Hellenic and Hellenistic, to the Muslim world was brought about by unusual historic factors. Among them, the following are of importance:

1. One important factor lies within Christian orthodoxy, which persecuted and excommunicated schismatic bodies separated from the mother church for reasons of doctrinal differences. Among such schisms in the Eastern church, the Nestorian and Monophysite dissenting sects should receive special attention. As these sects were persecuted, they

*All dates refer to A.D. unless otherwise specified.

were forced to migrate to more friendly cultures where they received protection and opportunities for self-perpetuation. Upon moving from centers of Nicene orthodoxy—Nestorians to the Persian empire, Monophysites to Persia and the Arab world—these hostile sects carried with them the Greco-Hellenistic heritage of learning, particularly in medicine, mathematics, astronomy, technology, and philosophy, and helped preserve them in foreign hands. This heritage was later returned to European schoolmen through Muslim channels.

When Muslim Arabs invaded the Roman and Persian empires, these minority sects welcomed the conquering Arabs as liberators and established friendly contacts with them from the very beginning. Unlike the Mongolian hordes of the thirteenth century, the Muslim invaders were tolerant of regional customs, religions, and cultures of the peoples they subdued; they left the traditions of learning undisturbed and protected them against internal persecution. Thus it seems obvious that orthodox persecutions within the Byzantine world led to the preservation and eventual transfer of the Greco-Hellenistic learning to the West in two ways: (a) By continuing this tradition in non-Christian cultures, particularly in the Zoroastrian-Sassanian cultures of Persia; and (b) by furthering it within the Byzantine and Persian world under Muslim protection and patronage during the early Muslim centuries.

Interest in neo-Platonism and Aristotelianism, though interpreted in Christian terms and adapted to Christian doctrines, nonetheless kept the Nestorians and Jacobites on a higher level of general education than the "Latin-speaking Christians of the West." With the Nestorians in particular, this Hellenistic interest was sustained for centuries, thanks to the protection given it first by the Sassanian Persians and later by Islam until the eleventh century and the ascendancy of the Turks. Indeed it was through the Nestorians that important elements of Greek thought, namely Aristotelian, were preserved in Greek and Syrian translations to become the backbone of Persian and Islamic intellectual life. [2]

Transmissions from classical cultures to the Muslims through these channels were largely of the following seven basic types: (a) Materials directly translated from Greek into Arabic; (b) materials translated into Pahlavi, amalgamated with Zoroastrian-Hindu (Buddhist) thought, and then transmitted through translation into Arabic; (c) materials translated from Hindu to Pahlavi, then into Syriac, Hebrew, and Arabic; (d) materials written within the Islamic period by Muslims but in effect borrowed from non-Muslim sources, with the line of transmission obscure; (e) materials which were mere commentaries or summaries of Greco-Persian works; (f) materials which were advances over pre-Islamic learning, but which would not have been developed in Islam except for the pre-Islamic foundations in Hellenistic, Syrian, Zoroastrian, and Hindu learning; and (g) materials which appear to arise purely from individual genius and national or regional stimulation, which would have developed regardless of pre-Islamic learning, although the form these original creations took might have been different if they had developed in a non-Islamic context or frame of reference.

2. Another important factor lies within the conquests of Alexander the Great and his successors, who spread Greek learning into Persia and India, where Greek science and philosophy were enriched with native ideas.

3. The third important factor, and the most significant, was the Persian empire's Academy of Jundi-Shapur, which developed a curriculum of studies patterned after the University of Alexandria and during the sixth century synchronized Indian, Grecian, Syriac, Hellenistic, Hebrew, and Zoroastrian learning. Jundi-Shapur encouraged translations of significant Greek classics in science and philosophy into Pahlavi and Syriac and became, in the early centuries of Islam, the central clearing house of ancient learning, transferring it to the Muslim world and the West, until this task was taken over by Baghdad in Eastern Islam and Sicily and Cordova in Western Islam.

4. The scholarly work of the Jews was another important factor. Hebrew translators were powerful instruments of this transfer because of their skill in languages, both in early Islam, when they translated Greek works into Hebrew and Arabic, and in the thirteenth century, when they translated these and other works from Arabic into Hebrew and Latin, or into Hebrew and from Hebrew to Latin.

The Syrian-Nestorian Background

The classical writings and teachings of Greek philosophers such as Aristotle and Greek scientists such as Galen and the whole complex of neo-Platonic learning and mysticism reached the Muslims largely by way of Nestorian and Jacobite teachers, Zoroastrian scholars of the Academy of Jundi-Shapur in Khuzistan, and the pagan teachers of Harran, whose beginnings and identity remain somewhat obscure. Nestorian and Jacobite interests in Hellenistic-neo-Platonic science and philosophy were sustained more by the support that Aristotelian logic gave to the theological doctrines of these two eccentric Christian groups than by an objective and detached interest in science and philosophy as such. Says H. G. Wells:

> The Nestorian Christians . . . seem to have been much more intelligent and active-minded than the court theologians of Byzantium, and at a much higher level of general education than the Latin-speaking Christians of the West. They had been tolerated during the latter days of the Sassanids [Persians], and they were tolerated by Islam until the ascendancy of the Turks in the eleventh century. They were the intellectual backbone of the Persian world. They had preserved much of Aristotle both in Greek and in the Syrian translations. They had a considerable mathematical literature. . . .[3]

In the year 363, which ended a long and relatively useless, indecisive war between the Persian and Byzantine empires, the city of

Nisibis was handed over to the Persians as one of the conditions of peace. The School of Nisibis, the intellectual pride of that city, was as a result of this political transfer moved to Edessa within the Byzantine empire soon to become the rallying place for the Nestorian schism against the doctrinal decisions of Ephesus. But Emperor Zeno in 439 closed the School of Edessa because of its Nestorian support and forced its members, led by Barsuma, to migrate to Persia, where the Persian monarch, Piruz, guaranteed them religious and intellectual freedom and protection.[4]

The School of Nisibis was re-opened under Nestorian control, and from there a Nestorian version of Christianity spread into the Middle East. There also the Nestorians developed a unique Christian theology, emphasizing the humanity of Jesus. Translations of Greek authorities were made into Syriac to sustain Nestorian versions of Christian theology and philosophy. In this manner the works of Aristotle and the neo-Platonists were translated into Syriac, and later through Nestorian translators into Arabic to become a part of the heritage of the Muslim world. But Hellenism remained more provincial than creative in Nestorian hands, producing an extensive educational system but showing no appreciable creative development.[5] D. L. O'Leary says:

> If we regard the main test of educational efficiency as being in its research product and not simply the promulgation of material already attained, then Nestorianism was not an educational success; and it seems that this should be the supreme test, for knowledge is progressive, and so the smallest contribution toward further progress must be of more real value than the most efficient teaching of results already achieved.[6]

Whether or not we are willing to agree completely with this statement, the fact is that Nestorians as translators and transmitters became, through the Syriac versions, an important medium through which Hellenistic learning was modified and channeled to the Muslim world.

The Alexandrian Background

During the Christian centuries, before the invasion of the Persian and Byzantine world by the Muslims, Alexandria had developed into a Christianized center of Greek learning. Schoolmen, such as Paul of Aegina (flourished in 625), Alexander of Tralles (525-602), Aetios of Arnida (flourished in 550), and Theophilos Protos-Patharios, had been expositors of Greek philosophy and science, particularly mathematics and medicine. They had written commentaries on the works of Aristotle, Ptolemy, Galen, Hippocrates, Archimedes, and others. But Alexandria abounded in occultism and mysticism, lacking scientific creativity and independent philosophic inquiry. The Greek tradition of dispassionate exploration and unhampered investigation was no longer an intellectual force. This task was assumed, as already noted, by Syrian scholars in Edessa and Nisibis, and at the Academy of Jundi-Shapur under Sassanian rulers of the fourth, fifth, and sixth centuries.

THE ACADEMY OF JUNDI-SHAPUR

Before the advent of Islam, Hellenistic, Alexandrian, Syrian, and Hindu philosophy and science had spread out to the Sassanian centers of learning within the Persian empire. When the tradition of Greek education had all but faded away in Europe in the early Christian centuries, when the Academy of Athens was closed in 529 by Emperor Justinian, and when the Nestorians were being driven from cities and academies that were under orthodox Christian domination, it was in Sassanian Persia under King Anushirwan the Just that Syrian, Alexandrian, and Jewish scholars found refuge. There they preserved these traditions, improved upon and added to them, and later passed them on through Islamic scholarship to European educators. Among these Persian centers of learning were Salonika, Ctesiphon,* Nishapur, and most particularly Jundi-Shapur.

It should be borne in mind that even in the pre-Sassanian centuries Persia had acquired a wealth of the sciences of Babylonia and India and had made important advancements in areas of mathematics and music. The libraries of Zoroastrian temples included many scientific and ethical books written in the Pahlavi (Middle Persian) language, many of which were later translated into Arabic, centuries later into Latin, and still later into other important languages in Europe. The Sassanian king, Ardeshir, commissioned special experts to India, Mesopotamia, and nearby Byzantine cities to gather works of learning, an effort which was continued by his successor, Shapur. These works were translated into Pahlavi under the patronage of these kings.[7]

Some authors, such as ibn-Khaldun, go so far as to say that it was perhaps through Persia that the Greeks had learned their first lessons in science and philosophy. Dr. Thabih-Allah Safa states (using ibn al-Ibri as his authority) that Shapur, the son of Ardeshir, brought Greek physicians to Persia to study medicine. It was also under him that many Greek works were translated and preserved in the library of the Academy of Jundi-Shapur, among them works on philosophy and logic.[8]

During its early centuries, a number of eminent Persian scholars were converted to Christianity. Some of them, as Farhad (Aphraate) and Pulis Irani (Paul the Persian), achieved high ecclesiastical posi-

*Ctesiphon was built on the left bank of the Tigris, 25 miles southeast of Baghdad. The city is mentioned by Polybius as early as 220 B.C. Ctesiphon was for a time the winter residence of the Parthian Arsacids after they conquered the region in 129 B.C., until it revolted from the Parthians in the first century A.D. With the founding of the Sassanian dynasty in the next century, the city developed into a metropolis with many impressive buildings. It was captured and plundered by Arabs in 637. When Baghdad became the capital of the Abbassides, Ctesiphon died away, save for a few surviving walls and a magnificent arch.

tions within the Christian church in Persia and elsewhere. These Persian Christian converts wrote interpretive works in Syrian for Khosru Anushirwan. Many returned to their homeland toward the end of the fifth century as a result of orthodox Christian persecutions and opened schools in Persian cities. One of them, the great scholar Narsi, opened a large academy at Nisibis in 457. It was through this school, and after orthodox Christian opposition to Nestorians was wiped out by armed assistance from the Persian monarch Firuz (459-483), that Nestorianism gained strength within the Persian empire and extended its religious and educational influences as far east as Herat, Marv, and Samarkand; but the main center was Jundi-Shapur. These educational Nestorian influences were mostly in the form of Hellenistic or Hellenized Syriac translations into Pahlavi. Many Nestorian scholars attached themselves to Persian academies as teachers and translators, largely of Aristotelian (Alexandrian) works. Nestorian, Syriac, and Hellenistic influences were further advanced as Nestorian teachers founded churches and schools in various Persian cities, developing Hellenized centers of learning.[9]

One of the important centers of Nestorian-Persian learning was *Beit Ardeshir* (The House of Ardeshir), known also as ***Riv-Ardeshir,*** or ***Rishahr,*** where special attention was given to translations and interpretations of the works of Aristotle as well as works in medicine, astronomy, and other sciences. There were other similar centers of learning, such as Ctesiphon, but none reached the fame and influence of the great Academy of Jundi-Shapur to which European medieval education owes a great debt as the first important channel of preservation and eventual transmission of Hellenistic, Hindu, and Persian learning to the Western world.[10]

The Academy of Jundi-Shapur was located in the city bearing that name in southeastern Persia (actually east of Shush or Saisanna, southeast of Dizful and northwest of Shushtar) where the present village of Shah Abad is located. It was referred to by Nestorians as the *Beit Labat* (House of Learning). The Arabs later called it Jandi-Sabur, or Jundaysabur, Arabized as Gundi-Shapur.*

---

*The origin and meaning of the phrase are somewhat obscure. According to Safa, the original name of this academy and of the city in which it was located was Weh-*Andev*-Shapur, which literally means better-than-Antioch-Shapur, or the-city-of-Shapur-which-is-better-than-the-city-of-Antioch, the word *Andeve* being the Pahlavi word for Antioch. Antioch (or Antakyyah) was a model city with well-engineered, straight streets. Other cities tried to surpass Antioch in engineering and beauty, and whether or not they succeeded in doing so, they boasted of their town as better-than-Antioch. So in naming their towns, they prefaced the names with the phrase, better-than-Antioch; hence the label *weh-andev i Shapur,* or better-than-Andev, or Antioch-Shapur; later called Gundi-Shah-Pur, and finally Jundi-Shapur, or Kundi-Shapur.[11] This method of naming cities was quite in fashion among the Sassanian Persians. Another example is that of a town built by Anushirwan called *Beh-az-andiv-i-Khasra,* or the-city-of-Khasra-better-than-andiv (Antioch).[12]

The city of Jundi-Shapur was founded by Shapur I (241-271), who, according to tradition, used Roman prisoners of war to lay the foundation of the famous city. The same tradition credits Shapur I with having ordered collections of Greek scientific-philosophic works and their translations into Pahlavi for the library of Jundi-Shapur. He also made the city the center of Hellenistic medical science.

Al-Ghafti relates a tale regarding the city which is of passing interest. In the *Akhbar-al-Hukama* (*The History of Men of Learning*, Cairo, 1326 Lunar Year, p. 93), he says:

> When the daughter of Caesar travelled to that city [Jundi-Shapur] there were quite a number of artisans representing various crafts whom she brought along from her own country, and whose skills she needed. Among them were learned physicians who established themselves in that city and began to instruct students, whose number kept constantly increasing.[13]
>
> . . . When Shapur, the son of Ardeshir, won victory over Syria and Antioch, he asked to marry the daughter of the Roman emperor. The emperor obliged and agreed to send his daughter to Shapur. Shapur built a city for her designed after Constantinople and that city is Jundi-Shapur.[14]

The city was invaded several times during the reign of Shapur II (310-379), who made it his headquarters.

Jundi-Shapur, unlike Edessa, was cosmopolitan both in taste and in the range of its intellectual interests. According to one unverified tradition, it had its origins in antiquity, being first known as the *Genta Shapirta* (the Beautiful Garden). However, it assumes historic significance from the reign of Shapur I (241-271), who rebuilt the city after the sack of Antioch and the defeat of the Roman Emperor Valerian by the Persian king. Shapur I romanized the city after his marriage with Aurelian's daughter.

When the city surrendered militarily to Islamic forces in 636, the university remained undisturbed. It continued a center of learning even after Baghdad had attracted its teachers as well as its intellectual traditions to that new Islamic city. Mention of Jundi-Shapur is made by Muslim writers, such as ibn Hawqal in 976, Yaqut, the encyclopaedist (died 1228), and al-Qazwini, as late as 1340.

From 531 to 579, during the reign of Anushirwan-i-Adel (the Just), the academy reached the peak of its development, bringing together for comparison and synchronism Hindu, Greek, Judaic, Syriac, Christian, and Persian learning. It became an important medical center. The hospital attached to the medical studies of the academy became a model for many built in the subsequent centuries throughout the vast cultural empire of Islam. This medical school survived until the end of the tenth century, and from the latter half of the eighth it exerted wide influence upon the science of medicine.[15] Jurjis ibn Bakhtishu (771), dean of the Jundi-Shapur hospital, and his descendants followed a brilliant medical tradition in Baghdad for some two and a half centuries.[16]

It was perhaps through Jundi-Shapur also that Hindu literary-ethical works were translated into Pahlavi. For example, *The Fables of Bed Pai* was translated from Sanskrit into Pahlavi during Anushirwan's reign. Both the original Sanskrit version and the Pahlavi translation were lost after the work was translated from Pahlavi into Arabic under the new title, *Kalila wa-Dimna,* by ibn al-Muqaffa, himself a Persian. Most of the original Sanskrit fables have also been preserved with many additions in the Hindu work *Panchatantra.* The Arabic *Kalila wa-Dimna* was translated into some forty European and other languages, including one in Icelandic and another in Malay.

One of the astronomical works of the period of Jundi-Shapur was a novel calendar which divided the year into twelve months of thirty days and each month into two seven-day and two eight-day weeks; then five intercalary days were added at the end of the year.[17]

Jundi-Shapur's Contributions to Western Education

The Academy of Jundi-Shapur is of interest to the historian of Western as well as Muslim education for two important reasons. First, the academy became an intellectual sanctuary in the sixth century for some of the great scholars of Greece and Syria who, in association with Hindu, Jewish, Persian, and perhaps even Chinese thought, carried on important elements of scientific (especially medical) and philosophical learning of classical cultures. Out of this scholastic association of minds a scientific synchronism arose which in many ways improved upon the scientific-philosophic conclusions of the separate cultures. The intellectual center of learning, which was once in Edessa (al-Ruha) and Harran and then transferred to Nisibis, was in the first half of the sixth century centered in this academy, which became the greatest institution of higher learning in the world.[18] In translating great scientific works, such as medical, mathematical, and astronomical works from Hindu and Greek into Pahlavi and Syriac (Aramaic) and by employing notable Syrian, Jewish, and Persian scholars and linguists to translate these works, the academy carried on, preserved, and improved upon these traditions.

The Greek teachers, who left the academy in Athens in 529, were Justinianos, Athenius, Proclus, Damascius, Simplicius, Eulamius, Priscianus, Diogenes, Isidorus. Among these, Priscianus was the monarch Anushirwan's favorite, with whom he carried on many inquiries in questions and answers. A partial translation of their Pahlavi original is preserved to the present day. The work contains discussions on psychology, care of the body, natural philosophy, astronomy, and natural history. An essay by Damascius has also survived.

Some interesting facts about the teachers of the Academy of Athens who taught briefly at Jundi-Shapur may be noted here.[19]

Damascius, formerly the head of the Academy of Athens from 511 until it was closed in 529, stayed at Jundi-Shapur from 531 to 533. He was a disciple of Proclus and author of a highly controversial work (*First Principles*), a biography of Isidorus, and some commentaries on Plato. Some have also ascribed to him the *Fifteenth Book of Euclid.*[20]

Simplicius, born in Sicilia, lived in Athens until 529 and stayed at Jundi-Shapur until 533. He was a student of Damascius and Anirnonius. He wrote several books on Aristotle, mostly commentaries, and a *Commentary on Book I of Euclid.* He was also a creative philosopher in his own right, explaining "the stability of the celestial bodies by the excess of their impetus over their gravity."[21]

Priscianus of Lydia remained at Jundi-Shapur until 533. Khosru Anushirwan engaged him in many discussions on philosophical questions, which are preserved as a collection of the philosopher's answers to the king's questions. Priscianus also wrote a commentary on Theophrastus' work on the senses. Unfortunately, his original *Greek Collection of Answers* is lost; however, a Latin translation of it appeared in the ninth century, ascribed to the philosopher John Scotus Erigena, known as *Solutiones Eorum de Quibus dubitavit Chosroes Persarum rex.*

Another Greek physician, Theodorus, lived from 309 to 379 in the Persia of Shapur II. He wrote a compendium of medicine in Pahlavi, which was translated later into Arabic and mentioned in ibn al-Nadim's *Al-Fihrist.*[22]

Anushirwan also welcomed scholar-refugees, mainly Nestorians from Edessa, who found Jundi-Shapur a cosmopolitan center of learning. During his reign (531-579), he encouraged Nestorians and neo-Platonists to use Syrian translations of Greek works in Jundi-Shapur and had Persian translations of the Syrian versions of Plato and Aristotle made under his personal supervision.

So great was Jundi-Shapur as a center of scholarship in philosophy, mathematics, astronomy, and medicine that after the Muslim conquest of Persia in the seventh century the academy flourished as an extensive intellectual reservoir having much influence on Islamic learning until the early eleventh century.[23]

The second reason for the interest of the historian of education in the Academy of Jundi-Shapur is that it continued as the scientific center of Islam throughout the Umayyad period (661-749). From this academy scholars, educators, and physicians went to the then Muslim capital, Damascus, and gave to Islam its first acquaintance with classical cultures. From it, or its alumni, the first Hindu, Persian, Syrian, and Greek works began to be translated into Arabic, a tradition which was transferred at the rise of the Abbassides in Eastern Islam about 750 to the new Muslim capital in Baghdad, where Islamic education and scholarship attained their highest peak. And to the extent that this new learning, this renaissance of translation, assimilation, and creative improvements and additions to the prevailing knowledge can be shown to have been stimulated and furthered by the example and contributions of the scholars of Jundi-Shapur, to that extent its importance for historians of Western education should be obvious. For Muslim scholarship preserved and enriched classical education and scholarship (mainly Greek, Syrian, Persian, and even Hindu) and transmitted it to Western schoolmen through Latin and Hebrew translations of Arabic works.

Insofar as the initial contributions of Jundi-Shapur are concerned, it is important to record that translations of Greek (and Hindu) classics into Arabic were resumed during the rule of the second Abbasside Caliph al-Mansur (754-775), mainly at the Academy of Jundi-Shapur. It was from the academy's famous hospital that Bakh-Tishu, its chief physician and dean, was summoned in 771 to the court of Abbasside Caliph al-Hadi (died 786) and the great Harun-al-Rashid (died 809).[24]

Bakh-Tishu is essential in any educational assessment of Jundi-Shapur because this Christian doctor's family produced distinguished physician-scholars for Islam for better than seven generations. It was through this family that the tradition of Greco-Persian-Hindu medical knowledge was conveyed to Islam, to be enriched and extended by its own scholars (mostly Persians, such as al-Razi from Rayy, Avicenna from Hamadan, and Haly Abbas the Magician) before its transmission to Europe.

The Academy of Jundi-Shapur disappeared as the center of intellectual influence in Islam in the late 880's, as scientific works which predominated in the Syriac and Pahlavi languages in the first half of that century gave way to more advanced scholarship in Baghdad and Samarra and still later to renewed Umayyad scholarship in Cordova and other Spanish and Sicilian academic communities.

During this long period of translation, which ended more or less about 900 A.D., Muslim science, particularly medicine, though both extensive in scope and intensive in substance, was founded nonetheless firmly upon Greek science and Persian and Indian thought and "experience." It produced great works formidable in scholarship but on the whole lacking originality. From the tenth century, however, Islam begins to rely more upon its own resources and to "develop from within" until the twelfth century. The sciences, particularly medicine, now pass rapidly from the hands of Christians and Sabians into the possession of Muslim scholars, mostly Persians.[25]

Elgood states in *The Legacy of Persia* that the first academic language employed in the hospital, medical school, and university of Jundi-Shapur was probably Sanskrit, and that Hindu medical knowledge flourished there until after 439, when the school of Edessa (al-Ruha) was closed in 439, bringing a large influx of Greek and Syrian teachers to the Persian scholastic center. The student of medical education interested in the traditions of his discipline would find the medical theory and practice at Jundi-Shapur hospital and school of medicine an interesting and important link in the chain of Greco-Hindu and Perso-Islamic medical innovations and development and the contributions of this medical synchronism at Jundi-Shapur to the development of medical education in both Eastern Islam and the West.

Buzurjmihr, the great court physician of Anushirwan the Just and tutor of his son, Hormuz, known to Western writers as Perzoes, was also one of the significant contributors to the medical school of Jundi-Shapur. On orders of the monarch, he went to India to secure a copy of the famed *Fables of Bed Pai.* Of special interest to the historian of education is the autobiography of Perzoes reproduced in the introduction of ibn al-Muqaffa's translation of the *Fables.*

A further incident may throw some light on the cosmopolitanism of Jundi-Shapur's medical school. Another royal physician of the court of Anushirwan, one Irian Durustpat, a Nestorian (and later Monophysite) Christian, also known as Jibra'il (Gabriel), is said to have cured the monarch's Christian wife, the favorite Shirin (Sweet), of sterility, and after Shirin bore a male child Jibra'il used his influence with the king to meddle in Nestorian church affairs.

TRANSLATIONS OF CLASSICAL WORKS INTO ARABIC

The Sassanian kings were patrons of learning. Even before them, the Hakhaminians had facilitated the assimilation and adaptation of Babylonian and Indian sciences—particularly mathematics, astronomy, and music – as well as the intellectual heritage of other Eastern cultures. However, Sassanian monarchs were more deliberate and systematic in their efforts to advance learning within their domains. Ardeshir Papakan, for example, sent learned men to India and the Roman Empire to procure scientific and philosophic works. He subsequently ordered their translation into Pahlavi, a task which was continued by his son, Shapur. Masudi concurs that the Persians were acquainted with some of the Greek philosophies and religions through similar communications with them.[26] Shapur himself, according to ibn al-Ibri, brought Greek physicians to his court to teach him medicine, perhaps at Jundi-Shapur, and ordered translations of Greek medical and other works into Pahlavi.[27]

In the fifth and sixth centuries many Zoroastrian scholars, who had adopted the Christian faith, kept Grecian science and philosophy alive in Sassanian and Syrian schools, particularly in the Persian school at Edessa. Among them were Farhad (Aphraate), who wrote in Syriac; Maraba the First, a Zoroastrian who, after adopting Christianity in 536, remained active in the Christian church; Paul (Paulus) the Persian of Nisibis, who wrote a book on Aristotelian logic in Syriac for Anushirwan. When the Persian school at Ruha was closed in 489, many of its scholars returned to Persia. They opened new schools within the Sassanian empire, advancing Greek (Aristotelian) and particularly Syrian philosophy and science and making new translations of them in

Pahlavi.[28] All these resulted in new institutions of learning in important Persian cities, such as Jundi-Shapur. Outstanding among these new schools was Beit Ardeshir (Riv-Ardeshir, or Rishahr), whose dean's (Maana Beit Ardeshiri, a native of Shiraz) translations of Syrian works were known even in India.[29] According to Yaqut, the historian, Maana's school developed into a prominent center of Hellenistic, Syrian, and Zoroastrian scholarship. Another such school opened near Ctesiphon with Maraba as its dean.

There is no doubt, however, that the focal point of Sassanian learning, insofar as Western education is concerned, was the Academy of Jundi-Shapur. It should be apparent that, prior to the advent of Islam, Sassanian education had achieved a high degree of maturity. There were important schools all over the empire; great teachers had established them or had been attracted to them. These were centers of translation of Greek and Hindu works of science and philosophy into Pahlavi, and it was also from these schools that some of the most important translations of Sanskrit, Pahlavi, Syrian, and Greek into Arabic emerged.

Most famous and productive among these Persian translators were the following:

George the son of Bakh-Tishu and his family of translators;[30] Abu Zakariyya Yuhanna ibn Musa, a physician of Jundi-Shapur who, during and following the reign of Harun al-Rashid, made important translations in Baghdad as head of the Dar al-Hikmah (the House of Learning);[31] Rabban al-Tabari of Marv (also called Sahl al-Tabari), who translated the Almagest into Arabic for the first time;[32] ibn al-Muqaffa, translator of Pahlavi works into Arabic;[33] Naubakht of Ahwaz, translator of Pahlavi mathematical works into Arabic;[34] Abu Sahl Khorshaz-Mah, translator of mathematical works into Arabic; Abu Hafz Umar ibn Farrukhan al-Tabari, head of a school of translators;[35] Ibrahim ibn Habib-al-Fazari, translator of the famous fifth century Hindu mathematical works (*Siddhanta*)—completed, according to Biruni, in 770-71;[36] Muhammad al-Fazari Ibrahim's son, translator of mathematical works from Indian into Arabic, including parts of the *Siddhanta*;[37] Musa ibn Khalid the Tarjuman (or "the great translator"), who translated Pahlavi and Greek works into Arabic, including Hunayn's Syrian version of Galen's works;[38] Isa Ben Chahar Bokht (or Sahar Bokht [meaning *Four Fortunes*]) of Jundi-Shapur, who also translated Galen into Arabic; Yusuf (Joseph al-Naqil), "The Story Teller" of Khuzistan, who made medical translations into Arabic; Ali ibn Ziad al-Tamimi, translator of mathematical works from Pahlavi into Arabic;[39] Istiphan al-Qadim, translator of works on chemistry at request of Khalid ibn Yazid ibn Muawiya (850); Maserjis, translator of the works of Aaron of Alexandria.

Abu Yahya al-Batriq translated Greek medical and philosophical works, particularly those of Aristotle and Hippocrates. His *Serrul Asrar (Secret of Secrets)* is an Aristotelian work on administration of government. This work, better known as *Secretum Secretorum,* he translated into Syriac at the beginning of the ninth century. Another translation of this work into Hebrew was made by Judab al-Harizi.[40] His translation of Ptolemy's *Quadripartium* is equally important. He was employed by al-Mansur to carry on the tasks of translation. His treatise on *Death* by Hippocrates and his *Meteorology* of Aristotle are among his basic translations.[41]

Hunain ibn Is'haq (died 264) was the greatest of all translators of classical works into Arabic. Among his translations were *Timaeus* of Plato; *Story of Sahlman and Isaal; The Aphorisms;* the important works of Galen; *Prognostics* and *On the Nature of Man* as well as other works of Hippocrates.[42]

Ghasta ibn Luka (Luke) al-Ba'labaki was another translator of Greek medical and mathematical works.[43] Among them were studies by Diophantus, Theodosius, Autolycus, Hypsicles, Aristarchus, and Heron. Later other translations were made into Spanish and Latin by Stephen Arnaldus.

Hubaish ibn-al-Hasan al-A'asam al-Damashqi translated Syrian and Greek works (Galenic) in medicine.[44] In addition to these, he completed a *Quaestiones Medicales* of Hunain.[45]

Thabit ibn Qurra al-Harrani (826-900) of Harran made many translations of Greek works on medicine and mathematics,[46] including the works of Apollonius, Archimedes, Euclid, Theodosius, Ptolemy, Galen, and Eutocius. The founder of a school of translators, he published solar observations and works on mathematics and anatomical and medical materials, and on astronomy.[47] Still other translators are Istiphan ibn Basil, a student of Hunain ibn Is'haq, translator of Greek medical books (Galenic works); Kanka the Hindu, translator of Hindu mathematical and medical works in the latter part of the eighth century and the first decades of the ninth; ibn Dehn, also from India, who made translations of Hindu medical works;[48] Theophilus of Edessa (known also as ibn Thuma and as Thomas of Edessa; died 785) who translated one of Galen's works into Syriac and perhaps some Greek or Syrian into Arabic;[49] ibn al-Tabari, a Jewish scholar from Tabaristan and one of the greatest theologian-scholars of the late decades of the eighth century and the early decades of the ninth who translated many books on medicine and mathematics from Syrian and Greek into Arabic;[50] Abu Zakariyya Yuhanna (or Yahya) ibn-al-Batriq, translator of medical and philosophical works during the reign of Caliph Ma'mun (813-833), including translations from Hippocrates and Alexander Tralles;[51] Hajjaj ibn Yusuf ibn Matr (or Matar) who made mathematical translations from Euclid during the reign of Harun-al-Rashid and Ma'mun; Isa ibn Asid al-Nasrani, a pupil of Thabit ibn Qurra, who made translations from Syrian into Arabic; Abu Is'haq Ibrahim al-Ghuwairi, who wrote commentaries in Arabic on Aristotle; Hilal ibn Abi Hilal al-Himsi, translator of the first four books of Apollonius from Greek into Arabic for Ahmad ibn Musa ibn Shakir; Isa ibn Yahya ibn Ibrahim, who translated various Galenic works, made a partial translation of Aribasius, and wrote some original medical works; Qawam-al-din (al-Fat'h ibn Ali ibn al-Fat'h al-Isfahani), who translated the *Shah Namah* of Firdawsi into Arabic for al-Mu'azzam, the Ayyubid ruler of Damascus (1218-1227); Yusuf al-Khuri, who translated Archimedes' lost work on triangles and Galen's *De Simplicium Temperamentis et Facultatibus* from Syriac versions into Arabic; ibn Sahda, translator of *De sectis* and *De Pulsibus Aditirones* into Syriac.

Other ninth- and tenth-century translators were* Zurba ibn Majuh al-Na'ami al-Himsi, Halal ibn Abi Halal al-Himsi, Abu al-Fath Isfahani (mathematics), Fethyun (or Fethum) al-Tarjuman, Abu Hasrawi (Kasrawi?) ibn Ayyub, Basil al-Mutran, Hairun (or Jairun) ibn Rabetch, Tazars' al-Sanghal, Abu Yusuf al-Katib (translations from Hippocrates), Gatha al-Rahawi, Mansur ibn Banas, Abdishu ibn Bahriq Mutram, Salam al-Abrash (translated some works from Aristotle), Ayyub, Sam'an, Abu Ruh al-Sabi (translated works from Aristotle), Abu Umar Yuhanna ibn Yusuf (translated from Plato), Ayyub ibn al-Qasim al-Rahhi (trans-

*The following Hellenistic authors were translated into Arabic during this period: Alexander of Aphrodisias, and Alexander of Tralles, Anazarbas, Apollonius, Archigenes, Archimedes, Aristarchus, Aristotle, Asclepius, Autolycus, Damascius of Damascus, Diophantus, Dracon, Erophile, Erasistratus, Euclid, Eudemus, Eutocius of Ascalon, Galen, Gregory of Nysse, Hipparchus, Heron of Alexandria, Hippocrates, Iambilichus, Jasides, Claudius of Alexandria, Theodosius, Theon of Alexandria, Theophrastus, and Thessalus.

lated *Isagogue* from Syrian into Arabic), Marlahi,[52] Abu Suhail Vikan ibn Rustam al-Kuhi, and Abdullah ibn Ali (translated the Hindu *Book of Sirak* into both Pahlavi and Arabic).[53]

TRANSLATIONS OF PERSIAN WORKS

It was first in Jundi-Shapur and later in Baghdad under al-Ma'mun and others that translations of many Persian scientific, moral, historical, and proverbial treatises were made into Arabic, which ultimately were transmitted through the Arabs to the Western world as part of the heritage of Western education.

Among the early patrons of Persian and other non-Arabic learning in Islam was the Shu'ubiya Party (the "Partisan of the Gentiles"), a society of many diverse peoples who combined their efforts in loosening the fibers of Arabian political and cultural supremacy in the Muslim world by reviving ancient cultures and standards. Although their chief war cry was *back to the Persian,* there were among the Shu'ubiya Party many Jews, Egyptians, Greeks, and even Spaniards. The society had many opponents, primarily the Arabs. Baghdad was the center of the Shu'ubiya activities, and their principal objectives were to demonstrate how much the Arab-Muslim culture owed to the contributions made to it by other races and nations, particularly to Persian models, and the Shu'ubi writers, with the Zoroastrian priest as their source of information. It was in him that the best of Iranian culture was preserved. Thus the Shu'ubiya Party promoted learning and played a vital role in the development of Muslim education.

In the last half of the tenth century, this zeal for Iranian revival was dimmed because of political disturbances, but the literary materials which the Shu'ubiya Party produced were preserved for a later renaissance. Translations were made into Arabic from Parsi sources by older circles of Muslim civilization sympathetic to Persian culture.

Some of the Persian educational writings of this century and the next which were either translated into Arabic or written in that language are the following:

Adab-al-Arab-i Wal-Ajam (*The Manners of the Arabs and the Ajam;* i.e., Persians). The works of the tenth and eleventh centuries contain a list entitled *The Manners of the Arabs and the Persians,* written by ibn Mushkuya, a Persian philosophical writer who was the treasurer and a close friend of the Buide Adud al-Dawla. Ibn Mushkuya used as the source of his work the three Persian treatises on manners called *Javidani Khirad* (*Eternal Wisdom*), *Pand-Namah* (*The Book of Advice*), and *Andarz* (*Advice*). In this period there were other works of this character such as maxims, proverbs, fables, morals, and the like.

Ibn al-Muqaffa, another great translator of Persian works into Arabic, whose important translation was the famous *Kalila wa-Dimna,* which introduced this set of Eastern stories to the Western world. (Of this book and the *Arabian Nights,* we shall speak later.) He translated also into Arabic other Persian works, written on the basis of Persian sources, such as: *Khudai Namah* (the official chronicle of Sassanian times), *Ain Namah* (the institutes of the time), *The Book of Mazdak, Book of Taj* (political), two books on *Adab* (manners), and *Al Yatima* (on morals in politics of the Sassanians).

Aban al-Lahiki, a poet who versified many Persian works into Arabic—for example, *Kalila wa-Dimna, The Book of Barlaam and Josaphat, The Book of Sindbad, The Book of Mazdak, The Book of the Acts of Ardeshir,* and *The Book of the Acts of Anushirwan.*

Taifur (Ahmad ibn Tabir Taifur) who wrote a treatise entitled *Book of Hormoz, Son of Kisra Anushirwan,* a Persian Sassanian emperor.

The family of Naubakht. Naubakht was Persia's leading astronomer of his time, and his son and grandson followed him in the profession with books on astronomy and jurisprudence.

Musa and Yusuf, brothers, sons of Khalid, who wrote treatises on astronomy.

Baladhuri, translator of the *Book of the Counsel of Ardeshir.*

Jabala ibn Salem, who wrote the book of *Rustam and Isphandyar* and translated the Persian history, *Khoday Namah.*

Tamimi (Abu al-Hasan Ali ibn Ziad), translator of *Zick al-Shahriyarvi* (*The Tables of Shahryar* [the king]).

Al Farrukhan (Omar ibn), who lived at the time of al-Ma'mun and Jafar Barmaki and was in close association with them. He translated *Kitab al-Mahasin* (*Book of Good Manners*). Others followed his example and wrote similar books, such as *Kitab al-Mahasin* (*Book of Good Manners*) by ibn Qutaiba, *Kitab Mahasin al-Akhlagh* (*Book of Good Morals*) by al-Ayashi, *Kitab al-Mahasin* (*Book of Good Manners*) by ibn al Hazm, *Kitab Mahasin Wal Masawi* (*Book of Good Manners and Their Likes*) by al Baihaqi, and *Kitab Mahasin Wal Azdad* (*Book of Good Manners and Their Opposites*) by Jahiz.

Is'haq ibn Yazid, translator of the *Khudai Namah.*

EXTANT TRANSLATIONS IN PRIVATE AND PUBLIC LIBRARIES

Probably the greatest translator of classical works, mainly Hellenistic, into Arabic, was Hunain ibn Is'haq,* whose translations are, per-

*Ibn al-Nadim considers ibn Luka (Ghasta ibn Luka al-Ba'labaki) as equal to, if not greater than, Hunain. Al-Nadim states in *Al-Fihrist:* "It was necessary to give priority to him [ibn Luka] because of his erudition, exalted position, and precedence to Hunain in the art of medicine, though some of my friends have urged me to give precedence to Hunain. Both of these are learned men. And Ghasta [ibn Luka] translated parts of ancient books, and he was accomplished in many fields of learning, among them medicine, philosophy, geometry, mathematics and music."[54]

haps, equal in importance and influence to Gerard of Cremona's translations of Arabic works into Latin during the second half of the twelfth century. Gerard, to be sure, was head of a school of translators, supervising and editing most of the translations, although, as we shall note later, he did a large number of them himself. Hunain's works of translation were carried on, on the other hand, by his son Is'haq ibn Hunain and the disciples of the latter and his father.

Of Hunain ibn Is'haq's translations which have survived, forty are listed by Safa, of which the following is a brief summary, with the libraries indicated in which these works may be located:

On Distinction Between Matter and Genus [Species] of Porphyry of Aphrodisias (No. 794 Escorial Library).[55]

Timaeus of Plato (No. 1933, Asad Effendi Collection of Arabic hand works, Constantinople).[56]

The Summaries [*Jawami,* or *Collected Statements*] of Aristotle's *Metaphysics [Athar al-Alawiyya* or *Heavenly Vestiges-Bodies]* (No. 153, Library, Ahmadiyya School, Mosul).[57]

Salaman and Ibsal (No. 14540,a,44, British Museum).[58]

On Spiritual Influences [*Fi Ta'sir al-Ruhaniyyat*] *of Pliny* (Asad Effendi Library).[59]

The Prognostics [Taghaddamat-al-Ma'rifa] of Hippocrates (Nos. 2835 and 2844, Paris; also at Aya Sufiyya Library; Nos. 1182 and 6227, Berlin Library; No. 152, Ahmadiyya).[60]

On Human Nature [Tahi-at-al-Insan] of Hippocrates (No. 2844, Paris; No. 6230, Berlin).[61]

Al-Kasr Wal Jabr of Hippocrates (Paris and Berlin).[62]

The Quadripartitum of Hippocrates (Paris and Berlin).[63]

The Aphorisms of Hippocrates (Berlin, Paris, British Museum).[64]

Al-Risalat-al-Ghabriyya of Hipprocates (No. 646, British Museum).[65]

Kitab al-Akhlat of Hippocrates (No. 277, Vol. iii, Meshed Library).[66]

Kitab al-Asabi [Septenaires] of Hippocrates as Interpreted by Galen (Paris and Munich).[67]

The Epidemics of Hippocrates as Interpreted by Galen (Paris and Milan).[68]

The Book of Water and Air [Risalat al-Ma'a Wal Hawa] (No. 4838, Aya Sufiyya).[69]

Amrath al-Haddeh of Hippocrates (No. 4838, Aya Sufiyya).[70]

Fargh al-Talat of Galen (No. 521, Madjlis Library, Teheran; Nos. 2859 and 2860, Paris; and Aya Sufiyya).[71]

Kitab al-Sanat al-Safhira of Galen [Medical Arts] (No. 521, Madjlis; No. 2860, Paris).[72]

Book of Pulse [Kitab al-Nabth] of Galen (No. 521, Madjlis; No. 2860, Paris).[73]

The Book of Galen (No. 521, Madjlis; No. 2860, Paris).[74]

The Book of the Elements [Al-Istiqsat] of Hippocrates from Galen's Sixteen Collections (Nos. 513 and 2847, Paris).[75]

The Book of Physical Health [Al-Mezaj] of Galen's Sixteen Collections (No. 2837, Paris).[76]

Galen's Seven Discourses [Commentaries] on Hippocrates (No. 2837, Paris).[77]

On Anatomy [De Anatomicis] of Galen's Sixteen (The Greek copy is lost). (No. 2851, Paris.)[78]

On Names of Bodily Organs [The Jawami al-Iskandaraniyyin] (Berlin).[79]

The Grand Method [Al-Sanat al-Kabira] of Galen's Sixteen (No. 2855, Paris).[80]

On Diseases and Symptoms [Al-Elal wal-Aaraath] of Galen (No. 2859, Paris).[81]

On Regulations of Health [Tadbeer-al-As-ha] of Galen's Sixteen (Aya Sufiyya).[82]

Kitab al-Sana [Medical Art] of Galen's Sixteen (Aya Sufiyya).[83]

Kitab al-Qawiyya-al-tabi'iyyah [Natural Faculties or Powers] of Galen's Sixteen (No. 6235, Berlin).[84]

On Types of Fevers [Kitab Asnaf al-Hamyat] of Galen's Sixteen (No. 6235, Berlin).[85]

The Five Discourses [Al-Maghalat al-Khams] of Galen's Sixteen (No. 6233 pm. 521, Berlin).[86]

The Major Book on Pulse [Kitab Nabq al-Kabir] of Galen's Sixteen (Aya Sufiyya).[87]

Book of Crisis [Kitab al-Buhran] of Galen's Sixteen (Aya Sufiyya).[88]

Kitab Ayyam al-Buhran [On Depressed Days] of Galen's Sixteen (Aya Sufiyya).[89]

On Description [Explanation] of Galen's Works.[90]

On Stars of Galen [Afthal al-Haiat] (No. 4838, Aya Sufiyya).[91]

On Pure Drugs [Kitab al-Adwiyyat-al-Mufrada] (No. 3572 and 4838, Aya Sufiyya).[92]

Book of Antidotes [Kitab al-Tiryagh] of Galen.[93]

Kitab al-Aatha-al-Alima [The Book of Types of Diseases] (Aya Sufiyya).[94]

Others whose extant translations are listed include the following (the number of works appears in parentheses): ibn al-Muqaffa (4), Abu Yahya al-Batriq (1), ibn al-Batriq (2), Is'haq ibn Hunain (11), Ghasta ibn Luka (7), Hubaish ibn al-Hasan-al-Aasani (5), Isa ibn Yahya (2), Hajjaj ibn Yusuf ibn Metran (2), Thabit ibn Qurra-al-Harrani (15), Abu Uthman Sa'id ibn Yaqub al-Damashqi (19), Istiphan ibn Basil (1), Astath (2), Abd al-Masih ibn Abdullah-al-Hams an-Na'imi (ibn Na'ima) (2), Abu Bashar Mala ibn Yunus al-Ghana'i (3), Abu Zakariyya Yahya ibn Ada (1), ibn Zara (1), Nadhif al-Ghas-al-Rumi (1), ibn Wah-Shiyijat-al-Kaldani (2), Hilal ibn Abi Hilal-al-Himsi (1), Basil al-Mitran (1), Tadhars al-Sanghal (al-Tathari) (1), Ibrahim ibn Abdullah-al-Nasrani al-Katib (2), Is'haq ibn Abi al-Hasan ibn Ibrahim (1), Sirjis (Sirgius) ibn Hulya (Elia) al-Rumi (1), Isa ibn Ibrahim al-Basri (1), Ahmad ibn Yusuf al-Misri al-Muhandis (1). These translations include the works of Aristotle (or Aristotelian) (12), Alexander of Aphrodisias (11), Euclid (4), Archimedes (of Syracuse) (4), Aristarchus (of Samos) (1), Theodosius (1), Ptolemy (of Alexandria) (3), Hippocrates (19), Meghnis al-Hamsi (Magnes, pupil of Hippocrates) (1), and Galen (in addition to others listed above) (5).[95]

AL-FIHRIST OF IBN AL-NADIM

From a historical point of view *Al-Fihrist* of Muhammad ibn Is'haq al-Nadim, better known as the *Index of Nadim,* is one of the most important documents in Islamic culture. Much of our knowledge of Islamic learning, both in translations of classical works into Arabic and in creative books, to the last decade of the tenth century, is based on information available in the *Index.* It is unfortunate for the English-speaking world that the *Index* is not as yet translated into English.

In the preface to the work al-Nadim describes the contents of his enormous undertaking as follows:

This is the Index of the books of all peoples Arabs and non-Arabs whereof somewhat exists in the language and script of the Arabs, on all branches of knowledge; together with accounts of their compilers and the classes of their authors, and the genealogies of these, the dates of their births, extent of their lives, the times of their deaths, the location of their countries, *and their virtues and vices,* from the time when each science was first discovered until this our age, to wit the year three hundred and seventy-seven of the Flight [987].[96]

It is a sad commentary on human disregard and intolerance of learning to note, as Browne says,

that sources of knowledge at once so numerous and so precious as were available when [al-Nadim] wrote should, for the most part, have entirely perished. Of authors who are known to us only by a few small fragments, he enumerates scores of works, but even these are the fortunate few, for the majority are known to us only or chiefly by his notices.[97]

The work of al-Nadim, compiled in Arabic, has fortunately survived to the present day and should be of interest to the student of history of education, if for no other reason, certainly for showing the extent and depth of scholarship, the variety of subjects, and the areas of knowledge, such as existed among the Muslims of the tenth and eleventh centuries of the Christian era and were available to students and scholars within and outside of the schools.

THE CONTENTS OF AL-FIHRIST

The following translation of the main divisions of the contents of the book shows the scope of the work:

First Discourse

Section i. Description of the languages of the different peoples, Arab and non-Arab, the characteristics of their writings, the varieties of their scripts, and the forms of their written character.

Section ii. On the names of the Books of the Law the Scriptures revealed to the different sects of Muslims, Jews, Christians, and Sabians and the different sects of those who follow them.

Section iii. Description of the Book "which falsehood approacheth not from before nor from behind, a Revelation from One Wise and Laudable" and the names of the books composed on the sciences connected therewith, with notices of the Readers, and the names of those who handed down their traditions, and the anomalies of their readings.[98]

Second Discourse on Grammarians and Philologists

Section i. On the origin of Grammar, with accounts of the Grammarians of the School of Basra, and the Stylists of the Arabs, and the names of their books.

Section ii. Account of the Grammarians and Philologists of the School of Kufa, and the names of their books.

Section iii. Account of a school of Grammarians who strove to combine the views of the two schools [above-mentioned] and the names of their books.

Third Discourse on History, Belles Lettres, Biography, and Genealogies

Section i. Account of the Historians, Narrators, Genealogists, Biographers and Chroniclers, and the names of their books.

Section ii. Account of the Kings, Secretaries, Preachers, Ambassadors, Chancellors, and Government Officials [who composed books], and the names of their books.

Section iii. Account of the Courtiers, Favourites, Minstrels, Jesters, and Buffoons [who composed books], and the names of their books.

Fourth Discourse on Poetry and Poets

Section i. On the groups of the Heathen Poets, and such of the Muslim poets as reached back to the Pagan Period [of the Arabs], and of those who collected their diwans (complete works), and the names of those who handed down their poems [till they were collected and edited].

Section ii. On the groups of the Muslim Poets, including the modern poets down to this our time.

Fifth Discourse on the Scholastic Philosophy and the Schoolmen

Section i. On the origin of the Scholastic Philosophy, and of the Schoolmen of the Mu'tazilites and Murjites, and the names of their books.

Section ii. Account of the Schoolmen of the Shi'ites, whether Imamis, Zaydis, or other of the Extremists [Ghulat] and Isma'ilis, and the names of their books.

Section iii. On the Schoolmen of the Predestinarians and the Hashwiyya, and the names of their books.

Section iv. Account of the Schoolmen of the Kharijites, their classes, and the names of their books.

Section v. Account of the wandering mendicants, recluses, devotees, and Sufis, who taught a scholastic philosophy based on their fancies and reveries, and the names of their books.

Sixth Discourse on Jurisprudence, and the Jurisconsults and Traditionists

Section i. Account of Malik and his disciples, and the names of their books.

Section ii. Account of Abu Hanifa al-Nu'man and his disciples, and the names of their books.

Section iii. Account of the Iman al-Shafi'i and his disciples, and the names of their books.

Section iv. Account of Da'ud 'Ali . . . ibn Khalaf al-Isfahani and his disciples, and the names of their books.

Section v. Account of the Shi'ite Jurisconsults, and the names of their books.

Section vi. Account of the Jurisconsults who were at the same time Traditionists and transmitters of Tradition, and the names of their books.

Section vii. Account of Abu Ja'far al-Tabari and his disciples, and the names of their books.

Section viii. Account of Jurisconsults and the names of their books.

Seventh Discourse on Philosophy and the Ancient Sciences

Section i. Account of the Materialist Philosophers and the Logicians, and the names of their books and their versions and commentaries of these, such as still exist, such as are mentioned but are no longer extant, and such as were extant but are now lost.

Section ii. Account of the Mathematicians, Geometricians, Arithmeticians, Musicians, Accountants, and Astronomers, and the makers of scientific instruments, and the Mechanics and Engineers.

Section iii. On the origins of Medicine, with accounts of the Physicians amongst the Ancients and the Moderns, and the names of their books, with their versions and commentaries.

Eighth Discourse on Legends, Fables, Charms, Magic, and Conjuring

Section i. Account of the Story-tellers, Saga-men and Artists, and the names of the books composed on Legends and Fables.

Section ii. Account of the Charm-mongers, Conjurors and Magicians, and the names of their books.

Section iii. On books composed on divers other topics, whereof the authors and compilers are unknown.

Ninth Discourse on Sects and Creeds

Section i. Description of the Sects of the Harranian Chaldaeans, called in our time Sabians, and the Sects of Dualists, Manichaeans, Bardesanians, Khurramis, Marcionites, Mazdakites, and others, and the names of their books.

Section ii. Description of sundry strange and curious sects, such as those of India and China, and others of other like peoples.

Tenth Discourse

Containing accounts of the Alchemists and seekers after the Philosopher's Stone amongst the Ancient and Modern Philosophers, and the names of their books.[99]

AL-FIHRIST'S LIST OF PERSIAN BOOKS

The translations of educational books from Persian into Arabic were mostly of a technical nature. They were, according to *Al-Fihrist,* books on warfare, on divination, on horse-breeding, on the training of other animals, on birds, on literature and history. There were also books of epic-historical content, such as the *Story of Bahram Gor,* writings on local history, tales and stories, *Hazar Afsana* used as source of *Arabian Nights,* Epic Tales of Western Persia, Stories of the Babylonian Kingdom, ethico-didactic works, the Pahlavi translation of *Kalila wa-Dimna, Hazar Afshan,* and books on good manners (*Adab*).*

---

*Out of a list of forty-four books in *Al-Fihrist* on this subject which are of Persian, Greek, Indian, and Arabic sources, fourteen are distinctly Persian. Of the remaining thirty, eleven belonged to Muslim periods but were written under Persian influences. Of the remaining nineteen, some were still of Persian origin, such as one written on "house building," and another on "good behavior," the book of the *Refutation of the Zandiqs* (dualists), book of the *Council of the Ancient Kings,* book of the *Questions to Certain Wise Men and Their Answers,* a book on ethico-didactics written by a Christian but drawn from Persian sources, and another by the author of *Al-Fihrist* on "classes." The remaining are of an anecdotal and didactic character, which were transmitted from Indian through Pahlavi literature into Arabic, such as *The Story of Despair and Hope, The Book of Hearing and Judgment, The Book of the Two Indians,* and the *Book of The Philosopher and His Experience with His Slave Girl Kaytar.* The first fourteen, which were distinctly Persian, were as follows: 1. Zadal Farrokh, a testament to his son; 2. Al-Mohedan; 3. Book of the testament of Khosro to his son Hormozd (still extant); 4. *Book of Counsels* of Kisra King Anushirwan to his son; 5. *Kisra* (a book similar to the one above); 6. *Book of Counsels* of Ardeshir Babakan to his son Shabur (Baladhuri made a verse translation of this book into Arabic); 7. A book of Mohedan Mobed (the high priest); 8. The correspondence between Kisra and Marzaban; 9 and 10. Books of questions directed from the emperor of Rome to Anushirwan and to another Persian emperor; 11. The order of Ardeshir for bringing out from the treasury books written by wise men on government; 12. Correspondence of a certain Kisra Anushirwan; 13. A book on gratitude written to a certain Kisra for public benefit; 14. A book of stories and anecdotes.[99] Refer to Appendix III for additional materials on *Al-Fihrist.*

We shall have occasion to refer to the labors of these translators of classical works into Arabic when we take up a brief survey of the creative centuries of Muslim learning, from the ninth century through the thirteenth, particularly through the ninth century and the first half of the tenth, when translations of classical works, or new translations of them, continued to appear, done by Muslim scholars and occasionally by non-Muslim scholars under Muslim patronage.

There follows a partial list of pre-Islamic and early post-Islamic writers and translators important to transmission of Hellenistic, Indo-Persian, and Syrian-Alexandrian learning to Islam through translations into Arabic, arranged according to (1) affiliation, (2) date, (3) field, and (4) writings.*

*Source: O'Leary, *Arab Thought and Its Place in History* (Trubner's Oriental Series), Kegan Paul, French Trubner and Co., N.Y., E. P. Dutton and Co., 1939.

The Bakh-Tishu Family

(Bokh-Tishu or Boktishu or Bokhtishu)

1. Bakh-Tishu I

2. Jurjis I
(Physician to al-Mansur, died 769)

3. Bakh-Tishu II
(Physician to al-Mahdi, al-Hadi, and Harun-al Rashid, died 801)

4. Jibra'il I
(Physician to H. al-Rashid, Al-Amin and al-Ma'mun, died 828)

5. Jurjis II

6. Bakh-Tishu III
(Physician to al-Mumtaz)

7. Ubayd-Ullah I
(Physician to al-Muttaqi)

8. Yuhanna

9. Jibra'il II
(Physician to Azud-ul-Doula, died 1005)

10. Bakh-Tishu IV
(Physician to al-Mughtadir, died 940)

11. Abu Sa'id Ubayd-Ullah
(died 1058)

Greek Learning

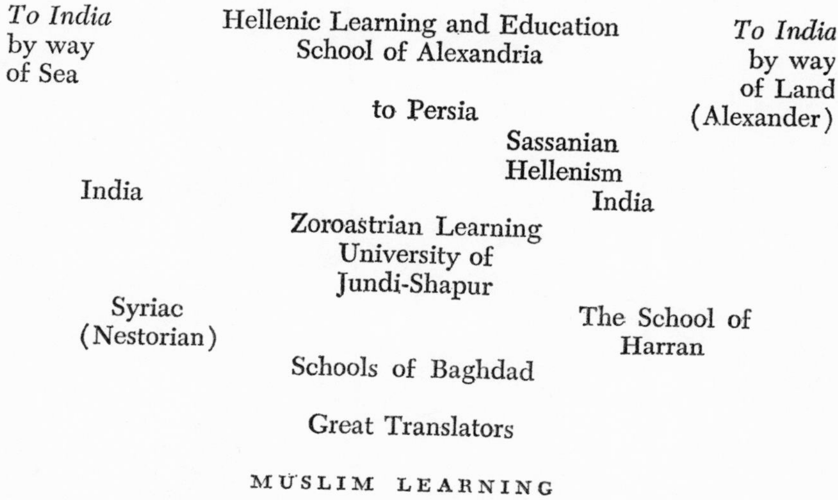

Point of Fusion of Arabic and Persian, and Its Development with Modern Persian

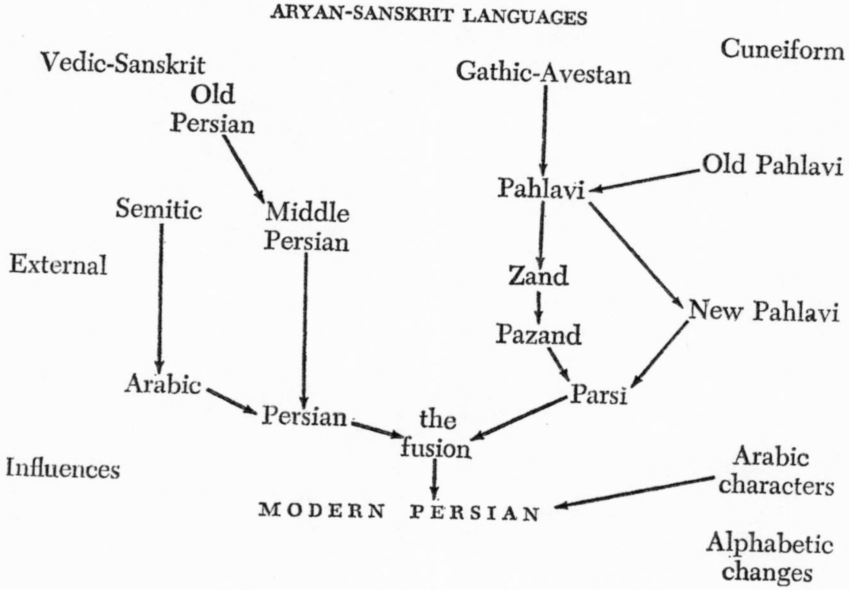

CHAPTER III *

THE NATURE AND SCOPE OF MUSLIM EDUCATION, 750-1350

EUROPE WAS IN ITS medieval period when the Muslims wrote a colorful chapter in the history of education. Many of their greatest contributions, particularly to Western education, have gone unnoticed because of religious prejudice, language barriers, the decline of Islamic culture, and inaccessibility of historic materials for Western historians of education. The Muslims assimilated through their educational system the best of classical cultures and improved them. Among the assimilated fields were philosophy and Hellenistic medical, mathematical, and technological sciences; Hindu mathematics, medicine, and literature; Persian religions, literature, and sciences; and Syrian commentaries on Hellenistic science and philosophy. By applying the classical sciences to practical pursuits, the Muslims developed the empirical-experimental method, although they failed to take full advantage of it. Later the method was adopted in Europe. They encouraged free inquiry and made available to the public the instruments of research and scholarship. They opened their public and even private libraries to public use, not only regionally but internationally. At a time when books were "published" only through the tedious labor of copyists, they made hundreds, even thousands, of copies of reference materials and made them available to all caring to learn from them. Often they allowed scores of books—sometimes more than a hundred per person—to be borrowed for an almost indefinite time for special studies and prolonged research. They provided food, lodging, and even incidental money for scholars from far away; they made their great teachers internationally accessible by encouraging the concept of the travelling scholar.

In the golden age (750-1150) of their cultural-educational activities they did not permit theology and dogma to limit their scholarship. They searched into every branch of human knowledge, be it philology, history, historiography, law, sociology, literature, ethics, philosophy, theology, medicine, mathematics, logic, jurisprudence, art, architecture, or ceramics. They respected learning; they honored the scholar. They introduced the science and philosophy of the Greeks, Persians, and

*All dates refer to A.D. unless otherwise specified.

Hindus to Western Christian schoolmen. But the story of Western education's debt to Islam is still to be written with fullness of knowledge and without prejudice and predetermination of results. What kind of education was responsible for so much in so short a time?

Muslim education went through two distinct periods. First was the period covering the ninth and tenth centuries, when schools developed spontaneously with private endowments interested in public enlightenment; and second the period beginning in the eleventh century and developing through the twelfth and thirteenth centuries, when education became the function of the state, and schools were institutionalized for purposes of sectarian education and political indoctrination.

Madrasahs and Nizamiyyas

A new type of school was conceived as a state institution to promote religious indoctrination of the Sunnite Islamic faith and political indoctrination of a Turkish-Persian style, aside from general learning and particular training. Nizam-al-Mulk (d. 1092; 485 A.H.), the founder and popularizer of these *madrasahs* (schools of public instruction), was a famous vizier (prime minister) in the administration of the Seljuq sultans in the eleventh century. He established the madrasah about the middle of that century, which, though not the first school in Islam, was the first system of special schools geared to that state and Sunnite Islam. The madrasahs had, aside from their zest for learning, both political and religious purposes—the moulding of public opinion in Sunnite orthodox Islam against the Shi'ah branch. Large sums of money were allotted for the establishment and maintenance of these schools with generous scholarships, pensions, and rations granted to all worthy students. In fact, Nizam arranged for regular stipends to all students. The schools were institutionalized under state control and support, and standardized madrasahs were established in all large cities within Islam, with the exception of Spain and Sicily. The greatest of these academies was the one established by Nizam in Baghdad, the famous *Nizamiyyah,* which opened for teaching in 1066-67 (459 A.H.) and continued as a center of learning for several centuries, motivated primarily by religious and literary pursuits. Altogether, Nizam-al-Mulk made the greatest single contribution to education in founding and extending an almost universal system of schools (madrasahs) throughout Eastern Islam.* He was one of the most learned

*Among the leading founders of schools in Islam should also be mentioned al-Ma'mun (d. 833; 218 A.H.), who supported and endowed the first great Muslim educational center in Baghdad, the famous *Bait-al-Hikmah,* and was instrumental in having Greek, Persian, and Hindu translations made into Arabic by the greatest scholars of the time; Nur-al-Din (d. 1173; 569 A.H.), the Sultan of the kingdom of Syria who, after the dissolution of the Seljuq Empire, founded schools in Damascus and throughout his kingdom, including Egypt; Saladin (d. 1193; 589 A.H.), who extended the school systems in Syria and Egypt.

men of his time, greatly versed in Muslim hadith, or tradition, and one of the great political theorists of Islam, as shown in his famous *Siyasat-Namah.* His passion for universal education was limited only by the means at his disposal. The schools he founded all over the empire were endowed generously. He supplied them with libraries, the best professors he could find, and a system of scholarships to aid all the students. Let us look into his educational enterprise in some detail.

Nizam-al-Mulk and Muslim Education

The opening of the first school carrying the name of the Persian statesman, Nizam-al-Mulk, took place in 1066 (459 A.H.). It marks the transition from the mosque schools and the beginning of a system of public schools, or madrasahs, throughout the vast area of the Muslim world, which was under strong Persian cultural and administrative influence. This influence continued, first under Arab political supremacy under the Abbassides from the middle of the eighth century to the ninth, and again during the long period of Turkish (Ottoman) politico-religious supremacy, to the early decades of the sixteenth century (1517). It is true that the earlier Turks had a simple culture and were given to warfare and conquest. But settling down to administer their empire, they learned from the superior cultures of the Persians and the Arabs, adopted the Arabic alphabet, and accepted Islam. In time they adapted the foreign cultures to their own needs and tastes, and encouraged the establishment throughout their empire of schools to perpetuate Sunnite Islam and Turkish politics and policies. Tarikh Zaidan, in his *Al-Tamaddun al-Islami* (*History of Islamic Civilization*), states that the Turkish princes encouraged learning and increased the number of schools in their empire, guided by three motives: The hope of heavenly reward; the fear of losing their fortunes to more greedy superiors or antagonists, so that they utilized their wealth in establishing schools; finally, but most important of all, the desire to indoctrinate religious beliefs of the founder and to combat opposing religious views.[1]

It was the employment of the school for sectarian indoctrination and political influence and propaganda that led the famous Seljuk Sultan Saladin to found madrasahs and also to close the college of Dar al-Ilm (The House of Learning) in Cairo in order to eliminate its Shi'ite influence. In fact it was not uncommon to dismiss professors during this period from the madrasahs because of their religious beliefs, particularly Shi'ite. Muslim scholasticism (*Ilm al-Kalam*) developed in these sectarian colleges of Sunnite or Shi'ite beliefs.

The Sunnite belief received its most sweeping expression under Nizam-al-Mulk. Before his day, there were several institutions of learning in the Islamic world which resembled a college, such as Al-Azhar in Cairo, Egypt, in the last quarter of the tenth century; Dar al-Ilm and Dar al-Hikmah, also in Cairo, in the early decades of the eleventh; Bait-al-Hikmah in Baghdad during the reign of al-Ma'-mun; and Baihaqiyyah at Nishapur in Khrasan, Persia.[2] But to Nizam-al-Mulk goes the distinct credit for having founded an institution for instruction and indoctrination under government and religious control, for political and religious ends—a sectarian system of public education with secular emphasis and political motivation.

With these objectives in mind, Nizam-al-Mulk established schools in every city and village of Iraq and Khorassan. Even a small place, such as "Kharn al-Jabal near Tus . . . had its teacher and school."[3] These schools were well distributed from Khorassan in the east to Mesopotamia in the west. These so-called madrasahs soon became standardized, and many of them were built after the example of the one in Baghdad, which was built by Nizam-al-Mulk himself, and named Nizamiyyah (or Nidhamiyyah) in his honor.

> Nizamiyyahs . . . were founded not only in Baghdad, but in Nisabur, Balkh, Herat, Isfahan, Marw, Basrah and Mosul. Not only did Nizam-al-Mulk establish these academies or colleges, but he endowed them. It is estimated that $1,500,000 was spent annually on educational, semi-educational and religious institutions.[4]

Nizamiyyah University, the most famous of the chain of madrasahs, was built in Baghdad in 1065 under the educator's personal supervision. The earliest account of this university is given by ibn Khaldun, the great Arab philosopher-historian, who says:

> Nizam-al-Mulk ordered that Abu Is'haq al-Shirazi should be its professor, but when the people were assembled to hear him he did not appear. He was searched for, but was not to be found; so Abu Nasir ibn-al-Sabbagh was appointed to the post. Later Abu Is'haq met his classes in his mosque, but his students showed their dissatisfaction with his action and threatened to go over to ibn al-Sabbagh unless he accepted the professorship at the Nizamiyyah. Finally he acceded to their wishes, and ibn al-Sabbagh was dismissed after having lectured for only twenty days.[5]

The chief reason for Abu Is'haq's refusal to teach at the Nizamiyyah was, according to ibn Khallikan, that he was "informed that the greater part of the materials employed in the construction of the college have been procured illegally."[6] But the foregoing quotation is of extreme interest for the information it gives us that the mosques were the chief places of learning before the foundation of universities. There were over one hundred such mosques in Baghdad alone.

The principal motive in founding the Nizamiyyah was religious. Its objective was the teaching of "The Shafi'ite (Sunni) school of law," its sole emphasis being upon the teaching of theology and Islamic law, and it stood as a university of Islamic theological learning for several centuries. The great mystic al-Ghazzali taught there twenty-five years after its founding. Al-Abiwardi (d. 1104; 498 A.H.) and ibn Mubarak (d. 1184; 580 A.H.) were associated with it. Ibn Jubair, who visited the school about the middle of the fourteenth century, said of it: "And in the midst of Suq al-Thalatha (Tuesday market) is the wonderful madrasah Al-Nizamiyyah, whose beauty has become proverbial."

Aims of Muslim Education

The aims of Muslim education in "medieval" times may be defined as follows:

1. Religious aims, based on (a) *Qur'an* as source of knowledge, (b) spiritual foundation of education, (c) dependence upon God, (d) sectarian morals, (e) subordination of secular subjects to religion, (f) equality of all men before God and man, (g) supremacy of Muhammad over all other prophets, (h) belief in the six articles of Imam or Creed (God, angels, scripture, prophets, judgment, decrees), and (i) belief (and application) in A'amal or religious duties, including confession of faith (There is no God but God), prayers, alms, fasting, and pilgrimage.

2. Secular aims, the importance of which is well suggested by a Muslim tradition, attributed to Muhammad, which says, "The best among you are not those who neglect this world for the other, or the other world for this. He is the one who works for both together."[7] Among these aims were pursuit of all knowledge, as the revelation of the nature of God; education open to all on equal terms, limited only by ability and interest; and guidance and teaching as essential to promote (initiate) knowledge and education.

The *Mutakallimun* (*Loquentes*), the Muslim scholastic teachers (speakers of truths), stressed the importance of teachers whose knowledge may be traced back to revelation or may have been made manifest directly by intuition. This was the view of the theologian-philosopher-educator al-Ghazzali, who believed in three degrees of knowledge: (a) Common-sense knowledge, restricted by undisciplined sense-experience and dependent upon external authority; (b) scientific knowledge; (c) intuitive knowledge.

It is of interest to note that al-Ghazzali's concept of scientific knowledge includes seven basic principles or conditions: Stimulation of the search for scientific knowledge; application of scientific arts; advancement of applied sciences and extensive application of them; development of laboratory and experimental pursuits; encouragement of arts and crafts (It was Aristotle in particular, from among the Greeks, who appealed to Islam. This was because of the Greek master's application of philosophy and science to the arts and needs of everyday living and because of the adaptability of his philosophic and scientific concepts to the art of living and the necessities of individual and civic life); encouragement of individual initiative and academic freedom for both teachers and pupils (in the college of Baghdad an inquiring student, who greeted the great teacher with devoted *salams* [bows], often ended the day with an intellectual fist fight with his master in defense of some principles, refutation of others, or hairsplitting argument over insignificant details); attainment of excellence, to produce great men of learning and leaders in public affairs. The pragmatic spirit of their education is indicated by development of textile fabrics, of irrigation systems, of iron and steel products, of earthenwares, and leather products, by architectural innovations, weaving of rugs and carpets, manufacture of paper and gunpowder, maintenance of a merchant marine of a thousand ships, and advancement of commercial activity.

Although Muslim education aimed at practical training, such training was as a rule based upon instruction in fundamental sciences. Thus, in the system, practice was sustained by theory; theory verified in practice. Even in commercial training, economics as a science was a foundational training.

It is of interest to note that as Islam began to decline after the end of the eleventh century, the number of its schools of higher learning increased and flourished. These colleges were, however, almost all denominational schools opened and supported by leaders of various Islamic religious factions. Each denominational college was open, with few exceptions, only to followers of a given sect. Religious and literary studies and Arabic language and grammar dominated the subject matter at the expense of philosophy, science, and social studies. The very abundance of these religious schools indicated the gradual decline which was under way. These colleges were intolerant of innovations, suspicious of secular studies, and aloof from creative scholars. Some of these colleges survived destruction by the Mongols in the thirteenth century and remained centers of dogmatic theological instruction to the fourteenth and fifteenth centuries.

There was competition among these denominational schools, particularly between the Shi'ite and Sunnite (Hanafite) religious factions. This competition proved healthy in the increase of these colleges and in their facilities, endowments, and the like, and would have been a tremendous educational power except for their limitations because of their religious nature.

It is of interest also to note that during this same period new universities were beginning to develop in western Europe, particularly in Italy, Germany, France, and England. But unlike the Islamic denominational schools, the Western universities were preserving the best intellectual elements that Islamic research and scholarship had developed during its creative centuries, from the ninth to the twelfth centuries. Islamic works were reaching Europe at about the same period (twelfth and thirteenth centuries) when secular learning was declining in Islam. The works of hundreds of translators not only enriched and created or enlarged many Western universities but brought about the Western Renaissance of the fourteenth and fifteenth centuries. One reason for this, of course, was the revival of secular interest and research in the West, which, though curtailed by religious passion until the seventeenth and eighteenth centuries, was left relatively free from then on to discover new knowledges and usher in the modern world.

In his *Tarikh Adabyyat Iran* (*A Literary History of Iran*), Volume II, Doctor Thabih Allah Safa states that these denominational colleges were spread all over Eastern Islam from Egypt to Transoxiana, most of them flourishing in such famous cities as Nishapur, Isfahan, Yezd, Marv, Kashan, Kirmanshah, Baghdad, Rayy, Qum, Basra, Balkh, Herat, Gorgan, Hamadan, Mosul, and Varamin. Whatever the weaknesses of these colleges, the fact that they flourished in such large numbers over vast areas of Eastern Islam would indicate the coexistence of sufficient elementary-secondary schools from which they drew their enrollments. The following table represents examples of some of the more important denominational colleges flourishing during this period in Eastern Islam and is based on those mentioned by Safa, whose main source appears to be a twelfth century work in Arabic entitled *Kitab-al-Naghth* (*Ba'dh Mathalit-ul-Nawasib fi Naghah Ba'dh Fadha'ih-al-Rawafidh*).

SHI'ITE AND SUNNITE MADHHABI (denominational) COLLEGES IN EASTERN ISLAM
(In vogue around 1050 to 1250 A.D.)

NAME OF COLLEGE	DENOMINATION	LOCATION
Shams-al-Islam Hasha (Hasan) Babuya	Imamiyyah Shi'ite	Rayy
Sadat Gilaki	"	"
Abu al-Futuh	"	"
Faqih Ali Jasti	"	"
Khawja Abd-al-Jabbar Mufid	"	"
Kooy Firuzeh	"	"
Khawja Imam Rashid Razi	"	"
Sa'd Selt	Shi'ite	Qum
Athir-al-Mulk	"	"
Saiyyid Aziz-al-Din Murtadha	"	"
Imam Zain-al-Din Amirah Sharaf Shah al-Husaini	"	"
Dhahir-al-din Abd-al-Aziz	"	"
Ustad Abu al-Hasan Kumaij	"	"
Shams-al-Din Murtadha	"	"
Saiyyid Murtadha Kabir Sharaf-al-Din	"	"
Sufiyyieh	"	Kashan
Madjdiyyieh	"	"
Sharafiyyieh	"	"
Aziziyyiah	"	"
Ezzol Mulki	"	Aveh
Arab Shahi	"	"
Radhawiyyieh	"	Varamin
Fathiyyieh	"	"
Nidhamiyya	Sunnite (Shafi'ite)	Baghdad
Tajiyyah	"	"
Nidhamiyya at Nishapur	"	Nishapur
Nidhamiyya at Basra	"	Basra
Nidhamiyya at Isfahan (Sadryya)	"	Isfahan

Nidhamiyya at Balkh	”	Balkh
Nidhamiyya at Herat	”	Herat
Nidhamiyya at Mosul	”	Mosul
Malik Shah	Hanafite	Isfahan
Khatun Mahd Araq	Sunnite (?)	Nishapur
Husain Baihaqi	”	”
Khurnu Gardi (Saif al-Din Abu Nasr Muhammad ibn Abi al-Khair)	”	”
Sarwiyya	”	”
Darwaza'i Araq	”	”
Nidhamiyya	Sunnite	Marv
Nidhamiyya	”	Shah Jahan
Mansur-al-Mustawfi	”	”
Gorgan	”	Gorgan
Khawja Najm-al-Din (Hasan Amidi)	”	Rayy
Malik-al-Umara (Jamal-al-Din)	”	Hamadan
Tughril ibn Muhammad Saljuqi	”	”
Arsalan ibn Tughril	”	”
Anushirwan ibn Khalid	”	Kashan
Khatun Saljuqi	”	Isfahan
Darb-i-Mahan	”	Kirmanshah
Arsalan Shah	”	”
Muhammad ibn Arsalan Shah	”	”
Abu Ja'far Ala' al-Dawlah Kalijar (Doe Menareh)	”	Yezd
Kyan Rosu	”	”
Ala Khan	”	”
Atabak Sam	”	”
Wardanrooz	”	”
Beltasiyyah	”	Baghdad
Talshiyyah	Hanafite	”
Suq-al-Amid	”	”
Mustansiriyyah	”	”

Elementary education was almost universal in Islam. The Abbasside caliphs were great patrons of learning and literacy. They insisted, beginning with Harun-al-Rashid, that every Muslim child have an opportunity to learn the fundamentals of reading, writing, computation, some elementary science, geography, history, and so forth. They attached, therefore, a primary school to every *masjid* (mosque), or place of worship. Skilled instructors taught the children of the rich and the poor on equal terms. Literacy was almost universal.

> It was this great liberality which the [Muslims] displayed in educating their people in the schools which was one of the most potent factors in the brilliant and rapid growth of their civilization. Education was so universally diffused that it was said to be difficult to find a [Muslim] who could not read or write.[8]

The education of women, however, followed the classical tradition, aiming at preparation for homemaking, although some Muslim women did become highly cultured members of their community. Among them were such poetesses as Badanuyyah, also a great expert on prose; Hafsa al-Rakuniyyah of Granada, a great teacher and poetess; Maryam bint Abi Ya'qub al-Awsari, another famous teacher and poetess; Safiyya of Seville, a distinguished poetess, orator, and calligrapher; Zainah bint al-Shari, a theologian; Unaidah, the grandmother of Abu al-Khair al-Aqta, a famous teacher; Taqiyyah Unim Ali Abi al-Faraji, a poetess; great singers, such as Jamilah, Dananir, Ulayyah, Mutayyam, Khadijah, daughter of al-Ma'mun, and Ubaidah al-Tamburiyyat; and famous physicians, such as Zainab of the Banu Awd and Unim al-Hassan (bint al-Qadi Abi Ja'far) al-Tanjali.[9] In general, however, the education of women was confined to elementary instruction, religious precepts, literature, music, and art.

The Organization of Muslim Schools

The Halqha (*Circle School*). The simplest type of early Muslim education was the *circle*. This was a unique educational experience in Islam and was known as *halqha*, which means a circular gathering. It was so named because the teacher was seated on a dais or cushion against a wall or pillar, and the students formed a semicircle in front of him. The circle was formed according to rank, the more advanced a student the closer he would be seated to the teacher, with the most advanced students or visiting scholars seated next to him. A predetermined area of the circle was always reserved for visitors.

Great teachers were symbols of learning and scholarship, and their utterances were meticulously recorded in notebooks by all listen-

ORGANIZATION OF MUSLIM EDUCATION, 750-1350

Known as *maktabs* or *kuttabs* (writing schools)	Known as 1) Mosque schools (*Masjid*) 2) Mosque *circles* (*Halqha*) 3) Madrasahs, outside of mosques, offering both secondary and college disciplines	1) Bait-al-Hikmas (Houses of Wisdom) 2) Bookshops as centers of research 3) Literary salons as centers of exchange of views and disputation of issues
5 or 6 to 14 Elementary Mostly outside the mosque in shops or tutors' houses	to 18 or above Secondary - College The transition from secondary to college was flexible and based upon individual initiative	University education and post-university education 4) Public libraries, semi-public libraries, and private libraries in homes of scholars, as centers of research and scholarship 5) Higher education also was carried on in some mosques exclusively, such as Al-Azhar

Note: The mosque circles (halqha) varied in content and approach, individuals belonging to circles according to the extent of their education. Standard depended on the quality of the teacher. Students were mobile in circles, looking for the right teacher and leaving him when he could not offer further enlightenment.

Pre-school education was accomplished in the home, sometimes under private tutors or moral guardians. There was no formal pre-school organization.

ers. These notebooks were sometimes examined closely by the teacher, who corrected and approved their use in teaching the subject to others. The circle was instruction through dictation (*imla*), the teacher lecturing and the student recording the lecture. When the material of a lecture series was available in part, students were urged to study and discuss its highlights with each other in order to have better orientation for advanced instruction in given areas. Advanced students, even new students and visitors, were encouraged to question the teacher on any point and feel free to disagree with his point of view or even to challenge and correct his statements. Disputes between students and teachers, therefore, were quite frequent and occasionally led to heated, abusive arguments. But all was done in the name and for the sake of investigation and scholarship.

Every subject was dealt with methodically by the teacher. First, he made a general survey of the subject. Then by connecting the day's lesson with previous lecture or lectures in order to develop a sense of continuity and comprehension, he allowed ample time for concentration on the more difficult disputed phases of the subject for illustration and clarification.

Students would often make long journeys to join the circle of a great teacher, or would move from circle to circle, sometimes at the cost of journeys to many distant cities, squeezing the scholar's lemon dry, so to speak, then moving on to others.

The *Maktab*, or *Kuttab* (*Writing School*). The *maktabs*, or places for teaching writing, existed in the Arab world even before Islam. It was actually a place to learn reading as well as writing, located in the teacher's house where pupils gathered for instruction. There were also other types of maktabs where, after the advent of Islam, instruction was exclusively in the *Qur'an* and religion.[10] Such maktabs as that of Abu al-Qasim al-Balkhi in Julfa (died 723; 105 A.H.) had as many as three thousand pupils. The tutors in these maktabs were called *Muallim*, or instructors.

The maktabs became the prevailing means of elementary education in early Islam in almost every town or village. In addition to the *Qur'an* and religion, poetry, horsemanship, swimming, famous proverbs, elementary arithmetic, elementary grammar, manners (*adab*), and penmanship were taught. These maktabs prevailed in Spain, Sicily, Africa, and the Middle East, though the contents of their curriculum varied and were adapted to local cultural-social interests and backgrounds.

The Palace School. These schools were conducted in royal palaces, and in addition to the curriculum of the maktabs, instruction was given in such social and cultural disciplines necessary to prepare for higher education, for polite society, and often for service in the government of the caliphs. In fact, the instructors in these palace schools were called *mu'addibs* from *adab,* or good manners, and one who modified his conduct by such manners was called *mu'addab,* or "of good manners." The art of oratory and good conversation, formal ethics, and some history and tradition were also in the curriculum.[11]

The Mosque School (Masjid). The most typical, and the one that lasted longest, of Muslim elementary education was the mosque school, encouraged by Harun-al-Rashid and promoted by the caliphs who followed him. Wherever Islam spread in the first century of its dramatic growth, the tradition of the mosque as a center of worship went along with it. Therefore, it was natural that the early caliphs (Abbassides) would in time see the significance of the mosque not only as a place of worship but as a center for instruction of the young. So numerous and widespread were the Muslim *masjids* that al-Yaqubi reports some 3,000 of them in Baghdad alone in the third century of the Hegira, or the first decades of the tenth century A.D. Alexandria claimed, according to ibn Jubair, some 12,000 mosques in the fourteenth century. Some were magnificent and costly enterprises. The mosque of al-Mansur, built during the reign of Harun-al-Rashid in Baghdad, is reported to have cost 18,000,000 dinars.[12] It became, like many others of its kind through Islam, and particularly in Egypt, Iran, Iraq, North Africa, and Spain, the center of learning for students from all over the Muslim world. The most famous mosques were those of Alhambra, Cairo, and Damascus, reputed to be among the unique wonders of the Middle Ages; and those in Isfahan, Mashhad, Ghom, and other cities of Persia.

The Bookshop Schools. In addition to the three types of writing schools—the maktabs, the palace (*adab*) schools, and the mosque (*masjid*) schools—there were other centers of education in Islam before the development of the public madrasahs by Nizam-al-Mulk. Most important among these centers were the bookshops, the private residences of great Muslim scholars, and the so-called literary salons.

During the Abbasside period, Muslim learning and scholarship rose to a high degree and inspired the rapid development of bookshops, book dealers, and copyists in all the important Islamic cities, particularly Baghdad, Cordova, Cairo, Mashhad (Meshed), and Damascus. Not only did the number of bookshops increase beyond expectation in Eastern Islam during the Abbasside period, and in Western Islam during the second (Spanish) Umayyad period, but with this increase came free access to the bookstores anywhere in Islam. Many a scholar spent long hours in these bookshops freely examining, browsing, and studying available books, or purchasing favorite selections for his private library. Some of the most learned men in Islam are known to have frequented these famous bookstores.

Bookdealers also contributed to the spread of learning by travelling to famous Muslim cities in search of rare manuscripts, either for private sale to interested collectors or scholars, or on order of caliphs, governors, and so forth, who were willing to pay almost any price to become the proud owner of a rare manuscript.

Many such manuscripts eventually found their way to the private libraries of Muslim scholars or rulers who were patrons of learning, only to be made readily available again to all who cared to study them. It was in one such library that ibn Sina spent a period of research which, by his own admission, contained manuscripts of medical and other subjects he had never seen before or since, and apparently they were the sources for much of the medical knowledge later incorporated in his monumental canon of medicine. Also, many of the great Muslim scholars, al-Ghazzali, al-Farabi, and Avicenna, to name a few who at one time or another taught in public schools, retired often to their private libraries and studies and made their homes centers of scholarly pursuits for those fortunate enough to be invited.

The Literary Salon. The literary salons, which developed around the learned caliphs and their scholarly companions, became meeting places for literary and scholarly exchange of ideas. "In the literary salons," says Shalaby, "foreign customs and civilizations manifested themselves; salons were highly prepared; only people of certain classes were permitted; the members had to come at fixed times and leave according to particular signs adopted by the califs; the califs and no one else would open the discussion."[13]

Those attending the literary salons were not only hand-picked but were instructed as to the style of dress they should wear and required to follow certain strict rules of general dignity and bearing. Everyone had a predetermined place to be seated, according to his class. Absolute silence and respectful attention were required when the caliph offered the opening statement to the discussion. The participants in the discussions were required to speak in refined language and in a quiet, measured voice. Interruptions were not allowed.

With all their formalities these literary gatherings were important centers of education. They attracted great scholars who debated and exchanged and communicated vast areas of knowledge and debated and clarified timely issues, thus becoming genuine centers of enlightenment and the pursuit of knowledge. The salons reached their height during the Abbasside period, under such caliphs as Harun al-Rashid. They used the salons for initiating debates on a wide variety of subjects between distinguished scholars, especially in areas of religion, scholastic theology, philosophy, rhetoric, grammar, and poetry. Al-Ma'mun, another enlightened caliph, encouraged scholarship by staging famous debates and disputes between opposing scholars in the philosophical and scholastic (Aristotelian and anti-Aristotelian) conflicts of the time. These debates included such topics as, "Is the *Qur'an* created or not created?" In this manner the courts of the caliphs and later of the Muslim kings served as centers of culture.[14]

One of the great debates in Islam took place in the court of Nizam-al-Mulk, where al-Ghazzali, after winning the debate, was appointed by the great vizier to professorship at the famous Nizamiyyah University of Baghdad.

The Madrasah (School of Public Instruction; literally, Place for Giving Lesson). The instruction provided in maktabs, palace schools, and mosque schools had definite educational limitations. The curriculum was limited, the schools did not always attract the best teachers, physical facilities were not conducive to the best educational environment; conflicts between educational and religious purposes within the mosques were almost irreconcilable, the former given to activity and noise, interfering with solemnities of worship. It became necessary, therefore, to relieve the mosques of as much of the responsibilities of secular-sectarian education as possible. Initiation of a new type of school, the madrasah was both natural and necessary. An external factor which also contributed to the development of this new concept was the fact that progress and diffusion of knowledge created a body of men who found it difficult to make a decent living through their abstract learning. (Not so different today!) It was partly to promote further study and provide sufficient stipends for such men that the madrasahs were really established.[15] Physical facilities of the madrasahs were, of course, quite different from locality to locality and from country to country, depending on geographic, economic, and cultural differences.

Although religious motives in the initial efforts of such patrons of education as Nizam-al-Mulk, Nur-al-Din, and others to establish the madrasahs universally in Islamic countries cannot be doubted, their insatiable passion for learning, scholarship, and general education were also among the important factors which culminated in the establishment of these schools.[16] The same factors motivated their zeal for establishing and endowing colleges and universities in such Islamic cultural centers as Nishapur, Baghdad, Damascus, Cairo, and Cordova and were responsible for opening the first madrasahs in other large cities within the domain. Shalaby lists by name fifteen such schools founded by Nur-al-Din in Damascus, Aleppo, and other Syrian cities, and over sixty schools established under the Ayyubid sultans, princes, princesses, amirs, ministers, and commoners in Egypt, Jerusalem, and Damascus.[17] He also gives a detailed description by ibn Jubair of one madrasah in the sixth century, as "one of the best colleges in the world." The school was established by Nur-al-Din in 566 A.H. (1170 A.D.) It was located in what is now called al-Khayyatin, about half a mile from the Mosque of Umar. The school consisted of a large lecture room (*qwan*), "8.25 m. long, 7.8 wide and 917 high," the mosque for students and public worship, quite remote from the lecture hall, the teachers' lounge, student lodges [eight], caretakers' lodges, the latrines of the building, the kitchen and dining hall, the food storeroom, and the general storage room.[18]

The University. The crown and glory of "medieval" Muslim schools were the universities, or research centers. We have already discussed the great University of Nizamiyyah in the section on Nizam-al-Mulk, but let us take as another illustration of the character of Muslim universities the great research center of *Mustansiriyyah.*

The Mustansiriyyah University came into existence to compete with and overthrow the Nizamiyyah. Of the origin and development of this university, the writer of *Baghdad During the Abbasid Caliphate* speaks as follows:[19]

Within the precincts and, as seems probable, immediately south of the Gharabah Gate [occupying some of the area formerly covered by the older Hasani Palace, for one of its walls was washed by the Tigris stream], stood the great College of the Mustansiriyyah. Of this college the ruins still exist [1900], while of the adjoining palaces of the Caliphs hardly a trace remains; but unfortunately, as the college was only completed in 631 [A.D. 1234], no mention of it occurs in Yakut, who had finished his great geographical dictionary shortly before this date, and therefore we do not know for certain on what grounds of the older precincts the college was actually built. Mustansir was the penultimate Caliph of the house of Abbas and the father of Mustasim, whom Hulagu put to death, and this Madrassah of the Mustansiriyyah was founded by him with a view to supplant and eclipse the celebrated Nizamiyyah College, which Nizam-al-Mulk had built nearly two centuries before.

We are told that in outward appearance, in stateliness of ornament and sumptuousness of furniture, in spaciousness and in the wealth of its pious foundations, the Mustansiriyyah surpassed everything that had previously been seen in Islam. It contained four separate law-schools, one for each of the orthodox sects of the Sunnis, with a professor at the head of each, who had seventy-five students [*Fakih*] in his charge, to whom he gave instruction gratis. The four professors each received a monthly salary, and to each of the three hundred students one gold dinar a month was assigned. The great kitchen of the college further provided daily rations of bread and meat to all the inmates. According to Ibn-al-Furat there was a library [*Dar-al-Kutub*] in the Mustansiriyyah with rare books treating of the various sciences, so arranged that the students could easily consult them, and those who wished could copy these manuscripts, pens and paper being supplied by the establishment. Lamps for the students and a due provision of olive oil for lighting up the college are also mentioned, likewise, storage places for cooling the drinking water; and in the great entrance hall [*Aywan*] stood a clock [*Sanduk-as-saat,* 'Chest of the Hours,' doubtless some form of clepsydra], announcing the appointed times of prayer, and marking the lapse of the hours by day and by night.

Inside the college a bath house [*Hammam*] was erected for the special use of the students, and a hospital [*Bimaristan*], to which a physician was appointed, whose duty it was to visit the place every morning, prescribing for those who were sick; and there were great store-chambers in the Madrasah provided with all requisites of food, drink, and medicines. The Caliph Mustansir himself took such interest in the work of the institution that he would hardly let a day pass without a visit of inspection; and he had caused a private garden to be laid out, with a belvedere [*Manzarah*] overlooking the college, whither it was his wont to come and divert himself, sitting at a window—before which a veil was hung—and which opened upon one of the college halls, so that through this window he could watch all that went on within the building, and even hear the lectures of the professors and the disputations of the students.

A century after its foundation, Ibn Batutah, who visited Baghdad in 727 [A.D. 1327], dilates on the magnificence of the Mustansiriyyah College, which had fortunately escaped destruction during the Mongol siege; and he describes it as situated at the further end of the Tuesday Market [*Suk-ath-Thalathah*], which was the commercial centre of Baghdad in his days. The law-schools in the Mustansiriyyah were then still frequented by students of the four orthodox Sunni sects, each sect or law-school having its separate mosque, and in the hall the professor of law gave his lectures, whom Ibn Batutah describes as 'seated under a small wooden cupola on a chair covered by a carpet, speaking with much sedateness and gravity of mien, he being clothed in black and wearing a turban; and there were besides two assistants, one on either hand, who repeated in a loud voice the dictation of the teacher.'

The Persian geographer Hamd-Allah, writing a dozen years later than Ibn Batutah, also refers to the Mustansiriyyah Madrasah as the most beautiful building then existing in Baghdad; and it appears to have stood intact for many centuries, for the ruins of the college, as already mentioned, still exist [1900], occupying a considerable space of ground immediately below the eastern end of the present Bridge of Boats. Mustansir likewise restored the great mosque of the palace [Jami-al-Kasr], originally built by the Caliph Ali Muktafi, and Mustansir set up four platforms [*Dikkah*] on the right or western side of the pulpit, where the students of the Mustansiriyyah were seated and held disputations on Fridays after the public prayers. The remains of this mosque also exist, at the present day occuying part of the Suk-al-Ghazl [the Thread Market], at some little distance to the eastward of the ruins of the Madrasah. When Niebuhr visited Baghdad in 1750 he found that the ancient kitchen of the Mustansiriyyah College was clearly to be recognized, being used in his day as a weighing house; and Niebuhr copied here the inscription which gives the name and titles of the Caliph Mustansir, with the statement that this Madrasah had been completed in the year 630 [A.D. 1233]. A similar inscription [also extant] was seen by Niebuhr in the ruined mosque, with the date of 633 [A.D. 1236], doubtless when the restoration by Mustansir was finished, for, as already said, the foundation walls in all probability are far older than this date, and belong to the great mosque of the Palace of the Caliph.[20]

This rather elaborate description of the Mustansiriyyah is fortunate for us today, not so much for what it tells us of the magnificence of an Islamic university at its best as for the fact that such universities shone like the morning star in the early part of the thirteenth century. It is perhaps of interest to compare Mustansiriyyah University with the oldest Christian universities of Bologna, Paris, Montpellier, and Oxford in the twelfth century for comparative merits and demerits, their similarities and differences, and their influences on one another.

In Spain the development of higher education began in the tenth century. The Moors (Berbers), and following them the Arabs, entered Spain in 712. By 756, the Umayyad Prince Abd-al-Rahman had defeated the army of the Abbasside Caliph al-Mansur and was made the Amir of Cordova. This initiated another Islamic golden age in southern Spain under the Umayyads which continued to the eleventh century. Meanwhile, the tenth century was the apex of intellectual development in Muslim Spain with Cordova as its center, and Seville, Toledo, and Granada less important by comparison. Al-Makkari's

History of the Muhammadan Dynasties in Spain contains a long list (some sixty pages) of this period's men of letters.[21]

Colleges provided higher education in Cordova (which was actually a university), Granada, Toledo, Marcia, Almeria, Seville, Valencia, and Cadiz. Elementary schools, charging tuition in contrast to schools in Eastern Islam, were open to large numbers of boys and girls, although some, as those patronized by Hakam II, were tuition free. Libraries were numerous—some seventy are known—attracting to them students and scholars in almost every field, be it art, music, literature, theology, philology, rhetoric, grammar, the sciences, or philosophy, indicating the varieties of informational materials in these libraries.

The Curriculum of Muslim Schools

The curriculum of Muslim education at that time reminds us in its extensive and intensive nature of curricular programs of modern advanced systems of education, particularly on higher levels of education. It was not unusual to find instruction in mathematics (algebra, trigonometry, and geometry), science (chemistry, physics, and astronomy), medicine (anatomy, surgery, pharmacy, and specialized medical branches), philosophy (logic, ethics, and metaphysics), literature (philology, grammar, poetry, and prosody), social sciences, history, geography, political disciplines, law, sociology, psychology, and jurisprudence, theology (comparative religions, history of religions, study of the *Qur'an,* religious tradition [*hadith*], and other religious topics). They offered advanced studies in the professions, for example, law and medicine.

Their vocational curriculum was varied and founded on the more general studies; in fact, it appears generally to have been as comprehensive as their education was universal. The extent and depth of Muslim curriculum can be detected by references to a number of encyclopaedias of general knowledge and specific disciplines, among them the celebrated *Encyclopedia of the Ikhwan al-Safa* (the *Brethren of Purity* or *Sincerity*), which was known to and respected by European schoolmen.

Another indication of the extent of Muslim curriculum is manifested in the fact that one Arabic dictionary contained sixty volumes, with an illustration for each definition.[22] Again, its richness may be determined by its practical and useful consequences, leading to such ventures as calculating the angle of the ecliptic, measuring the size of the earth, calculating the procession of the equinoxes, inventing the pendulum clock, explaining in the field of optics and physics such phenomena as "refraction of light, gravity, capillary attraction and twilight," using the globe in teaching the geography of a round earth, developing observatories for the empirical study of heavenly bodies, making advances in the uses of drugs, herbs, and foods for medication, establishing hospitals with a system of interns and externs, improving upon the science of navigation, introducing new concepts of irrigation, fertilization, and soil cultivation, discovering causes of certain diseases and developing correct diagnoses of them, proposing new concepts of hygiene, making use of anesthetics in surgery with newly innovated surgical tools, introducing the science of dissection in anatomy, furthering the scientific breeding of horses and cattle, and finding new ways of grafting to produce new types of flowers and fruits. In the area of chemistry, the curriculum led to the discovery of such substances as potash, alcohol, nitrate of silver, nitric acid, sulphuric acid, and corrosive sublimate. It also developed to a high degree of perfection the arts of textiles, ceramics, and metallurgy.

On the curriculum of Muslim higher education in the Abbasside period, the summation given by Abu Yahya Zakariyya is of interest.[23] It included such legal subjects [*shariyyat*] as jurisprudence, exegesis, and tradition; literary studies [*adabiyyat*] in philology, syntax, rhetoric, prosody, composition, reading, and history; mathematics [*riyadhiyyat*] including geometry, astronomy, arithmetic, algebra, music, politics, ethics, and domestic economy; rational [*aqliyyat*] studies in logic, dialectic, dogmatic theology, metaphysics, natural science, medicine, and chemistry; and such miscellaneous subjects were approved as surveying, veterinary, agriculture, phrenology, dream interpretation, astrology, and magic.

The greatest calamity which came to Muslim learning was the cataclysm of the Mongol invasion in the thirteenth century. The Mongols destroyed most of the great institutions of learning in Khurasan and Baghdad—the mosques, the universities, the libraries. After the Mongols, these Islamic universities never regained their old spirit and beauty.

Fortunately we have some definite information on the range and scope of Islamic learning in the latter part of the tenth century from three authentic sources. These are (1) the *al-Fihrist-al-Ulum* (*Index of the Sciences*) by ibn al-Nadim, 988; (2) the works of the Society of Encyclopaedists, known better as Ikwan al-Safa (Brethren of Purity), and (3) the *Mafatih al-Ulum* (*Keys of the Sciences*) by Yusuf al-Katib of Khwarizm (976).

In the treatises of the Ikhwan al-Safa which flourished in Basra in the second half of the tenth century, we have the following information compiled by Friedrich Dieterici from the fifty-one *Treatises* published by the fraternity:

Mundane studies: Reading and writing, lexicography and grammar, calculation and computation, prosody and poetic art, the science of omens and portents, the science of magic, amulets, alchemy and legerdemain, trades and crafts, buying and selling, commerce, agriculture and cattle farming, and biography and narrative.

Religious studies: Knowledge of the Scriptures (i.e., the *Qur'an*), exegesis of the Scriptures, the science of tradition, jurisprudence, and the commemoration of God, admonition, the ascetic life, mysticism (Sufiism), and the ecstatic or beatific vision.

Philosophical studies: Mathematics, logic, numbers, geometry, astronomy, music, arithmetical and geometrical relations; natural science and anthropology; matter, form, space, time and motion; cosmogony; production, destruction, and the elements; meteorology, mineralogy; the essence of nature and its manifestations; botany; zoology; anatomy and anthropology; sense-perceptions; embryology; man as the microcosm; the development of the soul (psychical evolution); body and soul; the true nature of psychical and physical pain and pleasure; diversity of languages (philology); psychology—understanding, the world soul, etc.; and theology—esoteric doctrine of Islam, the ordering of the spirit world; the occult sciences.

In the *Mafatih al-Ulum* (the *Keys of the Sciences*) of al-Katib, we find a somewhat similar scope but different grouping of knowledge, excluding the mundane studies. The sciences, "which are for the most part Greek or Persian," are divided into two main branches, as follows:

The Indigenous Sciences: Jurisprudence (*Fiqh*), principles and (*Furu'*) applications, such as legal purity, prayer, fasting, alms, pilgrimage, buying and selling, marriage, homicide, wounding, retaliation, compensation and bloodwit, etc. (eleven sections); scholastic philosophy (*Kalam*) "the various schools and sects of Muslims, Christians, Jews and Gentiles (Persians, Indians, Chaldeans, Manichaeans, Marcionites, Bardesanians, Mazdakites, Sophists, etc.), Arabian heathenism, and the first principles of religion" (seven sections); grammar (*Nahw*) (twelve sections); the secretarial art (*Kitabat*) . . . including explanations of all the technical terms employed in the various government offices (eight sections); prosody and the poetic art (*Arieth* and *Shi'r*) (five sections); history (*Akhbar*) "the history of Ancient Persian, Muhammadan history, pre-Muhammadan history of Arabia, especially Yaman, and the history of Greece and Rome" (nine sections).

The Exotic Sciences: Philosophy (*Falsafa*) (three sections); logic (*Mantigh*) (nine sections); medicine (*Tibb*)—anatomy, pathology, materia medica, therapeutics, diet, weights and measures (eight sections); arithmetic including algebra (*Hisab, Arithma'tighi*) (five sections); geometry (*Handasa, Jumetriya*) (four sections); astronomy (*Ilmu n'nujum*)—"planets and fixed stars; the composition of the universe according to the Ptolemaic system; judicial astrology" (four sections); music (*Musighi*) (three sections); mechanics, hydrostatics (*Ilmu'lhiyal*) (two sections); and alchemy (*Kimiya*) (three sections).[24]

There is no doubt that in the Islamic educational curriculum the religion of Islam and the religious book (the *Qur'an*) stood at the center of all learning activities, as stated by ibn Khaldun. Next to religion, a language proficiency was essential (as it is considered today), but then it was to achieve a better understanding of religion. This language was, of course, Arabic. In fact, the *Qur'an,* writing, and some arithmetic were the only studies considered in the elementary schools, or *maktabs* (writing schools).

Medical Education in Early Islam

The medical profession and medical education in the early centuries of Islam followed the pattern and standards of the Greeks, particularly as they were maintained and improved upon at the medical school of the Academy of Jundi-Shapur. The Greek educational influences through this medical school in Iran may be traced beyond the Sassanian period to the Achaemenians. The standards and traditions of the school of medicine of the Academy of Jundi-Shapur were transferred and developed further in Baghdad under the Abbasside caliphs, and many of the teacher-physicians of the school of Jundi-Shapur, mostly Nestorian Christians and Jews, carried the tradition to the Muslim hospitals in Baghdad where the foundations of Muslim medical education were laid.

Medical education began early in a student's academic career, usually between his fifteenth and seventeenth years, although ibn Sina began at eleven, and Hunain ibn Is'haq had already completed his basic medical education at Jundi-Shapur when he was seventeen.

Studies in music, astronomy, and geometry were among optional premedical courses: Music to develop appreciation for the "subtleties of the human pulse; astronomy to determine lucky and unlucky times; geometry to determine the shape of wounds, for round wounds heal with ease."[25]

Students learned medical theory and practices interdependently in small classes and, as a rule, under a senior practitioner. The most basic aspect of training was clinical instruction in hospitals, including attendance at operations "and of those things that are incumbent upon the profession."[26] In addition to observation and internship, students attended lectures given by senior practitioners in their homes or in public places. Students questioned their masters on minute medical and surgical points with complete freedom, even to pointing out any fallacies in the master's theory. When so cornered, the teacher was often forced to revise his outlook or write treatises proving his position against objections.[27] One such treatise, the *Cure Within an Hour,* was written by Barr'-al-Sa'at after being challenged by hecklers in his class for stating that "it was possible to disperse the *materies morbi* of certain diseases within one hour." The methodology of instruction and learning stated here regarding medical students was, with some modifications, the methodology of higher education in all branches of study in Islamic colleges and universities.[28]

In lecture rooms, in the practitioner's home, or at the mosque, students took their seats according to academic seniority, the advanced students being seated together and closer to the lecturer. These lectures were always based on some written medical document and were immediately open to questions for clarification of obscure points, or definition of medical terms used during the lecture and indication of their correct pronunciation. Lectures were held sometimes during the evening hours, particularly during the *Ramadhan,* the month of fasting. Students gathered around famed lecturers from all over the Muslim world, with complete freedom to go from center to center to listen to other important lecturers, or to move to another teacher when the first one's professional "lemon was squeezed dry," or seemed dehydrated from the outset. Some of these international gatherings of students were quite large; usually the more famous a professor, the larger his classes.[29]

The most frequently used medical texts and references were the following: *Aphorisms,* Hippocrates; *Questions,* Hunain ibn Is'haq; *Guide,* Razes; also his book of al-Mansuri, *Continens; Commentaries,* Abu Sahl al-Nile; *Treasury,* Thabit ibn-Qurra; *Aims,* al-Jurjani; *Hidaya* (*Guide*), Ajwini; *Kifaya* (*Sufficiency*), ibn Faraj; *Treatises,* Galen; *Liber Regius,* Haly Abbas; *Hundred Chapters,* Abu Sahl; *Canon,* ibn Sina; *Thesaurus,* al-Jurjani. It should be noted here that the bulk of this list, when translated into Latin during the twelfth to fourteenth centuries, constituted the basis for the medical curricula of European medical schools, such as that of the University of Paris.[30]

The Teacher in Muslim Education

The degree of respect (or lack of reverence) for the teacher in the early centuries of Muslim education depended upon two factors: (1) The place where he taught (in countries such as Persia, where reverence for the teacher had a long tradition in Zoroastrian education, this tradition continued into the Islamic period) and (2) the level at which he taught. Ordinarily, reverence for the teacher increased through secondary and higher education. Elementary teachers commanded less respect because of their modest learning, and because that level of education seems to have attracted mediocre minds. They were often, but often unfairly, targets of ridicule and jokes, described by the public and students as naïve, stupid, even immoral. One proverb reported by al-Jahim says, "Do not seek advice from teachers, shepherds, and from those who sit much among women." Another, "Stupidity is found in tailors, teachers, and weavers." One story about the naïveté of the teacher is proverbial even to this day in Muslim countries. The story goes that the pupils in a certain maktab plotted to delude the teacher into believing that he looked ill. As each pupil walked into the classroom he stared at the teacher and then sorrowfully asked what ailed him and counselled him to rest. The simple-minded teacher took the bait—hook, line, and sinker; so he gave the youngsters a holiday and went to bed. The truth of the matter, however, is that Muslim education reveals every evidence that students showed great devotion to teachers and often preferred direct intellectual association with them than with their writings.[31]

Types of Teachers. There were six types of teachers, the *muallim,* the *mu'addib,* the *mudarris,* the *shaikh,* the *ustad,* and the *imam,* not to mention private tutors and *muaiyyids,* or assistants (junior instructors). *Muallim* was usually a title for elementary instructors. *Mu'addib* (or *adeib*), literally meaning a man of letters or teacher of manners, was a title used for either elementary or secondary instructors. *Mudarris* was a professional title attached to the title of *mu'id* or helper. He was the equivalent of an assistant to a professor and helped students by explaining difficult points in a professor's lectures. *Shaikh,* or master teacher (master professor), was a special title given to indicate academic or theological excellence. The *imam* was the supreme religious teacher.

The Teacher's Garment. During the Abbasside rule, teachers followed the Persian style: The Persian headgear, wide trousers, "skirt, vest, and jacket," all covered by a *jubbah* or *aba,* an outer mantle, a turban, and a *taylasan* over the turban.

Teacher's Guild. The *niqabat* (guilds) were known in Islam. There were different guilds according to professors, including the teacher's guild, which mainly set scholastic and moral standards for the teachers. The guilds exercised great influence on the profession.

Guidance. Every teacher was a guide. This was the ideal of Muslim educational theorists, such as Avicenna and al-Ghazzali. Particularly was this true of pre-college education and in the choice of a career. Children, insisted Avicenna, should be trained in a profession for which they have talent and inclination and should not be encouraged to choose in imitation of their fathers, or from pure wish. "It is the duty of the teacher, then, to study the qualities of a student and direct him to the most suitable branch of learning."[32]

Academic Freedom. In the golden centuries of Islam, religion encouraged freedom of inquiry. Scholarship and intellectual excellence were regarded most highly. Students were encouraged to debate their views with their teachers. Libraries, both public and private, even the courts of the caliphs and the palaces of kings, were centers of open and free inquiry by scholars, who often received financial aid to pursue their interests.

Method in Muslim Education

The following methods of instruction prevailed in "medieval" Islam, though adaptations were made to meet the needs of different levels of instruction: Formal delivery of lecture with the lecturer squatting on a platform against a pillar and one or two circles (a circle within a circle) of students seated before him, was the prevailing method in higher levels of instruction. The teacher read from a prepared manuscript or from a text, explaining the material, and allowed questions and discussion to follow the lecture. Students were encouraged to question the teacher's statements and even to differ with him provided they brought evidence to support their position. To say, "I do not know," when you do not know is one-half, and the most important half, of learning.[33] Students took complete notes on each lecture, for the lecture had to substitute for a text which was, for lack of printing, scarce.

The *mu'id* (assistant) often helped students with the master teacher's lecture. The lecturer always began by seeking from God assistance and guidance that he might speak the truth. He never spoke of colleagues or of authority in a derogatory manner before students. He referred to the works of others frequently and with due respect; and he did not lose his poise when being heckled. He used three steps in his presentation, dealing with his subject first in general, somewhat briefly, and avoiding details. He then went over the same material in more depth. He would then go over each difficult point of his subject with necessary explanatory details and with elucidation of all the difficult portions. Lectures were generally held in the late hours of the morning and the early hours of the afternoon. They ordinarily lasted from one to two hours.

The principles of mastery employed by students included memorization, repetition of what is memorized, reflection on what is mastered and its application.[34] Other principles incorporated these concepts: Freedom from anxiety is conducive to learning; simple food in small quantity helps keep the mind clear;[35] motivation, encouragement, and praise of the work well done stimulate further learning; and physical punishment is considered necessary as a last resort.

Freedom from worldly cares, studying away from home, and the selection of the right teachers were three conditions of good education. Choosing a good teacher was taken very seriously by students of higher learning, who often travelled on foot for months from Khurasan in northeastern Persia to Baghdad or Cairo, seeking not only good teachers, but going from teacher to teacher.

In E. G. Browne's *Persian Literature in Modern Times* there is an excellent description of the methods through which a theological student of the Shi'ah Islam earned his education, a method which was not unusual during the history of Muslim education, including the golden age of Islamic learning. The passage from Browne, though referring to seventeenth century Muslim education, may equally apply to the "medieval" Muslim education, and is quoted in full because of the unusual information regarding the hardships which students of higher learning often suffered in pursuit of their studies.

Autobiography of a Student of Theology

It is the autobiography of this same Sayyid Nimatullah, as given in the Qisas ul-Ulama, which furnishes us with so unusually vivid a picture of the privations and hardships experienced by a poor student of divinity. He was born in 1050/1640-1 and wrote this narrative when he was thirty-nine years of age, 'in which brief life,' he adds, 'what afflictions have befallen me!'

This affliction began when he was only five years old, when, while he was at play with his little companions, his father appeared, saying, 'Come with me, my little son, that we may go to the schoolmaster, so that thou mayst learn to read and write, in order that thou mayst attain to a high degree.' In spite of tears, protests, and appeals to his mother he had to go to school, where, in order the sooner to escape and return to his games, he applied himself diligently to his studies, so that by the time he was aged five years and a half he had finished the Qur'an, besides learning many poems.

Tyranny of teachers:

This, however, brought him no relief and no return to his childish games, for he was committed to the care of a blind grammarian to study the Arabic paradigms and the grammar of Zanjani. For this blind teacher he had to act as guide, while his next preceptor compelled him to cut and carry fodder for his beasts and mulberry leaves for his silk-worms.

An ignorant professor:

He then sought another teacher with whom to study the Kefiya of Ibnu'l-Hajib, and found an imposing personage dressed in white with an enormous turban 'like a small cupola,' who, however, was unable to answer his questions. 'If you don't know enough grammar to answer these questions, why do you wear this great load on your head?' enquired the boy; whereupon the audience laughed, and the teacher rose up ashamed and departed.

'This led me to exert myself to master the paradigms of grammar,' says the writer; 'but I now ask pardon of God for my question to that believing man, while thanking Him that this incident happened before I had attained maturity and become fully responsible for my actions.'

Hardships of travel in search of knowledge:

After pursuing his studies with various other masters, he obtained his father's permission to follow his elder brother to Huwayza. The journey thither by boat through narrow channels amongst the weeds, tormented by mosquitoes 'as large as wasps' and with only the milk of buffaloes to assuage his hunger, gave him his first taste of the discomforts of travel to a poor student. In return for instruction in Jami's and Jarbardi's commentaries and the Shafiya, his teacher exacted from him 'much service,' making him and his fellow students collect stones for a house which he wished to build, and bring fish and other victuals for him from the neighboring town. He would not allow them to copy his lecture notes, but they used to purloin them when opportunity arose and transcribe them. 'Such was his way with us,' says the writer, 'yet withal we were well satisfied to serve him, so that we might derive benefit from his holy breaths.'

Study under difficulties:

He attended the college daily till noon for instruction and discussion, and on returning to his lodging was so hungry that, in default of any better food, he used to collect the melon skins cast aside on the ground, wipe off the dust, and eat what fragments of edible matter remained. One day he came upon his companion similarly employed. Each had tried to conceal from the other the shifts to which he was reduced for food, but now they joined forces and collected and washed their melon skins in company. Being unable to afford lamps or candles, they learned by heart the texts they were studying, such as the *Alfiyya* of Ibn Malik and the *Kafiyya* on moonlight nights, and on the dark nights repeated them by heart so as not to forget them. To avoid the distraction of conversation, one student would on these occasions often bow his head on his knees and cover his eyes, feigning headache.

From Basra to Shiraz:

After a brief visit to his home, he determined to go to Shiraz, and set out by boat for Basra by the Shattu'l-Arab. He was so afraid of being stopped and brought back by his father that, during the earlier part of the voyage, he stripped off his clothes and waded behind the boat holding on to the rudder. When he had gone so far that recognition was no longer probable, he re-entered the boat. Farther on he saw a number of people on the bank, and one of his fellow passengers called out to them to enquire whether they were Sunnis or Shia. On learning that they were Sunnis, he began to abuse them and invoke curses on the first three Caliphs to which they replied with volleys of stones.

At college in Shiraz:

The writer remained only a short while at Basra, then governed by Husayn Pasha, for his father followed him thither to bring him home, but he escaped privily with his brother, and as already narrated, made his way to Shiraz and established himself in the Mansuriyya College, being then only eleven years of age. He found one of the tutors lecturing on the Alfiyya Ibn Malik, who, on the conclusion of the lecture, questioned him as to his aims and adventures, and finally seizing him by the ear and giving it a sharp twist, said, 'O my son, do not make thyself an Arab Shaykh or seek for supremacy, and do not waste thy time! Do not thus, that so perchance thou mayst become a scholar.'

Sufferings from cold and hunger:

In this college also the life was hard and the daily allowance of food inadequate, and the writer's brother wished to return home. He himself determined to remain, copying books for a pittance and working almost all night through the hot weather in a room with closed doors while his fellow companions slept on the roof. Often he had neither oil for his lamp nor bread to eat, but must work by moonlight, faint with hunger, while in the winter mornings his fingers often bled with the cold as he wrote his notes. Thus passed two or three years more, and though his eyesight was permanently affected by the strain to which it was subjected, he began to write books himself, a commentary on the *Kafiyya*, and another, entitled, *Niftahul-Labib*, on the *Tahdhib* of Shaykh Bahaud-Din Muhammad. He now began to extend the range of his studies beyond Arabic grammar and to frequent the lectures of more eminent teachers from Baghdad, Al-Ahsa and Bahrayn, amongst them Shaykh Jafar al-Bahrani.

An exacting professor:

One day he did not attend this Shaykh's lecture because of the news which had reached him of the death of certain relatives. When he reappeared on the following day the Shaykh was very angry and refused to give him any further instruction saying, 'May God curse my father and mother if I teach you any more! Why were you not here yesterday?' And when the writer explained the cause of his absence, he said, 'You should have attended the lecture and indulged in your mourning afterwards.' Only when the student had sworn never to play the truant again whatever might happen was he allowed after an interval to resume his attendance. Finally he so far won the approval of this somewhat exacting teacher that the latter offered him his daughter in marriage an honour from which he excused himself by saying, 'If God will, after I have finished my studies and become a Doctor [*alim*], I will marry.' Soon afterwards the teacher obtained an appointment in India, at Haydarabad in the Deccan.

Life of a poor student at Shiraz:

Sayyid Nimatullah remained in Shiraz for nine years, and for the most part in such poverty that often he swallowed nothing all day except water. The earlier part of the night he would often spend with a friend who lived some way outside the town so as to profit by his lamp for study, and thence he would grope his way through the dark deserted bazaars, soothing the fierce dogs which guarded their masters' shops, to the distant mosque where he lectured before dawn. At his parents' wish he returned home for a while and took to himself a wife, but being reproached by a learned man whom he visited with abandoning his studies while still-grounded in the Science of Traditions, he left his parents and his wife [he had been married only for three weeks] and returned to the Mansuriyya College at Shiraz. Soon afterwards, however, it was destroyed by a fire, in which one student and a large part of the library perished, and about the same time he received tidings of his father's death. Those two misfortunes, combined with other circumstances, led him to leave Shiraz and go to Isfahan.

He wins the favour of Mulla Muhammad Baqir-i-Majlisi:

During his early days at Isfahan he still suffered from the same poverty with which he had been only too familiar in the past, often eating salted meat to increase his thirst, so that the abundance of water he was thereby impelled to drink might destroy his appetite for solid food. The change in his fortune took place when he made the acquaintance and attracted the notice of that great but fanatical divine Mulla Muhammad Baqir-i-Majlisi, perhaps the most notable and powerful doctor of the Shia who ever lived. He was admitted to the house of the famous man and lived with him for four years studying theology, and especially the Traditions. Yet in this case familiarity did not breed contempt, for as the author mentions in his Anwar-al-Nu'maniyya, though specially favored by this formidable 'Prince of the Church,' he often when summoned to his library to converse with him or to help in the compilation of the Biharul-Ansar, would stand trembling outside the door for some moments ere he could summon up courage to enter.

He obtains a lectureship at Isfahan:

Thanks to his powerful patronage, however, he was appointed lecturer [*mudarris*] in a college recently founded by a certain Mirza Taqi near the Bath of Shaikh-i-Bahai in Isfahan, which post he held for eight years, when the increasing weakness of his eyes and the inability of the oculists of Isfahan to afford him any relief determined him to set out again on his travels. He visited Samarra, Kazimayan and other holy places in Iraq whence he returned by way of Shushtar to Isfahan. In 1079/1668-9 his brother died, and ten years later when he penned this autobiography, he still keenly felt this loss. After visiting Mashad he returned to Huwayza, where he was living a somewhat solitary and disillusioned life at the time of writing (1089/1678-9). Of his further adventures I have found no record, but his death did not take place until 1130/1718, only four years before the disaster which put an end to the Safawi Dynasty. [Dates are A.H. corresponding with A.D.]

The document illustrates how closely Muslim methodology resembled that of the medieval European schools. We see the child prematurely torn from the games and amusements suitable to his age to undergo a long, strenuous, and arid course of instruction in Arabic grammar and philology, reading one grammar after another in an ascending scale of difficulty, with commentaries, supercommentaries, glosses, and notes on each; we see him as a boy, now fired with ambition, pursuing his studies in theology and law, half-starved, suffering alternately from the cold of winter and the heat of summer, ruining his eyesight by perusing crabbed texts by the fitful light of the moon, and his digestion by irregular and unwholesome meals, varied by intervals of starvation; cut off from home life and family ties; submerged in an ocean of formalism and fanaticism; himself in time adding to the piles of glosses and notes which serve rather to submerge and obscure than to elucidate the texts whereon they are based; and last, if fortunate, attracting the favorable notice of some great divine, and becoming himself a mudarris [lecturer], a mutawalli [custodian of the shrine], or even a mujtahid [chief priest].[36]

Some Muslim Contributions to Education

Before concluding this brief summary of "medieval" Muslim education, it may be well to point out some of its basic contributions to educational theory and practice, and state also its basic shortcomings.

1. Throughout the twelfth and part of the thirteenth centuries, Muslim works on science, philosophy, and other fields were translated into Latin, particularly from Spain, and enriched the curriculum of the West, especially in northwestern Europe.

2. The Muslims passed on the experimental method of science, however imperfect, to the West.

3. The system of Arabic notation and decimals was introduced to the West.

4. Their translated works, particularly those of men such as Avicenna in medicine, were used as texts in classes of higher education far into the middle of the seventeenth century.

5. They stimulated European thought, reacquainted it with the Greek and other classical cultures and thus helped bring about the Renaissance.

6. They were the forerunners of European universities, having established hundreds of colleges in advance of Europe.

7. They preserved Greco-Persian thought when Europe was intolerant of pagan cultures.

8. European students in Muslim universities carried back new methods of teaching.

9. They contributed knowledge of hospitals, sanitation, and food to Europe.

The strength of the Muslim educational system lay in the following areas: It produced great scholars in almost every field. It developed literacy on a universal scale when illiteracy was the rule in Europe. It transmitted the best features of classical cultures to the West. It led the way in the development of libraries and universities. Its higher education in its creative centuries was open to rich and poor alike, the only requirements being ability and ambition. It held teachers and books in reverence, particularly on higher levels of instruction. The teacher, the book, the lecture, the debate—these were the nerve centers of its educational system.[37]

The curriculum, which was in the early centuries balanced between sectarian and secular studies, became in the later centuries scholastic, making all or practically all secular studies subject to religious and theological approval. The curriculum became formal, fixed, traditional, religious, dogmatic, backward-looking. It encouraged static minds and conformity. It became authoritarian and essentialist.

Whereas in its early centuries Muslim education encouraged debates, experimentation, and individualism, in its later stages it encouraged formal methods, memorization, and recitation. A system which was in its early stages rather spontaneous and free, encouraging individuals to pursue learning and inspire others to enlightenment, lost in the later stages this sense of intellectual adventure and its direction became superimposed from the top (the state and church) rather than inspired by the people. This led in time to an elite and aristocratic concept of education, replacing its early democratic educational spirit. Muslim education did not, and with its scholastic disciplines could not, take advantage of the tools of science and experimentation which it had inherited and improved upon. Rather, it passed on these tools to European men of science, who utilized them effectively after the Renaissance and thus initiated and developed the modern world of science.

CHAPTER IV *

THE LIBRARY AS AN EDUCATIONAL CENTER IN ISLAM

All Muslims, rich or poor, rulers or commoners, Persian or Arab, young or old, entertained great reverence for the scholar and still greater reverence for works of scholarship or literary masterpieces. To them, at a time when books were hand-copied by special copyists, devotion to great books carried with it almost religious, even mystical, attachments. Muhyi-al-Din ibn al-Arabi states in the *Mahadurat al-Abrar* that a great book of historical or scientific nature expressing the best wisdom of the finest minds, sustained by past traditions, and representing the fruits of sound minds from many distant lands was indeed a treasure, easily and inexpensively procured when compared to other goods. In describing man's relation to such a book, he asks, "Who can have such another guest that may either make a short sojourn or stay with you as your own shadow or even as a very limb of your body?"[1] Al-Jahiz points out that "the book is silent so long as you need silence, eloquent whenever you want discourse. He never interrupts you if you are engaged, but if you feel lonely he will be a good companion. He is a friend who never deceives or flatters you, and he is a comrade who does not grow tired of you."[2]

Al-Arabi, in the source quoted above, compares a book to an orchard and a park, a tongue of the dead, the voice of the living—"an evening visitor who never sleeps until you sleep and never utters a word except what pleases you, never reveals a secret or abases a deposit. He is the most faithful neighbor, just friend, obedient companion, submissive professor, expert and useful comrade, with no desire to argue or to weary of his owner."[3]

It is, therefore, no wonder that with such reverence for books the Muslim libraries (and before them those of the Persians) became centers of learning wherever they were established. In fact, some of the early Muslim colleges, such as the Academy of Bait-al-Hikmah in Baghdad, were originally libraries which in the course of time evolved into colleges. Shalaby reports that such libraries as the Khizanah-al-Hikmah (The Treasure House of Wisdom) of al-Munajjim (888; 275

---

*All dates refer to A.D. unless otherwise specified.

A.H.) and others in Mosul and Basra were established by their patrons either as centers or were adjoined to centers of learning, open to the public from near and far.

Pinto, describing the facilities of a Muslim "medieval" library similar to those of Shiraz, Cordova, and Cairo, states that it contained

> . . . many rooms for different uses: Galleries with shelves in which the books were kept, rooms where the visitors could read and study, rooms set apart for those in charge of making copies of manuscripts, rooms which served for literary assemblies, and even in some cases rooms for musical entertainment. All rooms were richly and comfortably fitted. On the floor were carpets and mats, where the readers in Oriental fashion squatted with crossed legs reading and even writing. The windows and doors were closed with curtains, the chief entrance door having a specially heavy curtain to prevent the cold air from entering.[4] The library of Adud-al-Dawlah in Shiraz, "consisted of a long gallery with store rooms off it. Along the wall of the gallery and the store rooms, bookcases were placed which contained many shelves. The books were arranged on the shelves, and for every branch of learning there was a separate section."[5]

The large libraries carried catalogues of their collections. *Al-Fihrist* of ibn al-Nadim is reported to have been originally a catalogue of the author's private library. The library in Shiraz had separate catalogues for sections of its library; the library of al-Sahib is reported to have consisted of 10,000 volumes.[6]

Not only did scholars freely use the libraries as such and all their facilities for pursuing scholarly endeavors: In some of them food and lodging, writing materials, and other aids were provided for the convenience of those who came from distant lands in pursuit of knowledge. Books were also lent out generously (sometimes as many as a hundred to one scholar) but under a certain borrowing code which included extreme care in the use of the books. Among the rules were the following: No marginal notes; no lending of books to others by borrowers; no borrowed book to be used as security for private matters; all books to be returned immediately upon library or owner request; all books to be retained by borrowers for a specified time; returned books to be accompanied by a statement of gratitude for their use.

There were three types of libraries in the early centuries of Islam: Public, semi-public, and private. Public libraries were usually those associated with the schools, colleges, and mosques, but they were open to the public as well. The semi-public libraries, on the other hand, were open to a select group. Private libraries, as the title implies, belonged to scholars for their private use. All three types were to be found in abundance all over Islam. How many private libraries actually existed in Islam and what was the fate of most of them will never be known.

Shalaby's *History of Muslim Education* gives a partial list with accompanying descriptions of these three types of Muslim libraries, of which the more important ones merit our attention here. The public libraries listed are Bait-al-Hikmah, the Haidari Library of Najaf, ibn Sawwar's Library at Basra, the famous Khizanah Sabur Dar-al-Ilm Library in Baghdad, the Dar-al-Ilm of al-Sharif al-Radi, the Library of the Mosque of al-Zaid, the Dar-al-Ilm (or Dar-al-Hikmah), Library of Cairo, and a number of famous school libraries. Among semi-private libraries listed are those of al-Nasir al-Din Allah, al-Musta'sim bi'llah, and that of the Fatimid caliphs. The private libraries listed belonged to al-Fath ibn Khaqan (d. 861; 247 A.H.), Hunain ibn Is'haq (d. 877; 264 A.H.), ibn al-Khashshab (d. 1171; 567 A.H.), al-Muwaffaq ibn Matran (d. 1191; 587 A.H.), Jamal al-Din al-Quifri (d. 1248; 646 A.H.), Ufra'im ibn al-Zaffan (ca. 1106; 500 A.H.), Quad al-Din al-Isfahani. Some sources cited in Shalaby are ibn al-Nadim's, *al-Fihrist;* Khuda Bukhsh's Islamic Libraries; *Encyclopedia of Islam;* Yaqut, *al-Buldan*, and Irshad G. Zaidan's *Tarikh al-Tamaddun-al-Islami* III.[7]

Muslim caliphs and viziers encouraged learning in all important Islamic cities and made libraries available to all who cared to use them. Even monarchs opened their private libraries to public use, particularly the Samanids in Bukhara, the Hamdanids in Syria, and the Buyyids (or Buwaihids) in Shiraz. Avicenna (980-1037) reports the free use of Sultan Nuh ibn-Mansur's royal library in these words:

> I found there many rooms filled with books which were arranged in cases row upon row. One room was allotted to works on Arabic philology and poetry; another to jurisprudence, and so forth, the books on each particular science having a room to themselves. I inspected the catalogue of ancient Greek authors and looked for the books which I required; I saw in this collection books of which few people have heard even the names, and which I myself have never seen either before or since.[8]

Ibn Abbad not only allowed the free use of his famous library but gave each scholar up to 1000 dirhams and a garment to encourage learning and scholarship. The library of the poet ibn Hamdan was open to all students, and free paper was given to penniless scholars; that of Adud-al-Dawlah in Basra was open to scholars, and those who "read or copied" received a stipend. Another library is reported by Khuda Bukhsh to have been established for the use of students by a rich landowner in Isfahan.[9] The Qadi of Nishapur, ibn Hibban (d. 965), bequeathed his house to the city along with a "library and quarters for foreign students and provided stipends for their maintenance."[10]

The geographer Yaqut al-Hamawai (1178-1229) states that during his three-year stay in Marv the various libraries were most generous in lending him books. According to his own statement, "My house was never clear of 200 volumes, taken on loan, or more, and I had never to give a deposit though their value was 200 dinars."[11] Again, "I surely would not have left [the city] till death, because of the people's generosity, kindness, and sociability, and the multitude of sound fundamental books there. For when I left it there were in it ten endowed libraries, the like of which, in number of books, I had never seen. . . . There were [in one library] about twelve thousand volumes [books bound in skin]."[12] Yaqut mentions the names of several other libraries at Marv in his geography, among them (a) the Kamilliyyah, (b) the Sharaf al-Mulk Mustawfi, (c) the Nizam-al-Mulk library, (d) two libraries in the Amidiyya College, (e) the library of Myd-al-Mulk, the vizier, (f) the Khatuniyyah, a library in the mosque college, and (g) Damir monastery.[13]

The famous library (the "House of Science") of the Caliph al-Hakim in Cairo, located in the college and founded in 1004, had a large collection of books with an exaggerated estimate of 1,600,000 volumes. It was open to the public as a center of learning and research. Al Maqrizi says of it:

> On the eighth day of Jamadi II 395 A.H. [1004 A.D.], the building called the House of Wisdom [or Science] was opened. The students took up their residence. The books were brought from the libraries of the garrisoned castles [the residences of the Fatimid caliphs], and the public was admitted. Whoever wanted was at liberty to copy any book he wished, or whoever needed to read a certain book found in the library could do so. Scholars studied the Qur'an, astronomy, grammar, lexicography, and medicine. The building was, moreover, adorned by carpets, all doors and corridors had curtains, and manager, servants, porters and other menials were appointed to maintain the establishment. Out of the library of the Caliph al-Hakim . . . books were brought . . . in all sciences and literatures and of exquisite calligraphy such as no other king had ever been able to bring together. Al-Hakim permitted admittance to everyone, without distinction of rank, who wished to read or consult any of the books.[14]

In al-Hakim's academy, "poor students were supplied with free ink, inkwells, reed pens and paper, as was the case with most other Muslim institutions of learning."[15] Al-Hakim allowed a budget of more than 200 dinars a year for maintenance of this library, covering such items as paper for copyists, paper, ink, and pen for students, repair of damaged or over-used books, librarian's salary, and so forth. Al-Maqrizi states that:

> As in the other Islamic cultures, the Arabs cultivated the Greek Sciences, wrote original books, fostered learning, founded schools, and established colleges. In the school the curriculum included, besides religion, grammar and poetry, history and law, philosophy and natural science. Even women were educated. . . . Christian Spaniards who had become Arabized* neglected Latin in favor of Arabic literature; and some of them translated Latin works into Arabic.[16]

The ninth-century Christian ecclesiastic, San Alvaro of Cordova, wrote as follows:

> Many of my coreligionists read the poems and stories of the Arabs, and studied the writings of Muhammadans, theologians and philosophers, not in order to refute them but to learn to express themselves most elegantly and correctly in the Arabic tongue. Alas! All the young Christians who became notable for their talents know only the language and literature of the Arabs, read and study Arabic books with zeal and at enormous cost from great libraries, and everywhere proclaim aloud their literature is worthy of admiration.[17]

The Caliph al-Hakim II founded a great library in Cordova in the latter decades of the tenth century, enriched with the best books that a generous and lavish caliph could buy through book agents "in all the

*Muslim Arabs refer to Arabized Spaniards as *Musta'ribs.* The Spaniards Latinized the term into *mozarabes.*

bookmarkets of the Muslim world." The library was open to all who cared to use it; poor students and scholars in pursuit of knowledge received financial aid from the caliph, and the learned caliph was himself the library's best student and scholar. Legend has it that "not one book was to be found in al-Hakim's library, whatever might be its contents, which the caliph had not perused, writing on the flyleaf the name, surname and patronymic *Takhallos* of the author, that of the tribe to which he belonged, the year of his birth and death."[18] This, however, was quite an overstatement even for the learned Caliph al-Hakim, since his library contained around 600,000 volumes, and required 24 volumes to catalogue the titles and descriptions![19]

Important Islamic Libraries

Libraries in the East: Baghdad to Nishapur. Baghdad in its glory—that is, at the turn of the thirteenth century and the decades preceding the Mongol destruction of the great city—boasted of thirty-six libraries, among them the following: (a) The library of Umar al-Waqidi (736-811) estimated at one hundred and twenty camel-loads of books;[20] (b) al-Ma'mun's Bait-al-Hikmah, founded about 318; (c) Ardeshir's (the vizier) "House of Learning" (Dar-al-Ilm), about 991; (d) the Nizamiyyah College Library, carrying the name of its founder (1064); (e) the Mustansiriyyah School (madrasah) Library, in 1233; (f) the library of al-Baiqani (1033), consisting of "so many books that it required sixty-three hampers and two trunks to transport them"; (g) the library of Muhammad ibn al-Husain of Haditha, containing a collection of rare manuscripts kept under lock; (h) the library of ibn-al-Kami with 10,000 books. In addition there were more than 100 bookdealers in Baghdad, some of them hiring "a corps of expert copyists who worked in a *scriptorium*," literally publishing hand-copied manuscripts.[20]

Libraries in Persia. When Nuh ibn Mansur, himself the proud owner of one of the finest libraries of his time, asked ibn Abbad to become his chancellor, the latter refused the royal offer because it would have taken some 400 camels to transport his books to the capital.[21] The catalogue of his private library "filled ten volumes."[22]

The library of ibn-al-Amid (d. 971) in Rayy is described by ibn Miskawaih, his librarian, after ibn al-Amid's house was plundered by some wandering sectarians, as follows:

> His heart sorrowed for his books, for he loved them better than anything else. There were many of them, including the sciences and all the branches of philosophy and literature, over 100 camel loads. When he saw me he asked me about the books, and when I told him that they were safe, that no hand had touched them, he brightened up and said, "Thou art a child of fortune; all other things can be replaced, but not the books," and I saw that his face shone, and he said, "Bring them tomorrow to such and such a place;" this I did. The books were all that was saved from his property.[23]

The library of the poet ibn Hamdan (d. 935) in Mosul, attached to the college which he had founded in that city, contained books on all branches of learning.[24]

The library of Adud-al-Dawlah (d. 982) had two "branches." In addition to the one at Basra, he built a large library on the palace grounds in Shiraz, run by a librarian, a superintendent, and a director (*Hazin, Mushrif,* and *Wakil*). The library contained a wealth of scientific literature. Cyril Elgood states in *A Medical History of Persia*:

> The books were stored in a long, arched hall, with stack rooms on all sides. Against the walls stood book presses, six feet high and three yards wide, made of carved wood, with doors which closed from the top. Each branch of knowledge had separate bookcases and catalogues.[25]

In the thirteenth century just before the Mongol invasion there were at least ten other libraries, eight of them located in various colleges and two in mosques. Still others in Persia were those of Isfahan, Shiraz, Marv, Mosul, Basra, Ghazna, and Nishapur.

Libraries in North Africa. In Cairo, one of the three intellectual centers of Islam, there were, in addition to the previously mentioned "House of Science," a number of famous libraries, among them the four named below:

The library of the Bait-al-Hikmah ("House of Learning") was established by the Fatimid Caliph al-Aziz (975-96) in 988, contained not less than 100,000 volumes, perhaps as many as 600,000 bound books, including 2,400 *Qur'ans* illuminated in gold and silver and kept in a separate room. Again according to Cyril Elgood:

> The rest of the books—on jurisprudence, grammar, rhetoric, history, biographies, astronomy and chemistry—were kept in large presses around the walls, which were divided into shelves, each of which had a door with a lock. Over the door of each section was nailed a list of all the books contained therein, as well as a notice of the lacunae in each branch of knowledge.[26]

The library of al-Fadhil was robbed by the vizier Abu al-Faraj in 1068, who carried off twenty-five camel loads of the precious books, all of which were burned months later by Turkish soldiers. It took over a century to restore even a part of the great loss. In 1171, when Sultan Saladin entered Cairo, "he found a library of 120,000 volumes in the palace," and gave them to his "learned Chancellor al-Qadi al-Fadhil."[27]

The library of Prince Ben Fatik, a learned scholar and writer, is listed by ibn abi Usaibiyyah, in his history of Greek and Arabic physicians, among the private libraries in Cairo, both Jewish and Muslim.

The al-Ma'arrif library contained thousands of books on "every branch of learning," with fine sentences inscribed on the back of each volume, stating its contents, and each volume on medical and scientific books contained "handsome glosses and useful elucidations," inscribed in them by al-Ma'arrif.[28]

*Libraries in Spain and Sicily.** Of the more than seventy libraries in Muslim Spain, two may be specially noted here. The library of Caliph al-Hakim (d. 976) in Cordova contained perhaps around 600,000 volumes, carefully selected by expert bookdealers from all the book markets in Islam. It employed a sizable staff of librarians, copyists, and binders in the *scriptorium.*

The library of Abu-al-Mutrif, a Cordovan judge, contained mostly rare books, "masterpieces of calligraphy, employing six copyists at full-time employment." The library was sold at auction for 40,000 dinars after his death in 1011.

Jewish Libraries in the Islamic Context. Among Jewish libraries, several were significant for Islamic culture. Yaqub ben Yusuf ben Killis was in the service of the caliph in Cairo in 979, where, stimulated by Muslim scholarship, he "employed many copyists for the transcription of legal, medical, and scientific books, spending over 1,000 gold dinars a month in support of scholars and in wages to copyists and binders."[30]

The eleventh century physician, Ephraim, possessed a great collection of medical books. Ten thousand volumes of his collection were eventually transported to the library of Afdad, the son of the Amir al-Juyush, but some 20,000 volumes remained in his own collection.[31]

The physician Abraham ben Hillel (Abu al-Izz) possessed a large library containing the works of Maimonides, Galen, Hippocrates, and Averroes which was later sold at an auction.

Another Jewish physician, Leo Mosconi of Majorea (early fourteenth century), had a library of medical and other books, also sold later at auction, which included the works of Avicenna and Averroes as well as those of Greek and Hebrew authors, with treatises on "astronomy, anatomy, meteorology, medicine, physics, music, logic, ethics and grammar."[32]

The library of the physician David d'Estella in France (at the end of the fourteenth century) "included Aristotle, Galen, Averroes, and Maimonides."

Destruction of Muslim Libraries

The circumstances attending the destruction of Muslim libraries were varied, as the following instances show. The Muslim library in

*The Visigoths, before the Arabs, had not developed a deeply rooted culture in Spain. Byzantine influence was in the south. Jews were isolated communities with their Hebrew-Aramaic academies, and Catholicism was limited to Latin. The Arabs became patrons of culture in Spain as they were in the East, and their capital, Cordova, "became probably the largest city in Europe after Constantinople, possessing 200,000 houses, 600 mosques, and 900 public baths. The streets were stone-paved, and water was brought to the houses in conduits; public lighting illuminated the streets at night. The palace of the caliphs had 21 doors and was surrounded by 1,293 columns of marble and jasper with gilded capitals. It was illuminated by hundreds of silver lamps. To Christendom, Cordova was a marvelous, fabulous city, and it attracted many amazed travelers from northern Spain, France, Italy and even Germany."[29] It was a center of learning and a haven for bookdealers, having one of the largest bookmarkets in Spain.

Tripoli was destroyed by crusaders on command of a monk who was displeased at finding so many copies of the *Qur'an* there.[33] The great library of Sultan Nuh-ibn Mansur, described by Avicenna elsewhere in this section, was totally burned soon after the great philosopher had completed his research there. This fact brought about the later accusation that the scholar burned the library after assimilating much of its contents, particularly in medicine, in order to claim these areas of information as his own.[34] When the Mongol and Tartar hordes sacked the city of Baghdad in 1258, they burned all the libraries, using the manuscripts for fuel! Other cities and libraries met with a similar fate, from Samarkand and Bukhara to Baghdad.[35]

The Vizier Abu al-Faraj carried away from al-Hakim's library in Cairo in 1068 (sixty years after the library was established) twenty-five camel loads of books, "and sold them for 1,000,000 dinars to pay for his soldiery." A few months later the books fell into the hands of Turkish soldiers, who, after defeating the caliph and plundering his palace, "tore the fine leather binding off the books and made shoes of them."[36] The manuscripts were finally piled up into a heap and burned near Abyar, which then became known as the "Hill of the Books."[37]

The library of Prince Ben Fatiq, described by ibn abi Usaibiyyah in his history of Greek and Arabic medicine, met with a curious fate described by the author as follows:

> Prince Ben Fatiq was eager to master the sciences, and he possessed a library. No sooner would he alight from his horse than he would join his books and could not be torn away from them; he did nothing else but read and write, which clearly was most important to him. Now he had a wife, a noble woman, who also belonged to the ruling family. When he died, she went with her slaves into the library, and in her heart there was resentment against the books, because on account of them her husband had turned away from her. She began to sing the dirge of the dead for him, and while doing so she and her slaves were throwing the books into a large water basin in the house large enough to immerse 1000 books. Then the books were taken out of the water, but most of them had sunk in the meantime.[38]

In Spain all private and public libraries met an unfortunate end when the Moors were thrown out of that country by Christian princes in 1492 and thousands of Arabic books were burned. The Escorial, which was founded by Phillip II and contained a large number of Muslim manuscripts and books acquired in the capture of a Moroccan galley, was burned down in June, 1674, and 8,000 Arabic books were destroyed. "A century later when Michael Casiri began to catalogue the Arabic collection in the Escorial, he found only 1,824 manuscripts—forlorn survivors, perhaps, of the once great libraries of Cordova."[39]

The extent of the damage, permanent or otherwise, to the world of scholarship and education which may have been brought about by the destruction of the chief libraries of Islam by Mongols, crusaders, Western Christians, Turks, fanatic sectarians, or accidental fire, may have been exaggerated by historians for the following reasons:

As to the number of bound volumes, they included undetermined numbers of copies of the same materials, so that the destruction of a library with 100,000 volumes did not necessarily mean that 100,000 works of scholarship were lost to man. The number of *Qur'ans* in some libraries such as those of Baghdad and Cairo, for example, ran into thousands. Further evidence of this fact was the availability of specialized copyists and scriptoriums in large cities and in connection with large libraries. Here uncounted copies of fundamental works were produced not only for libraries but also for publishers and the public in general.

There were also many bookdealers in large Islamic centers who traded books or sold them to libraries and to scholars. Baghdad at its height, just before the Mongolian destruction of it, boasted over 100 such bookdealers. In Shiraz, Marv, Mosul, Basra, Cairo, Cordova, Fez, Tunis, and many other Islamic cities there were numerous bookdealers. Bargaining for books had developed in these cities into a skillful art. Hence many copies of important works were made available to private collectors, and the destruction of the large libraries did not necessarily mean the final extinction of these works. Many of them survived and have been preserved in private, and sometimes uncatalogued, collections in mosque libraries and elsewhere.

We should also remember that much that was worthwhile in Islamic learning had been translated into Latin and other European languages and had become part of the heritage of Christian Europe by the middle of the thirteenth century. Furthermore, long after the destruction of some of these Eastern libraries, Western Muslim scholars spent many years in the libraries of Egypt furthering scholarship, a practice which would appear puzzling had all the Eastern libraries been destroyed. Ibn Khaldun, for example, made frequent use of Egyptian libraries after the Mongolian invasions in the middle of the thirteenth century.

In *al-Fihrist,* ibn al-Nadim made a complete annotated list of all the works of merit that were available in Arabic toward the end of the tenth century. About this list the following observations are of interest:

The total number of titles listed in *Al-Fihrist* falls short of the estimates of the number of volumes available in some libraries. Moreover, statements made by some authors that not one in a thousand of the works listed by Nadim have survived leave two questions unanswered. First, if we take the list of surviving works and multiply it by 1,000, we shall have a list hundreds of times larger than the one in *Al-Fihrist*. Second, not until we have combed all the private libraries in Islam can we say with any reasonable certainty what has or has not survived of this list or of the works in Islamic learning in general.

We should also remember that many of the works of scholarship in Islam were translations of Greek, Persian, and Hindu classics, or commentaries, interpretations, and adaptations of them. If we therefore conclude that many of these translated or interpreted works were destroyed, the fact remains that many of the originals from which these were translated have survived.

Some private libraries had their titles catalogued, and these catalogues are reported to be in some cases as many as ten volumes. Evidently, these included lists of copies of the same work, since al-Nadim's *Index* shows a somewhat limited listing by comparison.

Many of the Islamic books on philosophy and science available in "medieval" libraries were copies of the same work; so the loss of many of them would mean at worst the loss of many copies of the same work. Furthermore, many of these works of philosophy and science (particularly medicine) were translated into Hebrew and preserved in medieval Jewish libraries. Later, hundreds of the best of them were translated into Latin and other languages and saved in this manner.

Fortunately, many of the basic works of the greatest scholars of Islam, such as Avicenna, Averroes, ibn Khaldun, Rhazes, Hafiz, Sa'di, Firdawsi, and others, have survived the destruction of libraries.

CHAPTER V *

MUSLIM EDUCATIONAL CLASSICS, 750-1350

EDUCATIONAL CLASSICS in the history of Islam from 700 to 1350 A.D., all in Arabic and Persian sources, deal largely with the aims of education, problems of method, theories of knowledge, the curriculum, moral and religious education, educational psychology, moral-educational counsel, educational equality, educational research, problems of discipline, educational organization, and educational administration.

Although each work is unique and contains helpful suggestions and concepts valuable to any culture, the appreciation of most of them would depend largely upon knowledge of social conditions of the time in which each work was written. Some are obviously regional in character or are adapted to Islamic concepts of education; some are very limited in the extent and scope of the questions and problems of education or deal with education in the context of a broader field of study, such as religion, or politics, or general culture. Others are definitely designed to appeal to religious groups—mystics, for example—or deal with moral considerations, implying their educational application. Still others are educational works in the sense of their tremendous and far-reaching educational influence, and in some instances they are quite comprehensive in the treatment of educational topics. All are written within the context of Islamic culture and religion; yet some are truly great literary and educational masterpieces worthy of translation into any language. Among these are the works discussed or outlined in this chapter.†

---

*All dates refer to A.D. unless otherwise specified.

†English translations of titles of books, though accurately worded to convey the original meanings, are occasionally abbreviated slightly or rearranged to make the English equivalent euphonious or simplified. In all such cases, a literal translation of the original title appears in the subsequent discussion of the work. The dates shown in this section do not always indicate the date of the writing of the book. Some may refer (or may have referred) to the author's birth or death; or they may refer to the date of the first appearance of the book, or to the date of a particular copy of the original text. The point of reference in each date is indicated whenever it has been reliably verified, or when the writer has been able to determine its intent. Nevertheless the dates should prove valuable, even

The ones chosen for a somewhat detailed analysis here have been selected partly because of their great educational importance in Islam and partly because of the writer's belief that all may prove valuable sources of information and guidance for Western students of the history of education and for teachers interested in the theoretical concepts in education. They are as follows: *Ghabus-Namah* of Washmgir, *Siyasat-Namah* of Nizam-al-Mulk, *Gulistan* and *Bustan* of Sa'di, *Fatihat-al-*

---

if not labeled, because they determine the century in which the author may have lived and, accordingly, the century in which the book may have been written.

I have also identified each work with its author's last name, or the nearest thing to it. The author's full name then follows in parentheses. This technique is used for purposes of quick identification and simplicity. In many cases the author's full name is too long, indicating in part his genealogy or affiliation with some monarch or prince, town or province, sect or cult.

Some authors (almost all Persian) wrote in both Arabic and Persian. In such cases their works are listed separately for each language. In some cases the author (for example, al-Ghazzali and ibn Sina) wrote the book originally in Arabic, and then rendered it more briefly into Persian, with adaptations to regional or national needs. European translations of these works were occasionally made in Latin during the medieval centuries. Others have been translated much later, some during the last two centuries, and mostly into German, French, and English—more in German than in either French or English. Some of these works, such as the *Gulistan* of Sa'di, the *Muqaddimah* of ibn Khaldun, the *Ghabus-Namah* of Washmgir or the *Siyasat-Namah* of Nizam-al-Mulk, have been translated into many European and Oriental languages.

It may be appropriate to observe here that the long list of Muslim education classics, along with the entire material covered in this study, should lead to some tentative suggestions on various methods and means of incorporating the areas of Islamic learning and education into our histories of education both in courses and in texts. Ten suggestions which should encourage historians of education and institutions of teacher-education are here suggested.

1. In texts on the history of education (particularly in the chapters dealing with education in the medieval periods) a proportionate section should be included on the development of Islamic learning, incorporating an adequate treatment of its origins, assimilation, innovations, and transmission to the Western world, with resulting contributions to Western learning and education.

2. Research studies in this field for term papers, panel reports, master's and doctor's theses, and for post-doctoral investigation should be encouraged.

3. Translations into English of important classics in Islam, particularly those available in Arabic and Persian, including the ones described here in special series for reference and research, should be made available for study alongside similar classics in Western education. There should also be translations into English of the important studies on Islamic learning and education which are available in German, French, Italian, and Russian, some of which (particularly in German and French) are important enough to be used increasingly by Muslim scholars themselves as source and reference materials for Islamic studies.

4. More extensive study should be advocated in the history of education of the Hellenistic and post-Hellenistic era with particular emphasis on Syrian, Persian (Pahlavi), and Hindu contributions to Western learning and education.

5. Special research in this area should be supported by such organizations as the History of Education Society, the Philosophy of Education Society, the Comparative Education Society, and various Oriental societies and institutes. Such societies can be instrumental in financing, through various foundations, in-

Ulum of Ghazzali, *Akhlaqi Nasiri* of Tusi, *Taharat al-A'araq* of ibn Maskuya, *Mantigh al-Tayr* of Attar, *Rasa'il* of Ikhwan al-Safa, and *Mafatih al-Ulum* of al-Katib.

1. Ghabus-Namah of Washmgir

The *Ghabus-Namah (The Book of Ghabus)* was written by Amir Kaikawus ibn Iskandar ibn Ghabus 'i Washmgir ibn Ziar, King of Tabaristan. Written toward the end of his life, the book was in the form of educational and moral exhortations to his son, Gilan-Shah. Amir Kaikawus was reputed in his time for his exemplary character and purity of spirit, and his book is perhaps one of the best educational-moral works produced in the Islamic culture. It covers the whole range of human conduct, dealing at considerable length with questions of education, problems of conduct, principles of friendship and love, wealth and contentment, marriage and family, contents of instruction, arts and sciences, education and vocations, and many other important topics. Its complete rendering into English would be an extremely valuable contribution to educational thought.

Amir Ziar ruled over Tabaristan (1049-1069), a mountainous area between the Caspian Sea and the Elborz Range, and between Gorgan and Gilan in northern Persia.[1] He completed the *Ghabus-Namah* in 1069 (462 A.H.), just before his death at the age of sixty-three. It apparently took the author, at most, five years to complete the work.[2]

It was a custom among the pre-Muslim Sassanian Persian kings to write a moral-educational book, counselling the heir to the throne on the proper education befitting a prince and on codes of conduct and political behavior appropriate for the ruler. A number of such didactic books had been written in Persia before Amir Ziar's *Ghabus-Namah*. Important among these was the lengthy educational counsel of Ardeshir to his son Shapur, as stated in the epic verse of Firdawsi in the *Shah-Namah* (*Book of Kings*).[3] The *Kalila wa-Dimna*, an ancient Indi-

---

vestigations in the surviving Islamic libraries in Spain, Egypt, Iraq, Iran, Turkey, and elsewhere for manuscripts of cultural-educational value for translation.

6. Instruction in Persian, Arabic, and Turkish as classical languages in more of our larger universities should be recommended in order to give American scholars who are interested in Islamic learning the linguistic tools for research.

7. Evaluations of Islamic (classical) educational theories and their historic theoretical comparisons with historic educational thought in Europe and the United States should be incorporated into our philosophies of education.

8. A comprehensive annotated bibliography of Islamic learning and its contributions to the West should be prepared, including books and periodicals in English, German, French, Russian, Spanish, Italian, Persian, Turkish, and Arabic.

9. Scholar-exchange between the United States and Islamic countries in the fields of history, pedagogy, philosophy, and anthropology should be stimulated and encouraged.

10. Our departments of history or of teacher-education in colleges and schools of education should offer a special course in the history of transmission of learning to the West, with a parallel course covering the East.

an book of fables, was translated by order of Anushirwan into Pahlavi by Burzuyah, his physician. The book was to be studied as a guide for good government.[4] Another similar work was the *Siyasat-Namah* of Nizam-al-Mulk, which will be explained in detail later. Still another was the *Nasihat-al-Muluk* (*Counsel to the Kings*)by Ghazzali in 1111, just before his death.[5]

Although *Ghabus-Namah* was similarly written by Washmgir ibn Ziar (Amir Ziar) as a didactic and moral guide, the Persian classic is more than a book of counsel from a royal father to his prince-son. It portrays better than any other work before the Mongolian invasions in the thirteenth century the conditions of educational, social, and moral life in northern Persia. The very selection of the areas for advice indicates the conditions of life which the author approves or criticizes, as will be noted by the translation of the titles of the chapters comprising the book. Moreover, the book can legitimately claim inclusion among the great Muslim and world classics because of the universality of its moral, social, and educational ideals, as noted by its translations into important European languages. Of special importance is the attention the author gives to conditions of education in his domain and the specific educational subjects which he treats. Also noteworthy are the chapters on religious education, medical science, geometry and astronomy, poetry, teaching, the relation of vocations to economic advantages, good and evil in speech, nurture of one's children, the art of writing, values of physical exercise, and commercial crafts.

The work is also known as *Andarz-Namah* or the *Book of Moral Counsel.* Translations of *Ghabus-Namah* into other languages include a German translation by V. Diez (Berlin, 1811); a French translation by Querry (Paris, 1886); and Russian and English translations about the same time. According to Richard Frye, an Arabic translation by Abd al-Majid Badawi and Muhammad Sadiq Nashat was made in Cairo in 1952. Persian editions include (1) that by Reza Ghuli Khan Hedayat, issued in 1868, 1890, 1901, and 1922, Habl-al-Matin Publishers, Isfahan; (2) a 1933 edition by the great Persian scholar Sa'id Nafisi. An abridged edition was made by the latter in 1941, and still another one after this date. Parts of *Ghabus-Namah* have also been published in Bombay in 1896, 1907 and 1912. A printed copy of a handwritten copy at the British Museum was made by Reuben Levy as E.J.W. Gibb Memorial Series, New Series XVIII; also Richard N. Frye, the *Andarz-Namah* of Kabus b. Iskandar b. Dabus b. Vashngir, Serta Cantabrigiensia A.D., 1954.[6]

The oldest, handwritten copy of *Ghabus-Namah* completed in 1090, is extant in three parts: One in the Fine Arts Museum in Sinsuatlee, one in Kurkian's collection in New York, with the precise whereabouts of the third in doubt, although it may be in Paris. This copy contains 109 miniatures, which are the oldest Persian miniatures in the world.[7]

The titles of these chapters, translated here by the writer, indicate the extensiveness of the coverage as well as the fine choice of topics.* It contains also fifty anecdotes on educational, ethical, and amusing events, many of them original.† In addition the book is rich with many pleasant proverbs, bits of humor, and shrewd, worldly maxims. At times it is "wonderfully modern" in its moral and educational views. The following are illustrative examples:

On modesty: Overmodesty is not a virtue but a handicap to success, and bashfulness prevents man from achieving his objectives.

On truthfulness: Truth is delightful. Be specious without being a liar. Develop such a reputation for speaking the truth that even if you would perchance tell a lie it would be accepted as truth. Avoid making statements, however true, that are likely to be disbelieved or cannot be proved easily. Never mind telling a truth that may take four months and two hundred respectable witnesses to prove!

On treatment of guests: Never apologize to your guests for the entertainment you offer them, for this will only embarrass them and

---

*God and Religious Duties, Parental Duties, Development of the Mind and the Powers of Expression, Maxims, On Youth and Age, Diet, On Drinking, On Entertaining and Games, On Love, On Life's Enjoyments, On Bathing, On Rest and Sleep, On Hunting, On Polo, On War, On Wealth, On Trusts, On Slaves, On Purchase of Property, On Purchase of Quadrupeds, On Marriage, On Education of Children, On Choosing Friends, On Handling Enemies, On Pardon, Punishment, and Favors, On Study and Legal Functions, On Business, On the Science of Medicine, On Astronomy and Mathematics, On the Arts of Poetry, On the Art of Minstrel, On Serving Royalty, On the Qualities of the Courtier, On the Secretarial Arts and State Secretaries, On Qualities and Duties of Prime Ministers, On Qualities and Duties of Generals, On Qualities and Duties of Kings, On Farmers and the Art of Agriculture, On Generosity.

†The rich and the poor pilgrims, The saving of a slave girl from drowning, The praising of Plato by a fool, The physician al-Razi and a madman's smiles, Anushirwan and his minister, Buzurjumihr, Inexpediency of improbable statements, Harun al-Rashid's dream and his interpretors, The remonstrance of a slave to a libertine master, Buzarjumihr's repartee to a woman on his inability to answer her questions, The Alawi and the Sunni, The tailor and his jar, The reply of the old hunchback to a youth who mocked him, The chamberlain and the horse, Isma'il ibn Abbas and his guest, Mughla and Mansur, How a man condemned to death by al-Mu'tasim saves his own life by a cup of water, The old woman and the prophet Muhammad, Anecdote of Ghabus ibn Washmgir, Anecdote of Sultan Mahmud of Ghazna, Anecdote of Amir ibn Laith, The murder of Ghabus-i-Washmgir, Honor among thieves, Anecdote of Ahmadi Farighun, On the advantages of swimming (autobiographical), Anecdote of Gushtasp, Anecdote of Shahrbanuya and Husain, On the Death of Socrates,[8] Anecdote of al-Muhallab, Sayyida, and Dhu al-Qarnain (instructions regarding his burial), Anecdote of Mu'awiya, A tree as a witness, A merchant and a dealer, The dishonest milkman, Anecdote of Fadlun, Anecdote of al-Ma'mun and the Judge, Anecdote of Isma'il-ibn-Abbas, Caliph al-Qadir's reply to Sultan Mahmud's threats, The discerning secretary, Anecdote of al-Ghasri, A Persian king and his minister, Anecdote of Fakhr al-Dawla and Isma'il-ibn-Abbas, Anecdote of Abu al-Fath al-Balami and Sahl, Anecdote of Tughril and Seljuq, Anecdote of Sultan Mahmud and al-Busti, Anecdotes of Sultan Mas'ud of Ghazna, Anecdote of Fakhr al-Dawla and Adud al-Dawla, Anecdote of Alexander the Great, Problems for thieves, The two mystics.

put them ill at ease with you; and never correct your servants' errors in the presence of your guests.

On money: Avoid playing games of chance with notorious gamblers for the sake of quick and easy money; nor lend money to friends unless you are prepared to make the loan a gift.

On drinking wine: It is best not to indulge in drinking wine, but if you cannot refrain, remember these rules: Avoid drinking in the morning (except on rare occasions), so that you may not forsake your prayers; get drunk in your own house to avoid scandal; avoid drinking on the eve of Friday (the Muslim sabbath); nor be riotous and offensive when drunk; it is a sin to drink, but if you must drink, do it with grace and pleasantness; drink the best wine your money can buy and listen to the best music when you drink; if you jest while drunk, do it well; and if you must ask a miser and avaricious person for a favor, do so when he is drunk, and he is more likely to be in a generous mood.

On love: To speak of love at first sight is to be absurd and foolish, for such love is impossible. Better to marry a good woman from an influential family.

On friends and enemies: It is wise to be friendly and polite to those we dislike and unwise to leave ourselves in the power of friends, for should they ever become hostile to us they are likely to use this power against us. Never rejoice over the death of your enemies, for such rejoicing is justified only if we have security against death ourselves. Do not pursue or overpress your foes, for they may turn at bay in desperation. It is wise to avoid the services of kings and the society of soldiers.

On youth and old age: My son, be old in understanding even if you are young in years. Cultivate self-control; avoid dissipation; the young are high spirited, and youth is, as Aristotle says, a kind of madness; enjoy life while young and take in your share of life's pleasures, for old age will reduce the fire of desire—as an aged man once well said, "When young I vainly sorrowed that, as I grow older, beautiful women may not care for me, but alas, now that I am old, I do not much care for them."

Proverbial sayings: (a) A man in his own home is a king in his own domain. (b) A house with two mistresses remains unswept. (c) Better a sparrow in the hand than a peacock on promise. (d) When the policeman should be watched, that is a disgrace. (e) Before indulging in whatever affair, first make certain how you may emerge therefrom. (f) It is foolish to trust the cat with the fat.

Examples of Anecdotes: The hunchback and the youth: A foolish youth, bent on teasing an old man whose back was bent double with age, said to him, "Aged sir, tell me what you have paid for your pretty bow (the hunched back) that I too may buy one for myself." "Young man," said the wise old man, "be patient long enough and fate will give you one for nothing."

The tailor and the pitcher: An old tailor in a certain city had his shop by the city gate, and there he hung a pitcher by a nail, casting into it daily one pebble for every corpse that was taken through the gate. At the end of each month, he counted the pebbles, threw them away and began the act all over again. The tailor passed away unnoticed, but a close friend, inquiring of his whereabouts from the neighbors, was informed by one of them that the tailor had finally gone into the pitcher himself!

On old age and death: Death will come to the aged as to the corn and fruits which fall when ripened. Decline follows fulfillment and exit the weakening of senses. And this is fortunate, for life will be stripped of enjoyment and can give no enjoyment to others when the gateways of the senses are shut upon life; when one becomes a source of trouble to others, then death is indeed a blessing. When old, therefore, forsake the exercises of youth, and the more so as you approach the end when your afternoon sun has reached the western horizon of life and is setting. When you are young have sympathy with the aged, for the old are seldom cheered by visits and have to endure the troubles of age. Every malady carries with it the hope of recovery, save old age, which daily increases the agony of deeper age. Man increases daily in strength and vitality until 34 years old. From 34 to 40, he lives on an even plane, without waxing or waning, as the sun which seems to be standing still in mid-heaven at noon, moving slowly but without detection. From 40 to 50, each year brings a new decline and decrease which passed unnoticed the year before. From 50 to 60, each month brings a decline undetected the previous month; 60 to 70, every week; 70 to 80, every day. Beyond 80, every hour carries an ache unlike the ones of the previous hour. Life is like a ladder. We ascend 40 years with pleasure and ease, followed by an inevitable return to the starting point.

In Chapter 27, Ghabus, speaking of his own education and the value of practical training, says:

> My father admired my teacher, saying, "You have done well with my son in all respects save one." "And what is the one respect in which I have failed?" inquired the instructor. My father replied, "Whatsoever you taught my son he could find someone else to perform for him, save one training which he alone can perform, but which you failed to teach him." "And what training is that?" the teacher asked. "Swimming," my father replied.

Elsewhere in the same chapter he states:

> Let knowledge and wisdom be the heritage of your father to you, and your heritage to your children. For no heritage is more fitting the sons of noblemen than culture, and to the children of the common folks than a trade. Yet if culture is preferred by the noblemen to a trade, a trade is, in my view, preferable to culture.[9]

2. Siyasat-Namah of Nizam-al-Mulk

The *Siyasat-Namah* (*Book of Statecraft*) of Nizam-al-Mulk (Ghawam-al-Din Abu Ali Hassan ibn Ali ibn Is'haq Khawja Nizam-al

Mulk) was written by the great vizier of the Seljuq Sultans Alp Arslan and Malik Shah toward the end of his life. He completed it in 1092, the year he was assassinated by the Ismailites. The work is also known as the *Sayr-al-Muluk* (*The Morals of Kings*), and *Panjahu-yak-Fassl* (*Fifty-One Chapters*), which is the number of chapters comprising the book; it was prepared at the request of Sultan Malik Shah as one of many such statements on good government.

On his last trip to Baghdad with Sultan Malik Shah, Nizam-al-Mulk left the final copy of the *Siyasat-Namah* with Muhammad Maghribi, the king's special secretary who preserved the royal books. The secretary was to prepare a clean copy from it to be presented to the king in the event of the vizier's death, and Nizam-al-Mulk was assassinated the same year. The present copy of the *Siyasat-Namah* is, therefore, the one copied from the original (which is in Nizam-al-Mulk's own handwriting) by Maghribi, probably during the reign of Abu-Shuja' (Ghiyath-al-Din Abu Shuja' Muhammad ibn Shah), Malik Shah's son, sometime between 1098 and 1117.[10] The introduction to the work, written by Maghribi and made part of the text, reveals Maghribi's hand in preparing the work as it has survived.

The *Siyasat-Namah* should be judged as a political and educational guide for good government, as its author intended. However, some historical statements in the book are inaccurate, and many of its religious views and admonitions are prejudiced in favor of the Sunnite Islamic doctrines which the vizier prescribed.

The extensiveness and variety of coverages of many topics in the *Siyasat-Namah* are indicated by the titles of some of the fifty-one chapters, as follows:[11] On Conditions of Men and Circumstances of the World, On Recognition of Gratitude of the Blessings of Almighty God, On Royal Justice and Noble Disposition in Judgment of Grievances, On Royal Inquiry on Conditions of Viziers (Ministers), On Tax Collectors (?) and their Treatment of Subjects, On Judges, Preachers, and Assessors' Briskness of their Work, On Marks of Statemanship and Inquiry into Conditions of Agent (Worker), Judge, and Chief of Police, On Examination of Religious Performance and Doctrine, On Inspectors (Controllers) and their Pittance, On Management of Government Affairs, etc., On Spies and Management of the Welfare of Government and Subjects, On Special Deputy and his Work, On King's Favorites (Jesters) and the Arrangement of their Work, On Consultation with Men of Learning and Wisdom, On Retired People and their Provision, On Speed in Government Affairs, On Worthiness of Employees and Public Servants, On the Treasury and Adherence to its Regulations, and On Maintenance of the Account of (each) Province and its Orderliness.*

---

*The foregoing historical account of the *Siyasat-Namah* is based on the Persian work, *Siyasat-Namah of Abu Ali Hassan ibn Ali Khawja Nizam-al-Mulk,* edited by Muhammad Qazwini, published (from Scheffer's copy, Paris 1891),

The work may be considered an educational classic in the sense that it deals with the education of a ruler. It is the first and one of the greatest of its type in the Muslim world, discussing character and education of rulers, their first ministers, judges, and other members of the ruling class within the ruler's immediate circle.[12]

Nizam-al-Mulk founded an extensive system of schools (madrasahs) in the Islamic world, and, although many schools were in existence in Islam before the days of Nizam-al-Mulk, such as Al-Azhar,[13] Dar-al-Ilm,[14] Dar al-Hikmah,[15] and Bait al-Hikmah,[16] he was responsible for a universal system of publicly endowed schools and colleges, which made basic contributions to the extensive development of learning and scholarship in Islam.

As he devoted a large section of his famous *Siyasat-Namah* to advocate Sunnite orthodox beliefs in Egypt, so also he used his new system of the madrasahs to promote Sunnite doctrines and repudiate Shi'ite dogmas. He endowed schools and spent annually considerable sums of money in maintaining and improving them,[17] and is reported to have established a school in every town in Khurasan and Iraq.[18] Yet, in spite of their sectarian ends under Nizam-al-Mulk, the schools became centers of scholarship in Eastern Islam, controlled and largely financed by the state. Famous were those schools that carried the prime minister's name, as the Nizamiyyah in Baghdad.[19]

3. Gulistan and Bustan of Sa'di

Sa'di was born in 1194 (571 A.H.), a short time after Saladin captured Jerusalem from the crusaders, in the celebrated city of Shiraz, seat of the Atabak rulers of Iran. The rule of the Atabaks, or Seljuq Turks, began in Iran about 1166 and came to an end by 1291, after 125 years. The first of these Atabaks was Tughlah (1194-1214; 571-591 A.H.), who was followed by his brother, Sa'd-ibn Zangi (1214-1246; 591-623 A.H.). Sa'di, therefore, born in the first year of the reign of Atabak Tughlah (Toklah), was fifty-two when the reign of Sa'd-ibn-Zangi came to a close in 1246 A.D. His poetic pen name, Sa'di, was either bestowed upon him by that monarch or adopted by the poet in order to receive the great ruler's patronage, which paid him generously through the major portion of the moralist's long life.[20] His real name is not known. Dawlat Shah[21] refers to him as *Mosleheddin* (Pacifier of Faith) and considers him an *Alawi* or a descendant of Ali. Jami the poet calls him *Sharafoddin Mosleh*[22] (Excellence of Faith—Pacifier).

Sa'di studied under a fellowship at the famous Nizamiyyah College of Baghdad, where later he also taught. At this college he studied science under the celebrated Abd al-Farah ibn Jawzi and theology under Abd al-Qadir of Gilan, with whom he made his first pilgrimage to

---

with introduction and notes by Murteza Modarresi Chahardahi, by Haidari Press, Teheran, 1334 A.H. (Solar). Scheffer's copy, on which all other copies have since then been based, was printed 1809.

Mecca.[23] It was after the poet had left Baghdad that the city was sacked in 1258 by Hulaqu Khan, the Tartar, the grandson of Ghengis Khan, and its caliph, Musta'sim, barbarously murdered along with a million and a half of the city's inhabitants.

Dawlat Shah, who lived some 200 years after Sa'di, divides the poet's life in the *Tazkarat-al-Shu'ara* into three formal periods, stating that

> The first thirty years of Sa'di's long life were devoted to study and laying up a stock of knowledge; the next thirty, or perhaps forty, to treasuring up experience and disseminating that knowledge during his wide-extending travels; and . . . the remainder of his life in the retirement of a recluse, when he was exemplary in his temperance and edifying in his piety.[24]

That Sa'di travelled extensively and for a long period is evidenced by references he makes in his works to the countries he had visited.[25] He travelled up to perhaps his seventies through Asia, Africa, and Europe, including all provinces of Iran, many sections of Turan and Tartary, Egypt, Abyssinia, Barbary, Syria and Palestine, Armenia, all of Asia Minor and Arabia, and beyond the Indus in India. He had resided in Baghdad, Damascus, Basra, Rudbar, and Mecca. He spoke and wrote in both Persian and Arabic and was acquainted with as many as eighteen dialects, some of which he employed to varying degrees in his writings.

It should be noted that Sa'di was more of an observer and thinker than scholar, and, although his works indicate acquaintance with Greek philosophy, Islamic tradition, Persian poetry, the Old and New Testaments, and even Hindu ritualism, his familiarity with these areas of culture is casual and his information sometimes inaccurate.

He knew so much not because he had read so extensievly but because he had lived so many lives, and always with an open eye and a receptive heart. We find him lecturing at the Nizamiyyah College of Baghdad, and preaching in the mosque of Damascus, and fighting in the crusades, where he was captured by the Franks from Tripoli and forced into slave labor. On the Island of Kish (Ghays), a trading center of the Persian Gulf during his time, we find him telling a merchant that only the dust of the grave can fill the eyes of a greedy man. We find him in India, in the temple of Kathiawar, criticizing idolatry at the risk of his life. We find him in Mecca laboring as a water-carrier in order to quench the thirst of his fellow pilgrims. He made the pilgrimage to Mecca fourteen times, mostly on foot, a holy duty which any Muslim would consider the richest experience of his entire life undertaken once. We find him on a street corner in bitter and eloquent dispute with a religious pretender defending the virtues of wealth and limitations of poverty.

To him existence was a mystery too lofty for frail human grasp, yet for those who possessed receptive hearts there was the presence of God in the rippling streams, blooming flowers, and chirping nightingales. For him faith filled the gap of longing that reflection left wide open. For him, if the essence of God was too subtle to be known, His goodness was obvious even in a single breath, which inhaled exhilarates our being and exhaled prolongs our lives. (*Gulistan;* Introduction.)

Sa'di's themes are universal, refreshing, and beneficial among any people and in any generation. He speaks in the *Scented Garden* (*Bustan*) of justice, beneficence, humility, love, compassion, good government, repentence, devotion, and contentment.

In the *Gulistan,* morals, maxims, aphorisms, and "sententious sayings" on statesmanship, contentment, education, love and youth, poverty, resignation, old age, religious devotion, and the like are intertwined with entertaining and instructive episodes, stories, and fables, derived mostly from his own experiences and observations, as well as what he had heard and read.

Sa'di died in Shiraz in 1291, a near-centenarian, mellowed in spirit by an exceptionally long life of searching study, inquisitive observation, and varied experiences, loved by the masses and respected by kings. His tomb is to this day a point of pilgrimage for lovers of poetry and wisdom.

Surprisingly, Sa'di is well balanced in the treatment of his many social-moral and educational themes. Whether he speaks of love and youth, wealth and poverty, or contentment and piety, he seems to be sure of his subject matter and clear in its treatment.

On Love: To Sa'di, love is an insanity of devotion. The lover forever gives, always adores, never makes demands upon the beloved, is not a fault-finder. The quality of human love is measured by the degree of its proximity with the mystical love of God. Just as in divine love the soul is absorbed into the substance of the Godhead, so also in human love the lover should seek complete fulfillment by virtue of complete denial. Sa'di warns that:

> He who is concerned with the safety of his life should not enter upon the path of love, for the thought of safety often diverts the heart from complete devotion to the object of affection. To be a slave to one's self turns the pursuit of love into sophistry. A true lover, though never attaining the goal of his affections, will forgetfully die in the effort. If you are a lover pursue your object, come what may, her sanctuary of bliss, or death at the gateway of longing.

On Silence: The chief defect of our tongue, says Sa'di, is that it is so often loose when it should be discreet; locked when it should be eloquent. Yet much as virtue in this respect lies in balance between speech and silence, wisdom lies by and large on the side of silence. When a shop is locked no one knows whether the merchant sells diamonds or cheap jewelry. To speak is to expose oneself. The fountain of words cannot rise higher than the level of thought. Words are exhibitions of the furniture of our minds. Therefore, he who is anxious to exhibit the contents of his being would do well to expend more energy in examining the quality and arrangement of the contents before they are displayed in public. Also, no matter how profound our thoughts, or how representative of them our words may be, two principles should ever guide the art of conversation: To think before we speak and to wind up the discourse before the listener cries, "enough!"

On Old Age: To Sa'di, every stage of life has its own pitfalls and riches. Therefore, no error in life is more fatal than the artificial and wishful effort to exchange the conditions and contents of one stage with another. Act your age. That is the secret. Just as it is unnatural to repress the impulses of youth in vain imitation of old age, so also it is unbecoming for an old man to demand the passions of yesteryears from a dissipated body.

> Now that you are old relinquish childishness and leave merriment and play to the young. Neither expect the gayeties of youth from old age, for the stream that has passed by shall never return, and corn when full grown can no longer rear its head. Even lions lose the sturdy grasp of their paws with age. An old woman may dye her grey hair by art, but cannot straighten her humped back.

On Piety: True piety, claims the poet, does not consist of saintly apparel or outward manifestations of sanctity. It is noted by the abandonment of the pomp and vanity of the world. "True piety," says Sa'di, "is in meditation, service, obedience, sacrifice, contentment, love of God, trust, submission and endurance. He who has these qualities has piety in the true sense."

The exhibition of physical symbols is no more the mark of the genuine devotions of the heart than cowardice can be converted into courage by putting on a suit of armor. Piety, so defined, becomes a mode of conduct shared equally by any heart receptive to it, whether the participant is king or beggar. Sa'di makes the substance of true piety crystal clear in the story of a man who saw in a dream a king who was enjoying the blessings of paradise and a beggar who was suffering the tortures of hell. Upon inquiry he was told: "This king is in heaven because of his affection for the needy, and that holy man in hell because of his connections with the rich."

On Contentment: Sa'di claims that "if the rich were just and the poor content, importunity would cease to exist." However, contentment should be distinguished from suppression. As a quality of being it stands halfway between excess and abstinence. Contentment is the regulation of natural impulses by impartial reason for the well-being of the individual as a whole. The body, and its corresponding passions and wants, is like a city in which good and evil compete for supremacy. It yields the satisfying fruits of balanced development if the soul assumes the rank of a king and reason that of a first minister. Left alone and unharnessed, lust leads to dissipation and with it comes the bitter experience of degeneration and eventual destruction. "I asked a philosopher," says Sa'di, "to interpret the saying, 'The most malignant of your enemies is the lust which abides within you.' He said, 'Every enemy upon whom you confer a favor might become a friend, save lust, which the more you gratify, the more hostile it becomes in demands.' "

To check such demands of lust by reason is the essence of contentment. If we nourish the whelp of excess, we shall soon face a full-grown wolf. The reply of Sa'di to the greedy merchant of his day holds a timely message for the materialism of our day which threatens to rob us of the higher values of life. Says Sa'di:

> A merchant who had amassed a fortune was surveying to me the prospects of his last enterprise before retiring. After boring me with an elaborate display of his present security, he continued, "I will now carry Persian sulphur to China, where the price is high, thence the porcelain of China to Rome, the Roman silk to India, Indian steel to Aleppo, and the Glassware of Aleppo to Yamin, and then return to Persia with Yamin's bordimani, and retire in a shop for life." I told him, "Alas that only the dust of the grave can fill the eyes of the greedy."

On Rulers: As did Plato, Sa'di considers the chief qualifications of ruling to be a combination of ability with justice, or wisdom with benevolence. Indeed, to him benevolence is born of wisdom, for it is wise to be good. Obviously, the surest guarantee for stability in government is the support it receives from satisfied citizens. Yet to keep the clashing and changing interests of individuals sustained is the very substance of justice in government and wisdom in statecraft.

The art of good government involves another difficult responsibility. Not only is it incumbent upon the ruler to smooth the path between the state and the citizens, but it is his added duty to keep the relation between governments, and therefore between nations, reciprocal and mutually complementary. Among the basic causes of friction between states Sa'di mentions greed as primary. "Ten beggars," he tells us, "can sleep on one mat, but two kings cannot live in the same kingdom." Again, "When the commander tolerates the plunder of five eggs, his troops will feast upon a thousand roasted fowls." Certainly in a world in which nations willingly work together for their mutual interests, the basic causes of friction, suspicion, hatred, prejudice, and the like would be minimized. "Three things," says Sa'di, "cannot last without three things: Wealth without trade; knowledge without debate; and government without policy." Policy, when coupled with indifference to trivialities, patience with differences, and firmness in safeguarding fundamentals, is the substance of wise statesmanship.

Sa'di sums up the end of good government magnificently in the statement: "Government is for the welfare of the people, and not the people for perpetuation of government."

On Teaching and Learning: The ever-renewed and often debated theme of heredity versus environment is also a central educational concern of Sa'di. It is natural that a man with the breadth of intelligence and depth of experience such as Sa'di should immediately recognize both the limitations as well as the assets of these twin conditions of education. He is, therefore, equally eloquent on the necessity of a good "nature" as he is on the indispensability of a desirable "nurture." Education cannot do the impossible. What we become in any environment depends largely on our potentialities and limitations.

> Whenever native capacities are good, education will make an impression, but no furbisher can give polish to iron of a bad temper. If you wash a dog in the seven seas, you cannot change his nature; and were you to take the donkey of Jesus to Mecca, upon his return he would still remain a donkey.[26]

On the other hand, the best of natures could be corrupted in a corrupt environment, just as a good environment can encourage and sustain the best that is within us, and develop it along proper channels. He tells us in a beautiful analogy:

> Once I received from a beloved's hand a ball of scented clay. I addressed it saying, "Your heavenly fragrance intoxicates me as would the perfumes of musk and ambergris." It replied, "Once I was a worthless piece of clay, but associated for a season with the roses, and the sweetness of my companions scented my essence; else I am the same humble clod I seem."[27]

When the choice is to be made between good capacities and the best of circumstances, Sa'di is decidedly on the side of heredity as Sa'di illustrates by the following story:

> A king turned his son over to a learned man telling him, "Educate him as you would one of your own." After many years of effort the prince had made no improvement while the sons of the preceptor excelled in knowledge and attainment. The king blamed the teacher for partiality in instruction, to which the preceptor responded: "Your majesty, instruction was equal in all cases, but capacities differed in each. And even though silver and gold are extracted from stone, not all stones carry gold and silver."

On Wealth and Poverty: To our poet, money is an instrument of welfare. Today it is in your hands and tomorrow in another's. But the trouble lies in the fact that as a rule too much of it falls in one hand and too little of it in another, with the consequent result of extreme poverty and prohibitive wealth. Yet both poverty and wealth force limitations upon conduct. Sa'di in his quarrel with a pretender states in the *Gulistan* that:

> Poverty ties the hands of ability, and wealth cripples the feet of inclination. . . . Men of liberality are often without means, and those who command opulence are as a rule without a spirit of liberality. . . . The spark of enthusiasm is extinguished when a man is starving, while the rich are concerned over hoarding their money and jealously watching over it while they live the life of sordid meanness. The poor fall into the well of wickedness out of necessity and give their otherwise fair reputations to the blast of infamy.[28]
>
> The rich are often a vain, conceited, fussy and overbearing group, being ever greedy after large possessions, ever ambitious of rank and dignity, whose speech is marked by insolence, and whose attitude is one of extreme contempt;

who call men of science beggars, and reproach beggars for their miserable raggedness; who consider themselves superior to all other men because of their riches and rank, their vanity and false pride; who never condescend to return a salutation.[29]

Having surveyed the evils of wealth and the limitations of poverty, the great philosopher finds the remedy in neither communism nor capitalism. He is neither an advocate of share-the-wealth nor an advocate of wealth without a share in responsibility and beneficence. Rather, he insists on the necessity of wealth in proper hands, hands that utilize it not as a means of subjugating their fellow men but as a tool for public welfare. Abundance should be coupled with beneficence. The wealthiest of men are those who sympathize with the sorrows of the poor, just as the most virtuous among those in humble circumstances are those who do not covet the society of the rich.

There is abundant material accessible in English, French, and German on the life and time of Sa'di. There are also many translations of his works, particularly of the *Gulistan* and the *Bustan*. *Bustan* alone has been translated into seventeen languages, the oldest in Latin, rendered by Thomas Hide.[30] Some of the early English translations of the *Gulistan* have been made in India.

None of the prevailing translations of Sa'di are of much value to the average English reader. The reasons for this failure are many. Some translations are too literal and technical. Others show clear evidence of failure to grasp the central ideas and meanings of the original. Most of them seem to have ignored the fact that the stories, fables, and experiences related by Sa'di are appreciated only by his fellow countrymen who are brought up in the atmosphere of Persian literature and history and the environment of Islamic faith and culture. These stories, taken away from their historic settings and cultural contexts are, as a rule, neither interesting nor instructive to the Western reader.

What is of universal value in the *Gulistan* and *Bustan* consists, as suggested above, of the sage sayings, the lofty morals, the exquisite maxims, the ever-refreshing aphorisms and sententious proverbs, the pleasing anecdotes and touching incidents with which all of Sa'di's works are saturated and which are the salt and essence of his writings. But even these immortal thoughts and ethical principles of the moralist poet lose their weight, if not their meaning, once they are rendered too literally into a foreign tongue.

In a real sense, the *Gulistan* is the greatest work on education ever to appear in Persia, and perhaps in all Islam, during the period considered in this study. Next in rank and influence is Sa'di's *Bustan*, which is divided into twenty chapters; the following titles of its first ten chapters indicate the educational concern of the book, which is written in verse: On Justice and Policy in Government, On Moral Goodness, On Love, On Humility, On Contentment, On Resignation and Satisfaction, On Education, On Thankfulness, On Repentence, and On Prayer.

Next in educational importance are Sa'di's *Risalat* (*Tracts*), which are not as well known in Persia and the Islamic world as *Gulistan* and *Bustan*. They are, nonetheless, educational essays with great depth of perception and are rich with stories, anecdotes, and proverbs. The six *Tracts* are Introduction, The Five-Fold Assemblies, On Interrogation, etc., On Reason and Love, On Counsel to Kings, and On Royalty.[31]

The educational maxims and stories, as said previously, are scattered throughout all his writings, appearing mostly in his *Gulistan* and to a lesser degree in the *Bustan* and the *Risalat*. The sections appearing in Chapter VI are translations by the writer of the most famous of these maxims and stories, rendered freely rather than literally into English to insure accuracy of the thoughts rather than the exact text in which they originally appear. The selections are made from his main works but organized largely under the titles which appear in the *Gulistan*.

4. Fatihat-al-Ulum of al-Ghazzali

Al-Ghazzali (Algazel) Imam Abu Hamid Muhammad, known also as al-Ghazali, was one of the greatest of Muslim theologians and mystics. He was born in 1058 or 1059 in the city of Tus in the northeastern Persian province of Khurasan. Nizam-al-Mulk gave him a professorship in the great Nizamiyyah College at Baghdad, a post which he left four years later to travel and write. Still later he taught briefly in the Nizamiyyah College of Nishapur but left for his native town of Tus, where he died in 1111. He wrote more than 70 books the greatest among them being the *Destruction of the Philosophies* (*Taha'fat al-Fala'sifa*), which led to ibn Rushd's (Averroes) great book in rebuttal to al-Ghazzali, named *Destruction of the Destruction* (*Taha'fat al-Taha'fat*).[32]

His masterpiece, the *Fatihat-al-Ulum* (*Introduction to the Sciences*), contains many views on problems of education which were improvements over the European pedagogy of the time; indeed some compare favorably with modern educational concepts. Among his views the following, on teacher-pupil relations, are worth noting:[33]

Teachers, he maintains, should have sympathy with students and treat them with kindness as though they were their own children (compare with Comenius): Be always perfectly honest with each student. See to it that no one becomes a candidate for a degree until he has proved himself worthy of it. Do not tolerate misconduct in students; when necessary exhort and rebuke them for it. Never abuse or speak unkindly of a fellow teacher to a student. Avoid teaching materials which are beyond the comprehension of pupils. Be always a good example of the precepts you teach lest your "deeds belie your words."[34] Always praise and encourage pupils when their deeds justify compliments. Overlook his first offense, but if the pupil persists in doing wrong reprimand him in private. Never employ nagging as a means of correction. Always keep him away "from evil companions," for this is most basic in his education.[35] Correct his motives and purify them, and his education will succeed in its functions.[36] Other educational doctrines of al-Ghazzali include: On the Virtues (Rules) of Scholarship (On Being a Student), On the Principles of Instruction and Guidance, Rational Proofs on Teaching as a Noble Profession, On the Divisions of Knowledge, and On the Responsibilities of the Teacher and the Student.

Another of Ghazzali's educational works is his *Mizan-al-Amal* (*The Rules of Conduct*), in which he develops an interesting associational psychology.[37] He argues that (a) the reasoning faculty abides in the center of the brain as a king would live amidst his kingdom, (b) the faculty of imagination is located in front of the brain, having a function similar to a postmaster in gathering and imparting news, (c) the retentive power is placed in the back of the brain (as a servant would stand behind his master), (d) the power of speech resembles an interpretor (of ideas), and (e) the five senses may be compared to spies, checking sources and verifying claims. Al-Ghazzali's best statement on the moral and practical foundations of education is perhaps his essay entitled *My Child,* from which the following quotations may be of interest to the reader.

My Child

In the name of God, the ever kind and ever pitying, (1) Know, my child and admired friend (may God prolong your life in His obedience and may He lead you on the path of His friends!). In the message of the Prophet (Whom God may bless with His grace) you will find many pearls of wisdom . . .; if you have his counsel you do not need mine, and if you have not been blessed with His wisdom what have you acquired during the past years?

(2) My child, above all that which the messenger of God . . . has told his people, cherish this word: It is a sign of God's alienation from His servant if His servant begins to be occupied with things which are not His; a man who has lost an hour of his life in something other than that for which he has been created will feel the biting of his conscience on the day of his resurrection; he who is more than forty and has not more good than evil on his side will have his place prepared in eternal fire. This counsel is enough for those who profess the true knowledge.

(3) My child, the counsel is easy but it is difficult to follow, for it is contrary to the taste of the man who follows his lusts; the things forbidden are dear to the heart especially of the one who seeks only the external side of knowledge, who is occupied with his own self, or who thinks of a great career as a judge and of the praise of the world. For such a man believes that mere erudition (without corresponding action) will be sufficient cause for his salvation and liberation; this is the belief of the philosophers . . . But, thus says the messenger of God (Whom God may bless with His Grace), more than all other men will be punished at the day of resurrection the learned man whose knowledge has not helped him in the eyes of the Almighty.

(8) My child, you may live as long as you wish yet your death will come; love what you wish, you will be separated from it; do what you wish, and you will have your reward for it. . . .

(9) My child, knowledge without action is insanity, but action without knowledge is not action. Know that all knowledge cannot save you from sin

and will not make you obedient, and will not free you from the fire of hell, unless you really act according to your knowledge.

(17) We say that those who walk the path of truth need four things: first, true faith in which there is no change; second, sincere repentance, after which there is no return to sinfulness; third, the satisfaction of one's enemies so that none of them can ask anything from you; fourth, the acquisition of the knowledge of the law in so far as it is necessary for the fulfillment of God's commandments. You ought also to know of the future world, for you need it for your salvation. More than this is not necessary.

(18) My child, if you act according to this tradition you do not need much knowledge, but contemplate (another story which is the following). Hatim the deaf was one of the companions of Shakik of Balch (may God have pity on each). Shakik asked him one day, "You have now been my friend for thirty years, what have you acquired during this time?" Hatim answered, "I have acquired eight useful insights which are sufficient for me because from them I expect my liberation and salvation." Shakik said, "What are they?" and Hatim replied, "The first useful insight is this: I have observed the people and have seen that each of them has one with whom he is friendly and loving: some accompany their friend through his last sickness and some to the edge of the grave. Then they all return and leave him single and alone, and none of them goes with him into the grave. I thought about it and said to myself: 'The best friend of man is one who follows him into the grave and stays there with him. I have found nothing but good deeds which I have chosen for my friends that they may be the light and friends in my grave and not desert me.'

"The second useful insight is this: I have seen men who follow their lusts and are anxious to satisfy their desires, and I thought about the word of God: 'But who fears the majesty of his Lord, and refrains his soul from lust, verily, he shall have the Paradise as his dwelling-place.' I understand that the Qur'an has the real truth; thus I prepared myself to oppose my emotions. I girded myself for the battle with them until they voluntarily submitted to the commands of God.

"The third useful insight is this: I have seen how everybody struggles to collect the goods of the world in order to preserve and keep them in his hand; then I thought about the words of the Lord: 'That which is with you will pass away, that which is God's will remain.' Then I turned my appetites away from the world toward the face of God the Highest and distributed my goods among the poor that they might serve me before God the Highest.

"The fourth useful insight is this: I have seen some who believe that nobility and honor are judged by the size of their people and tribe, and they are proud of it; others believe that nobility and honor depend on the wealth of goods and positions, and the number of children of whom they can boast; others believe that nobility and honor come from the exploitation of men, their suppression, and from shedding their blood; and others believe that nobility and honor may be acquired by spending and wasting one's goods. Then I thought about the word of the Highest: 'The most worthy in the eyes of God is he who fears Him most.' So I chose the fear of God; I believed that the Qur'an has a truth and that the opinions and illusions of men are vain and perishable.

"The fifth useful insight is this: I have seen that some criticize the others; one blackmails the other, and I have found that this springs from the envy of others' good offices and knowledge. Then I thought of the word of God the Highest; 'We have distributed their subsistence among them in this world's life.' Then I understood that the distribution from God the Highest comes from eternity and I envied nobody and was content with what God the Highest had given me.

"The sixth useful insight is this: I have seen that people make enemies for many causes and intentions. Then I thought of the word of God the Highest:

'Satan is your enemy and hold him for such.' And I knew that I was not permitted to make enemies except Satan.

"The seventh useful insight is this: I have seen how each of us labors and struggles for food and sustenance so that he falls into temptation and does deeds forbidden, humiliates himself, and degrades himself. Then I thought of the words of the Highest: 'There is no animal on earth whose food does not depend on God.' Then I knew that my food was with God and that He guarantees it, and I devoted myself to His service and cut off my greed for all which did not come from Him.

"The eighth useful insight is this: I have seen that each of us leans on one thing created, some on the world and money, some on gold and property, some on craft and art, and some on creatures of their own kind. Then I thought of the word of God the Highest: 'For him who puts his faith in God He will be all-sufficient, for God will attain His purpose, and God has assigned its destiny to everything.' Trust in God, He will not mislead thee, He will reward you."

Then Shakik said, "God has led you with His wisdom O Hatim; I have read the Pentateuch, the Psalms, the Gospel, and the Qur'an, and have found that these four books all turn around the same eight useful insights, and he who acts accordingly acts according to these four books."[38]*

We shall conclude al-Ghazzali's philosophy of education by summarizing the highlights of his educational views in his *Al-Ihya' al-Din* (*The Vivification of Faith*).

Parents are responsible for looking after their children properly. To their hands the innocent child is confided with his pure conscience and stainless soul. His heart resembling a mirror is ready to reflect anything put before it, and he imitates carefully whatever he watches. He may be an ideal citizen if he is educated well, and he may be a harmful person if he is ill-trained or neglected. His parents, relatives (relations) as well as teachers will share with him his happiness or suffer from his being evil. So it is the duty of parents or guardian to pay full attention to the child; teach him good behavior, edify him and keep him away from bad company.

He must be accustomed to rough and hard life and not luxury. Self respect, modesty and sincerity must be among his outstanding qualities. He should not be encouraged to be fond of money or material things as this is the first step toward useless quarrels.

When he is grown up he is due to be handed over to an excellent and good instructor to teach him useful and necessary learning, and to lead him by the right way to the right end.[39]

The attempt to teach ill-qualified persons is as unjust as to prevent the well-qualified from learning.[40]

Other Significant Educational Classics

1. THE ETHICS OF NASERI

The Ethics of Naseri (*Akhlaqi-Naseri*) of Nasir-al-Din al-Tusi is, in my opinion, greatly overrated among the Muslims, particularly among the Persians. The book has survived for centuries as a basis for courses in ethics in public schools in Persia to the present day, although its metaphysical and moral assumptions are partly derived

*The foregoing quotation is taken from the essay, *My Child*, by al-Ghazzali, translated by Robert Ulich, from Hammer-Purgstall, *O Kind! Die beruhmte ethische Abhandlung Ghasali's*, Arabisch und deutsch, Wien, Gedruckt bei U. Strauss'sel. 1838. Refer to note 38.

from Hellenistic-Aristotelian-Platonic views and partly based on Muslim theological and moral doctrines. Nonetheless, the work does contain some fair passages on the educational foundations of morality as well as the moral foundations of education, particularly the following selections:

Discourse One (On Purity of Conduct—Origins and Basic Aims of Conduct) Part II (On Basic Aims) Chapter 6: Distinction between Virtues and Whatever Appears as Virtues; Chapter 7: On the Superiority of Justice to Other Virtues, and a Description of Types of Justice and their Nature (This concept is definitely Platonic); Chapter 8: On Explanation of Manner of Acquisition of Virtues and Level of Happiness.

Discourse Two (On Home [Domestic] Management) Chapter 1: On the Necessity of Homes, the Knowledge of its Foundations, and Consideration of its Importance and its Pre-requisites; Chapter 2: On Management (Planning) and Government of Property and Provisions (Food, Shelter and Cover); Chapter 3: On Knowledge of Government and Planning of Members of Family; Chapter 4: On Knowledge of Government, Regulation and Bringing up of Children, and the Observance of the Rights of Parents (by Children).[41]

The book is dedicated to Abu Mansur, the Governor of Ghuhistan.[42] Tusi also wrote the *Safar-Namah* (*The Book of Travels*), a record of extensive travels in Islamic countries, with great educational value; the *Rawshanai-Namah*,[43] (*The Book of Enlightenment*); the *Sa'adat-Namah*[44] (*Book of Happiness*); and the *Diwan* (*Complete Poetical Works*).[45] The last work is listed because of its educational ideas on the use of language, the place of the *Qur'an* in education, the relation of knowledge to piety, the use of knowledge for religious development, universal intelligence, and the parts free will and predestination play in human life and vice versa.[46]

2. THE TAHARAT-AL-A'ARAQ OF IBN MASKUYA

Ibn Maskuya was a great historian, physician, moralist, theologian, and educator of Shi'ah Islam in the latter part of the tenth century and the beginning of the eleventh. He was, according to the historian Yaqut, a Zoroastrian convert to Islam.[47] He became one of the librarians of the private books of the vizier ibn-al-Amid and also served at the courts of Adud-al-Dawla Dailami and Samsam al-Dawla. Of the many works* written by him the greatest was the *Taharat-al-A'araq* (*Cleans-*

*The following may be noted here: *The Major Victory* (*Fa'iz-al-Azfar*); *The Order of Habits* (*Tarib-al-Adat*); *The Comprehensive Book* (*Kitab-al-Jami*); *Experiences of Nations* (*Tajarib-al-Umam*); *Singular Intimacy* (*Uns-al-Farid*) (containing proverbs and maxims); *Immortal Wisdom* (*Jawdani Kherad,* or *Jawdani-Feraz*); *The Book of Morals* (*Kitab-al-Siar*); *Purification of Conduct* (*Tahzib al-Akhlaq*); *Cleansing of the Foundations* (*Taharat-al-A'araq*); *The Manners of the Arabs and the Persians (Abad-al-Arab-i-Wal-Fars),* and *Relief from Sorrow—or Fear—From Death* (this book is also credited to ibn Sina).

ing of the Foundations [of Conduct]). Maskuya therein argues that human nature, though neutral at birth, is nonetheless bent upon either good or evil, depending primarily on the kind of education (nurture) that the native impulses receive. Like Aristotle, he defends the doctrine of inequalities of natures and is, therefore, a relativist rather than perfectionist. Since no one is capable of absolute goodness, the greatest good, resulting from mutuality and benevolence, is the ethical ideal. Mutual aid is the basis of moral life, and education is the only path to mutual life.[48]

The *Taharat-al-A'araq* deals, among others things, with the following: The seven-fold origins of morality, based on understanding of human nature[49] (as distinguished from animals[50]) by virtue of moral excellence[51] as the essence of humanity;[52] indifference to material interests as an approach to God;[53] happiness and unhappiness as derivatives of conduct[54] (i.e., mutuality[55]); the three natures of man, animal, rational and divine,[56] the four-fold virtues, wisdom, chastity, courage, justice, and each one of which is analyzed and discussed according to its various qualities;[57]* analysis of conflicting concepts of moral life;[62] instruction and education of children and the youth (education and human nature[49] (as distinguished from animals[50]) by virtue of moral (including types of happiness[69] as conditions within one's self[70]); marks of a perfect man—freedom from longing or desire, self-satisfaction, continuous effort in spreading knowledge and in guiding others, enjoyment of companionship of equals (in level of maturity) and fulfillment of the will of God[71] (including Aristotle's concept of the perfect man[72] in contrast with common folks[73]); on varieties of love;[74] ways to spiritual health;[75] the cure of carnal ills.[76]‡

3. THE MANTIQ AL-TAYR OF ATTAR

The *Mantiq al-Tayr* of Attar Nishaburi consists of 4,600 couplets. In the allegory the birds typify the Sufis (mystics). They make a pilgrimage to visit the Simurq, literally meaning the Thirty-Bird, a legendary bird signifying in this poem Truth, or God. In the forty-five dis-

---

*These qualities cover meanings of the seven-fold powers of wisdom, including intelligence, memory, reasoning, purity, perception, excellence of perception, ease of learning;[58] the twelve-fold virtues of chastity, modesty, patience, generosity, calmness of spirit, freedom of spirit, contentment, gentleness, orderliness, direction, tranquility, dignity, abstinence;[59] the seven-fold character of courage—magnanimity, self-reliance, ambition, steadfastness, patience, modesty, inflexibility, valour, endurance;[60] the twenty-one-fold qualities of justice, among them veracity, sociability, benevolence toward relatives, retribution, fair partnership, fair judgment and obedience to God.[61]

†The reference is essentially to the education of the young;[64] the education of the child's native powers;[65] degrees of human progress (development);[66] and happiness as a derivative of action.[67]

‡The foregoing outline is based on an anonymous translation of the Persian edition—ibn Maskuya, *Taharat-al-A'araq*, The Imami Printing Shop, 1368 A.H.

courses in which the allegory evolves, thirteen species of birds are urged by the Hoopoe (Hudhud, their leader) to make the pilgrimage to the abode of the Thirty-Bird. Each bird endeavors to excuse himself for a specific reason. The nightingale pleads its love for the roses. The parrot insists that he is confined to a cage because of his beauty and cannot be liberated. The peacock claims that he is unworthy of the journey because of his affiliations with Adam's expulsion from paradise. The duck quacks that he is unable to dispense with water. The partridge claims attachment to the mountains. The heron feels tied up to the lagoons. The owl indicates preference for the ruins. The huma "loves its power of conferring royalty." The falcon "cannot relinquish its place of honor on the king's hand." The wagtail "pleads its weakness."

The Hoopoe, noting the weakness of each position, rejects their excuses as mere expressions of their unwillingness to hazard the hardships of the pilgrimage. New excuses are advanced by twenty-two birds and answered by Hoopoe. At long last, those birds with sufficient courage to continue the quest endure the journey through the Seven Valleys, which are the valleys of search, of love, of knowledge, of independence, of unification, of amazement, and of destitution and annihilation.

Finally, so purified by the seven disciplines of the spiritual journey, they discover the Thirty-Bird in whose self, as though through a mirror, they see themselves. The Thirty-Bird was, therefore, none other than a reflection of the faces of the bird pilgrims. Each saw in himself the true image of the Thirty-Bird, i.e., of truth or God. "They perceived themselves to be naught else but the Simurq, while the Simurq was naught else than the Thirty-Birds," hence the destruction of plural selves into one all-embracing self.[77]

As Ralph Waldo Emerson puts it in *The Celestial Love*:

Higher far,
Upward into the pure realm,
Over sun and star,
Over the flickering Daemon film,
Thou must mourn for love;
Into vision where all form
In one only form dissolves;
In a region where the wheel
On which all beings ride
Visibly revolves;
Where the starred, eternal worm
Guides the world with bound and term;
Where unlike things are like;
Where good and ill,
And joy and moan,
Melt into One.

So the path to mystic realization is marked by *Search,* which is the unwavering desire for perfection; *Love,* which is a fixed attachment to the goal in view, forsaking all else; *Knowledge,* which means the relative progress of each seeker in accordance with the extent of his ability to know; *Independence,* which requires the complete abandonment of the world and the desires of the flesh; *Unification,* which enables the seeker to see God everywhere and to resolve the illusions (of "this" and "that"—"here" and "there"—"now" and "then"); *Amazement,* which is the state of glorious wonder, one in which the seeker realizes his own insignificance and loses it in wonderment; and *Annihilation,* which is marked by the final destruction of all passions and self-seeking, and the self, as Emerson says, "melts into one."[78]

4. RASA'IL OF THE IKHWAN AL-SAFA

The *Rasa'il* or *Treatises* of the Ikhwan al-Safa (the Brethren of Purity) is a most ambitious undertaking, perhaps the most extensive of its kind in the "medieval" Muslim culture. The work is comprised of fifty-one treatises in which the scientific-philosophic learning of the time (the last half of the tenth century)* is summarized as a popular encyclopaedia. Although all fifty-one treatises are anonymous, they were compiled by the Shi'ah religious fraternity of the Brethren of Purity, then flourishing in Basra. Some of the members of the fraternity were from Bust in far eastern Persia, from Zanjan in northwest Persia, and from Jerusalem; others were perhaps of Arabic extraction. A complete edition of the work was printed in Bombay in 1887-89 in four volumes. Frederich Dieterici indicates in his reference to the *Rasa'il* that an intelligent understanding of its contents presupposed on the part of the scholar a knowledge of the educational fundamentals as outlined in detail in this work.[79]

The *Rasa'il* of Ikhwan al-Safa is the first extensive attempt at a synthesis of all knowledge. Treatises XIV-XL, discussing philological and psychological subjects, should be of special interest to students of both education and psychology.[80]

5. MAFA'TIH AL-ULUM OF AL-KATIB

Mafa'tih al-Ulum or *Keys to the Sciences* was composed by Abu Abdullah Muhammad ibn Yusuf al-Katib (*al-Katib* means the *scribe*), a native of Khwarizm, in 976 and edited in 1895 in Leyden by van Vloten. Al-Katib divides the sciences into two main groups: *Native* (indigenous) and *external* (exotic), referring to areas of learning mainly of Persian and Greek origin.[81]

A Catalogue of Selected Other Muslim Educational Classics, Briefly Annotated

Western historians of education have long believed that Islam, in contrast with Western culture, has lacked classics in the field of education. The following partial list should discourage this point of view.

*First appeared in 360 A.H.

One hundred twelve titles are listed, not counting some works we have already discussed in some detail. Of course not all these works are completely on education, though they contain educational materials in the broadest sense. I have written brief commentaries on a few of them. Translations of titles of books, and so on, are mine. Some of these works are lost; some are listed in *Al-Fihrist* of ibn-al-Nadim. They are written in either Arabic or Persian, the Arabic titles being in the majority. Extant selections from this list, plus those already discussed at some length, would make excellent reading sources for students of the history of education, and await ambitious translators.

1. *Adab al-Muridin: On the Responsibility of Students* by al-Uthmani (1050 A.H.; 1640 A.D.). Author's full name: Taj al-Din ibn Zakariyya al-Uthmani. This book discusses eleven requirements of good teaching, eleven principles of efficient learning, and twelve rules of conduct for teachers.[82]

2. *Akhlaqi Muhseni: The Ethics of Muhseni,* edited by Husain Kashefi (written 900 A.H.; 1491 A.D.). The book deals with the foundations of good conduct, treating the subject in forty chapters.

3. *Al-Amir al-Daris fi'l-Ahkam al-Muta'alliqa bi'l Madaris: Forgotten Facts on the Administration of Schools* by ibn Atiyyah (936 A.H.; 1528 A.D.). Author's full name: Alwan ibn Ali ibn Atiyyah. The book deals with student responsibilities in schools and the teachers and their professional obligations.[83]

4. *Risalah fi'l-Siyasah: Discourse on Statecraft* by ibn Sina (428 A.H.; 1036 A.D.). This work emphasizes the need for vocational education. "When the boy has completed his *Qur'an* and has mastered the fundamentals of the Arabic language, his education should be focused on his future calling. This is to be conditioned, however, by the capacity of the lad, for he is to follow that profession for which he is naturally fitted and should not be guided by his whims."

5. *Andarzi Atripati Maraspandan: Precepts (Counsel) Concerning Religion and Worldliness* by Dasturan Dastur Adarbad Mahrespand to his son Zarthust. The book was written at the time of Hormozd Shapur, the grandson of the founder of the Sassanian Dynasty.[84]

6. *Hadiqat al-Haqiqa: The Garden of Truth* of Sana'i. It is an educational-moral-mystical work, divided into 10 books dealing with educational topics: On reason (book 3), On the excellence of knowledge (book 4), On carelessness (book 5), On philosophy (book 7), On love (book 8).

7. *Kalila wa-Dimna: The Book of Kalila and Dimna.* Originally of Indian origin, known as *Fables of Bed Pai,* the book was translated into the Pahlavi Persian, from the Persian into Syriac (570) and Arabic (750) versions; from the Arabic version of ibn al-Muqaffa into a large number of languages, among them Greek, Latin, Hebrew, Spanish, Italian, Turkish, Slavic, German, Danish, French, Dutch, English, and others between 750-1778. The Persian translation was made by Nizam al-Din Abd al-Hamid from ibn Muqaffa's Arabic version. The

book appears also in Persian verse by the poet Rudagi. Near the end of the fifteenth century the book appeared under the title *Anwar-i-Suhayli* by Husain Wa'idh-i-Kashefi, and later as the *Qyar-i-Danish* (*Cornerstone of Wisdom*) by Abu al-Fadhl. The Persian translator ibn Muqaffa (Abdullah), whose Persian name was Uruz-beh, was born in the province of Fars. Aside from the Pahlavi version of the *Kalila wa-Dimna,* ibn Muqaffa translated many other Pahlavi works into Arabic, although the *Kalila* was his best. It ranks to the present day as one of the finest literary and educational works among the Arabic-speaking nations. Both the Persian and Arabic versions include additional stories, poems, and anecdotes not found in the original Sanskrit.[85]

8. *Kitab al-Mu'allimin*: *The Book of Teachers* by al-Jahiz. He also wrote *Al-Bayanu wa'l-Tibyan: Explanation and Manifestation.* The book contains a chapter on the teacher's social status ("Bab fi dhikr al-Mu'allimin), and a chapter on remembrance or praise of teachers.[86]

9. *Lawami' al-Ashraq fi Makarim al-Akhlaq: The Book of Conduct of Jalali* by Jalal al-Din (died 1502). The book deals with rules of conduct, home management, and good government. It is, as the author admits, an imitation of the famous *Ethics of Naseri* (*Akhlaqi-Naseri*).[87]

10. *Shahar Maqalah*: *The Four Discourses* by Arudhi. Author's full name: Abu al-Hasan Ahmad Samarqandi Arudhi. The first of these *Discourses* deals with the conditions of secretaryship.

11. *Muqaddimah,* or the *Prolegomena* of the Arab historian ibn Khaldun. Author's full name: Abd al-Rahman Abu-Zaid Wali al-Din ibn Khaldun (808 A.H.; 1405 A.D.). The book contains extensive materials on the art of teaching, aims of education, and curriculum. Ibn Khaldun divides studies into two categories, some as means-to-other-ends, such as logic, arithmetic, and languages, and others as ends-unto-themselves, such as theology, dialectics, and so on. The *Muqaddimah* may be considered a book on education in the broadest sense, since it surveys all branches of Muslim sciences and culture with unsurpassed "depth of thought, clearness of exposition, and correctness of judgment." His philosophy of history is certainly in advance of his time. History is, to ibn Khaldun, the record of man's struggles for survival and should include the story of his political, religious, economic, and educational life—not merely a report of war and peace. (Check Index for more materials on his educational theories.)

12. *Nafa'is al-Funun fi Dra'is al-Uyun: Rare Areas of Arts and Sciences* by al-Amali. Author's full name: Muhammad ibn al-Amali (died 1352). Amali was a Persian. He visited all the important scholars of his time before undertaking this encyclopaedic work.

13. Part (Qism) I, section of listing 12, is divided into 36 groups dealing with literary, legal, musical, and conversational arts. Part II covers ethics, domestic economy, government, philosophy, logic, physics, mathematics, physical crafts, agriculture, geography, mechanics, and many derivative arts and sciences related to above areas. One hundred sixty arts and sciences are listed in all.[88]

14. *Nama'i-Danishvaran: The Book of Learned Men,* co-edited by Adib Abd al-Rahb Abdi. Although this work was written in Persian in the latter decades of the nineteenth century during the reign of Nasir al-Din Shah, it is important to list it here from the standpoint of our survey. The work is in 7 volumes. It surveys the life and teaching of some of the great Persian men of learning.

15. *Nuzhat al-Qulub: Delight of the Hearts* by Mustawfi (born 1281, still living in 1340). This is a scientific and cosmographical encyclopaedia, written in Persian. The work is divided into 5 parts, of which Part II should be of educational interest, dealing with man, his faculties, moral qualities, and so on.[89]

16. *Pand-Namah: Book of Moral Counsel* by Farid al-Din Attar (born in Nishapur between 1150 and 1155 ?, probably died 1222). Author's full name: Abu Talib Muhammad Farid al-Din Attar. Attar means perfume dealer. The book deals with the mystic rules of conduct.[90]

17. *Rashf al-Nasa'ih*: *Draughts* (Sips) *of Counsel* by Shihab al-Din Suhrawardi (born 1145, died 1234 or 1235). Author's full name: Umar ibn Muhammad al-Bakri Shihab al-Din Suhrawardi. The book deals with the mystic rules of conduct.[91]

18. *Riadat al-Muta'allimin*: *On the Instruction of Students* by Abu Abdullah ibn al-Zubair, who was an instructor in law in Baghdad and Basra. According to Hajji Khalifa, the same book, or one carrying the same title, may have been written by Hamzah ibn Yusuf al-Hainawi (670 A.H.; 1270 A.D.); another by Abu Abdullah ibn Sulaiman al-Ziri al-Basri; and still another by Abu Na'im Ahmad ibn Abdullah al-Isfahani (430 A.H.; 1032 A.D.) or ibn al-Sunni.[92]

19. *Rawdhat al-Anwar*: *The Garden of Lights* by Amir Khosrow, who was born in India (1253). He also wrote the *Kamil-Namah: Book of Perfection,* and the *Gho'har-Namah: Book of Gems* (Essences). All are educational and ethical in scope, containing rich passages on the religious way of life and the rule of reason. *The Garden of Lights* is divided into 20 discourses dealing with the following topics: On the reality of words, On the position of sages, On human perfection, On punishment and threats of punishment, On change of *status quo,* On knowledge and excellence, On condition of life, On the rule of love, On worldly interests, On appreciation of youth and qualities of old age, On condemnation of over-drinking (wine-worshipping) and excessive passions, On reason and modesty, On reproach and haughtiness, On generosity, On unity with God, On purification of the soul, On pride, On creation, On God, and On human qualities.[93]

20. *Sad Kalima: One Hundred Sayings* by Rashid-i-Watwat, whose full name is Muhammad ibn Abd al-Ali al-Umari, known also as al-Katib. There were apparently four series of "sayings" written by Watwat, the last being the *One Hundred Sayings of Ali.* He owned and donated to various libraries "some thousand fine manuscripts and rare books"

for the benefit of the public before his death in Khiva (Khwarizm) in 1182 or 1183.[94]

21. *Sifat al-Adab: On Rules (Qualities) of Conduct* by Shaykh Nadim al-Din Kubra. The book is an educational guide for the observance of mystic (Sufi) neophytes. The author perished in the 1221 sack of Khwarizm by the Mongols.[95]

22. *Tadabir al-Manazil: Plans for Homes* (or *Prudence and Destinations*) by ibn Sina. The book deals with parental responsibilities for the child's education, including both moral and physical education.

23.*Tadhkirat al-Sami' wa'l-Mutakallim fi Adab al-Alim wa'l-Muta'allim: A Memorandum for Students and Lecturers on the Responsibilities of the Teacher and the Pupil* by al-Kinani (733 A.H.; 1333 A.D.). Author's full name: Burhan al-Din Abu Is'haq Ibrahim ibn Sa'dullah ibn Jama'ah al-Kinani. The book was written in 1273. Totah states that he secured a photographic copy of this manuscript, written in "good and legible hand, dating from the year 1087 A.D." from the Berlin library. According to Totah, two of the chapters are missing. The table of contents indicates some interesting pedagogic topics, including the art of learning, teacher-student relations in the classroom, student-teacher and student-student conduct and relations, the fellowship of books, and the rules or etiquette of dormitory life in colleges.[96]

24. *Ta'lim al-Muta'allim: On Teaching the Pupil* by Burhan al-Din al-Zarnuji (600 A.H.; 1203 A.D.). This work was translated from Arabic into Latin with the new title *Enchiridion Studiosi* in 1709 by H. Reland, and again in 1838 by Caspari. It is probably the most famous work of its kind. Its contents are as follows: The essence and value of learning and jurisprudence; the motive of studying; the selection of the subject; professor, schoolmate, and adherence thereto; the reverence due learning and the learned; application, perseverance, and diligence; beginning, extent, and arrangement of a lesson; concentration, sympathy, and advice; the acquisition of knowledge; piety; causes of retention and forgetfulness and that which brings sustenance (spiritual and physical) given by God. As an example the following may be cited: "On the Causes of Retention and Forgetting—We retain that which we intend to use, and persevere in retaining materials motivated by prospective application. Moderation in food and the careful choice of diet also stimulate memory." Al-Zarjuni prescribes particularly drinking honey and eating twenty-one raisins daily before breakfast. Among the causes of forgetfulness he lists grief, worry, and eating coriander seeds. The material memorized is good only as an instrument of thinking and application. "The student," he tells us, "must reflect even when dealing with the most minute point of knowledge," for to understand, we must reflect; to reflect, we must verify. Thoroughness is the key to scholarship. Never leave a subject for the sake of another until the one at hand is mastered.

25. *Tarbih al-Ta'dib wa Irshad al-Daris fi Tawarikh al-Madaris: Student Guide and Teacher Directions in Histories of Schools* by Abd al-Qadir al-Mi'aimi (927 A.H.; 1521 A.D.). The book is a survey of the schools of Damascus, divided into eleven chapters dealing with different types of schools in that city.

The following are general educational works, not strictly on educational theory, listed in Shalaby. They contain interesting information on Islamic schools, teachers, libraries, and so on. (Some of these titles have already been discussed in this work.)

I. Travel Books

Author	Title
26. al-Yaqubi	*Kitab al-Buldan*
27. ibn al-Faqih	*Al-Buldan*
28. al-Maqdisi	*Ahsan-al-Taqasim*
29. ibn Jubair	*Al-Rihlah*
30. Yaqut	*Mu'jam-al-Buldan*
31. ibn Batutah	*Tuhfat al-Nuzzar*

II. Biographical Books

Author	Title
32. al-Isfahani	*Kitab al-Aghani* (*Book of Songs*)
33. ibn-al-Nadim	*Al-Fihrist* (*The Index*)
34. al-Aubari	*Tabaqat al-Udaba* (*Classification of Learned Men*)
35. al-Khatib al-Baghdadi	*Tarikh Baghdad* (*History of Baghdad*)
36. Yaqut	*Mu'jam al-Udaba*
37. ibn Khallikan	*Wafayat al-Ayun*
38. al-Kutbi	*Fawat al-Wafayat*
39. al-Safadi	*Al-Wafi*
40. al-Qifti	*Akhbar al-Hukama*
41. ibn abi Usaibiyyah	*Uyun al-Anba*
42. al-Subki	*Tabaqat-al-Shafiyya*
43. al-Makkari	*Nafh al-Tibb*
44. ibn Qadhi Shuhbah	*Manaqit al-Shafi'iwal Ashabiki*
45. al-Suyuti	*Akhbar al-Nisa*

Note: Al-Isfahani describes in *Al-Aghani* the literary salons and the education of women. Others, such as Yaqut, Qifti, and ibn Khallikan discuss teachers' salaries and social status, classroom sizes, and materials on student habits.

III. Works with Discussions on Education

Author	Title
46. ibn Sina	*Al-Qanun*
47. ibn Abd al-Barr	*Jami' Bayan al-Ilm*
48. al-Sabi	*Rusum Dar-al-Khilafah*
49. al-Ghazzali	*Al-Ihya'*
50. al-Abdari	*Al-Madkhal*
51. ibn Khaldun	*Al-Muqaddimah* (Discussed above)
52. al-Maqrizi	*Al-Kitab*
53. al-Suyuti	*Husu al-Muhadarah*

Note: The foregoing contain materials on the social status of teachers, the literary salons, and the curriculum of education of princes.

IV. Educational Treatises

Author	Title
54. ibn Juma'a	*Tadhkirat al-Sami' wa'l-Mutakallim* (*Book of Disciple and Teacher*)
55. ibn Shaddad	*Al-A'laq al-Khatirah*
56. al-Nu'imi	*Al-Daris* (*The Teacher*)
57. ibn Abdun	*Risalah* (*Essay*)
58. al-Jahiz	*Risalah-al-Mu'allimin* (*Essay on Teachers*)
59. al-Qabisi	*Al-Fudtah*
60. al-Qatmuni	*Tarqhib al-Nass ila'l-Ilm* (*Inclination of People Toward Learning*)
61. ibn Sahnen (Sahneh?)	*Adab al-Mu'allimin* (*Manners of Teachers*)
62. Abu Hanifah	*Nasihat* (?) (*Advice*)
63. al-Walid ibn Baku	*Al-Wijazah*
64. al-Zarnuji	*Ta'lik al-Muta'allim* (*Pupil Interest*)
65. al-Shahid	*Al-Munya*
66. Tash Kubri Zadah	*Risalah fi Ilm al-Adab* (*Essay on Science of Nurture*)

Note: Ibn Juma'a discusses intelligence tests and the classification of pupils on the basis of tested abilities. Al-Walid describes teaching certificates and special permits. Al-Jahiz describes the teacher's social status, and ibn Sahnen discusses the education of girls.

Other educational works which may have been lost or on which no information was available to the author include the following (some already discussed):

67. *Adab-al-Arabi wa'l-Ajam* by ibn Mushkuya. He used three original Persian treatises on manners for his source material. These were *Javidani Khirad* (*Eternal Wisdom*), *Pand-Namah* (*The Book of Moral Counsel*), and *Andarz* (*The Book of Counsel*).

68. *Adab al-Daris wa'l-Mudarris* by al-Nawawi (676 A.H.; 1278 A.D.). Author's full name: Muhyi al-Din ibn Sharaf al-Nawawi.

69. *Adab al-Bahth: On the Rules* (Manners) *of Discourse* by al-Shirazi (1281-1355). Author's full name: Adud al-Din Abd al-Rahman ibn Ahmad al-Shirazi, a Persian who wrote in Arabic.

70. *Adab al-Muridin: The Ways* (Manners) *of Students* by Abu al-Najib abd al-Qadir ibn Abdullah al-Suhrawardi (563 A.H.; 1169 A.D.).

71. *Adab al-Dunya wa'l-Din: Worldly and Religious Manners* (Habits) by al-Mawardi Abu al-Hasan Ali, who died in 1058. The book was in use for many centuries in both Egyptian and Turkish schools.

72. *Aql-Namah*: *Book of Reason* by Sana'i.

73. *Ahwal al-Muta'allimin wa Ahkam al-Mu'allimin*: *Conditions of Learners and Precepts of* (for) *Teachers* by al-Qabisi. Author's full name: Abu al-Hasan Ali ibn Muhammad al-Qabisi. Date of the manuscript is 706 A.H.; 1306 A.D.

74. *Al-Alim wa'l-Muta'allimin: The Teacher* (Sage) *and the Students* by Abu al-Hasan Ali ibn Isma'il al-Mursi ibn Sida (458 A.H.; 1066 A.D.).

75. *Al-Durr al-Nadir fi Adab al-Mufid wa'l-Musta'fid: On the Duties of the Instructor and the Learner*. Literal translation, *The Rare Pearl in the Manners of the Teacher and Instructed* by al-Qazzi (984 A.H.; 1576 A.D.). Author's full name: Abu al-Barakat Badr al-Din Muhammad ibn Ridha al-Din al-Qazzi. The manuscript was completed in 932 A.H.; 1555 A.D.

76. *Al-Imla' wa'l-Istimla': On Dictation and Note-Taking* by Abd al-Karim ibn Muhammad ibn al-Sam'ani (562 A.H.; 1166 A.D.).

77. *Al-Lu'lu' al-Nazim fi Ra'um al-Ta'allum wa'l-Ta'lim: Studded Pearls in the Art of Learning and Teaching* by al-Ansari (926 A.H.; 1520 A.D.). Author's full name: Abu Yahya Zakariyya al-Ansari.

78. *Al-Manhaj al-Mufid fima Yalzam al-Shaikh wa'l-Murid: Useful Rules* (Guides) *for the Teacher and the Pupil* by al-Sha'tibi (672 A.H.; 1273 A.D.). Author's full name: Muhammad ibn Sulaiman al-Afiri al-Sha'tibi.

79.*Al-Sifat wa'l-Adawat'al-Ladhi Yabladi bihal'l Ahdath: The Qualifications and Equipment with which Children Start* by Abdullah ibn Ali al-Harawi al-Mu'addib (489 A.H.; 1095 A.D.).

80. *Anwar al-Tahqiq*: *The Lights of Research* by Ansari (1006 to 1088 A.D.). Author's full name: Shaykh Abu Ismail Abdu'llah Ansari of Herat.

81. *Danish-Namah'i 'Ala'i: Book of Knowledge* by ibn Sina. The book was written by the great philosopher for Kakuya's son, Ala' al-

Dawla, hence Ala'i, or referring to Ala. The book is written in Persian, the author's native tongue.

82. *Desatir: The Teachers.* (Author not known to me.)

83. *Ganji-Shayagan: Worthy Treasure.* (Author not known to me.)

84. *Hidayat al-Muta'allim wa Umdat al-Mu'allim: The Learner's Guide and the Teacher's Fundamentals* (or mainstay)by Shihab al-Din (819 A.H.; 1416 A.D.). Author's full name: Ahmad ibn Muhammad ibn Sulaiman al-Zahid Shihab al-Din.

85. *Ihya al-Nufus fi San'ati Ilqa al-Durus: Vivification of the Mind in the Art of Lecturing* by al-Subki (756 A.H.; 1355 A.D.). Author's full name: Taqi al-Din Ali ibn Abd al-Kafi al-Subki.

86. *Is'haq Namah: Book of Love* by Sana'i.

87. *Jami' Bayan al-Ilm: The Whole Description* (Explanation) *of Learning* by Abu Umar Yusuf ibn Abd al-Barr al-Namari al-Qurtubi (463 A.H.; 1071 A.D.).

88. *Kar-Namah: Book of Deeds* by Sana'i.

89. *Kherad Nama'i Eskandari: The Book of Knowledge* (Learning) *of Eskandari* by Jami (918 A.H.; 1414 A.D.). Author's full name: Nur al-Din Abd al-Rahman Jami.

90. *Kimiya' al-Sa'adat: The Chemistry* (Alchemy) *of Happiness* (or Prosperity) by al-Ghazzali.

91. *Kitab al-Alim wa'l-Muta'allim: The Book of the Teacher and the Pupil* by Ahmad ibn al-Sayyid al-Luqawi al-Andalusi (382 A.H.; 991 A.D.?).

92. *Kitab al-Alim wa'l-Muta'allim: The Book of the Teacher and the Pupil* by Abu Hatim ibn Yahhan al-Busti (254 A.H.; 965 A.D.?).

93. *Kitab al-Ilm wa'l-Ta'lim: The Book of Knowledge* (Learning) *and Instruction* by Abu Zaid Ahmad ibn Sahl al-Balkhi (332 A.H.; 934 A.D.), who was a student of the philosopher al-Kindi and, himself, a schoolmaster.

94. *Kitab al-Madkhal: The Book of Gateway* (or Entrance) by Muhammad al-Abdari (737 A.H.; 1256 A.D.). It is in two volumes.

95. *Kitab al-Mahasin: Book of Virtues.* The title was used for similar works by ibn Qutaiba' al-Ayashi, ibn al-Harm, al-Baihaqi, and Jabiz (Jahiz?).

96. *Lata'if al-Ma'arif: The Fine Points of the Sciences* by Abu Mansur al-Tha'libi.

97. *Nasihat: Book of Moral Advice.* It was dedicated to Nizam-al-Mulk. (Author not known to me.)

98. *Nasihat: Book of Ethical Counsel* by Shaykh Abdullah Ansari.

99. *Nizam al-Amal: The Rules of Conduct* by al-Ghazzali.

100. *Sad Dars: Hundred Lessons.* Written in modern Persian.

101. *Shia' al-Muta'allim* (Mu'allim?) *fi Adab al-Muta'allim: On the Conduct of Students.* Literal translation, *The Recovery of the Sufferer Based Upon* (or in) *the Conduct* (or Manners) *of the Student*

by al-Maqdisi (856 A.H.; 1452 A.D.). Author's full name: Abd al-Latif ibn Abd al-Rahman al-Maqdisi.

102. *Taha'fut al-Taha'fut: The Destruction of Destruction* by ibn Rushd in reply to al-Ghazzali's *Tahafut al-Falasifa: Destruction of Philosophies.*

103. *Tahrir al-Maqal fi Adab wa Fawa'id Yahtaja Ilaiha Mu'addib al-Atfal: An Essay on Tutoring Children.* Literal translation, *Essay on Manners and Rules and Useful Information for which there Is Need by Tutors.*

104. *Talqin al-Mubtadi: Instruction of the Beginner* by Abd al-Haqq ibn Abdullah al-Ishbili (581 A.H.; 1185 A.D.).

105. *Talqin al-Muta'allim: Instruction of the Learner* by Abu Ubaidah Ibrahim ibn Muhammad (400 A.H.; 1009 A.D.).

106. *Talkhis: On the Nicomachean Ethics of Aristotle* by ibn Rushd (Averroes).

107. *Tariq al-Tahqiq: Paths of Research* by Sana'i.

108. *Zad al-Arifin: The Provision of the Learned* (Gnostics?).

109. *The Book of the Counsel of Ardeshir* translated by Baladhuri.

110. *The Ethical Anthology* by Muhammad ibn Ibrahim ibn Yahya al-Watwat (born 1235, died 1318 A.D.).

111. *Supreme Inquiry in the Requisite of Conduct* (Manner) *for the Master and the Pupil* by Ali ibn Khalil al-Marsifi (930 A.H.; 1524 A.D.).

112. *A Treatise on Education* by al-Uqsura'i (908 A.H.; 1502 A.D.).* (See Appendix on *Al-Fihrist* of al-Nadim for other titles on education.)

*Consult Hajji Khalifa, Vol. I, p. 214; Vol. III, p. 196; Vol. V, pp. 113, 119; Vol. VI, p. 22. Totah, pp. 68-75, 90. Ahlwardt, Vol. I, pp. 35, 53. al-Muqtalif, Vol. 57, p. 366. Brockelman, Vol. II, pp. 455-456. Yaqut, *Dictionary of Learned Men,* Vol. I, pp. 141, 364. E. G. Browne, *Literary History of Persia,* Vols. I and II. Shalaby. And al-Nadim's *Al-Fihrist.*

CHAPTER VI

SA'DI'S REFLECTIONS ON EDUCATION AND THE ART OF LIVING

IN THE PREVIOUS CHAPTER dealing with Muslim "medieval" classics in education, we discussed briefly the life and teachings of Sa'di, with particular reference to his masterpiece, the *Gulistan.* His far-reaching educational and moral influences throughout the past seven centuries, on Muslim societies in general and on Persian life in particular, may justify a closer look at his social outlook.

SELECTED MAXIMS, APHORISMS, ANECDOTES, SHORT STORIES, AND EXCERPTS FROM THE "KULLIYYAT" OF SA'DI

(Largely adapted from the *Gulistan,* the *Bustan,* and the *Risalat*)

The following selections have been brought together from Sa'di's various works and grouped by subject. My concern has been more with carrying the original meanings in the translations than with making them literal equivalents of the original narratives in Persian. In translation of passages many details have been omitted, consideration being given to the essence of a sentiment or substance of a thought or point of view. Since many selections are culled out of context, their choices have been guided by the universality of the thoughts or sentiments they express, as well as their appeal to the English reader.

Important English translations listed in the bibliography have been consulted constantly, though the responsibility for choice of words and phraseology is my own.

In the last passage of the *Gulistan* the poet, reflecting upon educational and moral precepts embodied in his great work, observes: "This can be said of Sa'di, that he mingled the bitter medicine of advice with the sweet honey of gentle words [delicate sayings] that receptive readers, though hurt momentarily by the truths they contain, would find them nonetheless acceptable."

I hope the following selections suggest to a small extent both the "bitter medicine of advice" as well as the poet's "sweet honey of gentle words."

I. *Sa'di On Limitations of Education*

(1) A nobleman had a stupid son whom he sent to a wise educator for instruction. After some time the teacher returned the boy to his father with a note saying, "Sire, your son is incapable of sanity and is driving me insane also."

(2) Whenever native capacities are good, education will make an impression, but no furbisher can give polish to iron of a bad temper. If you wash a dog in the seven seas, you cannot change his nature; and were you to take the donkey of Jesus to Mecca, upon his return he would still remain a donkey.

(3) A wise man exhorted his children, saying, "Dearly beloved ones, acquire knowledge, for there is no reliance upon worldly goods. Rank is not recognized away from home; silver and gold are exposed to the risk of plunder by thieves or gradual waste by its owner. But knowledge is a perennial spring and an enduring fortune. If a professional man loses a fortune he need not fear or entertain regret, for his knowledge is a lasting fortune; wherever a learned man 'sojourns,' he is met with respect and is ushered into the upper seat, while the ignorant may beg for food and suffer hardship."

(4) If you covet your father's heritage, acquire his knowledge (craft), for his fortune you may squander in ten days.

(5) I heard that once there happened an insurrection in Syria, and people fled in every direction for their lives. The learned sons of peasants were employed in other lands as ministers of kings, while the ignorant sons of noblemen begged for food in villages.

(6) A learned teacher was the tutor of a prince. He chastised the boy mercilessly and reproved him to no end. The prince, out of all patience, complained of his master's conduct to his father, and laid bare his bruised body before him. The king offended and in anger summoned the teacher and asked, "Why is it that you do not treat the children of my humblest subjects with such severity and discipline as you do my son?" The teacher replied, "To think before they speak, and to deliberate before they act, are duties incumbent upon all mankind, and more immediately upon rulers, because whatever they may do or say, the special deed or word will become the subject of public scrutiny or admiration; whereas any act or remark of the common man goes without notice. Let a beggar or tramp commit a thousand indiscretions, and not one will be noticed by his companions; but let the head of a state utter but one foolish word or give a slight indication of misconduct, and the indiscreet word or unbecoming deed will be echoed from continent to continent. Therefore, more pain should be taken in forming the morals of the prince than the sons of the common folks."

(7) A schoolmaster of extreme severity, in whose presence pupils dared not utter a word, was replaced by a meek and kindly instructor. The pupils soon forgot the awe in which they held their first master

and relying on the clemency of the new teacher became devilish, neglected their studies, and passed all their time at play and mischief. Later the townfolks discharged the sheepish teacher and restored the old master to his place. I kept wondering why the townfolks made the old devil the preceptor of angels again until an old and sagacious gentleman observed, "The severity of the master is more valuable to the child than the blind love of his parents."

(8) A king turned his son over to a learned man telling him, "Educate him as you would one of your own." After many years of effort the prince had made no improvement while the sons of the preceptor excelled in knowledge and attainment. The king blamed the teacher for partiality in instruction, to which the preceptor responded: "Your majesty, instruction was equal in all cases, but capacities differed in each, and even though silver and gold are extracted from stone, not all stones carry gold and silver."

(9) A learned teacher remarked to a disciple, "If the sons of Adam were as solicitous after providence as they are in securing worldly goods, they would surpass the angels in heaven."

(10) They asked the scorpion why he hides away during winter months. He replied, "Of what good am I to anyone in summer months that I may continue my presence in winter?"

(11) It is better for a woman to give birth to a snake than to an ill-disposed child.

(12) When I was an adolescent I asked a wise man, "What are the marks of adulthood?" He said, "It is agreed in common that the signs of adulthood are evidenced when you are of age, have wet dreams, and hair grows all over your body. But in reality maturity is measured by the degree of self-discipline, without which you will be counted an adolescent regardless of other symbols."

(13) A rich man mounted his camel and journeyed toward Mecca on pilgrimage. A fellow traveller remarked: "Your camel is a nobler pilgrim for he, the poor creature, eats the thistles of the desert and carries his load dutifully."

(14) When you know that the answer is unfavorable, do not ask the question.

(15) A fellow with eye trouble went to a horse doctor who applied to his eyes what he was accustomed to applying to the eyes of quadrupeds, and the man became blind. The case was brought before a judge who decreed: "This man has no amends, for had he not been an ass he would not have gone to a veterinarian."

(16) Do not entrust affairs of consequence to those lacking in ability and experience. Do not employ in a silk factory the "plaiter" of mats, even though he is a weaver.

(17) The son of a holy man died. They asked, "What shall we

inscribe on his tombstone?" The holy man replied: "No word should be written in places where time might efface, people tread upon, and dogs defile."

(18) A rich man's son standing by the tomb of his father was saying to a poor orphan: "My father's mausoleum is built of granite, the epitaph inscribed with letters of gold, the pavement and lining of marble "tessellated" with slabs of turquoise; and of what is your father's tomb constructed but a few bricks cemented together with a handful of mortar?" The poor boy replied, "I pity your father! For before he can force his way out of this heavy weight of stones, mine shall have reached heaven."

(19) Any foe may be converted into a friend through acts of goodness, save the carnal self with which the more moderately you deal, the more violent it gets in demands.

II. *Sa'di On The Wisdom of Living*

(1) Wealth is for the comfort of life and not life for the acquisition of wealth. They asked a wise man, "Who is fortunate and who unfortunate." He said, "Fortunate is he who sowed and reaped, and unfortunate he who died and left behind."

(2) Generosity without the hope of return makes the joy of giving its own reward. Would you be better for worldly possessions, be good to others as fortune has been good to you.

(3) Two persons toil in vain and labor without gain—the one who gathers without using, the other who learns without improving.

(4) A nation is beautified by its learned men, and a religion by its devout followers.

(5) Three things cannot last without three things: Wealth without trade; knowledge without debate; and government without policy.

(6) Kindness to the wicked is injustice to the good.

(7) Do not trust the generosity of the wealthy nor the sweetness of a child's voice. The first may change with a thought, the second with a nap.

(8) Do not display all your secrets before your friends, for some day they may become your enemies; and do not exercise all your meanness on your enemies, for some day they may become your friends.

(9) A thought which you wish to keep secret, tell no one, no matter how trusted—for if you cannot keep your own secret you should not expect others to be better in this regard. It is better to be quiet about one's intimacies than to tell others, then urge them to keep the matter under cover. Do not tell *anyone* what you do not want *everyone* to know—remember, the best place to stop a stream is at the fountainhead.

(10) A weak enemy who acts subordinate and shows friendliness

has only one aim in mind, namely, to become a strong enemy. It is said that one can hardly trust the sentiments of friends, let alone the enemy's wagging tail.

(11) Whoever underestimates a little enemy is like one who underestimates a little fire. If you do not like a big fire, extinguish the little one. If you do not wish to cope with a strong enemy, discourage the weak one.

(12) If enmity prevails between two men, speak of one to the other in such a manner that if they become friends you may not feel ashamed. For animosity between two men is like a fire to which the backbiter adds fresh fuel; and once their differences are cleared, the poor fuel-carrier would burn in the flames.

(13) Whoever cultivates friendship with the enemies of his friends is unfair to his friends.

(14) If you are in doubt about any decision or action, choose the side which seems to do less injury [and move].

(15) What you can accomplish with your money, do not endanger your life for its sake, and use your sword only when other means have failed.

(16) To accept advice from one's enemy is wrong, but to listen to it is right, that you may do otherwise, which is the thing to do.

(17) Anger in excess will bring fright, and kindness in excess will take away respect. Neither be so severe that they may tire of you, nor so kind that they may rule over you. Mix discipline and kindness like a surgeon, who first cuts, then medicates.

(18) Two men are the enemies of state and religion—rulers without humility, and devotees without knowledge.

(19) An ill-tempered man is in the hands of an enemy from whom he finds no escape wherever he may go.

(20) Ten mendicants can eat at one table, but two dogs seldom from the same dish. Give to the greedy the whole world and he is not satisfied, and give to the contented a loaf of bread and he is fortified.

(21) Whatever comes easily cannot last long. In China it takes forty years to mould a bowl, while in Baghdad they bake a hundred a day, and you know their difference in price [and quality]. The little chick once out of its shell picks its own crumbs, while the human infant is ignorant of distinction and reason. But the wit of the former does not go beyond its crumbs, while the wisdom of the latter unravels eternities. The real difference between glass and pearl is that the second is rare.

(22) For the ignorant nothing is better than silence—but if he knew this much he would not be ignorant.

(23) An ignoramus was preaching to a donkey when a wise man

passing by said, "The donkey will learn nothing from your sermon, but you may learn something from his silence."

(24) He who debates with those more learned than he in order to make an impression will convince others of his ignorance. When you face those who know more than you do, silence is the best speech to make.

(25) Those who are of base nature are jealous of those whose lives are noble, like the dogs of the street who, upon seeing a hunting dog, bark but keep their distance.

(26) Philosophers eat rarely; worshippers go half hungry; students eat until they are satisfied; young men until they become burdened; old men until they begin to sweat; but priests until there is no room for a breath in their system nor a grain of food on the table.

(27) The test of a good rose is in its perfume, not in what the gardener says. And a wise man is like a rose in blossom, though silent it spreads its fragrance; while the ignorant is like a drum, though making a loud noise, is empty within.

(28) If you hear of news which may "afflict" some heart, remain silent. Be like the nightingale who brings the good tidings of spring—leave evil news to the owl.

(29) Whoever advises a blockhead is himself in need of advice.

(30) Patience leads to success—haste to disappointment.

(31) Whoever knows but does not practice is like one who drives the oxen, but does not scatter the seed.

(32) The nightingale would lose its spirit were a crow its companion in the cage.

(33) They asked an old bachelor why he would not marry. He said, "I would feel no intimacy with old women." He was advised, "Being wealthy you should seek the companionship of a young wife." He observed, "If at my age I cannot feel attachment to an elderly dame, how would a young mistress cultivate a desire for me?"

(34) I asked a wise man to advise me. He said, "Watch how you commit yourself with the ignorant. For if you possess knowledge he considers you a dumb ass, and if you are without knowledge your folly will be still greater."

(35) The sorrow which you bear before enjoyment is better than the enjoyment which precedes sorrow.

(36) They asked a wise man, "Why is it that of all trees the cypress is nicknamed free?" He replied, "Because the cypress is not bound by the vicissitudes of seasons, always flourishing, and such should be the character of free men."

(37) Prostitutes repent when they age, and policemen reform when fired.

(38) Every man's teeth are "blunted by acid," save the mayor's which require sweets.

(39) No two complainants ever appeared before a judge to seek justice.

(40) Only those who are fearless of death and indifferent to reward are in a position to advise rulers.

(41) It is wisdom not to meddle with disagreements between two others.

(42) You get gold from a mine by digging in the earth, and from a miser by digging into his life.

(43) God hides our committed sins, and the neighbor exposes the uncommitted ones.

(44) The sky refreshes the earth with rain and gets dust in return.

(45) It is better to take warning from examples of your predecessors, than to have the rising generation take warning from your acts.

(46) The effect of a falsehood is like the cut of a sabre; the wound may heal but the scar remains.

(47) Whoever associates with the wicked will be accused of sharing their ways, even though he may not have been influenced by their character.

(48) It is a mark of good breeding to accommodate yourself to your host, or forego the invitation.

(49) Whatever you are sure you will know in time, do not question others about it.

(50) They asked a great philosopher, "How did you reach such a pitch of knowledge?" He replied, "Of whatever I was ignorant I was never ashamed to ask others."

(51) A scholar without diligence is like a lover without means; a traveller without scope is like a bird without wings; a knower without practice is like a tree without fruit; and a holy man without knowledge is like a house without an entrance.

(52) When you meet a starving man do not ask him how he is unless you can provide him with the means of sustenance.

(53) Misconduct is reprehensible in any man, particularly the learned. When an armed man is caught, the stain of his disgrace is deeper.

(54) To show clemency to the vulgar strengthens his vulgarity and lessens your self-respect.

(55) Intellect without firmness leads to "chicanery," and firmness without intellect to obstinacy.

(56) Reason enthralled by passion is like a helpless man in the hands of an artful woman.

(57) A learned man with a large family to support mentioned this

fact to a philanthropist. The benefactor, who had held the learned man in high regard, considered this complaint unbecoming of him, and though he added a little to his stipend [out of charity], he subtracted more from his respect for the learned man.

(58) Whoever does not listen to counsel cannot bear criticism.

(59) Yesterday has left you forever, and tomorrow is yet to be born; take advantage of what fortune offers you between unborn tomorrow and dead yesterday.

(60) You cannot break a broken man.

(61) Of all that one would remember, the reminiscences of a friend are the loveliest; and of all that the ears would hear, a message from a loved one is most satisfying to the heart.

(62) Since the body of man is exalted by his soul, a beautiful garment is no guarantee of manhood. If manhood were to be judged by the shape of eyes, ears, mouth and nose, where would lie the distinction between man and a painting on the wall? Be a man in reality, for I know a bird that can imitate you in words.

(63) The homeless regards the whole city as his home, and the beggar camps wherever the night falls.

(64) Relations of heart and mind are more binding than those of name and blood.

(65) Between two friends the privileges of association would be felt more deeply when they sever relations for a period and unite again.

(66) There is nothing in this world so dear for the want of which you should shed tears, or your heart should be troubled over its absence or overjoyed in its presence.

(67) Only those who can look down upon this handful of earth are truly men of generous hearts.

(68) If you must worship an idol, worship a living one.

(69) If your God is not pleased with you, the benedictions of the prophets will do you no good.

(70) Do not rejoice over the funeral of your enemy. Remember, they are preparing the same fate for you.

(71) Do not give your heart to one mistress, nor your loyalties to one location, for countless are mistresses, and extensive are lands and seas. Be free like the fluttering pigeons, not enslaved like the farm hen; fly in freedom like nightingales from branch to branch. If your path crosses a thousand beauties, give them a glance, move on, and leave your heart with none. Mix with everyone so you may laugh with all, nor be tied down with one for whose welfare you should ever shed tears. What need is there that there should be two under one roof, one joyous and the other in sorrow for her joy—one sleep in peace and the other in wakeful concern for her. Enjoy pretty dresses on shapely forms, but not too much, for the cloth is aplenty in the

market place. Why should a free body be left behind prison bars, or peace of mind exchanged with troubled thoughts? You submit and serve and get no recognition; you humble yourself for naught. Be wise. At night sleep tight with a mistress and at dawn move on.*

(72) Real wealth is not measured by possessions but by one's quality of life.

(73) Do not look with the eyes of greed upon worldly possessions, for many a snake that has a beautiful skin carries poison in its fangs.

(74) It is better to die trying than to sit idle. If the goal is not attained, there is the satisfaction of effort.

(75) If you are a man of a thousand talents and bad luck, your talents will be all but useless.

(76) I am like a compass: One foot on the ground of my beliefs, and one travelling.

(77) It is foolish to decorate a house that has a shaky foundation.

(78) The vice that appeals to the king becomes a virtue.

(79) Wherever the night falls is the beggar's camp.

(80) Do not be shocked at your caricature if your enemy is the artist.

(81) Enough mosquitoes can kill an elephant.

(82) He who throws a stone should expect a brick.

(83) If you expect to reach Mecca do not travel to Turkistan.

(84) Suffering is universal.

(85) He who expects wages should learn to work.

(86) Those who are rich in worldly goods are often poor in spirit.

(87) Patience is bitter but bears sweet fruit.

(88) When the host pays the bill, the guest is generous.

(89) Keep your place, even when your master is friendly.

(90) The secret of wealth is in learning to save (pennies).

(91) Do not harm the physician who cures you; you may need him at your bed again.

(92) Save your lamp until the night falls.

(93) You can hide your thoughts from others, but not your pale complexion.

(94) To a drowned man rain and sunshine are the same.

(95) If you are honest you need not fear the inspector.

(96) An iron nail cannot penetrate a stone, nor advice a selfish head.

---

*These sentiments are exceptions rather than basic convictions with Sa'di. He had a somewhat unhappy married life to which these reflections may be traced. (Read No. 40 "On the Requirements of Piety.")

(97) Do not judge yourself by your father's wisdom.

(98) Kindness will not turn your enemy into a friend, but will only add to his greed. . . . You cannot take rust off an old metal with a soft file.

(99) Sometimes a child unknowingly hits the target.

(100) If you go to battle ride on a lean horse, not a fat cow.

(101) When fortune closes one door, it opens another.

(102) Immortality is in words well expressed and work well done. Our joys would please and our griefs would pain us but for awhile, yet the reward of one's labor and the praise of one's good name continue.

(103) A man who is not skillful with his tongue should make better use of his ears.

(104) An act of goodness surpasses a thousand prayers.

(105) It is better to eat and share than to fast and hoard.

(106) The tragedy of life lies in the fact that so often men of a generous heart are afflicted with poverty, and those of vast riches and mean disposition lord it over their fellowmen.

(107) To the beggar the clatter of dishes is a sweeter sound than the smack of kisses.

(108) Those who promise but do not fulfill are like a drum—noisy but empty.

(109) In the hands of a miser gold is still in the ore. Consume what you gather before the worms of the grave devour you.

(110) You cannot conquer love by reason, nor kill a lion with bare fists.

(111) An ailing maiden was infatuated with a young and handsome physician. It proved to be a race between skill and desire. For, while the doctor applied his skill to cure and dispose of the patient, the patient nourished the ailment in order to call oftener on the object of her amour. [How modern!]

(112) Love is fire and advice is wind.

(113) Leave your jewels with the guards, but guard your own secrets.

(114) When a thought is not spoken you are its master, when uttered it wins mastery over you. A thought is like a captive demon, once released no "stratagem" can bring it back.

(115) Do not destroy your brother's reputation at the corner store if you do not want fortune to betray your good name in the market place.

(116) Two things are against reason: To eat more than one's share, and to die before one's allotted time.

(117) A man complained to me bitterly of the evil of envy in his

neighbor. I said, "One who disapproves of envy should not entertain slander."

(118) If you believe that your fellowmen are asses, remember that you too are a fellowman.

(119) Lend your tongue to praise, and your ears to good counsel.

(120) If you meet a man of brute force, save your tender fist.

(121) When you have exposed a villain, keep him powerless.

(122) If you have disturbed a beehive, run to another quarter or be overwhelmed. If you shoot an arrow against one more skillful in the art, gather your gown and flee. If you undermine a wall, do not stand beneath it.

(123) Make no effort to discover the concealed faults of your fellowmen. This may contribute to their ill-repute but will make you untrustworthy.

(124) Make your contribution now that prosperity is yours. Wealth is an instrument of good—today it is in your custody, tomorrow in another's.

(125) The speaker is not to blame if listeners are not receptive.

(126) A man of good reputation lives in the memory of his admirers, while one with ill reputation is already dead.

(127) Kissing the temple grounds is no gesture of devotion to God. Bring him an honest heart.

(128) Do not brag that you are alive. You have that in common with the jackass. Man's distinction is in reason and feeling.

(129) Deal with the good according to their goodness, and with the wicked in accordance with their wickedness. Be a rose among the roses and a thorn among the thorns.

(130) Do not open the secrets of your heart to your best friends, for they too may have many best friends.

(131) Never look down upon the masses, for many a friend of God is among the humble.

(132) Though the love of one's land is a noble tradition, it is not wise to suffer in any community because you were born in its midst.

(133) Take it easy. This handful of earth upon which you stand today will tread upon you tomorrow.

(134) Do not expect motherly sympathy from this old lady, destiny: She gives birth to myriads of children today in order to feast upon them tomorrow.

(135) If your income is meager, watch your expenses. Remember, if a roaring river is not fed by the mountain streams for a single season, it will turn into dry land.

(136) If your skirt is caught in thorns, disentangle it gently or you may tear it to shreds.

(137) If you respect yourself, others will respect you.

(138) In conversation remember two principles: Think before you speak; stop talking before they say, "Enough."

(139) It is better to be without a tongue than to own one and refuse to use it wisely.

(140) Silence is a virtue, but so is appropriate speech. It is unwise to remain silent when you should speak, as it is foolish to speak when you should remain silent.

(141) Gold is good if you spend it on yourself and others. For mere hoarding, stones will do.

(142) A face that is beautiful should be exposed. It delights the eyes of admirers without diminishing its beauty.

(143) If knowledge were to disappear from the earth, none would be aware of ignorance.

(144) He who knows and does not apply is like a blind man carrying a candle. He cannot find his path by its light but may burn his garment.

(145) Those of wealth are more in need of the counsel of the learned than the learned are of the abundance of the wealthy.

(146) Whoever fosters cruelty is the enemy of the oppressed.

(147) One who is a slave of his belly entertains two sorrows: Hunger and stomach-ache.

(148) Do not count as friends those who brag of love and kinship in your hour of success but are aloof in your hour of distress. Count as friends those who rejoice in your success and stoop to lift you when you are down.

(149) If you wish to escape the critic's lash, fling away your pen.

(150) A wise man with a short stature is preferable to a tall blockhead.

(151) Not all that is mighty in stature is superior in value. Of the mountains, Sinai is one of the least, yet it is the most mighty in the sight of God in dignity and stature.

(152) Notwithstanding his slim make, an Arabian horse is worth a herd of asses.

(153) A man's virtues and vices are hidden until he opens his mouth.

(154) In the day of battle, the lean steed serves you better than the fat oxen.

(155) To educate the blockhead is like throwing walnuts over a dome.

(156) Do not put out a fire and leave the embers, nor kill a viper and foster the young.

(157) You can never gather fruit from a willow twig even though the clouds pour down the waters of immortality.

(158) You can never extract sugar from a mat cane.

(159) If the whelp of a wolf is brought up in human environment, it will still grow into a wolf.

(160) A man of base birth can no more be educated into a noble character than a tempered sabre may be made from base iron. And rain, in the purity of whose nature there is no dispute, grows tulips in the garden and common weeds in the salt marsh. A briny soil can never be made to yield spekenard; to scatter seed upon it is to waste labor.

(161) A man's worth rests upon talents and not riches, and the mark of maturity is not in the number of one's years, but in the degree of one's good sense.

(162) The envious man carries within himself the cause of his malady.

(163) We are all members one of another and claim a common origin. When the little finger aches, a sympathetic pain vibrates through the body system. Therefore, he who is aloof to the afflictions of his fellowmen is not worthy of humanity.

(164) A fool who illuminates the day with camphorated candle will have no oil for his lamp at night.

(165) Preserve the dignity of your character, and leave buffoonery to jesters.

(166) Do not put your hand in a scorpion's hole if you cannot endure the pain of his sting.

(167) No one throws a stone at a tree that bears no fruit.

(168) The lion is the king of the animals, and the donkey the humblest, yet the burden-bearing donkey is superior to a man-eating lion.

(169) You may force a sharp bone down your throat, but you will also tear your belly.

(170) If you grapple with a steel-armed wrestler, you torture your own silver arm.

(171) The arrow issues from a bow, but the archer gives it its aim.

(172) Whoever forsakes the desire to live says openly whatever he thinks or feels.

(173) A lie which is intended to serve a good purpose is preferable to a truth which aims at malice.

(174) Quantity is no index of quality. It is better to be puny but intelligent than to be husky and foolish.

(175) Two beggars can sleep under one blanket—but two kings cannot rule over the same kingdom.

(176) The wise will speak and eat whenever silence may bring about injury and fasting may lead to starvation. Thus, appropriate speech is a mark of wisdom, and timely eating a contribution to health.

(177) A puny plant which has not taken roots may be uprooted with one hand, but if left to gain strength it may defy a windlass.

(178) Those whose natures are dull cannot gain light by association with the enlightened. To educate the feeble in mind is like placing nuts on a cupola.

(179) To be good to the wicked amounts to doing evil to the good.

(180) The test of genuine power is in accomplishment, not in wealth, and the greatness of man is measured by the quality of his thoughts rather than the number of his years.

(181) Those whose fortunes are little and whose characters are base wish the downfall of men of wealth and dignity.

(182) If you desire succor in calamity, be generous in prosperity.

(183) If you mistreat a slave, he will depart; and if you treat a free man well, he will voluntarily remain devoted to you.

(184) Satisfied subjects are the king's best soldiers.

(185) Someone saw the devil (Satan) in a dream with a stately countenance and a face shining as that of the sun. He asked, "Why is it that with such a handsome face you are drawn so ugly by mankind throughout the ages?" To which the devil replied, "O fool, these are not my likenesses, but alas the brush that has painted me has ever been in the enemy's hand."

(186) If you receive a rich inheritance, avoid the company of hoboes.

III. *Sa'di On Love And Youth (Mostly From His Ghazaliyyat Or Odes)*

(1) They asked a wise man, "How is it that Sultan Mahmud, who has so many attractive bondswomen, does not entertain such fondness for them as he does for Ayaz, who is inferior to them in beauty?" He said, "Whatever enters the heart looks lovely to the eyes. If you glance at angels with disparagement they appear homely, and if you look at demons with the eyes of desire they appear like angels."

(2) It is not easy to detect the faults of a loved one, for the hue of sentiment colors the object of desire. When you declare yourself a friend, expect no favors, for where amorous relations prevail, possessiveness is out of place.

(3) When the manager is in love with his secretary, the secretary is the management.

(4) Wherever the king of love appears, the strong arm of chastity is weakened. It is impossible to fall in mud and keep your skirt clean.

(5) When the charmer's eyes do not covet your gold, gold and dust will have the same value.

(6) Beauty has strength. Charmers overwhelm their lovers with their sheer loveliness, as warriors overcome their adversaries with brute power.

(7) Whoever is concerned with the safety of his life should not enter upon the path of love, for the thought of safety often diverts the heart from complete devotion to the object of affection. To be a slave to one's self turns the pursuit of love into sophistry. A true lover, though never attaining the goal of his affections, will forgetfully die in the effort. If you are a lover pursue your object, come what may—her sanctuary of bliss, or death at the gateway of longing.

(8) A darling once chastised her admirer: "So long as you are concerned with your own worth, you are incapable of viewing my merits."

(9) A man may have committed the *Qur'an* to memory, but when distracted with love forgets the alphabet.

(10) There was a teacher who was infatuated with the beauty of one of his pupils. He was inclined, as it is the weakness of human nature, to favor her with tender attentions discriminatory to other pupils. He would never admonish or correct her, but on the contrary, whenever he would find her isolated he would say, "O, celestial creature, I am so occupied with your loveliness that I forget my own presence when you are around. I could not help looking at your charms even if arrows were crossing my eyes." The pupil said, "O, teacher, if you would observe my conduct as you would my beauty, you might perchance offer me corrections that would improve my manners." To which the teacher replied, "O my lovely pupil, propose this duty to someone else, for the light in which I view you reflects nothing but good." If the charmer has one virtue and seventy faults, the lover discerns naught but the virtue.

(11) A friend whom I had not seen for some time told me, "We have been anxious to visit with you," to which I replied, "It is better to be eager to see me than to become weary of me." A beloved whom you seldom see is more desired than one with whose presence you are satiated.

(12) A friend of mine whom I had not seen for some time questioned me for not corresponding with him. I said, "I was vexed by the thought that the eyes of a courier should be delighted by your countenance while I was deprived of that joy."

(13) No matter how ill-tempered or ill-mannered your object of love, it is still less onerous to carry on the instinct of courtship than to deprive the heart of this fond exercise. For it is easier to bear violence than to live without love. Neither it is the quality of a lover to exact terms of his charmer. Relinquish your heart unreservedly to your beloved, whether she responds with kindness or harshness. At end you may declare with pride: "I have loved."

(14) The light of the sun is not diminished if the bat cannot keep company with the sun.

(15) One must taste adversity in order to relish prosperity.

(16) When you were flourishing with loveliness you drove me away, and now that your face is lined with age you seek my love.

(17) Courtship is sweet when mutual, and coquettishness when welcomed.

(18) The garden of your beauty is like a bed of roses, the more a lover crops it, the more it will shoot.

(19) A man asked a philosopher: "If an admirer is shut in with a lovely mistress and the doors are locked, the rivals asleep, the heart anxious, and passion overpowering, could he remain safe from indulgence by the strength of abstinence?" He replied: "He may remain safe from temptation, but not from condemnation of malicious neighbors."

(20) A parrot was shut up with a crow in the same cage. The parrot, affronted by the crow's ugly face, lamented, "What a detestable aspect is this, what a hideous shape and accursed appearance, and disproportionate figure. Ah, if I were as far from this raven of the desert as east from the west. A glance at his ugly features turns my day of delight into gloomy night. Would that a creature as hideous were to be his companion, if such another were to be found anywhere." Strangely enough, the crow was also fed up and "vexed" to the soul at the society of the parrot. Wringing his hands of chagrin and lamenting his misfortune, he kept saying, "What bad luck and ill fate to be caged with this conceited bird, than to strut along with falcons on the walls of gardens. Woe is me that my stars should in retribution lock me in this dungeon of 'calamity' in companionship with such a vain blockhead and moronic babbler." All of which goes to show that however men of learning despise the ignorant, the ignorant are many times more scornful of the learned. Like a mystic who, falling in company with "rogues," would prove to be as offensive to them as they appear unholy to him.

(21) A man was married to a beautiful woman who died, but her mother, who was a "decrepit" old dotard, remained with him. The poor man was irritated to death by her company, but was forced to put up with her because of the dowry. A friend came by to comfort him one day asking, "How are you doing since the loss of your dear wife?" To which he replied, "Alas, the absence of my wife is not so unbearable to me as the presence of the mother-in-law."

(22) It is easier to break with a thousand friends than to put up with one enemy.

(23) I beheld a "luminary" in the shadowed portico of a mansion, so splendid an object that the tongue of eloquence falls short in summing

her loveliness, such as the day dawning upon the dark night, or the fountain of immortality issuing from chaos. She held in her hand a goblet of snow-cooled water, into which she dropped some sugar and tempered it with spirit of wine; but I know not whether she scented it with attar of roses or sprinkled it with a few blossoms from her own rosy cheeks. I received the beverage from the idol-fair hand, and having drunk it found myself restored to a new life and said, "Happy is the eye that can contemplate your beauty every morning."

(24) If you seek safety do not follow the path of love. If you dread the waves, avoid the ocean. If you are seeking the society of the rose do not forget the "vexation" of the thorn.

(25) Give me a companion who has the self-same malady as I, and I shall chat the livelong day unfolding my tale. For two pieces of wood burning together burn all the brighter. Tell the anguish of your aches to a fellow-sufferer, for the healthy are oblivious to the cries of pain; and speak of the horrors of hornets to those who have been smarted by their stings.

(26) Those who are afraid of love should keep their eyes shut.

(27) Whoever has no face to save cannot save yours.

(28) You count it sin to look at a beauteous shape: I count it sin to turn my eyes away.

(29) If in the final judgment they ask me what I desire most, I would seek to abide with my beloved and leave the blessings of paradise to you.

(30) If desire invites suffering, and indifference peace of mind, I would rather suffer a thousand times with you, than enjoy tranquility without you.

(31) Her attractive personality could be viewed through her lovely shape, as shining wine may be seen through a clear glass.

(32) It is a necessity for a beautiful woman to remain reserved in public, else they may take her friendly smile as an invitation to courtship.

(33) A beautiful song enriches the soul, and a beautiful face excites the senses. What a sublime experience to hear a beautiful song from a lovely creature.

(34) For a beautiful face to crave notice is normal, and for an admiring eye to seek beauty is natural. Unnoticed beauty is therefore wasted, as unadmiring eyes are blind.

(35) The absence of a friend makes the heart grow fonder, just as the blessings of the water are better realized by a fish thrown on the shore.

(36) I would not leave you even if you were to drive me away, and if driven, I would keep on returning—like a fly who refuses to be chased away from sweets, and if driven would soon return.

(37) I thought I would reduce the agony of love's longing by patience. But as time goes on, I seem to have more of the agony of love and less of the virtue of patience.

(38) O Sa'di, you set your tent of dream in vain amidst the roses. The flower which delights your eyes grows elsewhere.

(39) Only those who know your beauty and my love can understand my agony.

(40) Many a time I have resolved to avoid love's embrace, and many a time the spell of a lovely shape has weakened my vow.

(41) How can you moan for a thorn which is in my feet? How can you sigh for a pain which is not in your heart?

(42) If you could only look at her beauty through the windows of my eyes, you would have a better grasp of my affections for her.

(43) Just as the light of one candle may light a thousand candles, so is your beauty native in you and imitative in others.

(44) If my eyes follow you around, do not blame my eyes; your beauty is the magnet and my heart the victim.

(45) Ah, if fortune would leave us together once without the neighbors knowing it.

(46) If the language of love makes no impression upon you, you are as good as dead.

(47) The meeting of my beloved is to me as rainfall to the thirsty in the desert.

(48) I am caught in the spell of your love as a pigeon in the claws of an eagle.

(49) I am so wrapped in thoughts of you that I forget to remember myself.

(50) Many a day I have waited for you in vain till eve, with the hope of spending one eve with you till daybreak.

(51) As a traveller loses his path when a lamp passes before his eyes, I lost my way when my beloved passed me.

(52) Do not seek union without the risk of separation. If you care to drink, expect the after-effect.

(53) O nightingale, keep on singing to the rose, for wherever there are fragrance and beauty there should also be songs.

(54) Any town can claim scores of beauties, but few beauties of spotless virtue.

(55) My heart carries the secrets of your love. Break it not, else they may fall in the hands of strangers.

(56) I had in mind to bring you my heart as a gift, were it not such a humble token.

(57) I can hide my troubled thoughts from you, but not my pale complexion.

(58) Now that we have a moment's peace let us walk together through the roses, before the floods of fate uproot the bushes and the winds of destiny put out the candlelight of our lives.

(59) Waste not your words. I have no listening ears, for one whose heart is torn with love is not receptive to advice.

(60) If you are disposed to cheer my heart, do it today, for tomorrow you may lay only flowers on my dust.

(61) Last night I heard my beloved telling me yes and no in one instant. Her eyebrows gestured me "no," her eyes signalled me "yes."

(62) A thousand times I tried to hide the secret of my love, but like a kettle left over the fire I could not help boiling.

(63) How unfortunate that the eyes that admire your beauty tonight should glance at anything tomorrow.

(64) If love were an ocean, the heart could drink it dry and still remain thirsty.

(65) It is futile to advise the lover; the one in need of counsel is the beloved.

(66) Love and reason can never be bedmates, for where there is one kingdom and two kings there is always trouble.

(67) It is easy for you to separate your heart from my love, but never your love from my heart.

(68) Love is immortal when the beloved is of a pure heart and the lover of clean eyes.

(69) I vowed to tell you the sufferings of my heart when I saw you again, but when I saw you, all agonies left my heart.

(70) Is it fair that a broken-hearted lover like I should flutter and burn like a moth by the candlelight of her beauty while she brightens the hearts of others with her luminary charms?

(71) I refrain from telling the tale of my love to others, jealous that they may share the beauty of my heart-felt story.

(72) How can I ever run away from you, since you are my refuge of hope.

(73) The proof of my love is in the sentiment, that while you broke away from me, I united with no other.

(74) A kiss may be a gift of sentiment or a commodity for sale; it is put on the market by some and given as a gift by others. I will squander my gold before you until I am penniless, and enjoy kisses from you until you refuse.

(75) If you refuse me your heart, send me the memory of our love to keep company with my secrets of you.

(76) You broke many a covenant with me; ah, if you were to keep one by error.

(77) If you do not pray for me, curse me; an utterance from your lips is transformed into sweetness regardless of contents.

(78) The light of your face dims the rays of the sun and moon, just as the miracles of Moses neutralized the magic of Pharoah.

(79) I cannot compare the light of your face to the sun, for this should flatter the sun, who is not worthy of this.

(80) The traveller who sees your beauty turns into a settler.

(81) If you ever enter the garden, roses will be ashamed to have opened their faces.

(82) There are many beauties in this world who disappear like stars when the sun of your beauteous face begins to shine.

(83) You are so settled in my heart that I feel you are in my arms.

(84) All nightingales sing near the roses save that of my heart, which remains silent in your presence.

(85) My heart cannot conceal its love any more than a clear flask can hide its contents.

(86) I took my case to a physician, saying that I stay awake all night dreaming. He said, "O Sa'di, your malady is love for which our profession offers no remedy."

(87) Love cannot open its mysteries to the eyes of lust.

(88) Were it not for beautiful shapes, the mystery of love would never have been born, and but for the presence of the roses, the nightingale would never sing the songs of joy and sadness.

(89) I thought the agony of love would come to an end; alas, each morning love declares a fresh beginning.

(90) You broke the tender flask of my heart; move with care—there are broken glasses on your path.

(91) As the day of union approaches, the flames of love rise higher.

(92) Alas that from a mouth so sweet should come words so bitter, and that behind breasts so ivory white there should be a heart so black.

(93) O doctor, a sickness which is of the heart cannot be cured by your pills, and would only give you a bad name.

(94) I began to tell you of the secret agony of my heart, and remembered that being in my heart you should be aware of my secret.

(95) All sentiments seem to mature in quality with age, save my love, which seems to increase in contents.

(96) At the moment of death I would be longing for you, and on the day of resurrection searching for you.

IV. *Sa'di On Benefits of Silence*

(1) I once remarked to a friend that my hesitation in discourse was due to the fact that in conversation one's judgment is apt to be

sound in some respects and faulty in others, and that the enemy's [critical] eyes are as a rule on the faults. He answered, "It is better that your enemies have no instinct to see the good, for the blindness of the bat would not diminish the light from the sun."

(2) A merchant lost a thousand dinars. He advised his son to mention the loss to no one. The son remarked: "I will abide by your wishes, but explain to me the wisdom of this secrecy." He said, "That I may not suffer two evils: One, the loss of my money, and another the malignant rejoicing of my neighbors."

(3) Do not relate your grievance to your rivals, for at best it delights their hearts.

(4) A youth who was known for his profound scholarship never uttered a word when he was in the society of the learned. On one occasion his father asked, "Why do you not also express an opinion in their company?" "Because," the son answered, "they may question me on what I do not know and put me to shame."

(5) So long as a man keeps silent others will leave him alone. But if he is disposed to pass judgment he should be prepared to show evidence and proof.

(6) A famous theologian fell in debate with an atheist. Finding him a formidable challenger he threw down the shield of submission and departed. Someone asked him why it was that with all his divine knowledge he failed to defeat an infidel in debate. He said: "My proof is the *Qur'an* in which he has no faith, and his creed is blasphemy for which I do not care."

(7) When you are unable to convince a man by the strength of your proof, wisdom is in silence.

(8) A wise man saw a learned man being beaten and insulted by a blockhead. He remarked, "Had this man been truly wise he would have known better than to get involved with a fool."

(9) When the sage meets the sage there is harmony; when the sage meets the fool there is discord; when the fool meets the fool there is destruction.

(10) An orator was known never to repeat the same word twice in his speech, and never to deliver the same speech again, on the evidence that repetition would diminish the value of the message and bore the audience.

(11) There is no better confession of ignorance than to interrupt while another is talking.

(12) An astrologer upon entering his home found his wife in the arms of a stranger. Cursing and beating followed the episode. A friend hearing of the incident remarked: "How can you read the signs of the stars if you are unaware of what goes on under your roof?"

(13) I am provoked at the flattery of those who make my vices

appear as virtues, my blemishes as excellences, my shortcomings as perfections, the thorn which is my conduct as jasmine and roses. Where is a frank and courageous rival to lay my faults bare before me?

(14) A muezin was chanting with so discordant a note that he drove the hearers insane. The attendant of the mosque, in order not to offend him, said, "Friend, since there are many meuzins of long standing in the mosque to each of whom I have allowed a monthly stipend of five dinars, I will offer you ten to go and chant elsewhere." The chanter agreed to this and left. After a while he returned saying, "Sire, you were unfair to prevail ten dinars upon me to leave you. The attendant of the mosque where I now chant offers me twenty to move to another temple, and I would not consent." The holy man replied, "Make a hard bargain, brother, for with the kind of voice which is yours, he will no doubt offer you fifty."

(15) A holy man with a grating voice was reading the *Qur'an* in loud tones. A passerby asked him, "What is your monthly stipend?" "Nothing," he replied. "Then why do you keep on reading?" "I am reading for the sake of God," he replied. "Then," said the passerby, "for God's sake do not read."

V. *Sa'di On Old Age And Senility*

(1) A centenarian was approaching death. I sat by his bedside and finding him in unbearable agony asked him consolingly, "How do you find yourself?" He replied: "You know what torture a man suffers from whose jaw they extract a tooth. Fancy how excruciating is the pain when the very dear life is being dragged out of the body." I said, "Banish the thought of death from your mind and allow no doubts to disturb your peace. For neither is vigorous health a guarantee of a long life, nor any sickness, however dangerous, a positive proof of immediate death."

(2) There was a holy tree to which pilgrims went to supplicate their wants. A rich old man once prayed at the foot of the tree for a son. Fortune made him the father of a handsome boy. I asked his son once what he desired most from life. He answered: "That I might discover that tree and pray for the death of this tedious old dotard, my father."

(3) An old man married a young and beautiful girl. He tried to win her heart by pleasantries and good humor, but to no avail. Once he exhorted her, saying, "To be wedded to an old man has its advantages. The old are mature because of age; they have seen much of the world, are rich in experience. They have tasted the bitter and the sweet of life, and have rubbed shoulders with good and evil; they are therefore appreciative of good company, and play the part of a faithful lover. They are tender and sympathetic, good-natured and sweet in conversation; they try to please even when tormented, never failing in devotion and heart-felt consideration. While the young are arrogant and self-

centered, quick-headed and light-footed; every moment they are of a new desire, and every day they make a new demand. Every night they sleep in different quarters, and every day they take a new mistress. They are like nightingales singing to many a rose; they excel in the strength of youth but are lacking in faith and fidelity." His spouse, unimpressed by his eloquent speech, sighed coldly and said: "As I was listening to your dissertation I happened to remember the shrewd advice my midwife gave me some years ago. 'It is better for a young girl to have a gun in her side than an old man beside her.'" In due time the two separated, as might be expected, and the girl was remarried to a young man, sour-faced, empty-handed and ill-mannered. I have heard that the lady uttered daily thanks for the good fortune of young companionship.

(4) To walk and halt is better than to run and break down; wishing to reach the end of your journey, do not hurry. The galloping horse wears out where the camel, with deliberate pace, moves on and completes the journey.

(5) Now that you are old relinquish childishness and leave merriment and play to the young. Neither expect the gayeties of youth from old age, for the stream that has passed by shall never return, and corn when full grown can no longer rear its head; and even lions lose the sturdy grasp of their paw with age. An old woman may dye her grey hair by art, but cannot straighten her humped back.

VI. *Sa'di On The Requirements of Piety*

(1) Be a saint at heart and wear what you please.

(2) Sanctity is not determined by change of dress, but by the abandonment of the pomp and vanity of the world.

(3) A coward cannot acquire courage by putting on a suit of armor.

(4) When a member of a sect commits an act of folly he disgraces the group.

(5) A holy man was the guest of a king. At the table he ate less than was his custom, and at prayer he said more than was his practice. When he returned home he asked his son to prepare him more food. His son inquired, "Father, did you not eat sufficiently at the palace of the king?" He replied, "Not enough to sustain my body." "Then repeat your prayers also," demanded the son, "for you did not say enough to sustain your soul."

(6) I spent one night in pious meditation while my companions were fast asleep around me. I remarked to my father, "It is a pity that my friends are dead asleep rather than in vigilant piety." He replied, "My son, better that you too had slept than calumniate the failings of others."

(7) On one occasion I was preaching to a congregation dead and

cold at heart. The logic of my discourse made no impression upon their deaf spirit, and the sparks of my argument struck no fire in their humid wood. I was weary of teaching brutes and holding up the mirror of truth to the assembly of the blind. As I was explaining this text from the *Qur'an,* "I (God) am nearer to you than the vein of your neck," a traveller, passing by, entered the mosque and the flame of my words lit upon him. He shouted so violently in response that the rawest in the assembly bubbled in unison. I exclaimed, "My Lord, those at a distance are near by virtue of awareness, and those who are near are far because of ignorance."

(8) The orator cannot strike the ball of eloquence if the hearer's field of understanding has no "scope." The vigor of genius in the speaker is wasted if the audience lacks comprehension.

(9) A wicked king asked a holy man, "Do you ever think of me?" He said, "Yes, whenever I am forgetting my God."

(10) A man in a dream saw a king in paradise and a holy man in hell. Puzzled by this mystery he heard a voice saying, "This king is in heaven because of his affection for the needy, and that holy man in hell because of his attitude toward wealth."

(11) They asked a wise man, "From whom did you learn manners?" "From the unmannerly," he said, "in that I was careful to detect whatever was not acceptable in their conduct and avoid it."

(12) A holy man was in the habit of eating ten pounds of food every night and reading the whole *Qur'an* by dawn. Once a shrewd observer remarked, "He would have been the holier had he eaten a piece of bread and gone to sleep."

(13) You can deliver yourself from the wrath of God by repentance, but you cannot escape the slanderous tongue of man.

(14) It is better to be good while people speak evil of you than to be an evil man with good reputation.

(15) I complained before a learned man that someone had accused me of corruption. He said, "Put him to shame by your good conduct."

(16) I was once intoxicated by the chirping of the morning birds. A friend remarked, "Why so distracted by the singing of a bird?" I said, "I am ashamed of my own silence while the birds are singing in the praise of God."

(17) Once a nightingale whispered to me at dawn, "What manner of man are you who are unaware of the ecstasy of love? Even camels are entranced by the song of the desert. If there is not as much in you, you are inferior to brutes."

(18) The twig of the ban-tree shakes in the zephyr, while solid rock remains still.

(19) The responsive heart is filled with divine mystery.

(20) Adversity brings pain and prosperity attachment, and thus the calamity in living is that we are disquieted in both poverty and wealth.

(21) If you covet wealth ask for contentment, which is a lasting treasure.

(22) Independence in the poor is of more merit than generosity in the rich.

(23) If you wish to strengthen the affection of your friends do not visit them too often. Remember that the sun is sought after during the winter months because we see its face less often.

(24) Better to be in chains with a friend than to walk in a garden with strangers.

(25) The ringlets of lovely damsels are traps on the path of reason and snares for the bird of wisdom.

(26) True piety does not require the "bread of consecration," just as native beauty is in no need of cosmetics and jewelry.

(27) A scholar annoyed by frequent visitors asked his father for a way to discourage their intrusion. His father replied, "To those who are poor lend money, and from those who are rich ask some in loan, and neither will trouble you again."

(28) The patched cloak of the mystic is the garment of resignation. Whoever wears it and cannot bear hardship is a hypocrite.

(29) A holy man saw a strong wrestler foaming at the mouth with rage because some one had given him a bad name. "What pity," he said, "that this paltry wretch is able to carry a ton of stones on his back but is unable to bear the weight of a few light words."

(30) It takes more courage for a strong man to utter kind words when he would be tempted to thrust his fist into another man's jaw.

(31) Only death can uproot a habit.

(32) A doctor of law wedded his homely daughter to a blind man. Soon after there arrived in town a physician who could restore sight to the blind. Someone asked the lawyer why he would not have the physician restore the eyes of his son-in-law. He said, "I am afraid to restore his sight and repudiate my daughter, for the husband of a homely woman should be blind."

(33) When the bride is devoid of symmetry, damask and brocade only add to her deformity.

(34) They asked a wise man which was preferable, wealth or courage. He said, "Whoever is wealthy is in no need of courage."

(35) You cannot awake your neighbor if you are asleep yourself.

(36) The hands of generosity are stronger than the arms of power.

(37) A scholar left the seminary for the college. Questioned on this change of heart he said, "Men of religion are concerned with saving

themselves from the waves, while the men of science have concern for saving the drowned."

(38) A king was in the habit of looking down at the fraternity of the hermits. One of them sensing his attitude said, "O king, in this world we are your inferiors in wealth, your superiors in happiness, your equals in death, and we will surpass you in the day of resurrection."

(39) True piety is in meditation, service, obedience, sacrifice, contentment, love of God, trust, submission and endurance. He who has these qualities has piety in the true sense.

(40) Once a friend redeemed me from captivity for ten dinars. Later he gave me his daughter in marriage with a dowry of a hundred dinars. The woman turned out to have a "perverse spirit and virulent tongue," and so "unhinged" all my domestic comfort. Once she told me, "Are you not the fellow whom my father redeemed from captivity for ten dinars?" "Yes," I replied, "and enslaved me to you for a hundred."

(41) Once a dispute arose between the curtain and the flag. Said the flag to the curtain, "We are both fellow servants at the royal court, yet I am never relieved from duty, marching early and late, falling into the hands of raw recruits, being rolled up on the army, marched and turned upside down. But you never experience any peril or siege. The dusts of whirlwinds never touch you, and the sands of deserts never fall upon your face. You are carried by his majesty's splendid youths and handled by the jasmine-scented damsels of the court. Why this discrimination?" The curtain replied, "Because I lay my head humbly at the threshold, and do not flare in the face of heavens like you."

VII. *Sa'di On Excellence of Contentment*

(1) If the rich were just and the poor content, importunity would cease to exist.

(2) Give me patience and contentment, for there is wisdom in the former and wealth in the latter.

(3) Contentment is the rarest wealth and patience the height of wisdom.

(4) The wealthy carry on the heritage of Pharaoh and Hamon, and the learned preserve the legacy of seers and prophets.

(5) Better be an ant tread underfoot than a hornet with agonizing sting.

(6) If you have no means of injuring your fellowmen, thank your destiny.

(7) It is better to be content with the dry crust of your own bread and a coarse woolen frock than to lay yourself under obligation to anyone! Better to die of want than to display your needs before others; better to endure the torment of hell than to go to heaven through the effort of your neighbor.

(8) The secret of a healthy belly lies in refusing to eat until hard pressed by hunger, and "relinquishing" the repast when there is still appetite.

(9) We suffer because of excess and endanger our lives because of abstinence.

(10) He who nourishes the whelp of excess will soon face a full-grown wolf.

(11) Eat to the point that supports you, but not to the extent that you would support what you eat.

(12) They asked a frustrated man, "What do you desire most?" He replied, "That I may desire no more."

(13) Those who are in the habit of temperance overcome hardships with ease, while those who are accustomed to luxury perish in straitened circumstances.

(14) Better to die of a surfeit than to starve.

(15) The conserve of roses in excess causes a "surfeit," while the dry crust of bread in moderation is relished as conserve of roses.

(16) Better to go without meat than to humor the butcher.

(17) To accept favors from the mean may sustain the body, but takes away from the soul.

(18) Do not exchange your self-respect for immortality. Better an honorable death than continuity in disgrace.

(19) A sinner who forgives is preferable to a holy man who holds a grudge.

(20) Relating your misfortune to friends endangers friendship.

(21) Speak of your misfortune with a cheerful and smiling face, for pleasantness is the first principle of good business.

(22) A man in distress went to a philanthropist for help. He found him a man of sour countenance with bitter lips, seated in "sullen" discontent. He left saying, "His gift is not worth his 'visage'."

(23) If the wretched cats were given wings, they would not have left a sparrow's egg on earth.

(24) I heard an Arab tell a circle of jewellers: "Once I lost my way in the desert, and consumed my provision and was preparing to die, when suddenly my eyes caught sight of a bag nearby. I shall never forget the joy with which I reached for the bag thinking that it contained parched grain, nor the bitterness I felt in discovering that it contained virgin pearls."

(25) I had shoes and complained until I beheld a man who had no feet.

(26) A merchant who had amassed a fortune was surveying to me the prospects of his last enterprise before retiring. After boring me with an elaborate display of his present security, he continued, "I will

now carry Persian sulphur to China, where the price is high, thence the porcelain of China to Rome, the Roman silk to India, Indian steel to Aleppo, and the Glassware of Aleppo to Yamin, and then return to Persia with Yamin's bordimani and retire in a shop for life." I told him, "Alas that only the dust of the grave can fill the eyes of the greedy."

(27) The greedy lifts his hands to heaven when in need and keeps them on his billfold when prosperous.

(28) A man deprived of hands and feet killed a millepede. I said: "The Lord be praised—when its fate was at hand, the millepede could not, even with its thousand feet, escape one without hand and foot!"

(29) The following are the assets of travellers: Wealth before which all men bow; learning which demands respect; beauty toward which admirers turn; a melodious voice (song) which captures the hearts of listeners; and a craft in demand which insures a livelihood.

(30) Ears can survive the absence of music, eyes the enchantment of beauty, nose the fragrance of the rose, sleep the absence of a soft mattress, and even the lover the departure of his mistress, but never a belly without food.

VIII. *Sa'di On Qualifications of Rulers*

(1) Ten beggars can sleep on one mat, but two kings cannot live in the same kingdom.

(2) Never consider a little foe helpless or abject, for a stream small at the fountainhead will carry away everything before it when turned into an overflowing river.

(3) Among the duties of a ruler one is generosity, that people may gather around him; and another is clemency that they may feel secure under him.

(4) A ruler given to tyranny undermines his own sovereignty.

(5) If you have been fair with your subjects you need not fear your enemies, for the shield of an upright prince is a satisfied army.

(6) Stand in awe of him who stands in awe of you, because the snake bites the herdsman's foot for fear of its own life, and a desperate man will charge at a tiger.

(7) A tyrant ruler asked a holy man, "What would be preferable to prayer?" He replied, "For you to remain asleep till mid-day that you might not 'afflict' mankind in that interval."

(8) When the king is slow in paying his troops, the troops are slow in handling their arms.

(9) Beware of the fickle disposition of rulers who are apt to take offense at a "salutation" and honor you with gifts for an act of rudeness.

(10) To serve the tyrant king offers a two-fold prospect, hope of a livelihood and fear of death.

(11) Four orders of people are ever in mortal fear of four others: The embezzler of government officials; the burglar of the policeman; the fornicator of the eavesdropper; and the adulteress of the censor.

(12) He whose account books are in good order should have no fear of the comptroller.

(13) Avoid extravagance and corruption while in office that the malice of your rival be circumscribed in settling your account.

(14) Avoid the service of rulers, for though the benefits of a sea voyage are many, safety is on the shore.

(15) If you wish to approach a man in high office, take along an introduction.

(16) The basis of oppression was in the beginning small. Each generation has added a little to it until it has reached its present proportions.

(17) When the commander tolerates the plunder of five eggs, his troops will feast upon a thousand roasted fowls.

(18) If you desire to shame your rival, speak well to his face whenever he slanders you behind your back.

(19) Disobedience to command means rejection.

(20) Government is for the welfare of the people, and not the people for perpetuation of government.

(21) A king ordered an innocent man to be put to death. Said the condemned, "O king, beware, for you seek your own hurt by giving way to anger." The king asked, "And how is that?" He replied, "The pain of death will last me but a moment, while the regret of injustice will endure with you forever."

(22) Overcome an evil act by forgiveness, but if you are bent on retaliation, see to it that you do not exceed the bounds. Otherwise, "debit" of injury will move to your side and the "credit" of complaint to that of the antagonist.

(23) There is more valor in patience than in fury.

(24) A man announced to a king that God had removed one of his enemies from the world. He said, "Has he also resolved that he will overlook me?"

(25) Do not rejoice over the death of your enemy, since your own life will not last forever.

(26) If fortune were to increase in proportion to knowledge, the share of the fool would be "scanty." But fortune sometimes bestows such wealth upon the ignorant that it would leave a learned man in astonishment.

(27) He is indeed base, ungrateful and of disrepute who, on a change of fortune, deserts his old benefactor and forgets the pleasures of many years of employment.

(28) Whoever has been "accessory" to dishonest acts trembles on rendering his account.

(29) Test a friend when you are in jail. Even enemies pretend friendship at your table.

(30) When a man has fallen, people tramp on his neck; when he is prosperous they are loud in his praise.

IX. *Sa'di's Quarrel With a Religious Pretender*

(Dialogue on Wealth and Poverty)

In its original form this work is a heated debate between Sa'di and a certain religious pretender, or modda'i, a man in the garb of holy men but lacking their qualifications. Sa'di's path happens to cross that of the modda'i as he is in full abuse and accusations against the rich, and his discourse has developed to this point:

"The hand of the poor man's ability is tied, and the foot of the rich man's inclination crippled. Men of liberality have no control over money, nor have the wealthy and worldly-minded a spirit of generosity."

Sa'di, who, as he admits, owed much for maintenance to the generosity of wealthy potentates, considers the argument of the modda'i unmerited and plunges head on into a passionate and, toward the climax, a hand-and-fist debate in defense of the rich. The quarrel ends before a ghazi, or judge, who points out the merits and weaknesses of both arguments, reconciles the two, and they kiss and depart. Sa'di, however, manages to keep the upper hand in his own report of the debate, which continues as follows:

Sa'di: "O my friend! The rich are the treasury of the poor, the granary of the hermit, the 'fane' of the pilgrim, resting place of the traveller, and the carrier of heavy burdens for the relief of their fellow-men. They eat when their servants and dependents are ready to partake with them, and the plentiful fragments of their tables they distribute among widows and the aged, their neighbors and kindred. The rich have their consecrated foundations, charitable endowments, rites of hospitality, their alms, offerings, manumissions, peace offerings and sacrifices. Whether in moral dignity or religious duty, the rich are at ease within themselves, for their property is consecrated by giving tithes, and their clothing hallowed by cleanliness, their reputations unblemished, their minds content. Reasonable men are aware that the zeal of devotion is warmed by good fare, and the sincerity of piety rendered more serene in a nicety of vesture; for it is evident what ardor there can be in a hungry stomach? What generosity in wretched poverty? What ability to travel with bare feet? And what readiness to give with empty hands? Uneasy must be the night slumbers of one whose provision for tomorrow is nil. It is clear that poverty and tranquility can never go together, nor have fruition and want the same position.

"While the wealthy composes himself for prayer, the poor is anxious and thinks on his supper. How then could anxiety ever compete with that? The man of wealth can fix his mind on God, but when a man's fortune is bankrupt, so is his heart. Accordingly, the devotion of the rich is more acceptable in the temple of God, because his thoughts are collected and his mind not distracted. He has laid up the conveniences of comfortable living and mastered at leisure the scriptural quotations. For there is a tradition of the prophet that 'poverty has a gloomy look in this world and in the next!' "

Modda'i: "Have you not heard, then, what the blessed prophet has declared? 'Poverty is my glory!' "

Sa'di: "Be silent, for the allusion of the prophet applies to those who are heroes in the field of resignation and are the devoted victims of their own fate, and not to those who put on the garb of piety to entitle themselves to the bread of charity. Being without divine knowledge, a poor man does not rest until his poverty settles into unfaithfulness; for he that is poor is close to being an infidel.

"Nor is it practicable, unless by means of wealth, to clothe the naked and to liberate the prisoner from jail. How then can such mendicants as we are aspire to the dignity of the wealthy; or what comparison is there between the arm of the lofty and the hand of the abject? Do you not see that the glorious and great God announces in the *Qur'an* that 'to this community, namely, the orthodox Muslims, a provision is allotted,' in order that you may understand that those who are solely occupied in looking after their daily subsistence are excluded from this portion of the blessed, and that the property of present enjoyment is sanctioned under the seal of Providence.

"To the thirsty it will seem in their dreams as if the face of the earth were wholly a fountain. You may observe everywhere that, instigated by his appetites, a person who has suffered hardship and tasted bitterness will engage in dangerous enterprises; and indifferent to the consequences and unawed by future punishments, he will not discriminate between the lawful and the forbidden. 'Should a clod of earth be thrown at the head of a dog, he would jump up in joy and take it for a bone; or were two people carrying a corpse on a bier, a greedy man would fancy it a tray of victuals.' Whereas the wealthy are regarded with the benevolent eye of Providence, and in their enjoyments of what is lawful are preserved from things illegal.

"Thus, having argued in detail and cited my proofs, I rely on your sense of justice for an equitable decree—whether you ever saw a felon with his arms pinioned, or a bankrupt immured in a jail, with the veil of innocence rent, or the arm mutilated for theft, unless in consequence of poverty! For lion-like heroes, urged on by want, have been caught undermining walls, breaking into houses, and getting themselves suspended by the heels. Moreover, it is possible that a poor man urged by an inordinate appetite may desire gratification of his lust and may fall victim of some doomed sin.

"Furthermore, of the manifold means of tranquility and enjoyment which are the lot of the rich, one is that they can command a fresh mistress every night and possess a new charmer every day such as must be the envy of the glorious dawn and stick the foot of the stately cypress in the mire of shame, so that it were impossible for them, with such lovely objects before their eyes, to desire what is forbidden or to wish to commit sin.

"In common, those who are in poor circumstances will contaminate the skirt of innocence with sin, and those who are suffering from hunger will steal bread. When a ravenous dog has found a piece of meat, he does not ask, 'Is this the flesh of the prophet Saleh's camel or Antichrist's ass?' Many a chaste person, because of poverty, has fallen into the sink of wickedness and given his fair reputation to the blast of infamy. The virtue of temperance cannot coexist with a state of being famished, and bankrupt circumstances will snatch the rein from the hand of temperance."

Modda'i: "You have so exaggerated in praise of the wealthy and amplified (their state) with such extravagance that we might fancy them an antidote to the poison of poverty and a key to the storehouse of Providence; yet they are a proud, self-conceited, fastidious and overbearing group, insatiate after wealth and property, and ambitious of rank and dignity; who do not exchange a word save to express insolence, or deign a look but to show contempt. They call the men of science beggars and reproach the poor for their wretched raggedness. 'Proud of the property they possess and vain of the rank they claim, they take the upper hand of all and deem themselves everybody's superior.' They never condescend to return anyone's salutation, unmindful of the maxim of the wise, that whoever is inferior to others in humility and superior in wealth, though he is rich in appearance, he is in reality a beggar. If a worthless fellow because of his wealth treats a learned man with insolence, reckon him an ass even if he is ambergris ox."

Sa'di: "Do not accuse the rich, for they are the sires of generosity."

Modda'i: "You mistake them, for they are slaves of dinars and dirams (dollars and cents). What matters if they are the clouds of the spring if they do not send us rain; or the fountain of the sun and shine upon no one; or though they are mounted on the steed of capability do not advance toward anybody? They will not move a step for the sake of God, nor bestow their charity without keeping you under obligation. They hoard their money with solicitude and watch it while they live with sordid meanness, and leave it behind them with bitter regret, which verifies the saying of the wise 'That the money of the miser is coming out of the earth when he is himself going into it.' One man hoards a treasure with pain and tribulation, another comes and spends it without tribulation or pain."

Sa'di: "You could have ascertained the parsimony of the wealthy only through the medium of your own beggary; otherwise to him who is not covetous, the generous man and the miser are alike. The touchstone can prove which is pure gold, and the beggar can say which is the niggard."

Modda'i: "I speak of the rich from experience. They station dependents by their doors and surly porters at their gates to deny admittance to the worthy and to lay violent hands upon the collars of the elect and say, 'There is nobody at home,' and indeed they tell the truth. For when the master is without reason or judgment, understanding or discernment, the porter reports right of him, saying, 'There is nobody at home.'"

Sa'di: "They can be excused since they are worried out of their lives by persistent memorialists and jaded to their hearts by indigent solicitors, and it is doubtful that the eyes of the greedy would be satisfied if the sands of the desert would be turned into pearls. The eyes of the greedy are not to be filled with worldly riches any more than a well would be replenished from the dew of night. And if Hatim Ta'i, who dwelt in the desert, had come to live in a city, he would have been overwhelmed with the importunities of mendicants, and they would have torn the clothes from his back."

Modda'i: "I pity their condition."

Sa'di: "Not so. But you envy them their property."

We were thus in heated argument, and both of us close engaged. Whatever chess pawn he might advance, I would set one in opposition to it; and whenever he put my king in check, I would relieve him with my queen; till he had exhausted all the coin in the purse of his resolution and expended all the arrows of the quiver of his argument. At last, with no more arguments to advance and crouched in mental submission, he stretched forth the arm of violence and began with vain abuse, as is the case with the ignorant who, when beaten by their antagonist in fair argument, shake the chain of rancor. Like Azor the idol-maker who, unable to contend with his son Abraham in words, fell upon him with blows. As the modda'i gave me abuse and I hurled back at him with asperity, he tore my collar, I plucked his beard. We had fallen upon each other, and a crowd had gathered round us enjoying the sport, yet astonished at what had taken place between us.

Finally we referred our dispute to the ghazi (judge) and agreed to abide by his equitable decree. The judge, surveying our faces and listening to our statements, after due consideration said,

Ghazi to Sa'di: "Let it be known to you, who were so lavish in praise of the rich and spoke disparagingly of the poor, that the rose has its thorn, intoxication is followed by a qualm, hidden treasures have their guardian dragons, where the imperial pearl is found there swims the man-devouring shark, the honey of worldly pleasures has the sting of death in its rear, and between us and heavenly happiness stands a frightful demon, Satan. Thus the rose and thorn, treasure and dragon, joy and sorrow, all mingle into one. As in the garden sweet-scented willows grow by the withered trunks, so among the classes of the rich some are grateful and some thankless, as among the orders of the poor, some are resigned and some impatient. Were every drop of dew to turn into a pearl, pearls would be as common as shells. The rich who are meek in spirit and the poor who are rich in resolution sit by the throne of the great and glorious Judge. The greatest among the wealthy are those who sympathize with the sorrows of the poor; and the most virtuous among the poor are those who do not covet the society of the opulent."

Ghazi to Modda'i: "And you who have charged the rich with sin and intoxication with forbidden things, there is indeed such a tribe as you have described, liberal in bigotry and stingy of God's bounty, who collect and hoard money but will neither use nor bestow it. If there were a drought or the whole earth were deluged with a flood, secure in their own abundance, they would not heed the poor man's distress, and . . . would exclaim, 'What does a goose care for a deluge?' Lolling in their litters and indulging in the easy pace of a female camel, they do not feel for the foot traveller perishing amidst overwhelming sands.

"There is such a tribe of rich men, but there is another class also, who spread the table of abundance and make public declaration of their munificence, and smooth the brow of their humility and are solicitous of reputation and forgiveness, and desirous to enjoy this world and the next."

Now that the ghazi had carried his harangue to such extreme and had galloped the steed of metaphor beyond expectation, we acquiesced in absolute satisfaction and apologized. Having reconciled, we laid the heads of reparation at each other's feet, mutually kissed and embraced, and as mischief fell asleep and war lulled itself into peace, I concluded the whole matter in this thought:

O poor man! Do not complain of the revolutions of fortune, for gloomy might be your lot were you to die in such sentiments. And O rich man! Spend and give away, that you may enjoy both this world and the next. (*Gulistan*)

X. *The Benedictions And Prayers of Sa'di*

(1) O Lord, be generous to me, a sinner, for thou hast been generous to the good in having made them good.

(2) Every breath that we inhale extends our lives, and as we exhale, exhilarates our being. In every breath, therefore, two benefits prevail, and to each a thanksgiving is due.

(3) He (God) directed his chamberlain, the breeze of the dawn, to cover the fields with an emerald carpet. He ordered his handmaid,

the vernal cloud, to nurse the daughters of young herbage in the cradle of the earth. He covered the bosom of the trees on the approach of spring with "mantles of verdant foliage," and crowned the infant twigs with "garlands of smiling blossoms." In his infinite power the plain juice of the (sugar cane) reed is turned sweet like virgin honey, and through his fostering care the kernel of the date has grown into a stately palm.

(4) The showers of His infinite mercy are sprinkled upon all, and the banquet of His generous bounty is spread forth everywhere.

(5) Once I received from a beloved's hand a ball of scented clay. I addressed it saying, "Your heavenly fragrance intoxicates me as would the perfumes of musk and ambergris." It replied, "Once I was a worthless piece of clay, but associated for a season with the roses, and the sweetness of my companion scented my essence, else I am the same humble clod I seem."

(6) In love one truth is clear, one fact is plain: That once consumed, my heart can nev'r explain Love's traceless cause. I am naught, and once expired, hear no sighs from lips of death again. If one were to ask me to reveal God's attributes, I would reply: "He is untraceable, and I incapable. The lover is ever extinct in the beloved's consuming presence, and the dead never speak again."

(7) O birds of the dawn, cease singing and learn the secret of love's ecstasy from the moth who laid its heart next to the candle light and was consumed without a sigh.

Seek His presence, oh my heart, in the sanctuary of silence, nor be deceived by the loud claims of pretenders, for once submerged into His sea of fullness, we do not emerge to relate our tale.

O Thou who towerest above all our dreams, reflections, logic and apprehension—above all that has been related, heard or pondered. Our days are consumed, and life's searching sojourn is ended, yet we thus remain at the threshold of your infinite attributes.

(8) O my heart, praise the Lord. For He is the omniscient Creator in whose grace all that lives and moves may flourish and evolve. He, the living Lord of strength, is sublime and all high. In Whose fostering care a beautiful personality is moulded in an esthetic form; Who in His foresight provided the fish of the sea for the fowl of the air; Who in remembering the needs of the eagle does not overlook the wants of a mosquito. He, Who knows and by anticipation provides in secret wisdom the subsistence of little ants, who live in caves of the earth under massive rocks. He, Who evolves life out of a sperm, and sugar out of a reed, fragrant leaves from a dry stem, and running water from lofty rocks; Who teaches the industrious bee to extract honey from growing foliage, and helps the kernel of the date to grow into a stately palm; Who is both self-sufficient and beneficent; hidden from everything and yet manifest in all things.

O my heart, praise the Lord. For His generous hands reach everywhere, of Whose infinite goodness the heart is incapable of thanks. He, Who beautified the canvas of existence in color and shape with varied paintings of infinite beauty; Who makes the stars of heaven a source of astonishment to the eyes of the thoughtful; Who responded to the needs of life in forming the seas, making the lands, fostering the ever-growing trees; Who divided time into seasons, Who makes the sun to enlighten the day, and the moon to brighten the night; Who founds mountains on the speck of earth, and establishes the earth over the face of waters; Who emerges in the heat of the sun, living trees from the substance of the earth, and glorifies them with sustaining fruits; Who nurses the infant bush in the cradle of barren land, and decorates it with scented flowers; Who carries allotted water to the thirsty roots of plants in the arms of clouds.

O heart, praise His excellence, and join the singing nightingale in hymns of thanksgiving.

O my heart, praise the Lord. He, Who is quick in forgiveness and slow in seeing our shortcoming; Who overlooks man's inequities; Who hides our mistakes, Who accepts sincere repentance with generous mercy; at Whose threshold the lofty heads of kings are laid in humble submission; Who does not punish the rebels in haste, nor does He chase away the mighty with the finger of oppression; He to whom existence is but a drop in the sea of wisdom; Whose table of mercy is spread out to friend and foe; to Whose will, matter and life move in humble obedience.

O heart, praise the Lord who is ancient and rich; Who sees the secrets of our breasts from behind the curtains of knowledge.

O my heart, praise the Lord!

CHAPTER VII *

THE CREATIVE-ADAPTIVE PERIOD OF MUSLIM EDUCATION

Preliminary Observations

THE PHRASE, *Muslim scholarship and learning*, is misleading if it implies that the faith created the scholar and determined the depth or scope of his scholarship. Nor can we refer to the scholarship under Islam as Arabian unless we imply only that it used Arabic as its medium of expression, a medium which by the end of the eleventh century was effectively challenged by the new Persian language after its revival by Firdawsi. Actually, the first Muslim conquerors were in no way patrons of learning.

The Umayyads, the first Muslim dynasty, ruling during the first century of expansion, were too preoccupied with the conquest, consolidation, and administration of a vast multi-national and multi-cultural empire to be concerned with the needs of the mind. They paid little attention to questions of education. Suspicious of learning, they were not interested in books or scholarship. They either burned or "drowned" many of the Hellenistic works in Alexandria and the Pahlavi works in Zoroastrian Persia.[1] When Amr ibn al-Ass conquered Egypt, he came upon the voluminous Alexandrian library and, hesitating to determine its fate upon his own initiative, asked Umar for instructions. Umar advised:

> As to the books about which you are inquiring, if there is to be found in them information which is in agreement with the Book of God [the *Qur'an*], such information is already available to us, and if there is in them materials that are contrary to the Book of God, there would be no need for them. In any event, proceed with their destruction.

Upon receiving this directive, the general distributed the famous library's books to the bathhouses of Alexandria, and, if we may trust Qifti's account, the new fuel kept the bathhouses heated for some six months. A similar fate awaited Persian libraries. When ibn Waqqas came and had access to them, he wrote Umar ibn-al-Khattab for further directions. Umar replied, "Drown them, throw them in the water, for if these works are to guide man, God has already guided us with a

*All dates refer to A.D. unless otherwise specified.

Book which is a more formidable guide, and if they are in essence to mislead man, God has made us free of them."[2]

On the other hand, there is some evidence—however doubtful—in Nadim's *Al-Fihrist* that the Islamic rulers who preceded the Abbassides did have a special interest in medical and alchemical works of classical cultures, mainly for practical applications.[3] Khalid ibn Yazid ibn Muawiya is reported to have engaged the services of Istiphan-al-Qadim and others to translate medical and perhaps chemical, pharmaceutical, and mathematical works into Arabic. Another ruler who showed some interest in translations of some of the works of scholarship in Alexandria and Antioch was Umar ibn Abd al-Aziz. Often, the translators were court physicians who had given special medical care to the prevailing ruler and were encouraged or ordered by him to make translations of medical works and prepare adaptations of them for the use of the other native physicians. Nonetheless, by reason of lack of academic backgrounds or scholarly interests in classical learning, and also for reasons of involvement in administering a vast empire, the Umayyad rulers were on the whole indifferent to educational advancement.

The Abbasside uprising, which had destroyed the Umayyads by 850, had originated in the northeastern Persian province of Khurasan as a fundamental reaction against the crude pragmatism of the Umayyads. With the coming of the Abbassides, the Muslim imperial administration was transferred largely from Arab to non-Arab people, primarily Persians. The Abbasside caliphs catered to Persian administrative traditions, adopted many of their court customs and left the management of the empire largely in the hands of Persian viziers. Most of these viziers came from Khurasan, which had instigated the overthrow of the Umayyads and brought about the Khurasanian Abbasside rule of Islam. It was under such Abbasside caliphs as al-Mansur and Harun-al-Rashid and his son, al-Ma'mun, that the task of translating the classical works in sciences and philosophy from Greek, Syriac, Sanskrit, and Pahlavi languages into Arabic began in earnest. This age of translation, roughly from 750 to 900, laid the foundation of a great renaissance of learning in Eastern Islam and brought about the golden age of Muslim education and creative scholarship which lasted through the tenth and eleventh centuries.

What stimulated these scholars was not so much their Islamic faith as the treasures of learning in sciences and philosophies which were altogether of non-Muslim origins. Islam, to its eternal credit, allowed the introduction of this classical knowledge through Arabic translations of these masterpieces. But the substance of this non-Islamic, basically Hellenistic learning, had already brought about an intellectual renaissance in the pre-Islamic Sassanian-Zoroastrian empire of Persia.* It had also reached India and stimulated the development of

*See chapters 4-8 in *The Heritage of Persia* by Richard N. Frye.

mathematics and astronomy among Hindu scholars after the Alexandrian conquest of western India.

The first wave of translations began under Caliph al-Mansur (753-774), but the wave turned into a flood under al-Ma'mun and continued with mounting force until the tenth century. The nerve center of this initial period of translation was the Bait-al-Hikmah (House of Wisdom) in Baghdad, which was in its beginnings a research and translation center, but which grew in time into a great academy. The first translators were largely Barmakites from Khurasan, Zoroastrians from other parts of Persia, and Nestorian Syrians who served the intellectual interests of Islam without abandoning their own Christian faith. The most active of these early translators in the Bait-al-Hikmah under Harun-al-Rashid and al-Ma'mun were Abu Sahl Fadhl ibn Naubakht, and Alan al-Shu'ubi, both Persians, and Yuhanna (John) ibn Masuya (Maskuya?), a Syrian.[4]

Creative activities in science and philosophy began with the second half of the eighth century, Jabir ibn Haiyyan being one of its distinguished men of learning.[5] This period was, politically, the age of Charlemagne in the Christian West and of Harun-al-Rashid in the Muslim East.[6]

All the basic contributions in mathematics and astronomy were made by Muslim scholars stimulated by Greek and Hindu works. Among these scholars was the mathematician Ibrahim al-Fazari, who constructed the first astrolabes in Islam. His son, Muhammad-al-Fazari,[7] translated the Hindu *Siddhanta* into Arabic by order of al-Mansur.[8] The engineering plans and measurements for building the city of Baghdad were undertaken by Mashallah,[9] the Jew, and Naubakht, the Persian, whose son, al-Fadhl, made astrological translations from Persian into Arabic.[10] But the creative period of Muslim scholarship began with the ninth century and moved ahead steadily until the end of the eleventh century and the beginning of the twelfth, as the following chart indicates. It is to this creative period that we now direct our attention.

Muslim Creative Works and Scholarship, 800-1000

The Caliph al-Ma'mun patronized men of science, philosophy, and letters and gathered around him in the scientific academy of Baghdad, which he founded, an impressive group of translators and creative writers. Among them were Yahya ibn al-Batriq, who translated many of the works of Plato and Aristotle into Arabic; al-Kindi, who wrote many scientific treatises; the three sons of Musa ibn-Shakir, who were responsible for collecting and translating a large number of Greek manuscripts into Arabic; and Ahmad ibn-Sirin, who wrote a treatise on the interpretation of dreams based largely on Hindu, Persian, and Egyptian ideas.

Also, during the ninth century the Isma'ili sect developed under

Islamic Renaissance

Ninth, Tenth and Eleventh Centuries

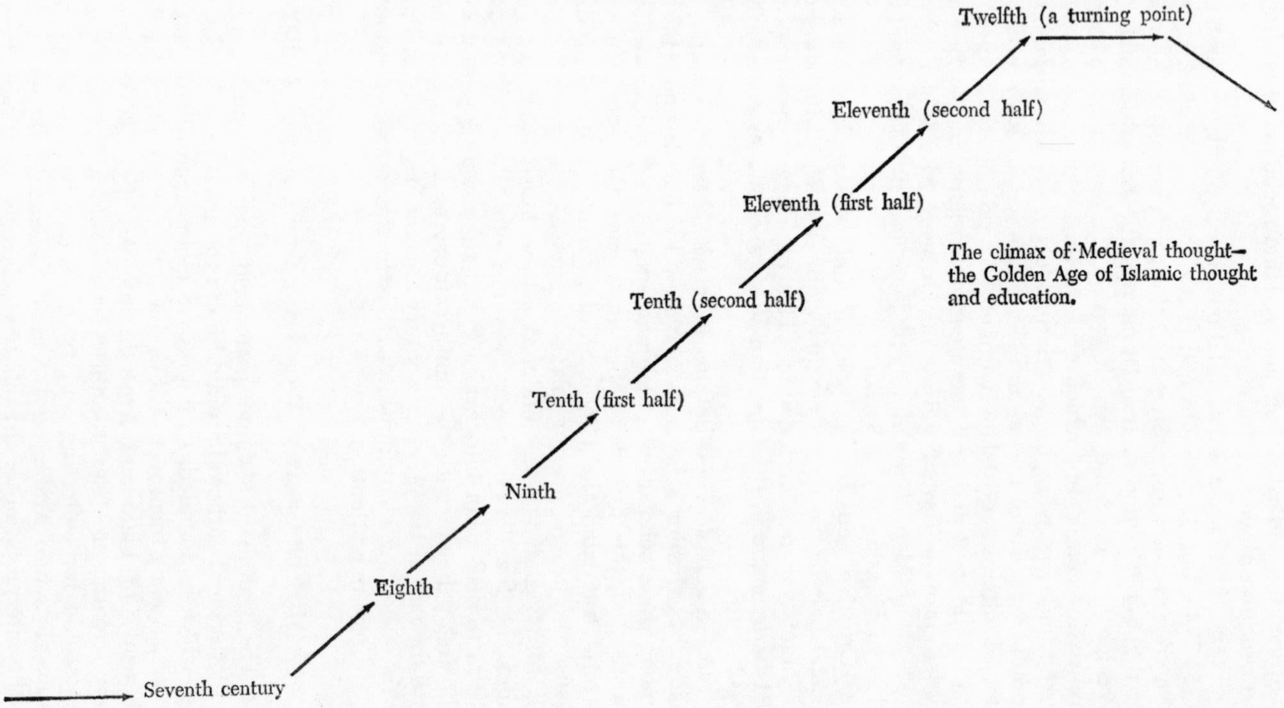

the influence of Abdullah ibn Maimun al-Qaddah, in the 860's, into a sect with considerable historic influence on scientific and philosophical-theological Islamic scholarship. Particularly was this true under the Qarmatians, a subsect within the Isma'ili group which was led by Hamdan Qarmat ibn al-Ash'ath.

Translations of classical learning, especially Greek, poured into Islam throughout the ninth century and included among them al-Mahani's commentaries on Archimedes and Euclid, al-Himsi's translations of the works of Apollonius, ibn-Yusuf's commentaries on the theorem of Menelaus, Nairizi's commentaries on Euclid and Ptolemy, and the work of Thabit ibn Qurra's school of translators, which rendered into Arabic the works of Euclid, Ptolemy, Archimedes, Apollonius, and Theodosius.

There were other translators in this period, such as Is'haq ibn Hunain, Isa ibn Yahya, Hubaish ibn al-Hasan, Musa ibn Khalid, Stephen, son of Basil, and Yusuf al-Khuri, although the translations of these scholars were minor ones when compared to the monumental translations of Hunain ibn Is'haq (Latinized Joannitius), which extended from 826 to 877. He combined in this art the tasks of direct translations from Greek works, supervision of other translators, and revisions of translations already made. Hunain and his school translated most of the medical works of Galen and Hippocrates into Syriac and Arabic. In addition to translations, Hunain wrote an introduction to Galen's *Ars Parva,* a treatise on ophthalmology, and prepared the earliest Syriac lexicons and grammar. He also compiled a catalogue of Arabic and Syrian versions of Galen's works available at that time.

Some of these scholars made creative contributions, such as al-Mahani's astronomical observations (855-866), al-Nairizi's treatises on the atmospheric phenomena and the spherical astrolabe and his astronomical tables, and Qurra's astronomical observations.[11] Al-Battani (Latinized Albategnius), the great Muslim astronomer, flourished in this century, and in 880 compiled a catalogue of stars based on his observations. His books on astronomy were authoritative in both Islam and Europe until the sixteenth century. Among his many contributions should be included the accurate determination of various astronomical coefficients and discovery of the motion of the solar apsides (or bits).

In the field of botany al-Dinawari's *Book of Plants* and in zoology al-Jahiz's *Book of Animals* constituted important sources of information and folklore. So also did ibn Khurdad-bih's *Book of Roads* and *Provinces* and al-Ya'qubi's *Book of the Countries.* Perhaps the greatest creative mind of this century was the Persian-Muslim Zakariyya al-Razi, "the greatest clinician of Islam and of the whole Middle Ages."[12] Aside from his extensive contributions in medicine, al-Razi was a great chemist and physicist as well. His greatest work was the *Al-Hawi* (*Continens*), an extensive encyclopaedia in medicine. In the field of history most historians of this period were Persians, such as al-Dinawari and al-Baladhuri; however, ibn Abd al-Hakam was an Egyptian historian. In the area of science the most important contributions were made by the Persians al-Razi, ibn Khurdad-bih, Yaqut, Nairzi, Hamini, ibn Qutaiba, and Baladhuri. Al-Haitham's (Muhammad ibn, the Alhazen of the Latin world, 965-?) *Kitab-al-Manazir* (*Book of Optics*) is perhaps the most scientific work produced by "medieval" Islam, and its subsequent translation into Latin constituted the most scientific treatise in Latin schools before Bacon, Witelo, Leonard, and Kepler. The work comprises a scientific study of the refraction of light through air and water and a new theory of perception of object as transmission of the form of the object by the transparent body to the eye—a theory which was the reversal of the theories of Ptolemy and Euclid. It contains an analysis of the correlation between "the weight and the density of the atmosphere and the effect of atmospheric density upon the weight of objects, the study of light's action on parabolic and spherical mirrors."[13]

During the tenth century, as in the ninth, Muslim learning and scholarship remained supreme in the areas of science as astronomy, trigonometry, algebra, and medicine. In the field of chemistry, examples of originality and creativity were fewer than some historians credit to Muslim education. In the fields of history, geography, historical biographies, travelogues, chronicles of kings, princes and other notables, Islam excelled during the tenth century, as indicated in the *Al-Fihrist* of al-Nadim. Not only had Muslim scholarship enriched the schools of Eastern and Western Islam with this new learning, but the results of scholarship in these areas had already reached European schools and were paving the way for the exciting period of translations of Muslim works into Latin.

Scholarship in the tenth century was not completely lacking among European schoolmen, but elements of novelty and originality were rare. Muslim works kept adding new concepts in mathematics, (trigonometry, geometry, and algebra) and in astronomy, particularly in astronomical studies resulting from new observations in the observatories of Baghdad, Rayy, and other centers. By the end of the century, Hindu numerals were being used in Egypt and Spain and had appeared in Latin in 976 in a manuscript written in Logrono. Muslim works also continued to be creative in medicine, particularly in clinical areas and in the making of new surgical instruments. So extensive had become scholarship in Islam, and so widespread its results in both the Muslim and Christian worlds, that Arabic had already been adopted as the language of research among both Muslim and European scholars. Jewish scholars as masters of Arabic, Hebrew, and Latin languages made fundamental and far-reaching contributions both in translation of Arabic works into Hebrew and Latin and in the interpretation of many Muslim works to Latin scholars.

It is interesting to note that Hebrew scholarship, which hitherto maintained its center of intellectual activities in the East—in Babylon, Baghdad, Cairo—had transplanted these activities during the last half of this century to Cordova, where Spanish learning had been ushered in during the progressive rule of Abd al-Rahman III, the eighth Umayyad caliph in Spain. Before Abd al-Rahman, the Umayyad caliph al-Hakam II (961-976) had patronized learning and, under his enlightened minister Hasnai ibn Shaprut, had paved the way for making Cordova the glory of Western Islamic learning, the "mecca of intellectual pilgrimage" from Europe. Thus, within the following century, Spain, particularly Cordova, under the Umayyad administration became the Western center of Islamic learning and education, and perhaps one of the greatest centers of civilization.

For the time being, however, Eastern Islam maintained its creative supremacy, with Iraq, Persia, and the lands to the east of it as great centers of learning, and with men of genius under Buwayhid princes, particularly the enlightened rulers Adud-al-Dawla (949-982) and his son, Sharaf-al-Dawla (982-989). Indeed, the most important creative works of the century—in both Europe and Islam—were accomplished by Persian Muslims, such as Abu al-Wafa, Khwarizmi Ali ibn Abbas (Haly Abbas), some members of the learned society of the Brethren of Purity, Kuhi, Sijji, Sufi, ibn Babuya, Khazim, Sagham, Khujandi, Buzurq ibn Shahryar, Abu al-Fath, Istakhri, Aham al-Tabari, ibn Miskawaih, Qumri, Hamzah, Ismail ibn Abbad, Janhari, and Abu Mansur Muwaffaq. Among these are also ibn al-A'lam, Muqaddasi, ibn Hawqal, ibn Jinni, and al-Tamaini (al-Tamami?), whose national origins remain in doubt. Some may have been of Persian origin.[14]

Although the tenth century belonged almost exclusively to Islam in accumulative and creative scholarship, the first half appears to have been more conservative and at points even reactionary in mood, while the century's last decades responded to the earlier "rest" period with a flurry of creative works in almost all areas of inquiry fashionable at the time.

For a closer look at some of the most important creative scholars of the tenth century, let us glance at authors and works in a selected number of fields—philosophy and theology, mathematics and astronomy, Persian literary men and works, and history.

Philosophy and Theology. In philosophy the greatest Muslim genius was perhaps the scholar-philosopher al-Farabi, who advanced upon the earlier labors of al-Kindi in harmonizing Hellenistic thought, principally Aristotelianism, with Muslim philosophy and theology. Although historians have referred to al-Farabi as of Turkish origin, ibn al-Nadim refers to him in *Al-Fihrist* as a native of Khurasan in northeastern Persia.[15] Aside from philosophic-theologic works, al-Farabi wrote on mensural music in advance of Europeans of his time.[16] He wrote altogether thirty-nine works—all commentaries on Aristotle, all of which have survived. His most original work is the *Madinat-al-Fadhila* (*The Ideal City*), a sociological study of urban life in which the author develops such concepts as natural self-determination as the law of survival. It recommends a theocentric monarchical society after examining such concepts as society by agreement and mutuality, and society by regimentation and power.[17]

Ibn Ya'qub al-Nadim, whose professional interests are in doubt, was unquestionably one of the great learned men of his time, being thoroughly familiar with men and works of scholarship in the Arabic language available to his time. He wrote the famous *Al-Fihrist* (*Index of the Sciences*) which we have already discussed briefly. The monumental encyclopaedic work of the semisecret learned fraternity, Brethren of Purity, may also be considered among the most significant philosophic achievements of that century. The encyclopaedia's fifty-one-volume *Rasa'il* (*Tracts*) is not only a well-organized summary of speculative knowledge of the time but is presented from the neo-Platonic-Muslim point of view. The work of the Brethren became one of the standard sources of reference in both Eastern Islam and Spain.

Another encyclopaedic-philosophic Muslim thinker of this century was al-Masudi, the "Pliny of Islam." Other semiphilosophic works of the century include ibn Tahir's encyclopaedia, *The Book of Creation and History;* ibn Miskawaih's ethical treatises; and al-Khwarizmi's (Muhammad ibn Ahmad) *Miftah al-Ulum* (*The Key of the Sciences*).

It was in this period also that al-Ashari founded Islamic scholasticism and gave to Sunnite orthodoxy its basic philosophic-theological foundations.

Mathematics and Astronomy. These disciplines in the early decades of the century claimed two Muslim mathematicians, both of great importance, Ibrahim ibn Sinan, who wrote commentaries on Apollonius, and the *Almagest,* and Abu Kamil, who perfected Khwarizmi's algebra. Others included ibn Amamur, who compiled astronomical tables between 885 and 933; and al-Hamdani, another compiler of astronomical tables. Also during this century al-Khwarizmi wrote important works in arithmetic and geometry;* al-Saqani wrote on the trisection of the angle; Abu al-Fath made improvements on Apollonius' *Conics* with commentaries on his first five books; al-Khujandi proved that the sum of two cubic numbers cannot be a cubic number; Abd al-Rahman al-Sufi made new illustrated catalogues of stars; Abu al-A'lam made new astronomical tables; al-Saqani made new astronomical instruments and helped, along with al-Kuhi and the astronomer Abu al-Wafa, in constructing the new observatory in Baghdad under Sharaf's direction; Jafar al-Khazin and Nasif ibn Yunus made new translations of Euclid's *Tenth Book;* Muslim ibn Ahmad made special studies of amicable numbers; and al-Khujandi made new astronomical observations in the city of Rayy (present ruins near the capital city of Teheran).

Persian Literary Men and Works. In Persia's numerous contributions to Islamic literature, Firdawsi's profound influence upon that

*Algorism is a Latinized corruption of his name.

culture's literary development for generations after the completion of the *Shah-Namah* are readily discernible and at the same time most significant. We shall bypass, for a short time, the chronological sequence of our survey and show the highlights of this post-Firdawsi development, which spans the entire period under discussion.

Firdawsi's familiarity with both Pahlavi and Arabian literature and general history made his voluminous (60,000 verses) epic poem, the *Shah-Namah* (*Book of Kings*), the inspiration for later epic, didactic, mystic, romantic, and lyrical poets. The story of Firdawsi's life is in itself a great poem. Flourishing during the reign of Sultan Mahmud of Ghazna, he was first presented to the sultan through his friend, Mahak, as the poet of Tus. His first court examination, so to speak, was passed when the king asked him about the origin of Tus, and the poet replied with a comprehensive account of the historical development of his own city.

As a reward for such erudition, he was admitted to the circle of the seven court poets. These court poets were engaged in the projected epic of Iran, which Daqiqi had started before his death. In fact, Firdawsi's appearance before the court of Ghazna had been for the sole purpose of impressing the sultan and thereby receiving his sanction for continuing Daqiqi's *Khudai-Namah* (*Book of Kings*). To gain this favor, Firdawsi composed a beautiful poem praising Ayaz, the sultan's favorite. According to one legend, the poem so pleased Mahmud that he bestowed upon the poet the pen name Firdawsi, which means "of paradise" and assigned to him later the long-coveted task of writing the *Shah-Namah*.

The Sultan of Ghazna had promised the poet sixty thousand coins of gold for his verses upon their completion, and for thirty-five years Firdawsi was engaged in the commission. Finally he completed the work and had it presented by Ayaz to the king, who at first was inclined to send him the promised gold coins but was persuaded by his treasurer to send sixty thousand silver ones instead. When the elephant and its cargo of silver reached Firdawsi's house, the poet at first received it with joy. But discovering its silver contents, he gave away, angrily, two thousand pieces to Ayaz, two thousand to a bathkeeper, and tipped a shopkeeper with the remainder for a glass of beer! Then he wrote one of the most bitter poems of satire and reproach in condemnation of the character of Sultan Mahmud—a poem which is today usually placed in the beginning of the *Shah-Namah*. Ayaz presented the poem to the sultan.

Firdawsi's remaining days were spent wandering from Mazandaran to Baghdad and other cities writing verses praising the notables of the day from whom he received generous support. It was in this period, and for the caliph of Baghdad, that he wrote his famous *Romances of Yusef-u-Zuleika* (the episode of the Biblical Joseph and Zolaikha). And it was not until many years later that the sultan decided to keep his early promise and send the poet his well-earned sixty thousand gold coins and a robe of honor. This time, however, the load was transported by slow-moving camels which reached the gates of the city—alas, too late! For Firdawsi died, at the age of eighty, before his promised reward arrived. The bitterness with which he responded to the thankless reception of his great masterpiece is evident in his poem, quoted below:

> Much toil did I suffer, much writing I pondered,
> Books writ in Arabian and Persian of old;
> For sixty-two years many arts did I study;
> What gain do they bring me in glory or gold?
> Save regret for the past and remorse for its failings.
> Of the days of my youth every token hath fled,
> And I mourn for it now, with sore weepings and wailings,
> In the words Khusrawani Bu Tahir hath said:
> "My youth is a vision of childhood in sooth
> I remember: alas and alas for my youth."*

As the early painters, weavers, and architects of Iran had established undisputed standards for their arts and traditions which would be followed by artists for centuries, so did Firdawsi, in his *Book of Kings*, set the inspiring standards for many eminent poets of the centuries which followed the age of Sultan Mahmud. In fact, one of the greatest characteristics of Iranian art, including its poetry, is its ability to emulate the good and improve upon that which has been imitated. In poetry this characteristic is evidenced by the innumerable *diwans* (collected works) of poets of the last ten centuries, who followed somewhat the same technical and topical standards of the early poets, whether they composed epic, lyric, elegiac, dramatic, romantic, moral, religious, or philosophical verses. It is, indeed, in reaction to this age-long imitation of classical standards that modern poets of the country, such as Iraj Mirza, Sa'id Nafisi, and Aref, to name but a few, are creating new poetic techniques and new poetic subject matters.

The *Shah-Namah* of Firdawsi has been the inspiration for at least three classes of Iranian poets: Epic writers, didactic and mystic writers, and writers of lyric and romantic fiction. As to the first class, we have in the centuries after Firdawsi's death a series of "books of kings" in which the character and the age of some contemporary monarchs are recorded in double-rhymed verse. Thus we have the *Taimur-Namah* (*Book of Tamerlane*), a record of Safawi rulers by Hatifi, 1521; the *Shah-Namah* of Shah Ismail and *Shah Tahmasp* by Khazimi, 1560; the *Shah-Namah Naderi* by Ishrati, 1749; and so on. In India, this style was followed by poets of both Iranian and Indian extractions.

As to the second class, didactic and mystic writers, the mystical passages of Firdawsi, such as the incident of the sudden and mysterious disappearance of Shah Kaikhusroe at the height of his glory and his reunion with heavenly spirits, along with the many other ethical reflections, moral exhortations, wise maxims and expressions of fatalism

*Translation by Edward Browne.

and despair, became not only an inspiration for the mystic writers of the country but also proved to be a most inspiring subject for great painters. In fact, the stories of *Shah-Namah* constitute one of the few sources of inspiration for the famous miniaturists and book designers of the country. The greatest post-Firdawsi mystics were Abu al-Khair, the writer of great quatrains; Nasir-i-Khusraw, the writer of the *Rushanai-Namah* (*Book of Enlightenment*) and other moral, ethical as well as mystical works; Ansari (1006-1089), the author of the Panghristic book called *Monajat* (*Innovations*); and Sana'i (1130), the creator of the *Hadiqat-al-Haqiqat* (*Garden of Truth*), which is one of the few textbooks in the Muslim world on mysticism.

Following these poets there were two other outstanding men whose writings became the inspiration for two new schools of literature. These were the mystic Rumi (1207-1273)* of Balkh in Khurasan and the immortal social-philosopher and mystic poet Sa'di (1292) of Shiraz. It is the strict mysticism and other-worldliness of Rumi's *Mathnawi* (40,000 double rhymed verses), and the human, readable style of Sa'di's *Gulistan* (*Rose Garden*) and *Bustan* (*Fruit Garden*) and other half-social, half-mystical works which established these writers as new models for artistic imitation.

Sa'di's genius and the enduring popularity of his works inspired two groups of followers. A few, of the *Bustan* school, were Nizami: *Dastur-Namah* (*Book of Exemplars*), 1320; Katibi: *Dah Bab* (*Ten Chapters*), 1434; Hairati: *Gulzar* (*Rose Bower*), 1554; and others. The leading representatives of the *Gulistan* group were Juwaini: *Negaristan* (*Picture Gallery*), 1335; and Jami: *Baharistan* (*Spring Garden*), 1487.

The two beautiful romantic fictions of Firdawsi, his story of *Yusef-u-Zulaikha* and the story of *Zal-u-Rudabeh*, provided the inspiration for the third class of Iranian poets, the lyrical fictional romanticists who rose to their highest under the Seljuk dynasty, especially in the reign of Sultan Sanjar. Some poets of this school were Nizami of Ganja (1141-1203), Sabir (1145), Jauhari Muizzi (1147), Watwat (1182), Anwari (1189), Faryabi (1202), Isfaranji (1262), Jami (1414), Hatifi, Maktabi, and Helali—all writers of romantic fictional poetry—and Hafiz (1389), Khujandi (1400), Maghribi (1406), Wali (1431), Feghani (1519), Lesani (1535), and Ahli (1535)—all writers of lyric verse.

---

*After Rumi and his beloved mystic creation, there is a long list of mystic works, the description of which is beyond the scope of this book. Here, however, is a list of the names and works of some of the outstanding Sufi poets, which the reader may wish to approach: Rumi (Jalal-al-Din): *Mathnawi*, 1207-1272; Attar: *Pand-Namah (Book of Counsels)*, 1230 and *Mantiq-al-Tair (Speeches of Birds)*, n.d.; Iraq: *Lama-at (Sparks)*, 1287-1318; Husaini: *Zad al-Mosaferin (Store of the Wayfarers)*, n.d.; Shabistari: *Gulshani-Raz (Rose Bed of Mystery)*, 1320; Awhadi: *Jam-i-Jam (Cup of Jamshid)*, 1338; Assar: *Mehr-o-Moshtari (Sun and Jupiter)*, 1376; Arifi: *Gui-o-Chaugan (The Ball and the Bat)*, 1438; Fattahi: *Husn-o-del (Beauty and Heart)*, 1448; Ahli: *Sham-o-Parvana (The Candle and the Moth)*, 1489; Helali: *Shah-o-Geda (King and Darvish)*, 1532; Amili: *Nan-o-Halva (Bread and Sweets)* and *Shir-o-Shakar (Milk and Sugar)*, 1621.

On our list, next to Sa'di, the names of Nizami, Jami, Anwari, and Hafiz stand out as the most popular poets of this class. Nizami's fame rests on his five great works of romantic fiction: *Khusroe and Shirin, Laila and Majnun, Haft Paikar* (*Seven Effigies*), *Iskandar-Namah* (*House of Alexander*) and *Makhzanol Asrar* (*Treasure House of Secrets*).

Khusroe and Shirin, the Romeo and Juliet of Iran, is the tragic story of the master builder Farhad and his love for Shirin (meaning *sweet*), the favorite of Khusroe. *Laila and Majnun* is another love story which is Nizami's version of the Arabian novel of *Majnun* (*love-crazy*), who was kept away from Laila by a family feud and longed for her during years of loneliness in the desert. The *Seven Effigies* contains stories about Bahram Gur, the most famous of which is that of Azada, the slave girl, who accompanied Bahram on his hunting expeditions. The *Iskandar-Namah,* as the title indicates, deals with the legendary adventures of Alexander the Great. The *Treasure House of Secrets* is a poem of ethical and mystical content. Nizami's *Khamsa* (*Five Books*), a collective title for all the foregoing works, stands today as the greatest romantic-epic fiction of Iran.

Jami, the fifteenth century poet, is famed, aside from his great odes and qasidas, for his version of Firdawsi's *Yusef-u-Zulaikha,* which, as mentioned before, is the legendary love story of the Biblical Joseph and Zolaikha. Anwari, the great astronomer and poet of the twelfth century, is important in Iran's literature not only for his genius, but because his satires became a fad among the poets who followed him, although with most of them the art degenerated into low parodies and travesties, cheap jocular poems, and pleasantries (*Hajvyyat*). Of such degenerate quality were some of the writings of Suzani and Shatranji of Samarkand, Khaqani, Faryabi (1202), Isfaranji (1267) and Lami of Bukhara. Some, however, used this art in writing humorous stories—for example, Zakani's *Mush-o-Gorba* (*Mouse and Cat*) and *Sang-Tarash* (*Stonecutter*).[18]

Hafiz of Shiraz wrote some of the most charming lyrical-mystical poems of Iran, or for that matter, of the world. Few poets have ever equaled the beauty of his expression and the wisdom of his perception. Wearing the simple woolen garment of the Sufis (mystics), he could walk with kings "without losing the common touch" and drink his wine without neglecting contemplation. His verses are saturated with so much of the natural gaiety of life blended with a deep religious sense that they are simultaneously hedonistic and divine. His expressions, both in variety and earnestness, are unsurpassed by any other literary work of the kind in Iran. Literary pilgrims visit his tomb in Shiraz today with reverence and read his verses with profound religious feeling. Because of their dual meanings, his verses are virtually impossible to translate successfully into any language.

History. In history, one of the Muslim men of scholarship in the tenth century was the Persian historian Abu Jafar Muhammad al-Tabari (835-923) who wrote an extensive history of man from early days to his own time. He wrote his monumental work, *Kitab Akhbar al-Rasul wa'l-Muluk* (*The Book of the Annals of Prophets and Kings*), a history of man to 913, in forty years. The work was apparently some one hundred fifty volumes of which only fifteen have survived.[19]

Another historian, Abu al-Hasan Ali al-Mas'udi, wrote *Meadows of Gold and Mines of Precious Stones*. The work is a condensation by its author of his original fifteen-volume encyclopaedia and compendium. It is a study of history in a sociological sense, covering religious traditions, social customs, arts, sciences and crafts, philosophy, and literature. He was one of the earliest Muslim writers to suggest the concept of the evolution of life from the physical (inanimate) plane upward to the plant, animal, and human planes.

Another great historian was the Persian Muslim Abu Rayhan al-Biruni (Muhammad ibn Ahmad, 973-1048), who lived during the reign of Sultan Mahmud of Ghazna. He was the most prominent figure among the encyclopaedists in the golden age of Islamic science and excelled in the fields of travel, geography, mathematics, astronomy, physics, poetry, philosophy, and medicine. His *Chronology of Ancient Nations* and some of his *Indian Studies* are available in English, but most of his works on mathematics and physics still await translation. His *Tarikhi Hind* (*History of India*) (1030), contains forty-two chapters on Hindu astronomy.[20] In this work he also attempts to show similarities among neo-Platonism, neo-Pythagorianism, Muslim Sufiism (mysticism) and the Hindu Vedanta* philosophy, and the *Bhagavat Gita* (*The Song Celestial*).[21] Biruni also gives one of the best "medieval" accounts of Hindu numerals, discusses the sphericity of the earth, formulates astronomical tables, and makes geological observations. His extensive studies of precious stones and metals include special researches on their density. He also made important contributions in astronomy, geometry, the astrolabe, planisphere, and armillary sphere, made observations on the speed of light in comparison with sound, and wrote extensively on geography and philosophy. In the *Athar-al-Baqiya* (*The Heritage [Vestiges] of the Past*) (1000), an impartial study of the world religions of his time, Biruni tells us in the preface that "we must clear our minds from all causes that blind people to the truth—old customs, party spirit, personal rivalry or passion, [and] the desire for influence" in order to be able to record historical events with a measure of objectivity and accuracy.[22] His greatest contribution, however, was in the field of geography of Muslim lands, a field in which Nasir-i-Khusraw also made important advances particularly in the archaeological and ethnological geography of Egypt. Biruni composed an astronomical encyclopaedia and made vital contributions in geometrical problems, referred to as the Albirnic problems.

*Vedanta: Veda anta, or end of Vedas, meaning the Upanishads.

As further evidence of the scholarly activity of this period, the following authors and their work may be briefly noted. The Hispano-Muslim Abu Bakr al-Razi wrote a history of Spain; Abu Mansur Mawaffaq wrote the first important work on preparation and properties of mineral substances; al-Istakhri introduced colored maps for various countries in his works on geography; Buzurg ibn Shahryar wrote *The Marvels of India,* a collection of sailors' tales; al-Muqaddasi wrote travelogues on his journeys through Muslim lands; ibn Sa'd compiled chronicles of Africa and Spain between 961-976; ibn al-Qutiya wrote a history of Andalusia from 711 to 893; Haly Abbas (Ali ibn Abbas) compiled a medical encyclopaedia entitled *The Royal Book;* Ahmad al-Tabari wrote a treatise on *Hippocratic Treatments;* Matta ibn Yunus and Yahya ibn Adi (both Christians) made new translations of Greek works into Arabic; Abu Uthman translated, among others, ten of Euclid's and Pappos' commentaries on Euclid; ibn Serapion wrote a geographical account of the world; ibn al-Faqih wrote *The Book of the Countries;* al-Jarhumi and Qudama wrote road books; ibn Fadlan in 921 wrote accounts of Russia; and al-Balkhi made new maps of parts of the world.

All in all, the tenth century was amazingly productive. The contributions it made within Islam were widespread geographically from Central Asia to Spain and came from Persians, Transoxianans, Arabs, Turks, Egyptians, and Spaniards. In terms of scholarly creativity, the century produced the greatest philosopher of the time, al-Farabi; the greatest mathematicians, Abu Kamil and Ibrahim ibn Sinan; the great encyclopaedist, Masudi; and the greatest historian, Tabari.[23]

The renaissance of learning, which was initiated in the eighth century and gained momentum during the ninth, developed extensively both in terms of subject matter and geographic distribution, and intensively in terms of research and creativity during the latter half of the tenth century, continuing through the next century, as we shall see in the following chapter. Indeed, the last decades of the tenth and the whole of the eleventh centuries may be regarded as the golden age of Islamic scholarship and creativity. This Islamic age claimed almost exclusively all that was creative in areas of basic sciences, particularly physics, astronomy, and mathematics; all the important comprehensive works in philosophy, theology, religion, history and law; all the important developments in the field of medicine and associated disciplines, to say nothing of art and literature and music, to which Muslim scholars also made significant contributions. The scholars who gave substance to this golden age were not only among the greatest intellectual giants that Islam has ever produced but were in their time among the greatest creative minds of the world; some of them, perhaps, of all ages.

Others who stood for creative scholarship during this age would have won greater fame and perhaps been responsible for further innovations in the realm of ideas had they lived in a period when competition with greater minds had not been so keen and the fruits of creative thought had not been so abundant. In such a position of relative honor should be placed Kushyar ibn Labban, the trigonometrist; Abu al-Jud, the mathematician; al-Karkhi, the algebraist; al-Bakri, the geographer and historian; ibn Sa'd, the historiographer; al-Khatib al-Baghdadi, the biographer; Nasir-i-Khusraw, the descriptive geographer of Muslim lands; Ali ibn Isa, the physician; Asadi, the philologist; al-Saffar, the author of improved astronomical tables; al-Zarqali, the compiler of the *Toledan Astronomical Tables;* ibn Hazm, the great interpreter of Islamic sects; ibn Tabir, author of the famous history of the "seven by three" Muslim sects; and al-Baquilani, Muslim scholastic and promoter of the al-Ashari theology.

Scholars from Spain included al-Karmani, the Spanish specialist in the encyclopaedic work of the Brethren of Purity and its promoter in Western Islam; ibn Abi-al-Rijal; al-Saffar, compiler of astronomical tables based on the Siddhanta method; ibn al-Samh, the mathematician; al-Bakri, the historical geographer.

Chronological Table of Muslim Political and Cultural Eras

622	The Hejira begins the Islamic era
661-750	The Umayyad Dynasty in Eastern Islam
750-854	Abu-al-Abbas al-Saffah exterpates the Umayyads
756-788	The beginning of Umayyad rule in Spain under Abd-al-Rahman, the Emir of Cordova
822-852	The reign of Abd-al-Rahman II in Cordova
852-886	The reign of Muhammad I in Cordova
888-912	The reign of Abdullah of Cordova
912-961	The reign of Abd-al-Rahman III of Cordova
961-976	Hakim I of Cordova
1027-1031	The reign of Hisham III—the last Umayyad ruler in Cordova
754-775	The Abbasside Caliph Abu Ja'far al-Mansur
775-785	al-Mahdi
786-809	The reign of Harun-al-Rashid and the flowering of Arabic literature
809-813	al-Amin
813-833	al-Ma'mun
833-842	al-Mu'tasim
842-847	al-Wathiq
847-861	al-Mutawkkil
861-862	al-Muntasir
862-866	al-Mu'tazz
866-869	al-Muhtadi
869-892	al-Mu'tamid
892-902	al-Mu'tadhid
902-908	al-Muktafi
908-932	al-Muqtadir (billah)
932-967	Mu'izz-al-Dawlah (guardian of the caliph)
932-934	al-Qahir
932-940	al-Radi
940-943	al-Muttaqi
943-946	al-Mustakfi
946-974	al-Muti'
974-991	al-Ta'i
991-1003	al-Qadir
1180-1225	Last on the Abbasside throne

(Refer also to the complete comparative chronology in Appendix I.)

CHAPTER VIII *

CREATIVE SCHOLARSHIP IN MUSLIM EDUCATION, CONTINUED TO 1300

Recapitulation and Introduction

During the period of the tenth and eleventh centuries some of the most creative scholars in Eastern Islam were, with but few exceptions, Persian authors who wrote in Arabic and frequently in their native Persian. Among these scholars in the tenth century were al-Farabi who was, according to *Al-Fihrist* of al-Nadim, from Khurasan; Abu Bakr-al-Razi from Rayy; Ahmad al-Khwarizmi from Khwarizm; some members of the Brethren of Purity; Abu-al-Wafa, who flourished in Baghdad; al-Khujandi from Khujand; ibn Shahryar from Khuzistan; Abu Sahl from Jurjan; and ibn Miskawaih of the court of the Buwayhid sultans. Important eleventh century scholars of Persian origin included such men as the epic poet, Firdawsi of Tus; al-Biruni of Khwarizm, ibn Sina of Afshana; Kushyar ibn Labban of Gilan; al-Nasawi of Khurasan; al-Ghazzali of Tus; Omar Khayyam of Nishapur; Nasir-i-Khusraw of Marv; Zarrin Dast of Gorgan; Nizam-al-Mulk of Tus; and Asadi, nephew of Firdawsi.

To be sure, the two centuries claimed some great original writers other than those in the Persian list. Among them were Mas'udi, a Mu'tazalite Arab; Ibrahim ibn Sinan and Sinan ibn Thabit, both of Baghdad; ibn Yunus of Egypt; ibn Haitham of Basra; ibn Haiyan and ibn Hazm, both of Cordova; and ibn Samh of Granada. But since, both in number of scholars and in supremacy of product, Persian authors dominated these two centuries, we may be justified in referring to these two centuries not only as the "Golden Centuries of Islam," but also as the golden age of Persian creative scholarship.

We have already indicated to what extent Persian scholars made outstanding contributions to the development of Muslim learning and scholarship in the first century and a half of Abbasside rule (750-900). The nerve-center of educational, intellectual, and literary creativity during the "medieval" period was Persia in Eastern Islam and Spain in Western Islam. These cultural centers resembled each other in a few respects but differed in many others. Among the common elements

*All dates refer to A.D. unless otherwise specified.

may be mentioned a deep sense of national pride and national identity predicated upon history and tradition, unique pride in their native language, a common dislike for the Arabs and disregard for native Arabian culture, and the ingenious adaptation of Islamic doctrines to cultural traditions.

But the differences seem to have overwhelmed the similarities. Persia was the geographic center of Islam in the East. Spain was the focal point of Western Islam. Spain reacted against Islam from its backgrounds of Latin Christianity. Islam took roots in Persia and replaced Zoroastrianism as the national religion. Islam never took root in Spain, and its temporary successes were swept away when the Muslims were expelled. Although the Muslims were not zealous in making converts, their missionary activities were more far-reaching in Persia. In Spain interest in making Muslim converts was secondary to political, economic, and cultural domination. In Persia, Muslim affairs were run by Persian political and intellectual leaders. In Spain control was largely in Muslim (Arab, Berber and Syrian) hands. In Persia scientific, philosophic, theological, artistic, and other creative works were dominated by Persian scholars. In Spain scientific and philosophic works were largely products of non-Spanish Muslim scholars. Many Muslim scholarly works were written in Persian, particularly during the eleventh and twelfth centuries, whereas few Muslim works were written in Spanish during the same or other periods. Muslim scholarship in Persia was not, on the whole, in touch with Muslim scholarship in Spain, but on the other hand, Spanish Islam was in touch with Muslim works in the East and was considerably stimulated by this contact. Many Persian works were translated into Arabic and reached Latin Europe through later translations. Few, if any, Spanish works reached Eastern Islam, particularly Persia. In literature, Persia influenced Islam. In literature, Islam influenced Spain. The Umayyads had a short political life in Persia, followed by the Abbassides, who were dominated by Persian leaders, whereas the Umayyads remained the main political and intellectual power in Spain, the Abbassides being without influence. Yet Spain rather than Persia was one of the main channels of the transmission of Muslim culture to Europe. Persia began with a well-established Hellenistic culture, particularly in Jundi-Shapur, whereas Spain began with native and Latin culture and depended on Islam for familiarity with Hellenistic culture. Persia developed its own political independence while under Muslim influence, but Spain depended on outside aid (Charlemagne) to attempt controlling Islam politically.*

---

*In Arabic literature and philology, Persian contributions were remarkable, but the golden age of Arabic literature, the period of the Abbassides (749-847), antedates the golden age of science by more than a century. Of forty-four literary writers in the Arabic language listed in Browne's *Literary History of Persia,* thirteen "of the most celebrated contributors" were writers of Persian extraction. They included ibn al-Muqaffa (died 757), the translator of the Pahlavi version of *Kalila wa-Dimna* into Arabic, to whom ibn Khaldun refers in the *Muqaddimah*

Mathematics and Astronomy. At the time of al-Mansur, the cultural center of the Islamic world shifted from the Byzantine to the Persian part of the empire, and Baghdad (founded in 762) became the new center of Muslim education. Among the men of learning flourishing in and around Baghdad there were many mathematicians, astronomers, and qualified engineers who helped in the planning of the city and in making it the queen of Eastern cities for several centuries. Construction of the city was planned by Arabs, Jews, Persians, and Indians. The Persians participating were Naubakht, the astronomer, and al-Farrukhan (815), who translated some Persian works and annotated Ptolemy's *Quadripartium.* Encouraged by al-Mansur and his successor, al-Ma'mun, scholars laid hold of Greek astronomical works and established observatories at Baghdad and Jundi-Shapur. With astronomy, flourished also arithmetic and algebra, and valuable contributions were made in all of these disciplines. Many of the mathematical thinkers were Persians, among them Omar Khayyam, Tusi, Banu Musa, and ibn Mashar of Balkh, in Khurasan. As Arberry states in the *Legacy of Persia*:

> From the beginning, it is to be remarked that the Persians approached mathematics from a different angle from the Greeks. The Greeks admired abstract philosophy and highly theoretical mathematics. They aimed at an intellectual training through speculation and imagination . . . . The Persians in the court of al-Ma'mun were asked to apply the result of their studies to astronomy, surveying, architecture, and the art of navigation. Even attention to smaller details was expected of them, such as the perfection of the calendar, determination of the direction in which Mecca lay, and an ability to measure time in order that the hour of prayer might not pass unnoticed. So it will be seen that running through the whole of Persian mathematical research is the craving not for precise knowledge but for precision in the application of knowledge.[3]

Among the great Persian mathematicians whose works made important contributions to Western education in this area was al-Khwarizmi of Khiva, who perhaps gave the West the term *algebra* (from *jabr*, meaning *reduction*).[4] In his systematic writings, Greek and Hindu mathematical sciences were brought together and synchronized. Also basic to Western education was his "contribution to the solution of linear equations."[5] The Brethren of Purity, as already noted, was a liberal religious sect with many Persian scholars and writers who together wrote a great encyclopaedia of sciences, a large part of it dealing with mathematics and astronomy.[6] Their writings included discussions of the nature and cause of sound, earthquakes, tides and eclipses.

Al-Biruni (973-1048) accurately determined latitudes and longi-

---

as one of the foremost masters of the Arabic language.[1] He also translated the *Khudai-Namah* (*Book of Kings*), one of the sources of the *Shah-Namah* of Firdawsi, from Pahlavi into Arabic. Others included Hammad ibn Sa'bur (Shapur) al-Rawiya (died 772 or 775), the collector and editor of the famous Arabic seven *Mu'allaqat* or *Hung* poems; ibn Qutaiba (died 828), the great historian and author of *Kitab al-Ma'arif* (*The Book of Sciences*), *Adab al-Katib* (*Manners of the Secretary*), and *Uyun al-Akhbar* (*Sources of Historic News or tradition*).[2]

tudes, correctly measured the specific gravity of eighteen precious stones and metals and explained the working of natural springs and artesian wells.

Another Persian mathematician-astronomer was the celebrated poet, Omar Khayyam, who not only was the greatest scientist of his time but sired the golden age of Persian and Islamic science.[7] Khayyam carried the science of mathematics beyond Khwarizmi, particularly in the realm of cubic equations, wherein he "applied the principle of intersecting conic sections in solving algebraic problems." He gave a complete classification of the forms of cubic equations and constructed a geometrical solution for each type.[8] He constructed a new era (*Jalali*), beginning with March 15, 1079, so accurately that "there is an error of only one day in 5,000 years."[9] Khayyam died in 1124 and may thus be considered not only the last great scholar of the eleventh century, but also a transitional figure, having done his work during the last decades of the eleventh and the first quarter of the twelfth centuries.

The last great Persian mathematician-astronomer of this period whose contributions reached the Western schoolmen was Abu al-Wafa (940-997). Arberry states in the *Legacy of Islam* that:

> He was probably the first to show the generality of the sine theorem relative to spherical triangles. He introduced a new method of constructing sine tables . . . made a special study of the tangents, calculated a table of tangents, introduced the secant and cosecant, and knew those simple relations between the six trigonometric lines which are now often used to define them.[10]

The study of mathematics led inevitably to astronomy. Heavenly bodies seem to have had a peculiar fascination for the Persians, though they studied the stars for pragmatic purposes, associating human behavior with the movements of celestial bodies, especially the sun.

Other mathematician-astronomers of Persian extraction were Abu al-Husain al-Sufi (903-986) of Rayy, the author of the *Book of the Fixed Stars*, one of the greatest Muslim works on observational astronomy; Habash al-Hasib of Marv, who determined time by developing the sundial and composed a table of shadows; al-Farghani of Transoxiana, who measured the earth's diameter, determined the distances between the planets as well as their diameter, and wrote on sundials; al-Fathl al-Nairizi, who wrote on atmospheric phenomena, spherical astrolabe and astronomical tables; Nasir al-Din al Tusi, compiler of the famous *Zij* (*Tables*), wrote extensively on astronomy and the calendar, mathematics and geomancy;[12] al-Muzaffar al-Tusi, the inventor of the linear astrolabe, known as Tusi's Staff; Qutb al-Din Shirazi (1236-1311) who wrote on the nature of vision, geometrical optics, and the rainbow; and Fakhr al-Din al-Razi, who was, among others, the author of an encyclopaedia of science.

Medicine. During the golden age of Muslim learning, the preeminence of Persian scholars in the assimilation and further development of Islamic medicine was obvious. Medical scholarship passed from the hands of the Christians and Sabians into the possession of Muslim scholars, mostly Persians.[13]

The greatest of these medical writers was al-Razi, better known as Rhazes (865-925), a Persian-Muslim scholar born at Rayy. Rhazes studied in Baghdad under the medical tradition of Hunain ibn Is'haq and mastered Greek, Persian, and Indian medicine. This all-embracing education is evidenced by his remarkable output of scientific works, totaling some two hundred, half of which dealt with medicine.[14] Of these, the best known is *Al-Hawi* in thirty volumes, *Al-A'sah* (*The Nerves*), and *Al Jami* (*The Universal*).[15] Some of his works were translated into Latin and later into other European languages, including English. Some of them were printed as many as forty times between 1498 and 1866. In addition to his works on medicine, Rhazes also wrote on philosophy, theology, mathematics, astronomy and the natural sciences.[16] Unfortunately, most of his writings have been lost.

Next to Rhazes is the Persian-Muslim physician ibn Sina, or Avicenna, of whom we have already spoken as a philosopher (980-1037). As a physician, his influence on European medical education was overwhelming. Avicenna developed upon the science of Hippocrates and Galen, as well as the philosophies of Aristotle and Plato, exercising an influence on the best brains of both the East and the West, not only during his lifetime but for many centuries after his death.[17] He handed over many ideas which became part of the stream of philosophical-educational thought in the West. Among these the most famous was his notion of the intelligibles, *intentio,* which was taken over by Albertus Magnus and became part of the scholastic tradition.[18] But it is in medicine that Europe and the Muslim world owe him an incalculable debt as the greatest clinical observer in Islam.[19] The first translations of his works were made in Latin between 1130 and 1150 by Archdeacon Dominic Gundisalvus and John Avendeath of Seville, at the order of Raymond, the Archbishop of Toledo.[20] His *Canon of Medicine,* an encyclopaedia of medical knowledge, was translated into Latin by Gerard of Cremona in the twelfth century and was reprinted fifteen times in the last decades of the fifteenth and twenty times in the sixteenth century. Besides his medical works, he wrote more than a hundred treatises on theology, philology, philosophy, and astronomy, and made special studies in music far ahead of Latin works and in the philosophy of mathematics along neo-Platonic lines.[21] The tomb of Avicenna at Hamadan in western Iran is visited today by natives and foreign visitors with pious veneration.

It is interesting to note that this was taking place in the Muslim world at a period when Saint Anselm was laying the foundations of Christian scholasticism in Europe at the School of Bec in Normandy and arguing his realist position on universals with Rocelin, the nominalist, and at a time when there was a neo-Platonic revival in Byzantine

Constantinople under Psello, a forerunner of the revival of Platonism in Florence four hundred years later.

Haly Abbas (994) was another Persian-Muslim physician well known among the Latins. His excellent and compact encyclopaedia on *The Whole Medical Art,* known in the Latin as *Liber Regius,* was twice translated into that language.[22]

Muwaffaq (ibn Mansur) was another famous Persian-Muslim writer on medicine (975). His most famous medical work is *The Foundations of the True Properties of Remedies,* in which the author describes some 585 drugs. It is a compact of Persian, Syrian, Greek, Arabic, and Indian knowledge.[23]

Geography. The vast empire of Islam in which Persia was one of the chief cultural centers was soon confronted with the problems of geographic knowledge for both territorial and commercial expansion. What was needed was not a series of theoretical treatises on climate, geography, race, social forces, and the like, but a practical knowledge for everyday purposes of the everyday man. Even before the tenth century, great travellers appeared on the scene who made practical and useful studies in commercial and territorial geography. These practical observations were soon combined with Hellenistic and Indo-Persian influences to produce some of the best geographical studies of the epoch. Ptolemy's geographical works as well as the Sassanian Persian views were soon combined, along with new observations, and the result was new knowledge in geography and further advance in the economic world.

At the opening of the tenth century, we find these combined geographical studies turned into a school of geographical thought which produced great men of merit, among whom some of the best were Persians. Important among these Persian-Muslim geographers were those mentioned below.

Al-Balkhi (934) was a leading scholar of the Samanid Dynasty in Khurasan, Persia. He wrote many books, among them some on geography which became the basis of principal geographical works written after him in the Islamic world by al-Istakhri (950), ibn Hawqal (975), and al-Maqdisi (985), forming a geographical school which inherited, at least in part, the Sassanian traditions.[24] Al-Hamdani wrote a geographical description of the Arabian peninsula which was one of the best studies of that region.[25] Al-Biruni wrote the famous description of India.[26] Nasir-i-Khusraw was an eleventh-century traveller and autobiographical-geographical writer of great merit. His home was in Khurasan, but he visited Egypt and Mecca and wrote the results of his observations. Some of his best works are his famous *Diwan, Safar-Namah* (*Book of Travel*) and his *Rawshanai-Namah* (*Book of Light*).[27]

Yaqut (1228) and al-Qazwini (1275) are famous for their elaborate dictionaries which contained geographical and biographical names in alphabetical order. The works of these men, along with those of other Muslim writers left direct impressions on European thought and education during the Middle Ages.

In the art of navigation it should be remembered that the Persian Gulf has been of great importance. The Gulf was linked through the River Euphrates to Baghdad, the center of the Islamic Empire, and through it to navigation of the Indian Ocean. Thus it was an instrument of world trade. Christian trade in this connecting line between India and the West was enhanced by Muslim (Turkish) pioneers during the crusades, and their search for a new route to India led to the discovery of America. After the Renaissance, the study of geography weakened in the Islamic world and was carried on by Italian and Spanish navigators and geographers.

Others among the Persian-Muslim scholars of the post-golden age of Islamic learning were al-Khazim (1200-?), who dealt with the specific gravity and weight of alloys, and the greater density of water as we reach nearer the center of the earth, a theory which Roger Bacon advanced upon later;[28] and Kamal al-Din, whose knowledge of mathematics, which he applied to the study of the path of the rays in the interior of a glass sphere, surpassed those of Euclid and Ptolemy.[29]

History. Muslim works in the area of history during the long period outlined in this chapter were quite extensive and represent philosophies of history ranging from extremely religious (spiritual and moral) to reasonably secular concepts. One of the greatest of Muslim historians and philosophers of history (also a great educational theorist), ibn Khaldun (1332-1406), is beyond the period to which this study is confined.*

---

*His *Muqaddima* is translated into English in three volumes by Franz Rosenthal in *An Introduction to History,* Bollingen Series XLIII, Pantheon Books, 1958.

Important educational passages in this English translation of *Muqaddima* are as follows:

On basic philosophy of education – Vol. 2, p. 140; vol. 2, p. 346; vol. 2, p. 419; vol. 2, p. 424 f.; vol. 1, p. 256 f.; vol. 1, p. 197; vol. 1, p. 184; vol. 2, p. 406; vol. 3, p. 281; vol. 3, p. 342; vol. 2, p. 411; vol. 2, p. 412; vol. 3, p. 307.

Methods of teaching – Vol. 1, p. 58; vol. 2, p. 346; vol. 3, pp. 290, 292, 300, 304, 307, 363, 392, 399.

The place of science among subjects – Vol. 2, pp. 426-428, 435.

School organization – Vol. 2, p. 430.

On religious education and instruction – Vol. 1, p. 260.

On curriculum – Vol. 2, p. 436; vol. 3, pp. 8, 111, 122.

On various subjects of study – Vol. 2, pp. 351, 355, 377; vol. 3, pp. 8, 34, 111, 118, 122, 147-152, 247, 318, 363, 392.

On teachers and teacher education – Vol. 1, pp. 58, 452.

Importance of research – Vol. 3, p. 288.

Methods of research – Vol. 3, pp. 284, 307.

On education and culture, civilization, and so forth – Vol. 3, pp. 114, 314.

Geographic factors in education, heredity, environment and education – Vol. 1, pp. 177, 253, 279, 292; vol. 2, p. 349.

Learning theory – Vol. 1, pp. 71, 76, 207, 209-212, 214; vol. 2, pp. 346, 355,

Of Persian historians, most of whom wrote during the Mongol period, Tabari (923) was among the best in the Islamic world. Born in Tabaristan, he flourished during the Samanid period. A prolific writer, he is reported to have written forty pages daily for forty years.[30] Although Western writers have listed, as a rule, the Muslim historians of the period between 650 to 1050 A.D. under the label "Arab," many of them were Persians employing the Arabic language, as shown by Brockelman, Browne and others.[31]

The Persian Firdawsi has already been discussed as a poet in some detail. He may well be called the "father of Persian history" and the first reviver of the Persian language as well. In fact he had no knowledge of Pahlavi and very little of Arabic, and the only sources of information for his book were in modern Persian. Consequently, the principal authority for his *Book of Kings* (*Shah-Namah*) was a translation of a Pahlavi text of the same title translated by Ibn Farrukh of Tus (full name: Abd al-Razzaq ibn Abdullah ibn Farrukh of Tus), the minister of Yakub ibn Laith Saffar, who commissioned him in 920 to make this translation with the help of four other Persians from Khurasan and Sijistan. This prose translation of the Pahlavi *Khudai Namah* (*Book of Kings*) was first attempted in poetry by Daqiqi for the Samanid rulers, but it was completed by Firdawsi for Sultan Mahmud of Ghazna. These facts are verified, according to Nariman, by the Persian-Muslim historian al-Biruni. We have dealt in some detail with Firdawsi in the previous chapter.

Muslim Scholarship in the Twelfth and Thirteenth Centuries

By the end of the eleventh century, Islamic learning had reached the pinnacle of its glory with the appearance in that century of such men as Biruni, Firdawsi, ibn Sina, Nasir-i-Khusraw, Nizam-al-Mulk, al-Ghazzali, and Omar Khayyam. As we look at the culture and the system of education which produced these men and their works, two facts stand out clearly. The first is that these scholars received their greatest stimulation from Islam's Greco-Hellenistic heritage of science and philosophy. The second, which is even more significant, is that Islam welcomed this heritage and encouraged within its schools, colleges, research centers, and libraries that spirit of free inquiry which is the lifeblood of creativity and progress. As long as this spirit prevailed, men's curiosity led to investigations, innovations, and vital advances in philosophy, science, literary creations, and the arts.

During the twelfth and thirteenth centuries this liberal spirit gradually gave way to orthodoxy of belief and fixed patterns of

357, 378, 386, 388, 411, 418; vol. 3, pp. 105, 137-140, 290, 281.

Origin of truth and knowledge – Vol. 1, pp. 184, 195-197, 306; vol. 2, p. 406; vol. 3, pp. 77, 281, 314, 342.

The nature of man – Vol. 1, pp. 197, 202, 291, 301; vol. 2, p. 416; vol. 3, p. 69.

Scholars – Vol. 3, pp. 308, 311.

thought; originality yielded to eclecticism; and second- and third-grade works appeared *en masse*, lacking the spark and spirit of the creative thinking that characterized the two previous centuries. Scholars of this period occupied themselves mainly with evaluations, canonizations, comments, and criticisms of the works of the golden age. As a result, with the fading of this liberal spirit, the decline of Muslim learning became evident: Muslim creative thinkers and writers were reduced in number and by the 1300's, save for the great historian-philosopher ibn Khaldun, had all but ceased to be.

By virtue, however, of the eleventh century's momentum and in spite of the obvious tendency toward a decline, the twelfth and thirteenth centuries still produced a few outstanding scholars, of whom the most important will be discussed briefly below.* Their main intellectual interests were directed toward philosophy, science and technology (including geometry, trigonometry, physics, and botany), geography, and medicine.

PHILOSOPHY, RELIGION, AND THEOLOGY

Of all the basic developments in the three interdependent disciplines of philosophy, religion, and theology, the most important during the twelfth and thirteenth centuries were the following:

In the twelfth century Abd al-Qadir Jilani founded the Qadari, or *Qadiriya dervish* order in Islam, somewhat similar to Christian monasticism. Shahrastani, the Asharite theologian, wrote the great history of the Muslim sects. Al-Ghazzali had already developed Muslim scholasticism and set the stage in his monumental repudiation of philosophy, *Destruction of Philosophy,* for ibn Rushd's (Averroes) famous refutation of al-Ghazzali, the repercussions of which controversy were felt in European philosophy, principally in St. Thomas Aquinas.

Al-Batalyusi and ibn Bajja (Avenpace) also wrote on philosophy in Western Islam, and the latter's *Tadbir al-Mutawahhid* (*The Guide of the Solitary*) influenced ibn Rushd (Averroes) and Albert the Great. Analysis of his *Risalat al-Wada* (*The Letter of Welfare*) also appeared in Hebrew. In Eastern Islam, Fakhr-al-Din al-Razi (Rhazes) and Nizami Arudhi were the outstanding philosophic thinkers, the latter for his views on natural evolution and the former for works in physics and philosophy.

---

*In addition, the following deserve mention: the physician ibn Zuhr (Avenzoar) of the Western Islam; the Persian grammarian Hariri, the Egyptian physician Abu-Salt, the Persian poet Nizami Arudhi, the Khurasanian geographer Tusi, the historian Baihaqi of the same province, the Persian philosopher-poet Farid-al-Din Attar, the Egyptian historian al-Qifti, the philosopher ibn Arabi of Murcia, the mathematician ibn Badr of Valencia, the great Persian poet Sa'di, the Persian mathematicians Ahmad al-Samarkandi and Abu Bakr al-Farisi, the mystic Jalal-al-Din Rumi, and the educator Muhammad al-Riquti of Murcia.

Ibn Rushd was one of the two greatest philosophers of the second half of the twelfth century (the other being ibn Tufail) and his influence, particularly in Latin philosophy, was felt to the end of the sixteenth century. His Aristotelian realism (universals), rationalism, scientific positivism, and sceptical attitude toward mysticism were the basis upon which he attacked al-Ghazzali's philosophy. His refutation of al-Ghazzali, entitled *The Destruction of the Destruction,* was quite offensive to Eastern Islam, particularly to al-Ghazzalites, although it played an effective role in Latin philosophy as Averroism.

The renaissance of Persian philosophic poetry in the thirteenth century, particularly during the second half, had far-reaching ramifications. The most significant of these poets were Sa'di, Jalal-al-Din Rumi, and Farid al-Din Attar.

Not much creative work was done in Spain at this time, however. Islam had already lost Spain: James I of Aragon had annexed Baleares in 1232 and Valencia in 1238; Frederick III of Castile took Cordova in 1236, Murcia in 1243, Jaen in 1246, and Seville in 1248. Nevertheless, two scholars should be mentioned: Ibn Arabi, who wrote within the framework of Cordova's Ishraqi Mystical School and composed the history of Augustinianism and neo-Platonism; and ibn Sabin, who wrote a famous work, *The Sicilian Questions,* consisting of answers to certain philosophical questions raised by Frederick II.

In the thirteenth century the Persian philosopher al-Mufaddal ibn Umar al-Abhari wrote the *Al-Hikmah* (*Guide to Wisdom*). The mathematician Nasir al-Din Tusi wrote influential works on logic, mathematics, metaphysics, ethics, theology, the limitations of human understanding, and the classification of knowledge. He was an astronomer during the troublesome period of the Mongol invasion and made new observations in Maragha in Asia Minor from an observatory founded there by the Mongol khans. In addition to compiling new astronomical tables entitled *The Ilkhanian Tables,* he edited many mathematical works of antiquity, including four works which constituted the fundamental scientific knowledge of the period. Tusi also wrote the *Treatise on the Quadrilateral,* which was edited with French translation by Caratheodory Pasha, Constantinople, 1891. The work deals with spherical trigonometry. Zakariyya ibn Muhammad al-Qazwini wrote an encyclopaedia of natural history and a popular book on geography.

SCIENCE AND TECHNOLOGY

Geometry. The interest of Muslim scholarship in Euclidian geometry continued throughout the twelfth century, as evidenced by the mathematical works of the School of Maragha that prepared, under Nasir al-Din Tusi and al-Maghribi, the *Kitab al-Mutawassitat* (*The Book of Triangles*), dealing among other things with the work of Apollonius and Theodosius. Other Muslim geometricians of this century were Kamal-al-Din ibn Yunus, Abd al-Malik al-Shirazi, who wrote on Apollonius's *Conics,* and Muhammad ibn al-Husain, who wrote a treatise on "the perfect compass by means of which every conic could be drawn."[32] Also, al-Hasan al-Marrakushi wrote on geometry and gnomonics.

Trigonometry. Islah al-Majisti's introduction to the astronomical treatise of Jabir ibn Aflah of Seville, written at mid-century, contained trigonometrical theories.

Hasan al-Marrakushi completed in 1229 in Morocco an astronomical treatise with trigonometrical information. His work contained "tables of sines for each half degree, also tables of versed sines, arc sines, and arc cotangents."[33]

Nasir al-Din Tusi's treatise on trigonometry and geometry, the *Kitab Shakl al-Qatt'a,* which remained a standard work in both fields until the sixteenth century, was written during the second half of the twelfth century. Another work bearing the same title, *Shakl al-Qatt'a* (*Treatise on Shapes*) was written by Muhyi al-Din al-Maghribi about the same time.

The Maragha Observatory, established in 1259 in the Persian Adharbayajan, became for a short period a famous and creative center of astronomical studies and new or improved astronomical instruments. The center attracted astronomers and instrument makers from Persia and Syria and probably China.[34]

The *Ilkhanian* astronomical tables of Nasir al-Din Tusi (1272) and the *Marw Tables* (one hundred fifteen of them) compiled by Khazimi, became very popular in the Muslim world, in the West, and in "Buddhist East." They were all Persian tables. Ibn Yunus, too, made improved astronomical tables, the *Hakemite Tables,* in honor of the sixth Fatimid ruler of Egypt, al-Hakim, in the observatory of the ruler's Academy of Dar-al-Hikmah (The House of Learning). He made significant contributions in trigonometry, "new solutions of spherical problems." Of the Islamic astronomical tables or *zijs* (from Persian *zig* or *zih,* meaning card), the *Jelali zij* was worked out by Omar Khayyam.

The largest number of tables (E. S. Kennedy lists one hundred nine) appeared in ninth-century Baghdad, except for a few scattered tables in other areas, during the Abbasside caliphates. Both geographically and nationally, the largest number was written by Persians, although most of them were greatly influenced by Hellenistic astronomy (mainly Hipparchus and Ptolemy), Babylonian and Hindu trigonometric methods, and Sassanian (Persian) astronomies. Thus Islam owed much to Hindu, Sassanian, Babylonian, and Hellenistic astronomy, all of which cultures—except Babylonion—leaned heavily upon Greek astronomical sciences, which in turn were influenced by Babylonian astronomy. Sassanian astronomy, on the other hand, appears to have been under direct Hindu influence.

Many Muslim astronomers made their tables from independent observations in widely diversified geographic areas, but as creative and independent as many of these studies were, "they made no advances comparable to those marked by the Ptolemaic and Newtonian systems." Islamic tables assimilated the substance of many pre-Islamic observations for which direct sources are either very scarce or lacking completely. Although the Muslims' astronomical advances were limited, translations of their works stimulated interest among European scholars of astronomy and awakened Europe to Newton and modern Western astronomy. Of the many Muslim *zijs*, only a few were based on Iranian and Hindu theories; the rest, largely on Ptolemy. Only the *Khwarizmi Zij* has been preserved from these few non-Ptolemaic observations.[35] Al-Kharaqi, a Persian, wrote a treatise on astronomy which was based on *Ibn Haithanus*. A Moroccan scientist, whose name isn't known, wrote around 1229 the great medieval text, the *Jami'al-Mabadi wal Qayat fi ilm al-Niqat* (*The Beginnings and Ends in the Knowledge of Time*).*

During the latter half of the thirteenth century, the Persian astronomers Ali ibn Umar al-Katibi and Qutb al-Din al-Shirazi had entertained, then rejected, the possibility of the rotation of the earth on the grounds that "sublunar motions cannot be circular."[36]

Music. Many musical treatises were written by the twelfth century leaders of the Maragha School, Nasir al-Din Tusi and Qutb al-Din al-Shirazi, but the most profound theorist of the time was another Persian, Safi-al-Din, "one of the founders of the systematist scale said to be the most perfect ever devised."[37]

Physics. The *Kitab Mizan al-Hikmah* (*The Scale of Wisdom*), written by Abd-al-Rahman al-Khazini in 1121, was one of the Middle Age's fundamental works in physics embodying "tables of specific gravities of liquids and solids and various physical facts and theories."[38]

Geography. The Persian Zamakhshari (died 1144) wrote *Kitab al-Amkina wa'l-Jibal wal-Mi'a* (*The Book of Places, Mountains and Waters*). Yaqut's *Mu'jam al-Buldan* (*The Persian Book of Places*), 1228, makes in alphabetical order an extensive list of geographical data, including facts on human and natural geography, archaeology, astronomy, physical and historical geography. Al-Qazwini's *Aja'ib al-Buldan* (*The Wonders of Lands*), 1262, was written in seven climatic divisions. Muhammad ibn Ali al-Zuhri of Spain wrote a treatise on geographic theory after 1140. Al-Idrisi of Sicily wrote for the Norman King, Roger II, an elaborate geographic description of the world as then known. He also composed a geographical encyclopaedia between 1154 and 1166 for William I. Al-Mazini of Granada wrote on the geog-

---

*The last word, *niqat,* I believe, should be *wiqat,* meaning *time* in Arabic.

raphy of Eastern Islam and the Volga region, both of which were based on his travels.

Al-Hasan al-Marrakushi wrote *Jami' al-Mabadi wa'l-Dhayat,* a treatise on mathematical geography, in 1229 which gave the coordinates of 135 places. This was the greatest work of its kind throughout the Middle Ages. Ibn Sa'id al-Maghribi's treatise on geography, which was written during the second half of the thirteenth century, contained a list of coordinates too but was based largely on Marrakushi's work. Materials on geography and cosmography were also covered in the *Chahar Maqala* (*Four Discourses of Nizami Aruzi [Arudhi]*), by Muhammad ibn Mahmud of Tus and in the collection of anecdotes of Muhammad al-Awfi.

Antidotes. Ibn Sarabi, Serapion the Younger, wrote a controversial treatise on simple chemical elements with Hebrew and Latin versions. The Latin translation (perhaps an adaptation or enlargement) proved to be more popular and influential than the Arabic original, which has survived only in part. Ibn al-Tilmidh, a Christian physician of Baghdad, wrote on antidotes in the first half of the twelfth century; and ibn Jami, an Egyptian Jew, wrote a treatise, *The Irshad,* later in the same century, which dealt in part with simple and compound medicines. Al-Qafiqi of Cordova wrote one of the best treatises describing simples. The geographer al-Idrisi described 360 simples in a work which was also of important botanical significance.

Botany. Abd-al-Latif of Baghdad's account of Egypt contains important botanical materials. Ibn al-Suri of Damascus made careful studies of plants in Damascus and the Lebanese mountains. Abd al-Abbas al-Nabati of Seville made exploratory studies of plants extending from Spain through North Africa to the Red Sea. Ibn al-Baitar of Malaga compiled the most important encyclopaedic work on the subject in the entire "Middle Ages" and brought together all that had been done in botany by the Greek, Persian, and Muslim scholars. The Egyptian Jew, al-Kuhin al-Attar, wrote a very popular work on pharmacopoeia, entitled *Minhaj al-Dukkan,* in the second half of the thirteenth century.

Medicine. Muslim commentaries on ibn Sina's *Qanun* (*Canons*) by Muwaffaq al-Din, the Samaritan, ibn al-Quffi, ibn al-Sa'ati, ibn al-Nafis, and Qutb al-Din al-Shirazi appeared during this period under consideration. Also, creative commentaries were written on Galen and Hippocrates by ibn al-Nafis, Yusuf ibn Hasda'i, ibn al-Quffi, and David ben Solomon. The *Zorihaguf* of Nathan ben Joel Falaquera, in Hebrew, containing medical extracts from Muslim and Hellenistic authors, and similar ones in Latin by William Corvi (*Aggregator Brixiensis*) and John of Saint Amands' *Revocativum Memoriose* were in popular use.

Numerous commentaries on Muslim medicine, including commentaries on Arabic translations of Greek works, were published by Taddeo Alderotti, Arnold of Villanova, and Peter of Spain.

"By the middle or end of the thirteenth century the same medical classics reached the libraries of Paris, Montpellier, Bologna, Salerno, Granada, Cairo, Damascus, or Baghdad."[39] By the end of the century, Greco-Muslim medical knowledge and art had reached and stabilized Latin and Hebrew medical skills and schools. Latin medical education for another two centuries or more remained predominantly Muslim—more accurately Greco-Zoroastrian-Hindu-Syriac—in theory and practice, save in surgery, in which Europe advanced upon Muslim practices.

Important among the Muslim medical scholars of the twelfth and thirteenth centuries were the following:

Sa'id ibn Hibat Allah al-Baghdadi, who wrote *Mughni fi Tadhir al-Amradh (A Discourse on Cure of Diseases);* Adnan al-Ainzarbi, who wrote *Kafi fi ilm al-Tibb (Sufficient Complete Discourse in the Science of Medicine);* ibn Hubal, author of *Mukhtar fi'l-Tibb* (*Authority on Medicine*); ibn al-Jawzi, author of the *Lughat al-Manafi fi'l-Tibb* (*Words of Advantages in Medicine*); Isma'il al-Jurjani, author of *Zakhira ye-Khwarizmshahi (A Storehouse Treasure of Khwarizmshahi),* a medical work dedicated to Khwarizm-Shah; Fakhr al-Din al-Razi, who wrote an encyclopaedia, including essays in medicine; Najib al-Din of Samarkand, who wrote *Kitab al-Asbab wa'l-Alamat* (the *Book of Causes and Symptoms of Disease*); ibn Jami and his son, Abu Tahir Isma'il, both Egyptian Jewish medical scholars, who wrote *Irshad al-Masalif al-Anfas wa'l-Ajsad* (*Instruction [Direction] for the Benefits of Souls and Bodies [Body and Mind]);* Maimonides, author of *Fusul fi'l-Tibb (Discourses [Chapters] on Medicine);* al-Kuhin al-Attar, an Egyptian Jew, author of *Minhaj al-Dukkan* (*The Manners [Ways] of Shops*); Solomon Cohen, an Egyptian Jew, author of *Al-Muntakhab* (*The Selected Works*); Abu al-Ala al-Zuhr, author of *Kitab al-Nukat al-Tibbiyya (The Book of Medical Subtleties [Minute Points];* Abu Marwan ibn Zuhr, "the Medieval Avenzoar," author of the *Taisir;* and ibn Rushd, the *Kulliyat (Complete Work).*

Muslim medical works and their Latin translations included lists (tables) of diseases and cures; anatomy, as in ibn Sina's *Qanun,* and the Egyptian Abd al-Latif's work; surgery; pulse and urine, as discussed in Is'haq al-Isra'il's *Kitab al-Baul* (the *Book of Urine*) translated into Latin by Constantine the African; blood-letting, the practice of which went back to the Greeks and Persians; midwifery; children's diseases; diseases of the eye, ophthalmology, as in *Nur-al-Uyun* (*Light of Eyes*), by the Persian Zarrin Dast, 1087; and the works of Ali ibn Rabban al-Tabari, Razi, ibn Masawaih, Khalaf al-Tuluni and Hunain ibn Is'haq (ninth century); Ali ibn Isa's *Tadhkirat al-Kahhalin* (*On Blindness*), Ammar ibn Ali al-Mawsili's *Muntakhab fi Ilaj Amradh al-Ain* (*The Cure of the Diseases of the Eye*) (eleventh century); Khalifa ibn Abi-al-Mahasin's *Al-Kafi fi'l-Kuhl* (*Book of Blindness*) and Salah al-Din's *Nur al-Uyun* (*Light of Eyes*) (thirteenth century); psychotherapy, as in the works of ibn Sina and Hebat Allah ibn Malka; hygiene; veterinary medicine; clinical-experimental medicine, as in the works of Abu al-Ala al-Zuhr, ibn Tilmidh and others, who wrote *Mujarrabats* (*Experimentations*); hospitals and bathing.

A Summation

The eighth and ninth centuries, particularly the period between 750 and 900, saw the introduction of classical learning, education, and refinement into the Islamic culture and schools. This epoch may be characterized by the initial organization, consolidation, adaptation, and assimilation of these classical elements. The tenth and eleventh centuries—the golden age of Islamic scholarship—were centuries of interpretation of classical thought (chiefly neo-Platonic and Aristotelian life and world views), criticism and further adaptations of these, and to some extent the adaptation of Persian and Hindu thought to Muslim theology and philosophy. Hellenistic, Persian, and Hindu sciences (mathematics, astronomy, trigonometry, algebra, technology, medicine and its associated disciplines), and other practical skills were introduced into Muslim schools. The application of these to the needs and interests of the Muslim world challenged the genius of many Muslim scholars. Finally, successful modifications of, and new and significant additions to, important areas of this classical cultural heritage were achieved—mainly in the fields of medicine, mathematical sciences, philosophical systems, and the social disciplines, such as geography, history, and educational theory.

The twelfth and thirteenth centuries were centuries of translation. They were marked on the one hand by the gradual and visible decline of Muslim creative scholarship and, on the other, by a steady flow of the results of Hellenistic-Hindu-Persian-Muslim learning in scientific, philosophic (and to some extent theological), technical, geographic, historical, esthetic, and other fields into the Hebrew and Latin Christian schools through the steady and systematic translations of the writings of the most eminent (even some lesser) Muslim thinkers and scholars from the Arabic (occasionally Persian) into Hebrew and Latin.

The decline of Muslim scholarship and creativity coincided, therefore, with the early phases of the European intellectual awakening, which was largely stimulated by the introduction of Muslim science, philosophy, and art into European society and educational institutions. The process had reversed itself, for the renaissance of Muslim learning had coincided during the earlier centuries of Islam with a period of relative intellectual inactivity and non-creativity in Latin Christianity brought about, in part, by the rejection of Hellenistic traditions of science and philosophy, more precisely, the Ionian experimental and inquiring spirit.

It is probable that as early as 1200, Islam had exhausted itself as a great world force; intellectual courage and innovation had sagged;

orthodox scholasticism, sustained by al-Ghazzali, had largely taken over and written off the fate of independent research.

As Islam was declining in scholarship and Europe was absorbing the fruits of Islam's three and a half centuries of creative productivity, signs of Latin Christian awakening were obvious throughout the European continent. These forerunners of what developed after the thirteenth century into a full-fledged European all-inclusive renaissance were such educators and scholars as (1) the French Roscelin of Campiegne, Odo of Meung, Gerald of Besancon, Franco of Liege, and Marbode of Augers; (2) the German Lambert of Hersfeld, Theophilus, Hermann of Reichenau, Adam of Bremen, Wilhelm of Hirsau, and Frutolf of Bemberg; (3) the Greek Christians, Paullus, Simeon Seth, Scylitzes, Atha-Liates, Xephilinus, and Theophylactus; (4) the Irish Marianus Scottas; (5) the Tunisian Jew al-Fasiq, the French Jew Raslu, and the Italian Jews Nathan ben Jehiel and Ahimaaz; (6) the Italian St. Anselm; (7) Constantine of Carthage; (8) the English Honorius Inclusus; (9) and others, as Papias the Lombard and Joannes Plalearius the Younger.

The twelfth century was one of intensified traffic of Muslim learning to the Western Latin and Hebrew worlds, which in itself helped Europe seize the initiative from Islam, when political conditions in Islam brought about indications of an intellectual decline in Muslim scholarship. By 1300, when all that was worthwhile in Muslim scientific-philosophic-social learning had been transmitted to European schoolmen through Latin translations, European scholars stood once again on the solid ground of Hellenistic thought, enriched or modified through Muslim efforts, and they were ready to pick up and continue the Greek spirit of inquiry which they had abandoned for centuries but which had been preserved and promoted, fortunately, during the early Christian centuries in the Syrian schools (Antioch, Nisibis, and Edessa) and in the Persian Sassanian Academy of Jundi-Shapur and, after the seventh century Islamic conquests, by Muslim scholarship.

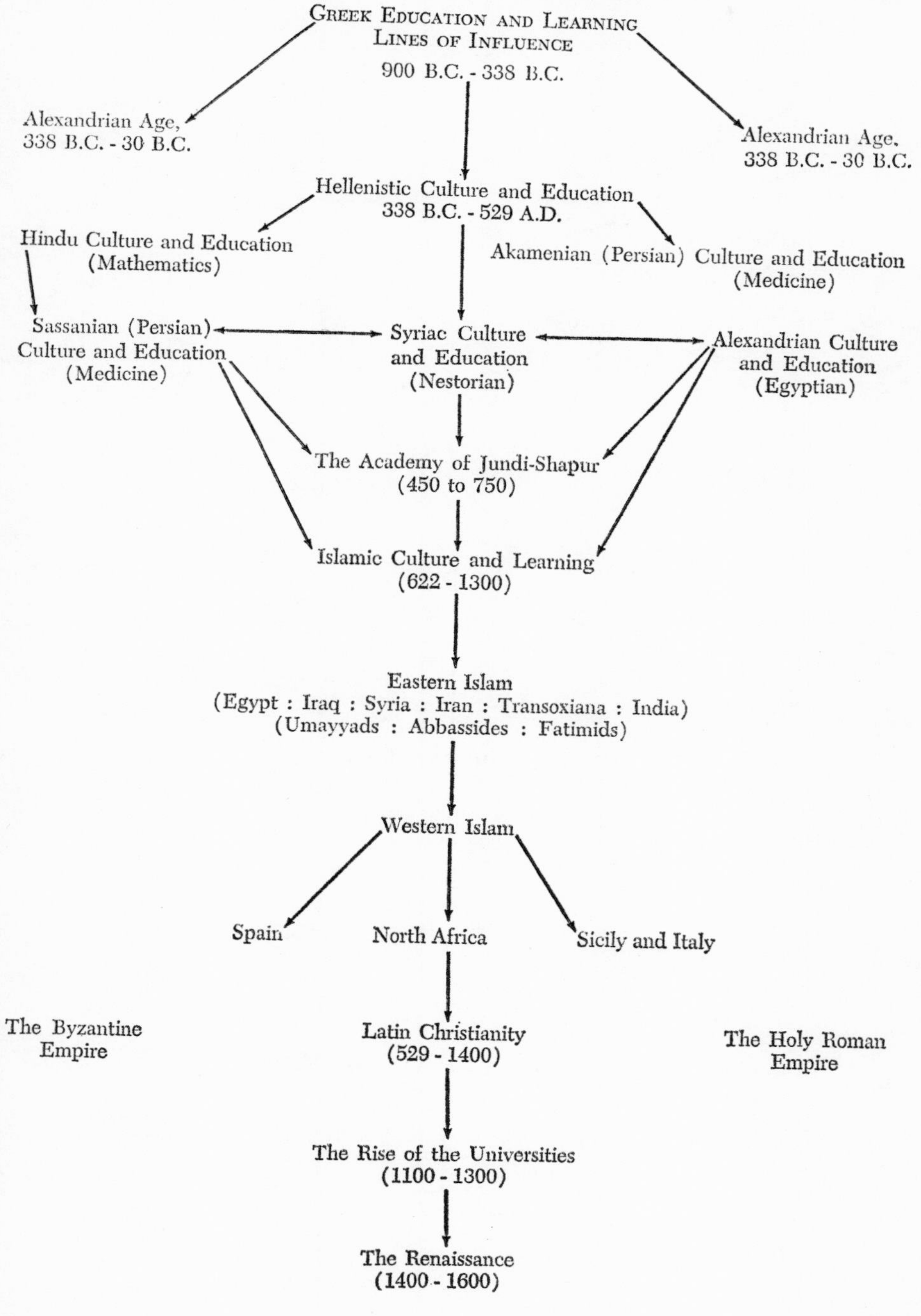
GREEK EDUCATION AND LEARNING
LINES OF INFLUENCE
900 B.C. - 338 B.C.
Alexandrian Age,
338 B.C. - 30 B.C.
Alexandrian Age,
338 B.C. - 30 B.C.
Hellenistic Culture and Education
338 B.C. - 529 A.D.
Hindu Culture and Education
(Mathematics)
Akamenian (Persian) Culture and Education
(Medicine)
Sassanian (Persian)
Culture and Education
(Medicine)
Syriac Culture
and Education
(Nestorian)
Alexandrian Culture
and Education
(Egyptian)
The Academy of Jundi-Shapur
(450 to 750)
Islamic Culture and Learning
(622 - 1300)
Eastern Islam
(Egypt : Iraq : Syria : Iran : Transoxiana : India)
(Umayyads : Abbassides : Fatimids)
Western Islam
Spain
North Africa
Sicily and Italy
The Byzantine
Empire
Latin Christianity
(529 - 1400)
The Holy Roman
Empire
The Rise of the Universities
(1100 - 1300)
The Renaissance
(1400 - 1600)

Islamic Learning and the West
Lines of Influence

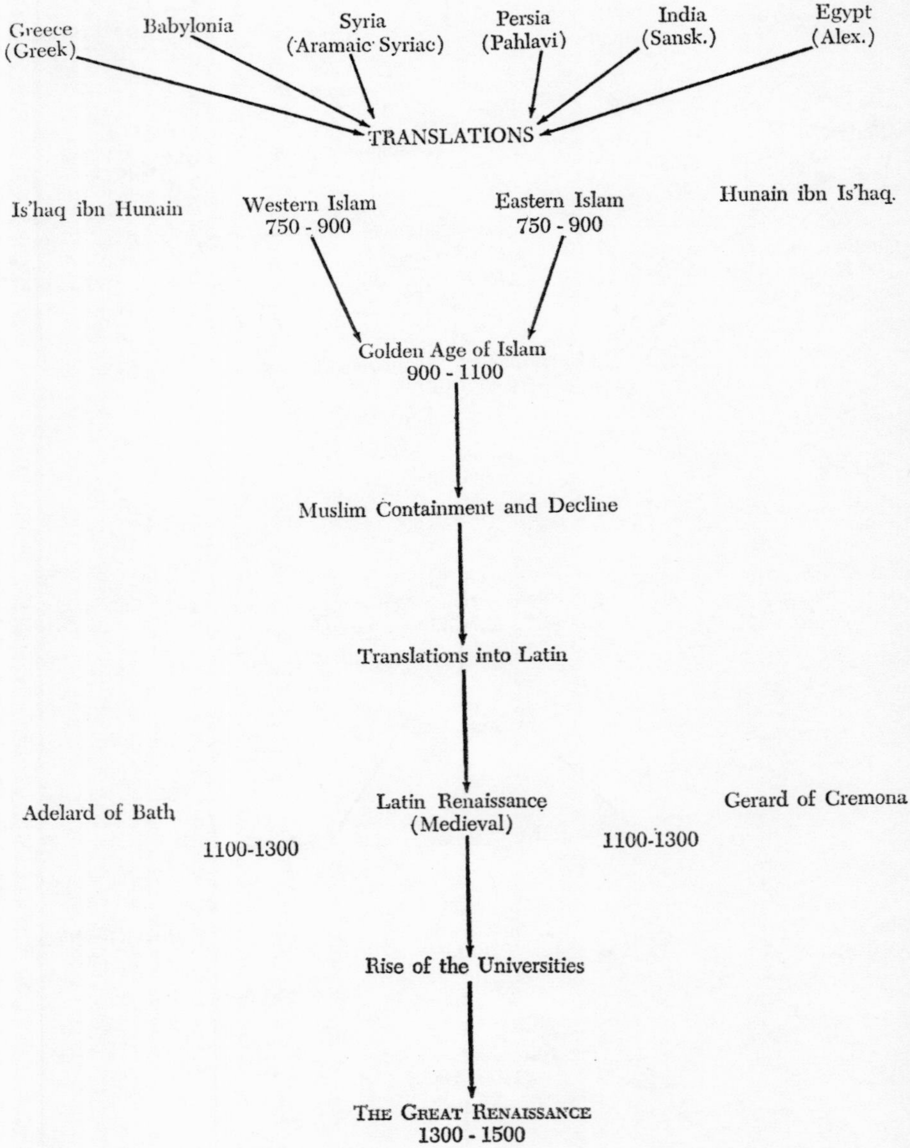

INFLUENCES OF MUSLIM PHILOSOPHY ON EUROPEAN PHILOSOPHY

			100 A.H.
718 A.D. Neo-Platonic	Augustinian-Hellenistic influences (Neo-Platonic)	ibn al-Muqaffa killed	140 A.H.
		Baghdad Founded	145 A.H.
			208 A.H.
		Decree that Qur'an is created	212 A.H.
		Bait-al-Hikma founded	217 A.H.
		al-Nazzam died	231 A.H.
		al-Bukhari died	257 A.H.
818 A.D. Scholasticism			
		al-Ashari professes Ortholoxy	300 A.H.
			306 A.H.
918 A.D.	Uncertain and undetermined Islamic Hellenistic influences	al-Matarich died	323 A.H.
	positive influence	al-Farabi died	339 A.H.
		Fatimites in Cairo, Egypt founded	388 A.H.
			409 A.H.
1018 A.D.	positive	ibn Sina died	428 A.H.
		Seljuk Turks in Baghdad	448 A.H.
		Asharites tolerated	455 A.H.
	negative influences	al-Ghazzali died	505 A.H.
			512 A.H.
1118 A.D. Aristotelian	College of Toledo: under Gondisawi (translators) sponsored by Raymond Archbishop of Toledo 1130-1150	ibn Bajja (Avenpace) died	533 A.H.
		Jehuda hal-Levi died	540 A.H.
	Arabic Philosophy and Science: al-Farabi Avicenna	Saladin in Egypt (end of Fatimites)	566 A.H.
	Special influence on John of Salisburg d. 1182	ibn Tufail died	581 A.H.
	University of Naples by Frederick II (devoted to transmission of Islamic science to Latin world)	ibn Rushd died	598 A.H.
		Maimonides died	601 A.H.
			615 A.H.
	Arabic science, philosophy Averroes	ibn Tumbus died	620 A.H.
		ibn Arabi died	638 A.H.
1218 A.D. Scholasticism	Special influence on: University of Bologna and Padua Avicenna - Averroes	Halagu takes Baghdad (end of Califate)	656 A.H.
	Albertus Magnus d. 1248 Thomas Aquinus d. 1274 Alexander Hales d. 1245	Fall of the Muwahhids in Spain	667 A.H.
	Averroism Special influence Dons Scotus d. 1308		
1268 A.D.	Peak of Scholasticism		

CHAPTER IX *

THE TRANSMISSION OF MUSLIM LEARNING AND EUROPE'S INTELLECTUAL AWAKENING

IN THE CHAPTER dealing with Muslim libraries, we have seen something of the great importance of both the public and private libraries as educational and research centers in Muslim cultures and noted particularly those in Persia, Iraq, Egypt, Sicily, southern Italy, North Africa and Spain. Unfortunately, many of these libraries, some historians say all, were destroyed in Eastern Islam in the Mongol invasions of the thirteenth century, others during the crusades, and those in Spain and North Africa by the Spaniards following their liberation from Muslim rule. The extent of this destruction, however, as previously noted, has been exaggerated by both Muslim and Western historians. Many of the Western libraries were out of reach of the early Mongol invaders and escaped destruction. Many private libraries owned copies of great books and managed to keep them out of the hands of invaders. However, and most important, the substance of the best of these works, as we shall show in the pages that follow, were saved for the Latin schoolmen of western Europe in the "nick of time," so to speak, through translations into Latin, Hebrew, Spanish, Italian, Greek, Catalan and other languages during the twelfth and thirteenth centuries just before the devastating Mongolian invasions.

How extensive and varied these translations were may be inferred from the list of translators and their works included in the Appendix. To indicate the extent of Muslim scholastic contributions to Western education and the European Renaissance, those resulting directly from these translations will be discussed in this final chapter. The labor of translation fell upon Jews, Nestorians, and Western Christians, mostly Englishmen but also Italians and others. Jews who migrated from Muslim into Christian lands found it necessary to translate Muslim works into Hebrew. These translations were predominantly Jewish works on various subjects which had been written originally in Arabic. Many of these were also translated later into Latin and other European

*All dates refer to A.D. unless otherwise specified.

languages. Persian literary works also found their way into Latin and Western literature with a marked influence.

Persian Literary Works

The Fables of Bed Pai is of Hindu origin and was translated from Sanskrit with some adaptations into Pahlavi in the sixth century. It was rendered into Arabic by the Persian ibn Muqaffa in the eighth century, and it is from this version that translations have been made into Latin and thirty-nine other languages.[1]

The Hazar Afsana, which was translated into Arabic, as *Alf-Lailatun wa Laila,* or *One Thousand Nights and One,* and later merely as *Arabian Nights,* was first referred to in Masudi's *Meadows of Gold and Fields of Gems,* in which he gives a description of the plan and theme of the book.[2] The original stories (or many of them) are of Hindu origin, although the *Hazar Dastan* makes generous adaptations of them in the Pahlavi edition as well as liberal additions and subtractions. In fact, there were so many varied selections and adaptations in the early collections of these tales that there is no way of ascertaining which are the originals among the tales of the present *Arabian Nights.* A sixteenth-century incomplete Arabic manuscript of the *Arabian Nights* was translated into French as *Les Mille et Une Nuits* by the Orientalist Antoine Galland and, thereafter, into scores of both European and Oriental languages. It is relatively safe to say that the *Fables of Bed Pai,* the *Arabian Nights,* and Omar's *Rubaiyyat* are among the most widely-read translated literatures of Muslim origin of the period under this survey in the non-Muslim world. What child does not know the "Story of Ali-Baba and the Forty Thieves," or "Sinbad the Sailor"! And what adult cannot recite some of Khayyam's quatrains—at least, "A book of verses underneath the bough. . . ."

Shah-Namah of the Persian poet-philosopher Firdawsi of Tus finds its inspiration and at least part of its historic-legendary materials in the poet Daqiqi's poem, the *Khudai-Namah* (*Book of Kings*), a collection of Persian legends gathered by Danishwar in the seventh century (651). Firdawsi's *Shah-Namah (Book of Kings)* was a monumental literary work comprising 60,000 couplets (120,000 lines). It was completed in the first decade of the eleventh century but only after thirty-five years of concentrated writing.[3] Translations or adaptations of it have been made in several European languages.

Omar Khayyam, the great "medieval" mathematician-astronomer of the eleventh-twelfth centuries, has already appeared in this study as a man of science. The *Rubai* is a poem of four lines which rhymes *a-a-b-a;* consequently the *Rubaiyyat* is a series of independent quatrains or four-line poems. Some twelve hundred such quatrains have been attributed to Omar, although the oldest known manuscript,[4] dating from 1460, lists only 158 stanzas.[5] The *Rubaiyyat* was translated into English quatrains, some faithfully, some liberally, and some in combinations of two or more original quatrains, and still some as sources of inspiration, by their greatest translator, Edward Fitzgerald in 1859, whose first translation consisted of seventy-five quatrains; the last one hundred ten quatrains.

The *Mathnawi* of Jalal-al-Din Rumi. Jalal-al-Din (Muhammad ibn Muhammad ibn Husain al-Balkhi) Rumi (1207-1273 A.D.) is the greatest Sufi or mystic poet of Persia. He was founder of the mystic society of dervishes known as the Maulawi. His greatest work, the *Mathnawi,* is a poem consisting of 40,000 double-rhymed verses arranged in six books, much of which was dictated by the poet to his disciple and assistant, Husam-al-Din. Translations of the *Mathnawi* into European languages were made during the nineteenth century.*

The *Gulistan* and *Bustan* of Sa'di. Sa'di has already been discussed at length as a moralist and educator. His two basic works, the *Bustan, Scented Garden,* (1257) and the *Gulistan, Rose Garden,* (1258), both dedicated to the thirteenth-century Persian monarch Atabak Abu Bakr Sa'd ibn Zanji, have enjoyed popularity both in Iran and in translations in Eastern and Western languages. The entire collection of Sa'di's works, the *Diwan,* was brought together and arranged between 726-734 A.H. (1326-1334 A.D.) by Ali ibn Ahmad ibn Bisutun. The best translations of Sa'di's *Bustan, Gulistan,* and selections from his other works (marathi's or elegies; ghazals or odes; mukatta'at or moral aphorisms and epigrams; rubaiyyat or quatrains; and mufarradat or distiches) into European languages took place during the nineteenth and twentieth centuries.†

Works on Mathematics

The Hindu numerals, explained by Khwarizmi in the ninth century and Biruni in the eleventh, were finally introduced into Latin Europe by Adelard of Bath and through an adaptation by Ibrahim ibn Ezra in the twelfth. They were then used together or in mixed forms with Roman numerals throughout the twelfth and thirteenth

*Important among these are a metrical version of the First Book of the "Mesnevi" by J. W. Redhouse, London, 1881; an abridged translation of the *Mathnawi* by E. H. Whinfield, 1898; selected translations of *Mathnawi* in German verse (*Diwan-i-Shams-i-Tabriz*) by V. von Rosensweig, Vienna, 1838.

†Among the earliest of these translations are Harrington's complete works (*Kulliyyat*) of Sa'di (edited) with English translations of selected prose treatises, Calcutta, 1791-1795; Graf's German translation of *Gulistan* (*Rosengarten*), Leibzig, 1846, and of *Bustan,* Vienna, 1850; another translation of *Bustan* by Schlechta-Wssehrd, Vienna, 1852; an English prose translation of *Bustan* by H. W. Clarke in 1879, and in verse by G. S. Davie in 1882; a French translation of *Bustan* by Barbier de Meynard in 1880; a translation of *Gulistan* into English by Eastwick in 1852 and by Platts in 1873, and the first four chapters in 1899 by Sir Edwin Arnold; a French translation of *Gulistan* by Defremery in 1858, and a German translation by Graf in 1846. (See S. Robinson's *Persian Poetry for English Readers,* 1883, pp. 245-366; and E. G. Browne, *Literary History of Persia,* pp. 525-539.)

centuries. Although these numerals were being used in northern Italy toward the end of the thirteenth century, the abacus (introduced into Europe by the Muslims) and other counting devices remained commonplace north of the Mediterranean. Hindu numerals were not employed universally for another three hundred years.

Latin Europe's first complete explanation of Hindu numerals was written by Bibonacci in a book entitled *Liber Abaci,* and the numerals were popularized further by Sacrabosso and Villedieu. They were referred to as Arabic—even Jewish numerals.[6] Decimal fractions, weights and measures had to wait much longer.

During the twelfth century these mathematical works were translated mainly into Latin; during the thirteenth cenutry, into Hebrew. Many of these were made from Spanish versions which were prepared by the group under the patronage of King Alfonso, but still later directly from Greek into Latin by William of Moerbeke. They were made from various versions of Arabic works or translations of Greek and Hellenistic authors.

Works on Medicine

The concept of the public hospital, says Elgood, is Persia's "greatest and most lasting legacy to Europe." The modern hospital is a direct growth from Persian foundations which were laid in the medical school of the University of Jundi-Shapur, dating back to the reign of Shapur I (died 271).[7] The hospital and the medical center combined Greco-Hindu principles with native efficiency, thereby developing, according to al-Qifti, "new methods in the treatment of disease along pharmacological lines so that their therapy was judged superior to that of the Greeks and the Hindus." The medical ideals of Jundi-Shapur corresponded with those of modern medicine, says Elgood, in the "study of current methods, modification through experience, and publication for the use of others."[8] The medical disciplines of Jundi-Shapur were transferred to the medical school and hospitals of Baghdad, where such practices as the in- and out-patient system prevailed, particularly in the more advanced hospitals such as the one founded by Adud al-Dawla.

Later in the Muslim period, two first-rank Persian physicians wrote encyclopaedic medical texts that became standard source-books in the medical schools of Europe until the close of the seventeenth century. They were al-Razi (865-925) or Rhazes, who pioneered the discovery of the contagious character of disease and gave the first clinical account of smallpox,[9] and Avicenna, who discovered the contagious character of disease through water.[10] The concepts of Rhazes and Avicenna on the nature of plague were carried further by ibn al-Khatib of Granada (1313-1374). Ibn al-Baitar (died 1248), one of the great Muslim pharmaceutists, wrote one of the most outstanding "medieval" books on botany in which he described some fourteen hundred medical drugs.

Ali al-Hasan ibn al-Haitham (965), known as Alhazen, wrote a great book on optics, *Opticae Thesaurus.* He corrected Euclid's and Ptolemy's theory "that the eye sends out visual rays to the object of vision," by postulating that "it is not a ray that leaves the eye and meets the object that gives rise to vision. Rather the form of the perceived object passes into the eye and is transmuted by its transparent body," or the lens. He also developed the theory of "focusing, magnifying, and inversion of the image."[11]

Works on Music

Islamic musical studies, as initiated by such theorists as Kindi, Avicenna, and Farabi, were translated into Hebrew and Latin as late as Europe's Renaissance period. Many Western writers and musicologists after 1200—Gundisalvus, Robert Kilwardi, Ramon Lull, Adam de Fulda, and George Reish and others—referred to the Latin translations of Farabi's musical writings. The two most frequently cited were his *De Scientiis* and *De Ortu Scientiarum.*

Muslim music was also disseminated over the European continent by the wandering minstrels of medieval times, and these troubadours introduced many Islamic instruments and musical elements.[12] The more notable instruments were the lute (*al-lud*), the pandore (*tanbur*), and the guitar (*gitara*). An important Muslim contribution to the musical heritage of the West was that of mensural music, including mensural values in the notes and rhythmic modes.[13] English Morris dances (Moorish) owe much to Moorish mentas (Morise). Spain adopted many musical models for rhyme and metre from Muslim culture.

Other Works

Although some of the most important scholars and creative minds of the Muslim world belonged to Eastern Islam, it was through Western Islam—Sicily and Spain in particular—that Latin Europe made considerable contacts with Islamic learning in the twelfth and thirteenth centuries, and to a smaller extent in the fourteenth. These contacts were made through two principal channels. One was the result of the flow of European students and scholars who studied in the Muslim colleges and universities of Spain, Sicily and southern Italy. The second came from the Latin scholars' direct contacts with original Muslim books and the eventual translation of the most significant of these into Latin as well as other European languages.

By the mid-1300's the number of these translated works had reached between twelve and fifteen hundred. Although many of them are now lost, we know that in the scope of their areas of learning these translations included studies in philosophy, theology, medicine, mathematics, astronomy, technology, history and historiography, natural sciences, biographies, fables, literary works, geography, music, and encyclopaedias. The translators were predominantly Sicilians, Spaniards, French, English, Germans, Greeks, Catalans, and Hebrews. An alphabetic catalogue of their names with the important translated works of the twelfth and thirteenth centuries, and of part of the fourteenth, appears in the Appendix. We shall summarize here the basic works of several of the leading translators.

Adelard of Bath translated, among others, Euclid from Arabic (1120), and al-Khwarizmi's astronomical tables (1126) which introduced Muslim trigonometry into Western curriculum. Our term logarithmic is a corruption of al-Khwarizmi. Aristippus of Catania (1156) in Sicily under the patronage of Frederick II translated Diogenes Laertius' *Lives of the Philosophers* and Plato's *Meno* and *Phaedo.*

Constantine Africanus of Carthage, a monk at Monte Cassino (died 1087), according to the historian Leo of Ostila was "the master of East and West." He translated works on Muslim medicine and other sciences which profoundly influenced the study of science in southern Italy. Among his translations were *Liber Experimentorum* of Razi (Rhazes), medical works of Isaac Judaeus, Arabic version of Hippocrates, *Aphorisms* by Hunain, and an Arabic version of Galen's *Commentary* by Hunain. Eugene of Palermo, in Sicily under the patronage of Frederick II, translated Ptolemy's *Optics* and cooperated with an unknown translator on an 1154 edition of the *Almagest.* Fara ben Salim of Girgenti, a Jewish scholar, translated al-Razi's *Liber Continens* under the patronage of Norman rulers.

Gerard of Cremona (died 1187) translated seventy-one works with the aid of some Christian and Jewish scholars during the last nine years of his life. Among them were Aristotle's *Posterior Analytics, On the Heaven and the Earth, On Generation and corruption, On Meteorology;* Alexander of Aphrodisias' *Commentaries;* Euclid's *Elements and Data;* Archimedes' *On the Measurement of the Circle;* Apollonius of Perq's (or Perga) *Conics;* Galen's eleven works; several works on Greek astronomy; four Greco-Arabic medical works; Avicenna's largest work, the *Canon;* al-Razi's largest medical work; al-Farabi's *On the Syllogism;* al-Kindi, three works; Isaac Israeli, two works; fourteen other works on Muslim mathematics and astronomy; three sets of astronomical tables and seven Muslim works on geomancy and astrology.

Gundisalvus translated some of the works that John of Seville had rendered into Castilian. He and Avendeath, together, translated into Latin Avicebron's *Mekor Hayim* (*Fountain of Life*) as *Fons Vitalis.* Avendeath (the Jew, John ibn David of Seville), who was in Gundisalvus' school of translators, rendered Arabic and Jewish versions of the works of ibn Sina, al-Farabi, al-Ghazzali, al-Khwarizmi, and the pseudo-Aristotelian work, *The Secretum Secretorum.* James of Venice, patronized by Norman rulers, translated Aristotle's *Topics* and *Posterior Analytics* before 1125.

John of Gorze, from a monastery in Lorraine, was commissioned by the German emperor, Otto the Great, to the court of Abd-al-Rahman III of Cordova on a diplomatic mission, where he spent three years learning the Arabic language. Upon his return to Germany he brought a horse-load of Arabic books on scientific and other subjects, perhaps introducing and extending the interest in and influence of Muslim learning "down the Rhine into Flanders."[14]

John of Seville (Arabic version of his name, ibn Da'ud, or Son of David) translated into Latin or Castilian a large number of the works of Avicenna both from Arabic originals and Hebrew translations, some of the works of al-Ghazzali, works of al-Farabi, works of al-Khwarizmi, and others. The latter translations were instrumental in introducing Hindu-Arabic numerals to the West.

Michael Scot worked under the patronage of Frederick II at Foggia. Among his translations were al-Bitruji's *Spherics* (a critique of Ptolemy) and Aristotle's *History of Animals* (from the Arabic version) including "On the Parts of Animals," and "On the Generation of Animals"; perhaps also his *Metaphysics, Physics, On the Heavens, Ethics* and *On the Soul.* Some of these works influenced the thinking of Roger Bacon and Albertus Magnus. Peter the Venerable, with the aid of his Christian and Arab associates, translated the *Qur'an* in 1141.

Plato of Tivoli translated in 1145 the mathematical work *Hibbur ha-Meshi hah* of the Jewish mathematician Abraham bar Hiyya. Plato laments the dearth of scientific knowledge in Latin, saying, "The Latins . . . have not a single author in astronomy. For books they have only foolish dreams and old wives' fables. This is the reason which has moved me, Plato of Tivoli, to enrich our tongue with that which it lacked the most, by drawing upon the treasures of an unknown language."[15] Just as the early Middle Ages had to digest the science contained in Pliny's *Natural History* and Seneca's *Natural Questions*, the later Middle Ages had to digest and to understand the new Greek-Arabic learning.[16]

Raymon of Toledo (1125-1155) was active in promoting translations of Muslim scientific books into Latin. There was "a wealth of Arabic books [in Toledo], and a number of masters of the two tongues [Arabic and Latin], and with the help of these Mozarabes, i.e., Arabized Christians and resident Jews, there arose a regular school for the translation of Arabic-Latin books of science which drew from all lands those who thirsted for knowledge."[17] Robert of Chester translated a Muslim work on chemistry and alchemy in 1144 and introduced both fields into Latin education for the first time.

William of Moerbeke, the Flemish archbishop of Corinth, in Sicily under patronage of Frederick II, translated Aristotle's *History of Animals*, "On the Generation of Animals," *Politics, Rhetoric, Metaphysics* (revision), *Meteorology* (revision), *On the Soul* (revision), perhaps also *Ethics, Commentaries* on Plato and Aristotle, Hippocrates' *Prognostics,* Galen's *On Foods,* Hero of Alexandria's *Physics,* and Archimedes' *Physics*. St. Thomas Aquinas was a Dominican friend of the archbishop, who made some of his translations at Aquinas' request. These, along with translations of Arabic works, were part of the source materials for Aquinas' great work, *Summa Theologica.*

Such translations as those mentioned above, and others made directly from Islamic works (see Appendix), not only enriched the curriculum of European schools (in some cases to the present day in both Europe and America) but revolutionized the thinking of educators and scholars. They stimulated scientific and humanistic inquiries and were largely responsible for the development of universities in Europe during the twelfth and thirteenth centuries. They expanded and deepened the mathematical disciplines, widened the theory and practice of medicine, disturbed Christian theology through conflicts with Muslim astronomy, put new life and material into branches of philosophic inquiry, and introduced new methodology into European instruction of the natural sciences. However, most important for the modern world, they stimulated—perhaps initiated—the tremendous social-cultural-educational awakening known as the European Renaissance.

Latin Translations of Muslim Works and the Rise of Western Universities

Latin education before the twelfth century was dominated by the disciplines known as the Seven Liberal Arts. These were the *trivium* or elementary training in language and literature, including grammar, dialectics, rhetoric, and logic; and *quadrivium* or the mathematical arts and sciences, including arithmetic, geometry, astronomy, and music. To these were added studies in fine arts and some training in industry, particularly in handicraft. Also literary classical studies, including some history and scholastic philosophy, were all geared predominantly to the study of law, theology, architecture, medicine, history, grammar (emphasizing proficiency in both written and spoken Latin), and literary appreciation through the study of Roman literary works. Rhetoric was mainly the study of the art of writing letters, the reading of epitomes of the subject, and the study of Cicero and Quintilian. Logic (Aristotelian) was the master study, overshadowing all other medieval intellectual disciplines. Music was dominated by a religious orientation. Arithmetic, geometry (with geography) and astronomy were rudimentary and of little consequence until the introduction of the Indo-Zoroastrian and Greco-Muslim mathematics and astronomy into the European curriculum in the twelfth and thirteenth centuries.

Indeed, the eleventh through thirteenth centuries—especially between 1050 and 1300—may be thought of as the renaissance of medieval learning, the intellectual, literary and esthetic flowering of the Middle Ages. In the area of intellectual revival, in science and philosophy, this early European Renaissance was stimulated largely by the influx of Greco-Muslim scholarship in an ever increasing number of translations from Arabic into Latin and Hebrew, or from Arabic into Hebrew or Spanish, and from these into Latin. Moreover, this passion for Greco-Muslim learning in a sense characterized the very nature of this early renaissance and gave this renaissance its intellectual-educational scope and direction. To receive and assimilate the substance of this Greco-Muslim thought became the dominant interest of intellectual life of the Latin-Christian world of that time, to which Latin scholarship throughout these two hundred years was devoted primarily. Its educational institutions and curricula were reconstructed and enlarged as this new knowledge became available to the scholar and the schoolman in abundance. The concepts of the Seven Liberal Arts gave way to an extensive system of new scientific knowledge and philosophic disciplines, modifying and replacing the traditional disciplines.

If the inspiration for this renaissance came from within the Latin-Christian world, certainly its stimulation—to a large extent its substance and intellectual direction—came from the Muslim world, which gave the European revival its form as well as content. What the European intellectual talked about, wrote about, and taught involved Indo-Persian, Greek, Syriac-Hellenistic, Chinese, and Muslim-Hebrew sciences and philosophies. Also included was the experimental spirit of observation and inquiry, which the Muslims had adapted from their Greek and Hellenistic teachers and transmitted to the Latin world without fully understanding or exploiting its far-reaching possibilities and promises themselves.

The translations of Greek, Persian, Hindu, Syrian, as well as purely Muslim works from Arabic into Latin introduced into European learning new concepts of scholastic research, such as the mathematical, historical, and experimental, and somewhat later the neo-Aristotelian logical methods of inquiry. It also introduced the art of translation itself, with its emphasis upon accuracy, thoroughness and faithfulness, disciplines which were not always adhered to even by the best translators of this period. Most important, these translations constituted the bulk of available Muslim and classical learning and literary masterpieces. Thus in time they were made accessible to European scholars, teachers and students.

Of prime importance also was the influence of Muslim philosophy both pure and scholastic, particularly the philosophical and/or theological systems of the intellectual giants of Islam—ibn Sina, al-Ghazzali and ibn Rushd—upon European philosophers, most of whom devoted much of their intellectual energies and talents to the repudiation of the philosophies of these Muslim thinkers. This attitude was particularly true of Albertus Magnus (1193-1280) and Thomas Aquinas, the former attacking largely the Aristotelianism of ibn Sina; the latter that of ibn Rushd.

The flowering of this renaissance of scholarship stimulated by Greco-Muslim sciences, literature and philosophies was the advent of a new institution of learning in Europe—the university. It was through this new center of learning that Greco-Muslim knowledge, methodology of research, technology, and the utilitarian arts, along with traditional humanistic studies, combined to initiate a scientific renaissance that was to expand into every field of knowledge in the centuries that followed. True, there had been available among Latin scholars translations from Greek into Latin of some of the works of Euclid and Galen, even of Plato's *Dialogues,* and perhaps other Greek authors. True also, some of these were more faithful translations of Greek works than the Latin translations of them or of other works from Arabic. But the dependence of twelfth and thirteenth century European scholars upon Muslim works was not altogether for the sake of reaching the Greek and Hellenistic sciences. It was to assimilate and utilize the monumental contributions of Muslim thought to science, philosophy and literature as well.

The first appearance of European universities coincided with the vast influx of translations, adaptations, and commentaries of Muslim works in sciences, technology, philosophy, and theology. Indeed, these universities were brought about as a result of this wholesale importation, whereby not only Muslim creative works but also Greco-Hellenistic, Syriac-Zoroastrian, and Hindu materials reached the Latin world of the West through these Arabic translations, commentaries, and adaptations. This inflow included also scientific and philosophic works which, although brought to Europe's attention through Latin versions of them as derived from Arabic translations, were being translated now directly from Greek.

The first European universities began to appear during the second half of the twelfth century. Prior to this period, the Academy of Jundi-Shapur, the Museum of Alexandria, the Bait-al-Hikmahs of Baghdad and Cairo, and the system of madrasahs (high schools and colleges) initiated by Nizam-al-Mulk were restrictive in aim and scope. From their usual position of being associated with or developed from important libraries which facilitated the tools of scholarly investigations, these academies were in some cases (Jundi-Shapur, the Museum of Alexandria and the Houses of Wisdom) research centers which were often motivated and sustained by the presence of famous scholars, only to disintegrate and disappear when these great masters left for another center or passed away. In the meantime, however, students and scholars alike flocked to these centers from all over Islam and remained long enough to empty the master scholar's "bag of knowledge." They would then move to other centers for further elaboration on what had been acquired, or throw new light on both old and new subjects. This was also the tradition which was followed in the early twelfth and thirteenth century European universities.

It should be noted, however, that European universities were more in line with the Greek lyceum and the academy and perhaps that of the Persian Jundi-Shapur than they were with the schools of higher learning in Muslim and Hebrew cultures. The beginnings of these early European universities—*studium generale*—are obscure. But by the end of the twelfth century there were five of them in existence: Salerno (basically a medical school) and Bologna (essentially a law school) in Italy; Paris and Montpellier in France and Oxford in England. The greatest of them was the University of Paris, of which Oxford was an offshoot and in turn "gave birth" to Cambridge in 1209. Other universities developing in the thirteenth century were Padua, 1222; Naples, 1224; Orleans, Angiers and Salamanca in Spain.

These early Western universities were created primarily to assimilate and utilize the new inflow of Muslim and classical learning which was available to Latin schoolmen and scholars in translations. The bulk of these, along with the creations of European scholars, dominated the European curriculum through to the end of the fifteenth century. In the words of Sarton, "Nothing can better illustrate the intellectual revolution caused in the Christian West by the sudden transmission of Greco-Arabic [Greco-Zoroastrian-Hindu-Muslim] culture" than the emergence of these early European universities. And, perhaps, nothing can show more clearly the original pragmatic motivation of a university than the demand of growing cities at this time for the acquisition and utilitarian application of these newly found knowledges and skills through these new centers of learning and teaching.

As we move into the thirteenth century the importance of these universities for both intellectual and general over-all progress becomes obvious to laymen and the elite. These institutions receive royal and ecclesiastical sanction and support, and the result is further curricular development within the early universities as well as the founding of new universities and special schools. For example, in Italy there were the following: Vicenza (1204) and Reggio (1210) Universities for general studies; the Arezzo Law School (1215); the Padua Studium Generale (1222); Naples (1224); the Papal University of Roman Curia (1244-45); the Siena School of Civil Law (1246, refounded by Charles IV in 1357); and the Piacenze Town School (1248). France developed the Orleans Law School (sanctioned by Clement V in 1306), Angiers (an older school reorganized as a law school in 1398) and the University of Toulouse (1230). England developed Balliol (1266), the Theological and Law University of Merton (1264 ?), University College (1280) and Peterhouse (1284). Spain developed the Cathedral School of Valencia (1212-14), Salamanca University (before 1230); Valladolid University (consecrated by Clement VI in 1346 but dating back to the mid-thirteenth century), the Seville School of Muslim Arabic Studies (one of a number of such schools in Murcia and in Tunis, its charter granted by Alfonso el Sabio in 1254) and the University of Lerida (1300. Portugal developed the University of Lisbon, founded in 1290 and moved to Coimbra in 1308-1309.

Translations of Muslim Works and Expansion of Europe's Curriculum

The results of translations of Muslim works upon the curriculum of Western Europe were revolutionary. This was particularly true in the reconstruction and enlargement of the curriculum of schools in such areas as mathematics, medicine, astronomy, philology, physics, chemistry, geography, history, music, theology and philosophy—a curricular transformation which no doubt shared in the twelfth and thirteenth century growth of European universities.[18]

It stimulated the further development of medical theory and practice, modified theological doctrines, initiated new worlds in mathematics, brought about new controversial philosophies and theologies.

Through Spain, which had itself assimilated the best of the Muslim East's learned contributions and made significant, varied additions of its own, much of Islamic science, philosophy, and art was introduced into Latin Europe. These materials, as stated previously, reached Europe through two main channels: (a) Through students and scholars from Western Europe studying in Spanish colleges and universities and (b) through translations of Muslim works from Arabic sources.

The intellectual ascendancy of Muslim Spain began in the tenth century, but its most significant contributions were made during the period from the latter half of the eleventh century to the middle of the thirteenth. We find such prominent men as the geographers al-Idrisi and al-Bakri, the great physician ibn Zuhr, the mystic ibn Arabi, the Jewish savant Maimonides, the traveller ibn Jubair, and the philosopher ibn Rushd. Europe absorbed the intellectual contributions of these men, along with those of Eastern Islam, when Toledo fell back into Christian hands in 1085, Cordova in 1236, Seville in 1248 and Granada in 1492.[19] Let us see what specific changes and additions the new learning made upon some aspects of the European curriculum.

Algebra. The science of algebra was transmitted to the West through Latin translations by Adelard of Bath, John of Seville, and Robert of Chester. (Plato of Tivoli also translated from Arabic into Latin the *Spherics* of Theodosius of Bythinia. It was further introduced through Febonacci's writings and Abraham bar Hiyya's Hebrew treatise translated into Latin by Plato of Tivoli in 1145.)

Geometry. Euclidean geometry reached Europe through Arabic translations and numerous commentaries (fourteen) on Euclid's books. Abd al-Baqi's *Commentaries on Euclid's Book X* was translated into

Latin toward the end of the twelfth century by Gerard of Cremona. Adelard of Bath made the first Latin translation of Euclid from Arabic in the second quarter of the twelfth century. It was reissued about a century later by Giovani Campano, and in 1482 the first printed edition of Euclid was made. It was reprinted in 1509.

Trigonometry and Astronomy. Most astronomical tables incorporated in their introductory statements the trigonometrical theories implied in their computations. The famous *Toledan Tables* of the Hispano-Muslim al-Zarqali were translated into Latin by Gerard of Cremona. Al-Khwarizmi's *Astronomical Tables* were revised by Maslama ibn Ahmad of Madrid in the tenth century, translated by Adelard of Bath and again by Hermann. A revised edition was made by Robert of Chester. Robert also made an adapted translation of al-Battani and al-Zarqali's *Tables* in 1149. Al-Battani's work had also been translated in 1145 by Plato of Tivoli. *Saphaea Arzachelis,* the name given to al-Zarqali's astro-table, was used in Spain at the beginning of the twelfth century and considerably later in the Latin world. Jacob ben Mahir and John of Brescia translated a description of it into Latin in 1263.

Astronomical translations from Arabic into Latin of the twelfth century included the tenth-century treatise of Maslama ibn Ahmad al-Majriti by John of Seville and again by Rudolf of Burges and the eleventh-century treatise of ibn al-Jaffar by Plato of Tivoli. The twelfth-century treatise of Jabir ibn Aflah, the *Islah-al-Majisti (Correction of the Almagest),* a semi-refutation of Ptolemaic astronomy, sustained also by ibn Tufail and al-Bitruji, was translated into Latin by Gerard of Cremona about 1187 and made a profound impression upon European schoolmen. A Hebrew translation of it was made about a century later. Jabir's views were carried to Egypt by Maimonides in 1165 and farther east by his disciple, Joseph ben Judah ben Aquin. Moses ben Tibbon, another Jewish linguist, translated the *Almagest* into Hebrew in 1274 and al-Bitruji's *Kitab al-Hai'a* (*Book of Astronomy)* in 1259, forty-two years after Michael Scot had translated it into Latin.*

The *Kitab al-Manazir* of ibn al-Haitham, dealing in part with optics, was translated into Latin by Gerard of Cremona, and the book became a basis for both Muslim and Latin opticians. An elaborate commentary on *Kitab al-Manazir* was written at the beginning of the fourteenth century by Kamal al-Din al-Farisi, a disciple of Qutb al-Din al-Shirazi, the author of *Nihayat al-Idrak* (*The End of Thought*) in which he gives an account of the rainbow.

*By 1231, Jacob Anatoli had translated the *Almagest* into Hebrew. Consequently, by the time the Muslims had outgrown the *Almagest,* the Latin world was beginning to read it. Gerard of Cremona tranlated it from Arabic into Latin about 1175, and a Latin edition prepared from Greek had appeared in Sicily fifteen years previously.

Music. The Islamic creation of mensural music had already reached Europe by the end of the eleventh century. One of the first Muslim treatises on music was translated into Latin by Adelard of Bath, and Abraham bar Hiyya translated another into Hebrew. Many monographs on music were written during this period.

Chemistry. Robert of Chester made a Latin translation from Arabic of *Liber de Compositione Alchemise.* About the same time Hugh of Santalla translated the *Emerald Table.* Gerard of Cremona later translated al-Razi's study of salts and alums, which "was a very valuable contribution in the right direction . . . a treatise on practical chemistry based on genuine experiments and describing the methods of preparation of many substances. The importance of al-Razi's treatise and of its impact upon Latin culture, e.g., through Vincent of Beauvais and Bacon, can hardly be exaggerated."[20] Alfred of Sareshel translated the alchemical part of the Persian physician ibn Sina's *Kitab al-Shafa* (the *Book of Healing*) toward the end of the twelfth century, a work which "exerted a deep and beneficial influence upon Latin writers."[21]

Gerard of Cremona translated *Kitab al-Tasrif* of Abu al-Qasim al-Zahrawi; Shem-tob ben Isaac, a century later, translated it into Hebrew, and other translations into Hebrew were made by Meshullam ben Jonah. Also, the medical section of *Tasrif* was rendered into Latin by Simon of Genoa and Abraham ben Shem-tob. Constantine the African translated into Latin ibn Jafar's *Zad-al-Musafi* (*Viaticum Peregrinantis*); another Latin translation was made by Stephen of Saragossa, and a Hebrew translation by Moses ben Tibbon. In addition, many treatises on Hippocrates were translated from Arabic into Latin by Gerard of Cremona and Marc of Toledo and into Hebrew by Shem-tob ben Isaac and Nathan he' Me'ati.

The important Arabic translations of and commentary on Galen during the second half of the ninth century by Hunain ibn Is'haq and his disciples were translated into Latin by Gerard of Cremona, Marc of Toledo and Faraj ben Salim, and into Hebrew by al-Harizi, Zerahiah Gracian, Nathan he'Me'ati, and Solomon ben Nathan, or from Hebrew into Latin by Armengand, son of Blaise. Ibn al-Wafid's treatise on drugs was translated by Gerard of Cremona in the first half of the eleventh century, and another study on the same subject by Masawaih al-Maridini was translated into Hebrew by Jacob of Capua about the same time. Ammar ibn Ali's works on eye diseases were translated into Hebrew by Nathan he'Me'ati. Ali ibn Ridivaus' *Commentary on Tequi* was translated into Latin by Gerard of Cremona and into Hebrew by Samuel ben Tibbon before the end of the eleventh century.

Ibn Sina's *Qanun (The Medical Encyclopedia),* the "bible of medieval medicine," was translated into Latin by Gerard of Cremona; in part into Hebrew by Zerahiah Gracian and Moses ben Tibbon. A complete Hebrew version was prepared in 1279 by Nathan he'Me'ati.

Ibn Sina's *Arjuza* and ibn Rushd's commentary on it were translated into Hebrew by Ayyub and Moses ben Tibbon and from Hebrew into Latin by Armengand.

Other translations during the twelfth and thirteenth centuries included ibn Zuhr's (Avenzoar) basic work *Taisir,* translated into Hebrew and from Hebrew into Latin by John of Capua and again by Parvicius and his other work, *Kitab al-Aqdiya,* translated into Hebrew by Nathan he'Me'ati. Ibn Rushd's *Kulliyat (Colliget: Complete Works)* —a medical encyclopaedia—was translated into Latin (or Hebrew) by Bonacosa almost a century after its appearance in Arabic. Finally, Maimonides' works which were written in Arabic were translated into Hebrew by Zerahiah Gracian, Moses ben Tibbon, and Nathan he'Me'ati and into Latin by John of Capua and Armengand.

One of the greatest alchemists of Islam who made extensive contributions to Latin chemistry was the druggist-physician Jabir-ibn Haiyan (702-765), the Latinized medieval Gebir. More than 100 works are attributed to him, and, although most of them belonged to other authors, many of them were translated into Latin carrying his name.

Literature. The contributions of Islamic literature in Spain from 1250 to 1600 are evidenced by the introduction of many Muslim literary works in Spanish translations. Among these were *Indian Fables* (*Disciplina Clericalis*) introduced by Petrus Alfonsi, a Spanish-Jewish convert to Christianity, and the translation of another book of Indian tales, the celebrated *Kalila wa-Dimna (Calila e Dimna)* about 1251 from an Arabic translation. *The Romance of the Seven Sages (Sindibad*) was translated from Arabic for Infante don Fadrique as *Libro de los Engannos e Asayamientos de las Mujeres (The Book of the Wiles and Deceptions of Women*) about 1251.* The *Libro de Exemplos por ABC* was a rendering of a lost version of the Buddhist *Barlaam and Josaphat* collected by Clemente Sanchez de Vercial. The *Libro de los gatos* (the *Book of Cats,* actually, *Book of Stories*). The *Legacy of Islam* states:

> Stories included in these collections are constantly recurring in Spanish literature down to the times of the dramatists of the seventeenth century. The greatest of Spanish plays, *La Vida Es Sueno (Life's a Dream)* is the story of Christopher Sly in *The Taming of the Shrew,* and *The Sleeper Wakened* in the *Thousand and One Nights* is derived ultimately from Barlaam.[22]†

---

*Edited by D. Comparetti, *Researches Respecting the Book of Sindibad* (London: 1882) and A. Bonilla y Zan Martin (Madrid: 1904), cited in *The Legacy of Islam,* p. 30.

†The writer is quite aware of repetitions of certain Muslim and Latin authors' translations and works in this and the previous chapter; but these repetitions are made in different contexts and for different purposes with the hope that they may be an added help for the beginning reader.

A Final Comment

In the universities of the twelfth and thirteenth centuries scholarship was based almost entirely on the writings of the Muslim and Greek authors as translated from Arabic or Greek sources. Muslim-Aristotelian science remained the core of the curriculum of the University of Paris until the sixteenth century. Roger Bacon and Albertus Magnus (Albert of Bollstaedt) lectured on Muslim sciences and acknowledged their debt to them, particularly to al-Hazin and Jabir. Not until the middle of the sixteenth century and the advent of Copernicus in astronomy, Paracelsus in medicine, and Vesalius in anatomy did Muslim-Hellenistic science give way to the new concepts of man and his world and bring about the decline of the medieval period.

To be sure, almost throughout the sixteenth century some translations of Muslim and Greek authors were still used, and the medical curriculum in Vienna and Frankfurt still depended on the works of Rhazes and Avicenna. They were still insisting upon and getting new translations of Muslim medical works. True also, the struggle between Muslim and Greek science went on in Italy until the seventeenth century, and Muslim pharmacology was respected in Europe until the nineteenth century.[23] But the handwriting of human progress was on the wall of time for those who would have the vision to see it. Muslim intellectual domination had exerted itself in Latin schools for some five hundred years, and what it had given European education was good, if only in awakening Europe from a millennium of intellectual standstill. Islam had given the West the best of what it had learned from classical cultures and what it had added by its own creative genius. Europe took over where Islam left off. The result has been the staggering progress in science and technology in the Western world which has characterized the last four centuries.

Only one debt remains partially unpaid. The Western mind, so generously enriched by the creative toil of five hundred years of Muslim scholarship, has been too slow, perhaps too reluctant, to acknowledge this indebtedness and render unto its givers an overdue expression of thanks. This work is a gesture in that direction.

On the unpredictable path of progress humanity runs an uneven and at times an uncertain and confusing race. Some groups or individuals crawl, while others walk; still others run full speed. Some are determined to move forward, and others are disposed to move backward. There are those who seem to move with zest but without covering distance in either direction. Yet, however important speed may be in this race, the torch which each runner carries and the direction in which he runs are what give substance and aim to the race and significance to the mobility of each participant. Unlike the Olympian torch, which each relay runner passes on to the next, the torch of culture which humanity passes on from one period to the next may generate glowing flames or be reduced to dying flickers, depending upon the quality or purity of the oil with which each torchbearing group sustains the torch.

Our analogy fails us at this point, for unlike the Olympian torch, the final value of the torch of human culture is determined and tested not so much by the hands that carry it or the hands that receive it, nor even by its substance, however pure it may be, but rather by the light it casts upon the path of human moral progress and by the comfort and well-being which its generating heat brings to those who walk in its light.

In the centuries that convenience calls medieval times, this torch was passed from classical hands to those of the Muslims. We have seen through the pages of this study how they preserved, improved and increased its substance, how they utilized its light and received comfort from its heat. And just as its light was beginning to dim and its substance to diminish, they passed it to other hands which were prepared to regenerate and resubstantiate it.

Islamic Philosophy and Science and Their Influences on Medieval Scholasticism and Modern Culture

I
Greco-Roman Background

Philosophy
Plato
Aristotle

Religion
Pythagorian
Gnostic

Science
Hippocrates
Gàlen
Diascorus

Christianity

Christian Gnosticism

Philonism

Apologists

Plotinus

(Neo-Platonism)
(5th Century)

System of St. Augustine

Dark Ages
(6th to 9th Century)

Greek Orthodoxy

Roman Orthodoxy

Closing of Schools of Athens
(529 A.D.)

Philosophy Moves East
(6th to 8th Century)

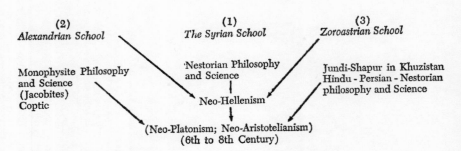

(2)
Alexandrian School

Monophysite Philosophy
and Science
(Jacobites)
Coptic

(1)
The Syrian School

Nestorian Philosophy
and Science

(3)
Zoroastrian School

Jundi-Shapur in Khuzistan
Hindu - Persian - Nestorian
philosophy and Science

Neo-Hellenism

(Neo-Platonism; Neo-Aristotelianism)
(6th to 8th Century)

Pre-Islamic Translators of Hellenistic Authors:

Plato *Aristotle* *Plotinus* Galen Hippocrates

II
Islamic Background

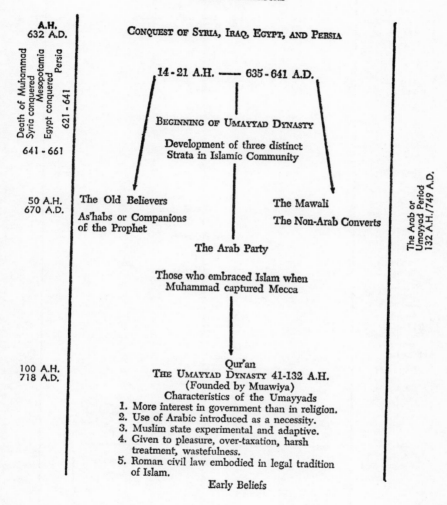

A.H.
632 A.D.

Death of Muhammad
Syria conquered
Mesopotamia
Egypt conquered
Persia
621 - 641

641 - 661

Conquest of Syria, Iraq, Egypt, and Persia

14 - 21 A.H. — 635 - 641 A.D.

Beginning of Umayyad Dynasty

Development of three distinct
Strata in Islamic Community

50 A.H.
670 A.D.

The Old Believers

As'habs or Companions
of the Prophet

The Mawali

The Non-Arab Converts

The Arab Party

Those who embraced Islam when
Muhammad captured Mecca

100 A.H.
718 A.D.

Qur'an

The Umayyad Dynasty 41-132 A.H.
(Founded by Muawiya)

Characteristics of the Umayyads

1. More interest in government than in religion.
2. Use of Arabic introduced as a necessity.
3. Muslim state experimental and adaptive.
4. Given to pleasure, over-taxation, harsh treatment, wastefulness.
5. Roman civil law embodied in legal tradition of Islam.

Early Beliefs

The Arab or
Umayyad Period
132 A.H./749 A.D.

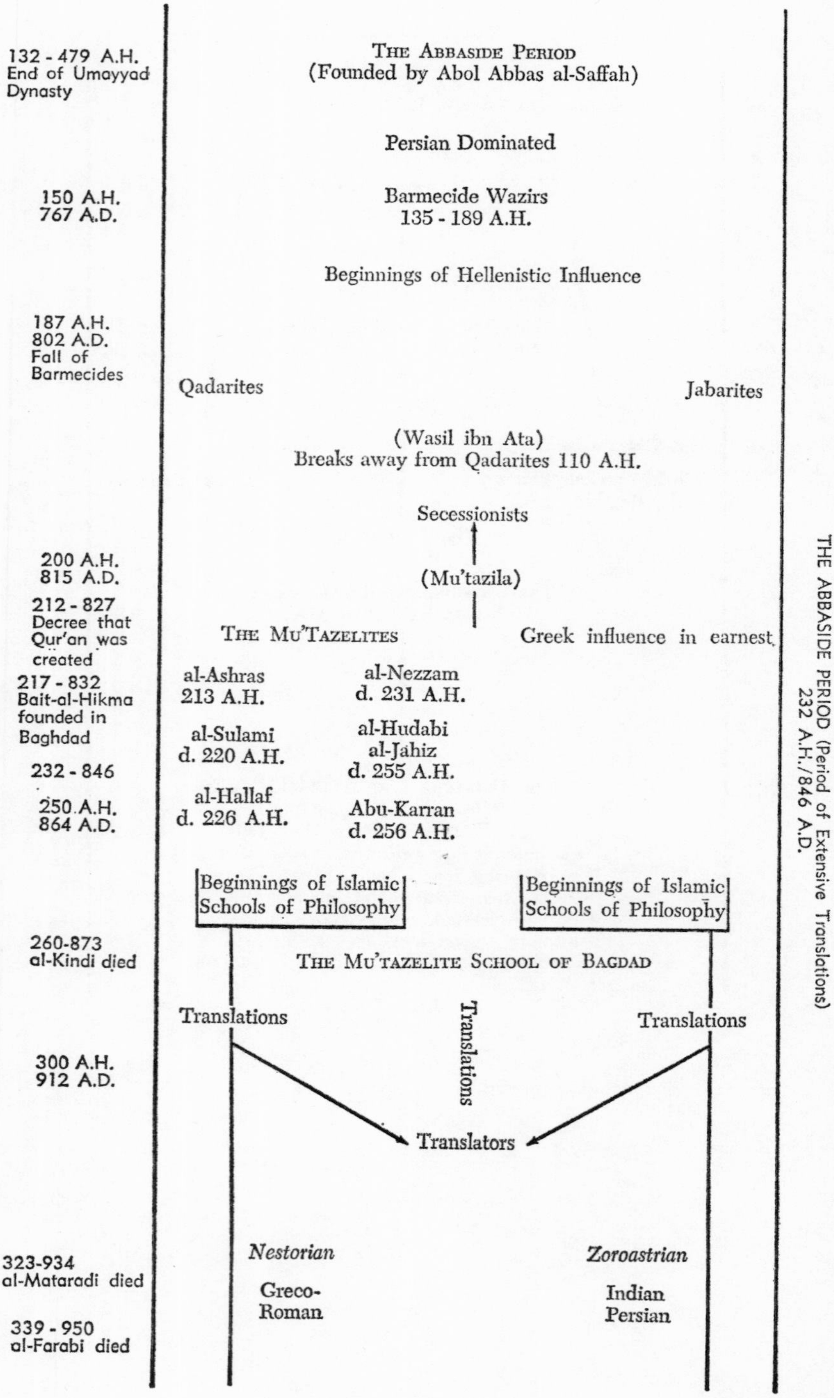
132 - 479 A.H.
End of Umayyad Dynasty
THE ABBASIDE PERIOD
(Founded by Abol Abbas al-Saffah)
Persian Dominated
150 A.H.
767 A.D.
Barmecide Wazirs
135 - 189 A.H.
Beginnings of Hellenistic Influence
187 A.H.
802 A.D.
Fall of Barmecides
Qadarites
Jabarites
(Wasil ibn Ata)
Breaks away from Qadarites 110 A.H.
Secessionists
200 A.H.
815 A.D.
(Mu'tazila)
212 - 827
Decree that Qur'an was created
THE MU'TAZELITES
Greek influence in earnest
217 - 832
Bait-al-Hikma founded in Baghdad
al-Ashras
213 A.H.
al-Nezzam
d. 231 A.H.
al-Sulami
d. 220 A.H.
al-Hudabi
al-Jahiz
d. 255 A.H.
232 - 846
250 A.H.
864 A.D.
al-Hallaf
d. 226 A.H.
Abu-Karran
d. 256 A.H.
Beginnings of Islamic Schools of Philosophy
Beginnings of Islamic Schools of Philosophy
260-873
al-Kindi died
THE MU'TAZELITE SCHOOL OF BAGDAD
Translations
Translations
Translations
300 A.H.
912 A.D.
Translators
323-934
al-Mataradi died
Nestorian
Zoroastrian
Greco-Roman
Indian
Persian
339 - 950
al-Farabi died
THE ABBASIDE PERIOD (Period of Extensive Translations)
232 A.H./846 A.D.

ISLAMIC

al-Muqaffa
Ruled 140 A.H.

Fables of Bed Pai
"Kalila wa Dimna"

Abu Mazar
d. 272

Razes
311 d. 923

Abu Zaraah
d. 398

al Ibadi
d. 263

Hunayn

Qurra
d. 289

Yunus
d. 328

Adi of Takhrit
d. 364

350 A.H.
961 A.D.

al Kindi d. 260 A.H.

Greatest Authors of Greco-Roman-Zoroastrian-Hindu Worlds

DEVELOPMENT OF ISLAMIC SCHOOLS AND PHILOSOPHIES

388 - 998
Rise of
Mahmud of
Ghazna

400 A.H.
1009 A.D.

(3)
Aristotelian
Tendencies

al-Kindi
260 A.H.

al-Farabi
339 A.H.

Akhawan al-Safa

"Brethren of Purity"
Encyclopaedia of
Philosophy and
Science in 51
epistles under
Zaid ibn Refa' and
collaborators

al-Busti
al-Zanjani
al-Mahrajani
al-Awfi

Opposed by
Aristotelian
Rationalists

(Doctrines of
Brotherhood
introduced by
Andalusi 395
influencing the
philosophers who
influenced Christian
Scholasticism)

(1)
Orthodox Development

Against

Orthodox Scholasticism
(Break away from
Mu'tazilites) become
anti-Hellenistic
(Qur'anic)
Traditional
Anti-innovation
al-Ashari
270-330 A.H.
al-Tahawi
al-Mataradi

Founds Orthodox
Scholasticism

Anti-Qur'anic Creation
Pro-beatific Vision
Pro-predestination

Asharite Scholasticism

DEVELOPED BY
AL-BAQILANI
d. 403

(2)
Neo-Platonic
Tendencies

Christian influences
before Islam

Arabian influences
before Islam

(Becomes prominent
in 3rd century)

Mostly in Iran

(a) Early Asceticism
to 200 A.H.

Opposed by extreme
orthodoxy
(Hambalites)

(b) New Sufism

Mazdakite Buddhist
Manichian Gnostic

Latter part of third
century A.H.

EASTERN
PHILOSOPHERS

428 - 1036 ibn Sina died	ibn Sina d. 428 A.H. (wrote on everything)	*Nizam-ul-Mulk,* the Wiziar to Alp Arsalan, founds Nizamiyyah Academy in Baghdad.		EASTERN PHILOSOPHERS (CONTINUED)
450 A.H. 1058 A.D.		It was a theological college of Asharite Teachings.		
455 - 1063 Asharites Accepted		Thus Asharites were established and Mu'tazilites became a minority. (Unwanted)		
	Yahya bin Jabirol (Avencebrol) 459 A.H. or 1058 A.D.			WESTERN PHILOSOPHERS
	ibn Bajja (Avenpace) 533 A.H. or 1138 A.D.	450 - 505 al-Ghazzali The St. Augustine of Islam		
500 A.H. 1106 A.D.	Avenpace	↓		
505 - 1111 al-Ghazzali died (al-Gazel)				
533 - 1138 ibn Bajja died (Avenpace)				
540 - 1145 Jehuda Hal-levi died	ibn Tufail 851 A.H. or 1185 A.D.	al-Gazalites and Anti-al-Gazalites in Spain		
550 A.H. 1155 A.D.				
581 - 1185 ibn Tufail died				
595 - 1198 ibn Rushd died (Averroes)				
600 A.H. 1203 A.D.	ibn Rushd Averroes 595 A.H.			
601 - 1204 Maimonides died 638 - 1240 ibn Arabi died				
620 - 1223 ibn Tumeus died				
650 A.H. 1252 A.D.	Averroism			
656 A.H. 1258 A.D. Halagu takes Baghdad				
667 A.H. 1268 A.D. Fall of Mawahhids in Spain				

APPENDIX I

AN ADAPTED MUSLIM-CHRISTIAN CALENDAR AND IMPORTANT ISLAMIC CULTURAL EVENTS AND POLITICAL DYNASTIES

(FROM 1 HEJIRA TO DEATH OF SA'DI, 691 HEJIRA)

	A.H.	*A.D.*
Beginning of Hejira	1	622
Muhammad dies	11	632
Mesopotamia and Syria conquered	17	638
(Muslim year begins January 2)	19	640
(Muslim year begins December 27)	20	640
Egypt is conquered	20	640
Cairo founded	21	641
Persia is conquered	21	641
Mosque of Amr Founded	22	642
Uthman becomes Khalif	23	643
Ali becomes Khalif	35	655
Mu'awiya I (Umayyads) becomes Khalif	41	661
Hindu numerals appear in Syria	42	662
Imam al-Hasan dies	49	669
(Muslim year begins January 8)	52	672
(Muslim year begins December 27)	53	672
Yazid becomes Khalif	60	679
al-Husain dies	61	680
Marwan becomes Khalif	63	682
Mu'awiya II becomes Khalif	64	683
Abd al-Malik becomes Khalif	65	684
Mosque of Damascus founded	86	705
al-Walid becomes Khalif	86	705
(Muslim year begins January 2)	86	705
(Muslim year begins December 23)	87	705
Sulaiman becomes Khalif	96	714
Umar II becomes Khalif	99	717
Yusuf II becomes Khalif	101	719
Hisham becomes Khalif	106	724
(Muslim year begins January 9)	119	737
(Muslim year begins December 29)	120	737
al-Walid II becomes Khalif	126	743
Yazid III becomes Khalif	127	744
Marwan II becomes Khalif	128	745
Umayyad dynasty ends	132	749
Abbaside Khalifate founded	133	750
al-Saffar becomes Khalif	133	750
al-Mansur becomes Khalif	136	753
Umayyads established at Cordova	138	755
Mu'tazilite philosophy begins	140	757

	A.H.	*A.D.*
ibn al-Muqaffa is killed	140	757
Baghdad is founded	145	762
Imam Ja'far al-Sadiq dies	148	765
(Muslim year begins January 4)	153	770
(Muslim year begins December 24)	154	770
al-Mahdi becomes Khalif	158	774
al-Hadi becomes Khalif	169	785
Blue Mosque of Cordova founded	170	786
Harun al-Rashid becomes Khalif	170	786
Idrisids are established in Morocco	172	788
(Muslim year begins January 10)	186	802
(Muslim year begins December 30)	187	802
Fall of Barmecides	187	802
The philosopher al-Kindi born?	188	803
al-Amin becomes Khalif	193	808
The scholar Hunain ibn Is'haq born	194	809
al-Ma'mun becomes Khalif	198	813
al-Shaf'i dies	204	819
Sicily conquered by Muslims	212	827
Qur'an decreed, created	212	827
Dar-al-Islam founded in Baghdad	215	830
Bait al-Hikmah is founded	217	832
al-Khwarizmi's algebra appears	215	830
al-Mu'tasim becomes Khalif	218	833
Muslim capitol is removed to Samarra	219	834
(Muslim year begins January 5)	220	835
(Muslim year begins December 26)	221	835
The philosopher al-Razi born	230	844
al-Nazzam dies	231	845
Attack on Rome by Muslims	232	846
al-Mutawakkil becomes Khalif	232	846
Mu'tazilite philosophy ends	233	847
al-Muntasir becomes Khalif	247	861
al-Musta'in becomes Khalif	248	862
al-Mu'tazz becomes Khalif	252	866
(Muslim year begins January 1)	254	868
(Muslim year begins December 20)	255	868
al-Muhtadi becomes Khalif	255	868
al-Mu'tamid becomes Khalif	256	869
Baghdad re-established as capital	256	869
The philosopher al-Farabi born	257	870
al-Bukhari dies	257	870
al-Kindi dies	260	873
The theologian al-Ashari born	260	873
Hunain ibn Is'haq dies	264	877
Mosque of Ibn Tulun founded in Cairo	265	878
Mu'tadid becomes Khalif	279	892
(Muslim year begins January 7)	287	900
(Muslim year begins December 26)	288	900
al-Muktafi becomes Khalif	289	901
al-Muqtadir becomes Khalif	295	907
Fatimites established at Kairawan	297	909
al-Ash'ari defends ortholoxy	300	912
Birth of historian al-Tabari? and poet al-Mutanabbi	303	915

	A.H.	A.D.
Death of al-Razi	314	926
al-Qahir becomes Khalif	320	932
(Muslim year begins January 1)	321	933
(Muslim year begins December 22)	322	933
al-Radi becomes Khalif	322	933
Poet Firdawsi born	323	934
al-Mataridi dies	323	934
al-Ashari dies	324	935
Buwayhids seize Baghdad	324	935
The mathematician Abu al-Wafa born	329	940
al-Muttaqi becomes Khalif	329	940
al-Mustakfi becomes Khalif	333	944
al-Muti' becomes Khalif	334	945
al-Farabi dies	339	950
The geographer al-Mas'udi dies	340	951
(Muslim year begins January 7)	354	965
(Muslim year begins December 28)	355	965
The poet Mutanabbi dies	355	965
al-Haitham, the physicist, born	355	965
Fatimites in Egypt	356	966
The Sufi poet Abu Sa'id born	357	967
al-Azhar Mosque founded in Cairo	360	970
The scientist al-Biruni born	363	973
al-Tai (Hatim) becomes Khalif	363	973
The poet al-Ma'arri born	363	973
The philosopher-physician ibn Sina born	370	980
Brethren of Purity established (Ikhwan-al-Safa)	373	983
Mosque of al-Hakim founded in Cairo 380-403 A.H. 990-1012 A.D.	380	990
al-Qadir becomes Khalif	380	990
Abu al-Wafa dies	388	998
Rise of Mahmud of Ghazna	388	998
(Muslim year begins January 3)	388	998
(Muslim year begins December 23)	389	998
Statesman-educator Nizam-al-Mulk born	408	1017
Epic poet Firdawsi dies	411	1020
(Muslim year begins January 9)	421	1030
(Muslim year begins December 29)	422	1030
al-Qa'im becomes Khalif	422	1030
ibn Sina dies (428-1036)	429	1037
The astronomer-poet Omar Khayyam born	430	1038
al-Haitham dies	431	1039
al-Biruni dies	440	1048
Abu Sa'id dies	441	1049
Saljuks in Baghdad	447	1055
al-Ma'arri dies	450	1058
The theologian-educator al-Ghazzali born	450	1058
Nizam-al-Mulk becomes prime minister (vizier) or Saljuk Court	454	1062
Ash'arites "tolerated"	455	1063
(Muslim year begins January 4)	455	1063
(Muslim year begins December 25)	456	1063
al-Muqtadi becomes Khalif	467	1074
Friday Mosque founded in Isfahan (Masjid Jam'a)	481	1088
The sect of Assassins founded (Hashishins)	483	1090
The physician ibn Zuhr born	483	1091

	A.H.	*A.D.*
Nizam-ali-Mulk dies	485	1092
al-Musta'thir becomes Khalif	487	1094
(Muslim year begins January 11)	488	1095
(Muslim year begins December 31)	489	1095
The geographer al-Idrisi born	494	1100
The philosopher ibn Bajja born?	500	1106
The philosopher ibn Tufail born	501	1107
al-Ghazzali dies	505	1111
al-Mustarshid becomes Khalif	512	1118
Omar Khayyam dies	517	1123
The philosopher ibn Rushd born	520	1126
(Muslim year begins January 6)	522	1128
(Muslim year begins December 25)	523	1128
ibn Tumart dies	524	1129
al-Rashid becomes Khalif	529	1134
al-Muktafi II becomes Khalif	530	1135
ibn Bajja dies	533	1138
Jehuda hal-Levi dies	540	1145
(Muslim year begins January 12)	555	1160
(Muslim year begins December 31)	556	1160
ibn-Zuhr dies	558	1162
al-Idrisi dies	562	1166
Saladin enters Egypt	566	1170
Fatimites end	566	1170
The geographer Yaqut born	575	1179
al-Nasir becomes Khalif	575	1179
The poet-moralist Sa'di born	580	1184
ibn Tufail dies	581	1185
The poet Nizami born?	584	1188
(Muslim year begins January 7)	589	1193
(Muslim year begins December 27)	590	1193
ibn Rushd dies	595	1198
The mystic poet Rumi born (Jalal-al-Din)	598	1201
Maimonides dies	601	1204
The biographer Abu Khallikan born	608	1211
Yaqut the geographer dies	617	1220
ibn Tumlus dies	620	1223
al-Zahir becomes Khalif	622	1225
al-Mustansir becomes Khalif	623	1226
(Muslim year begins January 2)	623	1226
(Muslim year begins December 22)	624	1226
ibn Arabi dies	638	1240
al-Musta'sim becomes Khalif	640	1242
Alhambra founded	646	1248
Abbaside Khalifate ends. Mongols sack Baghdad	656	1258
Halagu takes Baghdad	656	1258
Khalifate ends	656	1258
(Muslim year begins January 8)	656	1258
(Muslim year begins December 29)	657	1258
Muwahhid dynasty in Spain falls	667	1268
Rumi dies	672	1273
ibn Khallikan dies	681	1282
Sa'di the poet dies	691	1291

APPENDIX II

PARTIAL LIST OF EARLY TRANSLATORS OF GRECO-HELLENISTIC WORKS INTO SYRIAN, ARABIC, ETC.

THE SCHOOLS OF NISIBIS
Edessa, Harran, Jundi-Shapur
Nestorian-Zoroastrian-Hindu
(Between the two schisms and the Muslim Invasion)

Mar Abba, (1) head of school of Seleucia, (2) 550 A.D., (3) ?, (4) ?.

Hares C. Kalada, (1) Jundi-Shapur, (2) 7th century, (3) medicine, (4) translations of Indian works.

al-Nadr, (1) Jundi-Shapur, (2) 7th century, (3) medicine, (4) translations of Indian works.

Sharak, (1) Hindu, (2) 7th century, (3) medicine, (4) translations of Indian works.

Qolhoman, (1) Hindu, (2) 7th century, (3) medicine, (4) translations of Indian works.

Manka, (1) ?, (2) 7th century, (3) medicine, (4) translations of Indian works.

Ibas, (1) school of Edessa, (2) d. 457, (3) philosophy, (4) first translation into Syriac of Porphyry's Isagoge.

Barsuma, (1) refounder of school of Nisibis, (2) ?, (3) ?, (4) ?.

Probus, (1) presbyter of Antioch, (2) 5th century, (3) philosophy, (4) commentaries on Porphyry's Isagoge, on Aristotle's Hermeneutica, and on Sophistici Elenchi's Analytica Priora.

Paul the Persian, (1) Nestorian, (2) 6th century, (3) logic, (4) treatise on logic.

Henanieshu, (1) Nestorian, (2) 7th century, (3) logic, (4) treatise on logic.

Mar Abba III, (1) Nestorian, (2) 740 A.D., (3) commentator, (4) on Aristotelian logic.

Jeshudena, (1) Bishop of Basra, (2) latter 8th, (3) logic, (4) introduction to logic.

Jeshubokt, (1) metropolitan of Persia, (2) latter 8th, (3) commentator, (4) on Categories.

Hunayn ibn Is'haq, (1) formed college of translators in Baghdad under Khalif al-Ma'mun, (2) latter 8th, (3) translator, (4) Greek, Persian, and Hindu texts into Arabic.

Is'haq B. Is'haq, same as above.

Hubaish, same as above.

Hunain, (1) Nestorian, (2) latter 8th, (3) translator, (4) from Greek into Syriac, Porphyry's Isagoge, Aristotle's Hermeneutica. Part of Analytica, Metaphysics, also "Summa" of Nicolas of Damascus, commentary of Alexander of Aphrodisias, great part of Galen, (Dioscorides), Paul of Aegina, Hippocrates.

John Bar Masivai (or *Maswai*), (1) Syrian, (2) d. 857 A.D., (3) medicine, (4) medical work in Syriac and Arabic.

Denha, (1) Syrian?, (2) 9th, (3) commentator, (4) Aristotelian logical organon.

Abzud, (1) Syrian?, (2) 9th, (3) poetic philosophy, (4) poetical essay on division of philosophy.

Deonysius Bar Salibi, (1) Syrian, (2) 12th, (3) commentary, (4) on Isagoge, Categories, Hermeneutica, Analytica.

Yaqub Bar Shakako, (1) Syrian, (2) early 13th, (3) philosophy, (4) dialogues on logic, physics, mathematics, metaphysics.

George Bar Hebraeus, (1) Syrian, (2) 13th century, (3) philosophy, (4) "Book of Pupils of the Eye," Isagoge, Aristotle's Categories, Hermeneutica.

The Alexandrian School
Monophysites
(Jacobites)

(Between the two schisms and the Muslim Invasion)
(Philosophy, Theology, Medicine, Chemistry, Astronomy)

John Philoponus, (1) ?, (2) philosophy, (3) commentaries.

John the Grammarian, (1) 6th, (2) medicine.

Paul of Aegina, (1) 7th, (2) medicine.

Sergius of Rah-al-Ayn, (1) d. 536, (2) philosophy, medicine, astronomy, (3) translations parts of Galen in Syriac, new version of Porphyry and Aristotle's Categories. Wrote seven-volume treatise on logic.

Ahudemmeh, (1) Bishop of Tagrit, 559, (2) logic, philosophy, (3) treatises on logic, morals, and so on.

Severus Sebokt, (1) convent of early 7th century Densherin, (2) Aristotle, (3) commentary on Aristotle's Hermeneutica and other works. Also wrote on astronomy.

Athanasius of Baghdad, (1) Monophysite patriarch, 684, (2) Porphyry, (3) a new Syriac version of Porphyry's Isagoge.

James of Edessa, (1) d. 708, (2) philosophy, (3) "Enchiridion," a treatise on philosophy terms.

George, (1) Bishop of the Arabs, 686, (2) Aristotle, (3) translated the entire logical organon of Aristotle.

Early Important Translators Into Arabic

Greater part of the works of Aristotle and of leading Neo-Platonic commentators; some of the works of Plato; greater part of the works of Galen; also Greek, Hindu, and Persian scientific and other works.

Two periods of translation: From accession of Abbassides to accession of al-Ma'mun, 132-198 A.H.; under al-Ma'mun and his immediate successors centered in Baghdad's newly founded college, Bait-al-Hikma. Translators were largely Christians, Jews, and recent converts from other faiths.

First period of translation, 132-198 A.H.:

Abdullah ibn al-Muqaffa, (1) a Zoroastrian Zindiq (half convert), (2) d. 142 or 143 A.H., (3) translator, (4) Kalila wa-Dimna, and other works.

Ibrahim al-Fazari, (1) ?, (2) 152 A.H., (3) astronomy, (4) a Hindu astronomical work, Siddhanta (Sindhind).

Muhammad ibn Musa al-Khwarizmi, (1) Islam, (2) ?, (3) astronomy, (4) combined Greek and Indian systems of astronomy.

George Bokhtishu, (1) Nestorian physician from school of Jundi-Shapur, court physician in Baghdad to al-Mansur, (2) 148 A.D., (3) ?, (4) ?.

Isa ibn Thakerbokht, (1) Nestorian physician followed Boktishu as court doctor, (2) ?, (3) therapeutics, (4) wrote book on therapeutics.

Gabriel Bokhtishu, (1) connected with court of Harun al-Rashid, (2) 175 A.D., (3) medicine and philosophy, (4) wrote introduction to logic, a manual on medicine based on Galen, Deoscorus (Dioscorides), Paul of Aegina, medical pandects, a treatise on perfumes.

Second period of translation, after 198 A.H.:

John Bar Maserjoye, (1) Jewish Syrian physician, (2) ?, (3) head of medical school in Baghdad, (4) translated Syntagma of Aaron into Syriac.

Abu Bakr Muhammad ibn Zakariyya al-Razi (Rhazes), (1) ?, (2) d. between 311 and 320, (3) philosophy, medicine, music, literature, (4) medical pandects, etc. Works not well arranged.

al-Ma'mun, (1) Khalif of Baghdad, (2) 217 A.H., (3) founded the Bait-al-Hikma.

Yahya ibn Masawaih, (1) first head of Bait-al-Hikma, (2) d. 243 A.H., (3) medicine, (4) treatise on fevers, translated into Hebrew and Latin.

Abu Zayd Hunayn ibn Is'haq al-Ibadi, (1) Nestorian physician, (2) d. 264 A.H., (3) mathematics, (4) Arabic translations of Euclid, parts of Galen, Hippocrates, Archimedes, Apollonius, Plato's Republic, Laws, Timaeus, Aristotle's Categories, Physics, Magna Moralia, commentary of Themistius, Arabic translations of the Bible, medical pandects of Paul of Aegina.

Is'haq Hunayn, (1) son of al-Ibadi, (2) ?, (3) philosophy and medicine, (4) original works on medicine, Arabic version of Sophist of Plato, the Metaphysics and Hermeneutica of Aristotle, commentaries of Porphyry, Alexander Aphrodisias and Ammanius.

Questa ibn Luqa, (1) Syrian Christian, (2) ?, (3) translator, (4) ?.

Abu Bishr Matka ibn Yunus, (1) Nestorian, (2) d. 328 A.H., (3) translator from Syriac to Arabic, (4) Aristotle's Analytica Posteriora, also Alexander Aphrodisias' commentary on generation and corruption, also wrote commentaries on Aristotle's Categories and Porphyry's Isagoge.

Yahya ibn Adi, (1) Jacobite from Takrit (pupil of Hunayn), (2) d. 364, (3) reviser, (4) Aristotle's Categories, Sophistici Elenchi's Poetics and Metaphysics, also Plato's Laws and Timaeus, Alexander Aphrodisias' commentary of Categories, also Theophrastus' Moralia.

Abu Ali Isa ibn Zaraah, (1) Jacobite, (2) d. 398, (3) translator, (4) Categories, the natural history, de Particus Animalium, of John Philoponus.

APPENDIX III

THE *AL-FIHRIST* OF AL-NADIM

The *Al-Fihrist,* or *Index,* of al-Nadim is perhaps one of the most valuable documents in the Arabic language, and certainly in the entire "medieval" Islamic culture. By listing the names of all the authors, at least those known to him,* (whether translators or original writers) who had written works in Arabic up to the latter decades of the tenth century, the titles of their (more important) works, their nationality, the dates and places of their birth and death, and interesting bits of information on the character, scholarship, and life of some of these men, al-Nadim has provided in this *Index* materials of great historical importance to the medievalist, as well as the student of the Muslim world and the Western culture. The work indicates clearly the scope and extent of Muslim learning before the end of the tenth century, and in effect sets this period in contrast to the overwhelming creative scholarly Muslim works of the eleventh century. The *Index* also shows that scholarly interests in Islam before the eleventh century were predominantly religious, theological, philological, grammatical, moral, and philosophical. Though many works in science, mathematics, and technology are listed, their number and quality cannot compare to the original scientific works of the eleventh century which culminated in the astronomy and mathematics of Omar Khayyam.

In spite of its great historic importance, the *Al-Fihrist,* which has appeared in both German and French translations, has not been as yet translated in the English language. It has been my desire for many years to prepare an English translation of the *Al-Fihrist.* But such a translation should await examination of some earlier copies of *Al-Fihrist* which are available in Turkey, Iran, and India.†

The following partial list of abbreviated and somewhat phonetically transliterated names of the more important authors in the *Al-Fihrist* is based on the Arabic copy of the work entitled *Al-Fihrist L'ibn*

*In many instances throughout the *Al-Fihrist,* al-Nadim in discussing an author ends with the statement, "and among his works are," without listing the works.

†I have seen microfilms of an early copy of *Al-Fihrist* on a visit with Dr. Bayard Dodge, who is preparing a translation of the work in English. His translation will be an invaluable contribution to the English speaking world.

al-Nadim, published by the Rahmaniyyah Press (Al-Matba'at al-Rahmaniyyah), Egypt, 1348 Hejira. In many instances when an author's name was not shared by other authors, only the first name by which he was identified in the *Al-Fihrist,* has been listed.

The list may be of value to students of Muslim scholarship in the tenth century, and is, so far as I have been able to determine, the first of its kind prepared for the English speaking reader. The alphabetic arrangement of names is mine. Following the list of authors is also a list of some interesting topics and the number of works in each as they appear in the *Al-Fihrist,* along with a few selected titles of works on education.

List of Authors in The Al-Fihrist of Al-Nadim

Abad ibn Kasib
Aban (al-Aheqi)
Aban (al-Munajjim abu Mansar)
Aban (ibn Uthman ibn Affan)
Aban (ibn Taqlab)
Abbas (ibn al-Ahnaf)
Abbas (ibn Sa'id al-Mohari)
Abd (al-Hamid ibn Yahya)
Abd (Allah ibn Tahir)
Abd'ul (Aziz ibn Yahya)
Abd'ul (Hamid al-Hatli)
Abd'ul (Hamid ibn Sahl)
Abd'ul'lah (al-Abadhi)
Abd'ul'lah (ibn Abi Qibah)
Abd'ul'lah (ibn al-Hekam al-Mesri)
Abd'ul'lah (ibn al-Mubarak)
Abd'ul'lah (ibn al-Muqaffa)
Abd'ul'lah (ibn Amer al-Yaksabi)
Abd'ul'lah (ibn Bakir)
Abd'ul'lah (ibn Dawud)
Abd'ul'lah (ibn Hemad)
Abd'ul'lah (ibn Masrur al-Nasrani)
Abd'ul'lah (ibn Muhammad ibn Abi Ubainah)
Abd'ul'lah (ibn Yazid)
Abd'ul Malik ibn Abd al-Aziz
Abd'ul Munim ibn Idris
Abd'ul Rahman ibn Abi'l-Zenad
Abd'ul Rahman ibn al-Qasim
Abd'ul Rahman ibn Isa
Abd'ul Rahman ibn Isa'l Hamdani
Abd'ul Rahman ibn Zaid
Abd'ul Razzaq al-San'ani
Abd'ul Wahhab al-Ajli
Abd'ul Wahhab ibn Ali
Abhari
Abi (ibn Ka'b)
Abi (Muhammad ibn Yazid al-Mahabi)
Abi (Rafi)
Abi (Shiba)
Abi (Ubbad)
Abion al-Betriq
Ablonios
Absqolawos
Abu Abd'ul Rahman
Abu Abd al-Rahman Muhammad
Abu Abd'ul'lah al-Attar
Abu Abd'ul'lah al-Basri
Abu Abd'ul'lah al-Khawlani
Abu Abd'ul'lah al-Namiri
Abu Abd'ul'lah al-Shatwi
Abu Abd'ul'lah Harun
Abu Abd'ul'lah Harun ibn Ali
Abu Abd'ul'lah ibn Thawaba
Abu Abd'ul'lah Muhammad ibn Idris al-Shafe'i & Associates
Abu Adnan
Abu Ahmad al-Munajjim
Abu Ahmad ibn al-Halab
Abu Ahmad ibn Yazdad
Abu Ainat al-Mahlabi
Abu Ali al-Basir
Abu Ali ibn al-Junaid
Abu Arar
Abu Aruba
Abu Asidah
Abu Ayyub al-Madini
Abu Bakr al-Khaledyan
Abu Bakr al-Razi
Abu Bakr al-Sowli
Abu Bakr ibn al-Anbari
Abu Barzat al-Khatli
Abu Bashr
Abu Dulf (or Dalf)
Abu Dumash
Abu Hamed al-Qadhi
Abu Hamzat al-Sowfi
Abu'l Abbas (al-Samiri)
Abu'l Abbas (Muhammad ibn Khalaf)
Abu'l Abr al-Hashemi

Abu'l Aina Muhammad ibn al-Qasim
Abu'l Ala
Abu'l Anbari Muhammad Qasim
Abu'l Anbas
Abu'l Aqili
Abu'l Asadi
Abu'l Ash'ath
Abu'l Atahiyya
Abu'l Bukhari Wahb ibn Wahb
Abu'l Fahd
Abu'l Faraj
Abu'l Faraj (al-Isfahani)
Abu'l Faraj (al-Maleki)
Abu'l Fat'h
Abu'l Haitham al-Razi
Abu'l Handam
Abu'l Hasam (Muhammad ibn Ahmad)
Abu'l Hasan (ibn Khayran)
Abu'l Hasan (Ahmad al-Khamshalil)
Abu'l Hasan (al-Harani)
Abu'l Hasan (Ali ibn Harun)
Abu'l Hasan (al-Munajjim)
Abu'l Hasan (al-Nesaba)
Abu'l Hasan (ibn al-Namh)
Abu'l Hasan (ibn Ibrahim)
Abu'l Hasan (Muhammad ibn al-Hussain)
Abu'l Hasan (Muhammad ibn Ibrahim)
Abu'l Husain (ibn abi Omar)
Abu'l Husain (ibn Karnib)
Abu'l Husain (Thawaba)
Abu'l Jainus
Abu'l Jaish ibn al-Khurasani
Abu'l Jarud
Abu'l Jawd
Abu'l Kalabi
Abu'l Menhal
Abu'l Muhlim al-Shaibani
Abu'l Mun'im
Abu'l Najm al-Anbari
Abu'l Qanawi
Abu'l Qasim (abd al-Rahman)
Abu'l Qasim (Abd'ul'lah ibn Ali)
Abu'l Qasim (al-Hadithi)
Abu'l Qasim (al-Kufi)
Abu'l Qasim (Isa'bni Ali)
Abu'l Samh
Abu'l Shais
Abu Hanifa al-Dinawari
Abu Hasan al-Ziadi
Abu Hashim al-Jaba'i
Abu Hashisha
Abu Hasin Muhammad
Abu Hatem (al-Razi)
Abu Hatem (al-Sajastani)
Abu Hathem (al-Qadhi)
Abu Hesan al-Namli
Abu Isa Ahmad ibn Ali
Abu Is'haq (al-Attar)
Abu Is'haq (al-Fazari)
Abu Is'haq (ibn ali Owr)
Abu Is'haq (Ibrahim ibn Abbas)
Abu Ja'far (al-Khazen)
Abu Ja'far (al-Mansur)
Abu Ja'far (Muhammad ibn Ali)
Abu Kabir al-Ahwari
Abu Kamil Shuja'a
Abu Karkara
Abu Khaira
Abu Khalid al-Qanawi
Abu Khalifa
Abu Khithama
Abu'l Umaithal
Abu'l Wafa
Abu'l Wazir Omar ibn Mutrif
Abu'l Yaqthan al-Nesaba
Abu Mahduyya A'arabi
Abu Mansur al-Munajjim
Abu Mashal
Abu Ma'shar
Abu Muhammad (Abd'ul'lah)
Abu Muhammad (Qadhi)
Abu Mukhif Lut ibn Yahya
Abu Mushar
Abu Mu'shar
Abu Muslim Abu Taba Taba al-Alawi
Abu Na'eem ibn Dakin
Abu Namilat al-Namili
Abu Nowas
Abu Obaida
Abu Omar (al-Qabri)
Abu Omar (al-Zahid)
Abu Qur'an
Abu Rubahi
Abu Sa'd al-Makhzumi
Abu Sahl (al-Fadhl ibn Noe'bakht)
Abu Sahl (al-Nowbakhti)
Abu Sa'id (Abd al-Rahman)
Abu Sa'id (al-Sairafi)
Abu Sa'id (al-Sakri)
Abu Sa'id (ibn Tarath)
Abu Sa'id (Thanan ibn Thabit)
Abu Saleh (ibn Yazdad)
Abu Saleh (Abdul'lah ibn Muhammad ibn Yazdad ibn Suwaid)
Abu Shaibani
Abu Sulaiman (al-Nisaburi)
Abu Sulaiman (al-Sajastani)
Abu Tahir
Abu Talib al-Anbari
Abu Thamin al-Kalabi
Abu Thowr
Abu Turab
Abu Ubaid al-Qasem ibn Islam

Abu Uffan al-Muhzemi
Abu Uthman al-Khaledyan
Abu Yahya al-Marwazi
Abu Ya'qub al-Razi
Abu Ya'qub Is'haq
Abu Yazid al-Balkhi
Abu Yusef (Ya'qut ibn Ibrahim ibn Habib ibn Sa'd)
Abu Yusuf (al-Masis)
Abu Zaid
Abu Zakariyya
Abu Zia al-Nasibi
Adam ibn Abd'ul Aziz
Adami
Adli
Afar ibn Luqait
Aflatun (Plato)
Aqriton
Ahfash al-Saqir
Ahmad (ibn al-Taib)
Ahmad (ibn Hanbal)
Ahmad (ibn Harith al-Khazaz)
Ahmad (ibn Hatem)
Ahmad (ibn Muhammad al-Hasib)
Ahamd (ibn Muhammad ibn Sulaiman)
Ahmad (ibn Sahl)
Ahran al-Qis
Ailan Abu Marwan
Ajri Abu Bakr
Akhfash al-Basri
Akhmimi Uthman ibn Swaid
Akhu ibn Ramdhan
Alaba't al-Qalam
al-Ahwal
al-Ahwari
al-Akhfash al-Mujashe'i
al-Akhtal
Alam (or Elim) al-Sha'irah
al-Amawi
Alan al-Sha'ubi
al-Ashram ibn al-Muqira
al-Asma'i
al-Hazri
Ali (al-Razi)
Ali (al-Tamar)
Ali (ibn Ahmad al-Emrani)
Ali (ibn Asem al-Nasa'i)
Ali (ibn al-Madini)
Ali (ibn Dawud)
Ali (ibn Hamza't al-Kasawi)
Ali (ibn Hashim)
Ali (ibn Hesham)
Ali (ibn Isa'l Jarrah)
Ali (ibn Muhammad al-Sayeh al-Alawi)
Ali (ibn Musa'l Qomi)
Ali (ibn Ubaida't al-Rayhani)
Ali (ibn Zail)
al-Isphahani
Alwi al-Basri
Amdi al-Hasan ibn Bashar
Amgidoros
Amna bent al-Walid
Amni
Amnu ibn Sa'id
Amonious
Amra'al-Qais ibn Hajar
Amra'ul-Qais ibn Zaid Manat
Amru ibn Mas'adeh
Anan Jaria't al-Natefi
Antaki al-Mijtabi
Aram
Arastalis (Aristotle)
Arios al-Rumi
Aristorkhos
Arshmidos (Archimedes)
Arstaklos
Asadi (al-Asadi)
Ash'ari abu-Ja'far
Ash'hab ibn Abd'ul Aziz
Ashnandani (al-Ashnandani)
Ashnani al-Qathi
Asim ibn Behdeleh
Astanhari abu-Sa'id
Atabi (al-Atabi)
Atarud ibn Muhammad
Atbi
Athafroditos
Athram ibn Hani
Atologhos
Atoqios
Attwi
Awami
Awanat al-Kalbi
Ayyashi
Azraqi
Badroqoqia
Bah Abu Abd'ul'lah
Bahtari
Bakhtishu'
Bakkar
Bakr ibn Soad (So'ad?)
Bakri
Balwi
Bandaniji bent Ruh
Banu'l Mudabber
Baqwi
Barji
Barjlani
Barmaki
Barzukh al-Arydhi
Bash ibn Ali Sara
Bashar ibn Bard
Bashr (ibn al-Harith)
Bashr (ibn al-Walid)

Muhammad (ibn al-Sabbah)
Muhammad (ibn Dawul Abu Bakr)
Muhammad (ibn Dawud ibn al-Jarrah)
Muhammad (ibn Habib)
Muhammad (ibn Hajar)
Muhammad (ibn Isa)
Muhammad (ibn Is'haq al-Sarraj)
Muhammad (ibn Mukram)
Muhammad (ibn Rashid)
Muhammad (ibn Sa'd Katib al-Waqedi)
Muhammad (ibn Sahl ibn Marzaban)
Muhammad (ibn Sa'ib al-Kalbi)
Muhammad (ibn Salam)
Muhammad (ibn Yahya)
Muhammad (ibn Yazid Dubays) (or Dabis)
Muhammad (ibn Zakariyya al-Razi)
Muhammad (ibn Ziad al-Harethi)
Muhammad (Wikani)
Muhammad (Yadizi)
Muhli Abu'l Abbas
Mu'idi
Mujalid ibn Sa'd
Mukhnaf
Munajjim
Muqirah
Muqsim al-Zaba
Muradi
Mu'rij al-Sadusi
Murtis (or Muristis)
Musa (ben Abd al-Malik)
Musa (ben Isa'l Kasrawi)
Musa (ben Shaker)
Mus'ib ibn Abd'ul'lah al-Zabiri
Muslim (ibn al-Hajjaj)
Muslim (ibn al-Walid)
Mutin ibn Ayyub
Mutwaq
Nabiqat (al-Ja'di)
Nabiqat (al-Thibyani)
Nafi ibn Abd al-Rahman
Naftuyah
Nairizi
Najeeh al-Madani
Najjar
Namiri
Namr ibn Towlab
Naqad
Naqqash (Abu Bakr)
Naqqash (Abu'l Hasan)
Nasabat al-Bukra
Nasbi Hasan ibn Musa
Nasivi Abu'l Hassan
Nasr ibn Muzahim (Abul Fadhl)
Nasr (ibn Sayyar)
Nasr (ibn Yusuf)
Nasran
Natahat al-Anbari
Nazeer ibn Shameel
Niqulaos
Niqumakhis
Nisaburi (Abu Bakr)
Nu'man ibn Thabet
Obaid ibn Sharya't al-Jarahmali
Obaidul'lah (ibn Abdul'lah ibn Tahir)
Obaidul'lah (ibn Abi Tabir)
Obaidul'lah (al-Warraq)
Obaidul'lah (ibn Muhammad ibn Abdu'l-Malik)
Obaina't ibn al-Menhal
Obbad ibn Kaseeb
Olia bent al-Mahdi
Omar (ibn al-Farrukhan)
Omar (ibn al-Marwarudhi)
Omar (ibn Bakir)
Omar (ibn Shabeh)
Omayya't ibn Omayyah
Othman ibn Abi Shibah
Othman ibn Sowaid al-Akhmimi
Otioqias
Otoliqos
Owza'i
Ozdi
Qafal Abu Bakr
Qairawani
Qaisi
Qalabi
Qalib ibn Uthman al-Hamdani
Qalishtanis
Qanbara
Qaris al-Muqanni
Qartalusi
Qasan ibn Abd al-Hamid
Qasem (ibn Yusuf)
Qasem (ibn Mu'in)
Qasem (ibn Sayyar)
Qashani
Qatiba ibn Ziad
Qitwar al-Baboli
Qodama (ibn Ja'far)
Qomama (ibn Zaid)
Qomi
Qorais al-Maqni
Qorqi Zahir ibn Maimun
Qotrab
Qowairi
Qulam (al Abbari)
Qulam (Khalil)
Qulam Zahl
Qumi (Abu Ja'far)
Qumi (Sa'd ibn Ibrahim)
Qunya't Umm al-Haitham
Qurat ibn Qamit al-Harrani
Qusta ibn Tuma al-Ba'labaki

Qutra ibn al-Fuj'at
Rababi
Rabia't al-Basri
Rabia't al-Ra'i
Ramah ibn Muharrer al-Basri
Ramzi (al-Kabir)
Ramzi (al-Saqir)
Rawanedi
Razi (Abu Bakr Ahmad ibn Ali)
Razi al-Shatranji
Razi (Zakariyya Abu Bakr)
Razi (Ya'qub ibn Muhammad)
Riyashi
Rowass
Ru'bat ibn al-Ajjaj
Rufis
Sabh ibn Asem al-Naqit
Sabi' Ibrahim ibn Halal
Sabuya ibn Sahl
Sa'dan ibn al-Mubarak
Sa'di al-Qasir
Sa'eq
Safdi
Saffah
Sahar al-Abdi
Sahib (Abul Qasem ibn Ubad)
Sahib (ibn Abdu'l Malik)
Sahir
Sahl (al-Tastari)
Sahl (ibn Bashr)
Sahl (ibn Harun)
Sahl (ibn Muhammad al-Sajistani)
Sa'id (ibn Hamid Abu-Uthman)
Sa'id (ibn Hamid ibn al-Bakhtakan)
Sa'id ibn Harun al-Katib
Sa'id ibn Wahb
Saif ibn Umar al-Asadi
Sairafi
Saji
Sakit (and his son Ya'qub)
Sakmah bent al-Husain
Salam al-Qari
Salem Abu'l Ala
Salih (al-Hanafi)
Salih (al-Naji)
Salih (ibn Is'haq al-Bajli)
Salim ibn Qais al-Halali
Salm Sahib Bait al-Hikmah
Salma't ibn Asim
Salmuya ibn Banan
Salmuya ibn Salih al-Laithi
Samisati
Samka Muhammad ibn Ali
Sanan (ibn al-Fat'h)
Sanan (ibn Thabit)
Sanbliqios al-Rumi
Sand ibn Ali al-Yahudi
Sarakhsi (Abdul Aziz ibn Muhammad)
Sarakhsi (Abu'l Faraj)
Sarfnani
Sa'uda
Sayeh al-Alawi
Sefwan ibn Yahya
Sefyan al-Thowri
Serri
Sesat al-Hindi
Shabib al-Asfari
Shabil ibn Arara't al-Dhab'i
Shafe'i (and associates)
Shaibani
Shaidama
Shaitan al-Taq
Sharif al-Ridha
Sharq ibn al-Qatami
Shifyan ibn Ubaina't al-Halali
Shikal
Sho'bat ibn al-Hajjaj
Shukla't umm Ibrahim ibn al-Mahdi
Sibuyah
Sifwani
Soali Abu Bakr ibn Yahya
Sufi
Sufyan (al-Thowri)
Sufyan (ibn Abinah)
Sufyan (ibn Muawiyah)
Sukri (Abu Sa'ed)
Sukri (al-Hasan ibn Sa'id)
Sulaiman ibn al-Warid
Suraij
Susanjerdi
Tabari (and associates)
Tahawi
Tahir ibn al-Husain
Ta'i
Talhi
Talib ibn al-Azhar
Tamimi
Tamin (ibn Abi' Muqbil)
Tamin (ibn Marra)
Taqlabi Muhammad ibn al-Harith
Tarmah
Tarmathi
Tateri
Tawal
Thabit (ibn abi Thabit)
Thabit (ibn Qurra)
Thadhinos
Thahhak ibn Ajlan
Tha'lab Abu'l Abbas
Tha'lab (Ahmad ibn Yahya)
Thamar't ibn Thamra't al-Nah'shali
Thamestios
Thana al-Katebiyyah
Thawaba't ibn Yunus

Thawaha Abu'l Hussain
Thawen al-Iskandarani
Thawferestos
Theodoros
Thismos
Thoar ibn Yazid
Thoari
Thonnoon al-Mesri (Dhonnoon al-Nisri)
Thorthios
Tiadoros
Tinqrous al Baboli
Tuklous al Baboli
Tusi
Urnbasios
Wafrawandi
Wahb ibn Munbih
Wahq
Wahshi Abu Qurwan
Waki' (al-Qadhi)
Waki' (ibn al-Jarrah)
Waliba't ibn al-Hobab
Walid (al-Qumi)
Walid (ibn Muslim)
Walid (ibn Yazid)
Waqedi
Waseh
Waseti (and associates)
Washa'
Wasil ibn Hayyan
Yahya (al-Nahwi)
Yahya (ben Abi Mansour)
Yahya (ben Ada)
Yahya (ben Adam)
Yahya (ben al Fathl)
Yahya (ben Kamel)
Yahya (ben Khalid)
Yahya (ben Muath al-Razi)
Yahya (ben Sarrafiyyun)
Yahya (ben Zahedah)
Yahya (ibn Abi Hafsah)
Yahya (ibn Balal al-Abdi)
Yahya (ibn Ziyad al-Harethi)
Yahya (ibn Zakariyya)
Yahya'l Mouseli ibn Abi Mansour
Yamani
Yaqteen (A'li Yaqteen)
Ya'qub (ibn al-Sukait)
Ya'qub (ibn Nuh)
Ya'qub (ibn Tariq)
Yazdjird al-Kasrawi
Yazid (ibn al-Muhlib)
Yazid (ibn Muhammad al-Mahli)
Youhanna'l Qis
Younis (al-Katib)
Younis (ibn Abd al-Rahman)
Younis (ibn Habib)
Yousef (ibn Umar al-Thaqfi)
Yousif (al-Qawwah)
Yuhanna ben Masuya
Yusefi
Zabir ibn Bakkar
Zabiri
Za'edah't ibn Qaddama't al-Thaqafi
Za'edan
Za'farani
Zafr
Zahir (ibn Abi Salmi)
Zahir (ibn Maimun al-Hamdani)
Zahri
Zaid al-Khail
Zaidiyya
Zarara't ibn A'in
Ziad (Ibrahim ibn Sufyan)
Ziad (ben Umaiyyah)
Zubaidah bent Ja'far
Zujaj (ibn al-Laith)
Zujaj (ibn al-Sara)

Works Listed Under Different Fields

Arabs
Arts and Crafts
Beginnings (Awa'il)
Caliphs
Histories of Cities (Akhbar al-Buldan)
Histories of Poetry (Akhbar al-Shi'r)
Histories of Women (Akhbar An-Nisa)
Ignorance, Period of (Jahiliyya)
Jalinus, Works and Commentaries on Galen
Love and Lovers
Muhammad, the Prophet
Persian Translations
Poets
Prophet, The
Publishers (Musannefin)
Published Works
Qoraish Tribe
Qur'an's Interpretations, and so forth
Superstitions, and so forth
Tradition (Akhbar al-Asmar)
Tradition, Islamic
Tradition (Munafirat)
Victories (Fotuh)

Works on Education

It may interest the reader to know that al-Nadim frequently lists titles of books in the *Al-Fihrist* dealing with the broad area of education and psychology, as the following examples indicate.

1. *Kitab Khulq al-Insan (The Book of Human Disposition)* by al-Harmazi.
2. *Kitab al-Sifat al-Insan (The Book of Human Characteristics)* by al-Nadhir ibn Shamil.
3. *Kitab Khulq al-Insan (The Book of Human Disposition)* by al-Qatrab.
4. *Kitab Khulq al-Insan (The Book of Human Disposition)* by Asma'i.
5. *Kitab Mukhtasari Nahw al-Muta'allemin (The Book of Brief Grammar for Pupils)* by al-Jurmi.
6. *Kitab Khulq al-Insan (The Book of Human Disposition)* by Abi Khatim al-Sajastani.
7. *Kitab Adab al-Katib (The Book of Manners of Scribe)* by ibn Qutaibah.
8. *Kitab Khulq al-Insan (The Book of Human Disposition)* by ibn Qutaibah.
9. *Kitab al-Ma'arif (The Book of Education* [or *Sciences*]*)* by ibn Qutaibah.
10. *Kitab al-Mahasen (The Book of Good Deeds)* by ibn Qutaibah.
11. *Kitab al-Ilm (The Book of Knowledge)* by ibn Qutaibah.
12. *Kitab al-Fisahah (The Book of Eloquence)* by Abu Hanifa't al-Dinuri.
13. *Kitab Adab al-Katib (The Book of Manners of Scribe)* by Abu Bakr.
14. *Kitab Khulq al-Insan (The Book of Human Disposition)* by Muhammad Qasim al-Anbari.
15. *Kitab Khulq al-Insan (The Book of Human Disposition)* by Mufdhal ibn Salmah.
19. *Kitab Khulq al-Insan* (*The Book of Human Disposition*) by Nasr ibn Yuseff.
17. *Kitab al-Taharah (The Book of Cleanliness)* by ibn Ubaid Qasim ibn Salam.
18. *Kitab Khulq al-Insan (The Book of Human Disposition)* by Ali Umar al-Shaibani.
19. *Kitab Khulq al-Insan (The Book of Human Disposition)* by Nasr ibn Yuseff.
20. *Kitab Khulq al-Insan (The Book of Human Disposition)* by Abu Ziad al-Kalabi.
21. *Kitab Khluq al-Insan (The Book of Human Disposition)* by Abu Malik ibn Karkarah.
22. *Kitab Khluq al-Insan (The Book of Human Disposition)* by Abu Mulhim al-Shaibani.
23. *Kitab Khulq al-Insan (The Book of Human Disposition)* by al-Wah'shi.
24. *Kitab Khluq al-Insan (The Book of Human Disposition)* by Sa'd ibn al-Mubarak.
25. *Kitab Khluq al-Insan (The Book of Human Disposition)* by al-Zujaj.
26. *Kitab Showq al-Watan (The Book of Patriotism* [or *Citizenship*]*)* by al-Wahshi.
27. *Kitab al-Natiq (The Book of the Orator)* by al-Mubrad.
28. *Kitab Adab al-Katib (The Book of Manners of Scribe)* by ibn Darstuyah.
29. *Kitab Hubb al-Awtan (The Book of Love of Homelands)* by Musa bin Isa al-Kasrawi.
30. *Kitab al-Imtihan al-Katib (The Book of Examination for the Scribe)* by ibn Hamarah.
31. *Kitab Makarim al-Akhlaq (The Book of Ethical Ideals* [or *Moral Ideals*]*)* by ibn Abi'l Dunya.
32. *Kitab al-Adab (The Book of Good Manners)* by al-Atabi.
33. *Kitab al-Ilm wa Sharaf al-Kitabat (The Book of the Science and Excellence of Writing)* by ibn Abi'l As'haq.
34. *Kitab al-Ilm (The Book of Knowledge)* by ibn Abi'l Sarh.
35. *Kitab Khulq al-Insan* (*The Book of Human Disposition*) by al-Hamiz.

36. *Kitab al-Qara'at (The Book of Reading Methods)* by Ben Kisan.
37. *Kitab al-Hija' (The Book of Spelling Method)* by Ben Kisan.
38. *Kitab al-Tasarif (The Book of Grammars)* by Ben Kisan.
39. *Kitab al-Sifat al-Insan (The Book of Human Disposition)* by al-Isfahani.
40. *Kitab Khulq al-Insan (The Book of Human Disposition)* by al-Ja'd.
41. *Kitab al-Mukhtasar l'il Muta'allim (The Book of Summaries for the Pupil)* by Abu Tawab.
42. *Kitab Hedayah (The Book of Guidance)* by Abu'l Hassan.
43. *Kitab Adab al-Akhwan (The Book of Good Manners Among Brothers)* by Quraish.
44. *Kitab Adab al-Sima' (The Book of Listening Manners)* by Abu'l Faraj al-Isfahani.
45. *Kitab Adab al-Saqir (The Book of Good Manners for the Child)* by Abd'ul'lah ibn al-Muqaffa.

APPENDIX IV

PARTIAL LIST OF ISLAMIC SCHOLARS AND WORKS, 700-1350 A.D.

In the following lists of Muslim scholars and their main writings from about 750 to 1350 A. D., the items of information on each author are arranged in the following order:

(1) The author's full name exclusive of his last name
(2) Date of his birth and death, if determinable
(3) His nationality
(4) The languages in which he wrote
(5) His basic fields of interest
(6) His basic works.

Many of these authors have been known by different surnames, which appear in their full names. In preparing the alphabetic arrangements I have been guided by the last name of each author as it usually appears in basic texts. Some writers refer to these authors by their honorary titles of distinction, their first names, or the place of their birth. To have followed all these variations would have made the present alphabetic arrangement impossible, and I was unable to find any alphabetic arrangements of these names. Therefore, I take full responsibility for the present method of arrangement. The lists, including translations from Arabic into Latin, etc., are based on materials that were available to me and are incomplete, but I hope representative. They are based by and large on the following works, particularly those of George Sarton whose subject pattern, except for a few omissions, is alphabetically arranged in this and the following appendix:

1. Brockelman, Carl, *Geschichte der Arabischen Litterature,* Lg. 8 vols., 5 vols., E. J. Brill, Leiden, 1937-49. First ed. 2 vols.: Verlag von Emil Felber, Weimar, 1899-1902.

2. Brockelman, Carl, *Geschichte der Islamischen Volker und Staaten,* mit 8 karten. 2 aufl München und Berlin: R. Oldenbourg, 1943.

3. Browne, Edward Granville, *A Literary History of Persia,* Cambridge (Eng.): The University Press, 1930 4v.

4. *Encyclopedia of Islam,* A dictionary of the geography, ethnography, and biography of the Muhammadan peoples. Edited by M. T. Houtsma, T. W. Arnold, R. Basset, R. Hartmann, A. J. Wensinck, W. Heffening, E. Levi-Provencal, H. A. R. Gibb, Leiden: E. J. Brill, London: Luzac and Co., 1938 4v plus supplement, rev. ed. Vols. I & II.

5. Safa, Dr. Dhabih Allah, *Tarikhi Adabiyyat dar Iran,* (Literary History of Iran from the Middle of the Fifth Century to the Beginning of Seventh Century

Hejira), Vol. II, Teheran: Elmiyyah Islamiyyah Press, 1339 Shamsi Hejira (in Persian).

6. Safa, Dr. Dhabih Allah, *Tarikh Ulum Aqli dar Tamadduni Islami,* (History of Rational Sciences in Islamic Civilization), Vol. I, Teheran: Danishgah Press, 1336 Shamsi Hejira (in Persian).

7. Sarton, George, *Introduction to the History of Science,* Baltimore: The Williams and Wilkins Co., Vol. I, 1927; Vol. II Parts I and II, 1931; Vol. III Parts I and II, 1948.

The areas of arts, literature and poetry have been omitted since they do not have direct bearing on the main purpose of this study.

Astronomy and Mathematics

1. al-Abhari, (1) ?, (2) Died 1332 or 1333, (3) Persian, (4) Arabic, (5) Mathematics, (6) Fusul Kafiyya fi Hisab al-Takht Wal-Mil'—Arithmetic treatise.

2. al-Abuli, (1) Muhammad ibn Ibrahim, (2) Died after 1347, (3) Algerian, (4) Arabic, probably, (5) Mathematics, philosophy, science, (6) None.

3. ibn Aflah, (1) Jabir ibn Aflah, (2) Died middle 13th, (3) Hispano-Muslim, (4) Arabic, probably, (5) Astronomy, mathematics, (6) Kitab al-Hai'a—Astronomy.

4. ibn Ahmad, (1) Ata ibn Ahmad, (2) Flourished 1362, (3) Persian, (4) Arabic, (5) Astronomy, (6) Astronomical treatise with Lainar tables.

5. al-Ainzarbi, (1) Adnan, (2) Died c. 1153 or 1154, (3) Cilicia, (4) Arabic, (5) Medicine and astronomy, (6) Kitab al-Kafi fi Ilm al-Tibb—On medicine; Kitab fi Ma Yahtaj al-Tabib Min Ilm al-Falak—On astronomy.

6. ibn Ali, (1) Abd al-Qadir, (2) Flourished last quarter 14th, (3) Western origin, (4) Arabic, (5) Mathematics, (6) Commentary on Fi Hisab al-Yad by ibn al-Maghribi—Reckoning.

7. ibn Ali, (1) Abul-Taiyib Sanad, (2) Died after 864, (3) ?, (4) ?, (5) Astronomy and mathematics, (6) Compiled astronomical tables and wrote on astronomical subjects; Investigations on specific gravity; Constructed the Kanisa, an observatory in Baghdad.

8. al-Araj, (1) Nizam al-Araj, (2) Flourished end 13th, beginning 14th, (3) Persian, (4) Arabic, probably, (5) Mathematics and astronomy, (6) Qaraib al-Qur'an wa Raghaib al-Furqan—Commentary on Qur'an; Commentary on al-Shafiyya by ibn al-Hajib—Arabic grammar; Al-Risala al-Shamsiyya fi al-Hisab—Treatise on arithmetic; A commentary on the Almagest; Commentaries on various works of Nasir al-Din.

9. al-Asfuzari, (1) Muzaffar al-Asfuzari, (2) Died before 1122, (3) Khurasan, Persia, (4) ?, (5) Mathematics and physics, (6) Summary of Euclid's Elements, Ikhtisar li Usul Uqlidis, extending to Book xiv composed by Hypsocles (2nd century).

10. al-Asturlabi, (1) al-Badi al-Asturlabi, (2) Died c. 1139 or

1140, (3) Lived in Ispahan and Baghdad, (4) Arabic, probably, (5) Astronomy, (6) Mahmudic tables.

11. al-Asturlabi, (1) Ali ibn Isa, (2) Flourished c. 830, (3) Persian, (4) Arabic, (5) Astronomy, (6) "Wrote one of the earliest Arabic treatises on astrolabe."

12. al-Asturlabi, (1) Abu Hamid Ahmad ibn Muhammad al-Saqani, (2) Died 990, (3) Persian, (4) ?, (5) Mathematics and astronomy, (6) None.

13. ibn Badr, (1) ?, (2) Probably 13th, (3) Hispano-Muslim, (4) Arabic, probably, (5) Mathematics, (6) Compendium of algebra.

14. al-Baghdadi, (1) Abu Bakr Muhammad ibn Abd al-Baqi, (2) Flourished c. 1100, (3) ?, (4) ?, (5) Mathematics, (6) Possibly the author of a commentary on the tenth book of Euclid, Liber Jdei Super Decimum Euclids, translated by Gerardo Cremonese.

15. al-Bahaniqi, (1) ?, (2) Born 1355, (3) Egyptian, (4) Arabic, (5) Astronomy, (6) Risala fi al-Amal bil-Rub al-Muqni—Treatise on the use of the sufficient quadrant.

16. ibn Bajja, (1) ?, (2) c. 1138-1139, (3) Hispano-Muslim, (4) Arabic, probably, (5) Philosopher, scientist, physician and commentator on Aristotle, music, (6) Kitab Tadbir al-Mutawahhid—Philosophy; Risalat al-Wada—Philosophy; Treatise on music—Lost.

17. al-Balkhi, (1) Abu Zaid Ahmad ibn Sahl, (2) Died 934, (3) Persian, (4) ?, (5) Mathematics, (6) Suwar al-Aqalim—Figures of the climates.

18. al-Balkhi, (1) Abu Mashar Jafar ibn Muhammad ibn Umar, (2) Died 886, (3) Persian, (4) ?, (5) Astronomy, (6) Kitab al-Mudkhal Ila Ilm Ahkam al-Nujum—The great book of introduction to astronomy.

19. ibn al-Banna, (1) ?, (2) c. 1256-1321, (3) Moroccan, (4) Arabic, probably, (5) Mathematics and astronomy, (6) Talkhis fi Amal al-Hisab—"Summary of the operations of calculation derived from al-Hassar"; Risala fi Ilm al-Masaha—Geometry; Al-Maqalat fi al-Hisab—Arithmetic; Tanbih al-Albab—Arithmetic; Mukhtasar Kafi li'l-Muttalib—Arithmetic; Kitab al-Usul al-Muqaddamat fi al-Jabr wal-Muqabala—Algebra; Kitab fi al-Jabr wal-Muqabala—Algebra; Kitab Minhaj li Ta'dil al-Kawakib—Astronomy; Qanun li-Tarhil al-Shams wal-Qamar fi'l-Manazil Wa Ma Kifat Awqat al-Lail wal-Nahar—Astronomy; Kitab al-Yasar fi Taqwim al-Kawakib al-Sayyara—Astronomy; Treatise on the astrolabe; Madkal al-Nujum wa Taba'i al-Huruf—Astrology; Kitab fi Ahkam al-Nujum—Judicial astrology; Kitab al-Manakh—Calendar.

20. ibn Basa, (1) ?, (2) Died 1316 or 1317, (3) Spanish Muslim, may be Jewish, (4) Arabic, probably, (5) Theology, mathematics, astronomy, (6) He may have written a book on the astrolabe.

21. al-Bitruji, (1) ?, (2) Pupil of ibn Tufail, (3) Hispano-Muslim, (4) Arabic, probably, (5) Astronomy, (6) Kitab al-Hai'a—Configuration of heavenly bodies.

22. al-Buni, (1) ?, (2) Died c. 1225, (3) Algerian, (4) Arabic,

probably, (5) Occultism, (6) Shams al-Ma'arif wa Lata'f al-Awarif—Sun of knowledge; Kitab al-Khawasi—Book of magic properties; Sirr al-Hikam—Secret of the sciences.

23. al-Buzjani, (1) Abu'l Wafa Muhammad ibn Muhammad ibn Isma'il ibn al-Abbas, (2) 940-999, (3) Persian, (4) Arabic, (5) Astronomy, mathematics, translator, (6) Commentaries on Euclid, Diophantos, al-Khwarizmi (all lost); Astronomical tables—Zij al-Wadih; A practical arithmetic; Kitab al-Kamil—The complete book; Kitab al-Handasa—Book of applied geometry ("probably the work of a disciple").

24. al-Dahhan, (1) ?, (2) Died 1194, (3) Born in Baghdad, (4) Arabic, probably, (5) Law, arithmetic, astronomy, (6) Taqwim al-Nazar—Legal tables.

25. al-Dimishqi (or Dimashqi), (1) Abu 'Uthman Said Yaqub, (2) Flourished 908-932, (3) ?, (4) Arabic, (5) Mathematics, medicine, (6) Translated into Arabic works of Aristotle, Euclid, Galen on temperaments and on the pulse, and works of Porphyry; Translated Book X of Euclid, with Pappos's commentary on it.

26. al-Farqani, (1) Abu al-Abbas Ahmad ibn Muhammad ibn Kathir, (2) Still living in 861, (3) Persian, (4) ?, (5) Astronomy, (6) Kitab fi Rarakat al-Samawiyya wa Jawami' Ilm al-Nujum—Celestial motions and complete science of the stars.

27. al-Farisi, (1) Muhammad ibn Abi Bakh?, (2) Undetermined, c. 1231-1232, (3) Persian, (4) Persian, probably, (5) Mathematics and astronomy, (6) Nihayat al-Idrak fi Asrar Ulum al-Aflak—Spheres; Ma'arij al-Fikr al-Wahij—Astronomical tables; Ayat al-Afaq Min Khawass al-Aufaq—Magic squares.

28. al-Faziri, (1) Abu Abd Allah Muhammad ibn Ibrahim, (2) Died c. 796-806, (3) Persian, (4) ?, (5) Science and astronomy, (6) None.

29. al-Ghafiqi, (1) Abu al-Qasim Ahmad ibn Abdul'lah ibn 'Umar, (2) Died 1035, (3) Hispano-Muslim, (4) ?, (5) Mathematics and astronomy, (6) Treatise on the astrolabe; Compiled tables according to the Siddhanta method.

30. al-Ghalib, (1) Abu 'Ali al-Khaiyyat (the tailor) Yahya, (2) Died c. 835, (3) ?, (4)?, (5) Astronomy, (6) De Judiciis Nativitatum.

31. al-Ghaznawi, (1) Thahir-ud-din Abul Mahamed Muhammad ibn Mas'ud al-Mas'udi, (2) ?, (3) Persian, (4) Persian, (5) Astronomy, (6) Kefayat-al-Ta'lim—On instruction in the science of astronomy; Jahani Danish—The world of knowledge.

32. al-Ghuttan, (1) Ainuzzaman Imam Abu Ali Hassan ibn Ghuttan Marwazi, (2) Born 1072, (3) Persian, (4) Persian, (5) Astronomy, (6) Gayhan Shenakht—Knowledge of stars.

33. al-Ha'im, (1) ?, (2) Born 1352-1355, died 1412, (3) Egyptian, (4) Arabic, probably, (5) Mathematics, (6) Murshid al-Talib Ila 'Asna' al-Matalib—On arithmetic and inheritance problems; Al-Muqni'—Algebraic poem; Tarqib al-Ra'id fi'Ilm al-Fara'id; Al-Ma'una fi'Ilm al-

hawa'il—Mental computation; Qayat al-Su'ul fi-Iqrar bil-Majhul; Sharh al-Arjuza al-Yasminiya—Commentary on al-Yasmini's algebra.

34. ibn Hamid, (1) Muhammad ibn al-Husain, (2) Flourished 9th or 10th, (3) ?, (4) ?, (5) Astronomy, (6) Compiled astronomical tables.

35. al-Hanbali, (1) Taqi al-Din, (2) Before 1409, (3) Egyptian or Syrian, (4) Arabic, probably, (5) Mathematics, (6) Hawi al-Lubab Min 'Ilm al-Hisab—Treatise on arithmetic.

36. ibn Hani (or Haya), (1) Abu 'Uthman Sahl ibn Bishr ibn Habib, (2) First half 9th, (3) Persian ?, (4) Arabic, (5) Astronomy and mathematics, (6) Many treatises on astrology; Book on algebra.

37. al-Harrani, (1) Jabir ibn Sinan, (2) ?, (3) ?, (4) ?, (5) Mathematics, (6) None.

38. al-Hasib, (1) Ibrahim al-Hasib, (2) Flourished 1358, (3) Egyptian (4) Arabic, probably, (5) Astrology, (6) Commentary on Kitab al-Uluf wal-Adwar by Abu Ma'shar; Commentary on Kitab al-Qiranat by Abu Ma'shar; Commentary on Kitab al-Amthal by Abu Ma'shar.

39. al-Hassar, (1) Muhammad al-Hassar, (2) 12th or 13th, (3) Western Muslim, (4) Arabic, probably, (5) Mathematics, (6) Treatise on arithmetic and algebra.

40. al-Haufi, (1) Abu al-Qasim al-Haufi, (2) Died c. 1192 or 1193, (3) Hispano-Muslim, (4) Arabic, probably, (5) Law and arithmetic, (6) Kitab al-Farid—Division of inheritances.

41. al-Hilli, (1) 'Abd al-Aziz ibn Soraya, (2) ?, (3) Iraqi, (4) ?, (5) Astronomy, (6) Buruj al-Aflak—Musical astrology.

42. al-Husain, (1) Abu Ja'far Muhammad ibn, (2) 2nd half 10th, (3) Arabic, (4) ?, (5) Mathematics, (6) Memoir on rational right angled triangles; "Memoir on determination of two mean proportionals between two lines by a geometrical method."

43. ibn Husain, (1) Muhammad ibn al-Husain, (2) Between 1187 and 1193, (3) Eastern Muslim, (4) Arabic, probably, (5) Mathematics, (6) Risala al-Birkar al-Tamm (assisted by Kamal al-Din ibn Yunus).

44. al-Husaini, (1) Abu al-Qasim 'Ali ibn al-Husain al-'alawi al-Sharif al-Husaini, (2) Died 985, (3) ?, (4) ?, (5) Astronomy, (6) None.

45. al-Huwari, (1) 'Abd al-Aziz ibn 'Ali, (2) ?, (3) Moroccan, (4) Arabic, probably, (5) Mathematics, (6) Ghayat al-Kuttab—Commentary on al-Banna's arithmetical treatise; Talkhis fi A'mal al-Hisab—Summary, "operation of calculation."

46. al-Imrani, (1) 'Ali ibn Ahmad, (2) Died 955 or 956, (3) ?, (4) ?, (5) Mathematics and astronomy, (6) Commentary on Abu Kamil's algebra; Various astrological treatises.

47. ibn Iraq, (1) Abu Nasr Mansur ibn 'Ali, (2) ?, (3) Iraq, (4) ?, (5) Astronomy, mathematics, (6) Wrote improved edition of Menalaos's Spherica; Wrote on trigonometry and astronomy.

48. al-Isfahani, (1) Abu al-Fath Mahmud ibn Muhammad ibn

Qasim ibn Fadhl, (2) About 982, (3) Persian, (4) ?, (5) Mathematics, (6) None.

49. al-Jadari, (1) ?, (2) Died c. 1415-1435, (3) Arabic, (4) Arabic, (5) Astronomy, (6) Raudat al-Azhar fi 'Ilm Waqt al-Lail wal Nahar—Determination of time, day and night; Iqtitaf al-Anwar—Commentary on previous work; Tanhib al-Anam—Treatise on calendar; Commentary on calendar treatise by Abu Muqri'.

50. al-Jaghmini, (1) ?, (2) Died 1344 or 1345, (3) Persian, (4) Arabic, (5) Astronomy, medicine, (6) Al-Mulakhkhas fi'l-Hai'a—Astronomy; Qiwa al-Kawakib—Astrology; Qanunce—The small qanun.

51. al-Jauhari, (1) al-Abbas ibn Sa'id, (2) Flourished under al-Ma'mun, (3) Persian, (4) ?, (5) Mathematics, astronomy, (6) None.

52. al-Jazuli, (1) Muhammad ibn al-Jazuli, (2) Flourished c. 1344, (3) Moroccan, (4) Arabic, probably, (5) Astronomy, (6) Risala fi 'l-'Amal bil-Istarlab—Astrolabes; Risala fi'l'Amal bil Jaib al-Qaib—Quadrant with hidden sine; Risala fi Thumn al-Da'ira—Octant.

53. al-Jili, (1) Abu al-Hasan Kushyar ibn Labban ibn Bashari, (2) Flourished c. 971-1029, (3) Persian, (4) Arabic, (5) Mathematics, astronomy, (6) Compiled astronomical tables—Al-Zij al-Jami' wa'l Baliq; Astrological introduction; Arithmetical treatise.

54. ibn Jundab, (1) Abu Is'haq Ibrahim ibn Habib ibn Sulaiman ibn Samura, (2) Died c. 777, (3) Persian, (4) ?, (5) Astronomy, (6) Qasida—Poem on astrology; Various astronomical writings.

55. al-Jurjani, (1) Abu Sa'id al-Darir, (2) First half 9th, (3) Persian, (4) Arabic, (5) Mathematics, astronomy, (6) Treatise on geometrical problems; Treatise on drawing of the meridian.

56. al-Juzzani, (1) ?, (2) 1282-1343, (3) Turkoman, (4) Arabic, (5) Theology, astronomy, (6) Commentary on Kitab al-Tabsira fi 'Ilm al-Hai'a by al-Kharaqi—Astronomy.

57. al-Karaki, (1) ?, (2) ?, (3) Arabic, probably, (4) Arabic, probably, (5) Astronomy, (6) None.

58. al-Karkhi, (1) Abu Bakr Muhammad ibn al-Hasan (or Husain) al-Hasib, (2) Died between 1019 and 1029, (3) Baghdad, (4) ?, (5) Mathematics, (6) Al-Kafi fi'l-Hisab—Arithmetic; Al-Fakhri—Algebra.

59. al-Karmani, (1) Abu al-Hakam (Amr or 'Umar) ibn 'Abd al-Rahman ibn Ahmad ibn 'Ali, (2) Died 1066, (3) Spanish Muslim, (4) ?, (5) Mathematics, medicine, (6) None.

60. al-Kashani, (1) ?, (2) c. 1343, (3) Persian, (4) Arabic, (5) Mathematics, rhetoric, (6) Lubab al-Hisab—Book on arithmetic; Commentary on rhetoric of al-Sakkaki; Commentary on rhetoric of al-Samarqandi.

61. al-Khalili, (1) ?, (2) 1378-1408, (3) Syrian, (4) Arabic, probably, (5) Astronomy, (6) Al-Jadwal al-Afaqi—Tables to determine time; Jawal Fadl al-Da'ir wa'amal al-Lail wal-Nahar—Hour angles of sun and stars; Risala fil' Amal bil-Jaib'l-Qa'ib—Quadrants with hidden

sines; Risala bil 'Amal bil-Murabba—Sine quadrants; Al-Nujum al-Zahira—Sine quadrants.

62. al-Kharaqi, (1) Muhammad ibn Ahmad, (2) Died c. 1138 or 1139, (3) Persian, (4) Arabic, (5) Mathematics, astronomy, (6) Muntaha al-Idrak fi Taqsim al-Aflak; Kitab al-Tabsira fi Ilm al-Hai'a; Al-Risala al-Shamila (lost)—Both on astronomy; Al-Risala al-Maqribiya (lost).

63. ibn Khasib, (1) Abu Bakr al-Hasan, (2) ?, (3) Persian, (4) Persian and Arabic, (5) Astrology, (6) De Nativitatibus.

64. Abi'l Khayr, (1) Shahmardan, (2) ?, (3) Persian, (4) Persian, (5) Astronomy, (6) Rowzat-ul Munajjemin—On astronomers; Nizhat Nama'i Ala'i.

65. al-Khayyam, (1) Khawja Imam Hujjat-ul-Haqq Hakim Abul Fath Omar ibn Ibrahim al-Khayyam al-Nishaburi, (2) Died 1123 or 1131 or 1132, (3) Persian, (4) Persian, (5) Astronomy and mathematics, (6) Rubaiyyat—Quatrains; Noe-Rooz Namah—Book of the new year; Resalat dar Ilmi Kulliyyat—Essay on the science of the universe, also called Wojudiyyah (on existence); Khotbat-ul-Qarra—On divine unity (Khayyam translated this work of Avicenna from Arabic into Persian on request of some of his friends in the year 1079).

66. al-Khazin, (1) Abu Ja'far al-Khazin, (2) Died between 961 and 971, (3) Persian, (4) ?, (5) Astronomy, mathematics, (6) Commentary on the tenth book of Euclid; Other mathematical and astronomical writings.

67. al-Khujandi, (1) Abu Mahmud Hamid ibn al-Khidr, (2) Died 1000, (3) Persian, (4) ?, (5) Astronomy, mathematics, (6) None.

68. al-Khwarizmi, (1) Abu 'Abd Allah Muhammad ibn Musa, (2) Died c. 850, (3) Persian, (4) Arabic, (5) Astronomy and mathematics, (6) "Liber Ysagogarum Alchorismi in Artem Astronomicam a Magistro"; Compositus—"Deals with arithmetic, geometry, music, astronomy and is possibly a summary of al-Khwarizmi's teachings rather than original work"; Astronomical and trigonometric tables; Probably collaborated in the degree measurements ordered by al-Ma'mun; Improved Ptolemy's geography.

69. al-Kuhi, (1) Abu Sahl Wijan (or Waijan) ibn Rustam, (2) ?, (3) Persian, (4) ?, (5) Mathematics, astronomy, (6) Many writings on mathematics and astronomy.

70. al-Lith, (1) Abu-l-Jud Muhammad ibn al-Lith, (2) ?, (3) Persian, (4) ?, (5) Mathematics, (6) None.

71. ibn al-Lubudi, (1) ?, (2) c. 1210 or 1211, died after 1267, (3) Syrian, (4) Arabic, probably, (5) Medicine, mathematics, astronomy, philosophy, (6) Treatise on rheumatism; Treatise on Hippocrates' aphorisms; "Treatise on questions of Hunain ibn Is'haq; Collection of discussions on 50 physiological and medical questions; Commentary on generalities of ibn Sina's Qanun; An extract from Euclid; Explana-

tion of Euclid's postulates; An arithmetic textbook; Treatise dealing with essentials of Euclid; Treatise on algebra; An essay on magic squares; An essay on the art of astrological judgments; Compiled tables."

72. al-Maqribi, (1) Muhyi al-Din al-Maqribi, (2) Died after 1274, (3) Hispano-Muslim, (4) Arabic probably, (5) Mathematics, astronomy, (6) Kitab Shakl al-Qatt'a—Trigonometry; Euclid—Elements; Appolonius—Conics (numbers 2, 3, 4 all titled Tahdhib); Theodosius—Spherics; Khulasat al-Mijisti—Essence of the Almagest; Risalat al-Khita' wa'l Ighur—Chronology of Chinese at Maragha; Kitab al-Madkhal al-Mufid fi Hukm al-Mawalid—Astrology (birth); Kitab al-Nujum—Astrology (book of stars); Kitab al-Hukm 'Ala Qiranat al-Kawakib fi'l-Buruj al-Ithna Ashar—Astrology; Kaifiyyat al-Hukm 'Ala Tahwil Sini al-Alam—Astrology; Kitab al-Jami' al-Saqir—Astrology; Umdat al-Hasib wa Qunyat al-Talib—Astrology; Tastih al-Asturlab—Astrolabe; Taj al-Azzaj wa Qunyat al-Muhtaj—Astronomical, geographical, and chronological tables.

73. al-Mahani, (1) Abu 'Abd 'Allah Muhammad ibn 'Isa, (2) Died c. 874, (3) Persian, (4) ?, (5) Mathematics and astronomy, (6) Commentaries on Euclid and Archimedes; Improved Is'haq ibn Hunain's translation of Menelaos' spherics.

74. ibn al-Majdi, (1) ?, (2) 1358-1447, (3) Egyptian, (4) Arabic, probably, (5) Astronomy, mathematics, (6) Khulasat al-Aqwal fi Ma 'rifat al-Waqt wa Ru'yat Hilab—Use of sine quadrants; Al-Manhal al-'adhb al-Zulal fi Taqwin al-Kawakib wa Ru'yat al-Hilal (may be the same as above); Inshad al-Ha'ir Ila Takhtit Fadl al-Da'ir—Sine lines on the quadrants; Zad al-Musafir fi Rasm Khutut Fadl al-Da'ir; Risala fi 'l-'Amal bi Rub'al-Muqantarat al-Maqtu'—Use of Quadrant bearing projections of parallels of altitude; Irshad al-Sa'il Ila Usul al-Masa'il—Commentary on al-Maridini, use of the Dastur quadrant; Al-Raud al-Azhar—Use of "mushattah" quadrant; Tuhfat al-Ahbab fi Nasb al-Badhahanj wa'l-Mihrab—On erection of badhahanj and the mihrab; Al-Jami'al-Mufid fi'l-Kashf al-Usul Masa'il al-Taqwim wa'l-Mawalid—Principles of almanacs; Al-Durr al-Yatim fi Tas'hil Sina'at Taqwim—On compilation of the calendar; Al-Tas'hil wa'l-Taqrib fi Bayan Turuq al-Hall wa'l Tarkib—Methods of explaining and composition of tables; Qunyat al-Fahim wa'l-Tariq Ila Hall al-Taqwim—Method of explaining the calendar; Al-Kawakib al-Mudi'a fi'l-'Amal fi'l-Masa'il al-Dauriya—Concerning periodic motion of brilliant stars; Majmu' Mahlulat fi'ilm al-Nujum—Problems of stars; Jadawil al-Sumut—Table of Azimuths; Dastur al-Nayyirain—Table of sun and moon; 'Iqd al-Durar fil-'Amal fil-Qamar—Tables of the moon; Kashf al-Haqa'iq fi Hisab al-Daraj wa'l-Daqa'iq—Sexagesimal fractions; Al-Muftakara'l Hisabiyya—Computation; Ibraz Lata'if al-Qawamid wa Ihraz Sina'at al-Fara'id—Extraction on inheritance; Sharh Nazm al'La'ali fi'lfara'id of Salih ibn Thamir al-J'bari—A commentary on inheritance.

75. al-Majriti, (1) Abu al-Qasim Maslama ibn Ahmad, (2) Died about 1007, (3) Of Madrid, (4) ?, (5) Astronomy, mathematics, occultry, (6) Edited and corrected astronomical tables of al-Khwarizmi; Treatise on astrolabe; Commentary on Ptolemy's Planisphaerium; Al-mu'amalat—Book on generation of animals; Rutbat al-Hakim—Sage's step (alchemic); Qayat al-Hakim—Aim of the wise (alchemic).

76. ibn abi Mansur, (1) Abu Ali Yahya, (2) Died c. 831, (3) Persian, (4) Arabic, (5) Astronomy, (6) Compiled astronomical tables, so-called tested Ma'munic tables.

77. al-Marrakushi, (1) al-Hasan al-Marrakushi, (2) c. 1262, (3) Moroccan, (4) Arabic, probably, (5) Astronomy, mathematics, geography, theology, (6) Talkhis al-A'mal fi Ru'yat al-Hilal—Astronomy; Alat al-Taqwim—Calendar; Jami al-Mabadi wa'l-Qayat—Astronomical instruments and methods, trigonometry and gnomonics.

78. al-Maridini, (1) 'Abd Allah ibn Khalil, (2) Died 1406 or 1407, (3) Iraqi, (4) Arabic, probably, (5) Mathematics, (6) Al-Durr al-Manthur fi l-'Amal fi Rub' al-Dastur—Use of dastur quadrant; Al-Waraqat—Quadrant bearing parallels of altitude; Risala fi'l Amal bi'l Rub' al-Mujaiyyab—Use of sine quadrant; Al-Shabaka—Trigonometrical and astronomical tables; Qayat al-Intifa—On sine quadrant.

79. al-Marwarrudhi, (1) Khalid ibn 'Abd al-Malik, (2) Flourished under al-Ma'mun, (3) Persian, (4) ?, (5) Astronomy, (6) None.

80. al-Marwazi, (1) Ahmad ibn 'Abd Allah, (2) Died between 864 and 874, (3) ?, (4) ?, (5) Astronomy, (6) Compiled astronomical tables.

81. Mashallah, (1) ?, (2) Died c. 815 or 820, (3) Egyptian Jew, (4) ?, (5) Astronomy, astrology, (6) Earliest book on prices of wares; Treatise called The Twenty-Seventh.

82. ibn Matar, (1) al-Hajjaj ibn Yusuf, (2) Flourished 786-833, (3) ?, (4) Arabic, (5) Mathematics, (6) Many translations.

83. Mirak, (1) Shams al-Din Mirak, (2) Died c. 1339, (3) Persian, (4) Arabic, (5) Philosophy, astronomy, (6) Commentary on Tabsira fi 'Ilm al-Hai'a by al-Kharaqi—Astronomy; Commentary on Hidayat al-Hikma by al-Abhari—Logic, physics, theology; Commentary on Hikmat al-'Ain by al-Katibi—Logic, science, philosophy; Commentary on Manar al-Anwar fi Usul al-Fiqh by al-Nasafi; Ashjar wa Athmar—Astrological treatises; Perhaps several other important commentaries.

84. Misri, (1) Abu Ja'far Ahmad ibn Yusuf ibn Ibrahim ibn al-Daya, (2) ?, (3) Egyptian, (4) ?, (5) Mathematics, (6) Liber de Similibus Arcubus—Book on similar arcs; Commentary on Ptolemy's Gentiloquium; Liber Hameti de Proportione et Proportionalitate—On proportions.

85. al-Misri, (1) Abu Kamil Shuja' ibn Aslam ibn Muhammad ibn Shuja' al-Hasib, (2) Between 850-955, (3) Egyptian, (4) ?, (5) Mathematics, (6) Translations.

86. al-Misri, (1) Abu al-Hasan 'Ali ibn Abi Sa'id 'Abd al-Rahman ibn Ahmad ibn Yunus (or ibn Yunis) al-Sadafi, (2) Died 1009, (3) Egyptian, (4) ?, (5) Astronomy, (6) None.

87. al-Mizzi, (1) ?, (2) Died 1349, (3) Egyptian, (4) Arabic, probably, (5) Astronomy, (6) Al-Risala al-Istarlabiya—Astrolabe; Kashf al-Raib fi'l 'Amal bil-Jaib—Use of sines; Al-Raudhat al-Muz'hirat fi'l 'Amal fi Rub' al-Muqantarat—Use of quadrant with parallel circles; Al-Risala fi'l Mujannahat—Winged astrolabes; Nazm al-Lu'lu' al-Muhadhdhab fi'l'Amal bil-Rub al-Mujaiyyab—Sine quadrants; Risala fi'l'Amal bil-Rub'al-Musattar—Quadrant; Mukhtasar fi'l'Amal bil-Rub' al-Da'ira—Quadrant of the circle; Al-Muquntarat—Folded quadrant; Jadawil al-Hisas—Table for latitude of Damascus.

88. ibn Muhammad, (1) 'Abd al-Wahid ibn Muhammad, (2) Flourished 1394, (3) Persian, perhaps, (4) Arabic, (5) Astronomy, (6) Commentary on Risala'i Si Fasl by al-Tusi—Treatise on calendars in 30 chapters; Commentary on al-Mulakhkhas fi'l-Hai'a by al-Jughmini; Manzuma—On the use of the astrolabe.

89. Abu Muqri, (1) ?, (2) c. 1331, (3) Moroccan, (4) Arabic, probably, (5) Astronomy, (6) Arjuza—Poem on the calendar and astrology.

90. al-Mutamin, (1) Yusuf al-Mutamin, (2) ?, (3) ?, (4) ?, (5) Science, mathematics, (6) Istikmal—Bringing to perfection, a mathematical treatise.

91. al-Nahawandi, (1) Ahmad ibn Muhammad, (2) Died between c. 835 and 845, (3) Persian, (4) ?, (5) Astronomy, (6) None.

92. al-Nairizi, (1) Abu al 'Abbas al-Fadl ibn Hatim, (2) Died c. 922, (3) Persian, (4) ?, (5) Astronomy, mathematics, (6) Commentaries on Ptolemy and Euclid; Treatise on spherical astrolabe.

93. al-Naubakht, (1) ?, (2) Died between c. 767 and 777, (3) Persian, (4) ?, (5) Astronomy, engineering, (6) Kitab al-Ahkam—Book on astrological judgments.

94. ibn Naubakht, (1) Abu Sahl al-Fadhl ibn Naubakht, (2) Died c. 815 or 816, (3) Persian, (4) ?, (5) Astronomy, (6) Translations of Persian works into Arabic; Edited astrological treatises.

95. al-Qabisi, (1) Abu al-Saqr 'Abd al-'Aziz ibn Uthman ibn 'Ali, (2) ?, (3) ?, (4) ?, (5) Astrology, (6) Introduction to the art of astrology—Al-Madkhal ila Sina'at (ahkam) al-Nujum; Treatise on conjunctions of planets.

96. Abi al-Qasim, (1) Qaisar ibn abi al-Qasim, (2) c. 1178 or 1179 to 1251, (3) Egyptian, (4) Arabic, probably, (5) Mathematics, astronomy, engineering, (6) Treatise on Euclid's postulates.

97. ibn Qurra, (1) Abu Is'haq Ibrahim ibn Sinan ibn Thabit, (2) 908 or 909 to 946, (3) ?, (4) ?, (5) Mathematics, astronomy, (6) Commentaries on first book of Conics; Commentaries on Almagest; Many papers on geometrical and astronomical subjects.

98. al-Qustantini, (1) 'Ali ibn 'Ali, (2) c. 1360, (3) Spanish Muslim, (4) Arabic, probably, (5) Astronomy, (6) Astronomical poem with tables for a Moroccan ruler.

99. ibn al-Raqqam, (1) ?, (2) Died 1315, (3) Spanish Muslim, (4) Arabic, probably, (5) Medicine, mathematics, astronomy, (6) Fi 'Ilm al-Zilal—Discusses sundials; Various other writings, lost.

100. al-Razi, (1) Fakhr al-Din al-Razi (Rhazes), (2) 1149-1210, (3) Persian, (4) Arabic and Persian, (5) Philosophy, history, mathematics, astrological treatise; Sirr al-Maktum—Astrological treatise; Tarikh al-Duwal—Politics and history of first four caliphs; Manaqib al-Imam al-Shafi'i—A history of Shal'ite doctors; Mahsul fi Usul al-Fiqh—Jurisprudence; Mafatih al-Qaib (?)—Commentary on the Qur'an; Kitab al-Mabahith—Principles of physics and metaphysics; Jawami'al-Ulum—Encyclopaedia on science; Hada'iq al-Anwar fi Haqa'iq al-Asrar—Encyclopaedia on science.

101. ibn Rushd, (1) Averroes, (2) 1126-1198, (3) Hispano-Muslim, (4) Arabic, (5) Philosophy, medicine, astronomy, (6) These are only a few of his works: Commentary on the smaller physical writings of Aristotle, 1159; Kuliyyat before 1162; Jami, 1169; Generation of animals; Talkhis, 1170; Physics and analytics; Commentary on the De Coelo et Mundo, 1171; Jami, rhetoric and poetry, 1174; Talkhis on metaphysics, 1174; Talkhis on Nicomachean ethics, 1176; Part of commentary on De Substantia Orbis, 1178; Kitab al-Kashf an Manqij (?) al-Adilla fi Aqa'id al-Milla, 1179; Talkhis on De Anima, 1181; Tafsir on physics, 1186; Commentary on Galen's De Febribus, 1193; Questions on logic, 1195.

102. al-Sabi, (1) Abu 'Abd Allah Muhammad ibn Jabir ibn Sinan al-Battani al-Harrani, (2) 858-929, (3) Harranian, (4) ?, (5) Astronomy, (6) Commentary on Ptolemy's Tetrabiblon; De Scientia Stellarum and De Numeris Stellarum et Motibus—Treatise with tables.

103. Abu-l-Salt, (1) ?, (2) c. 1067 or 1068 to 1134, (3) Hispano-Muslim, (4) Arabic, probably, (5) Medicine, mathematics, astronomy, music, (6) Al-Rasa'il al-Misriyya—Essays on people in Egypt; Kitab al-Adwiyya al-Mufrada—Simple drugs; Taqwim al-Dhihn—Logic; Risala fi'l'Amal fi'l-Istarlab—Astrolabe; Risala fi'l'Musiqi—Music.

104. al-Samarqandi, (1) Muhammad ibn Ashraf, (2) c. 1276, (3) Persian, probably, (4) Arabic and Persian, (5) Mathematics, astronomy, logic, (6) Risala fi Adab al-Bahth—Dialectics; Kitab al-Qustas—Logic; Kitab 'Ain al-Nuzar fi'l Mantiq—Logic; Kitab Ashkal al-Ta'sis—Mathematics and astronomy; A'mal-i Taqwim-i Kawakib-i Thabita—Tables of stars; Kitab al-Saha'if—Dogmatics.

105. ibn al-Samh, (1) Abu al-Qasim Asbaq ibn Muhammad, (2) Died 1035, (3) Hispano-Muslim, (4) ?, (5) Mathematics, astronomy, (6) Treatises on commercial arithmetic—al-Mu'amalat; Hisab al-Hawa'i —Metal calculus; Many other treatises on nature of numbers, geometry,

astrolabe; Compiled astronomical tables according to the Siddhanta method, together with theoretical explanations.

106. ibn Sam'un, (1) Muhammad ibn Sam'un, (2) Died 1336 or 1337, (3) Egyptian or Syrian, (4) Arabic, probably, (5) Astronomy, (6) Al-Tuhfa al-Malikiyya fi 'l-As'ila wa'l Ajwiba al-Falakiyya—Treatise on astronomical questions; Kanz al-Tullab—Use of astrolabes.

107. ibn al-Shatir, (1) ?, (2) 1306-1375, (3) Syrian, (4) Arabic, probably, (5) Astronomy, (6) Rasd ibn Shatir—On his astronomical observations; Nuzhat al-Sam' fi'l Amal bil-Rub' al-Jami'—New quadrant; Al-Naf al-Amm fi'l Amal bil Rub' al-Tamm—New quadrant; Risalat al-Istarlab—Instruments; Mukhtasar fi'l-'Amal bil-Istarlab—Instruments; Idah al-Muqaiyyab fi'l Amal bil-Rub' al-Mujaiyyab—Instruments; Al-Zij al-Jadid—Astronomical problems and theories; Ta'liq al-Arsad—Ptolemaic astronomy; Nihayat al-Su'ul fi Tashrih al-Usul—Ptolemaic astronomy; Nihayat al-Qayat fi A'mal al-Falakiyat—Ptolemaic astronomy; Bi'l Nisba al-Sittiniyya—Sexagesimal fractions.

108. al-Shirazi, (1) Abd al-Malik, (2) 2nd half 12th, (3) Persian, (4) Arabic, (5) Mathematics, astronomy, (6) Summary of Apollonius' treatise on conics; Abridgment of the Almagest.

109. al-Shirazi, (1) Qutb al-Din al-Shirazi, (2) 1236-1311, (3) Persian, (4) Arabic, Persian, (5) Mathematics, astronomy, medicine, philosophy, (6) Yani Jami'—Persian translation of redaction of Euclid's Elements ascribed to al-Shirazi; Fi Harakat al-Dahraja wa Nis'h (?) Bain al-Mustawi wa'l-Numhani—Geometry; Nihayat al-Idrak fi Dirayat al-Aflak—Astronomy and geography and other fields; Ikhtiyarati Muzaffari—Astronomy; Kitab al-Tuhfa't al-Shahiyya fi'l-Hai'a—Astronomy; Kitab fi 'Altu Fala Talum fi'l-Hai'a—Astronomy; Kitab al-Tabsira fi'l-Hai'a—Astronomy; Sharh al-Tadhkira al-Nasiriyya—Astronomy, commentary; Kharidat al-'Aja'ib—Astronomy; Extract from Islah al-Majesti of Jabir ibn Aflah—Astronomy; Kitab Nuzhat al-Hukama wa-Rawdhat al-Atibba—Medicine; Risala fi Bayan al-Haja Ila'l Tibb wa Adab al-Atibba' wa Wasayahum—Medical deontology; Risala fi'l-Baras—Leprosy; Commentary on ibn Sina's "Arjuzat"; Treatise on eye diseases ("probably not his"); Durrat al-Taj li-Qurrat al-Dibaj fi'l Hikma—Encyclopaedic treatise; Sharh Hikat al-Ishraq—Philosophy, commentary; Fath al-Mannan fi Tafsiral-Qur'an; Fi Mushkilat al-Qur'an; Commentary on Kitab al-Kashshaf 'an Haqa'iq al-Tanzil of al-Zamakhshari.

110. al-Tabari, (1) Abu Bakr Muhammad ibn Umar ibn al-Farrukhan, (2) Beginning 9th, (3) Persian, (4) ?, (5) Astronomy, (6) Treatise on nativities.

111. al-Tabari, (1) Abu Hafs Umar ibn al-Farrukhan, (2) Died c. 815, (3) Persian, (4) Arabic, (5) Astronomy, architecture, (6) Translations; Wrote on astrological and astronomical subjects.

112. al-Tabari, (1) Sahl al-Tabari, also called Rabban al-Tabari, (2) Beginning 9th, (3) Persian, (4) Arabic, (5) Mathematics, (6) None.

113. ibn Tariq, (1) Ya'qub ibn Tariq, (2) Died c. 796, (3) Persian, (4) ?, (5) Astronomy, (6) Memoirs on the sphere; Wrote on division of Kardaja; Wrote on the tables derived from the Siddhanta.

114. ibn Tufail, (1) ?, (2) c. 1100-1110 to 1185 or 1186, (3) Hispano-Muslim, (4) Arabic, probably, (5) Philosophy, medicine, (6) Haiy ibn Yaqzar—Philosophy; Two medical treatises, lost; Commentary on Aristotle's Meteorologica.

115. al-Turki, (1) Abu al-Qasim 'Abd Allah ibn Amajur (or Majur), (2) c. 885-933, (3) Turkish, (4) ?, (5) Astronomy, (6) None.

116. al-Tusi, (1) al-Muzaffar al-Tusi, (2) Died 1213, (3) Persian, (4) Arabic, probably, (5) Astronomy, mathematics, (6) Treatise on the astrolabe; Treatise on the subdivision of a square into 4 parts; Treatise on algebra.

117. al-Tusi, (1) Nasir al-Din al-Tusi, (2) 1201-1274, (3) Persian, (4) Arabic and Persian, (5) Philosophy, mathematics, astronomy, medicine, science, (6) The Mutawassitat; Works on the following: Arithmetic, geometry, trigonometry, observatory and library of Maraqa, instruments used in Maraqa, astronomical tables, astronomical theories, calendar superstitions, optics, mineralogy, music, geography, medicine, logic and classification of knowledge, philosophy, theology, ethics, poetry.

118. al-Urdi, (1) ?, (2) Contemporary of Nasir al-Din, (3) Syrian, (4) Arabic, probably, (5) Astronomy, architecture, engineering, (6) Risala fi Kaifiyya al-Arsad wa Ma Yuhtaja Ila Ilmihi wa Amalihi min Turuq al-Muwaddiya Ila Ma'rifa 'Audat al-Kawakib—Instruments used at Maraqa; Risala fi Amal al-Kura al-Kamila—Spheres; On the determination of the distance between the center of the sun and the apogee.

119. al-Usquf, (1) Rabi' ibn Zaid al-Usquf, (2) About 961, (3) ?, (4) ?, (5) Astronomy, (6) None.

120. al-Wasiti, (1) Abu al-Rabi (Hamid ibn 'Ali), (2) ?, (3) ?, (4) ?, (5) Astronomy, (6) None.

121. ibn al-Yasmini, (1) ?, (2) Died 1204, (3) Berber, (4) Arabic, probably, (5) Mathematics, (6) Al-Arjuzza al-Yasminiya—Algebra.

122. ibn Yunus, (1) Kamal al-Din ibn Yunus, (2) 1156-1242, (3) Musul, (4) Arabic, probably, (5) Theology, mathematics, (6) Commentaries on the Qur'an and ibn Sina; Treatises on Arabic grammar, logic, astrology, arithmetic, algebra, square numbers, magic squares, heptagons, etc.

123. ibn al-Zarqala, (1) Abu Is'haq Ibrahim ibn Yahya al-Naffash, better known as ibn Zarqala, (2) 1029-1087, (3) ?, (4) ?, (5) Astronomy, (6) Toledan tables—Trigonometrical introduction.

124. ibn Zuraiq, (1) ?, (2) 14th, 15th, (3) Syrian, (4) Arabic, probably, (5) Astronomy, (6) Al-Raud al-'Atir—Summary of astronomical tables; Risala al-Nashr al-Mutaiyyab fi'l-'Amal bil-Rub' al-Mujaiyyab—Use of the sine quadrant; Talkhis al-'Ibarat wa Idah al-Isharat—On the binomial.

Chemistry

1. ibn al-'Adim, (1) 'Umar ibn al-'Adim, (2) 1192-1262, (3) Muslim-Syrian, (4) Arabic, probably, (5) Chemistry (perfume), history, (6) Buqyat al-Talib fi Ta'rikh Halab—History of Aleppo; Zubdat al-Halab fi Ta'rikh Halab—Abridgment of history of Aleppo; Kitab al-Wuslat Ila al-Habib fi Wasf al-Taiyybat wa'l Tibb—Guide to making perfumes.

2. Dhu-l-Nun, (1) Abu al-Fayd Thawban ibn Ibrahim al-Ikhmimi al-Misri (nicknamed Dhu-l-Nun), (2) Died 859 or 860, (3) Egyptian, (4) ?, (5) Alchemist and mystic, (6) Mujarrabat—Alchemical and magical treatise.

3. Geber (an unknown person), (1) ?, (2) Last of 13th, (3) ?, (4) Latin, (5) Chemistry, (6) Summa Perfectionis—Most important; Liber de Investigatione Perfectionis; Liber de Inventione Veritatis Sive Perfectionis; Liber Fornacum; Testamentum Geberis.

4. al-Harrani, (1) Abu Musa Jabir ibn Haiyan al-Azdi al-Tusi al-Tartus, (2) ?, (3) Sabian, (4) ?, (5) Chemistry (alchemist), (6) Book of the kingdom; Little book of balances; Book of mercury; Book of concentration; Book of Eastern mercury; The foregoing are Arabic "alchemical texts."

5. ibn Hayyim, (1) Abrahim ibn Hayyim, (2) Flourished 1240-1262, (3) Spanish or Portuguese Jew, (4) Portuguese and Hebrew, probably, (5) Colors, perhaps religion, (6) 'Ibbur—Calendar; Treatise on the use of colors; Treatise on adorning Hebrew characters.

6. al-Iraqi, (1) Abu al-Qasim al-'Iraqi, (2) Flourished 2nd part of 13th, (3) Iraqi ?, (4) ?, (5) Alchemy, (6) Kitab al-'Ilm al-Muktasab—The cultivation of gold; Zubdat al-Talab fi Zar'al-Dhahab—Gold (lost); Commentary on the diwan of alchemical poems; 'Arf al-Abir fi 'Ilm al-Iksir (elixirs); Kitab al-Durar al-Makhtum bi'l-Sur—Elixirs; Kitab al-Aqalim al-Sab'a fi'l-'Ilm al-Mausum bil-San'a—Social aspect of alchemy; 'Uyun al-Haqa'iq wa Idah al-Tara'iq—Magic and metals; Kitab al-Kanz al-Afkhar wa'l-Sirr al-A'zam fi Tasrif al-Hajar al-Mukarram—Alchemy; Kitab al-Najat wa'l-Ittisal bi 'Ain al-Hayat—Source of life, etc.

7. al-Jawbari, (1) ?, (2) About 1216-1231, (3) Damascus, (4) Arabic, probably, (5) Alchemy, technology, (6) Kitab al-Mukhtar fi Kashf al-Asrar wa Hatk al-Asfar—Exposure of alchemists, etc.

8. al-Jildaki, (1) ?, (2) Died 1342 or up to 1361, (3) Arabic, (4) Arabic, (5) Alchemy, (6) Al-Badr al-Munir fi Asrar al-Iksir—Secrets of elixir; Buqyat al-Khabir fi Qanun Talab al-Iksir—Wish of the expert; Al-Burhan fi Asrar'ilm al-Mizan—Alchemy, natural history, physics, metaphysics; Al-Durr al-Manthur; Al-Durr al-Maknun fi Sharh Qasidat Dhi al-Nun (Dhun'nun)—Commentary on alchemical treatise by Dhu'l Nun; Qayat al-Surur; Al-Ikhtisas wa Durrat al-Qawwas fi Asrar al-Khawass—Natural and occult properties of animals and stones; Kashf al-Sutur; Al-Misban fi Asrar 'Ilm al-Miftah—Secrets and history of

alchemy; Mukhammas al-Ma'al Waraqi—Quintessence of a work by al-Tamibi; Nata'ij al-Fikar fi Ahwal al-Hajar; Nihayat al-Talab fi Sharh al-Muktasab—Commentary on works about chemicals; Sharh Qasidat Abi al-Asba'—Commentary on alchemical poem by al-Iraqi; Sharh al-Shams al-Akbar li Balinas—Commentary on the greater sun of Apollonius of Tyona; Al-Taqrib fi'l Asrar al-Kimiya—Introduction to the secrets of alchemy.

9. al-Kashani, (1) Abd Allah ibn 'Ali, (2) 1300, (3) Persian, (4) Persian, (5) Alchemy, (6) Kitab Jawahir al-'Ara'is wa Ata'ib al-Nafa'is —On technique of glazing earthenware.

Education

(See Chapter V)

Geography

1. ibn Aban, (1) Sahl ibn Aban, (2) First half 12th, (3) ?, (4) Muslim, (5) Geography, (6) Author of nautical instructions; Compiled route books and sea voyages dealing with the Eastern seas.

2. al-Abdari, (1) Abu Muhammad ibn Muhammad ibn 'Ali, (2) Flourished 1289, (3) Hispano-Muslim, (4) ?, (5) Geography, (6) Al-Rihla al-Maqribiya.

3. ibn Ahmad, (1) Abu Muhammad 'Abd Allah ibn Ahmad al-Tijani, (2) Flourished 1306, (3) Tunisian, (4) ?, (5) Geography, (6) Rihla—Account of a journey; Tuhfat al-'Rus wa-Nuzhat al-Nufus—Gift of the bride and delight of the souls.

4. al-Aiyyubi, (1) Abu al-Fida' Isma'il ibn 'Ali 'Imad al-Din, (2) 1273-1331, (3) Syrian, (4) ?, (5) Geography, (6) Mukhtasar—Universal history; Taqwim al-Buldan—Treatise on geography.

5. ibn Amr, (1) Abu 'Ubaid 'Abd Allah ibn 'Abd al-'Aziz ibn Muhammad ibn Aiyyub, (2) Died 1094, (3) Hispano-Muslim, (4) ?, (5) Geographer, (6) Kitab al-Masalik wa'l Mamalik—Book of the roads and the provinces; Kitab Mu'jam ma'sta'jama—"Dictionary of ancient geography; Book on plants and trees of Andalusia" (?).

6. al-Ansari, (1) Muhammad ibn Ibrahim ibn Yahya al-Watwat Jamal al-Din al-Ansari al-Kutubi al-Warraq, (2) 1235-1318, (3) ?, (4) ?, (5) Geography, (6) Mabahij al-Fikar wa Manahij al 'Ibar—Encyclopaedia of natural science and geography.

7. al-Baghdadi, (1) Abu al-Faraj Qudama ibn Ja'far al-Katib, (2) 948 or 949, (3) ?, (4) ?, (5) Geography, accounting, (6) Kitab al-Kharaj—Book on land tax.

8. al-Baghdadi, (1) Abu Muhammad 'Abd al-Latif ibn Yusuf ibn Muhammad ibn Ali Muwaffaq, (2) 1162-1231, (3) Baghdad, (4) ?, (5) Geography, (6) Al-Ifadat wa'l-I'tibar fi'l Umur al-Mushahadat wa'l-Hawadith al-Mu'ayanat bi Ard Misr—Account of Egypt.

9. al-Bakawi, (1) 'Abd al-Rashid ibn Salih ibn Nuri, (2) Flourished

end 14th and later, (3) Caucasian Muslim, (4) ?, (5) Geography, (6) Talkhis al-Athar wa 'Aja'ib al-Malik al-Qahhar—General view of the monuments and marvels of the omnipotent king.

10. ibn al-Balkhi, (1) ?, (2) Born between 1107 and 1116, (3) Persian, (4) Persian, (5) Geography, (6) Fars Namah—Description of the province of Fars.

11. ibn Battuta, (1) Abu 'Abd Allah Muhammad ibn 'Abd Allah ibn Muhammad al-Lawati al-Hanji, (2) 1304-1377 or 1378, (3) Tangiers, (4) ?, (5) Geography, (6) Tuhfat al-Nuzzar fi Qara'ib al-Amsar wa 'Aja'ib al-Asfar—Gift to the observers dealing with the curiosities of cities and the wonders of journeys.

12. al-Dimashqi, (1) Shams al-Din Abu 'Abd Allah Muhammad ibn Ibrahim ibn Abi Talib al-Ansari al-Sufi, (2) Born 1256 or 1257, died 1326 or 1327, (3) Syrian, (4) ?, (5) Geography, (6) Kitab Nukhbat al-Dahr fi'aja'ib al-Barr wa'l-Bahr—Selection of the age of the wonders of land and sea; Kitab al-Siyasa fi 'Ilm al-Firasa—On Physiognomy in relation to government; On the signs of death according to Hippocrates; Jawab Risala Ahl Jazirat Qubrus—A defense of Islam against the Christians of Cyprus; Al-Maqamat al-Falsafiyya wa'l-Tarjamat al-Sufiyya—Treatise on mysticism.

13. (al-Din) Dhiya' (Dhiya al-Din), (1) Abu Muhammad 'Abd Allah ibn Ahmad ibn al-Baitar Dhiya' al-Din al-Malaqi, (2) Died 1248, (3) Hispano-Muslim, (4) ?, (5) Geography, medicine, (6) Descriptions of plants which grew in various parts of the Islamic world.

14. al-Fariqi, (1) Muhammad ibn Muhammad ibn Nubata, (2) 1287-1366, (3) Iraqi, (4) ?, (5) Law, sociology, (6) Many poems; Ta'liq al-Diwan—Collection of letters and compliments; Saj' al-Mutawwaq—Collection of letters and compliments; Treatise on the duties of princes —Suluk Duwal al-Muluk.

15. al-Fazari, (1) Burhan al-Din Abu Is'haq Ibrahim ibn 'Abd al-Rahman ibn al-Firkah al-Shafi'i al-Badri, (2) 1262-1329, (3) Syrian, (4) ?, (5) Geography, (6) Ba'ith al-Nufus Ila Ziyara al-Quds al-Mahrus —Guidebook for pilgrims to Jerusalem and Hebron; Al-I'lam bi-Fada'il al-Sham—Description of the beauties of Damascus; Al-Mana'ih li-Talib al-Said wa'l Dhaba'ihl—Ritual slaughter of animals; Hall al-Qina' 'an Hall al-Sama'—Loosening the veil concerning the solution of listening (to music).

16. al-Gharnati (al-Qarnati), (1) Abu Abd' Allah Muhammad ibn Abd al-Rahim ibn Sulaiman al-Qaisi al-Mazini al-Andalusi, (2) 1080 or 1081 to 1169 or 1170, (3) Granada, (4) Hispano-Muslim, (5) Geography, (6) Al-Muqrib' an ba'd 'Aja'ib al-Maqrib—Collection of singularities about some of the marvels of the Maghrib; Tuhfat al-Albab wa Nukhbat al-A'Jab—Gift to the hearts and choice of wonders.

17. ibn al-Ha'ik, (1) Muhammad al-Hasan ibn Ahmad ibn Ya'qub al-Hamdani, (2) Died 945 or 946, (3) ?, (4) ?, (5) Geography, archae-

ology, (6) Sifat Jazirat al-'Arab—Geography of Arabia; Al-Iklil—The crown, on histories and antiquities of Yemen; Compiled astronomical tables for Yemen.

18. al-Hamadhani, (1) Abu Bakr Ahmad ibn Muhammad ibn Is'haq ibn at-Faqih, (2) Flourished 903, (3) Persian, (4) ?, (5) Geography, (6) Kitab al-Buldan—Book of the countries.

19. al-Hamawi, (1) Abu 'Abd Allah Yaqut ibn 'Abd Allah Shihab al-Din al-Hamawi al-Baghdadi, (2) 1179-1229, (3) Asia Minor, (4) Arabic, (5) Geography, philology, (6) Geographical dictionary; Mu'jam al-Buldan; Kitab Irshad al-Arib Ila Ma'rifat al-Adib; Kitab al-Mushtarik Wad'a wa Mukhtalif Saq'a.

20. ibn Hammad, (1) Ahmad ibn Fadlan ibn 'Abbas ibn Rashid, (2) Living in 921, (3) ?, (4) ?, (5) Geography, (6) Earliest reliable account of Russia.

21. al-Hanbali, (1) Najm al-Din Ahmad ibn Hamdan ibn Shabib al-Harrani, (2) ?, (3) Iraqi, (4) ?, (5) Geography, (6) Jami' al-Funun wa Salwat al-Mahzun—Encyclopaedia of geography, natural history, folklore.

22. al-Hanbali, (1) Abu al-Fada'il Safi al-Din 'Abd al-Mu'min ibn al-Khatib 'Abd al-Haqq al-Baghdadi, (2) 1259 or 1260 to 1338 or 1339, (3) Baghdad, (4) Arabic, (5) Geography, (6) Compiled a geographical dictionary; Marasid al-Ittila' 'Ala Asma' al-Amkina wal-Biqa'—Summary of the great dictionary of Yaqut.

23. al-Harawi, (1) 'Ali ibn abi Bakh ibn 'Ali, (2) Died 1214 or 1215, (3) Musul, (4) ?, (5) Geography, (6) Kitab al-Isharat fi Ma'rifat al-Ziyarat—Indications for the knowledge of pilgrimages; Kitab al-'Aja'ib—Book of marvels.

24. ibn Hawqal, (1) Abu al-Qasim Muhammad ibn Hawqal, (2) 943-977, (3) ?, (4) ?, (5) Traveler, geographer, (6) Kitab al-Masalik wa'l-Mamalik—Book of roads and provinces.

25. ibn Isa, (1) Abu al-Baqa' Khalid ibn 'Ia, (2) ?, (3) Hispano-Muslim, (4) ?, (5) Geography, (6) Taj al-Mafriq fi Tahliyat 'Ulama al-Mashriq—Crown of the vortex on the description of the learned men of the East.

26. al-Istakhri, (1) Abu Is'haq Ibrahim ibn Muhammad al-Farsi, (2) Flourished 950, (3) Persian, (4) ?, (5) Geography, (6) Masalik al-Mamalik—Revised work of al-Balkhi on the figures of the climates.

27. al-Jaihani, (1) al-Jaihani, (2) Flourished 893-907, (3) Persian, (4) ?, (5) Geography, (6) Extensive road book (lost).

28. ibn Khurdadhbih, (1) Abu al-Qasim 'Ubaid Allah ibn 'Abd Allah, (2) 825-912, (3) Persian, (4) ?, (5) Geography, (6) Kitab al-Masalik wa'l Mamalik—Book of roads and provinces.

29. al-Kinani, (1) Abu al-Husain Muhammad ibn Ahmad, (2) 1145-1217, (3) Valencia, (4) Arabic, (5) Geography, (6) Rahlat al-Kinani—Kinani's journey.

30. al-Lakhmi, (1) Muhammad ibn 'Abd al-Rahman ibn al-Hakim Zubaidi al-Lakhmi al-Ishbili (or Ronda), (2) ?, (3) ?, (4) ?, (5) Geography, (6) None.

31. al-Maghribi (al-Maqribi), (1) Abu al-Hasan 'Ali ibn Musa ibn Muhammad, (2) 1208 or 1214 to 1274 or 1287, (3) Granada Hispano-Muslim, (4) ?, (5) History, geography, (6) Kitab Bast al-Ardh fi Tulha wa'l-'Ardh—Extent of the earth in length and breadth; Kitab al-Muqrib fi Akhbar Ahl al-Maqrib—Book of singularities concerning the people of the West; Kitab al-Mashriq fi Akhbar Ahl al-Mashriq—Book throwing light upon people of the East; Kitab Nashwat al-Tarab fi Tarikh Jahiliyyat al'Arab—On chronicles of the pagan Arabs.

32. al-Marrakushi, (1) Abu 'Ali al-Hasan ibn 'Ali ibn 'Umar, (2) Flourished 1262, (3) ?, (4) Moroccan, (5) Geography, mathematics, astronomy, (6) None.

33. al-Mas'udi, (1) Abu al-Hasan 'Ali ibn al-Husain ibn 'Ali, (2) Born before 912, died 957, (3) ?, (4) ?, (5) Geography, history, (6) Muruj al-Dhahab wa Ma'adin al—Jawahir—Historico-Geographical encyclopaedia; Kitab al-Tanbih wa'l Ishraf—Book of indication and revision, summary and revision of his life's work.

34. al-Muhaqqiq, (1) Abu Jafar Muhammad ibn Muhammad ibn al-Hasan Nasir al-Din al-Tusi, (2) 1201-1274, (3) Khurasan, (4) Arabic, (5) Geography, mathematics, astronomy, (6) Kitab Surat al-Aqalim—Persian translation of the Suwar al-Aqalim of al-Balkhi with good maps added; Tadhkira—Deals with geodesy and ends with a description of the seas, sea winds, etc.

35. ibn Rusta, (1) Abu 'Ali Ahmad ibn 'Umar ibn Rusta, (2) Flourished 903, (3) Persian, (4) ?, (5) Geography, (6) Al-A'laq al-Nafisa—The precious bags of traveling provisions, deals with celestial and terrestrial spheres, then describes countries.

36. al-Salmani, (1) Muhammad ibn Mahmud ibn Ahmad al-Tusi; (2) Flourished 1177-1194, (3) Persian, (4) Persian, (5) Cosmography, (6) 'Aja'ib al-Makhluqat—The marvels of creatures.

37. al-Saqali, (1) Abu Abd' Allah Muhammad ibn Muhammad ibn Allah ibn Idris al-Hammudi al-Hasani al-Qurtubi al-Saqali, (2) 1099 or 1100 to 1166, (3) Sicilian, (4) ?, (5) Geography, botany and materia medica, (6) Al-Kitab al-Rujari—The delight of him who desires to journey through the climates; Rawddha't al-Uns wa-Nuzhat al-Nafs—Pleasure of men and delight of souls, a geographical encyclopaedia.

38. ibn Sarafyun, (1) ?, (2) Flourished beginning 10th, (3) ?, (4) ?, (5) Geography, (6) Book of geography.

39. al-Shafi'i, (1) Ahmad ibn Muhammad ibn Hilal al-Maqdisi, (2) 1314-1364, (3) ?, (4) Arabic, (5) Geography, (6) Pilgrim book for Jerusalem.

40. al-Shafi'i, (1) Shihab al-Din Abu'l 'Abbas Ahmad ibn Yahya ibn Fadhl Allah al-'Umari al-Qurashi, (2) 1301-1349, (3) Damascus, (4) Arabic, (5) Geography, (6) Masalik al-Absar fi Mamalik al-Amsar—

Voyages of the eyes in the kingdoms of the main cities; Al-Ta'rif bi'l-Mustalah al-Sharif—Manual of chancellery or diplomatics.

41. al-Shafi, (1) Abu Hafs Zain al-Din 'Umar ibn al-Muzaffar al-Qurashi al-Bakri al-Ma'arri ibn al-Wardi, (2) Born before 1290, died 1349, (3) Syrian, (4) ?, (5) Historiographer, (6) Al-Tuhfa al-Wardiyya—Grammatical poem; Tatimmat' al-Mukhtasar fi Akhbar al-Bashar—Summary of the chronicle of Abu-l-Fida'; Al-Bahja al-Wardiyya—Treatise on another work; Al-Masa'il al-Mulaqqabat al-Wardiyya fi'l-Fara'id—Poem on the rules of inheritance; Al-Muqaddama al-Wardiyya—Interpretation of dreams; Shihab al-Thaqif wa'l-Adhab al-Waqif—Mystical treatise.

42. al-Shirazi, (1) Mahmud ibn Mas'ud ibn Muslih Qutb al-Din, (2) 1236-1311, (3) Persian, (4) Arabic and Persian, (5) Geography, mathematics, astronomy, (6) Nihayat al-Idrak fi Dirayat al-Aflak—Highest understanding of the knowledge of the spheres, partly geographical.

43. al-Sirafi, (1) Abu Zaid al-Hasan al-Sirafi, (2) Living 920, (3) ?, (4) ?, (5) Geography, (6) Akhbar al-Sin wa'l-Hind—Accounts of China and India.

44. Sulaiman, (1) Sulaiman the Merchant, (2) Flourished probably first half 9th, (3) ?, (4) Arabic, (5) Geography, (6) "Records the use of fingerprints as signature by the Chinese."

45. al-Tini, (1) Ahmad al-Tini, (2) ?, (3) Arabic (Egyptian?), (4) ?, (5) Geography, (6) Geographer, quoted by many authors.

46. al-Yanubu'i, (1) Abu Dulaf Mis'ar ibn al-Muhalhal al-Khazra, (2) Flourished 913-942, (3) ?, (4) ?, (5) Poetry, geography, (6) Aja'ib al-Buldan—Marvels of the countries.

47. al-Zuhri, (1) Muhammad ibn abi Bakr, (2) Wrote after 1139 or 1140, (3) Hispano-Muslim, (4) ?, (5) Geography, (6) Kitab al-Juqrafiya—Geography.

History

Histories of *Peoples, Places, Periods, Doctrines, Governments, Great Men* (Scholars, Poets, Statesmen, Theologians, Philosophers, and others) *Dynasties, Literary Works, Biographies, Chronicles, Biographical Dictionaries,* and so forth.

1. al-Abbasi, (1) Ahmad ibn abi Ya'qub ibn Ja'far ibn Wahb ibn Wadith, (2) Living 891, (3) Persian, (4) ?, (5) Historian, geographer, (6) Kitab al-Buldan—Book of the countries.

2. Abi-al-Fada'il, (1) Mufaddal ibn Abi-al-Fada'il, (2) Flourished at least to 1358, (3) Coptic, (4) Arabic, (5) Historiography, (6) Nahj al-Sadid wa'l-durr al-farid Fima ba'd Tarikh ibn al-'Amid—History.

3. al-Amid, (1) Jirjis al-Makim 'Abd Allah ibn Abi al-Yasir ibn abi al-Makarim, (2) 1205 or 1206 to 1273 or 1274, (3) Egyptian, (4) ?, (5) Historiography, (6) Kitab al-Majmu' al-Mubarak—The blessed collection, Muslim history.

4. al-Andalusi, (1) Abu 'Abd Allah Muhammad ibn 'Umar Muhib al-Din al-Sabti al-Fihri, (2) 1259-1321, (3) Moroccan, (4) ?, (5) Historian, traditionalist, geographer, (6) Rihlatani—Two itineraries, Spain and Africa; Kitab Silsilat al-Sama' wa Ifadat al-Nasib—Notes on the Spanish traditionists and legalists; Kitab al-Sanan al-Abyan wal-Mawrid al-Am'an—Lives of al-Bukhari and al-Muslim; Mal' al-'Aiba fi Ma Jama'a Bitul al-Qaiba fi'l-Rahla Ila Makka wa Taiba—Notices on the learned men who lived in Cairo and Alexandria in 1300.

5. al-Andalusi, (1) Abu-al-Qasim Sa'id ibn Ahmad ibn Abd al-Rahman ibn Muhammad ibn Sa'id al-Qurtubi, also called Qadi Sa'id, (2) 1029 or 1030 to 1070, (3) Spanish, (4) ?, (5) Historiography, (6) Kitab al-Ta'rif bi Tabaqat al-Umam—Summary of universal history; History of learned men (this may be part of the previous listing).

6. al-Baladhuri, (1) Abu-al-'Abbas Ahmad ibn Yahya Jabir, (2) Died 892 or 893, (3) Persian, (4) Arabic, (5) Historian, (6) Futuh al-Buldan—Conquest of the lands; Ansab al-Ashraf—Genealogies of the nobles.

7. al-Baghdadi, (1) Abu-al-Ma'ali Muhammad al-Baghdadi al-Katib Kafi-al-Kufat Baha al-Din, (2) 1102-1167, (3) Baghdad, (4) ?, (5) Historiography, (6) Kitab al-Tadhkira—The book of remembrance, 12 volumes.

8. al-Baghdadi, (1) Abu Bakr Ahmad ibn 'Ali ibn Thabit al-Khatib, (2) 1002-1071, (3) ?, (4) ?, (5) Historiography, (6) Tarikh Baghdad—History of learned men of Baghdad, 14 volumes; Kitab al-Kifaya fi Ma'rifat Usul 'Ilm al-Riwaya—Treatise on the criticism of traditions; Mu'tanif Takmilat al-Mu'talif wal-Mukhtalif—On the orthography of proper names; Many others.

9. al-Baghdadi, (1) Abu Mansur 'Abd al-Qahir ibn Tahir ibn Muhammad, (2) Died 1037 or 1038, (3) Muslim, (4) Arabic, (5) History, philosophy, theology, mathematics, (6) Kitab al-Farq Bain al-Firaq—Book on schisms and sects; Al-Takmil—The completion, book on arithmetic; Wrote on solution of inheritance problems.

10. al-Baghdadi, (1) Abu al-Faraj Muhammad ibn Is'haq ibn abi Ya'qub al-Nadim al-Warraq (better known as al-Nadim), (2) Died 995, (3) ?, (4) ?, (5) Historian, bibliographer, (6) Fihrist al-'Ulum—Index of the sciences.

11. Baihaqi, (1) Khawjah Abul Fadhl Muhammad ibn Hussain, (2) 995-1087, (3) Persian, (4) Persian, (5) History, (6) Tarikhi Baihaqi—History of Baihaqi; Zinat-ul-Kitab—On the art of writing.

12. al-Banakati, (1) Fakhr al-Din abu Sulaiman Da'ul ibn Muhammad, (2) Died 1329 or 1330, (3) Persian, (4) Persian, (5) Historiography, (6) Rawdhat-ul-Albab fi Tawarikh al-Akabir wa'l-Ansab—Garden of the intelligent on the histories of the great and on genealogies.

13. al-Basri, (1) Abu Muhammad Abd al-Malik ibn Hisham ibn Aiyub al-Himyari, (2) Died 833, (3) ?, (4) Arabic, (5) Historiography, (6) Sirat al-Rasul—Earliest biography of the Prophet.

14. al-Bayhaqi, (1) Abu-al-Hasan 'Ali ibn al-Imam abi-al-Qasim Zaid al-Bayhaqi Zahir al-Din, (2) 1106-1169 or 1170 or 1174, (3) Persian, (4) Arabic, probably, (5) Biographer, scientist, (6) Tarikh Hukama' al-Islam—History of the learned men of Islam; Siwan al-Hakma—Container of wisdom; History of Bayhaq, in Persian; Number of books on medicine, mathematics, astrology, various other subjects.

15. al-Bukhari, (1) Nur'ud-din-Muhammad ibn Muhammad Awfi, (2) End of 13th and beginning of 14th, (3) Persian, (4) Persian and Arabic, (5) Literary historian, (6) Jawami-ul-Hekayat wa Lawami-ul-Rawayat—Collection of stories; Lobab-ul-Albab—Selection of selections.

16. al-Dinawari, (1) Abu Hanifa Ahmad ibn Da'ud, (2) Born 815 to 825, died 895, (3) Persian, (4) Arabic, (5) Historian, lexicographer, botanist, astronomer, (6) Kitab al-Akhbar al-Tiwal—Book of long stories; Kitab al-Nabat—Book of plants; Astronomical and mathematical writings.

17. al-Dinawari, (1) Abu Muhammad 'Abd Allah ibn Muslim ibn Qutaiba, (2) 829-889, (3) Persian, (4) Arabic, (5) History, philology, writer, (6) 'Ulun al-Akhbar—Choice histories; Kitab al-Ma'arif—Treatise of history or book of general knowledge; Kitab al-Shi'r wa'l-Shu'ara'—Book of poetry and poets; Kitab Adab al-Katib—Accomplishments of the secretary; Two treatises on astrology.

18. ibn Faradi, (1) Abu-al-Walid 'Abd Allah ibn Muhammad ibn Yusuf ibn Nasr al-Azdi, (2) Between 926 and 963 to 1013, (3) Hispano-Muslim, (4) ?, (5) History, (6) Biographies of the learned Muslims of Spain.

19. al-Fasi, (1) Abu-al-Hasan 'Ali ibn 'Abd Allah ibn Abi Zar', (2) Died after 1325, (3) Moroccan, (4) ?, (5) Historiography, (6) Kitab al-Anis al-Mutrib bi Raud al-Qirtas fi Akhbar Muluk al-Maqrib wa Tarikh Madinat Fas (?).

20. ibn Futi, (1) Kamal al-Din abu al-Fada'il 'Abd al-Razzaq ibn Ahmad ibn Muhammad, (2) 1244-1323, (3) Iraqi, (4) Arabic, (5) Historiography, (6) Al-Hawadith al-Jami'a wa'l-Tajarib al-Nafi'a Min al-Mi'a al-Sabi'a—Dealing with the last Abbaside caliphs and the beginning of the Mongol domination to 1300; Majma't al-Adab fi Mu'jam al-Asma' wa'l-Alqab—Biographical dictionary; Mukhtasar Akhbar al-Khulafa' al-Abbasiyin—Collection of stories concerning the Abbaside caliphate; Many other works, historical and philological, completely lost.

21. ibn Haiyyan, (1) Abu Marwan Haiyyan ibn Khalaf ibn Husain, (2) 987 or 988 to 1076, (3) Hispano-Muslim, (4) ?, (5) History, (6) Kitab al-Matin, Liber Solidus—History of Spain, 60 volumes; Kitab al-Muqtabis fi Tarikh al-Andalus—Biographies of Hispano-Muslim scholars.

22. ibn 'Abd al-Hakam, (1) Abu-al-Qasim 'Abd al-Rahman ibn 'Abd Allah, (2) Died 871, (3) Egyptian, (4) Arabic, (5) Historian, (6) Futuh Misr wa'l-Maqrib—Earliest Muslim account of Egypt.

23. al-Halabi, (1) Abu-al-Mahasin Yusuf ibn Rafi' ibn Shaddad

al-Halabi Baha al-Din, (2) 1145-1234, (3) Musul, (4) ?, (5) Historian, (6) History of Salah al-Din; History of Aleppo; And others.

24. al-Halabi, (1) Abu-al-Walid Muhammad ibn Muhammad ibn al-Shihna, (2) 1348-1412, (3) Syrian, (4) ?, (5) Historiography, textbook writer, (6) Raudhat al-Manazir fi 'Ilm al-Awa'il wa'l Awakhir—Abridgment of the Mukhtasar Tarikh al-Bashar of Abal-Fida; Series of short textbooks.

25. al-Hamawi, (1) Abu Is'haq Ibrahim ibn 'Abd Allah ibn 'Abd al-Mun'im ibn Abi-al-Dam al-Hamdani Shihab al-Din, (2) 1187 or 1188 to 1244 or 1245, (3) Hamat, (4) ?, (5) Historian, (6) Tarikh—History of the Prophet and of the caliphs to 1231; Al-Tarikh al-Muzaffari—History of Islam, 6 volumes.

26. al-Hamadani, (1) Abu-al-Khair Rashid al-Din Fadl Allah ibn 'Imad al-Dawla (often called Rashid al-Din Tabib), (2) 1247-1318, (3) Persian, (4) Persian, Arabic, (5) Historiography, (6) Jami' al-Tawarikh—Collection of histories; Treatise on advantages and disadvantages of various kinds of food and clothing; Jami' al-Tasanif al-Rashidi—Encyclopaedia of Chinese medicine and government, 4 volumes; Biography of Hulagu Khan; Kitab al-Ahya wa'l-Athar—Book of animals and monuments; Tawdihat—Treatise on mystical theology; Miftah al-Tafasir—Key to the commentaries, a book on the Qur'an; Lata'if al-Haqa'iq—Subtle truths, 14 letters on theology; Al-Risala al-Sultaniyya—Account of a theological discussion; Bayan al-Haqa'iq—Elucidation of truths, letters on theology, smallpox, nature and kinds of heat, etc.; Collection of 53 letters addressed to his sons and other high officials.

27. ibn Hammad, (1) Abu 'Abd Allah Muhammad ibn 'Ali, (2) 1150-1230, (3) Bu-Hamra, (4) ?, (5) Historiography, (6) Akbar Muluk Bauk 'Ubaid Wa Siratutum—Account of the Fatimid rule in Africa; Chronicle of Bougie (Bijaya).

28. al-Hanafi, (1) Kamal al-Din Abu al-Qasim 'Umar ibn Ahmad ibn abi Jarada ibn al-Adim al-'Uqaili al-Halabi, (2) 1192-1262, (3) Aleppo, (4) ?, (5) Historian, (6) Buqyat al-Talib fi Tarikh Halab; Zubdat al-Halab fi Tarikh Halab; Kitab al-Wusilat (or Wasilat) Ila'l-Habib fi Wasf al-Taiyybat wa'l-Tibb.

29. Harwi, (1) Muhammad ibn Hussain ibn Omar, (2) ?, (3) Persian, (4) Persian, (5) History, (6) Translator from Arabic; Tarikhi-Baramekeh—History of the Barmakites.

30. al-Hisfani, (1) Hamza ibn al-Hasan, (2) Flourished 961, (3) Persian, (4) Arabic, (5) History, lexicography, (6) "Annals based essentially upon Persian sources; Work dealing with grammatical subjects and etymology."

31. al-Isfahani, (1) Muhammad ibn Muhammad 'Imad al-Din al-Katib, (2) 1125-1201, (3) Persian, (4) Arabic, (5) Historiography, (6) Kitab al-Fat'h al-Qussi—History of Saladin's conquest of Syria; Kitab Nusrat al-Fatra—Abbreviated translation of a Persian work by Anushir-

wan ibn Khalid; Kitab al-Barq al-Sha'mi (Shami'?)—Historical memoirs.

32. al-Hisfani, (1) Abu-al-Faraj 'Ali ibn al-Husain ibn Muhammad ibn Ahmad al-Qurashi, (2) 897 or 898 to 967, (3) Persian? Arab?, (4) Arabic, (5) Historiography, poetry, (6) Kitab al-Aqani—Book of songs.

33. ibn Is'haq, (1) Abu 'Abd Allah Muhammad ibn Is'haq, (2) Died 768 or 769, (3) Arabic, (4) ?, (5) Historian, (6) ?.

34. al-Ishbili, (1) Abu Bakr Muhammad ibn Khair ibn 'Umar ibn Khalifa, (2) 1108 or 1109-1179, (3) Hispano-Muslim, (4) ?, (5) Historiography, bibliography, (6) None.

35. al-Iskandari, (1) Muhammad ibn Qasim al-Nuwairi al-Maliki, (2) Flourished 1137-1174, (3) Egyptian, (4) ?, (5) Historiography, (6) Al-Ilmam bi'l-I'lam fima Jarat bihi al-Ahkam wa'l-Umar al-Maqdiyya fi Waq'at al-Iskandariya—History.

36. ibn Isma'il, (1) Shihab al-Din abu al-Qasim 'Abd al-Rahman, (2) 1203-1268, (3) Damascus, (4) ?, (5) Muslim historian, (6) Kitab al-Rawdhatain fi Akhbar al-Dawlatain—History.

37. al-Janadi, (1) Abu 'Abd Allah Muhammad ibn Ya'qub Baha' al-Din, (2) Died 1331 or 1332, (3) Arabian, (4) ?, (5) Historiography, (6) Kitab al Suluk fi Tabaqat al-'Ulama wa'l-Muluk—Local history of Yemen.

38. al-Jaziri, (1) Abu-al-Hasan 'Ali ibn Muhammad 'Izz al-Din ibn al-Athir al-Shaibani (best known as ibn al-Athir), (2) 1160-1233, (3) Mesopotamia, (4) ?, (5) Historiography, (6) Kitab al-Kamil fi'l-Tarikh—The perfect book of chronicles; History of the Atabeg rulers of Musul (1127-1211); Kitab Usd (?) al-Qaba fi Ma'rifat al-Sahaba—Alphabetic dictionary of the contemporaries of the Prophet; Lubab Kitab al-Lubab Mukhtasar al-Ansab li'l-Sam'ani—Abridgment of Kitab al-Ansab of al-Sam'ani.

39. al-Juwaini, (1) 'Ala al-Din 'Ata Malik ibn Muhammad, (2) 1233-1283, (3) Persian, (4) Persian, (5) Historiography, (6) Tarikh-i-Jahan Gusha—History of the Mongols; Tasliyat al-Ikhwan—Consolation of the brothers.

40. al-Kalbi, (1) Abu-al-Mundhir Hisham ibn Muhammad ibn al-Sa'ib, (2) Died 820, (3) Arab, (4) ?, (5) Historian, archaeology, (6) Kitab al-Nasab al-Kabir—Deals with genealogy of Arabs.

41. al-Katib, (1) Bahau'd din Muhammad ibn Hassan ibn Isfandyar, (2) Died 1220, (3) Persian, (4) Persian, (5) History, (6) Tarikhi Tabaristan—History of Tabaristan.

42. Khati'l, (1) al-Amir Rukn al-Din Baibars (or Bibars) al-Mansuri, (2) Died 1325, (3) Egyptian, (4) ?, (5) Historiography, (6) Zubdat al-Fikra fi Tarikh al-Hijra—General history of Islam to 1324, 11 volumes; Al-Tuhfat al-Mulukiyya fi'l-Daulat al-Turkiyya—History of Mamluk dynasty, 1250 to 1321.

43. ibn Khaldun, (1) Abu Zakariyya Yahya ibn Muhammad, (2) 1332-1406, (3) Tunisian, (4) ?, (5) Historiography, (6) Buqyat al-Ruwad fi Dhikr al-Muluk Min Bani 'Abd al-Was—History.

44. ibn Khaldun, (1) 'Abd al-Rahman ibn Khaldun, (2) 1332-1406, (3) Tunisian, (4) ?, (5) Historiography, (6) Muqaddima—Introduction to the following listing; Kitab al-'Ibar wa Diwan al-Mubtada' wa'l Khabar fi Ayyam al-'Arab wa'l 'Ajam wa'l Berber wa Man 'Asarahum Min Dhawi'l-Sultan al-Akhbar—"Instructive examples and collections of origins and information concerning the history of the Arabs, Persians and Berbers."

45. al-Khazraji, (1) Muwaffak al-Din Abu-al-'Abbas Ahmad ibn al-Qasim ibn abi Usaibi'a al-Sa'di, (2) 1203 or 1204 to 1270, (3) Syrian, (4) ?, (5) Physician, historian of medicine, historiography, (6) Collection of medical observations (lost); Kitab 'Uyun al-Anba' fi Tabaqat al-Atibba—Medicine and physicians.

46. al-Kirmani, (1) Afdhal'ud din Abu Hamed Ahmad ibn Hamed, known also as Afdhal-i-Kirman, (2) Latter part of 12th and beginning of 13th, (3) Persian, (4) Persian and Arabic, (5) History, (6) Aqd-al-Ula L'l Moaqif-al-A'ala—On the history of Kirman; Bada'yi'uz-Zaman fi Waqai-i-Kirman—History of Kirman.

47. al-Kutubi, (1) Muhammad ibn Shakir al-Halabi al-Dimashqi, (2) Died 1363, (3) Syrian Muslim, (4) ?, (5) Historiography, (6) 'Uyun al-Tawarikh—Sources of the histories; Fawat al-Wafayat—Continuation of the biographical dictionary, Wafayat al-A'yan of ibn Khalliqan.

48. al-Marrakushi, (1) Abu Muhammad 'Abd al-Wahid ibn 'Ali al-Tamimi al-Marrakushi Muhyi al-Din, (2) 1185-1224, or died later, (3) Marrakush, (4) ?, (5) Historiography, (6) Kitab Alumu'jib fi Talkhis Akhbar Ahl al-Maqrib—History of the people of Africa.

49. al-Marrakushi, (1) ibn al-'Idhari al-Marrakushi, (2) About end of 13th, (3) Moroccan, (4) ?, (5) Historiography, (6) Kitab al-Bayan al-Maqrib—History of Africa and Spain.

50. ibn Mashawayh, (1) Abu 'Ali Ahmad ibn Muhammad ibn Ya'qub, (2) Died 1030, (3) Persian, (4) Arabic, (5) History, medicine, philosophy, (6) Kitab Tajarib al-Umam—Universal history to 982 or 983; Kitab Adab al-'Arab wa'l Fars—Compilation on practical wisdom; Kitab Tahdhib al-Akhlaq—Treatise on the refinement of manners.

51. Minhaf-i-Siraj, (1) Abu 'Umar-i-'Uthman Minhaj-i-Siraj of Jurjan (?), (2) 1193, died after 1260, (3) Persian, (4) ?, (5) Historiography, (6) Tabaqat-i-Nasiri—General history of the Muslim dynasties of Asia to 1260.

52. al-Misri, (1) Ibrahim ibn Muhammad ibn Duqmaq Sarim al-Din al-Hanafi, (2) Died probably 1407, (3) Egyptian, (4) ?, (5) Historiography, (6) Nuzhat al-Anam fi Tarikh al-Islam—"Annals of Muslim Egypt to 1377"; Al-Jauhar al-Thamin fi Siyar al-Khulafa' wa'l Salatin—History of the Salatin of Egypt; Kitab al-Durra't al-Mudhi' fi Fadhl Misr wa'l Iskandariya—Account of two Egyptian capitals, Cairo and Alexandria; Nasm al-Juman fi Tabaqat As'hab Imamna al-Nu'man—

Biographical collections; Tarjuman al-Zaman fi Tarajim al-A'yan—Organization of the army; Fara'id al-Fawa'id—Treatise on interpretation of dreams.

53. al-Misri, (1) Abu-al-'Abbas Shihab al-Din Ahmad ibn 'Ali al-Qalqashandi (also called ibn abi Qudda and al-Qalqashandi), (2) 1355-1418, (3) Egyptian, (4) ?, (5) Historiography, encyclopaedist, (6) Subh al-A'sha fi Sina'at al-Insha—Dawn of the weak-sighted on the art of composition; Subh al-A'sha; Nihayat al-Arab fi Ma'rifat Qaba'il al-'Arab—"Genealogy and history of the Arab tribes before the time of Islam"; Qala'id al-Juman fi'l-Ta'rif bi Qaba'il 'Arab al-Zaman—"Supplement to previous listing."

54. ibn Munqidh, (1) Abu-al-Muzaffar Usamah ibn Murshid, (2) Died 1188, (3) Hamah, (4) ?, (5) Historiography, poet, autobiography, (6) Kitab al-I'tibar—Learning by example; Kitab al-Badi—Poems, treatise on rhetoric.

55. ibn al-Muthanna, (1) Abu 'Ubaida Ma'mar ibn al-Muthanna, (2) 725-825, (3) Jewish Persian, (4) ?, (5) Historian, philology, (6) Abundant works on history and philology; Kitab Aiyam al-'Arab—"Book of the days of battle of the Arabs"; Kitab al-Mathalib—The vices of the Arabs reprehended.

56. al-Nasawi, (1) Muhammad ibn Ahmad ibn 'Ali Shihab al-Din, (2) Died 1241 or later, (3) Khurasan, (4) Arabic, (5) Historian, (6) Biography of Sultan Jalal al-Din.

57. Nasir Khusru, (1) Hakim Abu Mu'in Khusru ibn Harith al-Qubadyani al-Balkhi al-Marwazi Hujjat, (2) 1003-1088, (3) Persian, (4) Persian, (5) History, biography, travel, (6) Mandhumat—Poems; Jami' ul-Hikmatain Zad ul-Musaferin—On Ismailite theology; Wajhi Din—On religion; Safar Namah—Travel book; Khani Akhwan; Goshayish wa Rahayish—Opening and release.

58. al-Nassab, (1) Abu al-Tasan 'Ali ibn al-Hasan ibn Wahhas al-Khazraji (also known as al-Khazraji), (2) Died 1409, (3) Yaman, (4) ?, (5) Historiography, (6) Kitab al-Kifaya wa'l-I'lam—Dynastic history; Tiraz A'lam al-Zaman fi Tabaqat A'yan al-Yaman—Biographical dictionary.

59. Nisibensis, (1) Elias Bar Sinaeus Episcopus, (2) 975-1049, or died later, (3) Syrian, (4) Arabic, (5) History, grammar, lexicography, theology, meteorology, (6) Kitab al-Burhan 'Ala Sahih—Demonstration of the truth of faith; Kitab al-Tarjuman fi Ta'lim Luqat al-Suryan—Arabic-Syrian vocabulary.

60. Qawam al-Din, (1) al-Fat'h ibn 'Ali ibn al-Fat'h al-Isfahani, (2) Flourished 1226, (3) Persian, (4) Arabic, (5) Muslim historian, (6) Abridgment of the history of the Saljuq rule by 'Imad al-Din al-Isfahani; Abridgment of the same author's Kitab al-Barq al-Sha'mi; Translation of Firdawsi's Shah Namah into Arabic.

61. al-Qibti, (1) Abu Shakir Butrus ibn Ali-al-Karam ibn al-

Muhadhdhib al-Ma'ruf ibn al-Rahib, (2) Flourished 1270-1282, (3) Egyptian, (4) Arabic, (5) Historiography, (6) Tarikh—Chronicle of Eastern history from the creation to 1259.

62. al-Quda'i, (1) Abu 'Abd Allah Muhammad ibn 'Abd Allah ibn Abi Bakr ibn al-Abbar, (2) 1199-1260, (3) Hispano-Muslim, (4) ?, (5) Historiography, (6) Kitab al-Sila of ibn Bashkuwal—A Continuation; Kitab al-Hulla al-Siyara.

63. al-Qurtubi, (1) Abu al-Qasim ibn 'Abd al-Malik ibn Mas'ud ibn Bashkuwai, (2) 1101-1183, (3) Hispano-Muslim, (4) ?, (5) History, (6) Tarikh 'Ulama' al-Andalus of ibn al-Faradi; Kitab al-Sila fi Akhbar A'immat al-Andalus.

64. al-Qurtubi, (1) Arib ibn Ea'd al-Katib, (2) ?, (3) Hispano-Muslim, (4) ?, (5) History, medicine, (6) Chronicle of Muslim Spain and Africa; Treatise on gynecology; Kitab al-Anwa'—Calendar.

65. al-Qustantini, (1) Abu al-Abbas Ahmad ibn al-Hasan ibn al-Khatib, known also as ibn al-Qunfudh, (2) Died 1407 or 1408, (3) Algerian, (4) ?, (5) Historiography, (6) Al-Farisiyya fi Mabadi al-Daulat al-Hafsiyya—History of the Banu Hafs; Sharh al-Talib fi Asna'l-Matalib—Obituaries of learned men; Uns al-Faqir wa 'Izz al-Haqir—"Biography of Abu Madyan Shu'aib ibn al-Hasan al-Tilimsani, a Spanish Sufi"; Tas'hil al-Matalib fi Ta'dil al-Kawakib—Commentary on the Talkhis of ibn al-Banna'; Commentary on the astrological poem of ibn Abi-l-Rijal; Kitab al-Wafayat—Probably identical with the second listing.

66. ibn al-Qutiyya, (1) Abu Bakr Muhammad ibn Umar ibn 'Abd al-'Aziz, (2) Died 977, (3) Hispano-Muslim, (4) Arabic, (5) History, grammar, (6) Tarikh al-Andalus—History of Andalusia; Kitab Tasarif al-Af'al—Conjugations of Arabic verbs.

67. al-Qurtubi, (1) Abu Ja'far Ahmad ibn Yahya ibn Ahmad ibn 'Umaira al-Dabbi, (2) Died after 1195, (3) Hispano-Muslim, (4) ?, (5) History, biography, (6) Kitab Bughyat al-Mutalammis fi Tarikh Rijal ahl al-Andalus—Desire of him who is anxious to know the story of the Andalusians.

68. al-Razi, (1) Shams-ud-din Muhammad ibn Qais, (2) 13th, (3) Persian, (4) Persian and Arabic, (5) Literary history, (6) Al-Mu'jam fi Ma'aiyyr Ash'ar al-Ajam—A comprehensive work on Persian literature.

69. al-Salmani, (1) Lisan al-Din Abu 'Abd Allah Muhammad ibn 'Abd Allah, (2) 1313-1374, (3) Hispano-Muslim, (4) ?, (5) Historiography, (6) Al-Hulal al-Marquma—"History of the caliphs East and West"; A'mal al-A'lam—Muslim history East and West; Al-Lumha al-Badriyya fi' l-Dawla al-Nasriyya—History of Granada to 1363; Al-Ihata bi Ta'rikh Qarnata—Collection concerning history of Granada; Al-Taj al-Muhalla—History of Spain since 1232; Mi'yar al-Ikhtiyar; Mufakharat Malaqa wa Sala—Rivalry between Malaga and Sala; Al-Hulal al-Maushiyya fi Dhikr al-Akhbar al-Marrakushiyya—Chronicle of Morocco; Nufadat al-Jirab fi 'Ulalat al-Iqtirab—Memoirs in Morocco; Khatrat al-

Taif fi Rihlat al-Shita wa'l-Saif—Journey in Eastern Granada; Raihanat al-Kuttab wa Nuf'at al-Muntab—Collection of models of letters; Manfa'at al-Sa'il 'an al-Marad al-Ha'il—Account of the plague which occurred in Granada in 1348; Amal man Tabba Li man Habba—Medical treatise; Manzuma fi'l-Tibb—Medical poem; Al-Usul li-Hifz al-Sihha fi'l-Fusul—Regimen for different seasons of the year; Al-Yusufi (?) fi Sana'at al-Tibb—Treatise on medicine; Other medical works.

70. al-Shafi'i, (1) Abu al-Fadl Ja'far ibn Tha'lab al-Adfuwi, (2) 1286-1347, (3) Egyptian, (4) ?, (5) Historiography, (6) Kitab al-Tali' al-Sa'id al-Jami' li'asma' Nujaba' al-Sa'id—"The auspicious star concerning the noble men of Sa'id"; Al-Badr al-Safir wa Tuhfat al-Masafir—Biographies of men of the 13th century; Al-Imta' bi-Ahkam al-Sama'—Music; Fara'id al-Fawa'id wa Maqasid al-Qawa'id—"Legal commentary on the book of al-Nawawi."

71. al-Shafi'i, (1) Abu al-Qasim 'Ali ibn abi Muhammad al-Hasan ibn Hibat Allah Thiqat al-Din ibn 'Asakir al-Shafi'i, (2) 1105-1176, (3) Damascus, (4) ?, (5) Muslim historian and traditionist, (6) Ta'rikh Madinat Dimashq—History of Damascus, 80 volumes.

72. al-Shafi'i, (1) Badr al-Din Abu Muhammad al-Hasan ibn 'Umar ibn Habib al-Dimashqi, (2) 1310-1377, (3) Syrian, (4) ?, (5) Historiography, (6) Durrat al-Aslak fi Mulk al-Atrak—History of Bahri Mamluk Dynasty; Juhainat al-Akhbar fi Muluk al-Amsar—History; Tadhkirat 'an Nabihi fi Aijam al-Mansur wa Banihi—History of Qala'um and his sons; Nasim al-Saba—"Description of natural and human scenes"; Kashf al-Murut 'an Mahasin al-Shurrut—Models of official letters.

73. al-Shafi'i, (1) Shams al-Din Abu'l Abbas Ahmad ibn Muhammad ibn Ibrahim ibn abi Bakr ibn Khallikan al-Marmaki (Barmaki?) al-Irbili, known as ibn Kallikan, (2) 1211-1282, (3) Persian ?, (4) ?, (5) Muslim historian, (6) Kitab Wafayat al-A'yan wa-Anba' Abna' al-Zaman—Deaths of great personages and histories of the leading people of the time.

74. al-Shafi'i, (1) Abu al-Fida' Isma'il ibn 'Umar ibn Kathir 'Imad al-Din ibn al-Khatib al-Busrawi al-Qurashi, (2) 1301-1373, (3) Syrian, (4) ?, (5) Historian and traditionist, (6) Kitab al-Bidaya wa'l Nihaya—The beginning and the end; Commentaries on the Qur'an, Muslim tradition, etc.

75. al-Shafi'i, (1) Salah al-Din Abu'l Safa' Khali ibn Aibak al-Safadi al-Shafi'i, known as al-Saqadi, (2) 1297-1363, (3) Palestinian, (4) ?, (5) Historiography, (6) Wafi bi'-Wafayat—Biographical dictionary; A'yan al-'Asr wa A'wan al-Nasr—Extract from previous listing; Masalik al-Absar fi Mamalik al-Amsar—Treatise on geography; Al-Tadhkira al-Salahiyya—Extracts from medical work, etc.; Law'at al-Shaki wa Dam'at al-Baqi—About male homosexuality; Kitab Kashf al-Hal fi Wasf al-Khal—About moles.

76. al-Shafi'i, (1) Shams al-Din Abu 'Abd Allah Muhammad ibn Ahmad al-Dhahabi al-Turkomani, (2) 1274-1348 or 1353, (3) Muslim

Turkish, (4) ?, (5) Historiography, (6) Al-Mushtabih fi Asma' al-Rijal —Alphabetical dictionary of proper names occurring in the Ahadith; Mizan al-I'tidal fi Naqd al-Rijal—Alphabetical dictionary of apocryphal or weak traditionists; Tajrid Asma al-Sohaba—Dictionary of the Prophet's companions; Tahdhib al-Kamal fi Asma' al-Rijal—"Correction of names in the traditions recorded in the six canonical books"; Mukhtasar li Tarikh Baghdad—Summary of history of Baghdad by Muhammad ibn Sa'id ibn al-Dubaithi; Mukhtasar Akhbar al-Nahwiyyin li ibn al-Qifti—Summary of the history of grammarians by ibn al-Qifti; Tarikh al-Islam —History of Islam; Al-Tibb al-Nabawi—Medicine of the Prophet.

77. al-Shahrastani, (1) Abu al-Fath Muhammad ibn 'Abd al-Karim al-Shahrastani, (2) 1076 or 1077 to 1153, (3) Persian, (4) ?, (5) History of religion and philosophy, (6) Kitab al-Milal wa'l-Nihal—Book of religions and sects; Tarikh al-Hukama; Kitab Musara'at al-Falasifa—Discussions of the philosophers; Kitab Nihayat al-Eqdam fi Ilm al-Kalam—The limit of diligence in the knowledge of scholastic theology.

78. al-Subki, (1) Taj al-Din Abu Nasr 'Abd al-Wahhab ibn 'Ali, (2) 1327-1370, (3) Egyptian, (4) ?, (5) Historiography, (6) Kitab Jam' al-Jawami' fi' l'Usul—"Collection of all collections concerning principles of Muslim jurisprudence"; Mu'id al-Ni'am wa Mubid al-Niqam—Restorer of favors and restrainer of chastisements; Tabaqat al-Shafi'iya—Biographies of Shafi'i theologians.

79. al-Tabari, (1) Abu Ja'far Muhammad ibn Jarir, (2) 838 or 839-923, (3) Persian, (4) Arabic, (5) Historiography, theology, (6) Kitab Akhbar al-Rusul wa'l-Muluk—Universal history of prophets and kings; Commentary on the Qur'an.

80. al-Tamimi, (1) Abu Sa'd 'Abd al-Karim ibn Muhammad ibn Mansur al-Tamimi al-Sam'ani Taj al-Islam, (2) 1113-1166, (3) Marv, (4) ?, (5) Historiography, (6) Kitab al-Ansab—Continuation of annals of Baghdad begun by al-Khatib.

81. ibn Tiqtaqa, (1) Abu Ja'far Jalal al-Din Muhammad ibn 'Ali ibn Tabataba, (2) Born 1262, (3) Iraqi, (4) ?, (5) Historiography, (6) Fakhr al-Din 'Isa; Kitab al-Fakhri fi'l-Adab al-Sultaniyya wa'l-Duwal al-Islamiyya—Political treatise.

82. al-Waqidi, (1) Abu 'Abd Allah Muhammad ibn 'Umar, (2) 747 or 748-823, (3) Medina, (4) ?, (5) Historian, (6) Kitab al-Maqazi —History of the wars, Muhammad's campaigns.

83. al-Wassaf, (1) 'Abd Allah ibn Fadhl Allah of Shiraz, generally called Wassaf, (2) Flourished 1303-1328, (3) Persian, (4) Persian, (5) Historiography, (6) Tarikh-i-Jahan Gusha—Continuation of the history of the Mongols by al-Juwaini.

84. ibn Wasil, (1) Abu 'Abd Allah Muhammad ibn Salim ibn Wasil Jamal al-Din, (2) 1207 or 1208-1298, (3) ?, (4) ?, (5) Doctor, historian, philosopher, mathematician, (6) Al-Impiruriyya; Kitab Mufarrij al-Kurub fi Akhbar Bani Ayyub—"The book which dispels sadness with

the tales of the Ayyubids"; Sharh al-Maqsad al-Jalil—Commentary on the treatise on prosody of ibn al-Hajib.

85. al-Yamani, (1) Abu Muhammad 'Umara ibn 'Ali ibn Zaidan al-Yamani Najm al-Din, (2) 1121 or 1122-1174, (3) Yemen, (4) ?, (5) Muslim historian, (6) Tarikh al-Yaman—History of Yemen; Qasa'id —Autobiography; Kitab al-Nukat al-'Asriyya fi Akhbar al-Wuzara' al-Misriyya—Contemporary subtleties concerning the viziers of Egypt.

86. al-Zuhri, (1) Abu 'Abd Allah Muhammad ibn Sa'd ibn Mani, (2) Died 845, (3) ?, (4) ?, (5) Historiography, (6) Kitab al-Tabaqat al-Kabir—Great book of the classes.

MEDICINE

1. al-Abrash, (1) Ayyub al-Ruhawi al-Abrash, (2) ?, (3) ?, (4) Syriac, (5) Medicine, (6) Translation of 35 Galenic works is ascribed to him.

2. al-Ainzarbi, (1) 'Adnan, (2) Died 1153 or 1154, (3) Sicilian, (4) Arabic, probably, (5) Medicine, astrology, (6) Kitab al-Kafi fi 'Ilm al-Tibb—The sufficient in medicine; Kitab fi ma Yahtaj al-Tabib Min 'Ilm al-Falak—Application of astronomy to medicine.

3. ibn al-Akfani, (1) ?, (2) Died 1348 or 1349, (3) Iraqi, (4) Arabic, probably, (5) Medicine, natural history, encyclopaedist, (6) Kashf al-Rain fi Ahwal al-'Ain—Treatise on eye diseases; Kitab Qunyat al-Labib fi Qaibat al-Tabib—Domestic medicine for use in doctor's absence; Nihayat al-Qasd fi Sina'at al-Fask—On bloodletting; Al-Nazar wa'l Tahqiq fi Taqlib al-Raqiq—Advice on slave buying; Kukhab(?) al-Ahakhir fi Ahwal al-Jawahir—Precious stones; Kitab Asas al-Riyasa fi'Ilm l-Firasa—On physiognomy.

4. Alcoatim, (1) ?, (2) Living 1159, (3) Hispano-Christian, (4) Arabic, probably, (5) Medicine (eye diseases), (6) Congregatio Sive Liber de Oculis—Eye diseases.

5. al-Aqsara'i, (1) ?, (2) Died 1368 to 1378, (3) Turkish, (4) Arabic, probably, (5) Medicine, theology, rhetoric, (6) Commentary on the Mujiz al-Qanun by ibn al-Nafis; Annotations of Qur'anic work; Commentary on rhetoric text.

6. al-Attar, (1) Zain, (2) 1329-1403, (3) Persian, (4) Persian, (5) Pharmacy, (6) Miftah al-Khaza'in—Medical work; Ikhtiyarat-i-Badi'i—New edition of the first listing.

7. ibn Sina (Avicenna), (1) Abu 'Ali al-Husain ibn 'Abd Allah, (2) 980-1037, (3) Arabic, (4) Arabic, Persian, (5) Physician, philosopher, encyclopaedist, astronomer, mathematician, (6) Many writings devoted to mathematical and astronomical observations; Translation of Euclid; "Studies of specific gravity, motion, contact, force, vacuum, infinity, light, heat; Autobiography; Kitab al-Shifa' Sanatio—Philosophical encyclopaedia"; Kitab al-Isharat wa'l-Tanbihat—Book of signs and admonitions; Qanun (Canon)—Medical work; Treatise on cardiac drugs.

8. ibn 'Abd al-'Aziz, (1) 'Abd Allah ibn 'Abd al-'Aziz, (2) Be-

ginning 14th, (3) Turkish, (4) Arabic, (5) Medicine, (6) 'Umdat al-Fuhul fi Sharh al-Fusul—Commentary on the aphorisms of Hippocrates.

9. ibn al-Baitar, (1) ?, (2) Died 1248, (3) Hispano-Muslim, (4) Arabic, (5) Botany, pharmacy, (6) Kitab al-Jami' fi'l-Adwiyya al-Mufrada—"Greatest Arabic and medieval treatise on simples"; Kitab al-Muqni fi'l-Adwiyya al-Mufrada—Therapeutical study of simples and vegetables.

10. ibn Bajja—See section on mathematics and astronomy.

11. ibn Bakhtyashu, (1) Abu Sa'id 'Ubaid Allah ibn Jibril, (2) Died 1058, (3) Persian-Syrian, (4) ?, (5) Medicine, (6) Tadhkirat al-Hadir—Philosophical terms used in medicine; Kitab al-'Ishq Maradhan—Treatise on love-sickness.

12. ibn Bakhtyashu, (1) Jibril, (2) Died 828 or 829, (3) Persian-Syrian, (4) ?, (5) Medicine, (6) Various medical works. (Perhaps same as 11.)

13. ibn Bakhtyashu', (1) Jirjis ibn Jibril, (2) Died 771, (3) Persian-Syrian, (4) ?, (5) Medicine, (6) Translated medical works into Arabic. (Perhaps same as above.)

14. al-Baladi, (1) Ahmad ibn Muhammad ibn Yahya, (2) ?, (3) Egyptian, (4) ?, (5) Medicine, (6) Kitab Tadbir al-Habala wa'l Atfal—Treatise on hygiene of pregnant women and babies.

15. ibn Bunan, (1) Salmawaih, (2) Died end of 839 or beginning of 840, (3) Syrian (Nestorian), (4) ?, (5) Medicine, (6) Helped translate Galen's Methodus Medendi.

16. ibn Butlan, (1) Abu-al-Hasan al-Mukhtar ibn al-Hasan ibn 'Abdun ibn Sa'dun, (2) Died after 1063, (3) ?, (4) ?, (5) Medicine, (6) Taqwim al-Sihha—Tables of health.

17. Ben Era, (1) Hasdai ibn Shaprut (alias Shabrut, Shafrut, Bashrut, Shprot) Abu Yusuf Ben Isaac, (2) 915-970 or 990, (3) Hispano-Jewish, (4) Arabic, (5) Medicine, translator, scientist, (6) Translator of Greek into Arabic; Patron of science; Physician to caliph.

18. al-Ghafiqi (al-Qufiqi), (1) ?, (2) Died 1165, (3) Spanish-Muslim, (4) Arabic, probably, (5) Medicine, botany, (6) Kitab al-Adwiyya al-Mufrada—On Simples; Treatise on eye diseases; Two abridgments on the first listing.

19. ibn Abi Hajala, (1) ?, (2) 1325-1375, (3) Algerian Muslim, (4) Arabic, probably, (5) Medicine, poetry, theology, letters, (6) Al-Tibb al-Masnun fi Daf'al-Ta'un—Medicine against plague; Jiwar al-Akhyar fi Dar al-Qarar—On the plague; Daf' al-Niqma fi'l-Slat 'Ala Nabi al-Rahma—Apropos of the plague; Kitab Anmudhaj al-Qital fi La'b al-Shatranj—On chess.

20. Haly Abbas, (1) 'Ali ibn 'Abbas al-Majusi, (2) Died 994, (3) Persian, (4) ?, (5) Physician, (6) Kitab al-Maliki—Medical encyclopaedia.

21. al-Harawi, (1) Abu Mansur Muwaffaq ibn 'Ali, (2) ?, (3) Persian, (4) ?, (5) Pharmacology, (6) Kitab al-Abniyya 'an Haqa'iq

al-Adwiyya—Book of the foundations of the true properties of the remedies by herbs.

22. ibn Hasda'i, (1) ?, (2) Living 1101-1130, (3) Hispano-Jewish-Muslim, (4) Arabic, probably, (5) Medicine, (6) The Ma'munic commentary on Hippocrates and Galen; Al-Sharh al-Ma'muni—Hippocratic oath; Sharh al-Fusul—Hippocrates' aphorisms; Fawa'id—Extracts from a commentary on Galen's treatise to Glaucon; Qual'ala Awwal Sana'ah al-Saqira—Commentary on first book of Galen's Ars Parva; Ijmal—Summary on logic.

23. ibn Akhi Hizam, (1) Abu Yusuf Ya'qub ibn Akhi Hizam, (2) ?, (3) ?, (4) ?, (5) Medicine, (6) Kitab al-Furusiyya—Horsemanship.

24. ibn Hubal, (1) , (2) 1117-1213, (3) Baghdad, (4) Arabic, probably, (5) Medicine, logic, (6) Kitab al-Mukhtar fi'l-Tibb—Treatise on medicine; Treatise on logic.

25. al-Ibadi, (1) Abu Zaid Hunain ibn Is'haq, (2) 809 or 810-877, (3) Nestorian, (4) Syriac, Arabic, Greek, (5) Medicine, (6) Treatise on synonyms; Explanation of Greek words in Syriac; Medical and astronomical writings; Introduction to Galen's Ars Parva; Translations.

26. al-Idrisi, (1) ?, (2) 1099 or 1100-1166, (3) Muslim (Sicily?), (4) Arabic, probably, (5) Geography, medicine, (6) Al-Kitab al-Rujari—Description of the world; Rawd al-uns Wa-Nuzhat al-Nafs—Geography encyclopaedia; Treatise on botany and medicine.

27. al-Iraqi, (1) Abu-al-Faraj 'Abd Allah ibn al-Taiyib, (2) Died 1043 or 1044, (3) Iraqi, (4) ?, (5) Medicine, (6) Commentaries on Greek medicine; Original memoirs on various medical topics; "Translations of pseudo-Aristotelian De Plantis."

28. al-Isra'ili, (1) Abu Ya'qub Is'haq ibn Sulaiman, (2) Died about 932, (3) Hebrew, (4) Arabic, (5) Medicine, (6) Kitab al-Mummayat— On fevers; Kitab al-Adwiyya't al-Mufrada wa'l-Aqdhiya—Book of simple drugs and nutriments; Kitab al-Baul—On urine, Guide of the physicians; Published classification of sciences.

29. al-Jawziyya, (1) ibn Qayyim al-Jawziyya, (2) 1292-1350, (3) Syrian, (4) Arabic, probably, (5) Theology, medicine, (6) Kitab al-Turuq al-Hikmiyya fi'l Siyasa al-Shar'iyya—On theology; Kitab al-Da'w al-Dawa—On remedy and sickness; Kitab al-Tibb al-Nabawi—Medical traditions traced to the Prophet; Kitab Tibb al-Qulub—Spiritual medicines; Tuhfat al-Mawdud bi-Ahkam al-Mawlud—Ritual care of newborn children; Hurmat al-Sama'—Listening to music; Zad al-Ma'ad fi Hadi Khair al-'Ibad—Book on manners and conduct of the Prophet.

30. ibn Jazi, (1) Abu 'Ali Yahya ibn 'Isa, (2) Early 14th?, (3) Syrian, (4) Arabic, probably, (5) Theology, medicine, (6) Taqwim al-Abdan fi Tadbir al-Insan—Tables of the bodies with regard to their constitutions; Minhaj al-Bayan fi ma Yasta'miluhu al-Insan—The pathway for explanation as to that which man uses; Dispositio Corporum de Constitutione Hominis—Description and treatment of diseases.

31. ibn Juljul, (1) Abu Da'ud Sulaiman ibn Hassan, (2) ?, (3) Muslim Arab, (4) Arabic, (5) Medicine, (6) Tarikh al-Atibba' wa'l-Falasifa—"Commentary on Dioscorides and supplement to it to determine the drugs dealt with by Dioscorides" (history of historians and philosophers).

32. al-Jurjani, (1) Abu Ruh Muhammad ibn Mansur ibn abi 'Abd Allah ibn Mansur al-Jamani, or al-Jurjani, (2) Flourished 1072-1092, (3) Persian, (4) Persian, (5) Medicine, (6) Nur al-'Uyun—The light of the eyes, on ophthalmology.

33. al-Jurjani, (1) Isma'il al-Jurjani, (2) ?, (3) Persian, (4) Persian, Arabic, (5) Medicine, philosophy, (6) Dhakhira al-Khwarizmshahi—First medical encyclopaedia written in Persian; Aghrad al-Tibb—The aims of medicine; Kafi 'Ala'i—Condensed edition of first listing; Tadhkira al-Ashrafiyya fi'l-Sina'a al-Tibbiyya—Medical repertory; Al-Munabbih—On philosophy.

34. al-Jurjani, (1) Abu Sahl 'Isa ibn Yahya al-Masihi, (2) Died 999 or 1000, (3) Arabic or Persian, (4) Arabic, (5) Physician, (6) Al-Kutub al-Mi'a fi'l-Sana'at al-Tibbiyya—Encyclopaedic treatise on medicine; "Various smaller treatises on measles, the plague, the pulse, demonstration of God's wisdom as evidenced in the creation of man, etc."

35. ibn Khatimah, (1) ?, (2) 1323 or 1324-1369, (3) Hispano-Muslim, (4) Arabic, (5) Medicine, poetry, (6) Al-Maziyyat Almeria 'ala Qairiha Min Bilad al-Andalusia—History of Almeria; Tahsil al-Qarad al-Qasid fi Tafsil al-Marad al-Wafidh—Treatise on the plague.

36. al-Khujandi, (1) Muhammad ibn Muhammad al-Khujandi, (2) Flourished 1304-1316, (3) Transoxian, (4) Arabic, (5) Medicine, (6) A super commentary on the Qanun of ibn Sina; Mukhtasar fi Sina'at al-Tibb—A brief medical book; Tarwih al-Arwah Min 'Ilal al-Ashbah—A medical book.

37. al-Kilani, (1) Ahmad ibn Muhammad al-Kilani, (2) ?, (3) Persian, (4) Arabic, (5) Medicine, (6) Arabic commentary on the aphorisms of Hippocrates.

38. ibn al-Kutubi, (1) ?, (2) Flourished 1311, (3) Iraqi, (4) Arabic, probably, (5) Medicine, (6) Ma La Yasa'u al-Tabiba Juhluhu—Treatise on simple drugs.

39. Abu al-Mahasin, (1) Khalifa ibn Abi al-Mahasin, (2) Flourished 1256, (3) Syrian, (4) Arabic, probably, (5) Medicine (eye specialty), (6) Kitab al-Kafi fi'l-Kuhl—Anatomy and treatment of the eyes.

40. al-Mahdi, (1) Muhammad al-Mahdi, (2) Died 1412 or 1413, (3) Bangali, possibly Hindu, (4) Arabic, (5) Medicine, (6) Kitab al-Rahma fi'l-Tibb wa'l-Hikma—Medical treatise.

41. ibn Mahmud, (1) Muhammad, (2) 1397, (3) Turkish or Caucasian, (4) Arabic, (5) Medicine, (6) Raudhat al-'Itr—Arabic pharmacopoeia.

42. al-Manbiji, (1) ?, (2) Writing in 1373, (3) Syrian, (4) Arabic,

probably, (5) Disease, (6) Tasliyat Ahl al-Masa'ib fi Mauta'l Awlad wa'l-Aqarib—The plague.

43. al-Malaqi, (1) Abu Muhammad 'Abd Allah ibn Ahmad ibn al-Baitar Dhiya' al-Din, (2) Died 1248, (3) Hispano-Muslim, (4) Arabic, (5) Medicine, botanist, pharmacist, (6) Kitab al-Jami' fi'l-Adwiyya al-Mufrada; Kitab al-Muqni fi'l-Adwiyya al-Mufrada—Both on drugs.

44. al-Mardini, (1) Masawaith, (2) Died 1015, (3) Iraqi, (4) ?, (5) Medicine, (6) "De Medicinis Laxativis—Purgatives and emetics; De Egritudinibus—Remedies relative to each disease; Antidotarium Sive Grabadin Medicamentorum Compositorum—Complete pharmacopoeia."

45. ibn Masawaih, (1) Abu Zakariyya Yuhanna ibn Masawaith (or Masuya), (2) Died 857, (3) ?, (4) Syriac, Arabic, (5) Medicine, (6) Daqal al-'Ain—Disorder of the Eye.

46. al-Mawsili, (1) Abu-al-Qasim 'Ammar ibn 'Ali, (2) ?, (3) Iraqi, (4) ?, (5) Medicine, occultry, (6) Kitab al-Muntakhab fi 'Ilaj al-'Ain—Treatment of the eye.

47. Mesue the Third, unknown Arabic surgeon, (1) ?, (2) ?, (3) ?, (4) Arabic, (5) Medicine, (6) Treatise on surgery (lost).

48. al-Misri, (1) Abu Hasan 'Ali ibn Ridhwan ibn 'Ali ibn Ja'far, (2) 998-1061 or 1067, (3) Egyptian, (4) ?, (5) Astrology, medicine, (6) Many writings; Commentaries on Galen, Hippocrates and Ptolemy.

49. ibn Muhammad, (1) Mansur, (2) 1396-1423, (3) Persian, (4) Persian, (5) Medicine, physician, anatomist, (6) Tashrih-i Mansuri—Illustrated treatise on anatomy; Kifayat-i-Mansuri—Medical treatise.

50. ibn Muhammad, (1) Muhammad of Almeria, (2) Died 1363, (3) Andalusian, Hispano-Muslim, (4) Arabic, (5) Medicine, letters, (6) Islah al-Niyyah—One of the earliest Arabic treatises on the plague; Poems on theology and rhetoric.

51. al-Muqaddasi, (1) Abu 'Abd Allah Muhammad ibn Ahmad ibn Sa'd al-Tamimi, (2) ?, (3) Palestinian, (4) ?, (5) Medicine, (6) Murshid—"Guide on materia medica"; Kitab al-Murshid Ila Jawahir al-Aqdhiyya wa Quwa al-Mufradat—On food and drugs.

52. ibn Murad, (1) Is'haq ibn Murad of Gerede, (2) Flourished 1388, (3) Turkish, (4) Turkish, (5) Medicine, (6) Khulasat al-Tibb—Medical summary; Khawass al-Adwiyya—"On herbs and other plants and products of animal and mineral origin."

53. ibn al-Nafis, (1) ?, (2) Died 1288 or 1289, (3) Egyptian or Syrian, (4) Arabic, probably, (5) Medicine, (6) Treatise on eye diseases; Kitab al-Mukhtar min al-Aqdiyya—Treatise on diet; Kitab Mujiz al-Qanun—Commentary on the Qanun; Sharh Tashrik ibn Sina—Commentary on anatomical rapt of Qanun.

54. Hajji Pasha, (1) ?, (2) Died 1417, (3) Turkish, (4) Arabic, (5) Medicine, theology, (6) Matali' al-Anwar fi'l-Mantiq of al-Urmawi —Notes to the commentary of Fakhr al-Din al-Razi on logic treatise; Commentary on Anwar al-Tanzil of al-Baidawi; Shifa al-Asqam wa

Dawa' al-Alam—Medical encyclopaedia on cure of diseases and remedies of pains; Ts'hil al-Tibb—Abridgment of first listing in Turkish for laymen; Muntakhab al-Shifa'—Abridgment of the third listing.

55. ibn al-Qifti, (1) ?, (2) 1172 or 1173-1248, (3) Egyptian, (4) Arabic, probably, (5) General scholarship, (6) Kitab Ikhbar al-Ulama fi-Akhbar al-Hukama—History of philosophers; Many other works.

56. ibn al-Quff, (1) ?, (2) 1232 or 1233-1286, (3) Karak, (4) Arabic, probably, (5) Medicine, (6) Kitab Jami' al-Qaradh fi Hifz al-Sihha wa daf'al Maradh—Preservation of health and avoidance of diseases; Kitab al-'Umda fi Sina'at al-Jiraha—Surgery; Kitab al-Usul fi Sharah al-Fusul—Commentary on Hippocrates' aphorisms—Commentary on the Qanun (lost); Commentaries on Kitab al-Isharat of ibn Sina (lost).

57. ibn Qurra, (1) Abu Sa'id Sinan ibn Thabit, (2) Died 943, (3) ?, (4) ?, (5) Medicine, mathematics, astronomy, (6) "Main title to fame is his brilliant administration of the Baghdad hospitals and his efforts to raise scientific standards of the medical profession."

58. al-Razi, (1) Abu Bakr Muhammad ibn Zakariyya, (2) Died 923 or 924, (3) Persian, (4) ?, (5) Physician, physicist, alchemist, (6) Kitab al-Hawi—Enormous encyclopaedia of medicine; Kitab al-Mansuri —Small compilation of 10 books on Greek science; Kitab al-Judari wa'l-Hasba—Monograph on chickenpox.

59. ibn Sahda, (1) ?, (2) Flourished beginning 9th, (3) ?, (4) Syriac and Arabic, (5) Medicine, (6) Translated Hippocrates into Arabic; Translated Galen into Syriac.

60. ibn Sahl, (1) Sabur, (2) Died 869, (3) Christian, (4) ?, (5) Physician, (6) Aqrabadhin—Antidotary, 22 books.

61. al-Samarqandi, (1) Najib al-Din, (2) Died 1222 or 1223, (3) Samarqand, (4) Arabic, (5) Medicine, (6) Kitab al-Asbab wa'l-'Alamat —Causes and symptoms of diseases; Various other unlisted medical works in Arabic.

62. ibn Sarabi, (1) ?, (2) First half of 12th ?, (3) Christian ?, (4) Arabic, (5) Medicine, (6) Kitab al-Adwiyya al-Mufrada—Treatise on simples.

63. ibn Sarafyun, (1) Yahya, (2) ?, (3) Christian, (4) ?, (5) Physician, (6) Medical encyclopaedia, one set in 12 books, the other in 7.

64. al-Shadhili, (1) ?, (2) Flourished second half 14th ?, (3) Egyptian, (4) Arabic, probably, (5) Medicine, particularly ophthalmology, (6) Kitab al-'Umda al-Kuhliyya fi'l-Amradh al-Basariyya—Treatise on ophthalmology.

65. al-Shafra, (1) Muhammad, (2) Flourished 1314-1322, (3) Hispano-Muslim, (4) Arabic, probably, (5) Medicine, surgery, (6) Kitab al-Itiqsa' (?) wa'l-Ibram fi'ilaj al-Jirahat wa'l-Awram—Treatment of wounds and tumors, "drugs used in surgery."

66. al-Shaquri, (1) Muhammad ibn 'Ali, (2) ?, (3) Andalusian

Muslim, (4) Arabic, probably, (5) Medicine, theology, (6) Tuhfat al-Mutawassil fi San'at al-Tibb—Treatise on medicine; Al-Jihad al-Akhbar —Medical experiments, holy wars; Qama'a al-Yahudi 'an ta' Adud al-Hudud—Errors of the physician and anti-Semitism.

67. al-Shirazi, (1) Mahmud ibn Iylas, (2) Died 1330, (3) Persian, (4) Arabic, (5) Medicine, (6) Kitab al-Hawi fi Ilm al-Tadawi—Medical encyclopaedia for householder.

68. al-Shirazi, (1) 'Abd al-Rahman, (2) Established 1170, (3) Persian, (4) Arabic, probably, (5) Medicine, (6) Kitab al-Irah fi Asrar 'Ilm al-Nikah—On married life; Kitab Raudhat al-Qulub wa Nuzhat al-Mahbub (?)—Medical matters; Kitab Khulasat al-Kalam fi Ta'wil al-Ahlam—Dream interpretation.

69. ibn al-Suri, (1) ?, (2) 1177 or 1178-1242, (3) Born at Sur, (4) Arabic, probably, (5) Botany, medicine, (6) Al-Adwiyya al-Mufrada—Treatise on simple medicines.

70. al-Tabari, (1) Abu-al-Hasan Ahmad ibn Muhammad, (2) ?, (3) Persian, (4) Persian, Arabic, (5) Physician, (6) Compendium of medicine.

71. al-Tabari, (1) Abu al-Hasan 'Ali ibn Sahl ibn Rabban, (2) Flourished 847-861, (3) ?, (4) ?, (5) Medicine, (6) Firdaus al-Hikma—"Paradise of wisdom, deals chiefly with medicine, but also with philosophy, meteorology, zoology, embryology, psychology, astronomy; The book of religion and empire—A defense of Islam."

72. ibn Tarkhan, (1) ?, (2) 1203 or 1204-1291 or 1292, (3) Syrian, (4) Arabic, probably, (5) Medicine, philosophy, (6) Tadhkirat al-Hadiyya—Medical treatise largely on drugs; Two abbreviated editions of the previous listing; Kitab al-Bahir fi'l Jawahir—Substances.

73. ibn al-Tilmidh, (1) ?, (2) Died 1164 or 1165, (3) Christian, (4) Arabic, (5) Medicine, (6) Aqrabadhin—An antidotary; Al-Maqala al-Aminiyya fi'l-Fasd—Treatise on bloodletting; Al-Mujarrabat—Collection of observations and experiments.

74. ibn abi Usaibi'a, (1) ?, (2) 1203 or 1204-1270, (3) Syrian, (4) Arabic, probably, (5) Medicine and medical history, (6) Collection of medical observations (lost); Kitab 'Uyun al-Anba' fi Tabaqat al-Atibba—History of Muslim medicine.

75. al-Zahrawi, (1) Abu al-Qasim Khalaf ibn 'Abbas, (2) Died 1013, (3) Zahra, near Cordova, (4) ?, (5) Medicine, (6) Medical encyclopaedia, 30 sections.

76. Ha Yehudi, (1) Asaph, (2) Flourished 9th or 10th, (3) Hebrew, (4) ?, (5) Medicine, (6) Treatise on medicine, probably oldest of its kind in Hebrew.

77. ibn Yusuf, (1) Salah al-Din ibn, (2) Flourished 1296, (3) Syrian, (4) Arabic, probably, (5) Eye Medicine, (6) Nur al-'Uyun wa Jami' al-Funun—Treatise on ophthalmology.

78. Zuhr, (1) Abu al-'Ala Zuhr, (2) Died 1130 or 1131, (3) Hispano-Muslim, (4) Arabic, probably, (5) Medicine, (6) Kitab al-

Khawass—Book of medical properties; Kitab al-Adwiyya al-Mufrada—Book of simple drugs; Kitab al-'Idah—Book of explanation; Kitab Hall Shukuk al-Razi 'Ala Kutub Jalinus—Solution of al-Razi's doubts regarding Galen; Mujarrabat—Medical observations; Maqala fi'l-Radd 'Ala Abu 'Ali ibn Sina fi Mawadi Min Kitabihi fi'l-Adwiyya al-Mufrada—Refutation of some of ibn Sina's book on simple drugs; Maqala fi Bahthi li Risala Ya'qub ibn Is'haq al-Kindi fi Tarkib al-Adwiyya—Develops al-Kindi's letter on drugs; Kitab al-Nukat al-Tibbiyya—Principles of medicine; Tadhkira—Identical to previous listing.

79. ibn Zuhr (Avenzoar), (1) ?, (2) 1091 or 1094-1161, (3) Spanish-Muslim, (4) Arabic, probably, (5) Medicine, (6) Kitab al-Iqtisad fi Islah al-Anas wa'l-Ajsad—Therapeutics, hygiene, psychology; Kitab al-Taisir fi'l-Mudawat wa'l-Tadbir—"Therapeutics, diet, pathological conditions"; Kitab al-Aqdhiya—Foodstuffs, drugs, hygiene.

Music

1. ibn Ghaibi (Qaribi), (1) 'Abd al-Qadir ibn Ghaibi, (2) Died 1435, (3) Persian, (4) Arabic, (5) Music, (6) Jami' al-Alhan—On melodies; Maqasid al-Alhan—Purport of melodies; Kanz al-Alhan—Treasure of melodies (lost); Sharh al-Adwar—Explanation of modes.

2. al-Hilli, (1) 'Abd al-'Aziz ibn Soraya, (2) 1278-1349, (3) Persian, (4) Arabic, (5) Music, poetry, (6) Fa'ida fi Tawallud al-Anqam Ba'daha 'an Ba'd wa Tartibiha; 'Ala al-Buruj—On musical astrology.

3. al-Irbili, (1) Khatiq, (2) Flourished 1329-1337, (3) Iraqi, (4) Arabic, probably, (5) Music, science, (6) None.

4. ibn Kara, (1) ?, (2) 1282-1358, (3) Egyptian, (4) Arabic, probably, (5) Music, (6) Qayat al-Matlub fi Fann al-Anqam wa'l-Durub—Treatise on music.

5. Safi al-Din, (1) ?, (2) Died 1294, (3) Baghdad, (4) Arabic, probably, (5) Music, (6) Kitab al-Adwar—Musical modes; Risalat al-Sharafiyya—Treatise on music; Fi 'Ulum al-'Arudh wa'l-Qawafi wa'l-Badi—Prosody, rhyme and rhetoric.

6. al-Shalahi, (1) Muhammad, (2) Writing 1221, (3) Hispano-Muslim, (4) Arabic, probably, (5) Music, theology, (6) Kitab al-Imta wa'l-Intifa fi Mas'alat Sama' al-Sima'—On hearing musical notes.

Natural History

1. al-Abbas, (1) al-Malik al-Afdhal al-'Abbas ibn 'Ali, (2) Ruled 1362-1376, (3) Yaman, (4) ?, (5) Natural history, (6) Buqyat al-Fallahin fi'l-Ashjar al-Muthmira wa'l-Rayahin—"The desired book of peasants on useful trees and aromatic plants."

2. ibn Arqam, (1) Abu Yahya Muhammad ibn Ridhwan, (2) Died 1356, (3) Spanish-Arabic, (4) ?, (5) Natural history, astronomy, (6) Manzum fi 'Ilm al-Nujum—Astronomical poem; Treatises on the

astrolabe—Risala fi'l-Istarlab; Shajara fi Ansab al-'Arab—Arabic genealogy; Kitab al-Ihtifal fi 'stifa' Tasnif ma li'l-Khail—Treatise on horses.

3. al-Baitar, (1) Abu Bakr ibn Badr al-Din al-Mundhir, (2) Flourished 1293-1340, (3) Egyptian or Syrian, probably, (4) ?, (5) Natural history, veterinarian, (6) Kashif al-Wail fi Ma'rifat Amradh al-Khail—Veterinary art and hippology.

4. al-Barjini, (1) Mahmud ibn Muhammad, (2) 3rd quarter 14th, (3) Turkish, (4) Turkish, (5) Natural history, (6) Baz-Nama—On falconry.

5. al-Damiri, (1) Abu al-Baqa Kamal al-Din Muhammad ibn Musa, (2) 1344-1405, (3) Egyptian, (4) ?, (5) Natural history, theologian, encyclopaedist on animals, (6) Al-Jauhar al-Farid fi 'Ilm al-Tawhid—On unity of God; Al-Najm al-Wihaj fi Sharh al-Minhaj—Commentary in 4 volumes on Shafi' law; Kitab Hayat al-Hayawan—The lives of animals, "para-zoological encyclopaedia."

6. ibn Da'ud, (1) al-Malik al-Mujahid 'Ali, (2) Ruled 1321-1362, (3) Yaman, (4) ?, (5) Natural history, (6) Kitab al-Aqwal al-Kafiyya wa'l-Fusul al-Shafiyya fi 'Ilm al-Baitara—Breeding, upkeep, and training of domestic animals.

7. al-Ghafiqi, (1) Abu Ja'far Ahmad ibn Muhammad, (2) Died 1165, (3) Spanish-Muslim, (4) ?, (5) Natural history, (6) Kitab al-Adwiya al-Mufrada—On simples.

8. al-Gharnati (Qarnati), (1) 'Ali ibn 'Abd al-Rahman ibn Hudhail al-Fazari al-Andalusi, (2) Flourished 2nd half of 14th, (3) Spanish-Muslim, (4) ?, (5) Natural history, (6) Kitab al-Fawa'id al-Musattara fi 'Ilm al-Baitara—Treatise on hippiatry; Tuhfat al-Anfas wa Shi'ar Sukkan al-Andalus—Treatise on horses; Hilyat al-Fursan wa Shi'ar al-Shuj'an—Abridgment of second listing.

9. al-Ishbili, (1) Abu Zakariya Yahya ibn Muhammad ibn Ahmad ibn al-'Awwam, (2) Flourished end of 12th, (3) Hispano-Muslim, (4) ?, (5) Natural history, agriculturalist, (6) Kitab al-Falaha—Treatise on agriculture.

10. ibn Juzayy, (1) Abu Muhammad 'Abd Allah ibn Muhammad ibn Juzayy (of Granada), (2) 3rd quarter 14th, (3) Spanish-Muslim, (4) ?, (5) Natural history, (6) Kitab Matli' al-Yumn wa'l-Iqbal fi Intiqa' Kitab al-Ihtifal wa Istidrak ma Fatahu min al-Maqal—On horses.

11. al-Mawsili, (1) Taj al-Din 'Ali ibn Muhammad ibn 'Abd al-'Aziz ibn al-Duraihim al-Tha'labi al-Shafi'i, (2) 1312-1360, (3) Iraqi, (4) ?, (5) Natural history, zoologist, (6) Qayat al-Maqnam fi'l-ism al-A'Zam—About God; Kitab Manafi' al-Hayawan—Treatise on animals.

12. ibn Mufarraj, (1) Abu al-'Abbas Ahmad ibn Muhammad, (2) Born 1165 to 1172, died 1239 or 1240, (3) Hispano-Muslim, (4) ?, (5) Natural history, botany, (6) Kitab al-Rihla—Account of his journey across North Africa; On Dioscorides; Treatise on the composition of drugs.

13. al-Nasiri, (1) Muhammad ibn Manqali, (2) 2nd half 14th, (3) Egyptian, (4) ?, (5) Natural history, (6) Ins al-Mala bi-Wahsh al-Fala—Religious duties of hunting men, etc.

14. al-Qabajaqi, (1) Bailak al-Qabajaqi, (2) 1242-1282, (3) Egyptian Muslim, (4) ?, (5) Natural history, mineralogist, (6) Kitab Kanz al-Tijar fi Ma'rifat al-Ahjar—"Treasure of merchants concerning the knowledge of precious stones."

15. al-Rammah, (1) Muhammad ibn Lajin al-Husami al-Tarabulusi, (2) Flourished 1372, (3) Syrian, (4) ?, (5) Natural history, (6) Buqyat al-Qasidin bi'l-Amal fi'l-Mayadin.

16. al-Shafi'i, (1) Abu Muhammad 'Abd al-Mu'min ibn Khalaf Sharaf al-Din al-Tuni al-Dimyati, (2) 1217-1306, (3) Egyptian, (4) ?, (5) Natural history, traditionist, writer, (6) Kitab Fadl al-Khail—Excellence of horses.

17. ibn al-Suri, (1) Mansur ibn Abi Fadhl ibn 'Ali Rashid al-Din (2) 1177 or 1178-1227, (3) Tyre, (4) ?, (5) Natural history, botanist, physician, (6) Al-Adwiyya al-Mufrada—Treatise on simple medicines.

18. al-Tifashi, (1) Abu al-Abbas Ahmad ibn Yusuf Shihab al-Din, (2) Died 1253 or 1254, (3) Flourished Egypt, (4) ?, (5) Natural history, mineralogist, wrote on erotics, (6) Kitab Azhar al-Afkar fi Jawahir al-Ahjar—Flowers of thoughts on precious stones; Matali' al-Budur fi Manazil al-Surur—Risings of the full moon over the abodes of joy; Nuzhat al-Albab fi ma la-Yujad fi Kitab; Ruju' al-Shaikh ila Sibah fi'l-Quwa 'Ala al-Bah; Risala fi ma Yahtaj Ilaihi al-Rijal wa'l-Nisa' fi 'Sti'mal al-Bah Mimma Yadurr wa Yanfa'.

19. al-Tujibi, (1) Abu 'Uthman Sa'd ibn Ahmad ibn Luyun, (2) Died 1349, (3) Spanish Muslim, (4) ?, (5) Natural history, (6) Ibda' al-Malaha wa Inha' al-Rajaha fi Usul Sina'at al-Filaha—"Poem in which Arabic agricultural writers are re-quoted."

20. al-Yunani, (1) Taiburqa ibn 'Abd Allah al-Ashrafi al-Baklamishi, (2) Died 1394 ?, (3) Turkish-Greek, (4) Arabic, (5) Natural history, (6) Buqyat al-Maram wa Qayat al-Qaram—On shooting with bow and arrows; Qunyat al-Tullab fi Ma'rifat al-Ramy bi'l-Nushb; Kitab fi'l-Jihad wal-Furusiya wa Funun al-Adab al-Harbiyya—On the arts of warfare.

Philology

1. ibn Ahmad, (1) Asadi of Tus, 'Ali, (2) Flourished 1056, (3) Persian, (4) Persian, (5) Philology, (6) Luqat-Furs—Persian lexicon; Transcribed Materia Medica of Abu Mansur Muwaffaq.

2. ibn Ahmad, (1) Khalil, (2) Died 791 or 792, (3) Arabian, (4) ?, (5) Grammarian, lexicographer, (6) Kitab al-Iqa' (lost)—Book of rhythm.

3. al-Anbari, (1) Abu al-Barakat 'Abd al-Rahman ibn abi al-Wafa' Muhammad ibn 'Ubaid Allah ibn Abi Sa'id ibn l-Anbari Kamal al-Din, (2) 1119-1181, (3) ?, (4) Arabic, (5) Philology, (6) Kitab al-Nuzhat

al-Dhibba' (?) fi Tabaqat al-Udaba—History of Arabic literature and philology; Kitab al-Asrar al-'Arabiyya—Secrets of the Arabic language, and grammar.

4. al-Azdi, (1) Abu Bakr Muhammad ibn al-Hasan ibn Duraid, (2) 837 or 838-933, (3) ?, (4) Arabic, (5) Philology, (6) Al-Jamhara fi'l-Luqa—The collection of words; Kitab al-Ishtiqaq—Treatise on genealogy of Arab tribes.

5. al-Baghdadi, (1) Safi al-Din 'Abd al-Mu'min ibn Faqir al-Urmawi, (2) 1st quarter 13th, (3) Baghdad, (4) Arabic, (5) Philology, (6) Fi 'Ulum al-'Arudh wa'l Qawafi wa'l Badi—On rhyming, etc.

6. al-Firuzabadi, (1) Abu al-Tahir Muhammad ibn Ya'qub Majd al-Din al-Shirazi al-Shafi'i, (2) 1329-1414, (3) Persian, (4) Arabic and Persian, (5) Philology, (6) Al-Qamus—The ocean, a dictionary; Other books dealing with Arabic lexicography.

7. al-Hariri, (1) Abu Muhammad al-Qasim ibn 'Ali ibn Muhammad, (2) 1054 or 1055-1122, (3) Arabian, (4) Arabic, (5) Philology, (6) Mulhat al-I'rab—Grammatical poem; Maqamat—Rhymed prose stories.

8. ibn Hisham, (1) Jamal al-Din Abu Muhammad 'Abd Allah ibn Yusuf, (2) 1309-1360, (3) Egyptian, (4) ?, (5) Philology, (6) "24 treatises, most of them on grammatical subjects"; Muqni al-Labib 'an Kutub al-A'arib.

9. al-Ifriqi, (1) Jamal al-Din abu al-Fadhl Muhammad ibn al-Mukarram ibn 'Ali ibn Mansur al-Ansari al-Khazraji, (2) 1232 or 1233-1311, (3) Egyptian, (4) Arabic, (5) Philology, (6) Lisan al-'Arab—Arab dictionary; Abstracted ibn 'Asakir's history of Damascus; Nidhar al-Azhar fi'l-Lail wa'l-Nahar—Anthology relative to night and day.

10. al-Jaiyyani, (1) Athir al-Din Abu Haiyyan Muhammad ibn Yusuf ibn Haiyan al-Qarnati al-Nafzi, (2) 1256-1344, (3) Spanish-Muslim, (4) Turkish, (5) Philology, (6) Al-Nudar fi Maslat 'an Nudat—"Pure gold on consolation for the loss of Nudar, an autobiography"; Al-Bahr al-Muhit fi Tafsir al-Qur'an al-'Azim—Commentary on Qur'an; Al-Mubin fi Tarikh al-Andalus—History of Spain, 60 volumes (lost); Shadhur al-Dhahab fi'l-Iliksir—Book on alchemy; Kitab al-Irtida fi Dad wa Za—Grammar; Al-Irtishaf al-Darab Min Lisan al-'Arab—Degustation of honey, concerning the language of the Arabs; Lamha fi'l-Nahw—Glance at syntax; Al-Nukat al-Hisan fi Sharh Qayat al-Ihsan—The excellent subtleties, a commentary; Nur al-Qabash fi Lisan al-Habash—Light of the end of the night, on the language of the Abyssinians; Five books devoted to Turkish matters.

11. Jamal al-Din, (1) Abu 'Amr 'Uthman ibn 'Umar ibn al-Hajib, (2) 1175, (3) Egyptian, (4) Arabic, (5) Philology, (6) Many treatises on grammar, prosody, law.

12. ibn Janah, (1) Abu al-Walid Marwan, (2) Born between 985 and 990, (3) Hispano-Jewish, (4) ?, (5) Grammarian, lexicography, medicine, theology, (6) Kitab al-Tanqih—Book of minute research.

13. al-Jawaliqi, (1) Abu Mansur Mauhub ibn Abi Tahir Ahmad ibn Muhammad ibn al-Khidhr, (2) Born 1073 or 1074, died between 1114 and 1145, (3) Baghdad, (4) Arabic, (5) Philology, (6) Kitab al-Mu'arrab min al-Kalam al-'Ajami—"Dealing with foreign words introduced into Arabic, a commentary"; Kitab al-Takmila fi ma Yalhanu Fihi al-'Amma—"Completion, dealing with the incorrect expressions of the vulgar, a supplement"; Kitab Asma' Khail al-'Arab wa Fursaniha—On names of horses; Kitab al-Mukhtasar fi'l-Nahw—Treatise on syntax.

14. al-Khwarizmi, (1) Abu Bakr Yusuf ibn abi Bakr ibn Muhammad Siraj al-Din, (2) 1160, (3) Khwarizm, (4) Arabic, Turkish ?, (5) Philology, (6) Kitab Miftah al-Ulum—On morphology, grammar, rhetoric.

15. al-Maidani, (1) Abu al-Fadhl Ahmad ibn Muhammad ibn Ahmad, (2) Died 1124, (3) Nishapur, (4) Arabic, (5) Philology, (6) Kitab al-Sami fi'l-Asami—The great book on words, a dictionary; Kitab al Hadi li'l-Shadi—"Guide for him who knows already a little, a treatise on Arabic syntax with Persian explanations."

16. al-Malati, (1) Abu al-Faraj Yuhanna ibn al-'Ibri, (2) ?, (3) Melitene, (4) Syriac, (5) Philology, (6) Kethabha Dhe-Semhe—Book of rays, grammar; Kethabha Dhe-Ghrammatiki—Grammar in verse; Kethabha Dha-Bhelesusitha—Book of the spark, grammar (incomplete).

17. al-Mausili, (1) Abu al-Fat'h 'Uthman ibn Jimmi, (2) 941 or 942-1002, (3) Muslim, (4) Arabic, (5) Philology, (6) Many writings of philosophical treatment of philology.

18. ibn Qanbar, (1) Abu Bishr 'Amr ibn 'Uthman, (2) Died 795, (3) Persian, (4) ?, (5) Philology, (6) Al-Kitab—"The book, earliest systematic presentation of philology."

19. al-Qazwini, (1) Jalal al-Din Abu al-Ma'ali Muhammad ibn 'Abd al-Rahman (called Khatib Dimashq al-Qazwini), (2) 1267-1338, (3) Turkish or Persian, (4) Arabic, (5) Philology, (6) Talkhis al-Miftah —"Summary of a book dealing with rhetoric"; Al-Idah (?) fi'l-Ma'ani wa'l-Bayan—On rhetoric.

20. al-Sanhaji, (1) Abu 'Abd Allah Muhammad ibn Muhammad ibn Da'ud, (2) 1273-1323, (3) Moroccan, (4) ?, (5) Grammarian, philology, (6) Al-Ajurrumiya—On grammar.

21. al-Shafi'i, (1) Ahmad ibn al-Hasan al-Jarabardi, (2) Died 1345 or 1346, (3) Persian ?, (4) Arabic, (5) Theologian, philology, grammarian, (6) Works on Arabic grammar; Commentaries on other works of grammar.

22. ibn Sida, (1) Abu al-Hasan 'Ali ibn Isma'il al-Mursi, (2) 1007 or 1008 to 1065 or 1066, (3) Spanish, (4) Arabic, (5) Philology, (6) Al-Kitab al-Mulakhkhas fi'l-Luqa—Great Arab dictionary; Kitab al-Muhkam wa'l-Muhit al-A'zam.

23. Tus, (1) Abu Mansur (or Nasr) Ali ibn Ahmad Asadi, (2) Died 1072, (3) Persian, (4) Persian, (5) Poetry and philology, (6) Loqati Fors—Persian words.

24. al-Zamakhshari, (1) Abu al-Qasim Mahmud ibn 'Umar, (2) 1075-1144, (3) Khwarizm, (4) Arabic, Persian, (5) Philology, (6) Kitab al-Kushshaf 'an Haqa'iq al-Tanzil—"The revealer of the truths of revelation, a commentary on the Qur'an"; Kitab al-Mufassal—Arabic grammar; "Compiled a number of lexicographical works"; Kitab Muqaddimat al-Adab—Introduction to literature; Kitab al-Amkina wa'l-Jibal wa'l-Miya—The book of places, mountains and waters, a geographical lexicon; Kitab al-Fa'iq—"A lexicon relative to the Hadith"; Kitab Asas al-Balaqa—Foundations of eloquence.

Philosophy

1. ibn 'Abbad, (1) ?, (2) 1332-1390, (3) Hispano-Muslim, (4) Arabic, probably, (5) Mysticism (philosophy), (6) Commentary on Kitab al-Hikam al-'Ata'iya by al-Shadhili; Al-Rasa'il al-Kubra (and others)—A collection of spiritual letters.

2. al-Abjari, (1) ?, (2) Died 1263, (3) Persian, (4) Arabic, (5) Philosophy, logic, mathematics, astronomy, (6) Hidayat al-Hikma—Logic, physics, theology; Kitab al-Isaquji—Summary of Porphyry's Isagoge; Al-Zij al-Shamil—Astronomical tables; Mukhtasar fi 'Ilm al-Hai'a—Astronomical summary; Risala fi'l-Asturlab—On the astrolabe; Kashf al-Haqa'iq fi Tahrir al-Daqa'iq; Zubdat al-Asrar—Philosophy; "There may be other astronomical treatises."

3. al-Amili, (1) Muhammad ibn Mahmud, (2) Died 1352, (3) Persian, (4) Persian, (5) Philosophy, an encyclopaedist, (6) Nafa'is al-Funun—Encyclopaedia of all sciences; Commentary of Kulliyyat of the Qanan of ibn Sina; Commentary on Kulliyyat of the Qanan of Sharaf al-Din al-Ilaqi; Commentary on Mukhtasar fi'l-Usul of ibn al-Hajib.

4. al-Amidi, (1) ?, (2) Died 1218, (3) Samarqand, (4) Arabic, probably, (5) Philosophy, (6) Kitab Mir'at (Hayat) al-Ma'ani fi Idrak al-'Alam al-Insani—"Comparison between microcosmos and macrocosmos"; Kitab al-Irshad—Dialectics; Kitab Haud al-Hayat—On talismans.

5. ibn Arabi, (1) ?, (2) 1165-1240, (3) Hispano-Muslim, (4) Arabic, probably, (5) Philosophy, theology, poetry, (6) Kitab al-Futuhat al-Makkiya (?); Kitab al-Isra Ila Maqam al-Asra—Treatise on mysticism; Kitab Tarjuman al-Ashwaq—Love poem; Kitab Dhaha'ir wa'l-Aqlaq—Love poem; Al-Durrat al-Fakhira—"Biography on Western scholars and saints."

6. ibn al-'Arabi, (1) ?, (2) 1076-1148, (3) Hispano-Muslim, (4) Arabic, (5) Law, theology, philosophy, education, (6) Commentary on Kitab al-Muwatta of ibn Anas.

7. ibn 'Asim, (1) ?, (2) 1359-1427, (3) Spanish-Muslim, (4) Arabic, probably, (5) Theology, (6) Tuhfat al-Hukkam fi Nakth al-'Uqud wa'l-Ahkam—Poem on principles of jurisprudence; Hada'iq al-Azahir—Collection of anecdotes.

8. 'Attar, (1) Farid al-Din 'Attar, (2) Died probably 1229 or 1230, (3) Persian, (4) Persian, (5) Poetry, (6) Tadhkirat al-Alwiyya (?)—

Memoirs of Sufi saints; Pand Nama—Book of counsel, poems; Mantiq al-Tayr—Logic of the bird, a mystical search for truth.

9. Averroes, (1) ibn Rushd, (2), (3), (4), (5), (6) See Mathematics and Astronomy Section.

10. al-'Awfi, (1) Muhammad al-'Awfi, (2) After 1206, (3) Persian, (4) Persian, (5) Letters, history, general scholarship, (6) Lubab al-Albab—History of 300 Persian poets; Jawami' al-Hikayat wa Lawami' al-Niwayat—Collection of stories, etc.

11. al-Baidawi, (1) ?, (2) Died 1286, (3) Persian, (4) Arabic, Persian, (5) Theology, history, (6) Anwar al-Tanzil wa Asrar al-Ta'wil—Commentary on the Qur'an; Minhaj al-Wusul Ila 'Ilm al-Usual—Metaphysics; Kitab Tawali'al-Anwar wa Matali'al-Anzar—Metaphysics; Nizam al-Tawarikh—History of the world.

12. Banu Musa, (1) ?, (2) Died in reign of al-Ma'mun, (3) Jewish, (4) ?, (5) Philosophy, (6) Fastun or Qarastun—Book on the balance; Book on measurement of the sphere, etc.

13. al-Batalyusi, (1) ?, (2) Born between 1049 and 1053 to 1127, (3) Hispano-Muslim, (4) Arabic, (5) Philosophy, theology, (6) Kitab al-Hada'iq (lost)—Theology and philosophy.

14. ibn Batriq, (1) Zakariyya Yahya, (2) Beginning 9th, (3) ?, (4) Arabic, (5) Philosophy, (6) None.

15. al-Biruni, (1) Abu Raihan Muhammad ibn Ahmad (or Bairuni), (2) 973-1048, (3) Persian, (4) Arabic, (5) Traveler, philosophy, mathematics, astronomy, geography, encyclopaedia, (6) Kitab al-Athar al-Baqiyya 'Ani al-Qurun al-Khaliyya—"Chronology of ancient nations, written in 1000"; Tarikh al-Hind—Account of India; Al-Qanun al-Mas'udi fi'l-Hai'a wa'l-Nujum—Astronomical encyclopaedia; Al-Tafhim Li-Awa'il Sina'at al-Tanjim—Summary of mathematics, astronomy, and astrology; Translated several works from Sanskrit into Arabic.

16. ibn Daniyal, (1) Muhammad ibn Daniyal, (2) 1265-1310 or 1311, (3) Christian or Jewish, (4) Arabic, probably, (5) Philosophy, dramatic poetry, (6) Taif al-Khayal fi Ma'rifat Khayal al-Zill—Ghosts of the imagination.

17. Emre, (1) Yunus Emre, (2) 1307, (3) Turkish, (4) West Turkish, (5) Poetry, (6) Diwan of Yunus Emre.

18. al-Farabi, (1) Abu Nasr Muhammad ibn Muhammad ibn Tarkhan ibn Uzlaq, (2) 950 or 951, (3) Turkish, (4) ?, (5) Philosophy, (6) Number of commentaries on Aristotle—Physics, meteorology, logical treatises, etc.; Commentary on Porphyry's Isagoge; Commentary on Ptolemy's Almagest; Risala Fusus al-Hikam—The bezels of philosophy; Risala fi Mabadi Ahl al-Madina al-Fadhila—The model city; Kitab Ihsa al-Ulum—"Treatises on classification and fundamental principles of science."

19. al-Ghazzali, (1) Hujjat-ul-Islam Abu Hamed Muhammed ibn Muhammad Ghazzali Tusi, (2) 1058-1111, (3) Persian, (4) Persian, (5) Philosophy and theology, (6) Kimyaya Sa'adat—The alchemy of

happiness; Nasihat ul Moluk—Advice to kings; Faza'el ul Anam, etc.—Collection of his Persian works.

20. al-Ghazzali, (1) Shaikh ul-Mashayekh Majd-ud-Din Abul Fat'h Ahmad ibn Muhammad Ghazzali—The youngest brother of the more famous al-Ghazzali, (2) Died 1126, (3) Persian, (4) Persian, (5) Philosophy, (6) Lobab-ul-Ahya'; Al-Thakhirah fi (ibn?) al-Basira—On the science of insight; Bahr-ul-Haqiqat—Ocean of reality; Restalat-ul-Ishqiyyah—Essay on love; Sawamah-ul-Ushshaq—The hazards or accidents of love; Makatib—Collection of Persian works.

21. Gulshahri, (1) ?, (2) 1317, (3) Turkish, (4) Persian, Turkish, (5) Poetry, (6) Mantiq al-Tayr by Farid al-Din 'Attar—Reasoning of the birds, translated from Persian to Turkish; Gulshan-Nama—Poems and treatise on theological terms; Falaknama—On firmament.

22. Hafiz, (1) Khauja Shirazi, (2) 1320-1389, (3) Persian, (4) Persian, (5) Poetry, (6) Diwan—Poems. (Lyric philosophical poems.)

23. ibn Hamid, (1) Abu Zakariyya Yahya ibn 'Adi, (2) 893-974, (3) ?, (4) Arabic, (5) Philosophy, (6) "Revised Matta's translation of Themistios's commentary on Aristotle's De Coelo"; "Translated commentary of Alexander of Aphrodisias of Aristotle's Meteorology."

24. ibn al-Hasan, (1) Abu al-Hasan Sa'id ibn Hibat Allah, (2) Died 1101 or 1102, (3) ?, (4) ?, (5) Philosophy, medicine, (6) Al-Muqni fi Tadbir al-Amradh wa Ma'rifat al-'Ilal wa'l A'radh—Symposium of medicine; Maqala fi Khalq al-Insan—Essay on human character (or on man's creation).

25. al-Hilli, (1) ibn al-Mutahhar al-Hilli, (2) 1250-1325, (3) Iraqian, (4) Arabic, probably, (5) Theology, (6) Nahj al-Haqq wa-Kashf al-Eidq—"Treatise against the Sunni school and al-Ash'ari"; Tahrir al-Ahkam al-Shar'iyya 'Ala Madhhab al-Imamiyya—Compendium of Imamiya law; Ida al-Ishtibah fi Asma' al-Ruwah—Biographies of doctors; "Apparently compiled a bibliography of his own and other writings."

26. al-Hindi, (1) 'Umar ibn Is'haq, (2) 1314-1372, (3) Hindu, probably, (4) Arabic, probably, (5) Theology, (6) Zubdat al-Ahkam fi Ikhtilaf al-A'im-ma al-A'lam—"Points of disagreement of the four schools of religious law"; Commentary on the Ziyadat of al-Shaibani; Aqidat Ahl al-Sunna wa'l-Jama'a of al-Tahawi; Hidaya of al-Marqinani—Two commentaries; Nazm al-Suluk of ibn l-Farid—Mysticism; Badi'al-Nizam fi Usul al-Fiq'h of ibn 'Ali ibn al-Sa'ati; Al-Muqni fi Usul al-Fiq'h of al-Khabbazi; Manar al-Anwar fi Usul al-Fiq'h of al-Nasafi; Al-Mukhtar li'l-Fatawa of al-Buldaji; Mystic verses of al-Yafi'i, called Tawa'ih al-Anwar fi'l-Radh'ala Man Ankara 'Ala 'Arifin Lata'if al-Asrar; Jam' al-Jawami' fi'l-Usul of 'Abd al-Wahhab al-Subki.

27. al-Hurufi, (1) Fadl Allah al-Hurifi, (2) 1339-1393 or 1394 or 1401 or 1402, (3) Persian, (4) Persian dialect and Arabic, (5) Theology, philosophy, (6) Jawidan-i Kabir—"The strange mixture of Arabic and Persian which influenced Baktashi mysticism in Turkey."

28. al-Iji, (1) ?, (2) Died 1355, (3) Persian, (4) Arabic, (5) Theology, (6) Kitab al-Mawaqif fi 'Ilm al-Kalam—"Summary of scientific knowledge and systematic philosophy"; Adab al-Bahth—On dialectics; Al-Risalat al-Wad'iyya al-'Adudiyya—On concepts; Al-Shahiyya fi 'Ilm al-Akhlaq—Compendium on practical philosophy; Al-'Aqa'id al-'Adhudiyya—On articles of faith; Al-Fawa'id al-Ghiyathiyya—Commentary dealing with rhetoric of al-Khwarizmi; Sharh Mukhtasar al-Usul—Commentary on Maliki law of ibn al-Hajib; Ishraq al-Tawarikh—"History of the patriarchs, the Prophet and his companions."

29. al-Isnawi, (1) Abd al-Rahim ibn al-Hasan, (2) 1305-1370, (3) Egyptian, (4) Arabic, probably, (5) Theology, (6) Various books on Shafi'i law; Tabaqat al-Shafi'iyya—Biography on Shafi'i doctors; Ankam al-Khuntha—On hermaphrodites; Tiraz al-Mahafil fi Alqaz al-Masa'il—Legal difficulties; Al-Kalimat al-Muhimma fi Mubasharat Ahl al-Dhimm—Against Christians.

30. al-Jahiz, (1) Abu 'Uthman 'Amr ibn Bahr, (2) Died 868 or 869, (3) Iraqi ?, (4) ?, (5) Philosophy, (6) Kitab al-Hayawan—Book of animals.

31. al-Jazari, (1) Muhammad ibn Muhammad, (2) 1350-1429, (3) Syrian, (4) Arabic, probably, (5) Theology, (6) Dhat al-Shifa' fi Sirat al-Rabi wa'l-Khulafa—Lives of the Prophet and four orthodox caliphs.

32. al-Jili, (1) Abd al-Karim al-Jili, (2) 1365-1428, (3) Persian, (4) Arabic, (5) Theology, (Commentary on Kitab al-Asfar by ibn 'Arabi); Commentary on al-Futuhat al-Makkiyya by ibn 'Arabi.

33. al-Jurjani, (1) ?, (2) 1340-1413, (3) Persian, (4) Arabic, Persian, (5) Philosophy, astronomy, theology, grammar, (6) Commentary on the Tadhkira fi 'Ilm al-Hai'a of al-Tusi—Astronomy; Commentary on al-Mulakhkhas fi'l-Hai'a of al-Jaqmini—Astronomy; Risala fi Taqsim al-'Ulum—Classification of science; Ta'rifat—"Definition of technical terms, especially Sufi terms"; Maqalid al-'Ulum fi'l-Hudud wa'l-Rusum—"Definitions, 21 branches of science."

34. al-Katibi, (1) 'Ali ibn 'Umar, (2) Died 1277, (3) Persian, (4) Arabic, (5) Philosophy, astronomy, (6) Kitab 'Ain al-Qawa'id fi'l-Mantiq wa'l Hakma—Logic, philosophy; Kitab Hikmat al-Ain—"Partial edition of above"; al-Risalat al-Shamsiyya fi'l-Qawa'id al-Mantiqiyya—Logic; Jami al-Daqa'iq fi Kashf al-Haqa'iq—Logic, physics and metaphysics.

35. Khalil, (1) Sidi Khalil, (2) Died 1365 or later, (3) Egyptian, (4) Arabic, probably, (5) Theology, law, (6) Mukhtasar—Maliki law textbook.

36. al-Khallal, (1) ?, (2) 1335, (3) Egyptian ?, Syrian ?, (4) Arabic, probably, (5) Divination, (6) Kitab al-Jafr al-Kabir—On Jafr.

37. al-Kindi, (1) Abu Yusuf Ya'qub ibn Is'haq ibn al-Sabbah (Latin name, Alkindus), (2) Beginning 9th, (3) ?, (4) Arabic, (5) Philosophy, (6) De Aspectibus—Treatise on geometrical and physiological optics; De Medicinarum Compositarum Gradibus.

38. al-Kindi, (1) Abu al-'Abbas Ahmad ibn Muhammad ibn al-Taiyib al-Sarahhsi Tilmidh, (2) Died 899 or 900, (3) Arabic, (4) ?, (5) Philosophy, (6) "Wrote large number of works on many subjects, but apparently none is extant."

39. al-Marghinani (Marqinani), (1) ?, (2) Died 1197, (3) Jaxartes, (4) Arabic, probably, (5) Law, (6) Kitab Bidayat al-Mubtadi—Treatise on law; Hidayat—Commentary on above.

40. al-Mu'aiyad Billah, (1) ?, (2) 1270-1348, (3) Yaman, (4) Arabic ?, (5) Theology, (6) Kitab al-Intisar—On Zaidi law.

41. al-Multani, (1) ibn al-Taj, (2) Flourished 1317-1333, (3) Hindu, (4) Arabic, Persian, (5) Theology, (6) Manasik al-Hajj—Arabic book on pilgrimage ceremonies; Khulasat al-Ahkam bi-Shara'it al-Imam wa'l-Islam—Arabic treatise on theology and jurisprudence; "Arabic and Persian abridgment of above treatise"; Khulasat Jawahir al-Qur'an fi Bayan Ma'ani Luqat al-Furqan—Persian explanation of terms in the Qur'an.

42. Mustawfi, (1) Hamdallah Mustawfi (often called al-Qazwini), (2) Born 1281, (3) Persian, (4) Persian, Turkish and Mongolian, (5) History, and encyclopaedist, (6) Tarikh-i-Guzida—History; Zafar Nama —Historical poem from days of the Prophet; Nuzhat al-Qulub—Cosmography and scientific encyclopaedia in Persian.

43. ibn al-Muzhir, (1) Abu Bakr ibn al-Muzhir, (2) Writing end of 12th, (3) Persian, (4) Persian, (5) Form of organic and inorganic world, (6) Farah-Nama-i-Jamali—"Organic and inorganic matter" (superstition).

44. al-Nawawi, (1) ?, (2) 1233-1277, (3) Damascus, (4) Arabic, probably, (5) Theology, law, general scholarship, (6) Minhaj'al-Talibin —Manual of Shafi'i law; Kitab al-Arba'in Hadith—The forty traditions; Tahdhib al-Asma' wa'l-Luqat—Biography of illustrious Muslims; Kitab al-Monthurat wa'Uyun al-Masa'il al-Muhimmat—Collection of his responsa.

45. al-Nazzam, (1) ?, (2) Died 845, (3) ?, (4) ?, (5) Mu'tazilite philosophy, (6) None.

46. al-Nizami, (1) Nizami Arudhi, (2) Living 1152, (3) Persian, (4) Persian, (5) Philosophy, (6) Chahar Maqala—Includes medical anecdotes, and many other subjects.

47. al-Nuwairi, (1) ?, (2) 1279-1332, (3) Egyptian, (4) Arabic, probably, (5) Historiography and encyclopaedist, (6) Nihayat al-Arab fi Funun al-Adab—An encyclopaedia.

48. al-Qaisari, (1) ?, (2) Died 1350, (3) Turkish, (4) Arabic, (5) Philosophy or theology, (6) Risala fi'l-Tasawwuf—Mystical treatise; Commentary on Manazil al-Sa'irin of al-Harawi; Commentary on Fusul al-Hikam of ibn 'Arabi; Commentary on Al-Ta'iyyat al-Kubra of ibn al-Farid; Commentary on Ta'wilat al-Qur'an of al-Kashani.

49. al-Qazwini, (1) ?, (2) 1203 or 1204-1283, (3) Persian, (4) Arabic, (5) Encyclopaedist, cosmology, geography, (6) 'Aja'ib al-

Makhluqat wa-Qara'ib al-Mawjudat—Cosmology; 'Aja'ib al-Buldan—Geography; Athar al-Bilad wa-Akhbar al-'Ibad—Enlarged geography listed above.

50. al-Qazwini, (1) Muhammad ibn Ahmad, (2) Lived 1132, (3) Persian, (4) Arabic, (5) Encyclopaedist, religion, ethics, politics, natural history, geography, history, (6) Mufid al-'Ulum wa Mubid al-Humum—An encyclopaedia.

51. al-Razi, (1) Imam Fakhr-ul-Din Abu Abd-Allah Muhammad ibn Omar ibn al-Hussain Tabari (better known as Tabari), (2) born 1209, (3) Persian, (4) Persian and Arabic, (5) Philosophy and mysticism, (6) Hada'iq-al-Anwar fi Haqa'iq-al-Asrar—Encyclopaedia of science; Usuli-Aqa'id—Principles of ideas; Resala'i Ruhyyah—A spiritual essay; Al-Ikhtyarat-al-Ala'iyyah—On astronomy. See also section on Mathematics.

52. al-Razi, see section on Mathematics and Astronomy.

53. ibn Rajah, (1) ?, (2) 1309-1393, (3) Syrian, (4) Arabic, probably, (5) Philosophy, theology, (6) Risala fi Ma'n al-'Ilm—On meaning of science; Kitab al-Tawhid—On unity of God; Ahwal al-Qubur—On the soul between life and death; Tabaqat As'hab al-Imam Ahmad ibn Hanbal—Biographies of Hanbali doctors.

54. al-Razzaq, (1) 'Abd al-Razzaq (many other names given him), (2) Died 1329 or 1330, (3) Iraqian, (4) Arabic, probably, (5) Philosophy, (6) Kitab Istilahat al-Sufiyya—Dictionary of technical terms used by mystical philosophers; Risala fi'l-Qada' wa'l-Qadar—Predestination and free will; Commentary on Manzil al-Sa'irin by al-Harawi; Commentaries on Mawaqi' al-Numum and Fusus al-Hikam by ibn 'Arabi; Commentary on the Qur'an.

55. Rumi, (1) Jalal al-Din Rumi, (2) 1207 or 1208-1273, (3) Persian, (4) Persian, (5) Philosophy, theology, poetry, (6) Mathnawi—Philosophical poem; Diwan—Collection of lyrical poems; Fihi Ma Fihi—What is written is within, treatise in prose.

56. Sa'di, (1) Muslihiddin Sa'di, (2) 1184-1284, (3) Persian, (4) Persian, Arabic, others ?, (5) Didactic and lyrical poetry, (6) Sa'di Nama—The Bustan, philosophic and didactic poem; The Gulistan—Collection of moral stories; Diwan—Collection of short odes; Pand-Nama—Collection of counsels; Many other poems, most in Persian but a few in Arabic; Kulliyyat—Complete works.

57. al-Sahrawardi, (1) Shahab-ud-Din Abul Fotuh Yahya ibn Habash ibn Amirak, (2) 1154-1191, (3) Persian, (4) Persian and Arabic, (5) Philosophy and mysticism, (6) Mantiq-ut-Talwihat; Kitab-al-Talwihat; Kitab-al-Mashari' wal Mutarihat; Kitab Hikmat-ul-Ashraq; Resalah fi I'tiqad-ul-Hokama—Doctrines of philosophers; Qissat-ul-Qurbtt-ul-Qarbbyah—Story of Western journey (?); Awazi Pari Jibrail—The song of Gabriel's wings; Resalat-ul-Ishq—Essay on love; Loqati Muran; Safari Simurq—Hooplo's journey; Translation of Resalat ul Tayr

of ibn Sina (?); Al-Lamahat; Al-Hayakil-al-Nuriyyah—Illuminated figures; Al-Alwah-al-Imadiyyah—Imadiyyah tablets (?); Al-Mabda' Wal Ma'ad—On beginning and end (?); Tawariq-ul-Anwar; Al-Bariqat-al-Ilahiyyah—God's blessing; Lawami-ul-Anwar; Aqli Surkh—Burning intelligence; Partoe Namah; Roozi ba Jama'ati Suffian—On Sufi ways; Yazdan Shenakht—On knowledge of God; Fi Halat-ut-Tofuliyyah—On childhood; Al-Tanqibat fi'l Hikma—On wisdom.

58. Shihab al-Din, (1) 'Ali ibn Shihab al-Din, (2) 1314-1383, (3) Persian, (4) Arabic and Persian, (5) Theology, (6) Commentary on the Fusus (?) al-Hikam of ibn 'Arabi.

59. al-Sibti, (1) Abu al-Abbas al-Sibti, (2) Flourished 2nd half 12th, (3) Ceuta (Moroccan ?), (4) Arabic, probably, (5) Astrology, magic, theology, (6) Za'irja al-'Alam—A magical table of the universe.

60. ibn Sirin (Shirin), (1) Ahmad ibn Sirin, (2) ?, (3) Persian ?, (4) Arabic, (5) Philosophy, (6) Treatise on oneirology.

61. al-Subki, (1) 'Ali al-Subki, (2) 1284-1355, (3) Egyptian, (4) Arabic, probably, (5) Theology, (6) Al-Saif al-Maslul 'Ala Man Sabba al-Rasul—The drawn sword against him who spurns the Prophet; Bai'al-Marhun fi Qaibat al-Madyun—Sale of mortgage in absence of debtor (may deal with veterinary art).

62. al-Suhrawardi, (1) Yahya al-Suhrawardi, (2) 1154-1191, (3) Persian ?, (4) Arabic, probably, (5) Philosophy, theology, (6) Kitab al-Alwah al-'Imadiyya—Infinity, the absolute, etc.; Kitab Hikmat al-Ishraq—Attack on peripatetic philosophy; Kitab al-Talwihat—"Elucidations"; Kitab al-Mashari' wa'l-Mutarrahat—Cross words and conversations; Kitab al-Lumahat fi'l-Haqai'q—Glimpses of truth; Kitab Hayakil al-Nur—Temples of light.

63. al-Suhrwardi, (1) 'Umar al-Suhrwardi, (2) 1144 or 1145 to 1234 or 1235, (3) Persian, (4) Arabic, probably, (5) Philosophy, mysticism, medicine ?, (6) Kitab 'Awarif al-Ma'arif—Benefits of knowledge; Kashf al-Fadha'ih al-Yunaniyya—Exposition of Greek shame.

64. al-Tabrizi, (1) Muhammad al-Tabrizi, (2) 2nd part of 13th, (3) Persian, (4) Arabic, (5) Philosophy, (6) Commentary on Maimonides' introduction to the second part of the Dalalat al-Ha'irin.

65. al-Taftazani, (1) ?, (2) 1322-1390, (3) Persian or Turkish, (4) Arabic, Turkish, (5) General scholarship, (6) Sharh Isaquji—Logic and theology, commentary on the Isagoge of Porphyry; Sharh al-Risala al-Shamsiyya—Commentary on the logic of 'Ali ibn 'Umar al-Katibi; Kitab al-Maqasid al-Talibin fi Usul al-Din (fi'l-Kalam), or Maqasid al-Kalam fi 'Aqa'id al-In'am; Tahdhib al-Mantiq wa'l-Kalam (Qayat Tahdhib al-Kalam fi Tahrir al-Mntiq); Summaries, translations, editions; Fadihat al-Mulhidin—Confusion of the heretics, mystic philosophy; Sharh al-Kashshaf—Explanation of the Qur'an; Al-Talwih Ila' Kashf Haqa'iq al-Tanqih—Law and theology; Sharh al-'Aqa'id al-Nasafiyya—Commentary on the Hanafi catechism of 'Umar ibn Muham-

mad al-Nasafi; Sharh al-Muqkhtasar fi'l-Usul—Commentary on the Muntaha, "the treatise on Maliki law of 'Uthman ibn 'Umar ibn al-Hajib"; Sharh al-Miftah—Compendium of Shafi'i law; Sharh Talkhis al-Jami' al-Kabir—Commentary on Hanafi law; Sharh Tasrif al-Zanjani—Grammar; Irshad al-Hadi—Grammatical guide; Al-Tarkib al-Jalil—On syntax; Sharh Talkhis al-Miftah—Rhetoric; Sharh Nawabiq al-Kalam—Commentary on proverbs; Tarkib Qarib Wa Tartib al-Ajib—On syntax.

66. al-Tahtani, (1) ?, (2) Died 1365, (3) Persian, (4) Arabic, (5) Philosophy, theology, (6) Muhakamat—Discussion of differences between Fakhr al-Din al-Razi and Nasir al-Din Tusi regarding the Kitab al-Isharat wa'l-Tanbihat of ibn Sina; Commentary on Kitab al-Kashshaf 'an Haqa'iq al-Tanzil, Qur'anic work of 'Umar al-Zamakhshari; Commentary on Risala al-Shamsiyya fi'l-Qawa'id al-Mantiqiyya of 'Ali ibn 'Umar al-Katibi al-Qazwini on logic; Commentary on Matali' al-Anwar fi'l Mantiq by Mahmud ibn abi Bakr al-Urmawion (?)—Logic.

67. al-Thani, (1) Sadr al-Shari's al-Thani, (2) Died 1346, (3) Persian, (4) Arabic, (5) Theology, encyclopaedist, (6) Ta'dil al-'Ulum—Encyclopaedia of philosophy and natural science; Tanqih al-Usul—Principles of jurisprudence.

68. ibn Tumlus, (1) ?, (2) Died 1223 or 1224, (3) Hispano-Muslim, (4) Arabic, probably, (5) Medicine, logic, (6) Kitab al-Madkhal Li Sina' fi'l-Mantiq—Introduction to the art of logic.

69. al-Turtushi, (1) Abu Bakr al-Turtushi, (2) 1059 or 1060 to 1126 or 1129, (3) Hispano-Muslim, (4) Arabic, probably, (5) Theology, (6) Siraj al-Muluk—Treatise on practical politics.

70. al-Wali, (1) Ni'mat Allah Wali, (2) 1330-1431, (3) Persian, (4) Persian, (5) Theology, (6) Diwan of mystic verse; Some 100 Sufi treatises.

71. al-Watwat, (1) ?, (2) 1235-1318, (3) Persian, (4) Arabic, probably, (5) Philosophy, religion, (6) Qurur al-Khasa'is al-Wadhi Wa'urur al-Naqa'is al-Fadhiha—An ethical anthology.

72. al-Yafi'i, (1) ?, (2) Died 1367, (3) Arabian, (4) Arabic, probably, (5) Philosophy, religion, (6) None.

73. ibn Yunus, (1) Abu Bishr Matta ibn Yunus, (2) Died 940, (3) ?, (4) Syriac, Arabic, (5) Philosophy, (6) Translated Themistios's commentary on Aristotle's De Coelo.

74. al-Zamakhshari, (1) ?, (2) 1075-1144, (3) Persian, (4) Arabic, Persian, (5) Grammar, lexicography, theology, (6) Kitab al-Kashshaf 'an Haqi'iq al-Tanzil—Commentary on Qur'an; Kitab al-Mufassal—Arabic grammar; Kitab Muqaddimat al-Adab—Lexicography; Kitab al-Amkina wa'l-Jibal wa'l-Miya—The book of places, mountains and waters; Kitab al-Fa'iq—Geographical lexicon; Kitab Asas al-Balaqh—Lexicon relative to the Hadith.

75. al-Zarnuji, (1) ?, (2) Flourished 1203, (3) ?, (4) Persian, probably, (5) Philosophy, education, (6) Ta'lim al-Muta'allim—On teaching the pupil, a philosophical primer.

Physics and Technology

1. al-Farisi, (1) Kamal al-Din al-Farisi, (2) Died 1320, (3) Persian, (4) Arabic, (5) Mathematics, physics, (6) Tadhkira al-Ahbab —On amicable numbers; Asas al-Qawa'id fi Usul al-Fawa'id—Commentary on arithmetic, geometry, etc. by ibn al-Khaddam; Tanqin al-Manazir—Correction of the optics; "6 smaller treatises on the work of ibn al-Haitham."

2. al-Jazari, (1) ?, (2) Flourished 1181-1206, (3) ?, (4) Arabic, probably, (5) Mechanician (physics), (6) Kitab fi ma 'Rifat al-Hiyal al-Handasiyya—Hydraulic apparatus and time.

3. al-Khazini, (1) ?, (2) Flourished 1115-1121, Greek Muslim (was a slave), (4) Arabic, probably, (5) Physics, astronomy, (6) Al-Zij al-Mu'tabar al-Sinjani—Astronomical tables; Kitab Mizan al-Hikma—On physics.

4. 'Abd al-Latif, (1) ?, (2) 1162-1231, (3) Baghdad, (4) Arabic, probably, (5) Science, philosophy, music, medicine, (6) Kitab al-Sama—On music; Treatise on ibn al-Haitham's views on space; Treatise on Hindu arithmetic; Treatise on medicine; Al-Ifadat wa'l-I'tibar fi'l Umar al-Mushahadat wa'l-Hawadith al-Mu'ayanet bi Ard Misr—On Egypt.

5. ibn al-Sa'ati, (1) ?, (2) Died 1223 or 1233, (3) Damascus, (4) Arabic, probably, (5) Mechanician, physician, (6) Commentary on ibn Sina's Qanun; Supplement on ibn Sina's treatise on grippe.

6. al-Sa'ati, (1) Muhammad al-Sa'ati, (2) 1146 or 1169 to 1184 or 1185, (3) Damascus, (4) Arabic, probably, (5) Clock making, (6) None.

Sociology and Law

1. al-'Abdwadi, (1) Abu Hammu Musa ibn Yusuf ibn Ziyan, (2) Ruled 1352-1386, (3) Algerian, (4) Arabic, (5) Law, sociology, (6) Wasitat al-Suluk fi Siyasat al-Muluk—"Treatise on the education of his son to make him a 'just and powerful ruler'."

2. al-Arabi, (1) Abu Bakr Muhammad ibn 'Abd Allah (called ibn al-'Arabi), (2) 1076-1148, (3) Hispano-Muslim, (4) Arabic, (5) Law, sociology, philology, (6) Commentary on Kitab al-Muwatta' of Malik ibn Anas, a fundamental treatise on Malikite law.

3. al-Baghdadi, (1) Abu Shuja' Muhammad ibn 'Ali ibn Shu'aib ibn al-Dahhan Fakhr al-Din, (2) Died 1194, (3) Baghdad, (4) ?, (5) Law, sociology, philology, (6) Taqwin al-Nazar—Legal tables.

4. al-Dimishqi, (1) Abu-al-Fadhl Ja'far ibn 'Ali, (2) ?, (3) Syria, (4) ?, (5) Law, sociology, economist, (6) Kitab al-Ishara Ila Mahasin al-Tijara wa Ma'rifa al-Jayyid al-A'rad wa Radiha wa Qushush al-Mudallisin Fiha—On commerce.

5. al-Haufi, (1) Abu-al-Qasim Ahmad ibn Muhammad ibn Khalaf, (2) Died 1192 or 1193, (3) Spanish, (4) ?, (5) Law, sociology, theology, (6) Kitab al-Fara'id—Treatise on division of inheritances.

6. ibn Hazm, (1) Abu Muhammad 'Ali ibn Ahmad, (2) 994-1064, (3) Hispano-Muslim, (4) Arabic, (5) Statesman, theologian, historian, (6) Kitab al-Milal wal-Nihal—Book of religions and sects.

7. al-Isfahani, (1) Abu Sulaiman Da'ud ibn 'Ali ibn Khalaf, (2) 814-883 or 884, (3) Persian, (4) ?, (5) Jurist, (6) None listed.

8. ibn Is'haq, (1) Abu 'Ali al-Hasan ibn 'Ali, (2) 1018-1092, (3) Persian, (4) Persian, (5) Politics, (6) Siyasat-Nama—Treatise on the art of government.

9. ibn Jama'a, (1) Abu 'Abd Allah Muhammad ibn Ibrahim, (2) 1241-1333, (3) Syrian, (4) ?, (5) Law, sociology, traditionist, government, (6) Tahrir al-Ahkam fi Tadbir Ahl al-Islam.

10. ibn Mammati, (1) Abu-al-Makarim As'ad ibn al-Khatir, (2) Died 1209, (3) Egyptian, (4) ?, (5) Law, sociology, Muslim statesman, (6) Kitab Qawanin al-Dawawin—Statutes of the councils of state; Kitab al-Fashush fi Ahkam Qaraqush—Weakmindedness in the judgments of Qaraqush.

11. al-Nasafi, (1) Hafiz al-Din Abu-al-Barakat 'Abd Allah ibn Ahmad, (2) 1284-1310 or 1311, (3) Samarkand, (4) ?, (5) Law, sociology, jurist, theologian, (6) Manar al-Anwar fi Usul al-Fiq'h—Beacon of light on the principles of law; Al-Wafi fi'l-Furu'—Compendium of Hanafi law; Kanz al-Daqa'iq fi'l-Furu'—Abridgment of above listing.

12. al-Mawardi, (1) Abu al-Hasan Ali ibn Muhammad ibn Habib, (2) Died 1058, (3) ?, (4) ?, (5) Politics, (6) Kitab al-Ahkam al-Sultaniyya—Book on the principles of government; Kitab Adab al-Dunya wa'l-Din—Treatise on ethics.

13. ibn Nasr, (1) Abd al-Rahman ibn Nasr, (2) Flourished 1169-1193, (3) Egyptian, (4) Arabic, probably, (5) Law, (6) Nihayat al-Rutbat al-Zarifat fi Talab al-Hisbat—Handbook for police officers.

14. al-Nawawi, (1) Abu Zakariyya Yahya ibn Sharaf ibn Mira al-Hizami al-Haurani Muhyi al-Din, (2) 1233-1277, (3) Damascus, (4) ?, (5) Law, sociology, (6) Minhaj al-Talibin—Guide of fervent believers, manual of Shafi'i law; Kitab al-Arba'in Hadithan—The forty traditions; Tahdhib al-Asma' wa'l-Luqat—"Correction of proper names and words, a biographical dictionary of illustrious Muslims"; Kitab al-Manthurat wa 'Uyun al-Masa'il al-Muhimmat—Collection of his responsa; Many works on traditions, law, religion, history.

15. al-Nisaburi (al-Nishabari), (1) Abu-al-Husain Muslim ibn al-Hajjaj al-Qushairi, (2) Born 817 to 823, died 875, (3) Persian, (4) ?, (5) Traditionist, (6) Al-Sahih—Collection of traditions.

16. Nizam-ul-Mulk (Nidham), (1) Sayyid-ul-Vozara Qavam ud-Din Abu Ali Hasan ibn Abul Hasan Ali ibn Is'haq ibn al-Abbas al-Tusi, (2) 1019-1092, (3) Persian, (4) Persian, (5) Law and education, (6) Siyasat Nama—Book of statecraft; Wasayaya Nizam-ul-Mulk—Nizam-ul-Mulk's testaments; Qanun ul-Mulk—Rules of government.

17. al-Rishtani, (1) Abu-al-Hasan 'Ali ibn Abi Bakr ibn 'Abd al-Jalil al-Farqani al-Marghinani, (2) Died 1197, (3) ?, (4) ?, (5) Law,

sociology, jurist, (6) Kitab Bidayat al-Mubtadi—Beginning of the beginner, a treatise on law; Hidayat—Guidance, commentary on previous listing.

18. ibn Sa'id, (1) Abu-al-Qasim Ja'far ibn Muhammad ibn Yahya ibn Sa'd (or Ja'far ibn al-Hasan ibn Ya'qub ibn Sa'id), (2) Died 1277, (3) Baghdad, (4) ?, (5) Law, sociology, theology, (6) Kitab Shara'i, al-Islam—The laws of Islam.

19. al-Shafi'i, (1) Abd al-Rahman ibn Nasr ibn 'Abd Allah ibn Muhammad al-Nabarawi, (2) Flourished 1169-1193, (3) Egyptian, (4) ?, (5) Law, sociology, (6) Nihayat al-Rutbat al-Za'ifat fi Talab al-Hisbat—"A handbook for police officers in charge of markets."

20. al-Turtushi, (1) Abu Bakr Muhammad ibn al-Walid ibn Muhammad ibn Khalar (surnamed ibn Abi Randaqa), (2) 1059 or 1060 to 1126 or 1129, (3) Hispano-Muslim, (4) ?, (5) Law, sociology, theology, (6) Siraj al-Muluk—Containing many historical anecdotes.

21. ibn Ziar, (1) Amir Unsur al-Ma'ali Kaikawus ibn Qabus ibn Washmgir, (2) Died 1098 or 1114 ?, (3) Persian, (4) Persian, (5) Law, education, (6) Qabus Namah—Book of Qabus.

Religion and Mysticism (Sufism), Including a Few Miscellaneous Works

1. Abid Allah, (1) Abu'l Ma'ali Muhammad ibn, (2) ?, (3) Persian, (4) Persian, (5) Religion, (6) Bayan-ul-Adyan—An exposition of religion.

2. al-Ansari, (1) Abu Yusuf Ya'qub ibn Ibrahim ibn Habib al-Kufi, (2) 731 or 732 to 798 or 799, (3) Arabic, (4) ?, (5) Theology, (6) Kitab al-Kharaj—Legal treatise on revenue.

3. al-Ansari, (1) Sheikh ul-Islam abu Ismail Abd-Allah ibn Muhammad, (2) 1006-1088, (3) Persian, (4) Persian, (5) Mysticism, (6) Munajat Namah—A litany; Zad'ul-Arefeen; Kanz ul-Salekin; Qalandar Namah—Book of vagabond; Muhabbat Namah—Book of love; Haft Hesar—The seven walls; Resla'i Dil-u-Jan—Essay on heart and soul; Rasalat Waridat; Elahi Namah—Book of the divine.

4. al-Asbani, (1) Abu 'Abd Allah Malik ibn Anas, (2) 715 or 716 to 795 or 796, (3) Medina, (4) ?, (5) Theology, law, (6) Kitab al-Muwatta'—The book of the beaten road, juridical traditions.

5. al-Ash'ari, (1) Abu al-Hasan 'Ali ibn Isma'il, (2) 874 or 875 to 935 or 936, (3) ?, (4) ?, (5) Theology, (6) None.

6. al-Balkhi, (1) Sultan 'ul-Ulama Baha'ul-Din Muhammad ibn Hussain Khatibi—Known also as Baha'd Din Walad, (2) Early 13th, (3) Persian, (4) Persian, (5) Mysticism, (6) Al-Ma'arif—Mystic knowledges.

7. Abu al-Baqa, (1) ?, (2) Writing 1221, (3) ?, (4) Arabic, probably, (5) Religion, (6) Kitab al-Bayan al-Wadih al-Mashud Min Fada'ih al-Nasara wa'l-Yahud—A refutation of Christianity and Judaism.

8. al-Baqilani, (1) Abu Bakr Ahmad ibn 'Ali ibn al-Taiyyb, (2) Died 1013, (3) Muslim, (4) ?, (5) Theology, (6) None.

9. al-Fanari, (1) ?, (2) 1350-1431, (3) Turkish, (4) Arabic, (5) Theology, encyclopaedist, (6) None.

10. ibn al-Hajib, (1) ?, (2) 1175-1249, (3) Egyptian, (4) Arabic, (5) Theology, law, grammar, (6) Al-Kafiya—Arabic Grammar; Al-Shafiyya—Arabic grammar; Kitab al-Maqsad al-Jalil fi'Ilm al-Khalil—On prosody; Muntaha al-Su'al wa'l-Amal—Maliki law; Mukhtasar al-Muntaha—Maliki law.

11. Hajwiri, (1) Abul Hasan Ali ibn Othman ibn Ali Jollabi Qaznawi, (2) Born 1072, (3) Persian, (4) Persian, (5) Mysticism, (6) Kashf-ul-Mahjub—Revelation of mystery.

12. Hamdani, (1) Ain-ul-Qudhat Abul Ma'ali Abd Allah ibn Muhammad ibn Ali Myanji, (2) Died 1075-1095 ?, (3) Persian, (4) Persian, (5) Theology and religion, (6) Resala'i Jamali; Zobdat-ul-Haqayeq—A compendium on reality.

13. ibn Hanbal, (1) Abu 'Abd Allah Ahmad ibn Muhammad, (2) 855, (3) ?, (4) ?, (5) Theology, law, (6) Compiled the Musnad, a collection of 30,000 traditions.

14. al-Islami, (1) Abd al-Haqq al-Islami, (2) Flourished last quarter 14th, (3) Moroccan Jew (converted to Islam), (4) Arabic, probably, (5) Religion, (6) Kitab al-Saif al-Mahdud fi'l-Radd 'Ala al-Yahud—"The sharpened sword to answer the Jews, using the gematria method in his argument."

15. al-Jili, (1) 'Abd al-Qadir al-Jili, (2) 1077 or 1078 to 1165 or 1166, (3) Jil, (4) Arabic, (5) Theology, letters, (6) "Many religious works, some the best in Arabic literature."

16. al-Ju'fi, (1) Abu 'Abd Allah Muhammad ibn Isma'il al-Bukhari, (2) 810-870, (3) ?, (4) ?, (5) Theology, law, (6) Kitab al-Jami' al-Sahib—Classified collection of traditions.

17. al-Mansur, (1) Abu Ja'far 'Abd Allah, (2) Died 775, (3) ?, (4) ?, (5) Statesman, (6) Many translations accomplished during his reign.

18. al-Mayhani, (1) Muhammad ibn al-Munawwar ibn Sheikh-al-Islam Abi Sa'd ibn Sa'd ibn Abi Tahir Sa'id ibn Abi As'id Fadhl-Allah ibn Abi'l Khayr, (2) ?, (3) Persian, (4) Persian, (5) Mysticism, (6) Asrar-ut-Toeheed—Divine secrets.

19. al-Nasafi, (1) 'Umar al-Nasafi, (2) 1067 or 1068 to 1142 or 1143, (3) Persian, probably, (4) ?, (5) Theology, (6) 'Aqa'id—"Catechism on fundamentals of faith."

20. al-Qarafi, (1) ?, (2) Died 1285, (3) Berber, (4) Arabic, probably, (5) Theology, law, science, (6) Various treatises on the defense of Islam; Kitab al-Istibsar fi ma Tudrikuhu al-Absar—Includes his explanation of the rainbow."

21. al-Qirqisani, (1) Abu Yusuf Ya'qub, (2) Flourished first half of

10th, (3) ?, (4) ?, (5) Theology, (6) Al-Riyadh wa'l-Hada'iq—"The gardens and orchards, applying scientific methods to religious matters"; Sefer ha-Gannim We-Pardesim or Sefer Ha-Nizzanim—Information on history of Qaraism.

22. Qushairi, (1) Abul Qasem Abdul Karim ibn Hawazen, (2) Died 1058, (3) Persian, (4) Persian, (5) Mysticism, (6) Resala-i-Qushairi—A treatise on Muslim mysticism.

23. ibn Sab'in, (1) ?, (2) 1217-1269 or 1270, (3) Hispano-Muslim, (4) Arabic, probably, (5) Theology, philosophy, metaphysics, music, (6) Kitab al-Ajwiba 'Ani al-As'ila al-Saqualiyya—Answers to the Sicilian questions; A metaphysical introduction; Asrar al-Hikma al-Mashraqiyya —Secrets of Eastern wisdom; Kitab al-Adwar al-Mansab—Book on musical modes.

24. ibn al-Salah, (1) ?, (2) 1181 or 1182-1245, (3) Kurdistan, (4) Arabic, probably, (5) Hadith (tradition), (6) Kitab Aqsa'l-Amal wa'l-Shauq fi'ulum Hadith al-Rasul—Work on traditions; Kitab Silat al-Nasik fi Sifat al-Manasik—Rites of the pilgrimage.

25. al-Shafi'i, (1) Abu Hamid Muhammad ibn Muhammad al-Tusi al-'Shafi'i al-Ghazzali, (2) 1058-1111, (3) ?, (4) ?, (5) Theology, (6) Ihya 'Ulum al-Din—Revivifying of the sciences of the faith; Kitab al-Durra al-Fakhira fi Kashf Ulum al-Akhira—Eschatological treatise; Kimiya Sa'adat—Alchemy of happiness; Mishkat al-Anwar—The niche for lights; Kitab Tahafut al-Falasifa; Kitab al-Munqidh min al-Dalal—The liberation from error. (See also al-Ghazzali under various titles.)

26. al-Shafi'i, (1) Muhammad ibn Idris, (2) Born 767 or 768, (3) ?, (4) ?, (5) Theology, law, (6) None.

27. Shahpur, (1) Imam Imad-ud-din Abul Muzaffar, (2) Died 1078, (3) Persian, (4) Persian, (5) Theology, (6) Tafseer Asfarayani, or Taj-ut-Tarajim—Commentary.

28. al-Shahrastani, (1) ?, (2) 1076 or 1077-1153, (3) Khurasan, (4) Arabic, probably, (5) Religion, history, philosophy, (6) Kitab al-Milal wa'l-ihal—Book of religion and sects; Tarikh al-Hukama—History of the philosophers; Kitab Musara'at al-Falasifa—Discussions of philosophers; Kitab Nihayat al-Iqdam fi'Ilm al-Kalam—Theology.

29. al-Sur-Abadi, (1) Abu Bakr Atiq ibn Muhammad al-Harwi, (2) Died 1060 to 1072 ?, (3) Persian, (4) Persian, (5) Religion and mysticism, (6) Tafseer—Interpretation of Qur'an.

30. ibn Taimiyya, (1) ?, (2) 1263-1328, (3) Syrian, (4) Arabic, probably, (5) Theology, (6) Kitab Sarim al-Maslul'ala Shatim al-Rasul —The drawn sword against the insulter of the Prophet.

31. ibn Tumart, (1) ?, (2) 1077 or 1087 to 1128 or 1130, (3) Berber-Muslim, (4) Berber, (5) Religious reformation, (6) Berber treatise on Tawhid, or monotheism.

32. Yazidi, (1) Yazidi Shaikh 'Adi, (2) Died 1162, (3) Ba'albek, (4) ?, (5) Religion, (6) Al-Yalvah—Yazidi sacred book.

Miscellaneous

Encyclopaedias, Mineralogy, Animals, Art, Agriculture, Lexicography, Oneirology, Military Science.

1. al-Asma'i, (1) Abd al-Malik ibn Quraib, (2) 739 or 740-831, (3) Arabic, (4) Arabic, (5) Animals, (6) Kitab al-Khail—On horse; Kitab al-Ibil—On camel; Kitab al-Wuhush—On wild animals; Kitab al-Sha'—On sheep; Kitab Khalq al-Insan—Making of man; Kitab al-Farq—Book of distinction.

2. al-Dinawari, (1) Abu Sa'id Nasr ibn Ya'qub, (2) ?, (3) ?, (4) Arabic, (5) Oneirology, (6) Kitab al-Qadiri fi'l-Ta'bir—Treatise on oneirology.

3. ibn Hajjaj, (1) Abu Umar ibn Hajjaj, (2) Flourished 1073, (3) Spanish, (4) ?, (5) Writer, (6) Al Kafi—The sufficient.

4. al-Hasib, (1) Utarid ibn Muhammad, (2) Flourished 9th, (3) ?, (4) ?, (5) Mineralogy, (6) Kitab Manafi al-Ahjar; "Author of oldest Muslim lapidary extant" on values of stones.

5. ibn Isa, (1) 'Ali ibn 'Isa, or Jesus Haly, (2) ?, (3) Arabic, (4) ?, (5) Occultist, (6) Risala al-Kahhalin—Ophthalmology.

6. al-Jauhari, (1) Abu Nasr Isma'il ibn Hammad, (2) Died 1002, (3) ?, (4) Arabic, (5) Lexicography, (6) Kitab al-Sihah fi'l-Luqa—Arabic dictionary, Book of the correct words of language.

7. ibn al-Jauzi, (1) ?, (2) 1115-1201, (3) Baghdad, (4) Arabic, probably, (5) Encyclopaedist—History, philology, biography, hadith, fiq'h, Qur'an, ethics, medicine, geography, etc., (6) Kitab al-Muntazam wa Multaqat al-Multazam—History of the world to 1180; Critical edition of al-Ghazzali's Ihya; Luqat al-Manafi fi'l-Tibb—A medical work.

8. al-Khwarizmi, (1) Abu 'Abd Allah Muhammad ibn Ahmad ibn Yusuf, (2) ?, (3) Persian, (4) Arabic, (5) Encyclopaedist, (6) Mafatih al-Ulum—Keys of the sciences (?).

9. al-Maqdisi, (1) Mutahhar ibn Tahir, (2) ?, (3) ?, (4) ?, (5) Encyclopaedist, (6) Kitab al-Bad' wa'l Tarikh—Book of the creation and of history.

10. al-Nabati, (1) Abu Bakr Ahmad ibn Ali ibn al-Wahshiyya al-Kaldani, (2) Born before 912, (3) ?, (4) ?, (5) Agriculture, (6) Kitab al-Falaha al-Nabatiyya—On agriculture.

11. al-Qumri, (1) Abi Mansur al-Hasan ibn Nuh, (2) 10th-11th, (3) Jibal Muslim, (4) ?, (5) Teacher of Avicenna, (6) Kitab Qina' wa Mana'—Treatise on medicine, the book of life and death.

12. al-Rammah, (1) al-Hasan al-Rammah, (2) Died 1294 or 1295, (3) Syrian, probably, (4) Arabic, probably, (5) Military subjects, (6) Kitab al-Furusiyya wa'l-Minasab al-Harbiyya—Horsemanship and war stratagems; Nihayat al-Su'ul wa'l-Umniyya fi Ta'allum A'mal al-Furusiyya—On the art of war and horsemanship.

13. al-Shafi'i, (1) Abu Muhammad al-Qasim ibn Muhammad 'Alam al-Din al-Birzali, (2) 1267-1339, (3) Hispano-Muslim, (4) ?, (5) His-

torian, (6) Tarikh Misr wa Dimashq—Collection of biographies, on the history of Egypt and Damascus; Mukhtasar al-Mi'a al-Sabi'a—"Obituaries and brief notes on main events of the period 1204-1335"; "At least two other writings."

14. al-Ramhurmuzi, (1) Buzurg ibn Shahriyar, (2) Flourished 912-1009, (3) Ramhurmuz, (4) Persian, (5) Sailor, (6) Kitab 'Ajayib al-Hind—Collection of sailors' tales on the marvels of India.

15. ibn Rukn al-Dawla, (1) Fana Khusraw Abu Shufa' ibn Rukn al-Dawla, (2) 936-983, (3) ?, (4) ?, (5) Patron of science, art, (6) None.

16. Shir Zayd, (1) Sharaf al-Dawla Abu al-Fawaris, (2) Ruled 982-989, (3) Persian, (4) ?, (5) Built an observatory, (6) None.

17. al-Talaqani, (1) Abu al-Qasim Isma'il ibn 'Abbad ibn al-'Abbas al-Sahib, (2) 936-995 or 996, (3) Persian, (4) Arabic, (5) Lexicography, (6) Kitab al-Muhit—Arabic dictionary, the comprehensive. See also*

*Sarton, Volume II, Book I, pages 161, 167-171, 173-179, 187-189, 206-208, 236-237. Volume II, Book II, pages 344-346. Volume II, Book III, pages 492, 555, 561-566, 579-581, 604-605, 648-649. Volume II, Book IV, pages 831-834, 842-854. Volume III, Book I, pages 426-438. Volume III, Book II, pages 1373-1377.

APPENDIX V

TRANSLATORS

– 1 –

Partial List of Translators of Scientific, Philosophical, and Literary Works From Arabic Into Latin Including Some Titles of Works and Dates of Translation

1. *Adelard of Bath* (also called Aethelhard, Alard, etc. Adelardus Bathoniensis),
   (1) Khwarizmi's astronomical tables, (1126).
   (2) Khwarizmi's mathematical treatise (liber ysagogarum alchorismi).
   (3) Euclid's Fifteen Books.[1]
2. *Alfred of Sareshel* (also known as Walafred, Alvred, Alphiatus, Sarewel, Sarchel, Serechel), end of the twelfth century and the beginning of the thirteenth century, translated.
   (1) De vegetabilibus of Nicolaus Damascenus (or Nikolaos Damaskenos) from the Arabic translation of Is'haq ibn Hunayn, made in the second half of the ninth century.
   (2) Alchemical part of ibn Sina's Shifa as Liber de congelatis, (1200).
   (3) De motu cordis, a treatise based on Greek, Muslim and Salernitan materials (c. 1210).[2]
3. *Armengandus,* son of Blaise (also known as Monspeliensis Hermengaldus, Armengand, Ermengard, etc.), translated.
   (1) Kitab Kifayata' al-Insan dhunubihi wa uyubihi (a treatise on man's good and bad qualities), a revision made by Hunayn ibn Is'haq of a translation of Galen made by Tuma al-Ruhawi (Thomas of Edessa).
   (2) Pseudo-Galen: Yconomica (second half of the fifth century).
   (3) ibn Sina al-arjuzat fi'l-tibb (1280-1284).
   (4) Maimonides: Maqala fi-tadbir al-sihha (a medical essay) (1290).
   (5) Maimonides: Al-sumum wal-mutaharriz, De venenis (1307).
   (6) Jacob ben Mahir, a treatise on quadrant translated by Jacob and Armengaud (1299).[3]
4. *Bonacosa* (also known as Tobiyah), translated 1255.
   (1) Kulliyat or complete works of ibn Rushd.[4]
5. *Constantinus Africanus* (or Afer), translated.
   (1) A great number of medical writings.
6. *Domigo Gundisalvo* or *Gonzalez* (Dominicus Gondissalinus, Gondisalvi, Gunsalvus). Archdeacon of Segovia. Spanish philosopher and translator from Arabic into Latin in collaboration with John of Seville.
   (1) De divisione philosophiae which is essentially derived from the Kitab ihsa al-ulum of al-Farabi (first half of the tenth century).
   (2) Arabic Euclid (the sections on arithmetic, music and medicine are partly of Arabic and partly of Latin origin).
   (3) Treatise de immortalitate animae (first half of the thirteenth century).

7. *Faraj Ben Salim* (Moses Farachi or Faragut, Fararius, Ferrarius, Farragius, Franchinus), translated 1279.
   (1) Kitab al-hawi of al-Razi. The Hawi was the largest encyclopaedia of Greco-Arabic medicine.
   (2) Pseudo-Galenic De Medicinis (Arabic version by Hunain ibn Is'haq).
   (3) ibn Jazla's Taqwim al-Abdan (second half of the eleventh century).
   (4) Mesue the Third's Treatise on Surgery (second half of the thirteenth century).[5]
8. *Gerard of Cremona* (also known as Gerardus Cremonensis, not Carmonensis), translated with his school of translators, second half of twelth century.
   (1) ibn Sina's Qanun.
   (2) Posterior Analytics with commentaries by Themistius and al-Farabi.
   (3) Aristotelian and pseudo-Aristotelian writings.
   (4) Philosophical treatises by al-Kindi, al-Farabi, Israili.
   (5) Mathematical treatises by Autolycus, Euclid, Archimedes, Apollonius, Hysicles, Theodosius, Menelaus, Ptolemy, Banu Musa, al-Khwarizmi, al-Farghani, Ahmad ibn Yusuf, al-Nairizi, Thabit ibn Qurra, Abul Kamil, Jabir ibn Aflah, al-Zarqali.
   (6) Physical treatises by Diocles, al-Kindi, Thabit and ibn al-Haitham.
   (7) Medical treatises by Galen, al-Kindi, ibn Masawaih, Yahya ibn Sarafyun, al-Razi, Abu-al-Qasim, ibn Sina, ibn al-Wafid, Ali-ibn Ridwan.
   (8) Alchemical writings by Haiyan and al-Razi.
   (9) Logic.
      a. Aristotle: Posterior Analytics, two books, from the Arabic version by Matta ibn Yunus (first half of the tenth century).
      b. Themistius (second half of the fourth century): "Commentary on the Posterior Analytics, one book, probably from the same Arabic version."
      c. al-Farabi (first half of the tenth century): De syllogismo. A part of his elaboration of Aristotle's Organon.
   (10) Philosophy (a. to g. the Aristotelian or pseudo-Aristotelian writings).
      a. De coelo et mundo, 4 books.
      b. De naturali auditu, 8 books.
      c. De generatione et corruptione.
      d. Liber meteororum from the Arabic version by Yahya ibn Batriq (books 1 to 3) (first half of the ninth century).
      e. Liber lapidum. "A work quoted by the German encyclopaedist Arnold of Saxony (first half of the thirteenth century)."
      f. De Expositione bonitatis purae—"the famous neo-Platonic Liber de causis—a work which cannot be anterior to Proclus" (second half of the fifth century).
      g. De elementis, or De proprietatibus elementorum.
      (h. to l. are Aristotelian commentaries by Alexander of Aphrodisius first half of the third century).
      h. De motu et tempore.
      i. De Sensu.
      j. De eo quod augmentum et incrementum fiunt in forma et non in hyle (?), from the Arabic version of Abu 'Uthman Sa'id al-Dimishqi (first half of the tenth century).
      k. De intellectu et intellecto from the Arabic version of Hunain ibn Is'haq (second half of the ninth century). Printed 1501.
      l. De unitate.
      (m. to s. are writings by al-Kindi, first half of the ninth century). The "Latin versions have been edited by Albino Nagy (Munster 1897), who would ascribe m. and n. to John of Seville."
      m. De quinque essentiis.

n. De somno et visione.
o. De ratione (or Verbum de intentione antiquorum in ratione).
p. al-Farabi (first half of the tenth century): Distinctio super librum Aristotelis de naturali auditu.
q. al-Farabi. De scientiis. "There is an earlier translation or adaptation by Gundisalvo (first half of the twelfth century). Gerard's version was published by Guilelmus Camerarius (Paris 1638); Gundisalvo's by Clemens Baeumker (Munster 1916; Isia, 4, p. 135). A Hebrew version was edited by Mich. Rosenstein (Breslau 1858)."
r. Is'haq al-Isra'ili (first half of the tenth century): De elementis. Printed in the Omnia Opera Ysaac (Lyon 1515).
s. Is'haq al-Isra'ili: De descriptione rerum et definitionibus earum et de differentia inter descriptionem et definitionem.

(11) Greek Mathematics and Astronomy.
a. Autolycus (second half of the fourth century B.C.): De sphaera mota. Arabic version by Is'haq ibn Hunain and Qustat ibn Luqa.
b. Euclid: Elements, XV Books. "Long believed to be lost, but A. A. Bjornbo discovered various MSS. in 1904 which he identified with Gerard's version."
c. Euclid: Data. Arabic version by Is'haq ibn Hunain; revised by Thabit ibn Qurra.
d. Archimedes: De mensura circuli.
e. Apollonius: Conics.
f. Hypsicles (first half of the second century B.C.). De ascensionibus. Arabic version by Is'haq ibn Hunain and Qustat ibn Luqa.
g. Theodosius (first half of the first century B.C.): De sphaeris.
h. Theodosius. De locis habitabilibus. Arabic version by Qusta ibn Luqa.
i. Ceminos (first half of the first century B.C.): Liber introductorius ad artem sphaericam.
j. Menelaus (second half of the first century): De figuris sphaericis.
k. Ptolemy (first half of the second century): Liber almagesti. "This translation was completed by Gerard at Toledo in 1175. Printed in Venice in 1515."

(12) Arabic Mathematics and Astronomy.
a. Banu Musa (first half of the ninth century): Liber trium fratrum. Edited by Max. Curtze (Halle 1885).
b. al-Khwarizmi (first half of the ninth century): De jebra et elmucabala. Edited by Guillaume Libri: Histoire des sciences mathematiques (Vol. 1, pp. 253-297, 1838).
c. al-Farghani (first half of the ninth century). De aggregationibus scientialibus stellarum et de principiis colestium motuum.
d. Ahmad ibn Yusuf (second half of the ninth century): De arcubus similibus. Edited by Max. Curtze.
e. Ahmad ibn Yusuf: De proportione et proportionalitate.
f. al-Nairizi (second half of the ninth century): Commentary on Euclid's Elements, Books I to X. Edited by M. Curtze.
g. Thabit ibn Qurra (second half of the ninth century): De figura alchata.
h. Thabit ibn Qurra: De expositione nominum Almagesti.
i. Thabit ibn Qurra: De motu accessionis et recessionis. Printed under the title De motu octavae sphaerae (1480, 1509, 1518).
j. Abu Kamil (first half of the tenth century): Liber qui secundum Arabes vocatur algebra et almucabala.
k. Abu 'Uthman (first half of the tenth century) or Muhammad ibn abd al-Baqi (second half of the eleventh century): Liber Judaei super decimum Euclidis.

l. 'Arib ibn Sa'd (second half of the tenth century): Libri anohe (anwa') "a Christian calendar containing astronomical and agricultural information. Edited by G. Libri, Liber anoe, in his Histoire des sciences mathematiques (Vol. 1, pp. 293-458, 1838)."
m. Jabir ibn Aflah (first half of the twelfth century): Gebri de astronomia Libri IX "in quibus Ptolemaeum emendavit (Nuremburg 1534)."
n. De practica geometrie. Unknown date and authorship.
o. Algorismus in integris et minutiis. Unidentified arithmetic; the translator is called Gernandus.
p. Liber coaequationis planetarum.
The following three are astronomical tables.
q. Liber tabularum iahen (?) cum regulis suis. Tabulae Jaen (?) (Jaen is an important town or district in Andalusia).
r. al-Zarqali (second half of the eleventh century): Canones Arzachelis.
s. Liber omnium sphaerarum coeli et compositionis tabularum.

(13) Physics and Mechanics.
a. Diocles (first half of the second century B.C.): De speculis comburentibus (Liber Tidei de Speculo). As transmitted by a commentary of Eutocios (first half of the sixth century), on Archimedes.
b. al-Kindi (first half of the ninth century): De aspectibus; "followed by De umbris et de diversitate aspectum. Very well edited by A. A. Bjornbo and Seb. Vogl (Leipzig 1912)."
c. Thabit ibn Qurra (second half of the ninth century): Liber charastonis (?).
d. ibn al-Haitham (first half of the eleventh century): De crepusculis et nubium ascensionibus. Printed in Lisbon in 1542, and in Basle in 1572.

(14) Greek Medicine.
a. Liber veritatis Hippocratis de istis qui laborant in agone mortis. Also called Liber sapientiae and Capsula eburnea. "There are various Arabic versions of this pseudo-Hippocratic treatise, one by Yahya ibn Batriq, another by Hunain ibn Is'haq. Printed together with Razi's Liber ad'Almansorem (1497, 1500)."
b to k are probably translations from Hunayn ibn Is'haq.
b. Commentary on Hippocrates' Regimen acutarum eagritudinum.
c. Commentary on Hippocrates' Prognostica. Same text previously translated by Constantine the African.
d. De elementis.
e. De secretis ad Monteum (apocryphal).
f. De complexionibus.
g. De malicia complexionis diverse (diversa).
h. De simplici medicina, or De simplicibus medicamentis.
i. De criticis diebus.
j. De crisi.
k. Tegni.

(15) Arabic Medicine.
a. al-Kindi (first half of the ninth century): De gradibus medicinarum, or De medicinarum compositarum gradibus investigandis. "Printed with the Latin translation of ibn Butlan's tacuinum (Strassburg 1531)."
b. ibn Masawaih (first half of the ninth century): Aphorisms.
c. Yahya ibn Sarafyun (second half of the ninth century): Breviarium. Practica Joannis Serapionis dicta breviarium (Venice 1497).
d. al-Razi (second half of the ninth century): Iiber Albubatri Rasis qui dicitur Almansorius.

e. al-Razi: Liber divisionum continens CLIV capitula cum quibusdam confectionibus ejusdem.
f. al-Razi: Liber introductionis in medicina parvus.
g. al-Razi: De juncturarum aegritudinibus.
h. Abu-l-Qasim (second half of the tenth century): Liber Azaragui de cirurgia. First printed together with Chauliac's Latin surgery (Venice 1498).
i. ibn Sina (first half of the eleventh century): Canonis Avicennae libri quinque. Milano 1473, Padua 1476, etc.
j. ibn al-Wafid (first half of the eleventh century): De medicinis et cibis simplicibus, or De simplicium medicinarum virtutibus. Printed with ibn Butlan's Tacuinum (Strassburg, 1531).
k. Ali ibn Ridwan (first half of the eleventh century): Commentary on Galen's Tegni. Haly Eben Rodan S. Rodoham Aegyptius: Commentarius in artem parvam (Venice 1496).

(16) Arabic Astrology.
a. Liber alfadholi. est arab de bachi. The author was possibly al-Fadl ibn Naubakht (second half of the eighth century), or al-Fadl ibn Sahl al-Sarakhsi (first half of the ninth century).
b. Mashallah (second half of the eighth century): De orbe, also De scientia motus orbis, De elementis et orbibus coelestibus, De ratione circuli coelestis, De natura orbium. "Printed in Nuremberg in 1504 and 1549."
c. Alchandrus, "Alcandrinus" (second half of the tenth century). Arcandam de vertitatibus et praedictionibus astrologiae (Paris 1542).
d. Liber in quo terrarum corporumque continentur mensurationes Abhabuchri, qui dicebatur Heus. Author unidentified.
e. Liber de accidentibus alfel. Alfel is a corruption of al-fal; "the word fal means augury, necromancy, anything taken as an omen."

(17) Arabic Alchemy and Geomancy.
a. Jabir ibn Haiyan (second half of the eighth century): Liber divinitatis LXX.
b. al-Razi (second half of the ninth century): De aluminibus et salibus.
c. Liber luminis luminum; Liber qui dictitur lumen luminum et perfecti magisterii. Also ascribed to al-Razi.
d. Liber geomantie de artibus divinatoriis.[6]

9. *Giovanni da Brescia, Joannes Brixiensis* (Brisciensis). Translated, 1263.
(1) "Treatise on the astrolabe" by al-Zarqali.[7]

10. *Gustav Flugel* (no complete translation in any language, and no translation in English, pp. 987-88 1871-72).
(1) Index of the Sciences or Fihrist al-ulum by Abu-l-Faraj Muhammad ibn abi Ya'qub al-Nadim al-Warraq al-Baghdadi (?).

11. *Herman the German "Hermannus Alemannus"* (or Teutonicus, Germanicus). Translated, Toledo 1240.
(1) Middle commentary on Aristotle's Ethics by ibn Rushd.
(2) Middle commentary on Aristotle's Rhetoric and Poetics (by ibn Rushd).
(3) Summa Quorundam Alexandrinorum, relative to the Ethics (1243-1244).
(4) al-Farabi: Commentary on the Rhetoric.
(5) Translated the Psalter into Castilian. (First half of the fifteenth century).[8]

12. *Herman the Dalmation* — also called Hermann the Slav or the Carinthian. Translated 1140. Printed under title Introductorium in astronomiam Albumasaris Alabachii.
(1) Kitab al-Madkhal ila ilm Ahkam al-Nujum by Abu Ma'shar (first half of the ninth century).
(2) Astrological treatise of the Jew Shal ibn Bishr (first half of the ninth century).
(3) About 1140, astronomical tables of al-Kwarizmi.

(4) About 1142, in Leon, two treatises against Islam: De generatione Muhamet et nutritura eius; Doctrina Mahumet. Printed in Bibliander's edition of the Latin Qur'an.
(5) Maslama ibn Ahmad al-Majriti (second half of the tenth century). Arabic translation of Ptolemy's Planisphaerium, with commentary.
(6) Al-Khwarizmi's astronomical tables (about 1140).

13. *Hugo Sanccelliensis* (Sanctallensis, Sandaliensis, Strellensis, de Satalia, etc.) Translated between 1119 and 1151.
(1) Commentary on the Astronomy of al-Farghani (first half of the ninth century).
(2) A pseudo-Aristotelian treatise entitled Liber Aristotelis de 255 Indorum voluminibus universalium questionum tam generalium quam circularium summam continens (1119 and 1151).
(3) Mashallah (second half of the eighth century).
(4) De nativitatibus; Liber imbrium (meteorological predictions).
(5) A treatise on geomancy and Muslim art, called in Arabic 'ilm al-raml, science of sand.
(6) Treatises on spatulamancy (two treatises).
(7) Liber Apollonii de principalibus rerum causis.
(8) Ptolemy's Centiloquium.
(9) The earliest Latin version of the alchemical text called the Emerald Table (tabula smaragdina, Lawh zabarjad).[10]

14. *John of Seville.* Translated.
(1) Treatise written by al-Kindi plagiarized by Abu Ma'shar. "(The Flores astrologiae seem to be an extract from the Magnae conjunctiones. Translated in Augsburg 1489, Venice 1515)."
(2) De nativitatibus et interrogationibus (1503) by "Umar ibn al-Farrukhan" (first half of the ninth century).
(3) Commentary on Ptolemy's Centiloquium by Ahmad ibn Yusuf ibn Daya (translated about 1130-1136).
(4) Liber de consuetudinibus in judiciis astrorum, printed with other works in 1493, 1507, 1533, by Al-Battani.
(5) De imaginibus astronomicis by Thabit ibn Qurra (second half of the ninth century).
(6) al-Madkhal ila sina'at ahkam al-nujum by al-qabisi (second half of the tenth century).
(7) De conjunctionibus planetarum in duodecim signis by al-Qabisi. Translated in 1485 in Venice.
(8) De astrolabio by Maslama ibn Ahmad al-Majriti (second half of the tenth century).
(9) Regulae utiles de electionibus by ibn abi-l-Rijal (first half of the eleventh century).
(10) Sir al-Asrar, Secretum secretorum (probably first half of the ninth century).
(11) Pseudo-Aristotelian De causis.
(12) De Intellectu. Edited by Albino Nagy: Die philosophischen Abhandlungen des al-Kindi (Munster 1897).
(13) al-Fasl bain al-ruh wal-nafs by Quata ibn Luqa: De differentia spiritus et animae. (Second half of the ninth century).
(14) Ihsa' al-ulum by al-Farabi. Translated into Liber Alpharibii de ortu scientiarum.
(15) al-Shifa by ibn Sina.
(16) Yanbu al-Hayat by ibn Gabirol.
(17) Maqasid al-falasifa by al-ghazzali (an encyclopaedia divided into three parts).
(18) al-Madkhal ila 'ilm ahkam al-njum by Abu Ma'shar. (Translated about 1133).

(19) Albohali de judiciis nativitatum liber unus by Abu 'Ali al-Khaiyat. (Translated 1153.)
(20) Kitab fi harakat al-samawiya wa jawami' ilm al-nujum by al-Farghani. (Translated about 1134-35.)
(21) Epistola de rebus eclipsium et de conjunctionibus planetarum (alias, de ratione circuli; de circulo et stellis) by Mashallah. (Translated in the second half of the eighth century.)
(22) Liber Alghoarismi de practica arithmetrice by Adelard of Bath, and later by a Muslim writer.[11]

15. *Joannes Saracenus Afflacius.*
(1) Surgical part of Ali ibn 'Abba's Maliki by Ali ibn Abbas. (Constantine translated first half of this work.)

16. *Marc of Toledo* (Marcus Toledanus) translated probably toward the end of the twelfth century.
(1) Galenic treatises of Arabic version of Hunain ibn Is'haq.
(2) The Qur'an.
(3) Hippocrates: De aeribus aquis locis.
(4) De utilitate pulsus.
(5) De motu membrorum.
(6) De motibus liquidis.
(7) Hunain ibn Is'haq.
(8) De tactu pulsus.
(9) Isagoge ad Tegni Galeni.[12]

17. *Michael Scot or Scott.* (Scotch philosopher, alchemist, astrologer, translator from Arabic into Latin.) Translated 1217.
(1) Astronomical treatise by al-Bitruji.
(2) First Latin translation of Aristotle's Historia animalium (15 books).
(3) Translation of Aristotle's De coelo et mundo, with ibn Rushd's commentary.
(4) Translation of Aristotle's De anima, with ibn Rushd's commentary.
(5) De generatione et corruptione.
(6) Meteora.
(7) Parva naturalia.
(8) De substantia orbis.
(9) Abbreviatio Avicennae de animalibus.
(10) Three popular treatises on astrology and general science. Posterior to 1228.[13]

18. *Moses of Palermo* (Moses Panormitanus). "Judeo-Sicilian translator of medical works from Arabic into Latin."
(1) Pseudo-Hippocratic treatise on veterinary medicine.

19. *Peter of Cluny,* Petrus Cluniacensis dictus Venerabilis (1094-1156) Translated.
(1) Qur'an.[14]

20. *Peter Gallego* translated.
(1) Aristotle's treatise on animals.
(2) A treatise on economy, "probably that of the pseudo-Galen."[15]

21. *Plato of Tiboli* (Plato Tiburtinus) translated 1134 to 1145 (?).
(1) Abu-Ali al-Khaiyat (first half of the ninth century): De nativitatibus or De judiciis nativitatum. "This was also translated by John of Seville in 1153. It is John's translation which was printed in Nuremberg in 1546 or 1549."
(2) In 1136, astrological aphorisms (fusul). "Alamansoris Judicia seu propositiones. . . , or, Centum propositiones. . . , or, Capitula stellarum oblata regi magno Saracenorum Alchacham (ab) Almansore astrologo filio Abrahae Judei."
(3) In 1138, Ptolemy's Quadripartitum. This book was translated again and again.

(4) Treatise on practical geometry: Liber embadorum by Abraham bar Hayya. (Translated in 1145).
(5) Theodosius of Bithynia (first half of first century B. C.).
(6) al-Battani (second half of the ninth century): De motu stellarum.
(7) Abu Bakr al-Hasan ibn al-Khasib (second half of the ninth century): De revolutionibus nativitatum.
(8) ibn al-Saffar (first half of the eleventh century): Liber Abulcasim de operibus astrolabiae.
(9) Unidentified treatise on geomancy: Alfakini arabici filii quaestiones geomanticae. Published in the Fasciculus geomanticus (Verona 1687; 1704).
(10) Aeneas de pulsibus et urinis. Aeneas might be Hunain ibn Is'haq (second half of the ninth century).[16]

22. *Philip of Tripoli* (Philipus Tripolitanus) translated at some time during the second quarter of the thirteenth century (c. 1243?).
(1) Manuscripts of the Sirr al-asrar, i.e., the pseudo-Aristotelian Secret of Secrets.[17]

23. *Rudolf of Bruges* translated.
(1) Treatise on the astrolabe of Maslama ibn Ahmad al-Majriti by Maslama ibn Ahmad al-Majriti.[18]

24. *Robert of Chester* (also known as Robertus Castrensis, Cestrensis, Retinensis, Ketenensis, Ostiensis, Astensis, Anglicus, Robert the Englishman, Robert de Retinus. Translated 1145).
(1) The first translation of the algebra by al-Khwarizmi.
(2) A translation of al-Kindi's (first half of the ninth century) Judicia.
(3) "The first Latin translation of the Qur'an, begun in 1141 and completed in 1143."
(4) Translation of a treatise on alchemy, Liber de compositione alchemiae.
(5) A treatise on the astrolabe in 1144.
(6) Astronomical tables for the longitude of London, 1149-1150.
(7) Revision for the meridian of London of the tables of al-Khwarizmi (first half of the ninth century), translated by Adelard of Bath.[19]

25. *Salio of Padua* translated in 1244, 1248, or 1218.
(1) An astrological treatise by Abu-Bakr.
(2) Treatise, De stellis fixis ascribed to Hermes Trismegistos.[20]
(3) Liber de nativitatibus (?).

26. *Stephen of Antioch* translated about 1127.
(1) Kitab al-Maliki by Ali ibn 'Abbas.[21]

27. *Stephanus Arnoldi,* Arlandi (or Orlandi) translated in the first quarter of the fourteenth century.
(1) Kitab al 'Amal bil-kurra al-fulkiya by Qusta ibn Luqa.
(2) Dietarium, or Translatio dietarii a Costa ben Luca compositi.
(3) Viridarium, id est expositio Antidotarii Nicolai Salernitani.
(4) Experimenta.
(5) De evacuatione.
(6) De febribus.
(7) Prognosticationes.
(8) Regimen contra defectum coitus.
(9) A treatise on cataract.
(10) Defensorium vitae.
(11) A treatise on bloodletting.
(12) Annotationes in Anatomiam Mundini.
(13) Isagoge in Hippocratis et Galeni physiologiae partem anatomicam.
(14) Ars medicinarum laxativarum tam simplicium quam compositarum.[22]

28. *Stephen of Saragossa* (Stephanus Caesaraugustanus civis Ilerdensis), translated in 1233.

(1) Kitab i 'timad fi-l-adwiya al-mufrada (treatise on simple drugs).
(2) De gradibus.[23]

29. *Theodore of Antioch* translated.
 (1) Moamyn's treatise on care of falcons and dogs.[24]
30. *Wilhelmus de Linis apud Neapolim* translated.
 (1) Commentaries on Aristotelian logic and Porphyry's interpretation of it by ibn Rushd.
 (2) Translated a book on algebra.[25]

—2—

List of Translators of Scientific, Philosophical and Other Works From Arabic or Greek Into Hebrew Including Titles of Works and Dates of Translations

1. *Abraham bar Hayya ha-Nasi* (often called Savasarda).
 (1) Treatise on music.[26]
2. *Abraham ben Meir ibn Ezra.*
 (1) Three treatises on grammar by Judah Hayyuj (second half of the tenth century), Rome 1140.
 (2) Two treatises on astrology by Mashallah, before 1148.
 (3) al-Biruni's commentary on al-Khwarizmi's tables, Narbonne 1160.[27]
3. *Abraham ben Nathan ha-Yarhi* (called Rabn for short).
 (1) Sefer ha-manhig (the guide) or Manhig 'olam (guide of the world) 1204. The Manhig is a guide divided into two parts, the first of which is a collection of his own responsa, the second a collection of extracts from the two Talmuds, the Midrashim, and many other works.[28]
4. *Abraham ben Samuel ibn Hasdai ha-Levi* (died in 1240).
 (1) Kitab al-tuffahah (book of the apple), a pseudo-Aristotelian philosophical dialogue.
 (2) Sefer ha-yesodot, translation of the treatise on the elements by Is'haq al-Isra'ili.
 (3) Mozene zedeq, translation of an ethical treatise by al-Ghazzali, Mizan al 'amal.
 (4) Two treatises by Maimonides, entitled Sefer ha-mizwot and Iggert Teman.
 (5) Story of Barlaam and Ioasaph.[29]
5. *Ahitub ben Isaac* translated toward the end of the thirteenth century.
 (1) Maimonides' logic, Maqala fi sina'at al-Mantiq; "this translation, Millot ha-higgayon, though superior in some ways to the earlier one by Moses ibn Tibbon (1254), did not supersede it."[30]
6. *David ibn Ya-ish* (also known as David ben Solomon ibn Ya'ish of Seville. Translated in the second half of the fourteenth century).
 (1) Seder hanagat ha-adam bebaithu, a treatise on domestic economy.[31]
7. *Isaac ben Nathan of Cordova* translated in 1347.
 (1) al-Ghazzali: Ma'amar bi-teshubot she'elot nisheal mehem.
 (2) Maimonides: Maqala fi-l-tawhid (On the unity of God), Ma'mar ha-yihud.
 (3) Joseph ben Judah ibn 'Aqnin: Ma'amar bi-mehuyab ha-mezyiut ve-ekut siddur ha-debarim mimenu (a treatise on existence).
 (4) Muhammad ibn Muhammad al-Tabrizi: Commentary on Maimonides' introduction to the second part of the Dalalat al-ha 'iron.[32]
8. *Jacob ben Abba Mari ben Simson* (or Simeon) *ben Anatoli* (Antoli, Anatolio) translated 1231-1235.
 (1) Ptolemy's Almagest from the Arabic—(Hibber ha-gadol ha-niqra).
 (2) ibn Rushd's intermediate commentaries on Porphyry's Isagoge, and on Aristotle's Categories, Interpretation, Prior and Posterior Analytics. "This

work was probably begun in Provence. It was completed at Naples in 1232. The first three books were translated from the Hebrew into Latin by Jacob Mantino (first half of the sixteenth century) and published in the editions of 1550 and 1553. Anatoli planned to translate other parts of ibn Rushd's commentaries but failed to do so."

(3) ibn Rushd's Summary of the Almagest. Translated in 1231 (or 1235) under the title Qizzur Alma gesti. "This text is known only in Hebrew."

(4) al-Farghani (first half of the ninth century): Kitab fi-harakat al-samawiya. The Hebrew translation also called Qizzur Almagesti.

(5) Muhammedis Alfragani chronologica et astronomica elementa (1590) was made from Anatoli's Hebrew version. "The Hebrew title, Yesdot ha-takunah, is a later one probably inspired by the Latin one, Elementa Astronomica."[33]

9. *Jacob ben Moses ibn Abbasi ha-Bedarshi* translated 1289-1297.
   (1) Maimonides' Kitab al-siraj, commentary on the third order (Seder nahim) of the Mishnah.[34]

10. *Jacob ben abi Abraham Isaac ben al-Carsono* (or Carsi, Corsono) translated in 1375.
    (1) Treatise on the astrolabe, Bi'ur 'Asiyot ha-azturlab, divided into eight chapters.
    (2) Alphonsine tables translated in Hebrew from 1336 to 1387.[35]

11. *Joseph ben Isaac Qimhi*, born about 1105 and died about 1170.
    (1) Kitab al-hidayat ila fara'id al-qulub by Bahya ben Joseph.
    (2) Sheqel ha-qodesh, a metrical version derived from a Hebrew translation entitled Mibhar ha-peninim.
    (3) Yesod ha-yirah (foundations of religious fear).[36]

12. *Joseph ben Joshua I ha-Lorqi* (also known as ibn Vives, Vivas, Bibas). He died before 1372.
    (1) Millot ha higgayon, of Maimonides' Maqalat fi sina at al-mantiq (1151).
    (2) Sefer ha-yesodot.

13. *Joseph ben Joshua II ha-Lorqi* (died before 1408).
    (1) He translated a part of the Qanun of ibn Sina before 1402, revised the translation of Nathan he-Me'ati and added a commentary, including a commentary on Shemtob ben Isaac ben Shaprut of Tudela.[37]

14. *Jacob ben Mahir ibn Tibbon* (died in 1304).
    (1) Astronomical tables for the longitude of Montpellier.
    (2) Be'ur ha-keli ha-niqra roba 'Yisrael, "a treatise containing the description and explanation of an instrument by him, the judaicus."
    (3) Autolycus (Autolykos) of Pitane (second half of the fourth century B. C.).
    (4) Euclid: Elements in 15 books. 1255.
    (5) Euclid: Data, translated into Hebrew, 1272, Sefer ha-mattanot.
    (6) Menelaus of Alexandria's Spherics, translated from the Arabic of Is'haq ibn Hunayn as revised by Thabit ibn Qurra.
    (7) Qusta ibn Luqa's Kitab al-amal bil Kurraat al fulkiyya (on celestial spheres), translated in 1256 as Sefar ha-ma'aseh be-kaddur ha galgal, divided into 65 chapters. (Qusta's work was also translated into Spanish by Judah ben Moses and John of Aspa in 1259.)
    (8) Ibn al-Haitham's Fi hai'at al-alam (on configuration of the world), translated as Sefer ha tekunah in 1271. This translation was translated into Latin by Abraham de Balmes about second half of the fifteenth century. The originl Arabic of ibn al-Haitham was translated into Spanish for Alfonso X by Abraham of Toledo.)
    (9) Ibn al-Saffar's Kitab al-amal al-asturlab (on astrolabe) was translated as Perush ha-azturlab. The original Arabic was translated into Latin about first half of the twelfth century by Plato of Tivoli. Also, al-Zarqali's Kitab al-amal bil-safihi al-zijyya (on zijs) was translated into

Latin in 1263 by ibn Mahir and John of Brescia in Montpellier. It was also translated into Spanish by Ferrando (Fernando?) of Toledo in 1255-1256. A second translation into Spanish was made in 1277 by Abraham of Toledo and Bernaldo. A Hebrew version, perhaps made from Latin by Jacob, was called Iggeret ha ma'aseh be-luah ha-niqra zofihah.

(10) Al-Ghazzali's Mizan al-amal (an ethical treatise) was translated into Hebrew as Mozene ha-iyyunim (balance of speculation).

(11) A partial translation of Jabir ibn Aflah's Islah al-majisti, revised by Ben Judah in 1335. (Another translation made in 1274 by Moses ibn Tibbon. The Arabic text was also translated into Latin by Gerard of Cremona.)

(12) Ibn Rush's (Averroes) Compendium of the organon, translated in 1289 (or 1298), was revised in 1329 by Marsilli Ben Judah as Qizzur ha-higgayon. This Hebrew version was translated into Latin about second half of the fifteenth century by Abraham de Balmes. Ibn Rushd's commentary on Aristotelian zoology (de partibus XI-XIX and de generatione animalum) was translated into Hebrew by Jacob ben Mahir in 1302. This Hebrew version was translated into Latin by Jacob Mantino as Paraphrasis Averrosis de partibus et generatione animalum. This version, along with a commentary by Levi Ben Gershon, was printed in Rome in 1521.[38]

15. *Judah ben Saul ibn Tibbon* (born in 1120, died after 1190).

(1) Kitab al-amanat wal-i 'tiqadat by Saadia ben Joseph (Faiths and Dogmas).

(2) Ibn Gabirol's Kitab islah al-akhlaq (on correction of manners) as Tiqqun middot ha-nefesh. (This work was printed in 1550 in Constantinople.)

(3) Ibn Janah's Kitab al-luma' as Sefer hariqmah about 1171.

(4) Ibn Janah's dictionary (Kitab al-usul) as Sefer ha-shorashim, about 1171. The work was edited in Berlin in 1896 by Wilhelm Bacher.

(5) Juda ha-Levi's Kitab al-hajjah, as Sefer ha-kuzari, 1167.

(6) Bahya ben Joseph's Kitab al-hidayat ila fara'id al-qulub, as Torat hobot ha-lebabot. This translation was begun in 1161.[39]

16. *Judah ben Solomon al-Harizi*

(1) Maqamat by al-Hariri.

(2) A pseudo-Galenic treatise on the soul, c. 1200, Sefer ha-nefesh.

(3) Hunian ibn Is'haq's Sayings of the Philosophers, as Musrehapilosofim.

(4) Ali ibn Ridwan: Iggert ha-mussar (letter on education).

(5) Partial translation of the Kitab al-siraj Maimonides' commentary on the Mishnah.

(6) Dalalat al-ha irin, Moreh nebukim.

(7) Ma'amar tehiyyot ha-metim. Essay on resurrection, translated into Hebrew by al-Harizi.

(8) Sheshet Benveniste (second half of the twelfth century): Segulah le harayon, a gynaecological treatise.[40]

17. *Jurad ben Solomon ibn Labi Benveniste della Caballeria* (flourished in 1380-1403 and died in 1411).

(1) Helped Meir Alguadez to translate the Nicomachean Ethics into Hebrew.

(2) Happalat ha-filisofim.

(3) Gerem ha-ma 'alot, a treatise on the powers and qualities of various foods and of simple and composite drugs.[41]

18. *Judah ben Solomon Nathan* (Maestro Bongodas, En Bongodas, Bongoes). Born in the first fifth of the fourteenth century.

(1) Umaiyya ibn abi'l Salt's Kitab al-adwiyyat al-mufrada (on drugs).

(2) Al-Ghazzali's Maqasid al-falasifa (aims of philosophers).

(3) Ibn Wafid's Kitab al-wisad (Book of pillow), a treatise on simples, as Mera'ashot ha-rosh, completed in 1352.

(4) Arnold of Villanova's De vino, a treatise on wines and their medical uses, translated (abridged) in 1358 as Ha-dibur bi-yenot.
(5) Treatise on fevers, compilation dated 1362. It is divided into 8 sections.[42]

19. *Moses ben Solomon of Beaucaire* (first quarter of fourteenth).
(1) Translated ibn Rushd's tafsir on Aristotle's metaphysics, Sefer mah Sheahar ha-teba.
(2) He wrote a Hebrew summary of ibn Rushd's tafsir or sharh on Aristotle's Physics.[43]

20. *Moses ibn Tibbon,* c. 1240-1283. He was a physician, mathematician, astronomer and translator.
(1) Physica auscultatio. Kitab al-sama al-tabi'i. Ha-shma ha-tib-i. Translated in 1250.
(2) De coelo et mundo, Kitab al-sama wal 'alam. Kelale ha-shemayim weha'olam.
(3) De generatione et corruptione. Kitab al-kawn wal-fasad. Sefer ha-hawayah weha-hefsed. Completed in 1250.
(4) Meteora. Kitab al-athar al'ulwiyat. Sefer 'otot 'elyonot.
(5) De anima. Kitab al-nafs. Kelale sefer ha-nefesh. Completed in 1244.
(6) Idem. Middle commentary completed by ibn Rushd in 1811. Hebrew version, Bi'ur sefer ha-nefesh, 1261.
(7) Parva naturalia. Ha-hush we ha-muhash. 1254.
(8) Metaphysica. Mah she-ahar ha-teba' Synopsis, 1258.
(9) Themistius, translated into Hebrew in 1255.
(10) al-Batalyusi (first half of the twelfth century): Kitab al-hadaiq. Ha 'agullot ha-ra 'yoniyyot. "Comparison of the world with an imaginary sphere."
(11) al-Farabi (first half of the tenth century): Kitab al-mabadi, a philosophical and political treatise translated in 1248 under the title Hathalot ha-namza'ot ha-tib 'iyyim.
(12) Kitab al-siraj, commentary on the Mishnah.
(13) Kitab al-fara'id, Sefer ha-mizwot. Translated very early, c. 1240.
(14) Maqala fi sina'at al-mantiq. Translated in 1254.
(15) Euclid: Elements. Hebrew version called Shorashim or Yesodot, or Uqlides. Translated in 1270.
(16) Geminos. Translated in Naples, 1246. Hokmat ha-kokabim, or Hokmat ha-tekunah.
(17) Theodosios of Bithynia's Spherics, translated into Hebrew in Montpellier, 1271.
(18) Jabir ibn Aflah (first half of the twelfth century): Kitab al-haia or Islah al-majusti. Translated into Hebrew in 1274.
(19) Muhammad al-Hassar. Treatise on arithmetic and algebra, translated into Hebrew, Montpellier, 1271. Sefer ha-heshbon.
(20) al-Bitruji: Kitab al-haia. Translated into Hebrew in 1259, Ma'amar be-tekunah.
(21) Aristotle's Problems. Translated into Hebrew in 1264, She'elot tib 'yot.
(22) ibn Sina (first half of the eleventh century): Canticum. Arjuzat with the ibn Rushd's commentary, 1260.
(23) ibn Sina: Al-qanun al-saghir. Translated in 1272—Ha-seder ha-qaton.
(24) ibn al-Jazzar: Zad al-musafir. Translated in 1259. Zedat ha-derakim.
(25) Hunain ibn Is'haq: Isagoge Johannitii ad tegni Galeni also She'elot.
(26) al-Razi (second half of the ninth century): Kitab al-aqrabadhin. Translated into Hebrew, 1257.
(27) al-Razi: Kitab al-taqism wal-tashjir. Translated into Hebrew in 1283. Ha-hilluq weha-hilluf.
(28) Maqala fi ta'dir al-sihha. Regimen addressed, c. 1198, to al-Malik al-Afdal. Translated in 1244.

(29) al-sumum wal-mutaharriz min al-adwiya al-qitalah. Translation under the title Ha-ma'amar ha-nikbad or Ha-ma'amar beteri 'aq.
(30) Commentary on Hippocrates' Aphorisms. Translated in 1257 or 1267.[44]

21. *Nathan ben Eliezer.* (Translated 1279-1283).
   (1) The Aphorisms of Hippocrates with Galen's commentaries by Hippocrates.
   (2) ibn Sina's Qanun.
   (3) The Muntakhab fi 'ilaj al'ain (a treatise on eye disease).
   (4) Maimonides' Aphorisms.
   (5) A treatise on vivisection by al-Razi, Ma'amar be-haqqazah.
   (6) ibn Zuhr's Kitab al-aghdhiya, Sefer ha-menzonot (on foods).
   (7) Qanun, completed in Rome in 1279.[45]
22. *Qalonymos ben David the Elder* (Qalonymos ben David ben Todros, or ha-Todrosi).
   (1) "Judeo-Provencal translator from Arabic into Hebrew. He flourished at Arles and translated ibn Rushd's treatise against al-Ghazzali, the Tahafut al-tahafut, under the title Happalat ha-happalo. This translation was probably made after 1318 and before 1328."
23. *Qalonymos ben Qalonymos* (born at Arles in 1286 or 1287).
   (1) Criticism of the Tirat kesef of Joseph Kaspi which was composed in 1317 and Qalonymos' criticism at Salon or Arles in 1318.
   (2) Sefer melakim, a treatise of arithmetic, geometry, algebra, and astrology.
   (3) Eben bohan which was first printed at Naples 1489.
   (4) Masseket purim, first edition, Pesaro 1507-1522.
   (5) Archimedes, treatise on the sphere and the cylinder.
   (6) Archimedes (Greek letters).
   (7) Appollonius (extracts from his geometry?).
   (8) Hypsicles, completed at Arles in 1309.
   (9) Nicomachus (Nikomachos) of Gerasa in 1316-1317 (Greek letters).
   (10) Ptolemy: Be 'inyane ha-kokabim ha-nebukim, 1317 (?).
   (11) Pseudo Ptolemy: Translated into Hebrew under the title Sefer ha-peri ha-niqra meah dibburim in 1314.
   (12) Galen: The Hebrew version, Sefer Galinus behaqna ube-gulga was completed in 1308.
   (13) Galen: Be-haqqazah, Arles, 1308.
   (14) Eutocius (Eutokios): Commentary on Archimedes.
   (15) Jabir ibn Haiyan, treatise on poisons translated probably in 1319.
   (16) al-Kindi: Igerret be-qizzur ha-ma'amar be-Moladot, short treatise on nativities. Translation completed in 1314.
   (17) al-Kindi: Iggeret be-illot, etc., in 1314.
   (18) al-Kindi: Iggeret be-lahyit ube-matar, or Iggeret masfiqet, undated.
   (19) Tabit ibn Qurra: Kitab fi shakl al-qat'a which has been translated into Hebrew called Sefer ha-temunah ha-hittukit (Kitab fi Shekl al-Qatta') completed in 1311.
   (20) Hunain ibn Is'haq translated into the Hebrew version, Mabo' ha-gadol le rufu-ah (Kitab al-mudkhal fil tibb).
   (21) al-Farabi translated into the Hebrew version, Ma'amar be-sekel veha-muskal (Kitab fi'l akl wa'l ma'kul) in 1314.
   (22) al-Farabi translated into Hebrew, Ma'amar be mispar ha-hokmot (Kitab ihsa al-ulum) was completed in 1314.
   (23) al-Farabi: Kitab fima yanbaghi an yuqaddama qabla ta'lim al-falsafat. Iggeret be-siddur queri 'at ha-hokmot, (Kitab fi ma yanbagi, etc.) undated.
   (24) Ikhwan al-safa translated into Hebrew, Iggeret ba'ale hayyim in 1316.
   (25) Ali ibn Ridwan translated into Hebrew, sefer ha 'ammud be-shoroshe ha-refuah (Kitab al-umud fi usul al-tibb) in 1307.

(26) ibn al-Samh, translated into Hebrew in 1312, Ma'amar be-iztawwonot ube-hiddudim.
(27) Jabir ibn Aflah: Ha-dibbur be temunah ha-hittukit.
(28) Priora analytica (extracts).
(29) Posteriora analytica (Bi'ur le sefer ha mofet).
(30) Sophistici elenchi. Bi'ur sofistiqi.
(31) Topica. Bi'ur tobiqi translation of the Talkhis, 1313.
(32) Physica. Translation of the Talkhis, Arles, 1316.
(33) Sefer ha-teba translated by Zerahiah Gracian in Rome 1284.
(34) Sefer ha-hawayh weha-hippased, translation of the Talkhis, Arles, 1316.
(35) Meteorologica. Sefer otot ha-shamayim. Translation of the talkhis, Arles, 1316.
(36) Metaphysica. Sefer ma sheahar ha-teba. Translation of the talkhis, 1317-1318.
(37) De plantis. Sefer ha-zamahim.
(38) Abu Sa'dan: Ha-dibbur ha-meshullash, treatise on the triangle, 1311.
(39) Sefer meshalim be-tishboraet translation, completed in 1311.[46]

24. *Salama.*
(1) "Egyptian theologian who was appointed metropolitan of Abyssinia and became the leader of the revival of Aethiopic literature in the first half of the fourteenth century. The Bible had been translated into Aethiopian in the fifth or sixth century. This text, which had gradually become corrupted, was revised by Salama."

25. *Samuel ben Jacob of Capua.*
(1) Treatise on purgatives and emetics written by Masawaih al-Maridini (Mesue junior, first half of the eleventh century).
(2) Canones generales.
(3) Simplicia.[47]

26. *Solomon ben Joseph ibn Ayyub ha-Sefardi.* Born or educated in Granada. (Translated in 1240).
(1) Maimonides: Kitab al-fara'id, Sefer ha-wizwot, the book of divine commandments.
(2) ibn Janah: Kitab al-tanbih (Book of admonitions).
(3) Kitab al-taswiya.
(4) ibn Rushd (1259) (Commentary on Aristotle's De coelo).
(5) ibn Eina: Arjuzat, Sefer ha-arguzah, medical poem (1262).[48]

27. *Samuel ben Judah of Marselle* (also known as Miles Benjudad, Baraveri, Barbavaire), born in 1294.
(1) Plato's Republic, that is, ibn Rushd's commentary on it. ("Translation completed at Arles in 1320 and revised in the prison of Beaucaire in 1321").
(2) Aristotle's Organon. (Translation of ibn Rushd's Jami).
(3) Aristotle's Organon.
(4) Aristotle's Ethics.
(5) Hypsicles, written in 1335.
(6) Ptolemy: ibn Rushd's commentary.
(7) Alexander of Aphrodisias in 1340.
(8) Abu Abdallah Muhammad ibn Mu'adh of Seville. Treatise of the solar system.
(9) al-Zarqali. Treatise on the movement of fixed stars.
(10) Jabit ibn Aflah: Islah al-majisti.[49]

28. *Samuel ben Judah ibn Tibbon.* Born in 1150, died in 1232.
(1) Aristotle: Meteorology by Yahya ibn Batriq.
(2) Ali-ibn Ridwan (first half of the eleventh century): Hebrew version, Melaka Qetana (Commentary on Galen's Tegni).
(3) ibn Rushd: "Three small treatises translated under the title Shaloshah Ma'amarim."

(4) Maimonides: Dalalat al-ha' irin (Guide of the perplexed).
(5) Maimonides: Treatise on resurrection under the title Iggeret, or Ma-'amar tehiyyat ha-metim.
(6) Maimonides: Mishna commentary on Pirqe abot, with psychological introduction called Shemonah peraqim.
(7) Maimonides: Thirteen articles, under the title Shelosh 'esheh 'iqqarim, or Yesodot.
(8) Maimonides: Letter to his disciple, Joseph ibn Aqnin.[50]

29. *Solomon ben Labi.*
(1) He translated the Kitab al-aqidah al-rafiah, a philosophical treatise of Abraham ben David ha-Levi of Toledo.[51]

30. *Solomon ben Pater* (also known as Solomon ben Pater ha-Kohen).
(1) Kitab fi haiat al 'alam (on the form of the universe) of ibn al-Haitham. This is an astronomical treatise.[52]

31. *Samson ben Solomon* (also called *ha-Qazin ben ha-Qazin*).
(1) Translated sixteen books of Galen into Hebrew in 1322.[53]

32. *Samuel ben Solomon ha-Me'ati* also known as Samuel ben Solomon ben Nathan ha-Me'ati.
(1) He completed the translation of Galen's commentary on Hippocrates' regimen in acute diseases, de diaeta acutorum, from the Arabic, Tafsir li-Kitab tadbir al-amradh al-hadda.
(2) He translated also a medical work of ibn Zuhr under the title Menorah ha-refuah (Lamp of Healing).[54]

33. *Samuel ibn Motot.*
(1) The Megillat setarim, a commentary on the Firush ha-Torah of Abraham ben Ezra written about 1380.
(2) Sefer yezirah and other commentaries.
(3) Abdallah ibn Muhammad al-Batalyusi: Kitab al-hadaiq (The orchard).
(4) Abraham ben David ha-Levi: Kitab al-aqidah al-rafiah (The Sublime Faith).
(5) Pseudo Abraham ben Ezra: Sefer ha-ezemim, book of substances.[55]

34. *Shem-tob ben Isaac* also called Babi ha-Tortosi. Translated in 1254-1258.
(1) Kitab al-tasrif by Abu-l-Qasim al-Zahrawi.
(2) Kitab al-Mansuri of al-Razi in 1264.
(3) The Tasrif.
(4) Hippocrates' Aphorisms was translated in 1267.
(5) Translated ibn Rushd's middle commentary on Aristotle's De anima, as Bi'ur sefer ha-nefesh.[56]

35. *Solomon Bonirac,* (also known as Boniac, ben Isaac).
(1) He translated Galen's Kitab fi-l-buhran known as Sefer buhran.[57]

36. *Todros Todrosi* also known as Todros ben Meshullam ben David Todrasi. Born in the beginning of the fourteenth century.
(1) al-Farabi: Kitab uyun al-masa'il including some 60 theses concerning Aristotelianism.
(2) ibn Sina: Kitab al-najat. A summary of Aristotelian philosophy.
(3) ibn Rushd: Translation of the Talkhis on Aristotle's Rhetoric.
(4) ibn Rushd: Translation of the Talkhis on the Poetics.
(5) ibn Rushd: Three dissertations, the first two dealing with ibn Sina's theory of the three modes of being. This was completed in 1340.
(6) ibn Rushd: Fragment of the treatise on the material intellect, translated under the title Ma'amar be-sekel ha-hayulani.[58]

37. *Zerahiah Gracian* also known as Zerahiah ben Isaac ben Shealtiel Gracian; Zerahiah Hen.
(1) He wrote commentaries on Job, on Proverbs (1288) and on Maimonides' Moreh nebukim.
(2) Aristotle's Physics (Sefer ha-teba).

(3) Metaphysics (Mah she-ahar ha-teba').
(4) De coelo et mundo (Ha-shamayim weha olam).
(5) De anima (Sefer ha-nefesh).
(6) Themistius' commentary on the De coelo.
(7) The neo-Platonic treatise De causis (Ha-bi 'ur ha-tob ha-gamur).
(8) al-Farabi's treatise on the nature of the soul.
(9) ibn Rushd's middle commentaries on Aristotle's Physics, Metaphysics, and De coelo.
(10) Galen's De causis et symptomatibus (Sefer he-halo 'im wtha-miqrim).
(11) Three chapters of this De compositione medicamentorum secundum genera.
(12) The first two books of ibn Sina's Qanun.
(13) Treatise on coitus (jima').[59]

—3—

List of Translators of Scientific, Philosophical, Literary, and Other Works From Arabic Into Spanish, and Some Dates of Translation

1. *Abraham of Toledo,* also known as Don Abraham Alfaquin. Translated into Spanish.
   (1) Treatise . . . on the configuration of the universe by ibn al-Haitham.
   (2) "A treatise of al-Zarqali on the construction and the use, chiefly astrological, of his astrolabe. Translated into Spanish in 1255 by Ferrando of Toledo."
   (3) "The seventieth chapter of the Qur'an, Surat al-Muarij. This same chapter was translated in 1264 from Spanish into French by Bonaventura de Sens."[60]
2. *Alfonso X the El Sabio,* also known as Alphonso X the Wise. Died in 1252.
   (1) Ptolemy: Tetrabiblon together with commentary by Ali ibn Ridwan translated into Spanish by an unknown translator.
   (2) al-Battani: Canones, by Isaac ibn Sid.
   (3) ibn abi-l-Rijal: Kitab al-bari fi ahkam al-nujum, an astrological treatise translated by Judah ben Moses in 1256.
   (4) ibn al-Haitham: Fi hai'at al alam. On the configuration of the world, by Abraham of Toledo.
   (5) "A series of astronomical works which were edited together by Alfonso's order in 1276-1277 under the collective title Libros del saber de astronomia. It is composed of eleven parts, of which the first is a sort of astronomical introduction dealing with the stars, and the ten following are devoted to a series of instruments."
   (6) Four books on stars. Derived from the Kitab al-kewakib al-thabit almusawar, by Abd al-Rahman al-Sufi translated in 1256 by Judah ben Moses and Quillen Arremon Daspa. This Spanish text derived from various Arabic sources was edited in 1276.
   (7) Book on celestial globe. Revised translation of the Kitab al-amal bilkura al-fulkiya by Qusta ibn Luqa. Translation completed in 1277.
   (8) "Two books on animals. Essentially derived from al-Zarqali but elaborated by the translator, Isaac ibn Sid."
   (9) Two books on the spherical astrolabe. Composed by Isaac ibn Sid.
   (10) Two books on the plane astrolabe. Source and translator unknown.
   (11) Book of atazir in two parts, composed by Isaac ibn Sid.
   (12) Two books on the universal plate.
   (13) Book of the saiha.
   (14) Two books on the plates of the seven planets (aequatoria). One was written by ibn al-Samh, the other by al-Zarqali at Seville, 1081.

(15) Book on quadrants. Composed by Isaac ibn Sid in 1277.
(16) "Five books on clocks. Four of these books were composed by Isaac ibn Sid and one by Samuel ha-Levi."
(17) Libro de las cruces (book of the crosses). "Elaborate treatise on judicial astrology, divided into 65 chapters."
(18) Libro de las formas et de las imagines que son en los cielos et de las virtudes et de las obras que salen de ellas en los cuerpos que philosopher antiquos. . . D. Alphonos (1276-1279) (an astrological work).[61]

3. *Dinis* (or Diniz), also known as Dionysios, Denis, etc. Born 1261, died 1325.
(1) He ordered the translation of many books from the Spanish, Latin, and Arabic into Portuguese. For example, the Cronica general of his grandfather (Historia geral de Hespanha).[62]

4. *Isaac ibn Sid* (Isaac ha-Hazzan), also called Rabbi Zag or Cag and Aben Cayut. Translated from Arabic into Spanish in Toledo c. 1263-1277.
(1) Canons by al-Battani.
(2) Alphonsine Tables, 1272.
(3) Author of at least nine translations and adaptations included in the libros del saber.
a. Two books on armils.
b. Two books on the spherical astrolabe.
c. Book of atazir.
d. Two books of the universal plate.
e. Book of quadrants, 1277.
f. Book on clocks.[63]

5. *Judah ben Moses.* Died after 1040.
(1) Al-bari fi ahkam al-nujum. Distinguished book on horoscopes from the constellations. This was written by Abu-l-Hasan Ali ibn Ali-I-Riajal al-Saibani al-Katib al-Maghribi. Translated from Arabic into Castilian.[64]

6. *Judah ben Moses ha-Kohen.* (Mosca el menor?) Translated from Arabic into Spanish in 1259.
(1) Treatise on the sphere by Qusta ibn Luqa.
(2) In 1256 the Libro complido was translated into Latin.
(3) ibn abi-l-Rijal. Kitab al-bari, libro complide, astrological treatise translated in 1256.
(4) Lapidary by one Abolays.[65]

7. *Samuel ha-Levi Abulafia.* Translated from Arabic into Spanish.
(1) He translated the anonymous works, fabrica y usos del relogio della condela (construction and use of the candle clock).
(2) The Fabrica y usos del instrumento del leva-mento que en Arabigo se llamaatazin. The translation is also ascribed to Isaac ibn Sid.
(3) In 1276 he helped Judah ben Moses to revise and elaborate the Spanish text of the book of stars of Abd al-Rahman al-Sufi.[66]

—4—

List of Translators of Scientific, Philosophical, and Other Works From Arabic Into Catalan and Translations From Persian Into Greek Including Titles of Works and Dates of Translations

Translations From Arabic Into Catalan

1. *Judah Bonsenyor* also known as Jafuda, Jaffuda Bonsenyor. Died before 1331.
(1) "Translated for Jacme II from the Arabic into Catalan a collection of proverbs entitled Libre de paraules e dits de savis e filosofs. This work was begun before 1298."

(2) Judah's collection was translated from Limousinian (Catalan) into Castilian by Jacob Cadique in Velez 1402 under the title Libro de dichos de sabios e philosophosos (Escorial MS).
(3) Jaume II ordered in 1313 the payment of a thousand solidos to Jahuda for his translation "de arabico in romancio" of a book of medicine called "halchahny."[67]

Translations From Persian Into Greek

1. *Gregorios Chioniades*
   (1) "He was the initiator of that short renaissance of Persian-Byzantine astronomical work which was freely translated from Persian into Greek by an unknown writer. The first date was given as 1323."
   (2) "There are some 16 letters of his (Cod. Vindob. theol. gr. 203) addressed to the emperor Alexios; to Hoannes XIII Glycys, patriarch from 1316 to 1320; and to Constantinos Lucytes (not Lyctes), protonotarios and protovestiarios at the court of Trebizond, and mathematician, who seems later to have inherited his library."
2. *Georgios Choniates*
   (1) Translated a treatise on antidotes from Persian into Greek. Date unknown. This is also the source for Gregorios Chioniades.[68]

NOTES

Consult the *General Bibliography* for full titles of works referred to in the following notes. Titles of Arabic, Persian, French, and German works are in the original language. In the case of Muslim classical and contemporary works, the author's last name, or the name under which the work is written, is used. Roman numerals indicate volumes. Whenever there is possibility of doubt or confusion as to the source, a fuller description is given.

Introductory Note

[1]Sarton, George, *Introduction to the History of Science*, 3 vols., Baltimore: The Williams and Wilkins Co., 1927-1948, Vol. I, pp. 16-18. Published for the Carnegie Institute of Washington, D.C.

[2]Arberry, A. J. (ed.), *The Legacy of Persia*, Oxford: Oxford University Press, 1952, Chapter 11.

Elgood, C., *History of Persian Medicine*, Elgood, C., *A Medical History of Persia and the Eastern Caliphate*, Cambridge (Eng.): The University Press, 1951, Oxford: Clarendon Press, 1931, pp. 377-378.

[3]Arnold, Sir Thomas Walker, and Guillaume, Alfred (eds.), *The Legacy of Islam* (Legacy Series. Oxford: Clarendon Press, 1931), pp. 377-378.

Chapter I

[1]Von Greenbaum, Gustave E., *Medieval Islam*, Chicago: University of Chicago Press, Third Impression, 1957, p. 43.

[2]*Ibid.*, pp. 44-45.

[3]*Ibid.*, p. 45.

[4]*Ibid.*, p. 47.

[5]*Ibid.*, p. 48

[6]Butts, *A Cultural History of Western Education*, pp. 76-79.

[7]The word "holy" (sacrum) was added officially in 1155 by Frederick Barbarossa.

[8]Durant, Will, *The Age of Faith*, pp. 528-529.

[9]*Ibid.*, p. 528.

[10]*Ibid.*, pp. 116-119.

[11]Hitti, Philip I., *History of the Arabs*, 3rd Edition, London: Macmillan & Co., 1946, Chapters X, XI, XII, XIII, XIV.

[12]*Ibid.*, pp. 606-614.

[13]*Ibid.*, pp. 508-511; Brockelman, pp. 181-221; Von Greenbaum, Chapter II.

[14]Reynold, *Europe Emerges.*

[15]Khadduri, Majid, *The Law of War and Peace in Islam*, London: Luzac and Co., 1941.

[16]Hitti, Philip K., *History of the Arabs,* Chapters X through XIV.
[17]Von Greenbaum, Gustave E., *Medieval Islam,* Chapter 1.
[18]Reynold, *Europe Emerges,* p. 299.

CHAPTER II

[1]Arnold and Guillaume, *The Legacy of Islam,* pp. 239-240.
[2]Wells, H. G., *Outline of History,* 1931, pp. 629-630.
[3]*Ibid.,* p. 629.
[4]Barsuma was a pupil of Ibas, the great teacher of the School of Edessa. Died 457.
[5]O'Leary, *Arabic Thought and Its Place in History,* p. 34.
[6]*Ibid.,* p. 34.
[7]al-Nadim, *Fihrist,* pp. 333-334.
Masudi, *Murawinij-u'Zhahab of Masudi,* p. 210.
Safa, *Tarikh Ulum Aqli,* pp. 94-95.
[8]*Ibid.,* p. 95.
[9]Christensen, Arthur, *L'Iran Sous les Sassanides,* p. 427.
[10]Safa, *Tarikh Ulum Aqli,* pp. 96-98.
[11]*Ibid.,* p. 98, using authority of *Mojmal-ut-Tavarikh,* p. 256; and Estakhri's *Masalik-ul-Mamalik,* p. 93.
[12]*Ibid.,* pp. 98-99.
[13]*Ibid.,* p. 93.
[14]Ghafti, *Akhbar-al-Hokama,* or *Annals of Learned Men,* p. 93. Translated from Persian as quoted by Safa, p. 99.
[15]Browne, *Arabic Medicine,* p. 23; Sarton, Vol. 1, pp. 435-436; Sykes, Sir Percy, *History of Persia,* Vol. I, 1915, pp. 40-41; Durant, pp. 246-258.
[16]Hitti, *History of the Arabs,* p. 309.
[17]O'Leary, *Arabic Thought,* pp. 41-42.
[18]Edessa was the intellectual headquarters of Christian-Syrian and Harran of non-Christian-Syrian, Sabians, or Sabi'uns.
[19]Safa, *Tarikh Ulum Aqli,* p. 103; Safa, *Hellenic Learning (Sciences) Among Sassanians,* pp. 27-28. In Persian.
[20]Heath, Th. L., *The Thirteen Books of Euclid's Elements,* Vol. III, Cambridge: 1908. Cited by Sarton, Vol. I, p. 421.
[21]Sarton, *Introduction to the History of Science,* Vol. I., p. 423. According to Sarton, "The Berlin edition of *Greek Commentaries of Aristotle* includes the following by Simplicios: In Vol. 2 *de anima,* edited by Nich Hayduck (375 pp., 1882); Vol. 7, *de Coelo,* edited J. L. Heibert (796 pp., 1895); Vol. 8, *Categories* edited Carl Kalbfleisch (1907); Vol. 9-10 *Physicorum libri* edited Hermann Diels (2 vols., 1,500 pp. 1882-1895)." Sarton, Vol. I, p. 423.
[22]*Ibid.,* Vol. I., p. 372; Browne, E. G., *Arabic Medicine,* p. 20.
[23]*Ibid.,* p. 23; Sykes, M., *History of Persia,* Vol. I, pp. 40-41. Browne, E. G., *A Literary History of Persia,* Vol. I, p. 4.
[24]Hitti, *History of the Arabs,* pp. 308-309.
[25]Arnold and Guillaume, *Legacy of Islam,* pp. 315-319.
[26]al-Nadim, *Fihrist,* pp. 333-334; Masudi, *Murawwij-ul-Thabab,* Cairo: p. 210.
[27]Safa, *Tarikh Adabiyyat,* p. 95.
[28]*Ibid.,* pp. 96-97.
[29]*Ibid.,* p. 97.
[30]Safa, *Tarikh Ulum Aqli,* pp. 52-56.
[31]*Ibid.,* pp. 61-62.
[32]Sarton, *An Introduction to the History of Science,* Vol. I, p. 565.
[33]Safa, *Tarikh Ulum Aqli,* pp. 56-58.
[34]*Ibid.,* pp. 58-59.

[35]*Ibid.*, pp. 87-88.
[36]*Ibid.*, p. 63.
[37]Sarton, Vol. I, p. 530.
[38]*Ibid.*, p. 613.
[39]Safa, *Tarikh Ulum Aqli,* p. 60.
[40]Sarton, Vol. I, p. 556.
[41]Safa, *Tarikh Ulum Aqli,* p. 62.
[42]*Ibid.*, pp. 63-71.
[43]*Ibid.*, pp. 71-73.
[44]*Ibid.*, pp. 73-74.
[45]Sarton, Vol. I, p. 613.
[46]Safa, *Tarikh Ulum Aqli,* pp. 75-79.
[47]Sarton, Vol. I, pp. 599-600.
[48]Safa, *Tarikh Adabiyyat,* pp. 108-114.
[49]Safa, *Tarikh Ulum Aqli,* p. 85.
[50]*Ibid.*, p. 60.
[51]*Ibid.*, p. 63.
[52]Sarton, Vol. I, pp. 562, 598, 600, 613; Vol. II, Book III, p. 686; Safa, *Tarikh Ulum Aqli,* pp. 79, 86.
[53]Safa, *Tarikh Ulum Aqli,* pp. 89-91.
[54]Inostrazen, *Iranian Influence on Muslim Literature,* Russian, translated by G. K. Nariman. Inostrazen's own sources of information have been chiefly the *Fihrist* of al-Nadim; *Ibid.*, pp. 54-61; Saba, Dr. Zabeh-al-lah, *History of Intellectual Sciences in Muslim Civilization to the Middle of Fifth Century Hejira* (about 1050 A.D.). (*Tarikhi Ulumi Aqli Dar Tamadduni-Islami*). University of Teheran Press, No. 157, Teheran (1329-1331), Vol. I, Appendix One, "Existing Works of Translators," pp. 328-372; Nadim, *Fihrist,* p. 410. Translation is mine.
[55]Safa, *Tarikh Ulum Aqli,* p. 333.
[56]*Ibid.*, p. 333.
[57]*Ibid.*, p. 333.
[58]*Ibid.*, p. 334, citing A. G. Ellis, *Catalogue of Arabic Books in the British Museum,* Vol. I, London: 1894, p. 662.
[59]*Ibid.*, p. 334.
[60]*Ibid.*, p. 334, citing *Aya-Sufiyya Catalogue,* p. 217; *British Museum Index,* p. 646.
[61]*Ibid.*, p. 334.
[62]*Ibid.*, p. 334.
[63]*Ibid.*, p. 335.
[64]Safa, citing Berlin, p. 495; Paris, p. 513; British, p. 643.
[65]Safa, p. 335.
[66]*Ibid.*, p. 335.
[67]*Ibid.*, p. 335.
[68]*Ibid.*, p. 335.
[69]*Ibid.*, p. 336.
[70]*Ibid.*, p. 336.
[71]*Ibid.*, p. 336, citing *Index of Madjlis Library,* II, 305-306; *Index of Paris,* p. 515; No. 214, *Aya-Sufiyya.*
[72]*Ibid.*, p. 336.
[73]*Ibid.*, p. 336-337.
[74]*Ibid.*, p. 337.
[75]*Ibid.*, p. 337.
[76]*Ibid.*, p. 337.
[77]*Ibid.*, p. 337.
[78]*Ibid.*, p. 337.
[79]*Ibid.*, p. 337.
[80]*Ibid.*, p. 338.

[81]*Ibid.*, p. 338.
[82]*Ibid.*, p. 338.
[83]*Ibid.*, p. 338.
[84]*Ibid.*, p. 339.
[85]*Ibid.*, p. 339.
[86]*Ibid.*, p. 339.
[87]*Ibid.*, p. 339.
[88]*Ibid.*, p. 339.
[89]*Ibid.*, p. 339.
[90]*Ibid.*, p. 339.
[91]*Ibid.*, p. 339.
[92]*Ibid.*, p. 340.
[93]*Ibid.*, p. 340.
[94]*Ibid.*, p. 340.

[95]*Ibid.*, pp. 62-119 and 328-372. The author refers to Muslim and European libraries, private or public, where these works are catalogued. These libraries include: (1) The Library of St. Joseph College in Beirut; (2) The Public Library in Paris; (3) Library of the British Museum; (4) The Cambridge University Library; (5) Eskrial Library; (6) S'ad Effandi Library (in Constantinople); (7) Library of Ahmadiyya School (in Musel); (8) Aya-Sufiyya Library; (9) Meshed Library (in Iran); (10) Madjlis Library (The Parliament Library in Teheran); (11) Berlin Library; (12) Kaditbuyya Library (in Egypt. There is also in the T. VIII, Session 1925-1926 of the *Bulletin of the Egyptian Institute* a list of 2,500 ancient literary and scientific manuscripts in Arabic and Syriac languages); (13) Fatheliyya Library; (14) The Library of the Association of the Ottoman Ministry of Education; (15) Baukipur Library.

[96]Browne, Vol. I, p. 384. The *Al-Fihrist* is edited by Flugel in 1871-72, based on two Paris MSS, and a Leyden MS containing mainly discourses VII-X.

[97]Browne, Vol. I, pp. 383-384.

[98]i.e., the Qur'an, whence (xli, 42) this phrase is taken.

[99]Browne, Vol. I, pp. 384-387; Nadim, *Fihrist,* Introduction, no page. And pages 3-5.

Chapter III

[1]Zaidan, *Islamic Civilization, Al-Tamaddun Al-Islami,* Vol. III, pp. 195-196; Totah, pp. 18-19.

[2]al-Subhi, Vol. III, p. 135 (in Totah, C.A.E., p. 20).

[3]*Ibid.*, Vol. III, p. 135 (in Totah, p. 24).

[4]*Ibid.*, p. 21 (Quoting Zaidan, *Tarikh Al-Tamaddin Al-Islami,* Vol. III, p. 195).

[5]ibn Khaldun, Vol. I, p. 382.

[6]C.A.E., p. 31.

[7]"Education and Philosophy," *The Year Book of Education,* World Book Company, 1957. Section I, Chapter Four, "Islam," by Sabba D. Djemal and George J. Tomeh, p. 69; Also read Section I, Chapter Five, "Philosophy of Muslim Education" by A. L. Tibawi; and Section II, Chapter Two, "Islamic Schools and Universities," A. Kh. Imami.

[8]Wilds, E. H., *The Foundations of Modern Education,* Rinehart & co., 1959, p. 216.

[9]al-Qhani, VII, pp. 31-38. *Legacy of Islam,* p. 358. Shalaby, pp. 193-201.

[10]Khaldun, ibn, *Moghaddimah,* p. 398; al-Baladhuri, p. 147; Hitti, *The History of the Arabs;* ibn Battuta, *Tuhfat-ul-Nazzar,* Vol. I, p. 213; Shalaby, *History of Muslim Education,* pp. 16-23.

[11]al-Isfahani, *Muhaddarat al-Udaba;* Shalaby, *History of Muslim Education,* pp. 23-26; Khaldun, Ibn, *Mugaddimah,* pp. 399-400; Yaqut, *Mu'jam el Udaba.*

[12]Yaqut, *Mu'jam al-Udaba* II, p. 234; Shalaby, p. 50.

[13]Sources cited by Shalaby: al-Iqd-al-Farid, Vol. IV, pp. 101 and 108; Nafh al-Teb, Vol. II, 1128; al-Khitat, Vol. I, pp. 385-386.

Al-Jahiz, *al-Taj fi Akhlaq al-Muluk,* 21, 119-130, 49-50.

[14]Shalaby, 32-40.

[15]Khuda Bukhsh, *Islamic Civilization,* 258. Quoted in Shalaby, 55.

[16]Murla'd-Din ruled from 541 to 569 A. D. in Syria.

[17]Shalaby, 59-63.

[18]*Ibid.,* 65-67.

[19]Yaqut, *Dictionary of Learned Men,* Vol. V, p. 231. Vol. VI, p. 343.

[20]Le Strange, O., *Bagdad During the Abbasid Caliphate,* Oxford, 1900, 240-266.

[21]Makkari, *History of the Muhammadan Dynasties in Spain,* trans. by de Cayangos, London, 1840, 2 v., VII, pp. 139-200.

[22]Shalaby, 217.

[23]*Al Lu'lu Al-Nazim fi Rawm al-Ta' Allum Wal-Ta'lim,* referred to in *Ahlwardt Verzerchmiss der Arabischen Haudschriften,* Vol. I, p. 28c. See Totah, p. 56.

[24]Browne, Vol. I, 377-390.

[25]Elgood, Cyril, *A Medical History of Persia,* Cambridge University Press, 1951, 234-235.

[26]*Ibid.,* 236.

[27]*Ibid.,* 240.

[28]*Ibid.,* 244.

[29]Hunayn, "The Examination of the Doctors" in *Mu'Allem al-Kubra* (*The Great Teacher*) by ibn al-Ukhawwa. Chapter 45. Geble Memorial Edition, cited in Elgood, *Medical History of Persia.*

[30]Elgood, Cyril, *A Medical History of Persia,* 234-260.

Browne, G. E., *Arabic Medicine.*

[31]al-Jahiz, *Al-Bayan Wa'l Tabyan,* I, 140-144.

al-Isfahani, *Muhadarat al-Udaba,* I, 30-31.

ibn Howghal, *Kitab Surat al-Arth,* I, 126.

Yaqut, *Mu'jam al-Udaba,* V. 636-697, cited in Shalaby, 120-123.

[32]Shalaby, 153-155.

[33]al-Makkari, Vol. II, 49.

[34]Zarnuji, *Ta'lim al-Muta'allim* (*Instruction of the Pupil*), 13-15.

Ghazzali, *Ih'ya Ulum al-Din'* (*Revivification of the Sciences of Religion*), Vol. I, 47.

[35]al-Zarnuji, 41-43.

[36]Browne, G. E., *Persian Literature in Modern Times,* 361-367.

[37]Haskins, *Medieval Science.*

Coulton, G. C., *Medieval Panorama.* Cambridge University Press, 1940.

CHAPTER IV

[1]Quoted in Shalaby, 75.

[2]In al-Hayanan, I, 50-51. Quoted in Shalaby, p. 75.

[3]In al-Musayarat. Quoted in Shalaby, p. 76.

[4]*Islamic Culture,* III, 1929, 227. Quoted in Shalaby, p. 79.

[5]*Ahsan al-Taqasim fi Ma'rifat al-Aqalim* by al-Maqdisi, I, 408.

[6]Yaqut, *Mu'jam al-Udaba,* II, 315.

[7]al-Maqrizi, *Al-Khitab* I. *The History of Islamic Civilization.*

[8]Thompson, James W., editor, *The Medieval Library.* Hafner Publishing Co., 1957, 352-353.

Nicholson, op. cit., 265-266.

[9]S. Khuda Bukhsh, "The Renaissance of Islam," *Islamic Culture,* IV, 1930, 295.

[10]S. Khuda Bukhsh, 297.
[11]Pinto, op. cit., 215.
[12]Yakut, *Geography,* IV, 509-519.
[13]*Ibid.,* 509-579.
[14]From al-Maqrizi, in Thompson, p. 357, who quotes from Pinto, op. cit., 227-228.
[15]*Ibid.,* 357.
[16]*Ibid.,* 360.
[17]Quoted by Thompson from Americo Castro, *Lingua ensenanza y Literatura.* Madrid, 1924, 135.
[18]Quoted by Thompson from ibn-al-Abar, quoted by al-Makkari, *The History of Mohammedan Dynasties in Spain,* tr. by P. de Gayangos, London, 1843, II, 170.
[19]ibn-al-Abar, quoted in al-Makkari, 168-169.
[20]Thompson, 351.
[21]*Ibid.,* 352-353.
[22]*Ibid.,* 353.
[23]*Ibid.,* 353.
Bukhsh, op. cit., 132, quoted above.
[24]*Ibid.,* 353.
[25]*Ibid.,* 354. Also Von Kremer, op. cit., II, 483-484.
Grohmann, op. cit., 436-437.
Pinto, op. cit., 228, quoted above.
[26]*Ibid.,* 356.
Grohmann, op. cit., 432. Quoted above.
[27]*Ibid.,* 358.
Poole, 193.
[28]*Ibid.,* 359.
[29]Adler, E. N. and Broyde, I., *An Ancient Booksellers' Catalogue,* F. Q. R., XIII (1901), 52-62, 550-551. Quoted in Thompson, page 342, footnote.
[30]*Ibid.,* 360.
[31]Thompson, 342-343.
[32]*Ibid.,* 343.
[33]*Ibid.,* 352.
[34]Browne, E. G., *Literary History of Persia.* London, 1909, II, 107.
[35]*Ibid.,* II. 12.
[36]*Ibid.,* 357.
[37]Poole, op. cit., 149.
[38]*Ibid.,* 358-359.
[39]*Ibid.,* 368.

Chapter V

[1]Badwi, 26.
[2]*Ibid.,* 88-104.
[3]*Shah-Namah,* Brukheim, p. 1994, referred to in Badwi, pp. 233-240.
[4]Badwi, 240-241.
[5]*Ibid.,* 245.
[6]*Ibid.,* 4, 84-88, 257.
[7]*Ibid.,* Preface, p. 12.
[8]Other ancient Greeks mentioned in the anecdotes are Pythagoras, Plato, Aristotle, Hippocrates, and Galen.
[9]The historical information of *Ghabus-Namah* and its author is based primarily on the work of Badwi, Amin, Abdul-Majir; *A Discourse on Bhabus Namah* and the *Text of Ghabus Namah;* the ibn Sina Book Store, publishers, 1956, Teheran, Iran. In Persian. The work is a doctoral thesis by Badwi completed at

the University of Teheran and is to my knowledge the most recent research on the history and contents of this Persian educational and moral classic; Other sources include the following: (1) Browne, Vol. II, pp. 276-288; Querry (translation) Paris, 1886; *Kitab 'i Amsal'u-Hikam*, or *The Book of Proverbs and Maxims* (4 volumes) by Ali Akbar Deh-Khod'a, The Madjlis (Parliament) Press, Teheran, 1310; *Tarikh'i Ad-a-biya't'i-Iran*, Or *History of Persian Literature* by Reza Zadeh Shafaq (2 volumes) Teheran.

[10]*Siyasat Namah*, int. by Chahardahi, p. 7.

[11]*Ibid.*, pp. 8-10; Safa, *History of Intellectual Sciences*, p. 136.

[12]Shafaq, p. 235.

[13]The oldest Muslim "university," founded in Egypt about a century before the age of Nizam-al-Mulk, i.e., al-Sunki, Vol. III, p. 135; Totah, p. 20.

[14]Early eleventh century A. D. in Egypt.

[15]Early eleventh century A. D. in Egypt.

[16]In Baghdad.

[17]Totah, 21.

[18]*Ibid.*, 24; ibn Khalliphan, Vol. I, 382.

[19]al-Subki, *Tabazhat al Shafi-Iyyah*, Vol. III, 135.

[20]The Takhallos, or poetic pen name, is ordinarily introduced by Persian poets in the Shah-Bayt (king-stanza), or the last stanza of their odes and occasionally other poems. It identifies the poem with its author and serves as a copyright, a practice which Emerson considers worthy of universal adoption. James Ross (*Gulistan*, pp. 3-4) reminds us in his essay on Sa'di of the imitation of this practice by a few Anglo-Saxon poets, among them Cowley:

> The wise example of the heavenly lark,
> Thy fellow-poet, Cowley, mark,
> Above the clouds let thy proud music sound,
> Thy humble nest build on the ground.

[21]In *Tazkartosh-Shoara*, or *Biography of Poets*.

[22]In *Nafhatol-uns*, or *Memoirs of Poets*.

[23]*Gulistan*, 2:21.

[24]*Gulistan*, 10-11. Translated by James Ross.

[25]*Bustan*, 5:2; 6:16. *Gulistan*, 3:28.

[26]*Gulistan*, "On Limitations of Education."

[27]*Ibid.*

[28]*Ibid.*

[29]*Gulistan*, "The Quarrel of Sa'di with Pretender."

[30]There are good translations of the *Gulistan* in Arabic, French, and German. Refer to: *Sa'di, Aphorismen und Sinngedichte* (*Sahibiyyah*), Strassburg, 1879; E. G. Browne, *Literary History of Persia*, pp. 525-539; also translations of parts of Sa'di's works into French by Defrémery (1858) and into German by Graf (1846).

[31]Shafaq, Vol. II, 248-263. Also *The Complete Works of Sa'di. Gulistan*, and *Bustan* (All in Persian).

[32]Browne, Vol. II, 293.

[33]A portion of this work is translated by al-Ghazzali in Persian entitled *Kimiya'ya Sa'adat, The Chemistry of Happiness.* Also in *Arab Fi'd-Din, Education in Religion*, al-Ghazzali sets 75 rules and precepts for the improvement of education and for the conduct of life. Five chapters of this book are devoted exclusively to problems and procedures in education.

[34]Totah, 63. In his *Kimiya' ya Sa'a'dat*, Tusi, Ministry of Education Press, Teheran, 1319 H. "The first aim of education is to protect the child from association with base company," p. 52.

[35]Totah, 64. Compare with *Akhlaghi Naseri* or the *Ethics of Naseri* by Nasir-ud-Din. Al-Ghazzali says, "The eyes of children are focused upon their teachers' behavior and their ears are ever open to the teachers' manner of speech. Whatever the teacher considers good and admirable is in turn considered admirable and good

by the pupil and is emulated by him; whatever the teacher condemns is likewise condemned by the student."

[36]*Fatihatu'l-Ulum,* Husainiyyah Press, Cairo, 1822 (?) H. Chapter 2.

[37]Cairo, 1910.

[38]From *Three Thousand Years of Educational Wisdom.* Selections from "Great Documents." Edited and commented upon by Robert Ulich, Harvard University Press, Cambridge, Massachusetts, 1959, pp. 193-198.

[39]al-Ghazzali, *Al-Ihya'ud-Din,* III, 57.

[40]al-I'hya', 47.

[41]Tusi, *Akhlaghi-Naseri,* 10-12.

[42]Translated by Schefer, Paris, 1881. In Browne, Vol. II, 220-221.

[43]Translated by Ethe in the A. D. M. G., 1879-1880. See Browne, Vol. II, 221.

[44]Published by Fagman in Z. D. M. G.

[45]A diwan is a complete collection of a given poet's verses arranged in alphabetical order according to the final letters of the rhyming words (see *Farhang* of Sulaiman Haim, Vol. I, 891).

[46]Browne, Vol. II, 224-232.

[47]Safa, *Tarikh Ulum Aqli*, p. 200.

[48]Taharat, 118-120.

[49]*Ibid.*, 21-23.

[50]*Ibid.*, 23-24.

[51]*Ibid.*, 24-25.

[52]*Ibid.*, 25-27.

[53]*Ibid.*, 27-28.

[54]*Ibid.*, 28-30.

[55]*Ibid.*, 30-31.

[56]*Ibid.*, 31-35.

[57]*Ibid.*, 35-38.

[58]*Ibid.*, 43-45.

[59]*Ibid.*, 40-42.

[60]*Ibid.*, 43-45.

[61]*Ibid.*, 46-61.

[62]*Ibid.*, 62-106.

[63]*Ibid.*, pp. 107-110.

[64]*Ibid.*, pp. 110-121.

[65]*Ibid.*, pp. 122-131.

[66]*Ibid.*, pp. 140-141.

[67]*Ibid.*, pp. 142-144.

[68]*Ibid.*, pp. 144-151.

[69]*Ibid.*, pp. 152-154.

[70]*Ibid.*, pp. 154-163.

[71]*Ibid.*, pp. 163-164.

[72]*Ibid.*, pp. 165-196.

[73]*Ibid.*, pp. 196-245.

[74]*Ibid.*, pp. 245-301.

[75]*Ibid.*, pp. 301-318.

[76]*Ibid.*, pp. 318-362.

[77]Browne, Vol. II, pp. 512-515.

[78]Shafaq, Vol. II, pp. 121-134.

[79]Friedrich Dieterici, *Seventeen Monographs on Moslem Philosophy in the 9th and 10th Centuries,* Berlin, 1858-1895, referred to by Browne, Vol. I, p. 379.

[80]Sources for the *Rasa'il*: Browne, Vol. I, pp. 378-380.

[81]Sources for *Mafatihu'l-Ulum*: Browne, Vol. I, pp. 378, 382-383; Vol. II, pp. 6-7; Totah, p. 72. See also al-Muqhtataf, Vol. XVII, p. 367, 1920; Sarton, Vol. II, Part II, p. 628.

[82]Ahlwardt, Vol. III, p. 155; Totah, p. 75; Browne, Vol. II, p. 289; *Catalogue*

des Manuscripts Arabes, Biblioteque Nationale, Paris, p. 730, No. 4595. "Regele de Conguite pour les eleve" in Totah, p. 62.

[83]Brockelman, Vol. 11, p. 133. Also French translation of the work of Sauvaire. *Le Journal Asiatique,* 9 serie, Vol. III and IV, (1894), referred to in Totah, p. 73.

[84]Pahlavi, educational work.

[85]Reza Shafaq, Vol. II, pp. 36, 53, 138, 232, 236-237, 243.

[86]Yaqut, *Dictionary of Learned Men,* Vol. VI, 76 ed. Margoliuth, Cairo, 1907, 6 vols.; al-Hajiz, *Al-Bayan Wa't-Tibyan,* Vol. I, p. 139, Cairo; Totah, footnote, p. 67; Browne, Vol. I, p. 354; II, p. 101.

[87]Shafaq, p. 334; Sarton, Vol. II, Part II, pp. 632-633. See Lithographic Teheran Editions, 2 vols., 1898-1899.

[88]Totah, p. 73.

[89]Sarton, Vol. II, Part II, pp. 630-631.

[90]Browne, Vol. II, pp. 506-515.

[91]*Ibid.,* pp. 496-497.

[92]al-Muqhtataf, Vol. LVII, p. 366; Haji Khalifa, Vol. III, p. 522, cited in Totah, page 68 edited by Flugel, 7 volumes, Leipzig, 1835-1858.

[93]Shafaq, pp. 289-299.

[94]Browne, Vol. II, pp. 330-333; Hajji Khalifa, Vol. I, p. 183; Ahlwardt, Vol. I, p. 53; Totah, p. 72.

[95]Browne, Vol. II, pp. 491-494.

[96]Totah, p. 7.

[97]Totah, pp. 60-65, 70-71.

CHAPTER VII

[1]Safa, *Tarikh Ulum Aqli,* pp. 33-34.

[2]*Kashfuth-Thonoon,* Vol. I, p. 446; Safa, *Tarikh Ulum Aqli,* pp. 33-34; Ghafti, *Akhbar-ul-Hokama, Chronicles of Wise Men,* Cairo, p. 233.

[3]Nadim, *Fihrist,* p. 430.

[4]Safa, *Tarikh Ulum Aqli,* pp. 42-50.

[5]Sarton, pp. 520-542.

[6]Harun-al-Rashid: Born 742, died 814. He too, like Harun, was a great patron of education and organized new schools under Alcuin. "He ordered the execution of great public works, introduced a new system of weights and measures, a new calendar, reformed the coinage," and advanced agriculture.

Important Muslim figures during the first half of the eighth century include Abu Hanifa (Nu'man ibn Thabit) 699-768, the grandchild of a Persian slave, and the founder of the Muslim Hanifite School, the earliest organized Muslim faction.

Imam Ja'far al-Sadiq, 699-765, the teacher of Jabir-ibn Hayyan (not verified). His full name is Abu Abd'ul'lah Ja'far al-Sadiq ibn Muhammad al-Baqir ibn Ali Zain al-Abedin ibn al-Husain ibn Ali ibn Ali Talih.

Hajjaj ibn Yusuf (Abu Muhammad), died 714. A grammarian, soldier, and governor of Iraq under Abd al-Malik.

[7]Born in Rayy, 763 or 766, and died in 809 in Tus. He was the fifth Abbasside monarch, and one of the greatest Muslim patrons of learning. He remained caliph from 786 to 809.

[8]The Hindu *Siddhantas* date back to the first half of the fifth century. They are mathematical works founded on Greek mathematics and astronomy with original ideas such as the nature of the sine. There are five *Siddhantas – Surya, Paitamah, Vasishtha, Paulisa, Romaka.* Sarton, 378, 386-387.

[9]The name means "Whatever God Wishes" (Arabic).

[10]The name means "New Fortune" (Persian).

[11]"He tried to improve the Ptolemaic theory of planetary motions by the addi-

tion of a ninth sphere to account for the imaginary trepidation of the equinoxes." Sarton, Vol. I, 585.

[12]Sarton, Vol. I, 587.

[13]Durant, 288-289.

[14]Sarton, Vol. I, 654.

[15]Nadim, ibn, *Fihrist*, 368.

Safa, *Tarikh Ulum Aqli,* 179-198, 373-375.

[16]Sarton, Vol. I, 621.

[17]O'Leary, Delacy, *Arabic Thought and Its Place in History,* London, 1929, 153.

[18]Sarton, Vol. I, 648.

[19]Tabari, *Chronique,* French translation by Zotenberg, Paris, 1867, i,I, cited in Durant, *Age of Faith,* page 238.

[20]Biruni, *Chronology of Ancient Nations,* translated by Sachau, London, 1879.

[21]Boer, T. J. De, *History of Philosophy in Islam,* London, 1903.

[22]Durant, 243.

[23]Sarton, Vol. I, 646-692.

Chapter VIII

[1]Arnold and Guillaume, *The Legacy of Islam,* 395-397; Arberry, *Legacy of Persia,* 306.

[2]Browne, E. G., *A Literary History of Persia,* Vol. I, 275-278.

[3]Arberry, *Legacy of Persia,* 297.

[4]Muhammad B. Musa — not to be confused with the Persian mathematician Abu Abd Allah Muhammad al-Khwarizmi, the author of the *Keys of the Sciences.*

[5]Arnold and Guillaume, *Legacy of Islam,* 581-585.

[6]Browne, E. G.

[7]Sarton, Vol. I, 759-761; Arberry, *The Legacy of Persia,* 300.

[8]Arberry, *Legacy of Persia,* 300.

[9]*Ibid.,* 305.

[10]*Ibid.,* 301.

[11]*Ibid.,* 303.

[12]*Ibid.,* 304.

[13]Arnold and Guillaume, *Legacy of Islam,* 322.

[14]*Ibid.,* p. 323.

[15]One of the best English sources on Razi's life and works is "The Life and Works of Rhazes," pp. 237-269, in *Transactions of the Seventeenth Congress of Medicine.*

[16]Arnold and Guillaume, *Legacy of Islam,* p. 325.

[17]*Ibid.,* pp. 329-330.

[18]*Ibid.,* p. 332.

[19]*Ibid.,* p. 257.

[20]Sykes, *History of Persia,* Vol. II, p. 133.

[21]Arnold and Guillaume, *Legacy of Islam,* pp. 257, 329.

[22]*Ibid.,* p. 331.

[23]An extra one is ms.

[24]*Ibid.,* 86-87.

[25]*Ibid.,* p. 87.

[26]*Ibid.,* p. 87.

[27]Browne, Vol. I, pp. 218-245.

[28]Arnold and Guillaume, *Legacy of Islam,* pp. 341-342.

[29]*Ibid.,* p. 345.

[30]I.I.M.L., p. 142.

[31]*Ibid.,* p. 142.

[32]Sarton, Vol. II, Book I, p. 10.

[33]*Ibid.,* p. 12.

[34]*Ibid.,* pp. 13-14.

[35]Kennedy, E. S., *A survey of Islamic Astronomical Tables,* The American Philosophical Society, 1956, pp. 124-137.

[36]Sarton, Vol. II, Book I, p. 22.

[37]*Ibid.,* p. 26.

[38]*Ibid.,* p. 26.

[39]*Ibid.,* pp. 67-68.

Chapter IX

[1]The Sanskrit original is lost.

[2]French translation by Sprenger, London, 1841, IV, p. 89.

[3]The poet's millennial anniversary was celebrated in 1934.

[4]Bodleian Library at Oxford.

[5]Nicholson, R. A., *Studies in Islamic Poetry,* England, Cambridge University Press, 1921, pp. 4-5; Weir, T. H., *Omar Khayyam the Poet,* 1926, p. 21.

[6]S.V.ABI, p. 5.

[7]Arberry, *Legacy of Persia,* p. 310.

[8]*Ibid.,* p. 311.

[9]Landau, p. 42.

[10]*Ibid.,* p. 42.

[11]*Ibid.,* p. 47.

[12]*Ibid.,* Chapter 13.

[13]*Legacy of Islam,* pp. 367-372.

[14]Thompson, J. W., *The Introduction of Arabic Science into Lorrain in the Tenth Century,* Isis, XII, 1929, pp. 184-194.

[15]*Ibid.,* p. 367.

[16]*Ibid.,* p. 367.

[17]*Ibid.,* p. 364; Hoskins, p. 52.

[18]Durant, p. 912.

[19]*Legacy of Islam,* pp. 4-11. Also, for inflow of Arabic words and phrases into Spanish language see pp. 19-27.

[20]*Ibid.,* p. 32.

[21]*Ibid.,* p. 32.

[22]*Ibid.,* p. 31. The prose of Infanti Don Juan Manuel (1282-1349?), and the poetry of Archpriest of Hita (died before 1351) show clear evidences of influences of Spanish translations of Eastern fables translated from Arabic. *Legacy,* pp. 35-37. On a detailed study of the influences of Muslim literature (mainly Persian and Arabic) in Sicily, Italy, Spain, and the rest of Europe before and after the Renaissance, read H. A. R. Gibb, "Literature" in *Legacy,* pp. 180-209. The period discussed in this article covers also the centuries following the thirteenth, which are not the concern of this study.

[23]The reprints of Baytar's *Simplicia* in 1758 and Mechither's work on medicine in 1832.

Appendix V

[1]Sarton, Vol. II, Book I, pp. 167-169.

[2]*Ibid.,* Vol. II, Book III, p. 561.

[3]*Ibid.,* Vol. II, Book IV, pp. 831-832.

[4]*Ibid.,* Vol. II, Book IV, p. 831.

[5]*Ibid.,* Vol. II, Book IV, pp. 833-834.

[6]*Ibid.,* Vol. II, Book II, Part I, pp. 338-344.

[7]*Ibid.,* Vol. II, Book IV.

[8]*Ibid.,* Vol. II, Book IV, pp. 832-833.

[9]*Ibid.,* Vol. II, Book I, pp. 173-174.

[10]*Ibid.,* Vol. II, Book I, pp. 174-175.

[11]*Ibid.,* Vol. II, Book I, pp. 170-171.

[12]*Ibid.*, Vol. II, Book III, p. 344.
[13]*Ibid.*, Vol. II, Book III, pp. 579-581.
[14]*Ibid.*, Vol. II, Book I, pp. 161-169.
[15]*Ibid.*, Vol. II, Book III, p. 562.
[16]*Ibid.*, Vol. II, Book I, pp. 177-179.
[17]*Ibid.*, Vol. II, Book III, p. 563.
[18]*Ibid.*, Vol. II, Book I, p. 177.
[19]*Ibid.*, Vol. II, Book I, pp. 175-177.
[20]*Ibid.*, Vol. II, Book III, p. 562.
[21]*Ibid.*, Vol. II, Book I, pp. 236-237.
[22]*Ibid.*, Vol. III, Part I, pp. 426-427.
[23]*Ibid.*, Vol. II, Book III, p. 562.
[24]*Ibid.*, Vol. II, Book III, pp. 648-649.
[25]*Ibid.*, Vol. II, Book III, p. 563.
[26]*Ibid.*, Vol. II, Book I, pp. 206-208.
[27]*Ibid.*, Vol. II, Book I, pp. 187-189.
[28]*Ibid.*, Vol. II, Book III, p. 555.
[29]*Ibid.*, Vol. II, Book III, pp. 563-564.
[30]*Ibid.*, Vol. II, Book IV, p. 588.
[31]*Ibid.*, Vol. III, Part II, pp. 1373-1377.
[32]*Ibid.*, Vol. III, Part I, pp. 436-437.
[33]*Ibid.*, Vol. II, Book III, pp. 565-566.
[34]*Ibid.*, Vol. II, Book IV, p. 853.
[35]*Ibid.*, Vol. III, Part II, pp. 1373-1377.
[36]*Ibid.*, Vol. II, Book II, pp. 344-345.
[37]*Ibid.*, Vol. III, Part II, pp. 1373-1377.
[38]*Ibid.*, Vol. II, Book IV, pp. 850-853.
[39]*Ibid.*, Vol. II, Book II, pp. 345-346.
[40]*Ibid.*, Vol. II, Book III, pp. 604-605.
[41]*Ibid.*, Vol. III, Part II, pp. 1373-1377.
[42]*Ibid.*, Vol. III, Part II, pp. 1373-1377.
[43]*Ibid.*, Vol. III, Part II, pp. 428-429.
[44]*Ibid.*, Vol. II, Book IV, pp. 847-850.
[45]*Ibid.*, Vol. II, Book IV, pp. 853-854.
[46]*Ibid.*, Vol. III, Part I, pp. 429-433.
[47]*Ibid.*, Vol. I, p. 728.
[48]*Ibid.*, Vol. II, Book IV, p. 485.
[49]*Ibid.*, Vol. III, Part I, pp. 435-436.
[50]*Ibid.*, Vol. II, Book III, pp. 564-566.
[51]*Ibid.*, Vol. III, Part I, pp. 426-438.
[52]*Ibid.*, Vol. III, Part I, pp. 436-437.
[53]*Ibid.*, Vol. III, Part I, pp. 428-429.
[54]*Ibid.*, Vol. III, Part I, pp. 436-437.
[55]*Ibid.*, Vol. III, Part II, pp. 1373-1377.
[56]*Ibid.*, Vol. II, Book IV, pp. 845-846.
[57]*Ibid.*, Vol. III, Part I, pp. 435-436.
[58]*Ibid.*, Vol. III, Part I, pp. 435-436.
[59]*Ibid.*, Vol. II, Book IV, pp. 846-847.
[60]*Ibid.*, Vol. II, Book IV, p. 844.
[61]*Ibid.*, Vol. II, Book IV, pp. 834-842.
[62]*Ibid.*, Vol. II, Book IV, pp. 844-845.
[63]*Ibid.*, Vol. II, Book IV, pp. 843-844.
[64]*Ibid.*, Vol. II, Book IV, pp. 715-716.
[65]*Ibid.*, Vol. II, Book IV, pp. 842-843.
[66]*Ibid.*, Vol. II, Book IV, p. 843.
[67]*Ibid.*, Vol. III, Part I, pp. 427-428.
[68]*Ibid.*, Vol. III, Part I, pp. 426-438.

GENERAL BIBLIOGRAPHY ON MUSLIM CULTURE BY TOPIC

The following topical bibliography has been selected, adapted, and alphabetized from *Index Islamicus 1906-1955,* compiled by J. D. Pearson. W. Heffer & Sons Limited, Cambridge, England (1958), and *Index Islamicus Supplement 1956-60,* compiled by J. D. Pearson. W. Heffer & Sons Limited, Cambridge, England (1962).

List of Contents

Glossary of Abbreviations

Act. Or. Hung.	Acta Orientalia (Academia Scientiarum Hungarica)
AI	Ather-e Iran
AJSL	American Journal of Semitic Languages and Literatures
BFA	Bulletin of the Faculty of Arts
Bull. J.R. Lib.	Bulletin of John Rylands Library
BM Qly	British Museum Quarterly
BSOAS	Bulletin of the School of Oriental and African Studies
Eg. Contemp.	L'Egypte Contemporaine
IC	Islamic Culture
IQ	Islamic Quarterly
JAOS	Journal of the American Oriental Society
JASB	Journal and Proceedings of the Asiatic Society of Bengal
JBBRAS	Journal of the Bombay Branch of the Royal Asiatic Society

JIH	Journal of Indian History
JQR	Jewish Quarterly Review
JRAS	Journal of the Royal Asiatic Society
MEA	Middle Eastern Affairs
MW	Muslim World
QJMS	Quarterly Journal of the Mythic Society
RSO	Rivista Degli Studi Orientali
SO	Studia Orientalia
WZKM	Wiener Zeitschrift fur die Kundi des Morgenlandes

I. Periodicals Dealing with Various Aspects of Muslim Culture

Figures in Arabic numerals represent volume numbers, those in Roman represent parts. The sign (//) means that the periodical is apparently dead.

Africa (Journal of the International Institute of African Languages and Culture), 1 (1928) - 30 (1960)

Allahabad University Studies, 1 (1925) - 34 (1953) Continued as University of Allahabad Studies (1954-58)

Annals of the Bhanarkar Oriental Research Institute, 1 (1918-19) - 40 (1959)

Annals of Medical History, 1 (April 1917) - 10; N. S. 1-10; 3sl-4 (Nov. 1942) //

Annals of Oriental Research, University of Madras, 1 (1935-37) - 16i (1959-60)

Arabica, 1 (1954) - 7 (1960)

Athar'e-Iran, 1 (1936) - 4 (1949)

Bulletin of the American Institute for Persian (Iranian) Art and Archaeology, 1 (1931) - 5iv (1938) //

Bulletin of the Faculty of Arts, Cairo University, 1 (1933) - 19i (1957), (5 Pt. II not published. European section only)

Bulletin Des Etudes Arabes, 2 (1942) - 12 (1952) //

Bulletin D'etudes Orientales, 1 (1931) - 15 (1955-7)

Bulletin of the Institute of Historical Research, 1 (1923) - 33 (1960)

Bulletin of the Institute of History of Medicine, 1 (1933) - 6 (1938); continued as Bulletin of the History of Medicine, 7 (1939) - 34 (1960)

Bulletin of the International Committee of Historical Sciences, 1 (1926) - 12 (1943) //

Bulletin of the School of Oriental and African Studies, 1 (1917) - 23 (1960)

East and West, 1 (1950-51) - 11 (1960)

Harvard Journal of Asiatic Studies, 1 (1936) - 21 (1958)

History of Education Journal, 1 (1949) - 10 (1958-9)

Indian Historical Quarterly, 1 (1925) - 36i (1960)

Indo-Asian Culture, 1 (1952-53) - 9ii (1960)

Indo-Iranica, 1 (1946-47) - 13 (1960)

International Social Science Bulletin, (1949) - 12 (1960)

Islamic Culture, 1 (1927) - 34 (1960)

Islamic Quarterly, 1 (1954) - 5 (1959-60)

Islamica, 1 (1924) - 7ii (1938) //

Journal Asiatique, 10 ser., 7 (1906) - 248ii (1960)

Journal of the American Oriental Society, 27 (1906) - 80 (1960)

Journal of the History of Ideas, 1 (1940) - 21 (1960)

Journal of the History of Medicine and Allied Sciences, 1 (1946) - 15 (1960)

Journal of the Middle East Society, 1 (1946-47) //

Journal of Near Eastern Studies, (formerly American Journal of Semitic Languages and Literatures), 15 (1956) - 19 (1960)

Journal of the Oriental Institute, Baroda, 1 (1951) - 10ii (1960)

Journal of Oriental Studies (Hong Kong), 1 (1954) - 4 (1957-58)
Journal of the Royal Anthropological Institute, 36 (1906) - 90 (1960)
Journal of the Royal Asiatic Society, (1906 - 1960) and Centenary suppl., (1924)
Medieval Studies, 1 (1939) - 22 (1960)
Middle East Journal, 1 (1947) - 14 (1960)
Moslem World; Continued as Muslim World, 1 (1911) - 50 (1960)
New Scholasticism, 1 (1927) - 34 (1960)
Philosophical Quarterly (St. Andrews), 1 (1950) - 10 (1960)
Philosophical Review, 15 (1906) - 69 (1960)
Proceedings of the Indian Historical Records Commission, 2 (1920) - 35 (1960)
Proceedings of the Iran Society; continued as Journal of the Iran Society, 1 (1936-38) - 3 (1947-48) - I1-iv (1950-54)
Studia Islamica, 1 (1953) - 13 (1960)
Studia Orientalia, 1 (1925) - (1960)

II. General Works on Islamic Culture

Amin Jung Bahadur, Nawab Sir Ahmed Hussain, What Is Culture in General and Islamic Culture in Particular? *IC* 17 (1943), pp. 15-24.

Bausani, A., Notes on the History of Arabic and Islamic Studies in Italy During the Middle Ages. *J. Pakistan Hist. Soc.* 3 (1955), pp. 174-185.

Buchthal, H., "Hellenistic" Miniatures in Early Islamic Manuscripts. *AI* 7 (1940), pp. 125-133.

Fulton, A. S., Arabic Medieval Manuscripts. *BM Qly* 11 (1937), pp. 81-83.

Gairdner, W. H. T., The Study of Islamics at Cairo. *MW* 12 (1922), pp. 390-393.

Greenslade, W. G., Roman Catholic Literature in Arabic on Islam. (Publications of the Jesuit Press in Beirut) *MW* 16.

Grunebaum, G. E., Islam in a Humanistic Education, *J. Gen. Educ.* 4 (1949), pp. 12-31.

Hitti, P. K., Arabic and Islamic Studies in Princeton University. *MW* 31 (1941), pp. 292-294.

Ivanow, W., A Notice on the Library Attached to the Shrine of Imam Riza at Mesched. *JRAS*, (1920), pp. 535-563; Errata, *JRAS*, (1921), pp. 248-250, 480.

Mackensen, R. S., Arabic Books and Libraries in the Umaiyad Period. *AJSL* 52 (1935-36), pp. 245-253; 53 (1936-37), pp. 239-250; 54 (1937), pp. 41-61; Supplementary Notes, 56 (1939), pp. 149-157.

Mackensen, R. S., Background of the History of Moslem libraries. *AJSL* 51 (1934-35), pp. 114-125; 52 (1935-36), pp. 22-33, 104-110.

Morgenstern, J., American Culture and Oriental Studies. *JAOS* 48 (1928), pp. 97-108.

Ogilvie, C. L., A Classified Bibliography of Books on Islam in Chinese and Chinese-Arabic. *MW* 8 (1918), pp. 74-78.

Oglu (1896-1949), Selected Bibliography. *AI* 15-16 (1951), pp. 267-271.

Pinto, O., The Libraries of the Arabs During the Time of the Abbasides. *IC* 3 (1929), pp. 210-243.

Social Science Periodicals Dealing with the Middle East. *Int. Soc. Sci. Bull.* 5 (1933), pp. 762-765. Social Science Periodicals Published in the Middle East. *Int. Soc. Sci. Bull.* 5 (1953), pp. 752-762. See also 3977, 9039, 10233, in Pearson's *Index Islamicus.*

Speiser, F. A., Near Eastern Studies in America, 1939-1945. *Arch. Or.* 16 (1948), pp. 76-88.

Torrey, C. C., The Outlook for American Oriental Studies. *JAOS* 38 (1918), pp. 107-120.

Witzmann, K., The Greek Sources of Islamic Scientific Illustrations. *Archaeol. Orient. in Memoriam E. Herzfeld,* (1952), pp. 244-266.

Zwemer, S. M., A Working Library on Islam. *MW* 2 (1912), pp. 32-36.

III. Collective and Commemorative Works on Islamic Culture

Avicenna: Scientist and Philosopher. A Millenary Symposium, ed. by G. M. Wickens, London, 1952.

A volume of Indian and Iranian Studies Presented to Sir E. Denison Ross on his 68th birthday, 6th June 1939. Ed. by S. M. Katre and P. K. Gode. (New Indian Antiquary, extra series, 2) Bombay, 1939.

A Volume of Oriental Studies Presented to Edward G. Browne on his 60th birthday (7 February, 1922), ed. by T. W. Arnold and R. A. Nicholson. Cambridge, 1922.

Semitic and Oriental Studies. A volume presented to William Popper on the occasion of his 75th birthday, October 29, 1949. Ed. by W. J. Fischel. Berkeley, 1951.

Islamic Research Association Miscellany. (Isl. Res. Assoc. Ser., 11.) Vol. 1, 1948. London, 1949.

Orientalia Neerlandica. A volume of Oriental studies published under the auspices of the Netherlands' Oriental Society (Oostersch Genootschap in Nederland) on the occasion of the 25th anniversary of its foundation (May 8th, 1945). Leiden, 1948.

Prof. Jackson Memorial Volume. Papers on Iranian subjects written by several scholars in honour of the late Prof. A. V. Williams Jackson. Bombay, 1954.

Roger Bacon: Essays contributed by various writers on the occasion of the commemoration of his birth. Collected and edited by A. G. Little, Oxford, 1914.

Studies in the History of Science, (Univ. of Pennsylvania Bicentennial Conference.) Philadelphia, 1941.

The Jews, Their History, Culture and Religion, ed. L. Finkelstein. 2 vols. New York, 1949.

IV. Education in Medieval Islam

Dar, Muhammad Ibrahim, Al-Ghazzali on the Problem of Education. *Shafi Press.* Vol. 1 (1955), pp. 33-50.

Fox, A. E., Islam and Modern Education, *MW* 23 (1933), pp. 29-37.

Hamidullah, M., Educational System in the Times of the Prophet. *IC* 13 (1939), pp. 48-59.

Jaffar, S. M., Islamic Education. *Shafi Press.* Vol. (1955), pp. 119-129.

Khuda Bakhsh, The Educational System of the Muslims in the Middle Ages. *IC* 1 (1927), pp. 442-472.

Mu'id Khan, M. A., The Muslim Theories of Education During the Middle Ages. *IC* 18 (1944), pp. 418-433.

Pedersen, J., Some Aspects of the History of the Madrasa. *IC* 3 (1929), pp. 525-537.

Pickthall, M., Muslim Education. *IC* 1 (1927), pp. 100-108.

Putney, E. S., Moslem Philosophy of Education. *MW* 6 (1916), pp. 189-194.

Renner, G. T., Arab Education in the Near East. *MEA* 1 (1950), pp. 215-224.

Sayili, Aydin, Higher Education in Medieval Islam. The Madrasa. *Ann. Univ. Ankara* 2 (1947-48), pp. 30-69.

Sayyidain, Kh. Ghulam., Iqbal's Educational Philosophy. *IC* 12 (1938), pp. 33-40, 334-351.

Tawfiq, M. A., A Sketch of the Idea of Education in Islam. *IC* 17 (1943), pp. 317-327.

Tibawi, Abdul-Latif, The Idea of Guidance in Islam from an Educational Point of View. *Islamic Qly* 3 (1956), pp. 139-156.

Tibawi, A. L., Muslim Education in the Golden Age of the Caliphates. *IC* 28 (1954), pp. 418-438.

Tibawi, A. L., Philosophy of Muslim Education. *IQ* 4 (1957), pp. 78-89.

Tibawi, Abdul-Latif, Some Educational Terms in Rasa'il Ihwan as-safa', *24 Int. Cong. Or.*, (1957), pp. 297-299. Also in *Islamic Q* 5. (1959), pp. 55-60.

Titus, M. T., A Study in Moslem Religious Education. *MW* 26 (1936), pp. 385-388.

Tritton, A. S., Arab Theories of Education. *JIH* 3 iii and 4 i (1925), pp. 35-41.

Tritton, A. S., Muslim Education in the Middle Ages (Circa 600-800 A. H.). *MW* 43 (1953), pp. 82-94.

V. History

Adolf, H., Christendom and Islam in the Middle Ages: New Light on "Grail Stone" and "Hidden Host." *Speculum* 32 (1957), pp. 103-115.

Ahmad, Fazal, The Islamic Interpretation of History. *Proc. Pakistan Hist. Conf.* 2 (1952), pp. 79-86.

Alam, Manzoor, Ibn Khaldun's Concept of the Origin, Growth, and Decay of Cities. *IC* 34 (1960), pp. 90-106.

Burns, R. I., Journey from Islam: Incipient Cultural Transition in the Conquered Kingdom of Valencia (1240-1280). *Speculum* 35 (1960), pp. 337-356.

Bury, W., Islam and Civilization. *MW* 3 (1913), pp. 140-146.

Chopra, Hira Lall, Indo-Iranian Relations Through the Ages. *Bull. Ramakrishna Mission Inst. Cult.* 10 (1959), pp. 212-215.

Darbishire, R. S., The Philosophical Rapprochement of Christendom and Islam in Accordance with Ibn Khaldun's Scientific Criticism of What Is Strange. *MW* 30 (1940), pp. 226-235.

Datta, K. K., A Brief Review of Works of Indian Scholars on the Medieval and Modern Periods of Indian History. *J. World Hist.* 6 (1960), pp. 380-402.

Dupree, L., Medieval European Feudalism and the Contemporary Middle East: a Clarification of Terms. *Report on Current Research*, (1957), pp. 47-55.

Fischel, W., Ibn Khaldun's Contribution to Comparative Religions. *24 Int. Cong. Or.*, (1957), pp. 334-335.

Fischel, W. J., Ibn Khaldun and Josippon. *Homenaje a Millas-Vallicrosa* I (1954), pp. 587-598.

Fyzee, A. A. A., Islamic Culture. J. K. R. *Cama Or. Inst.* 37 (1944), pp. 1-40.

Gibb, H. A. R., The Islamic Background of Ibn Khaldun's Political Theory. *BSOAS* 7 (1933-35), pp. 23-31.

Grunebaum, G. E. von., The Problem of Cultural Influence. *Charisteria Orientalia J. Rypka*, (1956), pp. 86-99.

Grunebaum, G. E. von., Toynbee's Concept of Islamic Civilization. *WZKM* 56 (1960), pp. 68-77.

Hamidullah, M., Islamic Culture as a Factor in World Civilization. *Sir W. Jones Bicentenary Commen.* Vol. (1948), pp. 124-132.

Husian, Mahdi, Cultural Aspect of Indo-Iranian Contacts. *Indo-Iranica* 9iv (1956), pp. 58-70.

Issawi, C., The Arabs and Islamic Civilization. *MW* 38 (1948), pp. 172-184.

Kabir, Mafizullah, Cultural Development under the Buwayhids of Baghdad. *J. Asiat. Soc. Pakistan* I (1956), pp. 25-45.

Khuda Bukhsh, Ibn Khaldun and His History of Islamic Civilization. *IC* I (1927), pp. 567-607.

Lewis, B., The Muslim Discovery of Europe. *BSOAS* 20 (1957), pp. 409-416.

Mirzoev, A. M., About the Author of the Shahanshah Nama. *24 Int. Cong. Or.* (1957), pp. 449-456.

Nashat, M. A., Ibn Khaldoun Pioneer Economist. *Eg. Contemp.* 35 (1944), pp. 377-490.

O'Leary, De L., The Sources of Arabic Culture. *JIH* 3iii and 4i (1925), pp. 23-34.

Prakash, Buddha, Ibn Khaldun's Philosophy of History. *IC* 28 (1954), pp. 492-508; 29 (1955), pp. 104-119, 184-190, 225-236.

Raad, Saeed, Islamic Contribution to the Study and Writing of History. *Proc. Pakistan Hist. Conf.* 2 (1952), pp. 53-59.

Rao, M. V. Krishna, Persia and India. *Studies in Education and Culture. In Honour of D. C. Pavate,* (1959), pp. 279-292.

Rosenthal, F. I. J., Ibn Khaldun: A North African Muslim Thinker of the Fourteenth Century. *Bull. J. R. Lib.* 24 (1940), pp. 307-320.

Saarisalo, A., Arabic Tradition and Topographical Research. *SO* 17iii (1952), 24 pp.

Saeed Sheikh, M., Ibn Khaldun. *Iqbal* 9 (1960), pp. 14-22.

Schmidt, N., Ibn Khaldun and His Prolegomena. *MW* 22 (1932), pp. 61-63.

Schmidt, N., The Manuscripts of Ibn Khaldun. *JAOS* 46 (1926), pp. 171-176.

Schoy, C., The Geography of the Moslems of the Middle Ages. *Geog. Rev.* 14 (1924), pp. 257-269.

Siddiqi, M. Z., The Criticism of Historical Reports Among the Muslims. *B. C. Law Vol. I.* (1945), pp. 695-700.

Spuler, B., Historiography in Muslim Persia. *J. Pakistan Hist. Soc.* 6 (1958), pp. 215-223.

Spuler, B., Iran: The Persistent Heritage. *Unity and Diversity in Muslim Civilization,* (1955), pp. 176-182.

White, H. V., Ibn Khaldun in World Philosophy of History. (Review Article) *Comp. Stud. Soc. Hist.* 2 (1959), pp. 110-125.

Zeki Validi, Ahmet, Islam and the Science of Geography. *IC* 8 (1934), pp. 511-527.

VI. Literature

Carelli, M., Persian Sidelights on Dante. *Indo-Iranica* 41v (1950-1951), pp. 23-28.

Goldziher, I., Arabic Literature in Western Islam. Trans. and enlarged by J. Somogyi. *IC* 32 (1958), pp. 135-152.

Grunebaum, G. E. von, Greek Form Elements in the Arabian Nights. *JAOS* 62 (1942), pp. 277-292.

Horovitz, J., The Origins of "The Arabian Nights." *IC* 1 (1927), pp. 36-57.

Inayatollat St., Dante and Islam. *IC* 12 (1938), pp. 461-465.

McDonald, D. B., The Earlier History of the Arabian Nights. *JRAS,* (1924), pp. 353-397.

VII. Medicine

Dunlop, D. M., Arabic Medicine in England. *J. Hist. Med.* II (1956), pp. 166-182.

Frame, J. D., Medicine in Persia. *MW* 6 (1916), pp. 415-418.

Galdston, I., Medical Explorers of Arabia. *Bull. of the New York Academy of Medicine* 13 (1937), pp. 512-538.

Gordon, B. L., Arabian Medicine in the Post-Koranic Period. *J. Mich. Med. Soc.* 55 (1956), pp. 1109-1116.

Gordon, B. L., Medicine in the Koran. *J. Med. Soc. N. J.* 52 (1955), pp. 513-518.

Haskins, C. H., The Reception of Arabic Science in England. *Engl. Hist. Rev.* 30 (1915), pp. 56-69.

Herrmann, E. T., Early Arabian Medicine. *Bull. Med. Libr. Assn. N.S.* 25 (1936-37), pp. 113-117.

Holmyard, E. J., Mediaeval Arabic Pharmacology. *Proc. Roy. Soc. Med.* 299 (1935-36), *Sec. Hist. Med.*, pp. 1-10.

Khairallah, A. A., Arabic Contributions to Anatomy and Surgery. *Annals of Medical History* 3rd ser., 4 (1942), pp. 409-415.

Khairallah, Amin A., and Hadded, Sami I., A Forgotten Chapter in the History of the Circulation of the Blood. *Annals of Surgery* 104 (1936), pp. 1-8.

Khairallah, A. A., Medicine's Debt to Syria. *Annals of Medical History* 3rd ser., 3 (1941), pp. 140-147.

Lichtwardt, H. A., Ancient Therapy in Persia and in England. Being Extracts from "Therapeutics of Joseph," Herat, 1511 A. D. and from John Wesley's "Primitive Physick," London, 1772. *Annals of Medical History N.S.* 6 (1934), pp. 280-284.

Meyerhof, M., An Early Mention of Sleeping-Sickness in Arabic Literature. *Proc. Roy. Soc. Med.* 30 (1937), pp. 670-671 (*Sect. Hist. Med.*), pp. 18-19.

Sa'di, Lutfi M., Glimpses into the History of Arabic Medicine. *Bull. Med. Libr. Assoc.* 46 (1958), pp. 206-218.

Saddiqi, M. Z., Indian Medical Science Among the Ancient Arabs. *Indo-Asian Culture* 5 (1957), pp. 374-386.

Wakim, Khalil G., Arabic Medicine in Literature. *Bull. Med. Libr. Assn. N.S.* 32 (1944), pp. 96-104.

Walsh, J. J., The Medical History of Two Crusades. *Contributions to Medical and Biological Research Dedicated to Sir W. Osler II*, (1919), pp. 796-805.

VIII. Music and Musical Instruments

Farmer, H. G., Byzantine Musical Instruments in the Ninth Century. *JRAS* (1925), pp. 299-304.

Farmer, H. G., Clues for the Arabian Influences on European Musical Theory. *JRAS*, (1925), pp. 61-80.

Farmer, H. G., A Further Arabic-Latin Writing on Music. *JRAS*, (1933), pp. 307-322.

Farmer, H. G., The Evolution of the Tanbur or Pandore. Trans. *Glasgow Or. Soc.* 5 (1923-28), pp. 26-28.

Farmer, H. G., Greek Theorists of Music in Arabic Translation. *Isis* 13 (1929-30), pp. 325-333.

Farmer, H. G., The Influence of Al-Farabi's "Ihsa' al-'Ulum" (De Scientiis) on the Writers of Music in Western Europe. *JRAS*, (1932), pp. 561-592.

Farmer, H. G., The Jewish Debt to Arabic Writers on Music. *IC* 15 (1941), pp. 59-63.

Farmer, H. G., The Lute Scale of Avicenna. *JRAS*, (1937), pp. 245-257.

Farmer, H. G., Maimonides on Listening to Music. *JRAS*, (1933), pp. 867-884.

Farmer, H. G., The Minstrels of the Golden Age of Islam. *IC* 17 (1943), pp. 273-281; 18 (1944), pp. 53-61.

Farmer, H. G., The Old Persian Musical Modes. *JRAS*, (1926), pp. 93-95.

Farmer, H. G., Oriental Influences on Occidental Military Music. *IC* 15 (1941), pp. 235-242.

Farmer, H. G., The Origin of the Arabian Lute and Rebec. *JRAS* (1930), pp. 767-783.

Farmer, H. G., The Science of Music in the Mafatih al-'ulum. *Glasgow Univ. Or. Soc.* Trans. 17 (1957-8), pp. 1-9.

Farmer, H. G., The Structure of the Arabian and Persian Lute in the Middle Ages. *JRAS*, (1939), pp. 41-51.

Gairdner, W. H. T., The Source and Character of Oriental Music. *MW* 6 (1916), pp. 346-356.

Imamuddin, S. M., Music in Muslim Spain. *IC* 33 (1959), pp. 147-150.

Sain, Kanwar, An Old Manuscript on Iranian Music. *Indo-Iranica* 8111 (1955), pp. 29-36.

Sykes, P. M., Notes on Musical Instruments in Khorasan, with Special Reference to the Gypsies. *Man* 9 (1909), pp. 161-164.

Worrell, W. H., Notes on the Arabic Names of Certain Musical Instruments. *JAOS*, 68 (1948), pp. 66-68.

IX. Philosophy

Abdul Hamid, Khwaja, Origin of Speculative Thought in Islam. *IC* 24 (1950), pp. 187-196.

Affifi, A. E., The Influence of Hermetic Literature on Moslem Thought. *BSOAS* 13 (1951), pp. 840-855.

Anisuddin, Ahmed, Rationalism in Islam. *13th All-India Or. Conf.*, (1946), Islamic Sec., pp. 1-5.

Ansari, M. Z. A., Anti-Aristotelian Thinkers of Islam. *Allahabad Univ. Studies* 12 (1936), pp. 85-116.

Calverley, E. E., A Brief Bibliography of Arabic Philosophy. *MW* 32 (1942), pp. 60-68.

Hourani, G. F., The Dialogue Between Al-Gazali and the Philosophers on the Origin of the World. Part II. *MW* 48 (1958), pp. 308-314.

Hourani, G. F., Ibn-Rushd's Defense of Philosophy. *The World of Islam. Studies in Honour of P. K. Hitti,* (1959), pp. 145-158.

Hourani, G. F., Two Theories of Value in Medieval Islam. *MW* 50 (1960), pp. 269-278.

Masumi, M. Saghir Hasan al-., Ibn Bajjah on Human End. *J. Asiat. Soc. Pakistan* 2 (1957), pp. 181-196.

Nadvi, Mawlana Saiyid Sylaiman, Muslim and Greek Schools of Philosophy. *IC* 1 (1927), pp. 85-91.

O'Leary, De L., The Influence of Galen on Arabic Philosophy. *JIH* 2, (1922-23), pp. 233-238.

O'Shaughnessy, T., St. Thomas and Avicenna on the Nature of the One. *Gregoriamun* 41 (1960), pp. 665-679.

Pandey, S. L., A Comparative Study of Indian and Persian Philosophy. *IC* 33 (1959), pp. 81-87.

Sadiq, 'Isa, Avicenna on Education. *Indo-Iranica* 9 iv (1956), pp. 71-77.

Shaikh, M. Saeed, Philosophy of the Ikhwan-us-safa. *Iqbal* 6 iii (1958), pp. 19-27.

Sharif, M. M., Muslim Philosophy and Western Thought. *Iqbal* 8 (1959), pp. 1-14.

Walzer, R., The Rise of Islamic Philosophy. *Oriens* 3 (1950), pp. 1-19.

Walzer, R., A Survey of Work on Medieval Philosophy, (1945-52), Part 1: Medieval Islamic Philosophy. (Philosophical Surveys, 8.) *Philos. Qly* 3 (1953), pp. 175-181.

Young, T. Cuyler, The Interaction of Islamic and Western Thought in Iran. *Near Eastern Culture and Society.* ed. T. Cuyler Young, (1951), pp. 130-147.

X. Religion and Sufism

Braumann, M. M., On the Spiritual Background of Early Islam and the History of Its Principal Concepts. *Museon* 64 (1951), pp. 317-365.

Darbishire, R. S., The Christian Idea of Islam in the Middle Ages, According to the "Chanson d'Antioch." *MW* 28 (1938), pp. 114-124.

Davis, G., Sufism: From Its Origins to Al-Ghazzali. *MW* 38 (1948), pp. 241-256.

Elder, E. E., The Conception of Universality in Early Islam. *MW* 17 (1927), pp. 11-30.

Foster, F. G., Is Islam a Christian Heresy? *MW* 22 (1932), pp. 126-133.

Hayes, H. E. E., Sufism in the West. *MW* 7 (1917), pp. 29-35.

Housseini, A. M. A. el-, The Origin of Early Islamic Mysticism. *J. Univ. Peshawar* 2 (1953), pp. 63-74.

Jeffery, A., Eclecticism in Islam. *MW* 12 (1922), pp. 230-247.

Macdonald, D. B., The Unity of the Mystical Experience in Islam and Christendom. *MW* 25 (1935), pp. 325-335.

Muhammad Ali, Universality of Islam. *IC* 2 (1928), pp. 445-452.

Pickthall, M., Islamic Culture. *IC* 1 (1927), pp. 151-163, 259-318.

Robson, J., "Islam" as a Term. *MW* 44 (1954), pp. 101-109.

Shushterry, M. A., History of Sufism. *Proc. 2nd All-India Conf.*, (1922), pp. 583-599.

Soorma, C. A., Islam and Intellectual Freedom. *MW* 24 (1934), pp. 26-32.

Sweetman, J. W., Sufism and Christian Teaching. *MW* 25 (1935), pp. 156-160.

Syrier, Miya, Ibn Khaldun and Islamic Mysticism. *IC* 21 (1947), pp. 264-302.

Watt, W. M., Ideal Factors in the Origin of Islam. *IQ* 2 (1955), pp. 160-174.

Wilson, C. E., The Common Ideals of Sufi and Western Poetry. *Islamica* 1 (1925), pp. 109-111.

Zaki, Ali, The Evolution of Islam. *IC* 11 (1937), pp. 433-443.

Zwemer, S. M., Islam: A Sevenfold Problem. *MW* 28 (1938), pp. 217-222.

Zwemer, S. M., Islam — Its Wroth and Its Failure. *MW* 19 (1920), pp. 144-156.

XI. Science and Mathematics

A. *Astronomy*

Ahmad, Nafis, Muslim Contributions to Astronomical and Mathematical Geography. *IC* 18 (1944), pp. 167-186.

Amir 'Ali, Sayid, of Lucknow, Modern Astronomy and Islam. *IC* 2 (1928), pp. 237-259.

Johnson, M. C., Manuscripts of the Bagdad Astronomers, 769-1000 A. D. *The Observatory,* 59 (1936), pp. 215-226.

Kennedy, E. S., The Sasanian Astronomical Handbook *Zij-i Shah* and the astrological doctrine of "transit" (Mamarr). *JOAS* 78 (1958), pp. 246-262.

Kennedy, E. S., Parallax Theory in Islamic Astronomy. *Isis* 47 (1956), pp. 33-53.

Kennedy, E. S., A Survey of Islamic Astronomical Tables. *Trans. Amer. Philos. Soc.* N.S. 46 (1956), pp. 123-127.

Khan, Mohammad Abdul Rahman, Muslim Contribution to Meteoric Astronomy. *IC* 20 (1946), pp. 353-361.

Nadvi, Sayyid Sulaiman, Muslim Observatories. *IC* 20 (1946), pp. 267-281.

B. *Biology*

Basu, K. K., Study of Zoology and Veterinary Science in Medieval India. *Proc. 8th Ind. Hist. Cong.*, (1945), pp. 126-129.

Glidden, H. W., The Lemon in Asia and Europe. *JAOS* 57 (1937), pp. 381-396.

Glidden, H. W., Some Supplementary Arabic Literature on the Lemon. *JAOS* 60 (1940), pp. 97-99.

Maswani, Aijaz Muhammad Khan, Islam's Contribution to Zoology and Natural History. *IC* 12 (1938), pp. 328-333.

C. *Chemistry*

Holmyard, E. J., A Critical Examination of Berthelot's Work Upon Arabic Chemistry. *Isis* 6 (1924), pp. 479-499; Letter, 7 (1925), p. 493.

Holmyard, E. J., Arabic Chemistry. *Nature* 109 (1922), pp. 778-779.

Holmyard, E. J., Chemistry in Islam. *Scientia* 40 (1926), pp. 289-296.

D. General Science

1. GENERAL

Bammate, N., The Status of Science and Technique in Islamic Civilization. *Philosophy East and West* 9 (1959), pp. 23-25.

Csillik, B., The Real 'Omar Khayyam. *Act. Or. Hung.* 10 (1960), pp. 59-77.

Ghani, A. R., Medieval Muslim Science: A Handlist of Indo-Pakistani References. *Pakistan J. Sci.* 6 (1954), 49-53.

Khan, Mohd. A. R., A Survey of Muslim Contributions to Science and Culture. *IC* 16 (1942), pp. 1-20, 136-152; Note by D. M. Dunlop 17 (1943), p. 330.

Sarton, G., Arabic Achievements of the Fifteenth Century; Their Decadence and Fall. *Homenaje a Millas-Vallicrosa* II, (1956), pp. 303-325.

Sarton, G., Arabic Scientific Literature. *Goldziher* Mem. Vol. I, (1948), pp. 55-72.

Siddiqui, M. Razi-ud-Din, The Contribution of Muslims to Scientific Thought. *IC* 14 (1940), pp. 33-44.

Winter, H. J. J., Science in Medieval Persia. *J. Iran Soc.* 1 (1950-), pp. 55-70.

2. GREEK AND LATIN SCIENCE IN ISLAMIC LEARNING

Arberry, A. J., An Early Arabic Translation from the Greek. *BFA* 1 (1933), pp. 48-76; 2 (1934), pp. 71-83.

Arberry, A. J., The Nicomachean Ethics in Arabic. *BSOAS* 17 (1955), pp. 1-9.

Levi, Della Vida, G., Two Fragments of Galen in Arabic Translation. *JAOS* 70 (1950), pp. 182-187.

Rosenthal, F., On the Knowledge of Plato's Philosophy in the Islamic World. *IC* 14 (1940), pp. 387-422.

Walzer, R., New Light on the Arabic Translation of Aristotle. *Oriens* 6 (1953), pp. 91-142.

3. TRANSMISSION OF GREEK SCIENCE TO THE ARABS

Clagett, M., The Impact of Archimedes on Medieval Science. *Isis* 50 (1959), pp. 419-429.

Dunlop, D. M., The Translations of al-Bitriq and Yahya (Yuhanna) b. al-Bitriq. *24 Int. Cong. Or.* (1957), pp. 303-305. Also in *JRAS* (1959), pp. 140-150.

4. TRANSMISSION OF GREEK SCIENCE TO THE WEST

Butler, P., Fifteenth Century Edition of Arabic Authors in Latin Translation. *Macdonald Presentation Vol.*, (1933), pp. 61-71.

Clagett, M., The Medieval Latin Translations From the Arabic of the *Elements* of Euclid, With Special Emphasis on the Versions of Adelard of Bath. *Isis* 44 (1953), pp. 16-42.

Dunlop, D. M., Arabic Science in the West. *J. Pak. Hist. Soc.* 5 (1957), pp. 1-22, 77-99, 129-150, 200-219.

Haskins, C. H., Arabic Science in Western Europe. *Isis* 7 (1925), pp. 478-485.

O'Leary, De L., Arabic Transmission of Science. *IC* 31 (1957), pp. 201-208.

O'Leary, De L., The Early Westward Drift of Science and Philosophy. *Philosophy East and West* iiv (1952), pp. 53-58.

Thompson, J. W., The Introduction of Arabic Science into Lorraine in the Tenth Century. *Isis* 12 (1929), pp. 184-193.

Welborn, M. C., Lotharingia as a Center of Arabic and Scientific influence in the Eleventh Century. *Isis* 16 (1931), pp. 188-199.

E. Mathematics

Cameron, J., The Origin of the Arabic Numerals. *Glasg. Or. Soc. Trans.* 4 (1913-22), pp. 9-13.

Clark, W. E., Hindu-Arabic Numerals. *Indian Studies in Honor of C. R. Lanman,* (1929), pp. 217-236.

Gandz, S., The Origin of the Term Algebra. *American Mathematical Monthly* 33 (1926), pp. 437-440.

Hill, G. F., On the Early Use of Arabic Numerals in Europe. *Archaeologia* 62 (1910), pp. 137-190.

Jenkinson, H., The Use of Arabic and Roman Numerals in English Archives. *Antiquaries Journal* 6 (1926), pp. 263-275.

Karpinski, L. C., Hindu Numerals Among the Arabs. *Bibl. Math.* 3.F., 13 (1912-13), pp. 97-98.

Karpinski, L. C., Hindu Numerals in the Fi'hrist. *Bibl. Math.* 3.F., 11 (1910-11), pp. 121-124.

Khan, Muhammad A. R., Muslim Contribution to Mathematics and Astronomy *Iqbal* 8 (1960), pp. 7-24.

Krishnaswami Ayyangar, A. A., The Hindu Arabic Numerals. *QJMS* 18 (1928), pp. 256-267; 19 (1928-29), pp.20-40, 115-133.

Lethaby, W. R., Some Arabic Numerals on the Sculptures on the West Front of Wells Cathedral Church. *Proc. Soc. Ant. London* 2 ser., 21 (1906-07), pp. 199-203.

Mitra, P. N., The Problem of Squaring the Circle and Iranian Contribution to It. *Indo-Iranica* 6i (1952-53), pp. 29-38.

F. *Science, Philosophy*

Abdul Hamid, Khwaja, The Philosophical Significance of Ibn Tufail's Haiy Ibn Yaqzan. *IC* 22 (1948), pp. 50-70.

Abid, Syed Abid Ali, Fresh Light on Avicenna. An Annotated Translation of the Autobiographical Fragment. *Iqbal* 7 i (1958), pp. 18-35.

Akhtar, Ahmedmian, A Tract of Avicenna Translated by 'Umar Khayyam. *IC* 9 (1935), pp. 218-233.

Arberry, A. J., The Achievement of Avicenna. *J. Iran Soc.* 1 (1950-), pp. 119-124.

Arberry, A. J., Farabi's Canons of Poetry. *RSO* 17 (1938), pp. 266-278.

Arberry, A. J., Avicenna: His Life and Times. *Avicenna: Scientist and Philosopher,* ed. G. M. Wickens (1852), pp. 9-28.

Asmous, V., Abu Ali Ibi Sina (Avicenna). *Europe* 30 No. 81 (1952), pp. 115-127.

Barani, S. H., Al-Biruni's Scientific Achievements. *Indo-Iranica* 51 v (1952-53), pp. 37-48.

Bell, R., A Moslem Thinker on the Teaching of Religion. Al-Ghazzali, A.D. 1058-1111. *Hibbert J.* 42 (1943), pp. 31-36.

Blumberg, H., Alfarabi's Five Chapters on Logic. *Proc. Americ. Acad. Jew. Res.* 6 (1934-35), pp. 115-121.

Carmody, F. J., The Planetary Theory of Ibn Rushd. *Osiris* 10 (1952), pp. 556-586.

Crombie, A. C., Avicenna's Influence on the Mediaeval Scientific Tradition. *Avicenna: Scientist and Philosopher,* ed. G. M. Wickens, (1942), pp. 84-107.

Darby, G. O. S., Ibn Wahshiya in Mediaeval Spanish Literature. *Isis* 33 (1941), pp. 438-443.

Ermatinger, C. J., Averroism in Early Fourteenth Century Bologna. *Mediaeval Studies* 16 (1954), pp. 35-56.

Dunlop, D. M., Al-Farabi's Aphorisms of the Statesman. *Iraq* 14 (1932), pp. 93-117.

Egginhausen, R., Al-Ghazzali on Beauty. *Art and Thought, Issued in Honour of A. K. Coomeraswamy,* (1947), pp. 160-165.

Falkenheim, E. L., Al-Farabi. His Life, Times and Thought. On the Occasion of the Millenary Anniversary of His Death. *Middle East Affairs* 2 (1951), pp. 54-59.

Falkenheim, E. L., A Treatise on Love by Ibn Sina. *Medieval Studies* 7 (1945), pp. 208-228.

Falkenheim, E. L., The Possibility of the Universe in Al-Farabi, Ibn Sina and Maimonides. *Proc. Amer. Acad. Jew. Res.* 16 (1946-47), pp. 39-70.

Faris, N. A., Al-Ghazzali's Rules of Conduct. Based on Al-Qawa'id al-'Asharah. *MW* 32 (1942), pp. 43-50.

Faris, N. A., Ghazzali's Epistle of the Birds. A Translation of the Risalat al-Tayr. *MW* 34 (1944), pp. 46-53.

Finkel, J., An Eleventh Century Source for the History of Jewish Scientists in Mohammedan Land (Ibn Sa'id). *JQR* N. W. 18 (1927-28), pp. 45-54.

Finnegan, J., Avicenna's Refutation of Porphyrius. *Avicenna Commem. Vol.*, (1956), pp. 187-203.

Foster, K., Avicenna and Western Thought in the 13th Century. *Avicenna: Scientist and Philosopher*, ed. G. M. Wickens, (1952), pp. 108-123.

Gai, B. M., Ibn Sina and Europe. *Avicenna Commem. Vol.*, (1956), pp. 15-19.

Gandz, S., The Sources of al-Khowarizmi's Algebra. *Osiris* 1 (1936), pp. 263-277.

Gruner, O. C., Avicenna's Canon of Medicine and Its Modern Unani Counterpart. *Univ. of Michigan Med. Bull.* 22 (1956), pp. 239-248.

Hare, T., Some Contributions to the Mediaeval Veterinary Science in the Kitab al-Falahah and in Fleta. *Proc. Roy. Soc. Med.* 28 (1934-35), pp. 1537-1544 (Section hist. med. pp. 27-34).

Hourani, G. F., The Chronology of Ghazzali's writings. *JAOS* 79 (1959), pp. 225-233.

Kazim, M. A., Al-Biruni and Trigonometry. *Al-Biruni Commem. Vol.*, (1951), pp. 161-170.

Kramers, J. H., Al-Biruni's Determination of Geographical Longitude by Measuring the Distances. *Al-Biruni Commem. Vol.*, (1951), pp. 177-193.

Law, B. C., Al-Biruni's Knowledge of Indian Geography. *Indo-Iranica* 7 iv (1954), pp. 1-26.

Levonian, L., The Ikhwan al-Safa' and Christ. *MW* 35 (1945), pp. 27-31.

Levy, R., Avicenna—His Life and Times. *Medical History* I (1957), pp. 249-261.

Meyerhof, M., Thirty-Three Clinical Observations by Rhazes (circa A.D. 900). *Isis* 23 (1935), pp. 321-356.

Miller, R., An Aspect of Averroes' Influence on St. Albert. *Mediaeval Studies* 16 (1954), pp. 57-71.

Mitra, P. N., Omar Khayyam the Mathematician. *Indo-Iranica* iii (1946-47), pp. 13-20.

Moody, E. A., Galileo and Avenpace: The Dynamics of the Leaning Tower Experiment. *Jl. Hist. Ideas* 12 (1951), pp. 163-193, 375-422.

Partington, J. R., The Chemistry of Razi. *Ambix* 1 (1938), pp. 192-196.

Rabin, C., Ibn Jami on the Skeleton. *Science, Medicine and History. Essays in Honour of C. Singer*, I (1953), pp. 172-202.

Rosenthal, E. I. J., The Place of Politics in the Philosophy of Al-Farabi. *IC* 29 (1955), pp. 157-178.

Rosenthal, E. I. J., Avicenna's Influence on Jewish Thought. *Avicenna: Scientist and Philosopher*, ed. G. M. Wickens, (1952), pp. 66-83.

Rosenthal, E. I. J., The Place of Politics in the Philosophy of Ibn Bajja. *IC* 25 (1951), pp. 187-211.

Rosenthal, E. I. J., The Place of Politics in the Philosophy of Ibn Rushd. *BSOAS* 15 (1953), pp. 246-278.

Rosenthal, F., A Short Treatise on the Meaning of the Names of Some Greek Scholars Attributed to Al-Farabi. *JAOS* 62 (1942), pp. 73-74.

Sa'di, Lutfi M., Ibn-al-Haitham (Alhazen), Medieval Scientist. *Univ. of Michigan Med. Bull.* 22 (1956), pp. 249-273.

Saidan, A. S., The Rasa'il of Biruni and Ibn Sina. (A rearrangement), *IC* 34 (1960), pp. 173-175.

Salmon, D., The Mediaeval Latin Translations of Alfarabi's Works. *New Scholasticism* 13 (1939), pp. 245-261.

Sayili, Aydin, Al Farabi's Article on Vacuum. *TTK Bulletin* 15 (1951), pp. 151-174.

Shafaq, S. R., Some Abiding Teachings of Al-Ghazzali. *MW* 44 (1954), pp. 43-48.

Sherwani, H. K., El-Ghazzali on the Theory and Practice of Politics. *IC* 9 (1935), pp. 450-474.

Sherwani, Harun Khan, Some Precursors of Nizamu'l-'Mulk Tusi. *IC* 8 (1934), pp. 15-38.

Sherwani, H. K., Al-Farabi's Political Theories. *IC* 12 (1938), pp. 288-305.

Smith, D. E., Euclid, Omar Khayyam, and Saccheri. *Scripta Mathematica* 3 (1935), pp. 5-10.

Spies, O., Al-Kindi's Treatise on the Cause of the Blue Colour of the Sky. *JBBRAS* N. W. 13 (1937), pp. 7-19.

Stephenson, J., The Classification of the Sciences According to Nasiruddin Tusi. *Isis* 5 (1923), pp. 329-338.

Tavadia, J. C., Al-Biruni and Firdausi. *Visvabharati Q.* N. S. 15 (1959-60), pp. 51-59.

Teicher, J. L., Avicenna's Place in Arabic Philosophy. *Avicenna: Scientist and Philosopher*, ed. G. M. Wickens, (1952), pp. 29-48.

Temkin, O., A Medieval Translation of Rhazes' *Clinical Observations. Bull. Hist. Med.* 12 (1942), pp. 102-117.

Tibawi, A. L., Ikhwan As-Safa and Their *Rasa'il.* A Critical Review of a Century and a Half of Research. *IQ* 2 (1955), pp. 28-46.

Tornay, S. C., Averroes' Doctrine of the Mind. *Philos. Rev.* 52 (1943), pp. 270-288.

Wali-Ur-Rahman, Mu'tazid, The Psychology of Al-Farabi. *IC* 11 (1937), pp. 228-247.

Walzer, R., New Studies on Al-Kindi. *Oriens* 10 (1957), pp. 203-232.

Wickens, G. M., The 'Persian Letters' Attributed to Al-Ghazali. *Islamic Q.* 3 (1956), pp. 109-116.

Wilcyznski, J. Z., On the Presumed Darwinism of Alberuni Eight Hundred Years Before Darwin. *Isis* 50 (1959), pp. 459-466.

Winter, H. J. J., and Arafat, W., The Algebra of 'Umar Khayyam. *JASB* Science ser. iii, 16 (1950), pp. 27-78.

Winter, H. J. J., and Arafat, W., A Statement on Optical Reflection and "Refraction" Attributed to Nasir ud-Din at-Tusi. *Isis* 42 (1951), pp. 138-142.

Worrell, W. H., An Interesting Collection of Tusi's works, Published at Hyderabad, 1939-40. *Scripta Mathematica* 9 (1943), pp. 195-196.

G. *Physics, Meteorology, Optics, Technology*

Kennedy, E. S., An Islamic Computer for Planetary Latitudes. *JAOS* 71 (1951), pp. 13-21.

Mayer, L. A., Islamic Astrolabists: Some New Material. *Aus der Welt der Islamischen Kunst, Festscrift E. Kuhnel,* (1957), pp. 293-296.

Neugebauer, O., The Early History of the Astrolabe. *Isis* 40 (1949), pp. 240-256.

Weibel, A. C., A Persian Astrolabe. *Bull. Detroit Inst. Arts* 25 (1946), pp. 59-61.

Winter, H. J. J., The Arabic Achievement in Physics. *Endeavour* 9 (1950), pp. 76-79.

SELECTED GENERAL BIBLIOGRAPHY

In the following Selected General Bibliography and in the General Bibliography on Muslim Culture by Topic, which follows, names of authors and titles of works, etc., are listed as they are spelled in English by the various authors.

Abdur Rahman, Khandkar M., "The Arab Geographer Yaqut al-Rumi," *JAS Pakistan* 3, 1958, pp. 23-28.

Abu Ali Sina, Sheikh Ra'is (Avicenna), *Resala'i Mantiq,* (An Essay on Logic), Teheran: Anjumani Asari Melli, 1331 Shamsi Hejira, 1371 Ghamari Hejira (in Persian).

Abu Ali Sina, Sheikh Ra'is (Avicenna), *Tab'iyyat: Danish-Nama'i Ala'i,* (On Natural Sciences), Teheran: Anjumani Asari Melli, 1331 Shamsi Hejira, 1377 Ghamari Hejira (in Persian).

Adams, George B., *Civilization During the Middle Ages,* New York: Scribner's Sons, 1894.

Adler, E. N. and Broyde, I., *An Ancient Bookseller's Catalogue,* F.Q.R., XIII, 1901.

Ahwani, Ahmad Fu'ad, *Al-Tarbiyah fi-al-Islam,* Cairo: Dar Ihya al-Kutub al-Arabiyah, 1955.

Alam, Manzoor, "Ibn Khaldun's Concept of the Origin, Growth, and Decay of Cities," *Islamic Culture,* 34, 1960, pp. 90-106.

Arberry, A. J., *Arab Contribution to Civilization,* San Francisco: American Academy of Asian Studies, 1958.

Arberry, A. J., ed., *The Legacy of Persia,* Oxford: The Clarendon Press, 1953.

Arnold, Sir Edwin, *Gulistan. The First Four Babs or Gateways,* New York: Harper and Bros., 1899.

Arnold, Sir Edwin and Alfred Guillaume, eds., *The Legacy of Islam,* London: Oxford University Press, 1931.

Arty, Frederick B., *The Mind of the Middle Ages A.D. 200-1500,* New York: Alfred Knopf, 1958.

al-Ash'ari, 'Ali ibn-Isma'il, *Al-Ibanah 'an Usul al-Diyanah,* tr. W. C. Klein, Washington: American Oriental Society, 1940.

Asin y Palacios, M., *Islam and the Divine Comedy,* London: publ not mentioned, 1926.

Attar, Nishapuri Sheikh Farid-ul-din Abu Hamed Muhammed ibn Abu Bakr Ibrahim ibn Ishaq, *Diwan Qasa'id wa Ghazaliyyat,* (Complete Lyrics), Teheran: Eqbal Press, 1219 Qamari (?) Hejira (in Persian).

Averroes, *A Decisive Discourse on the Relation Between Religion and Philosophy, and An Exposition of the Methods of Argument Concerning the Doctrines of Faith,* Baroda: publ not mentioned, no date.

Avicenna, *Scientist and Philosopher, a Millennary Symposium,* London: Luzac and Co., 1952.

Badwi, Amin Abdul-Majid, *A Discourse on Ghabus-Namah,* Teheran: ibn Sina Book Store, 1956 (in Persian).

Bafeqi Wahshi, Shams-ul-din Muhammad, *Diwan Kamel,* (Complete Works), Dei Mah: Piruz, 1335 Shamsi Hejira (in Persian).

al-Baghdadi, abu-Mansur ibn-Tahir, *Moslem Schisms and Sects,* tr. Kate C. Seelye, New York: Columbia University Press, 1920.

Bahay, Muhammad, "Al-Gassali fi-al-Falsafah al-Akhlaqiyah wa'l Sufiyah," *Majallat Risalat al-Islam,* no date, Vol. VII.

Baihaqi, *Al-Mahasin wal Musawi,* Libsick: 1320 Hejira (in Arabic).

Baihaqi, Dabir Khawja Abul Fadhl Muhammad ibn Hussein, *Tarikhi Baihaqi,* (History by Baihaqi), eds. Drs. Ghani and Fiadh, Teheran: Rangin Press and Bangi Melli Iran Press, 1324 Shamsi Hejira (in Persian).

al-Baladhuri, Ahmad, *The Origins of the Islamic State,* tr. P. K. Hitti, New York: Columbia University Press, 1916.

Balazs, E., "Marco Polo Dans La Capitale de la Chine," *Oriente Poliano,* 1957, pp. 133-154.

Balkhi, Ghadhi Hamid-ul-din Omar ibn Mahmud, *Maghamat i Hamidi,* Isfahan: Muhammadi Press, Mehr Mah 1339 Shamsi Hejira (in Persian).

Bar Hebraeus, *Historia Denostiarum* (History of Dynestus), Popock's ed., Oxford: 1663.

Barnes, Harry Elmer, *An Intellectual and Cultural History of the Western World,* Random House, 1937.

Beazley, C. R., *The Dawn of Modern Geography,* 3 vols., Oxford: 1897-1906.

Beagley, C. R., *Notebook on Medieval History,* 1917.

Becker, C. H., *Christianity and Islam,* London: publ not mentioned, 1909.

Beddie, J. S., *Books in the East During the Crusades,* VIII, no place or publisher given, 1933.

Bevan, E. R. and C. Singer, *The Legacy of Israel,* Oxford: The Clarendon Press, 1928.

Bhatnagar, R., "Madhyadesh in the Rehla of Ibn Battuta," *Saugar University Journal,* Vol. IV, Part I, 1955-1956, pp. 97-109.

Biblioteque, Nationale, *Catalogue des Manuscrits Arabes,* Paris: No. 4595.

Biruni, *Chronology of Ancient Nations,* tr. by Sachau, London: 1879.

Biruni, *Ketab ut-Tafheem of Biruni,* Teheran: Madjlis Press, 1316-1318 (in Persian).

Biruni, Ustad Abu Raihan Muhammad ibn Ahmad, *Kitab-ul-Tafhim li Awa'il Sana'at-ul-Tanjim,* (The Book of the Rational Introduction to the Science of Astronomy), Teheran: Madjlis Press, 1316-1318 Shamsi Hejira (in Persian).

Boer, T. J. de, *History of Philosophy in Islam,* London: publ not mentioned, 1903.

Brehaut, Ernest, *An Encyclopedist of the Dark Ages: Isidore of Seville,* New York: Columbia University Press, 1912.

Brentano, *The Middle Ages,* tr. by E. O. Hill, 1921.

Brockelmann, Carl, *Geschichte der Arabischen Litteratur,* Vol. I, Weimar: 1898. In German, Vol. II, Berlin: 1902. Supplement to Vol. I, Leiden: 1937. Supplement to Vol. II, Leiden: 1938. Supplement to Vol. III, Leiden: 1939-1942. *Geschichte der Arabischen Litteratur, Zweite den Supplement-banden angepasste Auflage,* Leiden: 1943. Vol. I, 1943. Vol. II, 1944-1949.

Brockelman, Carl, *Geschichte der Islamischen Volker und Staaten,* mit 8 karten. 2 aufl Munchen und Berlin: R. Oldenbourg, 1943.

Browne, Edward Granville, *A Iiterary History of Persia,* 4 vols. Cambridge (Eng): The University Press, 1908, reprinted 1909. Vol. I, *From the Earliest Times Until Firdawsi,* 1906, reprinted 1915. Vol. II, *From Firdawsi to Sa'di,* 1920, reprinted 1928. Vol. III, *Tartar Dominion*—1265-1502, 1924, reprinted 1928. Vol. IV, Modern Times—1500-1924.

Browne, Edward Granville, *Arabic Medicine,* Cambridge (Eng.): The University Press, 1921.

Browne, Lewis, ed., *The Wisdom of Israel,* New York: publ not mentioned, 1945.

al-Bukhari, Muhammad Ibn-Isma'il, *El-Bokhari, Les Traditions Islamiques,* tr. O. Houdas and W. Marcais, Paris: Imprimerie Nationale, 1906.

al-Bukhari, Shahab-ul-din Ama'q, *Diwan,* (Complete Works), Tabriz: Sharq, 1947 (in Persian).

Bukhsh, S. K., *The Orient under the Caliphs,* tr. from A. von Kremer's Kulturgeschichte des Orients, Calcutta: publ not mentioned, 1920.

Burton, Sir Richard, *Tales from the Gulistan of Sa'di,* London: Phillip Allen and Co., 1888.

Campbell, Donald, *Arabian Medicine and its Influence on the Middle Ages,* 2 vols., London: K. Paul, Trench, Trubner and Co., 1926.

Canard, M., "Quelques observations sur l'introduction geographique de la Bughyat at 'T'alab de Kamal Ad-Din Ibn Al'Adim d'Alep," *Annals de l'Institut des Etudes Orientalies,* Vol. XV, 1957, pp. 41-53.

Carmody, Francis J., *Arabic Astronomical and Astrological Sciences in Latin Translations,* Berkeley: University of California Press, 1956.

Chambers, E. K., *The Medieval Stage,* Oxford: The Clarendon Press, 1903.

Choudhuri, Roy, Makhanlal, "Persian Proverbs," *Indian Folk Lore,* Vol. II, 1959, pp. 179-181.

Christensen, A., *L'Iran Sous les Sassanides,* Copenhagen: Ejnar Munksgaard, 1944.

Clarke, H. Wilberforce, *Bustan,* London: publ not mentioned, 1879.

Cole, P. R., *Later Roman Education,* New York: Columbia University Press, 1909.

Compayre, Gabriel, *The History of Pedagogy,* tr. W. H. Payne, Boston: D. C. Heath, 1888.

Coulton, George C., *Life in the Middle Ages,* selected, tr. and annotated by G. C. Coulton, Cambridge (Eng): The University Press, 1930.

Coulton, George C., *Medieval Panorama,* Cambridge (Eng): The University Press, 1938.

Cranmer-Byng, L., *Rose Garden,* New York: Dutton and Co., 1912.

Crump, Charles G. and Ernest Fraser, eds., *The Legacy of the Middle Ages,* Oxford: The Clarendon Press, 1926.

Cubberley, E. P., *The History of Education,* Boston: Houghton Mifflin, 1920.

Cubberley, E. P., *Syllabus of Lectures on the History of Education,* New York: Macmillan Co., 1904.

Cutts, E. L., *Scenes and Characters of the Middle Ages,* London: Simpkin, Marshall, Hamilton, Kent and Co., 1926.

D'Arcy, M. C., *Thomas Aquinas,* Boston: Little and Co., 1930.

Davis, G., *Garden of Fragrance,* London: M. Paul Trench and Co., 1882.

De Boer, T. J., *History of Philosophy in Islam,* 2nd ed., London: 1933.

Deh-khoda, Ali Akhbar, *Kitab'i Amsal'u-Hikam,* (The Book of Proverbs and Maxims), Teheran: The Madjlis Press, 1310 (in Persian).

Demieville, P., "La situation religieuse en Chine au temps de Marco Polo," *Oriente Poliano,* 1957, pp. 193-236.

Destombes, M., "Fragments of two medieval world maps at the Topkapu Saray Library," *Imago Mundi* Vol. XII, 1955, pp. 150-152.

DeVaux, Baron Carra, *Les Penseurs de l'Islam,* 5 vols., Paris: publ not mentioned, 1921.

De Wulf, M., *History of Medieval Philosophy,* New York: Dover Press, 1952.

De Wulf, M., *Philosophy and Civilization in the Middle Ages,* tr. E. C. Messenger, Princeton: Princeton University Press, 1922.

Dhalla, Maneckji, *Zoroastrian Civilization,* New York: Oxford University Press, 1922.

Dieterici, Fredrich, *Seventeen Monographs on Moslem Philosophy in the 9th and 10th Centuries,* Berlin: publ not mentioned, 1858-95.

Dieterici, Frederich, *(Die) Naturanschauung und Naturphilosophie der Araber im X Jahnhundert,* 2 ed., Leipzig: Hinrichssche, 1876.

Dimand, M. S., *A Handbook of Muhammadan Art,* New York: Hartsdale House, 1947.

Dodge, Bayard, *Al-Azhar, A Millennium of Muslim Learning,* Washington: Middle East Institute, 1961.

Dozy, R., *Spanish Islam,* New York: publ not mentioned, 1913.

Draper, J. W., *History of the Intellectual Development of Europe,* 2 vols., New York: Harper and Bros., 1863.

Duggan, Stephen P., *A Students' Textbook in the History of Education,* New York: D. Appleton and Co., 1916.

Durant, Will, *The Age of Faith,* New York: Simon and Schuster, 1950.

Durnoulin, James, *Goolistan,* Calcutta: publ not mentioned, 1807.

Eastwick, Edward E., *Gulistan,* London: Trubner and Co., 1880.

Eby, Frederick, *The History and Philosophy of Education,* New York: Prentice-Hall, 1940.

Elgood, C., *A Medical History of Persia and the Eastern Caliphate,* Cambridge (Eng.): The University Press, 1951.

Ellis, A. G., *Catalogue of Arabic Books in the British Museum,* London: no publ mentioned, 1894.

Emerson, Mabel I., *The Evolution of the Educational Ideal,* Boston: Houghton Mifflin, 1914.

Encyclopedia of Islam, A dictionary of the geography, ethnography, and biography of the Muhammadan peoples. Edited by M. T. Houtsma, T. W. Arnold, R. Basset, R. Hartmann, A. J. Wensinck, W. Heffening, E. Levi-Provencal, H. A. R. Gibb, Leiden: E. J. Brill; London: Luzac and Co., 1938 4v plus supplement, rev. ed. vol. I & II.

Items Consulted:
Abbasides—inadequate; Afghanistan (civilization); Ahmad al-Badwi (Egyptian Saint); al-Akhtal (an Arabian Christian poet); Alf Laila Wa-Laila; Alger and Algeria; Alhambra; Allah; Arabesque (foliage ornament of Muslim art); Arabia (Muslim culture is included here); Architecture; Aristutales (Aristotle); Armenia (extensive bibliography); Arnauts (Albania); Astronomy; Baghdad (a cultural history); Batoeistan; Barmakids (a Persian family which produced the first Persian ministers of the Caliphate); Berbers; Bukhara; Cairo; China; Constantinople; Dhu'l; Nun (great early mystic); Djuwaim (Persian historian).

On Arab and Persian poets, minor Islamic religious sects and others:
Egypt; Falsafe (philosophy) links Arab philosophy to Greek and Christian Europe; al-Farabi (Islamic philosopher); Fatimids; Fikh (Islamic jurisprudence); al-Ghazzali (the greatest Muslim theologian); Hadith (tradition); Hafiz; Hanafis (Sunni followers of Abu Hanifa); ibn Hazm (Spanish scholar and historian); ibn Khaldun (Arab historian); ibn Rush, (Averroes); ibn Sina (Avicenna); Ikhwan al-Safa (an association of religious scholars of Albra-Shii views); India; Indies; Indo-China; Irak (Iraq); al-Iskandariya (Alexandria); Ka'ba; Kalila wa-Dimna; al-Kazwim (geographer); Khediw (Khediwes) of Egypt; al-Kindi (philosopher); Qur'an (great); al-Kuds (Jerusalem); Kurds; al-Madina; Maktab; Maui; Mantik (logic) (Greek Aristotelian influence); Marrakish (in Morocco—tells its political history); Masjid (Mosque); Mathnawi; Mazdak; Mecca (history); Meshed (Mashhad); al-Mizah (scale-balance); Mizmar (flute—nay); Moors (a social analysis); Morocco (social-cultural-history); Mughal (in India) empire; Muhammad (entire life); Muhr (seal); Musiqi (music); al-Mu'tazila (great theological school in Islam—dogmatic); Nasara (Christians); Nasir-i Khusraw; Nestorians (short section); Nizam al-Mulk Tusi (celebrated minister of the Saldjukid sultans Alp Arsalan and Malik Shah); Nizami; Firdawsi; Persia; al-Razi (physician and philosopher); Saba (people and culture of a kingdom in southwestern Arabia in first millennium B.C.); Sa'di; Samaritans; Samarkand; Sassanian; Shi'a; Sihr (magic); al-Tabari (historian); Tabriz; Tadj Mahal; Baba Tahir; Tarika (extensive outline of schools of Muslim mysticism—also see Tasawwuf); Teheran; Tunis and Tunisia; Turks (cultural, social and political); al-Tusi

(Nasir-al-Din—astronomy); Ud (Lut); Umayyads (East and Spain); Urmiya; Samaritan literature (by M. Gaster).

Encyclopedia of Religion and Ethics, 13 vols., New York: Scribner and Sons, 1927.

Eqbal, Abbas, ed., *Tarikhi Tabaristan,* (The History of Tabaristan), Teheran: no publ mentioned, 1941 (in Persian).

Faris, Nabih Amin, ed., *The Arab Heritage,* Princeton: Princeton University Press, 1944.

Fadhl, Mirza abu'l, *Sayings of the Prophet Muhammad,* Allahabad: Reform Society, 1924.

Farmer, Henry G., *Historical Facts for the Arabian Music Influence,* London: Luzac and Co., 1930.

Farmer, Henry G., *History of Arabian Music to the Thirteenth Century,* London: Luzac and Co., 1929.

Farmer, Henry G., *The Sources of Arabian Music, Annotated Bibliography of Arabic MSS,* Scotland: no publ mentioned, 1940.

Farrukhi, Hakim Seestani, *Diwan,* (Complete Works), Teheran: Eqbal Distributors, Sepehr Press, Esfand Mah 1335 Shamsi Hejira (in Persian).

Firdausi, Shah Namah, *Muntakhabi Shah Namah,* (Selections from Shah Namah) ed. by Muhammad Ali Forughi and Habib Yaghma'i, Teheran: Bangi Melli Press, 1321 Shamsi Hejira (in Persian).

Fischel, W., "Ibn Khaldun's contribution to comparative religions," 24th International Congress Orientale, 1957, pp. 334-335.

Flujel, Edward G., and R. A. Nicholson, *A Literary History of the Arabs,* Cambridge (Eng.): no publ mentioned, 1930.

Forget, J., *Le Livre des Theoremes et des Avellissements,* Leiden: no publ mentioned, 1892.

Frost, S. E., *Essentials of History of Education,* Brooklyn: Barron's Educational Series, 1947.

Frye, Richard N., *The Heritage of Persia,* Cleveland: The World Publishing Co., 1963.

Frye, Richard N., "Notes on the Renaissance of the Tenth and Eleventh Centuries in Eastern Iran," *Central Asiatic Journal,* Vol. 1, No. 2.

Garrison, F. H., *An Introduction to the History of Medicine,* London: W. B. Saunders Co., 1929.

Ghafti, *Akhbar-al-Hokama,* (Annals of Learned Men), Cairo: no publ mentioned, 1325 Shamsi Hejira (in Persian).

Ghazzali, *Ihya'i Ulum al-Din',* (Revivification of the Sciences of Religion), no date or publisher mentioned (in Arabic).

Ghazzali, *Nasihat-ul-Moluk,* (Advice to the Kings), Teheran: no publ mentioned, 1937.

al-Ghazzali, Abu Hamid, *The Alchemy of Happiness,* tr. by Field, London: Luzac and Co., 1910.

al-Ghazzali, Abu Hamid, *Some Religious and Moral Teachings,* tr. by Nawab Ali, Baroda: no publ mentioned, 1920.

al-Ghazzali, Abu Hamid, *The Confessions of al-Ghazzali,* tr. by C. Field, London: John Murray Co., 1909.

al-Ghazzali, Abu Hamid, *Ihya al-Ulum,* (Revivification of Sciences) Cairo: al-Maymuniyah Press, 1916 (in Persian).

al-Ghazzali, Abu Hamid, *Ih'ya Ulum ed-Din,* ed. G. H. Bousquet, no publ mentioned: Besson Press, 1955.

al-Ghazzali, Abu Hamid, *The Faith and Practice of al-Ghazzali,* ed. W. M. Watt, London: Allen and Unwin Co., 1953.

al-Ghazzali, Abu Hamid, *Ayyuha'l-Walad,* (Oh Child) ed. G. H. Scherer, Beirut: American Press, 1933.

al-Ghazzali, Abu Hamid, *Tahafut al-Falasifah,* (Revivification of Philosophy), tr. by Sabih Ahmad Kamali, McGill University Press, 1955.

Ghoshal, U. N., "Corroboration of Marco Polo's account of India from Indian sources," *Jadunath Sarkar Commem.* Vol. II, 1958, pp. 104-107.

Gibb, H. A. R., *Arabic Literature,* Oxford: Oxford University Press, 1926.

Gilson, E., *Reason and Revelation in the Middle Ages,* New York: C. Scribner's Sons, 1948.

Gladwin, Francis, *The Gulistan,* tr. by F. Gladwin, Boston: Ticknor and Fields, 1864.

Goldziher, "Muslim Education," *Encyclopedia of Religion and Ethics,* Vol. V.

Gottheil, R. J., ed., *The Literature of Persia,* 2 vols., New York: The Colonial Press, 1902.

Graves, Frank, *History of Education,* 3 vols., New York: Macmillan Co., 1909-13.

Grunebaum, Gustave E. von, *Medieval Islam – A Study in Cultural Orientation,* Chicago: University of Chicago Press, 1946.

Gruner, O. C., *Treatise on the Canon of Medicine of Avicenna,* London: Luzac and Co., 1930.

Guillaume, A., *The Traditions of Islam,* Oxford: The Clarendon Press, 1924.

Hafiz, Khawja Shams-al-din Muhammad Shirazi, *Diwan,* (Complete Works), Teheran: Brukheim Press, 1318 Shamsi Hejira (in Persian).

Ha'im, Sulaiman, *Persian-English and English-Persian Dictionary,* 4 vols., Teheran: Brukheim Press, 1312 Shamsi Hejira.

Haji, Khalifa, *Kashfu'dh-Dhunun an Asami'l-Kutub wa'l-Funun,* (Names of Books and Branches of Knowledge), Latin tr. by G. Flugel, Leipzig: no publ mentioned, 1825.

Haji, Khalifa, *Kashf-uth-Thonun,* Lipsick: 1825.

Halevi, J., *Kitab al Khazari,* tr. by Hirschfield, London: Luzac and Co., 1931.

Hamidi, *Maghamat of Hamidi,* Isfahan: Muhammadi Press, 1339 Shamsi Hejira (in Persian).

Hammond, Robert, *The Philosophy of Alfarabi and its Influence on Medieval Thought,* New York: The Hobson Book Press, 1947.

Hambis, L., "Le Voyage de Marco Polo en Haute Asie," *Oriente Poliano,* 1957, pp. 173-191.

Hampton, C. E., *Roses from Sa'di's Garden,* New York: Barse and Hopkins, 1913.

Hart, Joseph K., *Creative Moments in Education,* New York: Henry Holt and Co., 1931.

Harvard Theological Review, "Amphibolic Terms in Aristotle, Arabic Philosophy and Maimonides," 1938, p. 31.

Haskins, C. H., *Studies in the History of Medieval Science,* Cambridge: Harvard University Press, 1927.

Haskins, C. H., *Studies in Medieval Culture,* New York: F. Ungar Publishing Co., 1958.

Hatif, Isfahani, *Diwan,* (Complete Works), Teheran: Sharq Publishing Co., Mah 1332 (in Persian).

Hazai, G., "Les Manuscrits, conserves a Sofia, des Remaniements Medievals de Marvazi et Auff," *Acta Orientalia Academia Scientiarum Hungarica,* Vol. VII, 1957, pp. 157-197.

Hazard, Harry W., *Atlas of Islamic History,* Princeton: Princeton University Press, 1954.

Hearnshaw, F., *Medieval Contributions to Modern Civilization,* New York: Barnes and Noble, 1949.

Hell, Jos., *The Arab Civilization,* Cambridge (Eng.): The University Press, 1926.

Hitti, Phillip K., *The Arabs – A Short History,* Princeton: Princeton University Press, 1946.

Hitti, Phillip K., *History of the Arabs,* 6th ed., London: Macmillan Co., 1956.

Hulme, E. M., *The Middle Ages,* New York: Henry Holt, 1929.

Husain, Mahdi, "Manuscripts of Ibn Battuta's Rehla in Paris and Ibn Juzayy," *Journal of the Asiatic Society of Bengal,* Letters, Vol. XX, 1954, pp. 49-53.

Husik, Isaac, "An Anonymous Medieval Critic of Maimonides," *Jewish Quarterly Review,* (New Series), Vol. II, 1911.

Husik, Isaac, "Maimonides and Spinoza on the Interpretation of the Bible," in supplement to the *Journal Am. Orient Soc.,* 1935, p. 55.

Huskin, Isaac, *A History of Medieval Jewish Philosophy,* New York: The Jewish Publication Society of America, 1941.

ibn Abi Usaybi'a, Uyunul Inba' *'fi Tabaghat-il-Atibba,"* (Medical), Cairo: no publ mentioned, 1882 (in Arabic).

ibn al-Ambari, *Tabaghat ul Udaba,* (On Men of Letters), Cairo: no publ mentioned, 1926 (in Arabic).

ibn al-Athir, *Tarikh-al-Kamel,* (The Perfect History), Cairo: no publ mentioned, 1873.

ibn al-Balkhi, *Fars-Namah,* (The Persian Book) Teheran: no publ mentioned, 1313 Shamsi Hejira (in Persian).

ibn al-Jowzi, *Akhbar-al-Humgha wal Muqhfelin,* (On Fools and Negligent Men), Damascus: no publ mentioned, 1348 Shamsi Hejira (in Arabic).

ibn al-Nadim, Muhammad ibn Is'haq, *Al-Fihrist,* (The Index), Egypt: Rahmaniyya Publishers, 1348 Shamsi Hejira (in Arabic).

ibn Batuta, *Tuhfat-ul-Nathar,* Paris: no publ mentioned, 1853 (in Arabic).

ibn Howgkhal, *Ketab-i-Surat al-Ardh,* (On Geography) Leiden: no publ mentioned, 1938 (in Arabic).

ibn Khaldun, *The Muqaddimah,* (An Introduction to History), tr. by F. Rosenthal, 3 vols., New York: Pantheon Books, 1958.

ibn Maskuyah, *Akhlaq wa Rahi Sa'adati Bashar,* (Ethics and the Way to Human Happiness), tr. and gathered from Taharat-ul-A'araq, Teheran: Imami Press, no date (in Persian).

ibn Sahnum, *Adab-al-Mu'allemin,* (On manners of Teachers), Tunis: no publ mentioned, 1348 Shamsi Hejira (in Arabic).

ibn Yamin, *Diwan,* (Complete Works) ed. by Sa'id Nafisi, Teheran: Aban Mah 1318 Shamsi Hejira (in Persian).

Index Islamicus, compiled by J. D. Pearson, 1906-1955. with supp. 1956-1960, Cambridge (Eng.): W. Heffer and Sons Ltd., 1958.

Isbahani, al-abu-al-Faraj, *Kitab al-Aghani,* (Book of Songs), Cairo: Dar al-Tiba'ah, 1868.

Issawi, C., *An Arab Philosophy of History . . . selections from Ibn Khaldun,* tr. by C. Issawi, London: Murray, 1950.

Jackson, A. V. Williams, *Sa'di,* (in Library of the World's Best Literature, ed. by C. D. Earner), New York: 1897.

Jarrett, Bede, *Social Theories of the Middle Ages,* Westminster, Md.: The Newman Book Shop, 1942.

Kama Shastra Society, *Gulistan,* Benares: 1888.

Kashfuth-Thonoon, Vol. I.

Katy, Solomon, *The Jews in the Visigothic and Frankish Kingdoms of Spain and Gaul,* Cambridge: Harvard University Press, 1937.

Kennedy, E. S., *A Survey of Islamic Astronomical Tables,* The American Philosophical Society, 1956.

Khadduri, Majid, *The Law of War and Peace in Islam,* Baltimore: Johns Hopkins Press, 1955.

Khairallah, Amin A., *Outline of Arabic Contributions to Medicine and the Allied Sciences,* Beirut: no publ mentioned, 1946.

Khan, M., *Muslim Theories of Education During the Middle Ages,* publisher and place not known, 1944.

Khuda-Bakhsh, S., *Contributions to the History of Islamic Civilization,* Calcutta: publ not mentioned, 1905.

Khuda-Bakhsh, S., *The Islamic Libraries, Nineteenth Century,* LII, 1902.

Khuda-Bakhsh, S., "The Renaissance of Islam," *Islamic Culture,* Vol. IV, 1930.

Kibre, Pearl, *The Nations in the Medieval Universities,* Cambridge: Medieval Academy of America, 1948.

Kimble, G. H. T., *Geography in the Middle Ages,* London: Methuen and Co., Ltd., 1938.

Knight, E. W., *Twenty Centuries of Education,* New York: Ginn and Co., 1940.

Kubiak, W., "Some West- and Middle-European geographical names according to the abridgement of Idrisi's Nuzhat al-mustak—known as Makrizi's Gany al-Azhar min ar-rawd al-mi'tar," *Folia Orient,* Vol. I, 1959, pp. 198-208.

Laurie, S. S., *Historical Survey of Pre-Christian Education,* London: Longman Green and Co., 1900.

Lacroix, Paul, *Science and Literature in the Middle Ages,* New York: D. Appleton, 1878.

Lammens, Henri, *Etude sur le siecle des Omayyades,* publisher and location not known, 1930.

Lane, Edward, *Arabian Society in the Middle Ages,* London: Ward Lock and Co., 1883.

Leclerc, *Histoire de la Medicine Arabe,* Paris: 1876.

Lee, *Gulistan,* London: 1827.

Leng, Reuben, *Stories from the Boostan of Shaikh Sa'di,* New York: Frederick Stokes Co., date not mentioned.

Le Strange, G., *Baghdad During the Abbasid Caliphate,* Oxford: The Clarendon Press, 1924.

Levy, R., *An Introduction to the Sociology of Islam,* London: Luzac and Co., 1931.

Lewis, B., "The Muslim Discovery of Europe," *Bulletin of the School of Oriental and Asiatic Studies,* Vol. XX, 1957, pp. 409-417.

Macdonald, D. B., *Aspects of Islam,* New York: The Macmillan Co., 1911.

Macdonald, D. B., *Religious Attitude and Life in Islam,* Chicago: University of Chicago Press, 1909.

MacKensen, Ruth Stellhorn, *American Journal of Semitic Languages and Literature,* LI, LII, LIII, LIV, 1935-1937.

Mahmasani, Subhi, *Falsafat al-Tashri', fi al-Islam,* (Philosophy of Religion in Islam), tr. by Farhat Ziyadah, Leiden: Brill Press, 1961.

MacKensen, Ruth Stellhorn, *American Journal of Semetic Languages,* Vols. LI, LII, LIII, LIV, 1935-37.

MacKensen, Ruth Stellhorn, "Four Great Libraries of Medieval Islam," *Library Quarterly,* Vol. II, No. 3, July 1932, pp. 279-299.

Mahmoudi, Yaqut, *Mu'jam-ul-Buldan,* Cairo: no publ mentioned, 1906.

Mahmud, al-Alusi, *Tarikh-Masajid Baghdad,* Baghdad: no publ mentioned, 1346 Shamsi Hejira (in Arabic).

Makdisi, George, "Muslim Institutions of Learning in the 11th Century Baghdad," *Bulletin of the School of Oriental and Asiatic Studies,* Vol. XXIV, Part I, 1961, pp. 1-64.

al-Makkari, Ahmed, *History of the Muhammedan Dynasties in Spain,* 2 vols., tr. by de Gayangos, London: no publ mentioned, 1840.

Maqdisi, *Ahsan al-Taqasim fi Ma'rifat al-Aqalim,* Vol. I.

Maqrizi, *Al-Khitab I, The History of Islamic Civilization.*

Margoliouth, D. S., *Mohammed and the Rise of Islam,* New York: G. P. Putnam's Sons, 1905.

Ma'ruf, Naji, *Al-Madrasah al-Mustansiriyah,* (The Mustansiriyah College), Baghdad: Nasi al-Muthanna, 1935.

al-Masudi, Abu-l Hasan, *Meadows of Gold and Mines of Gems,* tr. Sprenger, London: no publ mentioned, 1841.

Masudi, *Murawinij-u'Zhahab,* Cairo: no publ or date.

Mayer, Frederick, *A History of Educational Thought,* Columbus: C. E. Merrill Books, 1960.

Melvin, Arthur G., *Education – A History,* New York: John Day Co., 1946.

Menasha, "Studies in Islamic Cultural History," *American Anthropological Association,* 1954.

Menasha, "Islam: essays in its nature and growth—a cultural tradition," *American Anthropological Association,* 1955.

Messenger, James F., *An Interpretive History of Education,* New York: Crowell Co., 1931.

Menage, V. L., "The Map of Hajji Ahmed' and its makers," *Bulletin of the School of Oriental and Asiatic Studies,* 1958, pp. 291-314.

Meyerhof, C., "Medieval Jewish Physicians in the Near East," *Isis,* Vol. XXVIII, No. 77, May 1938, pp. 432-460.

Mez, Adam, *The Renaissance of Islam,* tr. by S. A. Bukhsh and D. S. Margoliouth, London: Luzac and Co., 1937.

Miksa, Klein, *Juszuf Al-Baszir, Al-Kitab Al-Muhtavi,* Budapest, 1913.

Mo'in, Dr. Mohammad, ed., *Char-Ma-Ghalet Arudhi,* (Four Discourses of Arudhi), Teheran: no publ mentioned, 1954 (in Persian).

Monroe, Paul A., *A Cyclopedia of Education,* 5 vols., New York: Macmillan Co., 1911.

Monroe, Paul A., *Source Book in the History of Education for the Greek and Roman Period,* New York: Macmillan Co., 1901.

Monroe, Paul A., *Textbook in the History of Education,* New York: Macmillan Co., 1905.

Moore, Ernest C., *The Story of Instruction,* New York: Macmillan Co., 1936.

Moore, Ernest C., *The Story of Education; The Church, The Renaissance, and the Reformation,* New York: Macmillan Co., 1938.

Morgenstern, Erno, *Juszuf Al-Basir Al-Kitab Al-Muhtavi,* Budapest: no publ given, 1913.

Mulhern, James, *A History of Education – A Social Interpretation,* New York: Ronald Press, 1959.

Muller, Herbert J., *The Uses of the Past,* New York: Oxford University Press, 1952.

Nadim, abu-al-Faraj, Muhammad ibn-Ishaq, *Kitab al-Fihrist,* ed. by G. Flugel, Leipzig: Vogel, 1871.

Nadir, Albert N., *Le System Philosophique des Mu'tazila,* Beirut: Les Lettres Orientales, 1956.

Naseer-ul-din, Khawja, *Akhlaghi Naseri* (The Naseri Ethics), Teheran: Elmiyyah Islamiyyah Press and Khorshid Press, no date (in Persian).

Nakosteen, Mehdi, *In the Land of the Lion and Sun,* Denver: The World Press, 1937.

Nakosteen, Mehdi, "The Islamic World"—Approaches to an Understanding of World Affairs, ed. H. Anderson, *The Twenty-Fifth Yearbook of the National Council for the Social Studies,* Washington: 1954.

Nakosteen, Mehdi, "Religion and Scientific Education" in *The Challenge of Scientific Education,* ed. Joseph Roucek, New York: Philosophical Library, 1959.

Nakosteen, Mehdi, *Religions of Iran,* Denver: Western Publishing Co., 1937.

Nicholson, R. A., *The Mystics of Islam,* Cambridge (Eng.): Cambridge University Press, 1922.

Nicholson, R. A., *Studies in Islamic Mysticism,* Cambridge (Eng.): Cambridge University Press, 1921.

Nicholson, R. A., *Studies in Islamic Poetry,* Cambridge (Eng.): Cambridge University Press, 1921.

Nicholson, R. A., *Translations of Eastern Poetry and Prose,* Cambridge (Eng.): Cambridge University Press, 1922.

Nidhami, Arudhi, *Chahar Maghala,* (Four Discourses), London: Brown, Gibb, 1921.

Nidham-ul-Mulk, Abu Hassan ibn Ali Khawja, *Siyassat Namah,* (Book of Statecraft), Teheran: Eghbal Press and Haidari Press, 1334 Shamsi Hejira (in Persian).

Nilakanta, Sastri K. A., "Marco Polo on India," *Oriente Poliano,* 1957, pp. 111-120.

Nizami, Aruzi, *Chahar Maghala* (Four Discourses), Browne, Gibb Series, London, 1921.

Nizami, *The Diwan of Nizami* (in Persian).

O'Leary, Delacy L., *Arabic Thought and Its Place in History,* New York: Dutton, 1922.

O'Leary, Delacy L., *How Greek Science Passed to the Arabs,* London: K. Paul, Trench, Trubner and Co., 1939.

Olschki, L., "Marco Polo, Dante Alighieri e la cosmografii medievale," *Oriente Poliano,* 1957, pp. 45-65.

Onsori, *The Diwan of Onsori,* Teheran: Sherkat Press, 1363 Hejira (in Persian).

Padover, S. K., "Muslim Libraries," in J. W. Thompson, *The Medieval Library,* Chicago: 1939.

Palmer, E., *Harun-al-Rashid,* London: Marcus Ward, 1881.

Patton, Walter M., *Ahmad ibn Hanbal and the Mihna,* Brill Press, 1879.

Pinto, O., "The Libraries of the Arabs During the Time of the Abbasides," *Islamic Culture,* 1929, Vol. III.

Platts, J. T., *Gulistan,* London: 1873.

Poole, R. Lane, *History of Egypt in the Middle Ages,* London: publ not mentioned, 1901.

Pope, Arthur U., *Masterpieces of Persian Art,* New York: The Dryden Press, 1945.

Pope, Arthur U., *Survey of Persian Art,* Cambridge (Eng.): Oxford University Press, 1938.

Quardi, G., *Philosophie Arabe dens l'Europe medievale,* Paris: publ not mentioned, 1947.

Radhwan, abu-al-Futuh Ahmad, *Old and New Forces in Egyptian Education,* New York: Columbia University Press, 1951.

Randall, John H., *The Making of the Modern Mind,* Boston: Houghton Mifflin, 1940.

Rashall, Hasting., *The Universities of Europe in the Middle Ages,* Oxford: The Clarendon Press, 1936.

Rezwi, Zadah, *New Words in Old Persian,* Teheran: Tahan Press, 1318 (in Persian).

Riedel, John O., "Maimonides and Scholasticism," *New Scholasticism,* Vol. X, 1936.

Raihani, A., *The Quatrains of Abu-l Ala,* London: publ not mentioned, 1904.

Rivoira, G., *Moslem Architecture,* Oxford: The Clarendon Press, 1918.

Robinson, S., *Selections. . Persian Poetry for English Readers,* Glasgow: publ not mentioned, 1883.

Roolvink, E. R., *Historical Atlas of the Muslim People,* Amsterdam: Djambatan, 1957.

Rosenthal, E., "Maimonides' Conception of State and Society," *Moses Maibonides* VIII Centenary Volume, ed I, London: Epstein, 1936.

Rosenthal, Franz, *An Introduction to History,* 3 vols., Bollingen Series XLIII, Pantheon Books, 1958.

Rosenthal, Franz., "The Technique and Approach to Muslim Scholarship," *Orientalie,* 1947.

Ross, James, *Gulistan,* (Rose Garden), tr. by J. Ross, Boston: Ticknor and Fields, 1864.

Sa'di, *Boostan,* tr. by A. H. Edwards, London: publ not mentioned, 1911.

Sa'di, Sheikh Musleh-ed-din Shirazi, *Kulliyyat*, (Complete Works), publ and date not mentioned (in Persian).

Sa'di, Sheikh Musleh-ed-din Shirazi, *Gulistan* (The Rose Garden), tr. by L. Cranmer-Byng, London: publ not mentioned, 1919.

Sa'di, Sheikh Musleh-ed-din Shirazi, *Gulistan*, (The Rose Garden), Teheran: Majlis Press, 1319 Shamsi Hejira (in Persian).

Saeed Sheikh M., "Ibn Khaldun," Iqbal 9, 1960, pp. 14-22.

Safa, Dr. Dhabih Allah, *Danish-hayi Yunani dar Shahan Shahi Sassani*, (Greek Science in the Sassanian Empire), Teheran: Rangin Press, 1330 Shamsi Hejira (in Persian).

Safa, Dr. Dhabih Allah, ed., *Resala'i Akhawan-us-Safa*, (An Essay on the Bretheren of Purity), Teheran: no publ mentioned, 1330 Shamsi Hejira (in Persian).

Safa, Dr. Dhabih Allah, *Tarikhi Adabiyyat dar Iran*, (Literary History of Iran from the Middle of the Fifth Century to the Beginning of Seventh Century Hejira), Vol. II, Teheran: Elmiyyah Islamiyyah Press, 1339 Shamsi Hejira (in Persian).

Safa, Dr. Dhabih Allah, *Tarikh Ta'lim-o-Tarbyat dar Iran*, (History of Education in Iran), in Mehr, Vol. IV No. 1, no date.

Safa, Dr. Dhabih Allah, *Tarikh Ulum Aqli dar Tamadduni Islami*, (History of Rational Sciences in Islamic Civilization), Vols. I and II, Teheran: Danishgah Press, 1336 Shamsi Hejira (in Persian).

Sa'id, Nafisi, *Diwan*, (Complete Works), *of Attar Nisha'buri*, Teheran: Eqbal Bookstore and Press, 1319 Shamsi Hejira (in Persian).

Saliba, D., *Etude sur la Metaphysique d'Avicenna*, Paris: no publ mentioned, 1926.

Sarton, George, *The Appreciation of Ancient and Medieval Science During the Renaissance*, Philadelphia: University of Pennsylvania Press, 1955.

Sarton, George, *A Guide to the History of Science*, Waltham (Mass.): Chronica Botanica Co., 1952.

Sarton, George, *Introduction to the History of Science*, Baltimore: The Williams and Wilkins Co., Vol. I, 1927; Vol. II Part I and II 1931; Vol. III Part I and II, 1948.

Sauvaget, J., *Introduction a l'histoire de'l'orient musulman*, Paris: Adrien-Maisonneuve, 1946.

Schacht, Joseph, *The Origins of Muhammadan Jurisprudence*, Oxford: The Clarendon Press, 1950.

Shafaq, Reza Zadeh, *Tarikh'i Adabiyyati Iran*, (History of Persian Literature), 2 vols., Teheran: no publ mentioned, no date (in Persian).

al-Shahrastani, Muhammad ibn-'Abd-al-Karim, *Kitab al-Milal wa'l-Nihal*, Part II, ed. W. Cureton, Leipzig: Harrassowitz, 1924.

Shalaby, Ahmad, *History of Muslim Education*, Beirut: Dar al-Kashshaf, 1954.

Shiloh, Ailon, "The System of Medicine in the Middle East Culture," *The Middle East*, 1961.

Shoup, William J., *The History and Science of Education*, New York: The American Book Co., 1891.

Smith, Margaret, ed., *The Persian Mystic: Attar*, London: Luzac and Co., 1932.

Smith, Wilfred Cantwell, *Islam in Modern History*, Princeton: Princeton University Press, 1957.

Spengler, O., *Decline of the West*, New York: A. A. Knopf, 1939.

Strong, D. M. and Simla J. Elston, eds., *Selections from the Boostan of Sa'di*, no publ or location mentioned, 1872.

Subhi, *Afsanehai Kohan*, (Ancient Folklore), Murdad Mah: Piruz Press, 1334 Shamsi Hejira (in Persian).

Subki, *Tabazhat* (Tabaqat?) *al Shafi-Iyyah*, Vol. III.

Sweetman, J. W., *Islam and Christian Theology,* 3 vols., no publ mentioned, 1945-52.

Sykes, Sir Percy M., *History of Persia,* 2 vols., London: Macmillan, 1930.

Tabari, *Chronique,* tr. by Zotenberg, Paris: no publ mentioned, 1867.

Tabrizi, Homan-al-din, *Diwan,* (Complete Works), publ not mentioned, 1333 Shamsi Hejira, (in Persian).

Talas, Asad, *La Madrasa Nizamiyya et son Histoire,* no place given: Geuthner, 1939.

Tarn, W. W., *Alexander the Great,* Cambridge (Eng.): The University Press, 1948.

Tarmadi, Adib Saber, *Diwan,* (Complete Works), Teheran: Farwardin Bros. and Khawar, 1331 Shamsi Hejira (in Persian).

Taylor, Eva G., *Ideas on the Shape, Size and Movements of the Earth,* London: Luzac and Co., 1943.

Taylor, H. O., *The Medieval Mind,* 2 vols., New York: Macmillan, 1925.

Theological Review, "The Internal Senses in Latin, Arabic and Hebrew Philosophic Texts," 1935, p. 28.

Thompson, J. W., "The Introduction of Arabic Science into Lorrain in the 10th Century," *Isis,* Vol. XII No. 38, 1929, pp. 184-193.

Thompson, J. W., *The Middle Ages,* 2 vols., New York: Macmillan, 1931.

Thompson, J. W., *The Medieval Library,* Chicago: University of Chicago Press, 1939.

Thorndike, L., *The History of Medieval Europe,* Boston: Houghton Mifflin Co., 1917.

Thorndike, L., *University Records and Life in the Middle Ages,* New York: Columbia University Press, 1944.

Tisdall, W., *Original Sources of the Qur'an,* no date or publ mentioned.

Totah, K. A., *The Contributions of the Arabs to Education,* New York: Columbia University Press, 1926.

Tritton, A. S., *Islam: Belief and Practices,* no publ or location mentioned, University Library, 1951.

Tritton, A. S., *Materials on Muslim Education in the Middle Ages,* London: Luzac and Co., 1957.

Toynbee, Arnold J., *A Study of History,* 6 vols., London: Oxford University Press, 1934.

Ubaid Zakani, *Kulliyyat,* (Complete Works including Eshq-Namah, or Book of Love; Akhlaq-ul-Ashraf, or Manners of Noblemen; Reesh-Namah, or Book of Beard; Sad-Pand, or Hundred Councils; Resala'i del-Gosha; Musho-Gorbeh, or Mouse and Cat; and Sangtarash, or Stone Cutter), Teheran: Eqbal Press, 1334 (in Persian).

Ulich, Robert, *The Education of Nations,* Cambridge (Mass.): Harvard University Press, 1961.

Ulich, Robert, *Three Thousand Years of Educational Wisdom,* Cambridge (Mass.): Harvard University Press, 1947.

Unsori, Abul Ghasem ibn Ahmad, *Diwan,* (Complete Works), Teheran: Sherkati Tab'i Kitab, 1325 Shamsi Hejira, 1363 Qamari Hejira (in Persian).

Von Greenbaum, Gustave E., *Medieval Islam,* Chicago: Chicago University Press, 1950.

Wallbank, T. Walter and Alastair M. Taylor, *Civilization—Past and Present,* Vol. I, Chicago: Scott Foresman and Company, 1942.

Walsh, J. J., *The Thirteenth: the Greatest of Centuries,* New York: Catholic Summer School Press, 1920.

Washmgir ibn Ziar, Amir Unsur-ul-Ma'ali Kei Kawus ibn Eskander ibn Qabus ibn, *Ghabus Namah,* (The Book of Qabus), Teheran: Ateshkadeh Press, 1335 Shamsi Hejira, 1956 A.D. (in Persian).

Watt, W. Montgomery, *Free Will and Predestination in Early Islam,* London: Luzac and Co., 1948.

Wells, H. G., *The Outline of History,* New York: Garden City Books, 1949.

White, H. V. "Ibn Khaldun in world philosophy of history," *Comparative Studies in Society and History,* 2, 1959, pp. 110-125.

Wickens, G. A., ed., *Avicenna: Scientist and Philosopher, A Millenary Symposium,* London: Luzac and Co., 1952.

Wilds, Elmer H., *The Foundations of Modern Education,* New York: Farrar and Rinehart, 1942.

Williams, Samuel G., *A History of Medieval Education,* New York: C. W. Bardeen Co., 1903.

Wittkower, R., "Marco Polo and the pictorial tradition of the marvels of the East," *Oriente Poliano,* 1957, pp. 155-172.

Wolfson, Harry A., "The Classification of Science in Medieval Jewish Philosophy," in *Hebrew Union College Annual,* I, Cincinnati: 1925.

Wolfson, Harry A., "The Problem of the Origin of Matter in Medieval Jewish Philosophy," in Proceedings of the Sixth International Congress of Philosophy, no location given: 1926.

Yaghami, Habib, *The Sa'di Namah,* (Book of Sa'di), Teheran: Khodkar-u-Iran Press, 1316 Shamsi Hejira (in Persian).

Yaqut, *Dictionary of Learned Men,* ed. D. S. Margoliouth, Cairo: no publ mentioned, 1907.

Yaqut, *Mu'jam al-Udaba,* Vol. II.

Yearbook of Education, "Education and Philosophy—Islam," (Chap 4), Yonkers-on-Hudson: World Book Co., 1957.

Young, T. C., *Christendom's Cultural Debt to Islam,* no publ or location, 1945.

Zaidan, Tarikh, *Al-Tamaddun al-Islami,* (History of Islamic Civilization) Vol. III, Cairo: no publ mentioned, 1920 (in Arabic).

Zarnuji, *Ta'lim al-Muta'allim,* (Instruction of the Pupil), Constantinople: no publ mentioned, 1292 Shamsi Hejira (in Arabic).

INDEX